Diversity and Multiculturalism

PETER LANG
New York • Washington, D.C./Baltimore • Bern
Frankfurt am Main • Berlin • Brussels • Vienna • Oxford

Diversity and Multiculturalism

A Reader

EDITED BY
Shirley R. Steinberg

PETER LANG
New York • Washington, D.C./Baltimore • Bern
Frankfurt am Main • Berlin • Brussels • Vienna • Oxford

Library of Congress Cataloging-in-Publication Data

Diversity and multiculturalism: a reader / edited by Shirley R. Steinberg.
p. cm.
Includes bibliographical references.
1. Multicultural education—United States. 2. Multiculturalism—United States.
3. Critical pedagogy—United States. I. Steinberg, Shirley R.
LC1099.3.D5794   370.1170973—dc22   2008042739
ISBN 978-1-4331-0346-9 (hardcover)
ISBN 978-1-4331-0345-2 (paperback)

Bibliographic information published by **Die Deutsche Bibliothek**.
Die Deutsche Bibliothek lists this publication in the "Deutsche
Nationalbibliografie"; detailed bibliographic data is available
on the Internet at http://dnb.ddb.de/.

Cover art, "Notre Sur" (Mural; [10mx12m] 120 Duluth E. Montreal, PQ, Canada, 2008),
by Shalak and Guko. Photo by Indiefotog.
Cover design by Joshua Hanson

The paper in this book meets the guidelines for permanence and durability
of the Committee on Production Guidelines for Book Longevity
of the Council of Library Resources.

October 20, 1989

Excuse me, I overheard you saying you had worked on a reserve in Southern Alberta?

I did, I was on the Standoff Reserve

I worked on the Rosebud Sioux Reservation in South Dakota

Where's your accent from?

Tennessee

Hey, are you married?

No

Are you gay?

No

Who was right? Neil Young or Lynyrd Skynyrd?

Neil Young

And that is when I fell in love with Joe L. Kincheloe, a man who loved rock n' roll more than Marx

    —Shirley

Contents

Section One: Doing Diversity and Multiculturalism

Section Two: Placing Whiteness *within* Diversity

Section Three: Race and Ethnicity

Section Nine: Diversity, Multiculturalism, and Leadership

Preface

Diversity? Multiculturalism?
Moving Tolerance and Tokenism to a Critical Level

Understanding that curriculum in school must be inclusive, educators have spent decades attempting to define just what diversity and multiculturalism mean. Diversity education or multiculturalism has often included activities such as eating tacos on *Cinco de Mayo,* acknowledging that President Franklin D. Roosevelt was confined to a wheelchair, and posting photos of famous African Americans and heroic women. Educational organizations have created myriads of unit or lesson plans calling for tolerance. We now find ourselves in the latter part of the first decade of the third millennium, and, as educators, we question whether any progress has been made in creating a truly diverse society. I would argue that we have not made a lot of progress: We've created a lot of school plays, spent lots of money infusing diversity and multiculturalism into the curriculum, and eaten a lot of tacos, but these attempts have merely been tokens that re-enforce the dominant culture.

Posting yet another Martin Luther King bulletin board in February, giving kids who play Native Americans in the Thanksgiving play more lines, celebrating women in March—these are tokenistic attempts to *show* diversity. However, these attempts sustain a dominant culture of whiteness, of maleness, of ableness, of heterosexualness, and of English languageness as the *real culture*—the token cultures are always the *other culture.* School programs that claim tolerance actually sustain the notion that the dominant culture must tolerate those who are *other.* Being tolerated, being tokenized, is not enough. No one deserves merely to be tolerated, or to be described as a token. Individuals are diverse and consequently must be understood and accepted as diverse.

Over the past couple of decades, Western societies have debated the question of multiculturalism with surprisingly little agreement over the meaning of the term. Because of this disagreement, educators have devised multicultural educational programs that have differed widely. The authors in this book take seriously the notions of diversity and multiculturalism and go beyond the food, festivals, and folk tales of limited and outdated twentieth-century curricula. They demand that educators understand that a critical diversity and multiculturalism must be established to break down a dominant culture that continually reasserts a status quo of marginalization and othering.

Section One proposes that we understand diversity and multiculturalism by identifying the inadequate ways curricula have been written and taught, and by redefining the field with an equitable lens, and overthrowing a dominant cultural curriculum. Section Two of the book, we then problematize the issue of whiteness, which is not simply the opposite of blackness or "person-of-colorness." Rather, whiteness is a meta-description for our dominant culture. We must include whiteness as a *part* of the whole that makes up difference, *instead* of making whiteness the context to which we measure *everything else*. Whiteness becomes another "category" within diversity and multiculturalism—not *the* category.

Section Three addresses race and ethnicity in the context of diversity and multiculturalism. Race and ethnicity are not synonyms; they reflect on one another and, depending upon which discipline is establishing a discourse, they can be more or less than their popular definitions. Section Four highlights sexuality and gender as essential to creating a critical diversity and multiculturalism. Although issues of gender are often addressed within traditional curricula, choices involving sexuality are suppressed. The majority of attention to diversity and multiculturalism lies in the racial, ethnic, and gender dynamics of human relationships.

The authors in Section Five articulate issues and concerns about social and economic class. Interestingly, students are not often taught to include poverty and lack of cultural capital as topics in diversity. In fact, in a first world context, *being poor* is usually not even discussed. This reflects the usual and dominant cultural educational assumption that *if it is not taught or not addressed. . . then it doesn't exist.*

Section Six discusses religion, a topic often avoided in school discourse. The chapters in this section position religion as another expression of diversity, an important part of many individuals' lives, and something that should be understood equally along with other notions of diversity and multiculturalism. Section Seven presents physical diversity as a diverse and multicultural aspect. Often physical diversity is separated into forms of special education, disability, or inclusion, categories that label differences as either physical or mental. The authors argue that physical diversity is social and cultural and must be included within our critical discourse. Section Eight authors discuss the diverse and multicultural nature of rural and urban geographic locations. Geographic difference is rarely included in mainstream educational conversations. The authors argue that the reality of being urban is completely different from that of being rural, and that consideration for geographic place must be included within the context of diversity. Diversity and multiculturalism vis-à-vis leadership completes this collection. The chapters in Section Nine, written by critical scholars of leadership and administration, advocate consideration of diversity education within the curriculum as necessary for schools and teacher education.

Originally I titled this book *Diversity: A Reader;* however, after reviewing current school and teacher education curricula, I realized that the word "multiculturalism" still needs to be included in the title. By placing diversity as the first descriptor, I am advocating that we turn to diversity as a more inclusive and critical term. Multiculturalism implies that some cultures may not be included, while diversity equalizes categories. In a critical diverse context, I suggest that categories eventually need to be dropped, and educators create an infused curriculum that gives equal attention and depth to all contexts. This would require the total re-working of all existing curricula and the absence of dominant cultural curricula as the bar with which *everything else* is measured. I don't think we are quite ready for this. So. . . small steps. And with these small steps, we create equity. In order to understand equity and social justice, however, we must accept that equity and social justice do not currently exist in school curricula, and that we—teachers and instructors—are the agents of social and cultural change.

It is with gratitude and respect that I thank the contributors to this volume. Each author was invited as a result of her or his commitment to critical diversity and social justice within teaching and schools. I appreciate them, and the time and care they contributed to this book. I also want to thank Victor Goebel, my exceptional assistant, for his engagement and care in assembling *Diversity and Multiculturalism: A Reader*. And, words alone cannot thank my partner in scholarship, and in life, Joe Kincheloe, for his mind and his heart. He was the love of my life.

I invite your critique and thoughts as you use this book, and also appreciate any suggestions or queries you or your students may have.

In solidarity for a diverse and just world,
Shirley R. Steinberg

About the Contributors

Liz Airton is a graduate student in the Department of Integrated Studies in Education and Women's and Gender Studies at McGill University, Montreal. Her research interests include gender theory and queer theory in educational research, teacher education, autobiography in research and pedagogy, feminist theory and research methods in education, and critical childhood studies. Liz's thesis research focuses on gender, discourse, and the development of teacher education students' professional identities and knowledges.

Gary L. Anderson is a professor in the Steinhardt School of Culture, Education and Human Development at New York University. He is a former high school teacher and principal. His latest book is the three-volume *Encyclopedia of Activism and Social Justice*. His new book, *Advocacy Leadership*, will be published in early 2009.

Susan Baglieri is an assistant professor in Adolescence and Special Education, as well as area coordinator in Special Education at Long Island University's Brooklyn Campus, New York. She is a board member of the Society for Disability Studies and an active participant in the Disability Studies in Education Special Interest Group of the American Educational Research Association. Her work has been published in the *Journal of Learning Disabilities* and *Disability Studies Quarterly*. Her areas of interest include inclusive education and teacher education, positioned through a disability studies orientation.

Kathleen S. Berry is a professor at the University of New Brunswick, Canada, where she teaches critical and literacy studies. She has published many chapters on critiques of dominant discourses in education including educational psychology, research methodologies, and literacy. Her books include *The Dramatic Arts and Cultural Studies* and, with Joe L. Kincheloe,

Rigour and Complexity in Educational Research: Conceptualizing the Bricolage. Presently she is working on a book about literacy studies and critical pedagogy.

Russell Bishop is a foundation professor for Maori Education in the School of Education at the University of Waikato, Hamilton, New Zealand. His research experience is in the area of collaborative storying as Kaupapa Maori research, having written a book *Collaborative Research Stories: Whakawhanaungatanga.* He has co-authored, with Ted Glynn, *Culture Counts: Changing Power Relationships in Classrooms,* which demonstrates how the experiences developed from within Kaupapa Maori settings. Other books include *Pathologising Practices: The Impact of Deficit Thinking on Education,* co-authored with Carolyn Shields and Andre Mazawi, and *Culture Speaks,* co-authored with Mere Berryman. He is currently the project director for Te Kotahitanga, a large New Zealand Ministry of Education funded research/professional development project that seeks to improve the educational achievement of Maori students in mainstream classrooms through the implementation of a culturally responsive pedagogy of relations.

Spencer Boudreau is an associate dean of Teaching, Learning and Students in the Faculty of Education at McGill University, Montreal. He has been involved in education in Quebec since 1968 and taught at the secondary, CEGEP (junior college), and university levels, in French and English, and in private and public institutions. As a secondary teacher he was seconded by the Ministry of Education for five years to work on pedagogical guides for the moral and religious education programs for secondary schools. For the past twenty years he has been at McGill in the Faculty of Education as an instructor, director of the Office of Student Teaching, and presently as an associate dean. His area of expertise includes the formation of education students to teach in the areas of ethics and, in particular, religion.

Paul R. Carr is an assistant professor in the Beeghly College of Education at Youngstown State University, Youngstown, Ohio, where he teaches at the undergraduate and graduate levels on the sociology of education. In addition to a number of articles on social justice and democracy in education, he has recently co-edited two books with Darren E. Lund: *The Great White North? Exploring Whiteness, Privilege and Identity in Education* and *Doing Democracy: Striving for Political Literacy and Social Justice.* Originally from Toronto, Paul previously worked for a number of years in the area of educational policy with the Ontario government.

David J. Connor is an associate professor in the Department of Special Education at Hunter College (CUNY) and the Disability Studies Program of the Graduate Center. He is the author of two books, *Reading Resistance: Discourses of Exclusion in Desegregation & Inclusion Debates* (co-authored with Beth A. Ferri), and *Urban Narratives: Portraits in Progress, Life at the Intersections of Learning Disability, Race, and Social Class* (both published by Peter Lang). His research interests include learning disabilities; social, cultural, and historical understandings of disability; disability studies in education; qualitative research; urban education; and issues of race, gender, social class, sexuality, and disability.

Larry Daffin is a doctoral student and graduate assistant in the Educational Leadership program at New York University. Larry served as a high school administrator in Houston, Texas, and as a math teacher and coach in San Antonio, Texas. He graduated from the United States Military Academy with a bachelor's degree in American Legal Studies (FOS) and earned a master's degree in Educational Administration from Texas A&M University, Kingsville. Larry is a decorated Iraqi war veteran and is married with twin girls and a son. His research interests are privatization and the achievement gap.

R. Deborah Davis is currently an assistant professor at State University of New York-Oswego, School of Education in Curriculum and Instruction, where she teaches culturally relevant teaching and foundations of education courses. She also serves as the diversity coordinator for recruitment in the School of Education. Davis received her Ph.D. in Higher Education Administration at Syracuse University. Her primary areas of research are: school climate; persistence to graduation for African American/ethnic students; and socialization in a racist society. She has worked in administrative capacities where she served as liaison to the black communities and constituent organizations. Dr. Davis is the author of *Black Students' Perceptions: The Complexity of Persistence to Graduation at an American University.*

Rona M. Frederick is currently an assistant professor in the Department of Education at The Catholic University of America, Washington, D.C. She has dedicated her life to research on black education, culturally relevant instruction, and meaningful uses of computer technology. She earned her bachelor's degree in psychology from Hampton University, master's degree in Africana studies from Cornell University, and Ph.D. in curriculum and instruction from the University of Maryland, College Park.

C. P. Gause is a former public school teacher, social service worker, and K–12 school administrator. He is an assistant professor of Educational Administration in the Department of Educational Leadership and Cultural Foundations at the University of North Carolina-Greensboro. He is co-editor of *Keeping the Promise: Essays on Leadership, Democracy and Education,* which earned the 2007 American Educational Studies Association Critics Choice Award. His new book, *Integration Matters: Navigating Identity, Culture and Resistance* has just been released. He served as the guest editor of the special issue "Edutainment" for the *Journal of School Leadership* and his work has also appeared in *Taboo: The Journal of Culture and Education.* His research interests include gender and queer studies, black masculinity, cultural studies, critical race theory, critical spirituality, and collaborative activism.

Jaime Grinberg is a professor of Educational Foundations and co-director of the Jewish American Studies Program at Montclair State University, New Jersey, where he teaches the history and philosophy of education, globalization, and social and educational analysis. Born in Argentina, he grew up in Uruguay and has lived in Israel, Michigan, and New Mexico before moving to New Jersey. His writings are on topics such as socio-historical analysis of schooling, the colonizing aspects of bilingual and ESL education, Latina/o students and their teachers' education, the disciplining and normalizing aspects of teacher education and "partnerships," or critical theories. He has published numerous books and articles in many academic journals. He is the author of *Teaching Like That: The Beginnings of Teacher Education at Bank Street.*

Judy Helfand has a master's degree in American Studies and Cultural Studies. She teaches American Cultures and World Humanities at Santa Rosa Community College, Santa Rosa, California, where her students give her hope for a future of social justice. They also inspire her to keep asking the hard questions as they join her in facing the many manifestations of global suffering and greed while celebrating the beauty of life. Her books include *Identifying Race and Transforming Whiteness in the Classroom* (Peter Lang, 2004), co-edited with Virginia Lea, and *Unravelling Whiteness: Tools for the Journey* (2008), with co-author Laurie Lippin.

Wade Herley is a doctoral student in the Adult and Higher Education program at the University of South Dakota.

Christie Ivie is a sociology major at Illinois Wesleyan University with an interest in early childhood education in developing countries.

Brian C. Johnson is committed to fostering intercultural relationships and community development. He is the founder and chief motivational educator for Manna Unlimited Motivations, specializing in diversity education. Having earned both the bachelor's and master's degrees in English from California University of Pennsylvania, Johnson has completed all coursework toward the doctor of education degree at Nova Southeastern University in the field of children, youth, and family studies. His research is in the area of racial identity development. Johnson is also an ordained minister and serves on the ministry team at Revival Tabernacle in West Milton, Pennsylvania. He is the co-author of *Reel Diversity: A Teacher's Sourcebook,* with Skyra C. Blanchard.

Joe L. Kincheloe was the Canada Research Chair of Critical Pedagogy at the McGill University Faculty of Education, Montreal. He was the founder of the Paulo and Nita Freire International Project for Critical Pedagogy. He was the author of numerous books and articles about pedagogy, education and social justice, racism, class bias, and sexism, issues of cognition and cultural context, and educational reform. His books included: *Teachers as Researchers; Classroom Teaching: An Introduction; Getting Beyond the Facts: Teaching Social Studies/Social Sciences in the Twenty-first Century; The Sign of the Burger: McDonald's and the Culture of Power.* His co-edited works with Shirley Steinberg include *White Reign: Deploying Whiteness in America* (with Shirley Steinberg et al.) and the Gustavus Myers Human Rights award winner: *Measured Lies: The Bell Curve Examined.*

Virginia Lea is an associate professor of education at Sonoma State University, Sonoma, California, and executive director of the California non-profit organization, the Educultural Foundation. She is the author (with Judy Helfand) of *Identifying Race and Transforming Whiteness in the Classroom.* Her most recent book with Erma Jean Sims is titled *Undoing Whiteness in the Classroom: Critical Educultural Teaching Approaches for Social Justice Activism.* She sees her research and teaching as a means of developing greater understanding of how hegemony contributes to global inequities. She tries to actively live a commitment to greater socio-economic, political, and educational justice.

Darren E. Lund is an associate professor in the Faculty of Education at the University of Calgary, where his research examines social justice activism in schools and communities. Darren formed the award-winning Students & Teachers Opposing Prejudice (STOP) program as a high school teacher in Red Deer, Alberta. In addition to a number of articles and book chapters, and creating the popular on-line Diversity Toolkit http://www.ucalgary.ca/~dtoolkit, he has recently co-edited with Paul R. Carr two books: *The Great White North? Exploring Whiteness,*

Privilege and Identity in Education, and *Doing Democracy: Striving for Political Literacy and Social Justice*. Darren has been recognized with a number of honors, including being named a Killam Resident Fellow, Exemplary Multicultural Educator of the Year, a Red Deer Top Educator of the Century, and a *Reader's Digest* National Leader in Education.

Curry Stephenson Malott works and lives in Buffalo, New York, where he teaches the philosophical foundations of education at D'Youville College. He publishes in related areas such as curriculum, cognition, cultural studies, world history, and critical pedagogy. He is the co-author (with Milagros Pena) of *Punk Rockers' Revolution: A Pedagogy of Race, Class, and Gender*. His most recent books include *A Call to Action: An Introduction to Education, Philosophy, Native North America*, and with Bradley Porfilio, *The Destructive Path of Neoliberalsim: An International Examination of Urban Education*.

Elizabeth J. Meyer completed her Ph.D. at McGill University, Montreal, on the topic of gendered harassment in secondary schools. She is a researcher at Concordia University in Montreal, Quebec. Her teaching and research interests include: critical pedagogy, diversity issues, teacher education, school law, bullying, harassment, youth culture, and new technologies. Her new book is *Gender, Bullying & Harassment: Strategies for Ending Sexism and Homophobia in Schools*.

sj Miller is an assistant professor of Secondary English Education at Indiana University of Pennsylvania. sj has published widely in journals and, most notably, won the 2005 Article of the Year Award from the *English Journal* for "Shattering Images of Violence in Young Adult Literature: Strategies for the Classroom." Most recently sj published (co-authored with Linda Norris) *Unpacking the Loaded Teacher Matrix: Negotiating Space and Time Between University and Secondary English Classrooms*, which received the Richard A. Meade award from NCTE, and co-authored *Narratives of Social Justice Teaching: How English Teachers Negotiate Theory and Practice Between Preservice and Inservice Spaces*. Current research interests are in unpacking English teacher identity in spacetime as pre-service teachers experience the larger matrix of the teaching world.

Erica Mohan is a doctoral student in the Educational Studies Department at the University of British Columbia. Her doctoral research examines the influence of K–12 schooling experiences on the identity construction processes of multiethnic students. Her broader research interests include multicultural, antiracist, and social justice education. Erica has taught in both the Department of Foundations, Leadership and Policy Studies and the Department of Sociology at Hofstra University.

Fernando Naiditch is an assistant professor in the Department of Curriculum and Teaching at Montclair State University, Montclair, New Jersey. He has been teaching for over twenty years and has taught not only in his native Brazil, but also in Israel, Argentina, Uruguay, England, and the United States. He holds a Ph.D. in Multilingual Multicultural Studies from New York University. Dr. Naiditch has done research and published in the field of TESOL, bilingual education, and critical second language pedagogy. His dissertation, a study on the pragmatic features of Brazilian ESL learners, received the Outstanding Dissertation Award at New York University. He is also the recipient of the 2003 James E. Weaver Memorial Award given by New York State TESOL for his work with and contribution to English language learners in the New York City public schools.

Jeremy N. Price is a professor of education and chair of the Educational Foundations at Montclair State University, Montclair, New Jersey. His research interests focus on the potential of transformative pedagogies in schools and teacher education and issues of power, identity, and knowledge in the lives of students and teachers.

Elizabeth P. Quintero has been involved with education programs in the United States and internationally as teacher, program developer, and curriculum specialist, and is particularly interested in programs that serve families in multilingual communities that represent a variety of cultural and historical backgrounds. She is a professor of Education at California State University Channel Islands. Her book publications include: *Refugee and Immigrant Family Voices: Experience and Education* (in press), and *Problem-Posing with Multicultural Children's Literature: Developing Critical, Early Childhood Curricula.* Betsy is a frequent contributor to international journals and has authored chapters in many books.

Nelson M. Rodriguez is an assistant professor of Women's and Gender Studies and Critical Theory in Education at The College of New Jersey, Ewing, New Jersey. His most recent book, with William F. Pinar, is *Queering Straight Teachers: Discourse and Identity in Education.* He is the co-editor (with Leila Villaverde) of *Dismantling White Privilege: Pedagogy, Politics, and Whiteness.* His forthcoming book (with John Landreau) is *Queer Masculinities: A Critical Reader in Education* (Dordrecht, The Netherlands: Springer).

Özlem Sensoy is an assistant professor of Critical Social Education in the Faculty of Education at Simon Fraser University. She teaches courses in social education, cultural studies, and critical anti-oppression theories and pedagogies. She has published in the *Journal of Intercultural Education, Taboo: The Journal of Culture and Education, Radical Pedagogy,* and in *Discourse.* She (with Christopher Stonebanks) is co-editor of the forthcoming book, *Muslim Voices in School: Narratives of Identity and Pluralism.* She is completing, also with Christopher Stonebanks, *Teaching Against Islamophobia.*

Carolyn M. Shields is a professor in the Department of Educational Organization and Leadership at the University of Illinois Urbana-Champaign. Prior to taking a university position, Dr. Shields worked for eighteen years as a teacher and teacher-leader in numerous cultural settings in K–12 school systems. She has served on several ministerial advisory boards and completed terms as president of the Canadian Association for Studies in Educational Administration and as Canadian representative to the Board of the Commonwealth Council for Educational Administration and Management—a council that honored her by electing her a fellow in 2004. She teaches courses and engages in research related to leadership for academic excellence and social justice. She has published seven books and over ninety articles and monographs. Her books include: *Bakhtin: A Primer,* and *Courageous Leadership for Transforming Schools: Democratizing Practice.*

Kmt G. Shockley is assistant professor of education at George Mason University in Arlington, Virginia. He has authored two books and several articles, mainly focusing on Africentric education. Kmt Shockley is officially designated as a "Living Legend" in Cincinnati, Ohio, for his years of work and positive impact in that region. He has traveled throughout West Africa,

China, and North and South America for his African-centered, humanistic and commonsensical approach to true education and personal transformation.

Timothy J. Stanley is vice-dean (Academic Programs) in the Faculty of Education, University of Ottawa, where he teaches antiracism education and the social foundations of education. He has published numerous journal articles and book chapters on the history of anti-Chinese racism in Canada and on the role of constructions of historical knowledge in contemporary racisms.

Christopher Darius Stonebanks is an associate professor in the Department of Education at Bishop's University. He has published extensively in the areas of applying methods of critical and cultural pedagogy, as well as in looking at developing strategies that encourage teachers to use classrooms as locations for social transformation, student empowerment, and social justice. He has been invited to speak at a number of academic settings on topics including qualitative research, media, multiculturalism, and critical pedagogy. Chris is the author of *James Bay Cree Students and Higher Education*. He is also co-editing *Muslim Voices in School: Narratives of Identity and Pluralism*, with Özlem Sensoy.

Melanie Stonebanks has been a teacher for the elementary grades for the past fifteen years. Presently she is working as a member of an English Language Arts team for Ministère de l'Éducation, du Loisir et du Sport and as a sessional lecturer for McGill University's Department of Integrated Studies in Education. She is currently a graduate student at McGill University in the Faculty of Education. A frequent collaborator with Chris Stonebanks, Joe Kincheloe, and Shirley Steinberg, this is her first published piece of writing.

Paul Theobald holds the Woods-Beals Chair in Urban and Rural Education at Buffalo State College in Buffalo, New York. He has published widely in the area of community- and place-based education and is probably best known as the author of *Teaching the Commons: Place, Pride, and the Renewal of Community* (Westview, 1997).

Gerald Walton is a recipient of a doctoral fellowship from the Social Sciences and Humanities Research Council of Canada. Currently, he is an assistant professor in the Faculty of Education at Lakehead University in Thunder Bay, Ontario. He teaches courses in education on sociology, moral and social philosophy, educational law and human rights, and diversity and the range of "-isms." His research focus is on educational policy related to "safe" schools, social privilege, and media's (mis)representation of issues related to sexuality, diversity and gender variance.

Linda Ware is an associate professor in the Ella Cline School of Education at the State University of New York (Geneseo). Her research and scholarship have appeared in *Hypatia, The International Journal of Inclusive Education, The Journal of Teacher Education*, and others. She has authored numerous chapters that explore exclusion as a given in educational contexts. She edited *Ideology and the Politics of In/Exclusion*, which probed educational exclusion in international contexts.

Venus Evans-Winters is an assistant professor of education and sociology at Illinois Wesleyan University. Her areas of teaching and research interest are urban education, feminisms, critical pedagogy, and school resilience. She is also the author of *Teaching Black Girls: Resiliency in Urban Classrooms*.

About the Editor:

Shirley R. Steinberg teaches in the McGill University Faculty of Education in the Department of Integrated Studies in Education. She is the director of the Paulo and Nita Freire International Project for Critical Pedagogy. She is the author and editor of numerous books and articles and co-edits several book series. The founding editor of *Taboo: The Journal of Culture and Education*, Steinberg's most recent books are: *Christotainment: Selling Jesus Through Popular Culture* (with Joe Kincheloe), *Media Literacy: A Reader* (with Donaldo Macedo) and *The Encyclopedia of Boyhood Culture*. Steinberg has also edited *Teen Life in Europe;* and with Priya Parmar and Birgit Richard *The Encyclopedia of Contemporary Youth Culture* (Library Reference Award Winner). She is the editor of *Multi/Intercultural Conversations: A Reader*. With Joe Kincheloe she has edited *Kinderculture: The Corporate Construction of Childhood* and *The Miseducation of the West: How Schools and the Media Distort Our Understanding of the Islamic World*. She is co-author of *Changing Multiculturalism: New Times, New Curriculum*, and *Contextualizing Teaching* (with Joe Kincheloe). Her next two projects are co-authored with Joe Kincheloe: *Writing and Publishing: A Primer*, and *Bricolage* and *Research: A Primer*, both due out in 2009. Her areas of expertise and research are in critical media literacy, cultural studies, diversity education, social drama, and youth studies.

One

Smoke and Mirrors
More Than One Way to Be Diverse and Multicultural

Shirley R. Steinberg and Joe L. Kincheloe

When entering into a conversation about critical diversity and multiculturalism, we are unable to ignore how power operates and the social, cultural, political, and economic forces that shape each person and/or how that person is perceived. When educators entered into the multicultural curricular trend in the late twentieth century, the mainstream intent was to *include* everyone—somehow. Early multiculturalists didn't discuss equity, or even social justice; the first work done in the area simply added on bits and pieces of information about *other* people while primarily discussing the white, dominant culture. As multiculturalism became more associated with the politics of education and not just another content area subject, teachers and scholars began to call for an examination of multiculturalism as a discipline unto itself. Calling it into question allowed us to all ask what *exactly* we (and schools) meant by diversity and multiculturalism. One of our favorite spots on the *Late Show with David Letterman* is the "Is this anything?" segment. Dave and Paul Schaeffer are given a short narrative and then are asked *if it is anything*. They quickly discuss the issue, then each of them pronounces if, indeed, it is anything. Just because something is *called* multicultural or diverse, indeed, doesn't mean *it is anything*.

The most apparent facet of diversity and multiculturalism is—there isn't one. There isn't one paradigm, nor one taxonomy, nor one way of diversifying and multiculturalizing citizens and school curricula. It became important for us to look at different manifestations of diversity and multiculturalism; by doing this, we are able to determine how the work was created, why, and by whom—thus asking essential questions: What is the purpose of this diversity and multiculturalism agenda? What are the forces that shaped this agenda? Who was involved in its creation? To whom is it addressed? Who does it serve? What, if any, social changes will be made in light of its implementation? By interrogating the forms of diversity and multiculturalism we are able to identify the political and social underpinnings. In our work, we find that, generally speaking, five positions emerge in public discourse about multicultural education and its pedagogy (Steinberg 2001; Kincheloe and Steinberg 1997; Kincheloe, Steinberg et al. 1998). By critically analyzing these positions, we find, indeed, if they establish socially just, critical, and equitable views of diversity and multiculturalism. . . *are they anything?* We present the five positions and their highlights in the following.

Tentative Positions of Diversity and Multiculturalism

(1) Conservative diversity practice and multiculturalism or monoculturalism:
- Tends to believe in the superiority of Western patriarchal culture.
- Promotes the Western canon as a universally civilizing influence.
- Has often targeted multiculturalism as an enemy of Western progress.
- Sees the children of the poor and non-white as culturally deprived.
- Attempts to assimilate everyone capable of assimilation to a Western, middle-/upper-middle-class standard.

(2) Liberal diversity practice and multiculturalism:
- Emphasizes the natural equality and common humanity of individuals from diverse race, class, and gender groups.
- Focuses attention on the sameness of individuals from diverse groups.
- Argues that inequality results from a lack of opportunity.
- Maintains that the problems individuals from divergent backgrounds face are individual difficulties, not socially structured adversities.
- Claims ideological neutrality on the basis that politics should be separated from education.
- Accepts the assimilationist goals of conservative multiculturalism.

(3) Pluralist diversity practice and multiculturalism:
- Is now the mainstream articulation of multiculturalism.
- Shares many values of liberal multiculturalism but focuses more on race, class, and gender differences rather than similarities.
- Exoticizes difference and positions it as necessary knowledge for those who would compete in the globalized economy.
- Contends that the curriculum should consist of studies of various divergent groups.
- Promotes pride in group heritage.
- Avoids use of the concept of oppression.

(4) Left-essentialist diversity practice and multiculturalism:
- Maintains that race, class, and gender categories consist of a set of unchanging priorities (essences).
- Defines groups and membership in groups around the barometer of authenticity (fidelity to the unchanging priorities of the historical group in question).
- Romanticizes the group, in the process erasing the complexity and diversity of its history.
- Assumes that only authentically oppressed people can speak about particular issues concerning a specific group.

- Often is involved in struggles with other subjugated groups over whose oppression is most elemental (takes precedence over all other forms).

(5) Critical diversity and multiculturalism:
- Draws upon the evolving theoretical position emerging in the Frankfurt School of Critical Theory in the 1920s.
- Focuses in this *critical* context on issues of power and domination.
- Grounds a critical pedagogy that promotes an understanding of how schools/education works by the exposé of student sorting processes and power's complicity with the curriculum.
- Makes no pretense of neutrality, as it honors the notion of egalitarianism and the elimination of human suffering.
- Rejects the assumption that education provides consistent socioeconomic mobility for working-class and non-white students.
- Identifies what gives rise to race, class, and gender inequalities.
- Analyzes the way power shapes consciousness.
- Formulates modes of resistance that help marginalized groups and individuals assert their self-determination and self-direction.
- Is committed to social justice and the egalitarian democracy that accompanies it.
- Examines issues of privilege and how they shape social and educational reality.

As with any typology, we tend to set it up to privilege our own embrace of critical diversity practices and multiculturalism. Obviously, with our concern with power and oppression, we find a critical form of multiculturalism preferable to the other positions. In an educational context, critical multiculturalism names the power wielders who contribute to the structuring of knowledge, values, and identity—a trait, we might add, that makes the position quite unpopular in some circles. The power of white supremacy is an important target of critical multiculturalism, with its phenomenal ability to camouflage itself to the point of denying its own existence. Whiteness presents itself not only as a cultural force or a norm by which all other cultures are measured, but as a positionality beyond history and culture, a non-ethnic space. Thus, in a culture where whiteness as an ethnicity is erased, critical multicultural educators receive strange looks when they refer to their analyses of white culture. Liberal and pluralist multiculturalists may include non-dominant cultural analyses in their curricula, but generally they do not examine the cultural dynamics of whiteness. In the same way, references to people of color, but not to white people, as "ethnics" tacitly imply that ethnicity does not influence the identities and lifestyles of whites. In this way, issues of race are seen as having little to do with white people; race concerns non-whites and ethnics, and the problems caused by their difference—from white people (Frankenberg 1993).

Race, Class, and Gender as Functions of One Another

An important feature of critical multiculturalism involves its ability to examine the domains of race and white supremacy, gender and patriarchy, and socioeconomic class and middle- and upper-class privilege in relation to and as functions of one another. Important strides have been made over the last fifteen years to understanding the ways race, class, and gender interact to shape our education and our lives in general. In the everyday politics and interactions of schools and workplaces, however, such understanding is all too rare. Mainstream conservative, liberal, and pluralist multicultural educators have been relatively uninterested in probing the connections that unite the spheres of politics, culture, and the economy with education. Without such study, multicultural educators and educational leaders view their task as merely addressing prejudicial attitudes toward women and minorities. Social life from these modernist perspectives is seen in fragmented segments—education here being isolated from politics, economics, and culture. In this context conservative and liberal analysts see "unattached individuals" who are unaffected by their membership in racial, gendered, or class collectives or groupings. Critical multiculturalists maintain that such fragmentation distorts our view of how schools and society operate. When conservative and liberal scholars fail to account for power dynamics in schools, workplaces, and the socioeconomic context that shapes them, specific processes of domination and subordination of students as individuals cannot be exposed. In the place of such specific exposure, the individual behavior of irrationally prejudiced men and women is embraced as the cause of unfair treatment. While such isolated irrational acts of prejudice certainly occur, they are not responsible for most of the oppression of racial, sexual, and economic "outsiders." To reach the point where we can explain the particular processes of subordination, educators must understand not only the dynamics of race, class, and gender but the ways their intersections in the lived world produce tensions, contradictions, and discontinuities in everyday lives (McCarthy and Apple 1988; Amott and Matthaei 1991).

In this context Carol Gilligan (1981) was on the right track in her study of taxonomies of moral reasoning and the ways they privilege male over female approaches. Subsequent analysis, however, indicated that gender is just one of the plethora of social categories that shape how individuals engage in moral reasoning. When race and class (as well as geographic place, national origin, religion, and other categories) are added to the social cauldron, we discover that women from different social locations reason differently. In this circumstance, gender analysis alone is insufficient; we must examine the way gender interacts with other social categories to get a deeper and richer picture of moral reasoning (Stack 1994). Such understandings are important in our efforts to grasp why different individuals engage with schooling in divergent ways. Such awareness can help us distinguish between being different or being deficient—a distinction that left undefined can perpetuate forms of institutional racism, sexism, and class bias.

Our position is simple: racial, sexual, and class forms of oppression can be understood only in a structural context—but these structures are never permanent and the way they interact with lived reality is never linear and static (a concept we will discuss later in more detail). Gender bias, for example, plays out on the terrain of economic and patriarchal macrostructures. An economic macrostructure might involve white male domination of the highest salary brackets in American economic life. A patriarchal macrostructure might involve the small percentage of upper-level corporate managers who are women or, in a domestic context, the high range of spousal abuse perpetrated by American males. Differences in men's and women's lives in general and economic opportunities in particular revolve around inequalities of power. For example, African American women, Latinas, Asian American women, and Native American women experience gender as one aspect of a grander pattern of unequal social relations. Indeed, the way one experiences race, class, and gender is contingent on their intersection with other hierarchies of inequality—other hierarchies in which the privileges of some grow out of the oppression of others (Zinn and Dill 1994; Zinn 1994; Amott and Matthaei 1991).

Let us focus for a moment on the ways gender intersects with race and class. Some intersections create privilege; if a woman marries a man from the upper class, gender and class intersect to create privileged opportunities for her. On the other hand, however, if the wife is Haitian American, forms of racial prejudice will exacerbate the ways in which she experiences gender bias. Thus, whether it be through subordination or privilege, race, class, and gender dynamics affect everyone—not just those at the bottom of the status hierarchy. The problem is that those at the top of these hierarchies often do not understand the ways in which the intersections of these axes affect them. The economic divisions of class serve to structure the ways race and gender manifest themselves. Though we understand that connections among race, class, and gender exist, we never can predict the effects of the interactions. Racial and gender hostilities, of course, can subvert class solidarity, and class solidarity can undermine gender-grounded networks. Working-class women, for example, have rarely felt a close affinity to the middle- and upper-middle-class feminist movement (Zinn 1994; Amott 1993).

As these race, class, and gender forces interact—sometimes in complementary and sometimes in contradictory ways—the school experience cannot be viewed simply as an uncomplicated reflection of social power. The school experience is exceedingly complex and while there are general patterns of subjugation that occur, such patterns play out in unpredictable ways with particular individuals. Cameron McCarthy and Michael Apple (1988) maintain that school mediates rather than imposes its power upon students. This means that students from lower-socioeconomic class backgrounds are not simply classified and relegated to low status classes and ultimately to low status jobs; instead, forces of race, class, and gender create a multi-level playing field on which students gain a sense of their options and negotiate their educational and economic possibilities. Race, class, and gender dynamics combine to create a larger playing field with more options for some and a smaller, more limited field for others. Thus, students struggle to make sense of and deal with triple or quadruple or more divisions of the social gridiron—they wrestle with fractious social classes, genders, and racial and ethnic groups.

Because it integrates and connects the study of race, class, and gender to the nature of consciousness construction, knowledge production, and modes of oppression, critical multiculturalism embraces a social vision that moves beyond the particular concerns of specific social groups. While these concerns are important and must be addressed in a critical pedagogy, we ultimately embrace a democratic politics that emphasizes difference within unity. The unity among different racial, ethnic, class, and gender groups can be constructed around a well-delineated notion of social justice and democratic community. Within this critical context the need for separatist, integrationist, and pluralist moments is appreciated. Indeed, there is a time for African Americans to study Afrocentrism, women to study feminism, and working people to study labor's continuing struggle for economic justice. Concurrently, there is a need for such groups to join together in the mutual struggle for democracy and empowerment. Critical scholars seek a multiculturalism that understands the specific nature of differences but appreciates our mutual embrace of principles of equality and justice (Kincheloe 2008; Collins and Sandell 1992).

Multiculturalism and Power

Though the nature and effects of power constitute the topic of contentious debate, rarely does anyone take the time to define the subject of the debate. In recent years a consensus seems to be emerging around the notion that power is a basic reality of human existence. Consensus, however, dissolves at this point, with various scholars running like quail in diverse theoretical directions. Critical multiculturalism contends that power is a fundamental constituent of human existence that works to shape the oppressive and the productive nature of the human condition. Scholars from the cultural studies tradition tend to accept the fundamental-constituent-of-reality thesis; they contend that power is embedded in the social frameworks of race, class, gender, occupations, and everyday interaction and communication. Post-structuralists such as Michel Foucault agree, maintaining that power is present in all human relationships, be they the interactions of lovers, business partners, or researchers and the researched. Indeed, Foucault concluded, after reading Nietzsche, that like the existence of capillaries in the circulatory system, power is inseparable from the social domain. As to the form of this ubiquitous social dynamic, Foucault never offered a definition more specific than that the exercise of power is a way in which particular actions modify others or guide their possible conduct. Because power is everywhere, it is therefore not something that can easily be dispensed with or overthrown. Simplistic politics or pedagogies that propose to put an end to power relations do not understand its relation to the web of reality (Kincheloe 2008; Musolf 1992; Cooper 1994).

Critical multiculturalists understand that there is nothing simple about the workings of power, that power is not simply the unchanging exercise of a binary relationship: A exercises its power over B and B responds by formulating acts of resistance against A. In its complexity and ambiguity, power is deployed by both dominant and subordinate individuals and groups; it is not the province of only one group. Indeed, we are all empowered and we are all unempowered, in that we all possess abilities and we are all limited in the attempt to use our abilities. Thus, conceptions of power that depict it as a one-directional, unified force with standardized outcomes miss important aspects of its nature. For example, when advocates of free market capitalism argue that the market works to satisfy consumer needs—that is, that consumer power flows in one direction toward the producers of goods to shape their production decisions—they fail to understand the two-way (and more) flow of power in the circumstance. Consumer power is not sufficient to thwart the producer's ability to hide information concerning safety, environmental aspects of production, exploitation of labor, etc. . . . that would drastically change the behavior of many consumers. Thus, power flows in a variety of directions, often behind the curtain of surface appearances (Cooper 1994; Rorty 1992; Bizzell 1991; Keat 1994). Power is nothing if not complex, ambiguous, and perplexing—indeed, that is part of its power. In contemporary hyperreality with its information saturation and global media networks, power wielders are invisible. As remote social actors, power forces are absent from everyday interactions; in this context the ambiguity of power becomes even more pronounced, thus enhancing power's power.

Defining Power Blocs in a Multicultural Context

John Fiske (1993) uses the term "power bloc" to describe the social formations around which power politics operated in Western societies in the late twentieth century. Employing the term as did Antonio Gramsci, the Italian political theorist, and Stuart Hall, the British cultural studies scholar, Fiske argues that power wielders do not constitute a particular class or well-defined social category. The power bloc, he contends, is more like an ever-shifting set of strategic and tactical social alliances. Such alliances are arranged unsystematically whenever social situations arise that threaten the "allies'" interests. Power blocs are historically, socially, and issue(s) specific as they come and go in relation to changing cultural arrangements. Power blocs are often created around social formations involving race, class, gender, or ethnicity in the pursuit of privileged access to particular rights or resources. For Fiske, power "is a systematic set of operations upon people that works to ensure the maintenance of the social order. . . and ensure its smooth running" (Fiske 1993, p. 11). It stands to reason that those individuals and groups who benefit the most from maintenance of this social order align their interests with those of the dominant power system and work to keep it running smoothly. Fiske concludes that the power bloc can be described better by "what it does than what it is." In this configuration the notion of "the people" includes those who fall outside the power bloc and are "disciplined" by it. Falling outside the power bloc does not mean that such an individual has no power; the power such outsiders hold is a weaker power (Fiske labels it a localizing power) than that of the power bloc. Indeed, it is a power that can be cultivated, strengthened, and sometimes successfully deployed. Along lines of race, class, and gender, individuals can simultaneously fall within the boundaries of one power bloc and outside another. While no essential explanation can account for the way an individual will relate to power blocs vis-à-vis their race, class, or gender, such dimensions do affect people's relationship to power-related social formations. In most cases individuals are fragmented in relation to power. An African American male may be disempowered in relation to the racial category of white supremacy yet may enjoy the political benefits of being a male in a patriarchal power bloc or an upper-middle-class male in the economic power bloc. Thus, individuals move in and out of empowered and disempowered positions. In our critical multiculturalist perspective, such fragmented power-related understandings are central, yet at the same time we maintain a keen sense of awareness of the human suffering caused by life outside of particular power alignments. Critical multiculturalists understand that there is little ambiguity to the pain, degradation, and horror that women experience from their batterings by men acting in complicity with the patriarchal power bloc, or that the poor experience as the result of the economic power bloc's insensitive fiscal politics, or that African Americans experience as a result of the white-supremacist power bloc's racism.

In these painful examples, a basic aspect of power is starkly illustrated: power produces inequities in the ability of human beings to delineate and realize their material and emotional needs. Teachers and other cultural workers who do not recognize the political dynamic will always be limited in their attempts to understand, provide for, and help empower their marginalized students and clients. The power bloc works consistently to obscure such appreciations; indeed, it labors to fix any violation of its borders by localizing powers. Such violations of the boundaries of power blocs have become common fare in Western societies. Public debates over affirmative action, minimum wage legislation, universal health care, sex and violence in TV and movies, and multicultural curricula all constitute skirmishes at the doorstep of the power bloc. The reaction of the power bloc as expressed in the forceful pronouncements of the conservative monoculturalists indicates a sense of threat; from a racial perspective, it reveals white perception of a challenge to racial supremacy. Conservative multiculturalism, with its monoculturalism, singularity of standards of excellence, and one-truth epistemology, is a quintessential representation of a power bloc that is resisting challenges to its previously unquestioned authority.

In the late 1990s one formation of the contemporary power bloc united several groups:

(1) dominant economic and political elites concerned with building good business climates to enhance corporate profits;

(2) white working-class and middle-class groups who sense their white privilege under attack by minority groups and who are uncomfortable with what conservative leaders refer to as an attack on traditional values like the family—such threats are perceived as coming from immoral African American welfare recipients, homosexuals, and feminists;

(3) social Darwinist conservatives with free market economic perspectives and guardians of Western cultural values who advocate a return to "standards of excellence" and discipline in schools; and

(4) upwardly mobile members of the new middle class who may not be comfortable with the other groups represented in this power bloc but who join the alliance because of their desire for professional advancement—such advancement is possible only if they buy into the corporate management procedures and non-controversial identities.

While such a power bloc constantly aligns and realigns itself depending on the issue in question, some groups obviously are more predisposed to alliance than others (Macedo 2006; Fiske 1993).

Critical Multiculturalism Studies Interacting Power Blocs

Critical multiculturalists are concerned particularly with the power blocs formed by the axes of power associated with class, race, and gender: class elitism, white supremacy, and patriarchy. Thus, for example, they study white supremacy by way of whiteness, focusing on its privilege, normativity (its ability to designate itself as the standard), and its erasure. In this context a critical multicultural pedagogy induces white people to rethink their understanding of their own ethnicity and the construction of their consciousness. It asks white people to reformulate whiteness in a critical multicultural context that values justice, egalitarianism, and community. At the same time, critical multiculturalists analyze and rethink maleness in much the same way as they approach whiteness. How are male privilege, normativity, and erasure accomplished within education and society? While critical multiculturalists understand the extreme importance of previously ignored questions of women's cultural production, they also focus on male supremacy (or patriarchy) and the ways it subordinates women and renders them passive, creates a male-dominant knowledge base, and promotes the male ways of seeing as the norm. The same factors are at work in the critical study of class, as the privilege, normativity, and erasure associated with class elites are analyzed. Focus on these power blocs and their interaction moves critical multicultural scholarship to a new level of insight. A more detailed examination of the three power blocs is in order.

Class Elitism—The Class Elitist Power Bloc

The first power bloc formed around our three axes of power is class elitism. Most forms of multiculturalism ignore questions of class and the ways class intersects with issues of race and gender. However, critical multiculturalists appreciate the centrality of class in any effort to understand the nature of social diversity in America and the racism, gender bias, and power inequalities that accompany it. The concept of class is extremely ambiguous and complex and must be used very carefully in any multicultural analysis. We assume that economic and occupational location in a social order is one of many factors that help construct consciousness, perception of others, and relation to power. In this context socioeconomic class is defined in relation to the labor process that is always changing as it interacts with social and cultural dynamics. Thus, all institutions (including work but not limited to it) are structured as hierarchies of inclusion and exclusion that shape individual and group power relations. Undoubtedly, class inequality is intensifying in Western societies—a fact that makes the inclusion of class elitism in the study of multiculturalism more important than ever.

Our conception of class is intimately tied to our understanding of power blocs. Expanding that understanding, we see the class elitist power bloc not as a social class per se—such a definition would inscribe it with a fixity and permanence that distorts the concept. The power bloc is an ever-shifting alignment that seeks to maintain dominant power relations in regard to particular issues. As John Fiske (1993) puts it, the power bloc is better conceived in relation to what it does than what it is. Like Fiske's power blocs, socioeconomic classes are always in process, taking shape and disintegrating around particular axes of power and specific contextual dynamics. Unlike previous notions, our concept of class does not involve empirically defined social groups with a shared monolithic view of the world. Thus, traditional depictions of the ruling class and proletariat give way to descriptions of shifting power blocs and disempowered peoples who are class-inscribed by their relationship to practices of inclusion and exclusion and their respective access to sociopolitical and economic mechanisms to promote their interests (Young 1992; Aronowitz and DiFazio 1994; House and Haug 1995; Fiske 1993).

When modern science was deployed by economic and political groups to produce unprecedented power, a major alignment of the class elitist power bloc was created. Though it would continue to shift, break apart, and realign across the decades in relation to diverse issues, the power bloc has worked to consolidate power in fewer and fewer hands. The technological advances of the late twentieth century have been employed to catalyze the consolidation of corporate power, in the process moving democracy and social justice farther out of reach. Indeed, the last three decades of the twentieth century have witnessed a class elitist-inscribed, conservative retrenchment—a call back to white supremacy, corporate power, and patriarchy. The gains of the 1960s in areas of race, gender, and the regulation of corporations signaled a threat to those who had traditionally held power.

By 1980 academic conservatives intent on protecting Western civilization from attacks by feminists, African Americans, and the political left joined with Republican business leaders and fundamentalist Christians to elect Ronald Reagan and scores of other conservative politicians. The new class elitist coalition accepted economic and political inequality as well as racial and gender discrimination as acceptable features of modern life. Once in power this conservative alliance undertook a massive redistribution of wealth in American society. It is important to note that not everyone aligned with the class elitist power bloc was from the upper-/upper-middle class or even the middle class. Many poor people aligned themselves with the power bloc not because of economic interests but because of the power bloc's deployment of white supremacy and patriarchy. Such deployments played on many individuals' fears and prejudices, inducing them to align with a power bloc that didn't serve their economic interest. Without an understanding of the interaction of race, class, gender, and the ever-shifting power blocs that grow up around them, an analyst would be hard-pressed to explain these dynamics.

As a result of the formation of the new class elitist power bloc in the 1980s, low-income families lost $23 billion in income and governmental benefits while high-income families gained $35 billion. The standard of living for middle-class Americans declined during these years while a new underclass emerged with homeless men and women living in the streets. Health care systems broke down; farm bankruptcies increased, and the federal deficit grew at an unprecedented rate (Grossberg 1992; Kellner 1989). Conservative economists boasted of the massive job growth of the 1980s and early 1990s. Upon closer examination this job growth turned out to be primarily an increase in so-called secondary jobs. Such jobs require virtually no training and demand little commitment to the work itself. Workers "put in time," viewing the job not as an end in itself but as a means to some other goal. Not only were many of the jobs secondary, but a large percentage were part-time, which are almost always of low status, as they deny individuals the possibility of promotion. Suffice it to say, the job expansion and other efforts of the class elitist power bloc of the 1980s and early 1990s did little to help its poor and the working-class allies (Falk and Lyson 1988; Block 1990).

The work of the class elitist power bloc of the last two decades has been frightening but fascinating to observe. As part of their successful effort to win consent to their domination, leaders of the bloc have worked to convince the U.S. population that anyone who has the ability and exerts the effort can make it in Western capitalist societies. Those who don't, they argue, are held back by their lack of morals and family values. Such talk ignores thousands of poor people who embrace the work ethic, labor year upon year with hardly a break, and still remain at the bottom rung of the economic ladder. Those who make this "character" argument often refuse to address the social context with its political and economic structures that work to privilege the privileged and punish the poor. Concurrently, they refuse to discuss the nature of white racism, sexism, and class bias—such talk, they confide, induces the poor to see themselves as victims, not agents. While the purpose of empowerment involves the ability to move beyond victimization and to take charge of one's own destiny, the way to do it does not involve the denial of history (West 1992; Jennings 1992). Social, political, and historical analysis grounds our understanding of the forces that overtly and covertly undermine socioeconomic mobility.

The class elitist power bloc's ideological vilification of the poor is grounded on the notion that the poor are not only dumb but are socially pathological as well. A major cause and effect of this pathological behavior, the argument goes, involves the absence of strong family values—middle-class family norms in particular. The "model" middle-class family existed at one point in our golden past, the class elitist narrative reads, but has dissolved due to welfare and "giveaway" programs. Such actions, by providing something for nothing, so reduced self-initiative that the poor have subsequently refused to work. In the "golden past" mothers were totally available to their children and intensely intimate with their husbands—a construction that placed so much pressure on women in the 1950s that thousands of them were driven to therapy, tranquilizers, and alcohol. Ignoring the mid-century problems, conservatives of the 1990s ascribe a large part of the blame for deteriorating family values on women's embrace of feminism.

If the class elitist power bloc is able to maintain the notion that the poor are debasing our society, then few will be able to challenge its domination. Its success in portraying the poor as dangerous welfare cheats who must be disciplined and punished for their transgressions is amazing. Contemporary observers rarely, if ever, witness explanations on network or cable TV or in the mainstream printed press of why most poor people turn to welfare. Maria Vidal (1996) writes that the realities of low pay for low-skilled work and the absence of affordable child care and health care push many people onto public assistance. Having nothing to do with the effort to vilify the poor, such realities are rarely referenced in the public conversation about poverty at the end of the century. Also absent is information on the market forces that are shaping class divisions in contemporary society (Lincoln 1996). Flagrant efforts to redistribute wealth began to take place in the Reagan and Thatcher eras in the United States and Britain. Distribution policies took from the poor and gave to the rich—like anti-matter Robin Hoods. Accompanying such redistribution policies have been offensives against labor unions, adoption of exploitative labor practices such as the utilization of part-time and labor from under-developed countries (usually women and minorities), the reestablishment of patriarchal sweatshops and domestic piecework, and the extensive use of subcontracting. Such policies have undermined the stability of the middle class, as an ever-increasing percentage of new jobs are low wage. A growing number of people are marginal to the work force, as they accept "contingent employment" in jobs with few benefits and no assurance of security (Grossberg 1992; Block 1990). As post-Fordist changes moved workers from industrial and agricultural jobs to service and information employment, many men and women watched their middle-class status disappear. Workers with jobs in the industrial sector were displaced by new technologies, computerization, and automation. These "deindustrialization" strategies affected middle-level and semi-skilled jobs (jobs paying $9 to $12 per hour in particular), resulting in further economic bipolarization (Kellner 1989; Rumberger 1984).

Indeed, the more vile the class elitist power bloc's portrayal of the poor, the more corporate profits increase—who cares about the rights and needs of such sociopaths? After all, the ideological narrative reads, the incompetent poor have caused our social ills; only bleeding heart fools would want to help these people. The new class war carries the battle against immigration, genetic inferiority, and issues of reproduction within poor communities. How dare these inferior poor people seek equality, the power bloc asks, when what they need is to be more effectively controlled. Democracy just may not work with these types of people. Indeed, the democratic effort to bring them into schools has been a tragic failure, many leaders of the power bloc argue. Their presence has undermined educational standards—dumbed schools down—and in the process spoiled education for the educable. Schools need more efficient testing practices that allow educators to track bright children into advanced classes and remove those deemed unable. Perhaps they could be funneled into expanded special education programs that teach discipline and low expectations. The poor in such circumstances could learn their place in a meritocractic society. After graduation they could possibly be corralled, as Richard Herrnstein and Charles Murray (1994) suggested in their intellectual justification for class elitism, *The Bell Curve: Intelligence and Class Structure in American Life,* and placed on a "high-tech Indian reservation." Critical multiculturalists are dedicated to the exposure of these and other activities of the class elitist power bloc.

White Supremacy—The White Supremacist Power Bloc

The white supremacist power bloc assumes its power from its ability to erase its presence. As the measure of all others, whiteness is unhyphenated, undepicted in "cultures of the world," in no need of introduction, and absent in most multicultural texts. Undoubtedly, it is one of the most powerful "nothings" we can conjure. Toni Morrison (1993) refers to the nothingness of whiteness as "mute, meaningless, unfathomable, pointless, frozen, veiled, curtained, dreaded, senseless, implacable" (59). Again, it is important to specify that the white nothingness we are describing does not imply that white people are not seen as white. Instead, it asserts the inability of individuals to understand exactly what whiteness entails. It is the nature of whiteness and its effects—for example, its status as power bloc, as norm and the privilege it bestows—that are invisible in end-of-century Western societies. In the Western white collective (un)consciousness, whiteness has been used not so much to signify a culture but rather the nonpresence of a culture, the absence of a "distasteful and annoying" ethnicity. In this same collective (un)consciousness, Stephen Haymes (1996) astutely observes, this white nothingness assumes a superior shadow that transforms it into whiteness as a "transcendental consciousness." Such a higher order of being, Haymes continues, involves at some level the privileging of reason over culture. Like the science that grounds white reason, this white consciousness has been so far unable to reflect upon its own origins, to confront its own particular assumptions (Mcintosh 1995; Frankenberg 1993; Nakayama and Krizek 1995; Morrison 1993; Stowe 1996).

This power of white nothingness reveals itself in everyday life, casual conversations, and political discourses. When Republican politician Patrick Buchanan implores his audience to "take back our cities. . . take back our culture, and take back our country," the "our" in question signifies whites. When George W. Bush, Dick Cheney, and William Bennett refer to family values, they are speaking of a white entity, a white norm missing in non-white homes. Television reporting of politics refuses to engage questions of whiteness in relation to such public pronouncements. Indeed, schooling and cultural pedagogy in general provide no lessons on the existence, not to mention the effects, of the white power bloc on life in Western culture. Even some forms of academic anti-racist multiculturalism fall victim to the power of whiteness, as they fail to appreciate the ways academic discourse is structured by Western forms of rationality—white reason. Whiteness is further erased in schools by the reticence of many teachers to discuss whites as a racialized group and white racism. Many teachers see value in multicultural education workshops and seminars only if such programs provide new information about minority groups they didn't already know—the study of privilege(s) makes no sense to them. Many complain that they already know about minority groups such as blacks and Latinos—a comment that grants insight into their theoretical schemas regarding multicultural education.

Faced with teachers who many times are reluctant to speak of whiteness and whose conceptual mapping of multiculturalism induces them to see no value in such a pedagogy, critical multiculturalists have a terrific task in front of them. Though it will be difficult, critical educators must be intellectually equipped to make a convincing case for the need to expose the fingerprints of the white power bloc on the academy. The white power of nothingness must no longer be allowed to tacitly shape the knowledge production and the academic canon of Western schooling. In this context a critical pedagogy of whiteness produces a counter-history grounded on the deconstruction of a whitewashed official history. Such a counter-history opens questions for discussion and research—questions about the deracialization of early Christianity; the possible whitening of ancient Egypt with its appropriation of the culture's innovations in writing, medicine, mathematics, and religion into a white European framework; and the bleaching of particular authors of African descent in the European literary canon, including Alexandre Dumas, Spinoza, and Aesop. Such historical whitewashing conveys debilitating messages to contemporary blacks and other non-whites, teaching them to believe that they are intellectually inferior to whites. In addition to the specific understandings about black contributions to history, Western white history in particular, counter-historical study engages students in an analysis of the hegemonic process of the white supremacist power bloc.

Such an analysis is central to a critical diversity and multiculturalism, as it focuses the attention of student and teacher on the subtle ways racism works to shape our consciousness and produce our identity—whether we are marginalized or privileged. Indeed, no matter what one's racial/ethnic background, such a process is complicit in the construction of subjectivity. Indeed, it can be argued that the conversation about education in Western societies has always, at one level, been about whiteness, in the sense that education was geared to make an individual more rational and to separate him (traditionally a male) from the uneducated, unreasonable other. The academic whitewashing of the white power bloc allows the white magic of nothingness to rob non-whites of their culture, contributions, and identities—a historical process that holds significant contemporary consequences. Recognizing these socio-pedagogical dynamics, critical multiculturalism's whiteness education works to produce counter-hegemonic identities among whites and non-whites alike. Such identity production is a crucial step in the development of an anti-racist counter-future that refuses to allow whiteness to continue its role as an oppressive hidden norm (Fiske 1993, 1994; Mcintosh 1995; Sleeter 1993; Tanaka 1996).

As the erased norm, whiteness and the white power bloc hold the peculiar privilege of constituting both the dominant culture and a nonculture. Within this contradiction resides the basis of white power: whiteness can be deployed differently depending on the contextual dynamics it encounters. Students of whiteness can zealously chronicle the workings of whiteness, though not in some complete way, because it is always developing new methods of asserting itself. Our concern here is not to explore white power as it pertains to the Aryan Nation or white militias, although these are very disturbing expressions of white power and merit detailed treatment. Our purpose here is to focus more on a mainstream, homespun, "good taste" white power that tacitly shapes everyday life—the white power bloc is nothing if not socially acceptable. Dean MacCannell (1992) provides insight into how the white power bloc shapes the way the social world operates. He describes an article in the real estate section of the *Los Angeles Times* about the Cahuilla Indians and their ownership of land around Palm Springs. The piece (by D. Campbell) describes how the tribe leases land on the reservation to white investors to build condominiums and resorts. The article speaks of the "crazy quilt" legal complexity of the division of land ownership, characterizing it as "half Indian controlled, half free."

The discursive use of "free" emerges unfiltered from the white unconsciousness—an unintentional rhetorical device to erase white ownership in particular and the white power bloc in general. In the newspaper article, the Cahuilla are variously described as falling into the "catbird seat," "forty rag-tail Indians," irresponsible in their handling of money, "living in complete isolation from any large group of civilized humans," and "primitive." Such discursive positioning of the Cahuilla puts them in an unusual position as landowners. According to Campbell: (1) even though they live in a money economy that values profit making, the Cahuilla don't deserve to make a profit from their land; (2) maybe white renters should not honor their debts to the Indians because their fiscal irresponsibility is so pronounced that they probably wouldn't know what to do with the cash once they procured it. The power of whiteness permeates this article given that the Cahuilla are positioned as the primitive, irrational "other." Without referring overtly to whiteness, the author makes it clear that whiteness is the powerful norm from which judgments about the Indians' unwarranted financial position can be issued. Speaking from the mountaintop of civilization, the author deploys his or her whiteness as a means of declaring the Indians uncivilized. Readers can discern traces of the white-supremacist power bloc's white rationale that justify unequal treatment of those who fall too far from the Enlightenment tree of rationality.

Thus, any analysis of white power should recognize the privileged social position whites occupy. As the advertisement for the luxury cruise line teases its privileged potential customers with the notion that "the rules are different here," we gain insight into the fact that the rules are different for whites, whether they are dealing with irresponsible Indian landlords or attempting to secure a home loan from the bank. White power exists; it may be at times rhetorically or discursively masked, but it is still quite apparent to anyone who cares to look. Whites—and white males in particular—control Western finances, information, corporate boards, unions, police departments, and officer ranks in the military. White males make up the majority of doctors and lawyers and occupy most political offices. There's nothing too complex about these data—the white power bloc rules. Yet, despite this obvious reality, whiteness maintains the ability to erase itself, even at times portraying itself as a position of victimization by a politically correct cadre of multiculturalist zealots. As the dominant culture, whiteness is capable of sophisticated measures of self-justification that work best when social inequities within the power of various groups are hidden from view—inequities from which whites profit unjustly (Jordan 1995; Fiske 1994; Nakayama and Krizek 1995; Merelman 1995).

The white power bloc develops a bag of tricks to mask its social location, making use of disguises, euphemisms, silences, and avoidances. Knowing this, it makes more sense when whiteness uses concepts such as equal opportunity, assuming that the term in no way challenges white supremacy. In this situation whites can speak publicly (in racially mixed groups) about their belief in granting everyone a fair chance at success, but understanding all the while at a tacit level that such assertions are "just talk." In reality they know that whites will always be better qualified—or at least appear better qualified and more comfortable to work with than non-whites. This tacit dynamic of whiteness works because whites continue to hang on to negative stereotypes about non-whites. A majority of whites believe that African Americans, for example, are more violent, less intelligent, and not as hard working as whites. In this articulation of white power the reason for white racism toward non-whites is the behavior of non-whites themselves. Of course, African Americans take special blame for such white perspectives, as the horror after all is Africa. In this context whiteness not only fears Africanism but is particularly terrified by the Africanism within itself. Modernist whiteness, buoyed by its white reason, is afraid of Africa's signification of the instinctual, the libidinal, the primitive (Rubin 1994; Merelman 1995; Gresson 1995).

Patriarchy—The Patriarchal Power Bloc

The diversity and multicultural focus on patriarchy and the patriarchal power bloc is important because it asserts that gender inequality is a pervasive feature of contemporary society. To invoke patriarchy is to problematize the social construction of gender and gender relations in a way that moves us to consider what constitutes a just and democratic academic curriculum, politics, and social consciousness. Any critical multiculturalist approach to patriarchy must draw upon a critical postmodern feminist theory for academic sustenance. Critical postmodern feminism posits that humans are social constructions—not entities determined by innate, biological, universal characteristics. Such a position should not be taken to mean that biology plays no role in the production of humans or that we can change who and what we are simply by wishing it so. The theoretical position *does* imply that the potential of humans is far more open-ended than traditionally believed and that we should not blame our dispositions merely on biological or psychological determinism.

Although a critical multicultural analysis of patriarchy relies on critical postmodern feminism, it is very careful (especially when theorists happen to be men) to consider the political dynamics of using feminism as it does. Too often men's engagement with feminism can be perceived to be or actually be an appropriation of such scholarship and political work for purposes not consonant with the feminist project. For example, patriarchal theorizing can serve to return the focus of scholarly attention to men in the process of helping to recover the authority of the patriarchal power bloc. Given this possibility any attempt to analyze patriarchy must carefully examine the danger of appropriation. Any critical multicultural attempt to redefine masculinity without a humble nod to feminist theory and the help of women in general collapses into traditional patriarchy's male bonding rituals—activities that always involve exclusion of women. The form of patriarchal analysis and political practice delineated here takes place in the presence of and with the collaboration of women (Fox 1988; McLean 1996a; Gore 1993).

In the spirit of this nod to feminist theory, a critical multicultural analysis of patriarchy and the patriarchal power bloc is informed by postmodern feminism's politics of difference that actually works to subvert traditional notions of gender difference in patriarchal societies. Such a traditional notion of difference divides individuals neatly into males and females and unequally distributes power to men. A critical analysis of patriarchy emulates postmodern feminism's efforts to subvert this system and to end the exploitation of both women and traditional patriarchy's disowned sons—gay men and non-white men. A critical multicultural analysis of patriarchy begins to rethink notions of gender, subjectivity, and sexuality, setting the stage for a reinvention of masculinity. Operating in this manner, theorists have come to realize that the essentialization of male and female difference precludes the recognition that men who reject dominant notions of patriarchal masculinity and who struggle against race, class, and gender domination, are ideologically closer to feminists than are women who unquestionably accept traditional notions of gender difference.

Such understandings hold dramatic implications. Indeed, a critical analysis of patriarchy demands nothing less than a questioning of comfortable assumptions about everything from

male/female differences to the gender inscriptions of social institutions and the power relations that sustain them. For example, our theory of patriarchy understands the ways that
the Western intellectual tradition has developed in the soil of the patriarchal power bloc. Such a
realization doesn't mean that we simply dismiss the entire Western canon, but it does induce
us to examine and develop alternatives to the epistemological assumptions that ground the
tradition. A key function of our multicultural work—the function that earns it the label "critical"—involves analysis of the ways that power shapes knowledge forms, the definition of
truth, and the rules of academic and other cultural discourses. It is easy to trace the ways our
three power blocs intersect in this knowledge/truth production process. Western democratic
societies find this power dynamic hard to fathom, bathed as they are in a liberal ideology of
equal opportunity, a just world, and egalitarian social relations. Understanding this social tendency, a critical diversity/multicultural analysis of patriarchy works hard to demonstrate the
ways society is structured by collective power differences that are constructed along lines of
race, class, gender, ethnicity, and sexual preference. If the construction of masculinity and the
oppression of women are to be understood, such a process will take place only in the context
provided by an analysis of structured power relations (Ebert 1991; Clough 1994; Gore 1993;
Hedley 1994; McLean 1996a; Walby 1990; McLean, Carey, and White 1996).

Gender in our critical conceptualization is a structural system of power and domination,
and masculine identity is a socially constructed agent of this power. The social construction of
patriarchy helps shape men's self-interest that, in turn, structures their dominant relationship
to women. Unlike more liberal gender perspectives that position male–female relations and
gender identities as contained within individuals, a critical analysis of patriarchy sees notions of
masculinity implanted throughout powerful social institutions, including education, the welfare
establishment, the police, the military, the legal system, the media, etc. Indeed, corporations,
colleges, and sports organizations are shaped by the patriarchal power bloc's values of Social
Darwinism and success for those who conform. The liberal notion of individualism champions the problematic belief that "personal problems" such as spousal abuse, violence, and
misogynistic attitudes can be solved by appeal to individuals. Our critical multicultural analysis
of patriarchy contends that such problems demand both personal and social solutions. Men's
oppressive relationship with women cannot be understood until we expose the ways various
social institutions attempt to socialize men and women and shape their gender identities in a
manner saturated by patriarchy (McLean 1996b).

Any emancipatory transformation in the attitudes and behaviors of men will take place
only in a situation where these social institutions are challenged. Male employees who confront the implicit patriarchal values of the corporation may lose their jobs, and male students
who confront the tacit androcentric knowledge of the academy may fail—these are the stark
prospects that face those who would challenge the power bloc. Critical scholars of patriarchal
power must gain insight into the ideologies and discourses that constitute ever-changing articulations of patriarchy and the ever-shifting nature of the patriarchal power bloc. By ideology
we do *not* mean a misrepresentation of what is "real" in society. Rather, we use the term in a
postmodernist sense to define a process involving the maintenance of unequal power relations
by mobilizing meaning in a way that benefits the dominant group, the patriarchal power bloc.
Thus, a patriarchal ideology in this articulation involves a tacit process of meaning-making and
mobilization of affect that induces women to accept a passive view of their femininity and

men to embrace unproblematically their gender privilege. All of this takes place in ever-changing ways and in a variety of social venues in a manner that camouflages gender antagonisms and conflict. Patriarchal forms of discursive power work through what are often perceived as neutral conduits of language to produce a set of tacit rules that regulate, in the context of gender, what can and cannot be said, who speaks with the blessing of authority and who must listen, and whose social constructions are scientifically valid and whose are unlearned and unimportant. Discursive analysis disputes the traditional assumption that individuals possess stable properties such as attitudes and beliefs. In our patriarchal context, language is viewed as a sociopolitical arena where gender identity is continuously renegotiated.

Understanding how patriarchal power works allows us to gain insight into methods of interrupting oppressive patriarchal practices. It prepares us to understand the pain that many heterosexual white men claimed to experience in the late 1990s without ignoring men's privilege and dominant gender position. These theoretical assertions understand that both masculinity and the patriarchal power bloc are ever mutating as they react to challenges from feminists, gay rights advocates, and other individuals and groups. In the same way, this critical multicultural understanding of patriarchy views masculinity as possessing multiple and ambiguous meanings and different expressions in different contexts. Indeed, masculinity is not the same for all men, and, as a result, our analysis of patriarchy refuses to essentialize or universalize the concept. Operating without the crutch of a universalized masculinity, our patriarchal analysis induces teachers to study the conflicting stories a culture tells itself about men and the ideological and discursive dynamics that help construct and frame these narratives. As we examine these stories the question we seek to induce various individuals to ask is: What is masculinity (Hedley 1994; McLean 1996a)?

In many ways asking such a question represents a potential radical act. Naturalized assumptions are opened to analysis and negotiation in an unprecedented manner, and the historical existence of "other masculinities" confronts those who would repress awareness of their reality. In the men's movements that have emerged in the last decade or so the question, "What is masculinity?" has often been answered with a set of assumptions very different from those embraced by the critical patriarchal theory. Men's movement leaders have often sought a "true masculinity." But a more critical and emancipatory search might involve an analysis of the effects of men's narratives and beliefs about masculinity on both themselves and women; or, in this same spirit, does the adoption of an alternative nontraditional masculinity result in the forfeit of patriarchal privilege? Can a critical theory and pedagogy of patriarchy help men who seek alternative masculinities understand gender power dynamics in a way that induces them to resist complicity with a power bloc noted for oppression of women and gay males and that allows them to reconceptualize patriarchy in a different but still hegemonic manner? In this situation, such men must seek the help and support of women, gay men, and non-white men and their insights for dealing with asymmetrical power relations.

In an educational context, how does a critical multicultural analysis of patriarchy help us teach boys to step away from dominant masculinity and the power bloc that supports it? Educational institutions in this culture unfortunately have rarely considered such a question; in fact, they have traditionally taught boys to embrace a patriarchal masculinity. The patriarchal nature of mainstream education—taught by both male and female teachers as surrogates for absent patriarchs—reproduces unequal gender relations. Such an education teaches young men to join in the power struggle that surrounds dominant notions of masculinity and the sacrifice of humanness that accompanies it. Educational institutions that "make men out of boys" often brutalize young men, use homophobia to induce them to conform to an insensitive masculinity, de-emotionalize them, and train them to physically and emotionally abuse one another. Those young men who do not internalize these messages and gain significant validation for mastery of the masculinity curriculum must live in the shadow of self-doubt and male inadequacy the rest of their lives. Our critical multicultural analysis of patriarchy and the ever-shifting patriarchal power bloc can help teachers make sense of and intervene in these oppressive pedagogical practices.

The Study of Privilege in Diversity and Multicultural Education

These brief comments were designed to propose to multicultural educators the need for studying power and privilege within a critical multicultural curriculum. Such analysis changes our orientation to multicultural education so that we study not only the effects of oppression on the oppressed, but its impact on the privileged as well. Such a curricular addition is not meant to imply that we abandon the inclusion of the cultural productions of non-whites, women, and the poor—not at all. It does mean that we see all human beings as shaped by race, class, and gender inscriptions of power. Indeed, part of what we would define as a characteristic of a critically educated person is consciousness of the way the power dynamics of race, class, gender, and other social dynamics operate to produce an individual's identity and consciousness. In this context, therefore, multicultural education becomes much more than a detour through diversity and a mere acquaintance with cultures and experiences other than one's own.

Note

Parts of this chapter appeared in Steinberg, S. *Multi/intercultural Conversations: A Reader.* New York: Peter Lang, 2001.

References

Amott, T. 1993. *Caught in the crisis: Women and the U.S. economy today.* New York: Monthly Review Press.

Amott, T., and J. Matthaei. 1991. *Race, gender, and work: A multicultural economic history of women in the U.S.* Boston: South End Press.

Aronowitz, S., and W. DiFazio. 1994. *The jobless future: Sci-tech and the dogma of work.* Minneapolis: University of Minnesota Press.

Bizzell, P. 1991. Power, authority, and critical pedagogy. *Journal of Basic Writing* 10 (2):54–70.

Block, F. 1990. *Postindustrial possibilities: A critique of economic discourse.* Berkeley: University of California Press.

Clough, P. 1994. The hybrid criticism of patriarchy: Rereading Kate Millett's sexual politics. *The Sociological Quarterly* 35 (3):473–86.

Collins, G., and R. Sandell. 1992. The politics of multicultural art education. *Art Education* 45 (6):8–13.

Cooper, D. 1994. Productive, relational, and everywhere? Conceptualizing power and resistance within Foucauldian feminism. *Sociology* 28 (2):435–54.

Ebert, T. 1991. The difference of postmodern feminism. *College English* 58 (8):886–904.

Falk, W., and T. Lyson. 1988. *High tech, low tech, no tech: Recent industrial and occupational change in the South.* Albany, NY: SUNY Press.

Fiske, J. 1993. *Power plays, power works.* New York: Verso.

Fiske, J. 1994. *Media matters: Everyday culture and political change.* Minneapolis: University of Minnesota Press.

Fox, B. 1988. Conceptualizing patriarchy. *Canadian Review of Sociology and Anthropology* 25 (2):163–82.

Frankenberg, R. 1993. *The social construction of whiteness: White women, race matters.* Minneapolis: University of Minnesota Press.

Gilligan, C. 1981. *In a different voice: Psychological theory and women's development.* Cambridge, MA: Harvard University Press.

Gore, J. 1993. *The struggle for pedagogies: Critical and feminist discourses as regimes of truth.* New York: Routledge.

Gresson, A. 1995. *The recovery of race in America.* Minneapolis: University of Minnesota Press.

Grossberg, L. 1992. *We gotta get out of this place.* New York: Routledge.

Haymes, S. 1996. Race, repression, and the politics of crime and punishment in *the bell curve.* In *Measured lies: The bell curve examined,* ed. J. Kincheloe, S. Steinberg, and A. Gresson. New York: St. Martin's Press.

Hedley, M. 1994. The presentation of gendered conflict in popular movies: Affective stereotypes, cultural sentiments, and men's motivation. *Sex Roles* 31 (11/12):721–40.

Herrnstein, R., and C. Murray. 1994. *The bell curve: Intelligence and class structure in American life.* New York: The Free Press.

House, E., and C. Haug. 1995. Riding *The bell curve:* A review. *Educational Evaluation and Policy Analysis* 17 (2):263–72.

Jennings, J. 1992. Blacks, politics, and the human service crisis. In *Race, politics, and economic development: Community perspectives,* ed. J. Jennings. New York: Verso.

Jordan, J. 1995. In the land of white supremacy. In *Eyes right: Challenging the right wing backlash,* ed. C. Berlet. Boston: South End Press.

Keat, R. 1994. Scepticism, authority, and the market. In *The authority of the consumer,* ed. R. Keat, N. Whiteley, and N. Abercrombie. New York: Routledge.

Kellner, D. 1989. *Critical theory, Marxism, and modernity.* Baltimore: Johns Hopkins University Press.

Kincheloe, J. 2008. *Critical pedagogy primer.* New York: Peter Lang.

Kincheloe, J., and S. Steinberg. 1997. *Changing multiculturalism: New times, New curriculum.* London: Open University Press.

Kincheloe, J., S. Steinberg, N. Rodriguez, and R. Chennault. eds. 1998. *White reign: Deploying whiteness in America.* New York: St. Martin's Press.

Lincoln, Y. 1996. For whom the bell tolls: A cognitive or educated elite? In *Measured lies: The bell curve examined,* ed. J. Kincheloe, S. Steinberg, and A. Gresson. New York: St. Martin's Press.

MacCannell, D. 1992. *Empty meeting grounds.* New York: Routledge.

Macedo, D. 2006. *Literacies of power: What Americans are not allowed to know.* Boulder, CO: Westview.

McCarthy, C., and M. Apple. 1988. Race, class, and gender in American educational research: Toward a nonsynchronous parallelist position. In *Class, race, and gender in American education,* ed. L. Weis. Albany, NY: SUNY Press.

McCarthy, T. 1992. The critique of impure reason: Foucault and the Frankfurt School. In *Rethinking power,* ed. T. Wartenburg. Albany, NY: SUNY Press.

Mcintosh, P. 1995. White privilege and male privilege: A personal account of coming to see correspondences through work in women's studies. In *Race, class, gender: An anthology,* ed. M. Anderson and P. Collins. Belmont, CA: Wadsworth.

McLean, C. 1996a. The politics of men's pain. In *Men's way of being,* ed. C. McLean, M. Carey, and C. White. Boulder, CO: Westview.

McLean, C. 1996b. Boys and education in Australia. In *Men's way of being,* ed. C. McLean, M. Carey, and C. White. Boulder, CO: Westview.

McLean, C., M. Carey, and C. White. 1996. Introduction. In *Men's ways of being,* ed. C. McLean, M. Carey, and C. White. Boulder, CO: Westview.

Merelman, R. 1995. *Representing black culture: Racial conflict and cultural politics in the United States.* New York: Routledge.

Morrison, T. 1993. *Playing in the dark: Whiteness and the literary imagination.* New York: Vintage.

Musolf, R. 1992. Structure, institutions, power, and ideology: New directions within symbolic interactionism. *The Sociological Quarterly* 33 (2):171–89.

Nakayama, T, and R. Krizek. 1995. Whiteness: A strategic rhetoric. *Quarterly Journal of Speech* 81:291–309.

Rorty, A. 1992. Power and powers: A dialogue between buff and rebuff. In *Rethinking power,* ed. T. Wartenburg. Albany, NY: SUNY Press.

Rubin, L. 1994. *Families on the faultline: America's working class speaks about the family, the economy, race, and ethnicity.* New York: HarperCollins.

Rumberger, R. 1984. The growing imbalance between education and work. *Phi Delta Kappan* 65 (5):342–46.

Sleeter, C. 1993. How white teachers construct race. In *Race, identity, and reproduction in education,* ed. C. McCarthy and W. Crichlow. New York: Routledge.

Stack, C. 1994. Different voices, different visions: Gender, culture, and moral reasoning. In *Women of color in U.S. society*, ed. M. Zinn and B. Dill. Philadelphia: Temple University Press.

Steinberg, S. 2001. *Multi/intercultural conversations: A Reader.* New York: Peter Lang.

Stowe, D. 1996. Uncolored people: The rise of whiteness studies. *Lingua Franca* 6 (6):68–77.

Tanaka, G. 1996. Dysgenesis and white culture. In *Measured lies: The bell curve examined*, ed. J. Kincheloe, S. Steinberg, and A. Gresson. New York: St. Martin's Press.

Vidal, M. 1996. Genetic rationalizations and public policy: Herrnstein and Murray on intelligence and welfare dependency. In *Measured lies: The bell curve examined*, ed. J. Kincheloe, S. Steinberg, and A. Gresson. New York: St. Martin's Press.

Walby, S. 1990. *Theorizing patriarchy.* Oxford: Blackwell.

West, C. 1992. Nihilism in black America. In *Black popular culture*, ed. G. Dent. Seattle: Bay Press.

Young, I. 1992. Five faces of oppression. In *Rethinking power*, ed. T. Wartenberg. Albany, New York: SUNY Press.

Zinn, M. 1994. Feminist rethinking from racial-ethnic families. In *Women of color in U.S. society*, ed. M. Zinn and B. Dill. Philadelphia: Temple University Press.

Zinn, M., and B. Dill. 1994. Difference and domination. In *Women of color in U.S. society*, ed. M. Zinn and B. Dill. Philadelphia: Temple University Press.

Two

"Doing Diversity" with Film

Brian C. Johnson

For the greater part of four decades, educational researchers have documented the value of addressing diversity issues in the classroom. Their findings indicate that students are much better prepared to be global citizens in a multicultural society when they have been taught to think critically about issues of difference. Educational excellence is born of a search for knowledge, but that knowledge should be tempered by wisdom, which can be defined as knowledge rightly applied. When based on an understanding of the complexity of the issues of life, academic success can be marked by the ability to acknowledge and comprehend multiple perspectives and solutions. Helping students to ponder differing worldviews is crucial in preparing them for productive and reflective lives of leadership, achievement, and service to others.

Despite the heralded benefits of attending to diversity concepts (which affect both teaching and learning), "diversity" has become little more than a buzzword; few institutions have not claimed to be addressing "it." Unfortunately for our students, both the teaching faculty and administrators have approached diversity as a problem that needs to be solved rather than an opportunity to significantly benefit student engagement and learning outcomes. In educational circles, diversity is perceived from a deficits base—most teacher-preparation programs use the "at-risk" language when teaching pre-service students about "different" students. While many newer textbooks have sections that provide students with diversity connections, the section on diversity is almost certainly not the focus of the curriculum and thus, it is more often skipped than utilized. If a goal of education is to produce citizens who are global thinkers, how much longer can eliminating this element from the curriculum be acceptable? At the end of the first year of teaching, most new teachers complain that their preparation for understanding the critical issues of diversity (identity, culture, power) has left them under-skilled and unprepared for "real world" teaching. This is especially important to note because new teachers often find themselves in "at-risk" schools and classrooms.

In some ways, the difficulty of "doing" diversity is semantic; there is a diversity of opinion about how diversity is defined. The Council for the Advancement of Standards has identi-fied eight dimensions of diversity that ought to be addressed: race, ethnicity, religion, gender, sexual orientation, national origin, socioeconomic class, and ability. These dimensions are in-dividually unique and nuanced but are also interconnected and complex. Both teachers and learners come to understand their world through the lens of these identity constructs. In a classroom of twenty students and one teacher, there is a likelihood of twenty-one differing worldviews colliding with one another; this conflict need not be negative—if harnessed, it can actually improve the learning of all participants.

To be knowledgeable and wise, students will need a truly multicultural education, one that teaches them to be self-aware of beliefs, biases, and values; to be aware of the different cul-tural perspectives around them; to have factual knowledge about others (rather than generali-zations); and to have the competency and skills to tailor their behavior to fit and accommodate differing experiences and vantage points. This competency enables students to be prepared to interact and navigate the changing demographic tide in our world.

K-12 schooling in America has been in need of significant reform for many years, es-pecially in the area of teaching about diversity and multiculturalism. We have minimized the effects of colonialization, especially the violence towards, oppression of, and expulsion of hundreds of thousands of people of racial minority. The colonizers and settlers are heralded as heroes, while targeted group members are vilified. The traditions, customs, religious prac-tices, values, and mores of the targeted groups are often made invisible in deference to the values and beliefs, and traditions of the predominant group. The missing pieces have negative societal and personal effects; the predominant group appears more valuable, and the targeted groups face discriminatory behaviors.

Our textbooks are virtually devoid of the horrors of American history. We recognize, for instance, that telling the story of the American slave trade is necessary, but the version we teach is whitewashed for the collective benefit of the dominant society (perhaps to assuage the blood-guilt). Black American history, as currently revealed in our textbooks, went something like this: blacks "magically" appeared in chains; Abraham Lincoln signed the Emancipation Proclamation; Martin Luther King proclaimed "I Have a Dream." A 400-year history summed up in fewer than twenty-five words. Depending upon the text, there may be a mention of Frederick Douglass as a former slave and abolitionist and a brief mention of Rosa Parks' re-fusal to give up her seat on the bus. Largely, however, the systemic abuses by white colonizers are left out of the discourse. There are fewer lessons on the legalities of racial prejudice and the denial of the human rights supposedly afforded to all in the founding documents. There is even less information revealed about the significance (and regularity) of slave resistance and revolution. What has resulted is an inaccurate historical image of a "happy savage" who is satisfied with forced servitude, and an "average citizen" who has earned a superior status through meritocracy and birth. Dominance and oppression have become, then, a major fac-tor in American culture and society, and from a racial perspective, whiteness has taken on a superior position. The belief in inherent black criminality, the over-representation of blacks in special education, and the racial disparity in economics, wealth, and poverty all have roots in white dominance. (Additional examples can be found in the experiences of the Japanese internment, the Chinese Exclusion Act, and the extermination and removal of indigenous populations from the homelands to reservations.)

Current conversations about diversity consist of arguments about identity politics, and while these subjects are important, to truly understand *difference*, we must explore these matters from a systemic perspective. To effectively teach about issues of difference, teachers need to be willing, then, to examine the structural and societal implications in addition to the personal dimensions of race, gender, ethnicity, nationality, language, ability, sexual orientation, religion, as well as the intersections of the above concepts. Remember, for there to be a minority, there must be a majority, and significant time must be spent understanding and deconstructing predominance to better explain the minority experience. The goal of this type of systemic study is to encourage students to become actively engaged in social justice—acting on the behalf of the rights of the oppressed. Finding the "right" method of educating contemporary students who, for the most part, are disconnected from the truth of history is difficult work. Teaching diversity concepts through mainstream American film provides teachers with a medium and instructional strategy for connecting with the technologically advanced and visually stimulated students of today.

Why Use Film?

Each person's individual identity is shaped by a number of different forces, including, but not limited to, parents and other family members, peer groups, social and religious organizations/leaders, educational providers and institutions, communities, and media messages. These forces, in many ways, dictate particular meanings and interpretations of the world around us. In your life, what have these forces taught you about who you are, and what have they said about people who are not like you?

Many times, these messages are not communicated verbally; they are often embedded in traditions, behaviors, activities, and the like. Of the above list of cultural shapers, few send more powerful messages (subtle and overt) than the *Hollywood machine*. The movie industry spends billions of dollars to produce films for all ages, and reaps billions in return from a public that is thirsty for the next big hit. Our national economy, in many ways, is supported by this industry, and in like manner, our cultural identities are influenced by Hollywood images.

Due to the relatively easy access to movies, the medium has become the visual aesthetic that students today continue to admire. Students watch movies on VHS (though this medium is quickly dying), DVD, the internet, on cellular telephones, and in handheld formats. This medium quenches the students' increasing needs for visual stimuli and can be used as a productive and efficient tool for teaching, despite the common misconception that students want to watch movies because they do not want to read.

Most people do not think about how movies shape our beliefs and worldview. Specifically, our individual cultural identities are continually shaped, changed, and sometimes distorted by what is seen in movies. Giroux adds that "films appear to inspire at least as much cultural authority and legitimacy for teaching specific roles, values, and ideals as do the more traditional sites of learning such as the public schools, religious institutions, and the family." (Giroux, 1997, p. 53).

Generally speaking, movies have a knack for creating, maintaining, and inverting social issues in America, and the consequences are often played out in the classroom. The line between entertainment and educational message is often blurred, and students use the "knowledge" gained from the movies as fact, thus creating difficulties and controversies. Students often take at face value those films that are "based on a true story," without critically evaluating the liberties that studios take with stories for dramatic effect. Teachers can use movies to begin productive conversations about diversity issues. Teachers, however, often feel ill-equipped to teach diversity issues, as they are either uncomfortable, fear being offensive or stereotypical, or are just plain unknowledgeable. Moreover, teacher education programs rarely prepare students to actually teach and explore diversity issues.

Jowett and Linton (1980) argue that movies create a type of "visual public consensus" (p. 75). They speak to the power of film to bypass traditional methods of teaching (family, church, school) and establish immediate relational contact with the watcher. In what ways do the studios, directors, actors, and the action of the films determine and reflect our national opinion, our personal values, and how do they enforce cultural ideals? Media literacy explores the ways in which our individual and societal psyches are impacted by cinematic expression. What determinations can we make about race, ethnicity, gender, and sexual orientation as they are defined by Hollywood standards?

Limitations of Teaching with Film

Although movies are a great place to start a diversity dialogue, they do have limitations. First, students are often not equipped to view movies critically, as this medium is usually a subject of entertainment, not education. Before educators can begin teaching students through the use of film, they must introduce students to the concept of critically analyzing film in order to get the most from the experience—to become media savvy and literate. Thus, this means that teachers themselves need to first learn how to view movies critically. Second, teachers often do not have time to show complete films. One of the most significant challenges to using film for instruction is the limited time available to view entire films in one setting. Secondary teachers, especially, face shorter time frames which makes viewing films an arduous task, so it is up to them to find the best parts of movies to maximize both their time and their objectives for their lessons. Furthermore, teachers must believe in the legitimacy of film as a cultural educational medium. In addition, they should understand how the film medium is appealing to students.

Students have not been trained in the skills of media literacy either. Media-literate students must recognize two essential foundations: all film is political in that it has a message, and there are no *mistakes* in films. The editorial process is such that multiple people must approve the film's content before it is released to the general public—this includes those *ad libbed* moments. In addition to critiquing the entertainment value of a film, students must be challenged to meaningfully discuss the film's values, historical significance, or the qualities that make it worthy of consideration. The study of film becomes a vehicle to sharpen critical thinking skills and develop an understanding of historical, socio-cultural, and personal contexts and their influence. For an in-depth discussion on the techniques of media literacy, visit the website of the Center for Media Literacy (http://www.medialit.org). Two electronic resources are available for download:

- *Literacy for the 21st Century: An Overview and Orientation to Media Literacy Education (2005)*
- *Five Key Questions That Can Change the World: Classroom Activities for Media Literacy Education (2005)*

Mainstream films, then, can be seen as a "reflector" of our national opinion, and because we live in a culture of instant gratification, film producers must offer easily reproducible, formulaic content. The studios are often at the mercy of a public that is satisfied with familiar themes, clearly identifiable characters, and expected conclusions. Film audiences seem to prefer what is repackaged, old, familiar, and comfortable. If the film strays too far from convention, the audiences generally boycott and don't show up to see the film. (We must remember, after all, that movies are made to make money.) For an example of the formulaic conventions, take films like *Dangerous Minds, Freedom Writers,* and *The Blackboard Jungle.*

Here's the equation: Take one urban high school, add a bunch of rowdy, undisciplined, poor, drug dealing, violent, functionally illiterate black and Latino students, and then add an unqualified, first-time white teacher who is from a privileged background, and *voila*—an instant box office smash! Yes, there are films like *Stand and Deliver* and *Lean on Me* that feature black and Latino school leaders, but the usual discourse is still there. What meaning, then, does the non-critical viewer take from the multiplicity of films like this, most of which are "based on true stories"? The formula remains—black and Latino kids are deviance-prone animals in need of a savior (who is usually white).

This impoverished and violent racial phenomenon played out in school-centered films related to blacks and Latinos is juxtaposed against the films focused on the white experience in schools where the overwhelming pattern is affluence, private education that is centered on learning the classics, preparation for college admission, marriage, careers in government and industry, and a legacy of power passed from generation to generation. Films such as *Dead Poets' Society, The Emperor's Club, The Skulls, Mona Lisa Smile, School Ties, The Great White Hope, Finding Forrester, O,* or even trivial comedies such as *Van Wilder, Road Trip, Animal House,* and so many others, show Hollywood's belief in the academic excellence and socioeconomic prowess of whites.

Interestingly enough, there is a scene in *Dangerous Minds* where the filmmakers revealed the racialized formula. Ms. Johnson (Michelle Pfeiffer) is talking with the tough student leader Emilio (Wade Dominguez), after she "saved" him from being arrested. She seeks to understand Emilio's experience—why he is the way he is—and asks about his family background and history of violence. Emilio retorts—"So, now you're gonna try and psychologize me. You're gonna try to figure me out. Let me help you—I come from a broken home and we're poor, alright. . . I've seen the same movies you did."

Guidelines for Teaching Diversity

In an article titled "Deconstructing Whiteness as Part of a Multicultural Educational Framework: From Theory to Practice," Anna Ortiz and Robert Rhoads (2000, *Journal of College Student Development,* pp. 81–93) created a multicultural education framework that insists that those "learning" diversity become astute in understanding culture (self and others), deconstructing white culture, and developing a multicultural outlook that leads to an action orientation. Becoming a critical "reader" of movie texts is an important task in both understanding American culture and being able to educate students about diversity concepts.

We are accustomed to talking about what is above the surface, what is easily observable and measurable. That is where "typical" diversity lives. A person talks about belonging to a particular cultural group or identity but rarely is able to discuss what it means to belong to that culture. Instead, the focus will primarily be on clothing, food, and music styles; but what gets forgotten or minimized are the beliefs, values, and assumptions of a culture that motivates the manifested behavior above the surface. A beneath-the-surface cultural exploration will include an explanation of the reasons why and how a particular culture eats a particular food or dresses in a particular style. It includes the epistemology or the philosophy by which a person or group determines worldview and culture.

In addition, our traditional diversity discourse does not include the systemic nature of oppression or the inherent power dynamics that prevail. Today's student will look at our textbook images of enslaved people in chains and of groups behind the fences of internment camps, and at the archival images from the 1950s and 1960s, and suggest that "we've come so far" and "things aren't as bad as they used to be." They will argue that racism is a thing of the past because they do not see lynching on a regular basis or because Eminem is on the rap charts and Usher is singing on the pop charts, thereby ignoring the systemic and systematized ways that minority groups are often ignored, exploited, and oppressed on a daily basis.

Without critical examination, the ills of society become the "fault" of the victim. Let's use a film example: in most movies that focus on the issue of rape, the alleged perpetrator inevitably suggests that the victim was "dressed like she wanted it," was "out late at night" in a particular location, was acting seductively, or that she "led me on." What is ignored is how the notion of male dominance has created a sexist system whereby women are objectified by their sexuality and commoditized for male use and abuse. It is this same belief in male dominance that inhibits male victims of rape from coming forward.

Critical engagement with diversity and multiculturalism, then, becomes an opportunity for teachers and learners to challenge ethnocentric assumptions and the manners in which we have been shaped by educational institutions, religious traditions, community leaders, family systems, and yes, the mass media. We ardently support the notion that creating a multicultural outlook is an important component of a "getting a good education," as it helps to build critical thinking and decision-making skills, and it provides opportunities for intercultural and cross-cultural interactions and relationship building. Critical multiculturalism is not about being "politically correct" nor about labeling all persons who identify as majorities as enemies or bad people. In fact, we believe that critical multiculturalism must welcome the vantage points of all members of the classroom community, while continuing to seek to ensure that minority groups have the equitable opportunity to be full-fledged members of the learning community. This type of education encourages teachers and learners to move beyond a mere "celebration of diversity" toward a better understanding of difference, particularly those differences that work to reproduce inequalities in the United States and their local communities and school settings. Since most of us have had our lives shaped by/among homogenous groups, we have consequently grown up with biases we have never learned to question. This chapter is about learning to question our cultural shaping by examining contemporary mainstream films.

Film literacy and multicultural literacy become, then, opportunities for students to engage important cultural subjects. Exploring these cultural ideals frees educators and students to ask questions about how films are created, their representations, their makers, and how we make meaning individually and as a collective audience. Both literacies require examination of the credentials and biases of the directors and writers and actors, the verisimilitude of the voices and action, and the apparent assumptions that are being made by the creators *about* the audiences as movie watching is an interactive and circular exchange between the studios and the audience.

Dealing with Diversity Tensions

When hot moments and conflicts inevitably arise, teachers should directly confront the issue or offensive remark. They must think rationally, remain neutral, and find teaching opportunities in the occurrence. If a teacher cannot find a workable position in the conflict, she or he recognizes it but puts it to the side for later processing. The deferment allows both the facilitator and the participants to calm down and plan strategies to effectively confront the topic. Before the end of the session, the group should return to the moment and deal with it, exploring the differing viewpoints surrounding it. No hot moment is ignored or not discussed.

It is important very early in a diversity course to develop an atmosphere of trust and sensitivity, not the faux sensitivity of political correctness, but the ability to speak freely among colleagues. (This freedom does come with responsibilities.) These types of courses can be highly emotional, can produce anxiety and fear, and can be frustrating for learner and teacher. Setting the tone for amicable dispute and discussion is important. Students need to be invited to be able to ask critical and challenging questions of one another. This cannot happen in a classroom of strangers. Considerable effort must be taken in the first several classes to lessen the strangeness between the individuals in the class. The more you break down the barriers and fears of multicultural engagement, the greater your ability to get into the "nitty-gritty" of the material.

It is also important to point out that deep discussions around diversity issues are best dealt with when students have relationships with one another. This is an important ingredient that allows for foibles and mistakes without major explosions. There are several assumptions that must be made if you are going to deal with these issues in your classroom:

- Many people internalize anger, fear, contempt, and guilt about both their ignorance of certain terminologies and how they express them in unhealthy and unproductive ways in school and the workplace.
- Blatant and subtle forms of racism, sexism, and other "isms" exist in daily interactions, media portrayals, and cultural institutions.
- Diversity engagement addresses these emotions and behaviors by providing a place for them to be expressed, confronted, corrected if necessary, and overcome.

Teachers must be aware that we must engage dialogue with the understanding that the process of dialogue itself can reproduce inequality unless participants recognize that we come to the table with unequal relations of power and privilege. Creating opportunities to discuss these assumptions requires teachers and students to learn how to honestly communicate with each other.

Breaking the Communication Barrier

One of the most important steps to take in diversity education is to ensure that all participants in the dialogue share a common lexicon or language about diversity. Teachers who wish to explore deeper levels of diversity dialogue have a responsibility for increasing access to that dialogue. Many times, students do not have the lexicon to participate freely; fear of "saying the wrong thing" is often very significant, especially for majority students. This reticence is a major deterrent to speaking about difference. In his book, *Frames of Mind*, Howard Gardner suggests, "[T]hose with keen understanding of their strengths and needs are in much better position than those with limited or faulty self-knowledge."

Diversity educators often talk about the necessity of cross-cultural competencies or having cultural awareness (of self and others), factual knowledge about the cultural traditions and mores of others, and the behavioral skills necessary to navigate cross-cultural situations. In their book, *Multicultural Competence in Student Affairs*, Pope and Mueller (2004) have identified the ability to communicate across lines of difference as paramount to achieving competence. What traditional foci on differences have created are chasms that are difficult to cross. Students need to be able to have significant conversations about relationships, ethnicity, activism, and outlooks on life.

Students fail to move into deeper engagement with the issues mainly because of a lack of preparedness for such conversations. Majority students, in particular, have difficulty approaching the topics because they have been left out of the dialogue for so long. Diversity has been a predominantly minority-based discourse, and majorities feel like they are encroaching on a territory that is not their own. What we have, then, is an opportunity to demonstrate that to have a minority means to have a majority—opening the access to a dominance discourse that is so necessary in truly engaging the issues of difference. Engaging with diversity and inclusion often means focusing on the "minority," with little to no attention paid to the predominant group and the opportunities they have to create change. Individual majority persons (heterosexuals, Christians, Americans, males, whites, etc.) are typically marked as enemies and bad people (often unwarranted), and are rarely invited to the multicultural table. Most students (majority and minority) do not possess the lexicon to contribute to the discussion in meaningful ways, and many retreat altogether, citing "I'm tired of all this diversity stuff." To understand the majority side of difference, we have to be willing to engage the minority experience. We must help students become cognizant and competent in understanding the facts of under-representation, the power of social contexts, and the systemic nature of oppression (the real enemy).

It is necessary that all students and educators "speak the same language," and all work from a common lexicon. There are numerous different opinions about the meaning of diversity, especially how different groups experience difference in society, underscoring the rationale to have common definitions that set the stage for your instruction. The definitions should focus attention on the systemic and structural treatment of difference. The Southern Poverty Law Center's *Teaching Tolerance* website offers a list of twenty-five definitions that attempt to raise awareness of difference, power, and discrimination. Visit http://www.tolerance.

a variety of scenes that highlight teaching opportunities. Each clip is based upon one of the definitions from the *Teaching Tolerance* website earlier mentioned.

Each illustration gives a brief statement on the content rating of the movie. Most of the lessons are written in a way that assumes that the movie clip will not be shown—providing necessary plot summary and describing the crucial scene concretely—but does include elapsed times so the instructor can locate the scene easily if the film is actually used (highly recommended).

These clips are designed to complement your instruction about the issues of difference. Teaching diversity concepts is often controversial, and, as stated earlier, students do not often possess the cross-cultural awareness, knowledge, and skills to be successful in these types of discussions. To effectively harness the power of these visual images, the teacher must prepare the students for what they might see and what they should be on the lookout for. This preparation should include providing information that is necessary for comprehension, including ensuring that students understand key terminology. Providing students with an overall context of the film is important, as is helping them to understand how a particular clip fits into the film's action and storyline.

So that the lessons are useful and useable for a variety of age groups from high school through adult learners, we have taken on the additional challenge of trying not to use scenes that contain objectionable elements, although it is difficult to find something that is not objectionable to anyone. In other words, we illustrate from PG-13 and R-rated movies but do not necessarily use PG-13 or R-rated scenes. Thus, most of the illustrations will not contain profanity or nudity because we want all learners, no matter the age, to be able to watch the clips. As the instructor, however, you must decide which clips are most suitable for your audience. You are responsible for ensuring that the content is developmentally appropriate for your students, and that you have appropriate permissions to use film in your classroom.

The Birdcage
COMPULSORY HETEROSEXUALITY/ HETEROSEXISM/ OUT-GROUP/ INVISIBILITY

In an adaptation of La Cage aux Folles, *a gay cabaret owner and his drag queen companion agree to put up a false straight front so that their son can introduce them to his fiancée's right-wing moralistic parents.*

This scene begins with a crowd of people helping to remove furniture and art from Armand's home; they are removing items that reflect a gay lifestyle. Val (Dan Futterman) questions why someone put copies of *Playboy* in the restroom; one guy says, "It's what they [heterosexuals] read." Val argues, "Don't add, just subtract." Meanwhile, Armand (Robin Williams) is trying unsuccessfully to keep Albert (Nathan Lane) from going home while the workers make the place "respectable." When Albert learns that Val and Armand "thought it would be better if you [Albert] weren't here" when the Keely family arrived, Val contends that "It's just for tonight," to which Albert responds, "I understand. Just while people are here. . .The monster, the freak is leaving. You're safe," and walks out the door. Armand follows, trying to console Albert, and offers to let him stay. Albert declines, stating, "I won't stay where I'm not wanted. Where I can be thrown out on a whim without legal rights." The scene ends when Albert faints outside a restaurant.

Elapsed time: This scene begins at 00:43:55 and ends at 00:48:20 (DVD Scene 12)

Rating: R for language.

Citation: *The Birdcage* (United Artists, 1999), screenplay written by Elaine May, directed by Mike Nichols

Falling Down
IN-GROUP

A divorced engineer for the defense industry gets stuck in Los Angeles traffic and finally snaps. He gets out of his car and begins a walk through central Los Angeles, where he encounters various levels of harassment, which he learns to deal with by acquiring weapons along the way. His actions attract the attention of a retiring cop, and he gets involved with the case, following the engineer's path toward Venice, where his daughter is having a birthday party.

Fresh from an altercation with a group of Latino gang members (where Bill managed to secure their duffle bag full of guns), Bill (Michael Douglas) is hungry and enters the local Whammy Burger, a fast-food restaurant. Bill wants to order breakfast but is told by the server, Sheila, that breakfast is no longer available as it is lunchtime. Bill again mentions that he wants breakfast and immediately asks to speak to the manager, Rick, who repeats the same. Bill scolds himself for using Rick and Sheila's first names although he does not know them—Bill states, "I don't want to be your buddy. I just want a little breakfast." Rick mentions that Whammy Burger stops serving breakfast at 11:30 a.m.; Bill looks at his watch and the time reads 11:33 a.m. Bill is particularly incensed when his claim that "the customer is always right" is refuted as not Whammy Burger policy. Again, Bill states that he does not want lunch, he wants to have breakfast. Rick apologizes, and Bill responds, "Yeah, well, hey, I'm really sorry too!" Bill reaches into the duffle bag, brandishes a machine gun, and holds the entire restaurant hostage until he is served properly. The gun accidentally fires, which shocks both the customers and Bill, who now demands to be served lunch instead of breakfast—not by Sheila, but by the manager, Rick. When he receives the food, Bill rants about the quality, stating that the food he received does not look as fresh as what is pictured on the menu. The scene ends when Bill questions if "anybody knows what's wrong with this picture."

Elapsed time: This scene begins at 00:41:01 and ends at 00:45:43 (DVD Scene 12)

Rating: R for violence and strong language

Citation: *Falling Down* (Alcor Films, 1993), written by Ebbe Roe Smith, directed by Joel Schumacher

Happy Feet
SOCIAL JUSTICE

Mumble, the young penguin, faces the ire of his entire village of emperor penguins. All of the other penguins love to sing, but not Mumble; he is a dancer. When he is kicked out of Emperor Land, Mumble sets out on a journey to prove the importance of being yourself, even in the face of opposition.

In nature, after the female penguins lay eggs, it is the male penguins who keep them warm until the eggs hatch. As this scene begins, the male penguins have gathered together as they face the cold and bitter night winds and are trying to keep their eggs warm. The leader of the village coaches them to stick together to bear the winds of the cold: "When all others leave, we remain. When the sun vanishes, we remain." He instructs them to "Heed the wisdoms, brothers! Make a huddle. Share the cold. Share the cold. Each must take his turn against the icy blast [on the outside of the circle where the harsh winds are strongest] if we are to survive the endless night."

Elapsed time: This scene begins at 00:02:40 and ends at 00:05:35 (DVD Scene 2)

Rating: G for all audiences

Citation: *Happy Feet* (Kingdom Feature Productions, 2006), written by John Collee and Warren Coleman, directed by George Miller and Warren Coleman

Harry Potter and the Chamber of Secrets
ETHNOCENTRISM / CLASSISM

It's year two at Hogwarts, and Harry Potter, Ron, and Hermione are back. Members of the school are turning up petrified and bloody writing is appearing on the walls, revealing to everyone that someone has opened the chamber of secrets. The attacks continue, forcing the possibility of the closure of Hogwarts. Harry and his friends must secretly uncover the truth about the chamber before the school closes or any lives are taken.

Harry and company are leaving the Flourish and Blotts bookshop, where they have just met and had pictures taken with famed wizard, Gilderoy Lockhart. Harry, Ron, and Ginny are stopped by their nemesis, Draco Malfoy, who is jealous of Harry's popularity: "Famous Harry Potter. Can't even go into a bookshop without making the front page." Draco's father, Lucius, steps in and tells Draco to "play nicely." Lucius mentions Harry's legendary scar and the fame of the wizard, Voldemort, who gave him the scar. Harry mentions that Voldemort murdered his parents. Lucius refers to each of the others as members of a particular class or group—speaking to Hermione, he calls her parents, "Muggles." He looks at Ron and states, "'Let me see, red hair, vacant expressions, tatty second hand book; you must be the Weasleys." In a very condescending tone, he speaks to Mr. Weasley about his low-paying job—Lucius says, "I do hope they are paying you overtime, but judging by the state of this [book], I'd say not." Lucius continues talking to Weasley, "What's the use in being a disgrace to the name of wizard if they don't even pay you well for it?" Arthur Weasley retorts, "'We have very different ideas about what disgraces the name of wizard, Malfoy." Lucius continues his rant by saying "Associating with Muggles. And I thought your family could sink no lower," and the Malfoys exit the bookstore.

Elapsed time: This scene begins at 00:19:40 and ends at 00:22:14 (DVD Scene 6)

Rating: PG for scary moments, some creature violence, and mild language

Citation: *Harry Potter and the Chamber of Secrets* (1492 Pictures, 2002), screenplay written by Steve Kloves, directed by Chris Columbus

Knocked Up
DOMINANCE

After a night of drunken passion, Alison and Ben find out that they are expecting a baby. The next nine months are a roller coaster for Ben, who has spent his entire adulthood drinking and getting high, and Alison, an up-and-coming star on E! Entertainment Network. Can they work through their differences to make a life for themselves and their baby?

Throughout the pregnancy, Ben has been a bit of a slacker. He had refused to stop drinking and partying with his buddies, and he has not been very involved in preparations for the baby. As the scene opens, Ben is frantically searching for Alison who is taking a bath. Her contractions are seven minutes apart, and she is nervous and afraid. Ben is trying to calm her fears and show that he can be responsible. He promises to take care of everything. At the hospital entrance, Ben parks in a handicapped parking space. When Alison questions the appropriateness of parking there, Ben whips out a handicapped parking decal that he stole from his friend's grandmother. Alison smiles and says, "That was really sweet of you," and Ben thanks her.

Elapsed time: This scene begins at 01:49:33 and ends at 01:54:25 (DVD Scene 17)

Rating: R for sexual content, drug use, and language

Citation: *Knocked Up* (Universal Pictures, 2007), written and directed by Judd Apatow

Maid in Manhattan
INVISIBILITY/OUT-GROUP

Marisa Ventura (Jennifer Lopez) is a single mother born and bred in the boroughs of New York City, who works as a maid in a first-class Manhattan hotel. Through a twist of fate and mistaken identity, Marisa meets Christopher Marshall (Ralph Fiennes), a handsome heir to a political dynasty, who believes that she is a guest at the hotel. Fate steps in and throws the unlikely pair together for one night. When Marisa's true identity is revealed, the two find that they are worlds apart, but the power of love prevails.

Marisa has been masquerading as a rich socialite and has captured the attention of political mogul, Chris Marshall. They have had several intimate moments, but the ruse has been found out and Marisa has been fired from the hotel. As this scene opens, Marisa is at the security checkpoint where she is surrendering her hotel identification. Lionel, her supervisor, stands next to her and begins to take off his identification as well. Marisa is incredulous as Lionel admits that he quit because, "Sometimes, we're forced in directions that we ought to have found for ourselves." Lionel continues, "To serve people takes dignity and intelligence, but remember, they're only people with money; and, although we serve them, we are not their servants. What we do, Miss Ventura, does not define who we are. What defines us is how well we rise after falling." Moments later, Chris is questioning Marisa about her duplicity. Marisa asks, "Who's kidding who here? Do you think you would have looked at me if you knew I was the maid? Come on, with respect for your big-hearted politics, I don't think so." Chris responds, "You stand on your soapbox, judging everyone, so sure they're judging you." She explains how, on the one hand, most people treat her poorly as a maid, "a stereotype they make fun of," and, "the other half of the time, I'm invisible" to her rich clients (Chris himself did not "see" her at their first introduction). Chris continues to push for an explanation; Marisa responds, "There was a part of me that wanted to see what it felt like to have someone like you look at me the way you did—just once. The scene ends when Marisa walks away from Chris.

Elapsed time: This scene begins at 01:22:36 and ends at 01:26:28 (DVD Scene 22)

Rating: PG-13 for some language/sexual references

Citation: *Maid in Manhattan* (Revolution Studios, 2002), written by John Hughes and directed by Wayne Wang

Malibu's Most Wanted
CO-OPTION

A senator arranges for his son, a rich white kid who fancies himself black, to be kidnapped by a couple of black actors pretending to be gangsters to try and shock him out of his plans to become a rapper.

Brad "B-Rad" Gluckman (Jamie Kennedy) has been required to undergo psychiatric counseling. B-Rad is white but argues that he is really black. He refuses to answer to his "slave name," Bradley. He mentions his dreams of being a successful gangster rapper and demonstrates his ability to rap about anything. He explains how his parents neglected him and how his black maid was the only one who raised him. After Bradley leaves the room, the therapist diagnoses him with "the most advanced case of gangstaphrenia I have ever treated." Mr. Gluckman (Ryan O'Neil), who is running for governor, sees B-Rad's behavior as a liability to his campaign. His African American campaign manager, Mr. Gibbons (played by Blair Underwood), and the staff have devised a plan to "Give him a taste of what the thug life is really like. It might just scare the black out of him [B-Rad]" by hiring actors to play gangsters who will kidnap B-Rad and take him into the ghetto. The hired actors are given instructions to "scare him into acting like a white boy." At the close of the scene, the actors are complaining about their "roles," indicating, "After all of our years of training and studying, they continue to give us the parts of gangbangers. Just once I'd like to play someone who speaks with proper grammar and doesn't wear those Timberlands with the laces undone; it's so sloppy."

Elapsed time: This scene begins at 00:06:31 and ends at 00:14:42 (DVD Scene 3)
Rating: PG-13 for sexual humor, language, and violence
Citation: *Malibu's Most Wanted* (Warner Bros., 2003), written by Fax Bahr and Adam Small, directed by John Whitesell

Pleasantville
DOMINANCE

A brother and sister from the 1990s are sucked into their television set and suddenly find themselves trapped in a Leave It to Beaver-style 1950s television show, complete with loving parents, old-fashioned values, and an overwhelming amount of innocence and naiveté. Not sure how to get home, they integrate themselves into this "backwards" society and slowly bring some color to this black and white world. But as innocence fades, the two teens begin to wonder if their 90s outlook is really to be preferred.

This scene begins when George Parker (William H. Macy) walks in the door with the familiar greeting, "Honey, I'm home," but realizes that no one is home, which is highly unusual. This has never happened before. Things have been changing in Pleasantville—teenagers are being sexually rebellious, it is raining for the first time ever, and wives are abandoning their traditional duties, such as making dinner. Most of the teenagers are excited about the new changes going on, but the patriarchs and male civic leaders of the town are at the local bowling alley and begin talking about their fears associated with these changes. They do not want things to change. They live in a town where every man picks up the dreaded 7–10 split at the bowling alley. The men are in shock when George explains that there is "real rain" outside and that his wife did not make his dinner. Big Bob, the mayor, tries to console George, "It's gonna be fine, George. You're with us now." One man mentions that his wife scorched his shirt with an iron because she was "thinking," which causes several of the men to wince. At the end of the scene, the men pledge to fix their problems and begin to chant "together, together, together."

Elapsed time: This scene begins at 01:13:10 and ends at 01:20:45 (DVD Scene 28)
Rating: PG-13 for some thematic elements emphasizing sexuality and for language
Citation: *Pleasantville* (New Line Cinemas, 1998), written and directed by Gary Ross

Transformers
SOCIAL JUSTICE

The 1980s cartoon characters come to life as the Autobots and Decepticons, two warring factions of robots that can change shape into automobiles and flying machines, are fighting their ancient war here on earth. Each is hoping to obtain a powerful ancient relic that will give the user the power to take over the world. Human beings become the collateral agents of the action as the Decepticons are hell-bent on human annihilation.

In answer to the question, "Why are you here?" Optimus Prime, leader of the Autobots, tells the story of how the Transformers come to Earth and the purpose of their search for Sam. He explains that their planet "was once a powerful empire, peaceful and just," until Megatron, leader of the Decepticons, took over and obliterated anyone who did not agree with him. Optimus explained how the "war finally consumed the planet." The Autobots and Decepticons are sworn enemies, and each is trying to find the All Spark, a source of great power, which has fallen to the earth. Megatron and the Decepticons "will use its power to transform Earth's machines and build a new army, and the human race will be extinguished." Sam Witwicky (Shia LaBeouf) is the grandson of the explorer who found the location of the All Spark. Optimus explains that the fate of human existence relies on Sam helping the Autobots find the All Spark.

Elapsed time: This scene begins at 01:04:03 and ends at 01:06:44 (DVD Scene 11)

Rating: PG-13 for intense sequences of sci-fi action violence, brief sexual humor, and language

Citation: *Transformers* (DreamWorks, 2007), written by Robert Orci and Alex Kurtzman, directed by Michael Bay

V for Vendetta
OPPRESSION

A young woman named Evey (Natalie Portman) is rescued from a life-and-death situation by a masked vigilante, known only as "V," who ignites a revolution when he detonates two London landmarks and takes over the government-controlled airwaves, urging his fellow citizens to rise up against tyranny and oppression. As Evey uncovers the truth about V's mysterious background, she also discovers the truth about herself—and emerges as his unlikely ally in the culmination of his plot to bring freedom and justice back to a society fraught with cruelty and corruption.

V (Hugo Weaving) is revealing the secret past of the government to two authority figures. He meets the men at the memorial commemorating those fallen in deadly biological attacks. He describes the government as cruel and oppressive. He begins the story by describing "a young, up-and-coming politician. He's a deeply religious man and a member of the Conservative Party. He's completely single-minded and has no regard for the political process. The more power he attains, the more obvious his zealotry and the more aggressive his supporters become." This leader began to exploit his power "in the name of national security." He begins to tell how this particular politician rose to fame and how he captured the favor of the public by "finding" a cure to a dreaded virus that is killing thousands of people. What the public doesn't know is that he is responsible for the targeted release of that virus as a means of social control. He argues that the political leader's "true goal of this project is power—complete and total hegemonic domination." To accomplish this, V says, "three targets are chosen to maximize the effect of the attack: a school, a tube station, and a water-treatment plant." V also describes how the media frenzy helped to stir public outcry, but the media were actually working in tandem with the governmental leader. "Fear," V says, "became the ultimate tool of this government." The scene ends with the pronouncement of the leader as the "High Chancellor."

Elapsed time: This scene begins at 01:32:20 and ends at 01:35:20 (DVD Scene 24)

Rating: R for strong violence and some language

Citation: *V for Vendetta* (Silver Pictures, 2005), written by Andy and Larry Wachowski, directed by James McTeigue

Welcome to the Dollhouse
OPPRESSION/INVISIBILITY

A tragic tale of 11-year-old Dawn Wiener and her experiences as an unpopular pre-teen in junior high school. Dawn is teased by her classmates, faces the daily threat by the school bully, and has a secret crush on her older brother's friend.

Mr. and Mrs. Weiner, Dawn's parents, are planning their twentieth wedding anniversary party. It will be held in their backyard. Mrs. Weiner wants Dawn to tear down her tree house in the back yard, where Dawn holds meetings of her "Special People Club." In this scene, the Weiner family is having dinner. When Dawn refuses again to tear down her clubhouse, Mr. Weiner tells her, "Be smart. Make things easy on yourself." Mrs. Weiner returns to the table with chocolate cake for everyone but refuses to give Dawn her piece. Instead, she divides Dawn's piece between her other two children. She then asks them (Mark and Missy) to help her tear down the clubhouse.

Elapsed time: This scene begins at 00:45:33 and ends at 00:48:01 (DVD Scene 13)

Rating: R for language

Citation: *Welcome to the Dollhouse* (Suburban Pictures, 1995), written and directed by Todd Solondz

Note

Certain selections excerpted from Johnson, B.C. and Blanchard, S.C. *Reel Diversity: A Teacher's Sourcebook* New York: Peter Lang, 2008.

References

Giroux, H. (1997). Are Disney movies good for your kids? In S. Steinberg & J. Kincheloe (Eds.), *Kinderculture: The corporate construction of childhood* (pp. 53–68). Boulder, CO: Westview.

Jowett, G., & Linton, J. (1980). *Movies as mass communication*. Newbury Park, CA: Sage.

Pope, R., Reynolds, A., & Mueller, J. (2004). *Multicultural competence in student affairs*. San Francisco: Wiley.

Section Two

Including Whiteness *within* Diversity

Three

The Unspoken Color of Diversity
Whiteness, Privilege, and Critical Engagement in Education

Paul R. Carr and Darren E. Lund

For the past few decades, the issue of diversity has become increasingly relevant within the educational context (James, 2003). Whereas the formal recognition of pluralism was once contested as being inconsequential to educational success, educators, researchers, decision makers, activists and others have now made diversity a fundamental component of the educational experience (Banks, 2006). It would be unusual for schools, teachers' associations, ministries and departments of education, teacher-educator programs and other entities involved in education *not* to endorse a commitment to diversity. In the same way that it would be difficult to oppose democracy, it is equally problematic to fail to embrace diversity. In this chapter, we challenge the traditional conception of diversity and the way it is understood within the educational context, arguing that teaching and learning in relation to diversity must be tethered around a core belief in the need to advance social justice (Carr, 2007). Our central concern relates to the notion of whiteness and how white power and privilege can diminish the problematic of diversity to nothing more than a superficial manifestation of potentially stereotypical gestures and exchanges.

The foundation for this chapter is based on a book that we co-edited, *The Great White North? Exploring Whiteness, Privilege and Identity in Education*, published by Sense (Carr & Lund, 2007). The process of coordinating and writing the book, along with the numerous presentations, articles and interviews that have buttressed the dissemination of the concept of whiteness, ultimately became more of a project than a discrete published contribution to the literature. As two white males from Canada, one from Toronto and the other from Calgary, who have been involved in anti-racism education for a number of years, the challenge of discussing, researching, learning about and teaching on whiteness has been enlightening and, in some ways, transformative. We have concluded that it is problematic and perhaps even counter-productive, at times, to entertain diversity without a solid comprehension of whiteness. Our project concerns a critical engagement toward social justice, and we have found that whiteness, despite being a concept and subject that many people wish to avoid, provides an effective platform to frame and analyze the lived experience of being part of a diverse, heterogeneous society (Sleeter, 2005).

This chapter contains three sections: the first will expose some of the ideas, debates and questions raised through *The Great White North?* project; the second will propose some strategies, thoughts and cautionary notes in relation to teaching on whiteness; and the last will involve a brief discussion of the problematic, concerns and consequences of whiteness for society and education systems that must meaningfully deal with diversity.

Whiteness and *The Great White North?* Project

The Great White North? begins by providing a philosophical, historical, conceptual, cultural, and political framework of whiteness. The various contributors make reference to the myriad metaphors, analogies, images, and cultural landmarks that all speak to the sanctity, beauty and hypnotic predominance of the color white in the Western world. Not merely the opposite of black, white has been a signifier for global racial supremacy—good against evil, lightness versus darkness and benevolence over malevolence—and in English, it symbolizes cleanliness, kindness, serenity, and youth. White is associated with Europe, the conqueror, while black is inexorably fused to colonial notions of the "dark continent" of Africa.

While the book is written and edited by Canadians—white, racially minoritized and Aboriginal women and men from across the country—about the problematic of whiteness in Canada, it also clearly applies to an international audience, as whiteness does not merely exist in Canada, but in all jurisdictions. Canada is an interesting starting point because of the entrenched national narrative of an expansive, decent nation, characterized by multiculturalism (Henry & Tator, 2005). One feature that defines the Canadian experience is the complex and often antagonistic relationship Canada has had with the United States since before Confederation. A common sentiment that binds Canadians together is the self-assured notion that Canada does not suffer from the same racial problems as in the United States. Canadians see themselves as less segregated, less discriminatory, less racist, and less divided, as we often remind ourselves. The Americans, on the other hand, have endless visible warts, including a long history of racial tensions and civil rights struggles, and we strive to convince ourselves that we Canadians have not followed their destiny (Lund, 2006c). As educational researchers interested in the sociology of "race" and identity in education, we have become aware of the intricate, systemic, and pervasive nature of racism in Canada. Recent books have included a more frank look at Canada's racist past (Baergen, 2000; Kinsella, 2001). Many strong anti-racism scholars have begun the work of acknowledging and documenting this racist past and present and its impact on education (e.g., Dei, Karumanchery, & Karumanchery-Luik, 2004; Fleras & Elliot, 2003; Henry & Tator, 2005; James, 2003; Solomon, Portelli, Daniel, & Campbell, 2005; Trifonas, 2003). Starting with the first European contact with the Aboriginal peoples, through the existence of slavery in Canada—about which many Canadians have no information—to the undulating waves of immigration, through the razing of Africville in Halifax, to the internment of Japanese Canadians during the Second World War, through the experience of Jamaican Canadians in Toronto and Haitian Canadians in Montreal, the history of racism in

Canada is as rich as it is shrouded with resistance and denial (Lund, 2006a, 2006b). While there have been hundreds of studies on race relations and racism in Canada, there had been few, if any, scholarly collections exclusively dedicated to exploring whiteness in Canada.

We realize that the oversimplification entailed in placing into one white category such heterogeneous ethnic, cultural, linguistic, religious, and other groups is problematic (Fine, Weis, Powell Pruitt, & Burns, 2004). Certainly, there are myriad international examples of nuanced experiences of oppression and struggle within and across nations of white people. For example, Francophones have historical differences with Anglophones in Canada, the Catholics and the Protestants have been at loggerheads for years in Northern Ireland, the Hungarian minority has not had a favorable experience with the majority Romanian population, and the Basque population has been involved in a separatist movement in Spain for generations, with all of these conflicts, struggles and complexities involving white people. It would seem extremely unusual, and perhaps even unacceptable to most people, to hear news anchors speak of "the white community" during a daily newscast in North America, yet we commonly refer to the "black community," the "Asian community," the "West Indian community," and so on, as if these racialized groups can so easily be confined within a tightly defined and coded category of identity and social experience.

Are people generally overtly racist? While it is unlikely that blatant racist behavior is currently condoned or tolerated by most Canadians, there is ample evidence that widespread systemic racism is a reality (Dei, 2008). Part of the problem in documenting trends is the absence of useful data collection. For a variety of reasons, many people resist indicating their racial origin on census forms. People from racialized minority groups know that a chance at employment may later be tainted with the accusation that the employer simply wanted to "fill a quota." Playing the proverbial "race card" is perhaps most insidious when considering the trivialization and maligning of employment equity in Canada (Klassen & Cosgrove, 2002) and affirmative action in the United States. (Feagin & O'Brien, 2003). At some level, racial identity is obvious to everyone and, at the same time, is obscured by the false notion that human rights legislation, common decency and religion all negate its existence. Where people live, the positions they ultimately attain, who they may befriend, employ, and marry, the types of associations, clubs, and organizations they belong to and other markers of social integration all may have a racialized component. Who most often attends private schools, private golf clubs and private business circles, has traditionally depended on, among other things, unspoken racial categories. How people choose to understand their own implication in racism relates to privilege and power, and, ultimately, whiteness is shrouded with justifications and denials that allow people to avoid discussion of how oppression continues to benefit white people in Canada (Henry & Tator, 2005).

Therefore, we accept the premise that "race" and racial identities are highly contested and problematic ideas for our consideration. Just as with politics and religion, these diversity-themed topics are not usually addressed openly in polite company. For this project, we insist that Canadian society (and that of the United States as well as others) cannot be understood without stripping away the layers of the race onion. Clearly, social relations are infinitely more complex than race relations. The social construction and intersectionality of identity provide a medium in which whiteness can be deconstructed and problematized. Whether we are speaking about sexual orientation, ability, religion, gender identity, cultural group membership, or some other aspect of our identities, the racial template always affects the power relations inherent between groups and individuals (McLaren, 2007). For instance, when a marginalized person is also a person of color, that individual's lived experience can become more complex.

Even before the launch of the edited collection (Carr & Lund, 2007), we were surprised at the strong reaction of some people to the notion of our studying whiteness as a way of explaining and challenging racism in Canada. In fact, when a *Globe and Mail* newspaper reporter wrote an article (Church, 2007) covering a recent presentation about our research at a national conference, the reader responses were immediate and vociferous. In less than twenty-four hours, over 160 written items were posted to the newspaper's "Comments" on-line forum, most of them expressing what many would consider to be racist, xenophobic, or otherwise hateful viewpoints. In the following months, throughout a series of radio interviews, we were able to learn of a number of issues that people have in relation to race and, importantly, how whiteness is considered to be an offensive concept for many whites in society. These experiences and observations reinforce our contention that education should be the forum for a more meaningful and critical engagement on diversity and the general theme of social justice (Howard, 1999; Banks, 2006; McLaren, 2007).

Teaching about Whiteness

Most teachers in North America are white, whereas an increasingly diverse demography is flourishing in schools and communities, most predominantly in urban centers, but also edging into suburban and rural areas (Banks, 2006). We could interrogate why members of racialized minorities are not drawn to teaching in the same numbers as whites, which could include an analysis of systemic barriers, the perception of teachers and teaching, the experience of minorities in education and the power structure overarching the decision making processes in education, but our focus here is on the reality of how faculties of education and educational institutions, in general, can seek to address social justice throughout the educational programs.

How can we teach about whiteness without alienating white students and without placing racial-minority students in an uncomfortable, marginalized position? Is it possible to teach about whiteness without being disruptive or causing paralyzing white guilt? What type of preparation do whites need in order to engage in whiteness? (Sleeter, 2005). These questions frame the examples of activities below that we believe are an effective way to start the process of critical reflection and then move toward action, in relation to whiteness. It is necessary to highlight that there is no single list that can be magically produced to remedy the problems emerging around social justice, multiculturalism or diversity themes. Rather, we advocate an approach whereby students are engaged in critical reflection of their own identities and experiences and then aim to draw them into a more dynamic, multi-faceted, dialectal dialogue and process with other identities and experiences (James, 2003). Underpinning this philosophy and conceptual approach is a belief in Paulo Freire's (1970) understanding of education being intertwined with the political, economic and socio-cultural milieu. In sum, education is politics (McLaren, 2007).

The first activity we recommend as a way of commencing the dialogue relates to a critical self-reflection on identity. It is important for education students to tease out their own educational experiences so as to be able to appreciate what led them to desire to become teachers.

One activity that Carr has used with his undergraduate education classes involves students writing a short paper on five personalities, experiences, factors, issues and/or events that have shaped their educational experience. When students present their papers in class, it proves to be extremely powerful to discover that the context is as important, if not more so, than the content in documenting students' experiences. Students start to make linkages with each other and also can see how peoples' identities are often fundamental in determining educational success. Many students had unfavourable elementary and secondary school experiences, and it is important to deconstruct, contextualize and critique the meaning of the social context in shaping one's educational experience.

Students can start to see trends in relation to how some were marginalized, ignored and diminished, whereas others seemed to have benefited from a relatively fluid, profitable and enjoyable experience. The process of documenting what shaped one's educational experience is powerful, especially as future teachers, in that students can start to connect the relevance of identity and cultural capital with the actual experience in the educational context. During this process, we also interrogate what diversity looked and felt like. We quickly learn that, if it was dealt with at all, diversity was often approached in a superficial manner and the absence of an explicit and/or implicit approach to social justice can be extremely traumatic for some and neutralizing for others. One of the focal points here is to determine how diversity shapes the educational experience and, moreover, how being white is not a neutral, raceless identity.

This activity allows us to engage in a discussion of the lived experiences for people from a range of identities and, significantly, to problematize whiteness, even if we start to do this through an analysis of social class and poverty. Ultimately, this exercise, when framed with critical questions about the pertinence of the sociology of education (the context being as important as the content in the educational experience), can lead to a demystification of the notion that people succeed in education merely based on effort. The social construction of identity does, indeed, flavour the educational experience, and it also plays a role in affecting attitudes and behaviours, the organization of the school culture, the decision making processes and the fundamental relationships that students develop in their formative years. One cautionary note here is that it is necessary to avoid passing judgement on how students formulate the key events, personalities, issues, factors and/or experiences they have highlighted. What is more important is to extract an analysis and to seek a more critical vantage point, which will be indispensable in guiding these students as they become teachers.

The second strategy that could be used involves multicultural surveys, such as those developed by Paul Gorski (2008), a multicultural education activist and scholar, that could be used to stimulate discussion on what we do and do not know and why. It is important for students to work first in small groups, debating issues and trying to work through what the answers to questions about diversity should be and then come together as a group to discuss the answers one after another. One technique Carr has used is to get one group to read a question and then have another group give their response with a justification. Other groups would then be invited to contribute, offering their analyses before the instructor reads the answer. From Gorski's basic multicultural quiz with twenty questions, the entire activity might take an hour to complete. The instructor should leave time after each answer is revealed to seek out a critical interpretation of how we came to believe, if that is the case, another conceptualization of reality. This exercise allows us to critique what we learn in schools as well as elsewhere, including through the media, that lead to certain stereotypes, fictitious images and shortcomings in relation to diversity. In relation to whiteness, it is important to consider how whites are portrayed, in general and how being white needs to be part of the equation of addressing racial discrimination. While this activity serves as a friendly and innocent ice-breaker, it can also reinforce the salience of knowledge construction and the epistemology of identity. When does identity matter and when does it not matter? How and why do we maintain that we are color-blind when there is so much evidence of racial discrimination and injustice?

The third activity relates to the media and aims to heighten awareness of importance of media (and political) literacy. Do we teach about and for media literacy in our schools? What are the implications? How do the media pervade what we know and how we think? Do we critically analyze the media? The media can have the effect of creating a normative, universal presence for whites and, as a corollary, may serve to further enhance stereotypes and discrimination. By not talking about white privilege, one might conclude that it does not exist. The activity is structured as follows: the class is broken down into five smaller groups, each with a different task (one watches the news, one times and documents everything, one focuses on the political messages, one monitors the news readers, journalists and others on the screen and the last group focuses on race); the class then watches the thirty-minute nightly news. It is important to point out that it does not make much of a difference what channel or jurisdiction is selected. After watching the news, each group, in the order outlined above, gives a report on what they saw. It is important to multi-layer the observations and analysis that each group comes up with and to not engage in a plenary discussion until each group has provided its input.

What Carr has found when using this activity with graduate students at the Master's level is that students are generally surprised, and also disheartened, to see how little analysis is provided in the news and moreover, how much it resembles entertainment more than a critical inquiry into what is important. Students start to question how the stories are selected and presented and why they are not critiqued, differentiated or contextualized in any meaningful way. Students can also observe a clear racialized organization to the news regarding who delivers the news and how, the angle selected, the lack of any critical discussion of race and the reinforced image that whiteness constitutes the norm. Students are then able to make the connection with their classrooms and how they address pivotal issues such as war, conflict, poverty and injustice, among others. Lund uses a similar media activity with the local daily newspaper, leading students through an analysis of the photos of people appearing throughout the entire edition. Whose faces do we see and what roles do they play in our community? How fairly do these statistics reflect the community's demographics? Invariably, the predominant images are of white people, shown in a wide range of roles in the city and around the globe, while non-white images appear mainly in the sports and entertainment section, or in stories as the exotic "other" or positioned as criminals. These activities also raise questions as to why so much time is expended in the media on trivial matters, most typically about which Hollywood star has been seen with whomever. By leading our students through these exercises, we can start to assemble a picture of how racialized power works and, significantly, how white power and privilege are maintained in some very explicit and complex ways.

Lund has adapted a privilege activity developed by his colleague Dr. David Este at the University of Calgary. It can be a powerful exercise that should be thoroughly debriefed by a skilled instructor. Participants should be led to the exercise site silently, hand in hand, in a line. At the site, participants can release their hands but should be instructed to stand shoulder to shoulder in a straight line, without speaking. You may have them close their eyes. Participants should be instructed to listen carefully to each sentence and take the step required if the sentence applies to them. They may be told there is a prize at the front of the site that everyone is competing for. Ask participants to remain in their positions and to look at their position at the site and the positions of the other participants. Ask participants to consider who among them would probably win the prize.

Students should then be read a number of sentences that ask them to take a certain number of steps forward or backward based on their experiences. Many of the questions address issues of race, class, gender, and sexual orientation and can be adapted for specific instructional purposes. For example, questions based on the following may be read slowly and separately and followed by "take one (or more) step(s) forward": if you graduated from high school, if you were encouraged to attend college or university by a parent, if there were more than fifty books in your house when you grew up, if a parent told you that you could be anything you wanted to be, if you have ever inherited money or property, if there were people of colour who worked in your household as servants, cleaners, nannies, gardeners, if one or both of your parents were professionals, if you studied the culture of your ancestors in elementary schools, and so on.

Other questions requiring at least one step back are: if you believe you have ever been followed by store personnel because of your race; if you were ever ashamed of your clothes, house, car, or other such things; if you were raised in an area where there was prostitution or drug activity; if you believe you were ever denied employment because of your race, ethnicity, gender or sexual orientation; if your parents did not grow up in Canada; if your home language was other than English; if you had to rely primarily on public transportation; if you often saw members of your race, ethnic groups, gender or sexual orientation portrayed on television in degrading roles; if you believe you have every been paid less or treated unfairly in a workplace because of your race, class, gender or sexual orientation; if you were ever stopped or questioned by the police because of your race, ethnicity, gender or sexual orientation; if you were ever called names because of your race, class, ethnicity, gender or sexual orientation; if you have ever tried to change your appearance, mannerisms, or behaviour to avoid being judged or ridiculed; if you were ever discouraged from pursuing academics or certain jobs because of your race, class, ethnicity, gender or sexual orientation; if you have ever felt uncomfortable about a joke related to your race, class, ethnicity, gender or sexual orientation but felt unsafe to confront the situation and so on.

When they open their eyes, it is impossible to ignore who is far ahead at the front of the room and who remains at the back, perhaps even behind the starting line. It reveals much about how privileges operate and how complex these issues are. As you might imagine, the front-runners typically include the white, straight, able-bodied males, but there are also some interesting anomalies and surprises that refute our assumptions about people's identities. After the activity, I ask my students questions such as: What happened here? How did this exercise make you feel? What were your thoughts as you did this exercise? What have you learned from this experience? As a graduate student, educator, or community worker, what can you do with this information in the future? It is an activity that has offered a rich window into privilege, but there is a great deal of potential emotional risk in using an activity such as this one, and so caution is recommended.

Conclusion: Whiteness and Diversity

Why focus on whiteness? One of the reactions to *The Great White North?* project has been: "This is very interesting, but will white people ever agree to share power?" As Paulo Freire (1970) has instructively pointed out, there must be hope in the proposition of educational transformation. Education is the core of societal hope, and not to desire social justice through education is to admit openly that empowerment, engagement and social change are undesirable. It is important to acknowledge the numerous barriers—historic, cultural, economic and political—that frame any discussion on education for social change. We acknowledge that, within in the context of neoliberalism, it is increasingly difficult to undertake meaningful social justice work that may challenge the balance of power (McLaren, 2007). However, to fail to problematize whiteness is to reinforce it, and this is the reason it is essential to attempt to address white power and privilege (Sleeter, 2005). The educative approach becomes extremely important, and poorly conceived or ineffective efforts at understanding, addressing and engaging in whiteness may result in adverse effects (McCarthy, Crichlow, Dimitriadis, & Dolby, 2005). It is, therefore, essential to focus on whiteness in order to seek the truth; to provide a legitimate moral foundation of knowledge; to provide hope to those marginalized by it; to empower whites to be sensitized to their relationship to their racial origin; to give meaning to human rights, constitutions and grand narratives espousing equality; to challenge the willing and unwilling complacency of those preaching a philosophy of color-blindness and in, finally, to be able to strive for social justice (Sullivan, 2006; Dei, 2008; Dei, Karumanchery, & Karumanchery-Luik, 2004). If the qualitative experience of education does not include the tangible expression and representation of democracy, citizenship and social justice, then educators might question the relevance of merely stocking up on knowledge and skills, as exemplified by Freire's critique of students being perceived as empty vessels (1970).

Whiteness is problematic for many reasons. That many white people do not see themselves as white, while simultaneously seeing non-whites as people of "color" and further, perceiving themselves as being "good," is problematic. There is a fear of being labelled racist, juxtaposed against an inability or unwillingness to become engaged, despite the preponderance of church and community groups that highlight the goodness and equality of all people. One student commented to Carr that, "Sunday is the most racist day of the week because that is when we all go to our separate churches." Some white people are led to become fearful of the "other" based on the endless replaying of media and societal programming, not actual lived experiences, all of which often reinforces the entrenched sentiments that some hold. In the United States, for example, it is not uncommon to see large racial-minority populations living in poorer conditions in the inner city with white populations living in relative harmony in "better" suburban neighbourhoods ringing the minority areas.

How should we consider "white flight," when white people leave a neighbourhood because black people have moved in, and, importantly, how should we learn to be together, to confront challenges collectively, to denounce inequitable situations and to create a more decent society, if we refuse to understand racism in a more collective sense? Individuals who choose to use the "N word" have faced public trauma and denunciation because of this. For example, in the past few years, three prominent white Americans (Michael Richards from *Seinfeld*, Don Imus of radio fame and Duane Chapman, who is *Dog, The Bounty Hunter* on the popular television show of the same name) have been the targets of the media for their overt expressions of racism. However, what is being done to understand that the individual acts are somehow connected to broader systemic, institutional and cultural practices, policies, programs and manifestations of racism? It would seem that education is the key piece to the puzzle in order to address, throughout myriad experiences, activities, courses, events and teaching and learning, what whiteness is and how it can best be addressed.

Teaching for social justice requires a critical interrogation of the world around us (Solomon, Portelli, Daniel, & Campbell, 2005). Is it purely a coincidence that all of the Canadian prime ministers and U.S. presidents (until 2009) have been white? What did each of them do to acknowledge and dismantle whiteness? Why do we think of Canada and the United States as being white, European, Christian countries? How do our schools reconcile the obvious reality that Aboriginal peoples were on these lands for thousands of years before the white man "discovered" them? We teach not only about what we know but also, importantly, about what we do *not* know, and the students form their opinions, ideals and values, in part, based on knowledge from schools. While we should expect resistance, rejection and cynicism from white students when teaching about whiteness, educators need to be vigilant, prepared, engaged and critical in demonstrating the transformative possibilities of being immersed in such an endeavor. Because this can be a disruptive and uncomfortable process, confrontation should be approached with caution as some students may not be sufficiently engaged to continue their reflection.

Dismantling whiteness is not easy because it straddles the line of innocence and decency. It is much easier to argue that times have changed and that "we can't be blamed for what our ancestors did." We do know that having the "right" parents is a key ingredient to success in education and that living in more well-off areas renders the schooling experience more enjoyable and less taxing than it is in poorer urban areas. White people, as Peggy McIntosh (1988) has effectively pointed out, need not reflect on their whiteness in a range of daily activities, ultimately demonstrating the unearned privileges of being white. White people may reject their own implication in social justice, but this comes at a cost in terms of the impact on all learners and those involved in education.

Finally, white power and privilege is intertwined with neoliberalism and the political systems that maintain hegemony. The notion of accountability, a major plank in educational reforms such as the *No Child Left Behind Act* in the United States, does not willingly embrace the concept of social justice. Critically interrogating whiteness, inequity, discrimination, marginalization and social justice, is often considered an "extra" duty, something that falls outside of the purview of the teacher who must, in the words of some critics, "teach to the test." One comment we often received when teaching for social justice is, "How will we have time for that with so much else to cover?" This is where our understanding that teaching about and for social justice, with an aim to addressing whiteness, is an ongoing process. It is not a list, and meaningful, sustained and critical engagement must be the cornerstone. The benefits to unmasking these concepts, regardless of the subject area or the cultural and institutional milieu, are numerous, and educators will find that the teaching and learning experience is enhanced, not diminished, by taking on such issues. Importantly, white people are uniquely positioned to play a crucial role in challenging white power and privilege.

Note

Parts of this chapter were inspired by a manuscript we wrote for *Directions: Research and Policy on Eliminating Racism* produced by the Canadian Race Relations Foundation (Lund & Carr, in press).

References

Baergen, W. P. (2000). *The Ku Klux Klan in central Alberta*. Red Deer, AB: Central Alberta Historical Society.

Banks, J. A. (2006). *Race, culture, and education: The selected works of James A. Banks*. New York: Routledge.

Carr, P. (2007). Educational policy and the social justice dilemma. In H. Claire & C. Holden (Eds.), *Controversial issues in education*. London, UK: Trentham.

Carr, P., & Lund, D. E. (Eds.). (2007). *The great white north? Exploring whiteness, privilege and identity in education*. Rotterdam, NL: Sense.

Church, E. (2007, May 31). White people need to face role in racism, academics say. *Globe and Mail*, A5.

Dei, G. J. S. (2008). *Racists beware: Uncovering racial politics in the post modern society*. Rotterdam, The Netherlands: Sense.

Dei, G. J. S., Karumanchery, L. L., & Karumanchery-Luik, N. (2004). *Playing the race card: Exposing white power and privilege*. New York: Peter Lang.

Ellsworth, E. (1997). *Double blinds in whiteness*. In M. Fine, L. Weis, L. Powell, & M. Wong (Eds.), *Off white: Readings on race, power, and society* (pp. 259–269). New York: Routledge.

Feagin, J., & O'Brien, E. (2003). *White men on race: Power, privilege, and the shaping of cultural consciousness*. Boston: Beacon Press.

Fine, M., Weis, L., Powell Pruitt, L., & Burns, A. (2004). *Off white: Readings on race, power, and society (2nd ed.)*. New York: Routledge.

Fleras, A., & Elliot, J. L. (2003). *Unequal relations: An introduction to race and ethnic dynamics in Canada* (4th ed.). Toronto, ON: Prentice Hall.

Freire, P. (1970). *Pedagogy of the oppressed*. New York: Continuum.

Gorski, P. (2008). *EdChange: Professional development, scholarship and activism for diversity, social justice, and community growth* [on-line resource]. St. Paul, MN: Author.

Henry, F., & Tator, C. (2005). *The colour of democracy: Racism in Canadian society*. Toronto, ON: Nelson Thompson.

Howard, G. R. (1999). *We can't teach what we don't know: White teachers, multiracial schools*. New York: Teachers College Press.

James, C. E. (2003). *Seeing ourselves: Exploring race, ethnicity and culture* (3rd ed.). Toronto, ON: Thompson.

Kinsella, W. (2001). *Web of hate: Inside Canada's far right network* (2nd ed.). Toronto, ON: HarperCollins.

Klassen, T., & Cosgrove, J. (2002). *Ideology and inequality: Newspaper coverage of the employment equity legislation in Canada* (Working Paper Series No. 28). Toronto, ON: Centre for Research on Work and Society at York University.

Lund, D. E. (2006a). Everyday racism in Canada: Learning and teaching respect for Aboriginal people. *Multicultural Education, 14*(1), 49–51.

Lund, D. E. (2006b). Rocking the racism boat: School-based activists speak out on denial and avoidance. *Race, Ethnicity and Education, 9*(2), 203–221.

Lund, D. E. (2006c). Waking up the neighbors: Surveying multicultural and antiracist education in Canada, the United Kingdom, and the United States. *Multicultural Perspectives, 8*(1), 35–43.

Lund, D. E., & Carr, P. R. (in press). Exposing the great white north: Tackling whiteness, privilege and identity in Canadian education. *Directions: Research and Policy on Eliminating Racism*.

McCarthy, C., Crichlow, W., Dimitriadis, G., & Dolby, N. (2005). *Race, identity and representation in education* (2nd ed.). New York: Taylor & Francis.

McIntosh, P. (1988). White privilege and male privilege: A personal account of coming to see correspondences through work in women's studies. Wellesley, MA: Wellesley College Center for Research on Women (Working Paper No. 189). Retrieved on March 4, 2008, from http://www.feinberg.northwestern.edu/diversity/uploaded_docs/UnpackingTheKnapsack.pdf

McLaren, P. (2007). *Life in schools: An introduction to critical pedagogy in the foundations of education* (5th ed.). Boston: Pearson Education.

Sleeter, C. E. (2005). How white teachers construct race. In C. McCarthy, W. Crichlow, G. Dimitriadis, & N. Dolby (Eds.), *Race, identity and representation in education* (2nd ed.). New York: Routledge.

Solomon, R. P., Portelli, J. P., Daniel, B-J., & Campbell, A. (2005). The discourse of denial: How white teacher candidates construct race, racism and "white privilege." *Race, Ethnicity and Education, 8*(2), 147–169.

Sullivan, S. (2006). *Revealing whiteness: The unconscious habits of racial privilege.* Indianapolis, IN: Indiana University Press.

Trifonas, P. P. (Ed.). (2003). *Pedagogies of difference: Rethinking education for social change.* New York: RoutledgeFalmer.

Willinsky, J. (1998). *Learning to divide the world: Education at empire's end.* Minneapolis, MD: University of Minnesota Press.

Four

Unmasking Whiteness in the Teacher Education College Classroom
Critical and Creative Multicultural Practice

Virginia Lea

WE

I am the white guy you see
who wishes to be seen for what I am
a potential friend.
You curse my privilege;
I am inclined to agree. After all I made it
here in spite of me.
You suspect narrow mindedness;
it's not true. The opinion I seek
belongs to you.
You judge that I don't care,
but you don't know. I seek the other
because I yearn to grow.
My color erects a wall that hides
the true me. To you I am only that
color that you see.
We're both white so you share a joke
about ghetto life. I guess you've
yet to meet my wife?
My children won't be white like
me. Their un-whiteness is all that
society will see.

The above "I-Poem" was written by a twenty-something, white, male student-teacher as part of the cultural portfolio I assign to the student-teachers in my Multicultural Pedagogy course. The "I-Poem" assignment, like the other assignments that make up the portfolio, is designed to help students identify the discourses/cultural scripts—the ways of thinking, feeling, believing and acting—they embody. In this way they become more critically conscious of the often unconscious discourses that shape their actions in the classroom. At the end of a recent semester, another of my students expressed her enhanced consciousness as follows:

> Before taking this class, I always tried to convince myself that I treat everyone equally and that I did not give into society's petty stereotypes. Perhaps this hardening of my heart and inability to be truthful and humble derives from growing up in a school system that tried to ignore these stereotypes for so long. However, I quickly realized just how much I have let society influence my perception of different cultures, races, classes, and gender. I first came to this realization when doing my *culture shock exercise*.

I shall return to the culture shock exercise later in this chapter.

For the past ten years, I have been teaching two educational foundations courses for the multiple subjects credential program at a California State University. The population of my classrooms is almost entirely made up of students of European American and Jewish/Middle-Eastern origin, categorized in this society as "white." As a person who also falls into this category, I try earnestly to work on the same assignments I give my students. I recognize that my partial Arab ethnicity in no way disrupts the white privilege I gain daily because of my physical appearance as a woman socially classified as white. It does nothing to interrupt the advantage I gain from speaking English with an English accent, or from my knowledge of the norms and values of the corridors of power, both in the United States and in Western Europe. While I am aware of the reality that "race" is socially constructed, I am also aware that race is "real in its consequences" (Thomas, 1923). It will take a long time and a considerable conscious commitment from large numbers of people before race no longer defines in important ways the lives of U.S. citizens. One cannot easily abolish race (Ignatiev & Garvey, 1996; Roediger, 1991), or the ways in which it continues to influence our lives in the United States, Western Europe, and beyond. Claiming color blindness will not abolish this impact (Bonilla-Silva, 2006).

In what follows, I explore how whiteness as hegemony operates in the field of education, particularly in the United States. More specifically, I offer answers to the following questions of critical importance to educators working in the field of critical multicultural, anti-racist, post-colonial education, interspersing my answers with reflections on some of the course assignments that have empowered my student-teachers to interrupt their own whiteness en route to becoming critical multicultural educators:

- What is whiteness?
- What is hegemony?
- How does whiteness as hegemony prevent most schools from empowering their students to become critically, creatively, and multiculturally literate?
- How can whiteness be unmasked and rendered visible? How can college students be empowered to develop the critical and creative multicultural practice denied to so many students in K-12 and college classrooms?

What Is Whiteness?

Whiteness involves what we look like—the color of our skin, the texture of our hair, the breadth of our noses, the shape of our backsides, all codes for race in the United States. However, whiteness is not only about race. It concerns more than our symbolic capital (Bourdieu, 1993):

> Whiteness is a complex, hegemonic, and dynamic set of mainstream socioeconomic processes, and ways of thinking, feeling, believing, and acting (cultural scripts) that function to obscure the power, privilege, and practices of the dominant social elite. Whiteness drives oppressive individual, group, and corporate practices that adversely impact schools, the wider U.S. society and, indeed, societies worldwide. At the same time, whiteness reproduces inequities, injustices, and inequalities within the educational system and wider society. We use the term whiteness rather than hegemony alone to signal these processes because a disproportionate number of white people have benefited, to greater or lesser extent, from whiteness. However, it is not our intention to continue to center whiteness. As a set of processes, whiteness recenters itself, and as such needs to be identified and transformed. (Lea & Sims, 2008, pp. 2–3)

The white male student-teacher who wrote the poem above was rare in his desire to cross race, class, and cultural borders and understand the process of whiteness that kept him from doing so. He was also rare in that he was married to a woman of color and thus, his motivation for understanding whiteness was deeply personal and emotional. Within the field of critical multicultural education, Ladson-Billings (1994), Nieto and Bode (2007), and Valenzuela (1999) among many researchers have shown that cultural, linguistic, and personal relevance are necessary to engage students in a curriculum. This was certainly true for this student. His poem, written at the end of the semester, suggests that fifteen weeks of the Multicultural Pedagogy course helped him relate to his own experience in gaining a greater understanding of his own white privilege. In his final reflection on the course, he wrote:

> This class has forced me to work outside my comfort zone more than any other class with the exception of speech class. I feel that I have come away with a better understanding of the place I occupy within society. I see that I am part of the dominant portion of society that gets to set the rules. As I made my mask I found that there were many things that would work for the side depicting how others see me. But when I tried to find images representing how I see myself I had a hard time. Part of the problem is that I feel unique and I feel that the mainstream media tends to dehumanize its subjects. I should not have been surprised that I have trouble finding images of "me" in glossy magazines.

The Mask is another course assignment that makes up the cultural portfolio. It is based on the theoretical idea that those of us who find meaning and support in our social groups do not question the authenticity of our identities. However, our identities are far from fixed. They are constituted by the discourses within which we live, work and play (Rabinow, 1984). As Stuart Hall (1993) told us:

> identity is not only a story, a narrative which we tell ourselves about ourselves, it is stories which change with historical circumstances. And identity shifts with the way in which we think and hear and experience them. Far from coming from the still small point of truth inside us, identities actually come from the outside, they are the way in which we are recognized and then come to step into the place of the recognitions which others give us. Without the others there is no self, there is not self-recognition. (p. 8)

In addition, our identities are complex. When we leave home to attend college, we often develop new identities, constituted by the new discourses we encounter at school. Returning home, we may find that old identities feel like badly fitting coats, hanging uncomfortably on the outside of new clothes. In my case, resisting the identity I was expected to inhabit as a child and young adult meant traveling six thousand miles from home to live freely with the new sense of who I was. Nevertheless, shedding the skins of old identities is never complete. "Our new skins always bear the marks of their predecessors" (Sumara & Davis, 1998).

The Mask assignment is designed to help students recognize the extent to which we are "designed" by the discourses/cultural scripts within which we are socialized. If teachers are to be able to develop their own voices in the service of educational social justice, they need to become aware of the ways in which public hegemonic discourses have shaped their identities. They need to recognize the extent to which they are seen by others in terms of these discourses and to which they actually identify with these discourses. This awareness is gained through the process of constructing their masks.

Students decorate the outside of their masks with images reflecting how they think others see them; they decorate the inside with images that reflect how they see their complex selves. The assignment helps student-teachers discuss whether, given the opportunity to step outside the discourses that define us, they would express more diverse selves. Creating their masks helps students recognize the ways in which they differ from the stereotypes others associate with their physical appearance—a process many low-income students, especially those of color, find particularly meaningful. Students also like the fact that the juxtaposition of their private and public selves opens up a space in which they can reflect critically on the discourses/cultural scripts that have impacted their lives. This is difficult when one is immersed in these discourses. As Clyde Kluckhorn wrote, "The fish would be the last creature to discover water" (Maxwell, 2004, p. 153).

Exercises like the Mask help us to see the water and explore the suggestion that nothing can be done to interrupt the deterministic power of cultural history. The dialogical act of juxtaposing our public and private selves allows us to step out of the water onto the banks from where we may gain a better view of the discourses that tell us what these selves are all about. Strengthened by this critical consciousness, we can better understand how the discourses of whiteness are embedded in our private as well as our public selves. As yet another of my students wrote in her end of semester reflection:

> My two favorite activities were the *Mask* and *I-Am Poem*. I believe these were my favorite and the most effective for me because I tend to express myself artistically. While writing my poem, I was astonished to find that I predominately related myself to the ocean. In the process of relating myself to the ocean, I found myself referring back to myself being caught in the waters of whiteness (a concept which I remember most from the readings). I began to realize how much this class has helped reshape my perception of culture and has taught me the importance of stepping outside the waters of whiteness in order to discard my former prejudices and stereotypes. Lastly, the mask allowed me to think critically about how I believe other people see me from the outside versus how I see myself on the inside. Doing this activity forced me to examine the ways in which my prejudices and stereotypes have outwardly affected the people I come in contact with on a daily basis. Doing this activity made me more aware of how people view me and made me want to change some of those things so that I, as an individual, can create a better, more culturally accepting, and peaceful society to live in. I definitely believe that the things which I have learned in this class as well as the tools I have been given have instilled a passion and desire inside of me to promote a multicultural education and in turn, touch the lives of all the children I come in contact with. *(White, female)*

Once critically aware of the ways in which whiteness has constituted us as subjects who are complicit in reproducing the increasingly hierarchical, capitalistic, neo-liberal state in which we live, we will be better able to see how whiteness works through us as a set of systematizing, normalizing, and disciplinary technologies that we impose on students in the classroom. In fact, over the last 500 hundred years, so-called Western states, including the United States, have been developing ever more effective technologies to shape their citizens who will work and live most effectively within evolving and increasingly corporatized socio-economic structures (Rabinow, 1984). Yet this process by which we are made in the image desired by the state is not wholly deterministic. Michel Foucault wrote: "Nothing is fundamental.... There are only reciprocal relations and the perpetual gaps between intentions in relation to one another." (Foucault, in During, 1993, p. 164.). We can unmask and interrupt this reciprocity and its function as whiteness, by recognizing the nature of our different relations and intentions and stepping into the gaps between them.

Unmasking whites and interrupting his reciprocal relations with other white people in his life was exactly what my white, male student was exploring in his poem. In the poem, he sees that his *color erects a wall that hides the true me.* He recognizes that other whites only see his persona of whiteness. He is able to engage in a racist joke, secure in the knowledge that he must reciprocate their assumptions about people of color: *"To you I am only that color that you see. We're both white so you share a joke about ghetto life."* Then, he points out that the presence of his wife would interrupt this reciprocity, this mutual acceptance of the process of whiteness— *"I guess you've yet to meet my wife?"* He is fully aware that racism and whiteness will mean that his children will not be able to experience this reciprocity based on mutual whiteness. His children will experience life on the downside of white privilege: *"My children won't be white like me. Their un-whiteness is all that society will see."*

Liberation from the whiteness discourses that most of us learn as part of our discursive communities from birth to death is a painful process. In fact, we do not usually have a chance to question this whiteness from alternative perspectives. Yet, engaging in a questioning process is essential if student-teachers are to become reflective educators, conscious of the lenses of whiteness through which they view the world—lenses that may potentially oppress their students. In dialogue, a few of my students tell me that they feel that their white privilege came at a price. While it continues to give white people—even poor whites—a social advantage, it locks them into a stereotypical box that limits how they are seen and expected to think, feel, believe, and act. It also confines them in a hierarchical dualistic relationship with people of color that precludes their working together to interrupt the laws and policies that have oppressive socio-economic consequences on the lives of all low-income people. It should be noted that rigid cultural expectations are also associated with gender, sexual orientation, linguistic, age, ability, and other complex socio-cultural discourses.

Some whites perceive that their privilege comes at a cost. They give up their diversity— ethnic and socio-economic class—in order to gain the advantage of whiteness. Some people of color also give up, at least publicly, their ethnic diversity and assume the cultural trappings of whiteness in order to be successful in the social hierarchy. However, the trade-off made by people of color has a more serious impact on them as a group. If whites want to remain within the mainstream of whiteness, they are limiting the discourses/cultural scripts available to them; their self-perception, their relationships with people of color, and the categories of knowledge they are likely to explore (Foucault, in Rabinow, 1984). However, given their numbers and relative power, they are not limiting their access to other whites. On the other hand, people of color, while limiting their self-perception, and the categories of knowledge they are likely to explore, are also limiting their relationships with a majority of people of color who do not embrace an upwardly mobile frame of reference (Ogbu, 1995). Even facing these trade-offs, it is understandable that people of color as well as whites would embrace many of the cultural norms and values of whiteness in order to be successful within the existing socioeconomic structure. It is hard to escape whiteness; it is the "best game" in town. In spite of this possibility for human agency and resistance, (we should) "not deny that (people) are often duped by culture" (Grossberg, in Giroux & McLaren, 1994, p. 6)—in this case the cultural process of whiteness as hegemony.

What Is Hegemony?

Hegemony is the process through which this duping takes place. As a social process, hegemony is a broader concept that includes ideology in terms of its impact on society. Ideology has been defined as "shared ideas or beliefs which serve to justify the interests of dominant groups" (Giddens, 1997, p. 583). Ideology is disseminated through all of the major institutions in the United States. Those in positions of corporate and/or political power disseminate ideology in order to have a conservative and/or self-serving impact on relations of power. People who manipulate ideology aim to reproduce their own interests.

> Hegemony combines ideological power with the consent of the people. Gramsci meant the permeation *throughout* society of an entire system of values, attitudes, beliefs and morality that has the effect of supporting the status quo in power relations. Hegemony in this sense might be defined as an "organising principle" that is diffused by the process of socialisation into every area of daily life. To the extent that this prevailing consciousness is internalised by the population it becomes part of what is generally called 'common sense' so that the philosophy, culture and morality of the ruling elite come to appear as the natural order of things. (Boggs, 1976, p. 39)

While members of dominant groups may be very sincere in their beliefs or ideas, they may be seen by those of us occupying alternative ideological territory as manipulating common sense public narratives or blatantly distorting reality to achieve their ends. By its nature, hegemony masks the origins of the ideological discourses it represents. It "bamboozles" us into thinking its processes are grounded in truth and are natural and normal. For example, the 2002 Elementary and Secondary Education Act, was dubbed "No Child Left Behind" (NCLB). Yet it is my contention, whether they were all aware of it or not, the authors of NCLB never intended to "leave no child behind." Public schools today are pursuing the same agenda as those of the common school in the nineteenth century. Joel Spring (2008) has clearly articulated that the main agenda of the common school when it was developed in the United States in the nineteenth century was to domesticate those students who met citizenship requirements into acquiring the cultural norms and values that would enable them to serve the nascent corporate, capitalist, "Christian" political economy. Spring and others (Kumashiro, 2008; Emery & Ohanian, 2004) argue that the public school agenda was, and remains, to prepare these students to fill the positions required by an increasingly hierarchical economy, requiring, in order to be functional, a significant redundant prison worker population. Thus, schools may be seen as functional when they *do* produce high school dropouts.

In *American Education* (2007), Spring asks the following questions and offers a significant response:

> How did educating workers for a global economy get translated into core high school curriculum of only four years of English and four years of math consisting of algebra I and II, geometry, and data analysis and statistics? Why aren't other subjects included in the core curriculum such as history, civics, art, physical education, and science? The answer is that communication skills and math, along with a good work ethic, are the main concern of employers filling entry-level jobs.

In spite of its proclaimed goal of improving educational achievement and reducing the "achievement gap"—or the "wealth gap" as Kitty Kelly Epstein calls it (Epstein, in Pollick, 2008)—between white and Asian students on the one hand, and students from African American, Latino, and Indigenous backgrounds and children from low-income backgrounds on the other,

> after six years, there is overwhelming evidence that the deeply flawed "No Child Left Behind" law (NCLB) is doing more harm than good in our nation's public schools. NCLB's test-and-punish approach to school reform relies on limited, one-size-fits-all tools that reduce education to little more than test prep. It produces unfair decisions and requires unproven, often irrational "solutions" to complex problems. NCLB is clearly underfunded, but fully funding a bad law is not a solution.
>
> Public recognition of the law's ill effects has produced a growing consensus in favor of a fundamental overhaul. It's time for a new conception of the federal role in education—beyond standards, tests and punishments—in order to strengthen schools and truly leave no child behind. (Pytel, 2007)

Hegemony also plays out in teachers' responses to NCLB. While the act has restricted the practices of teachers in elementary and secondary schools, turning them into technicians, obliged to teach to a script associated with high stakes tests (FairTest, 2008; Sleeter, 2004), the vast majority of educators go along with the increasingly standardized teaching practices that NCLB mandates (Pytel, 2007).

How does whiteness as hegemony prevent most schools from empowering their students to become critically, creatively, and multiculturally literate?

Whiteness, as hegemony, works in powerful ways to curtail genuine educational opportunities for low-income students, who are disproportionately of color. Research indicates that among the most economically challenged social classes, socio-economic and cultural factors, particularly family and neighborhood influences—not genetics—are strongly associated with academic performance (Berliner & Nichols, 2007; Steinberg & Kincheloe, 2007; Bowles & Gintis, 1976). However, the current reductive curriculum and the hierarchical evaluation system by which California schools and students are being assessed provide modern-day deficit theorists with a great deal of hegemonic ammunition for their classist, racist, and sexist explanations of why some children fail to meet the standards of "hyper-accountability" in public schools (Epstein, 2006; Mansell, 2007; See Ryan, 1971, for a critique of deficit theory.) Given the longevity of hegemonic racism and classism in the United States, punctuated by pseudo-scientific race theory constructed to legitimize the socio-economic system of slavery and legal segregation, we should not be surprised that white people, who have not been encouraged to engage in assignments designed to unmask whiteness, still hold deficit views about people of color. Nor should we be surprised at the tenacity of internalized racism experienced by students of color who live in a discursive system in which whiteness, as hegemony, conceals the awful details of slavery, and the genocide of native people, and uses school to gain the consent of citizens to a kinder version of "American history." In her excellent analysis of "post traumatic slave syndrome," Dr. Joy DeGruy Leary (2008) "traces the history of African Americans from slavery through their virtual re-enslavement by Peonage, Black Codes, Convict Lease and Jim Crow segregation to contemporary problems facing African Americans today." In spite of their extraordinary resiliency, African Americans, Indigenous people, Latinos/as and others whom John Ogbu (1995) termed "caste minorities," have experienced officially sanctioned oppression and genocide, the details of which are still missing from most text books (Loewen, 1995). Howard Zinn's and Rebecca Stefoff's (2007) new *Young Peoples' History of the United States* redresses this issue and is a timely addition to available historical texts for children.

In pursuing their analysis, deficit theorists, then, harness historical U.S. hegemonic mechanisms. Consciously or unconsciously, or what Joyce King called "dysconsciously" (1991)—when we seek to avoid discomfort by relegating a matter to a place just below consciousness—deficit theorists do not recognize and/or they personally benefit from the oppressive bias in their analysis and practice. They have been successful over the years in colonizing public educational space with Eurocentric, competitive, and rationalistic values and cognitive processes that define the assessment measures by which students and schools are judged. For example, Ruby Payne's (1995), *A Framework for Understanding Poverty,* is a deficit prescription for ameliorating the limited school achievement and success of poor students within the rules of a cultural game, designed in the nineteenth century to domesticate those students who met citizenship requirements into acquiring the cultural norms and values that would enable them to serve the nascent corporate, capitalist, "Christian" political economy (Spring, 2008; 2007; Kumashiro, 2008; Emery & Ohanian, 2004).

Payne herself has little or no idea that her own "whiteness" is driving the prescription she is advocating for the schooling of generationally poor students (Payne, 2006). She validates, without question, the cultural space that is typically considered to be normal in school. She describes poor students in terms of deficit stereotypes instead of framing the reality faced by generationally low-income students as one of being in a vulnerable, powerless position in relation to the privileged school culture, with which they are often unfamiliar. She argues that these students need to reject the "hidden rules" associated with the norms, values, and relationships familiar in their class and/or ethnic backgrounds in order to be successful in school (Payne, 1995). Unlike Igoa (1995), who told us that her newcomer students needed to have their home cultures integrated into and validated by the classroom culture in order to feel "alive and whole in the world," Payne's message is clear: the mainstream, white, middle-class school culture is the only one of value.

The pedagogical space considered valid by Payne is colonized by the hegemony of whiteness. As Dyer told us many years ago, whiteness has "colonized the definition of normal" (Dyer, 1988). Unless our student-teachers, who are disproportionately white, have interrogated their own whiteness (Lea & Helfand, 2004; McIntosh, 1989) and are able to engage in praxis—reflecting on their own whiteness in the classroom as it emerges and acting to transform it—they are likely to continue to reproduce the status quo in which whites and some Asians are most successful in school. Moreover, as suggested, this transformation is not just about teachers working on their own whiteness. Whiteness is encoded in how and what we teach. As we have learned from Michel Foucault (Rabinow, 1984), controlling ideas and relations of domination inform most of our present-day patterns of social, economic and political organization, social policies, and dominant ideological positions. These same patterns are present and may be unveiled in the field of education:

> [These] "dividing practices" are clearly central to the organizational processes of education in our society. These divisions and objectifications are achieved either within the subject or between the subject and others. The use of testing, examining, profiling, and streaming in education, the use of entry criteria for different types of schooling, and the formation of different types of intelligence, ability, and scholastic identity in the processes of schooling are all examples of such dividing practices. In these ways, using these techniques and forms of organization, and the creation of separate and different curricula, pedagogies, forms of teacher-student relationships, identities and subjectivities are formed, learned and carried. Through the creation of remedial and advanced groups, and the separation of the educationally subnormal or those with special educational needs, abilities are stigmatized and normalized. (Ball, 1990, p. 4)

How can whiteness be unmasked and rendered visible? How can pre-service teachers be empowered to develop the critical and creative multicultural practice denied to so many students in K-12 and college classrooms?

> We need to provide [student-teachers] with opportunities to identify the hegemonic practices that divide us and that constitute us as ideal subjects that reproduce the status quo. We need to help [student-teachers] to question the dominant categories of knowledge that those in positions of corporate and political power consider acceptable and appropriate. The dam that prevents counter-hegemonic knowledge from reaching the mainstream could theoretically burst if more of us joined the already growing number of individual and group activists to plan, organize, and work in solidarity to publicly challenge the whiteness hegemony that is being practiced in our names—from the standardized testing and tracking practices in schools to the imperialist policies abroad. (Lea & Sims, 2008, pp. 191–192)

The I-Poem and the Mask are both assignments that have helped my student-teachers to "identify the hegemonic practices that divide us and that constitute us as ideal subjects that reproduce the status quo" (Ibid). Through these and other assignments, some of which are outlined below, my student-teachers develop critical, multicultural, and creative consciousness that will theoretically serve them well in the quest to facilitate critical, multicultural, and creative consciousness in their own students. I am currently undertaking research to find out how new teachers fare once they leave college in terms of implementing a critical social justice curriculum in which whiteness is unmasked in an ongoing basis. Data suggest that many new teachers struggle to maintain the teaching agenda to which they appeared committed while they were in my class—one that includes developing critical, multicultural, and creative consciousness in their own students from a young age. Most new teachers find themselves in school cultures that validate the hegemonic mainstream. They find themselves swimming upstream. As a result, while we need to continue to develop assignments that help student-teachers (and ourselves) to unmask whiteness and empower critical and creative multicultural practice, we must also work with and connect communities and institutions outside of the college to support and further our students' goals.

In my teacher education courses, I strive to present *education* as the process by which we develop critical consciousness and understanding, from multiple perspectives, of how our world and society work, and of how we think, feel believe and act in that society and world. To be educated is to become more and more liberated. "Liberation is a praxis: the action and re-flection of men (and women) upon their world in order to transform it" (Freire, 1993/1970, p. 62). To be educated requires that we reject the idea that education is a one-way street in which the teacher chooses and deposits knowledge in his/her students, controlling their behavior and responses, treating his/her students as appropriately meek objects of her authority.

> Throughout much of my educational years, I have suffered under what we call the "banking concept of education" (Freire, 1993/1970). Teachers and former professors would continuously pour out various facts and dates that I was expected to memorize and regurgitate in the form of a written test. Overtime, I began to see this method as ineffective and unbeneficial not only to my education, but to my overall development of an individual of society. While reflecting back upon this whole process (of the Multi-cultural Pedagogy course), I have come to realize how much richer and beneficial my education could have been had my teachers and professors put more emphasis on a multicultural education. *(White, female student-teacher)*

In traditional hegemonic terms, the good student is a "docile body" (Foucault, in Rab-inow, 1984). In critical multicultural terms, the good teacher engages in "problem-posing education" in which content scripted by a state increasingly interwoven with corporate interests is replaced with "the problems of men (and woman) in their relations with the world" (Freire, 1993/1970, p. 63). Problem-posing education is the development of critical, emotional, and spiritual literacy through dialogue. It is the process by which we construct our own knowledge in response to the contradictions and tensions of our everyday experiences. It is meta-con-sciousness. It is the development of critical, emotional, and spiritual literacy through dialogue. It is the process by which we construct our own knowledge in response to the contradictions and tensions of our everyday experiences. It is, as we learned from the insights of Paulo Freire (1993/1970), the ability to be able to "read the word and the world," and act on it justly and humanely.

While my students in the Educational Foundations and the Social Studies methods courses that I teach gain insights into how whiteness, as hegemony, operates through school through, for example, role plays, critiques of official texts, videos and DVDs, the following represents the main assignments in the Multicultural Pedagogy course:

1. **The Cultural Portfolio (including narratives (Lea, 2004), I-Poem (Lea & Sims, 2008), Mask, and Imaging Whiteness (Lea & Sims, 2008) assignments:** This assign-ment is designed to help student-teachers become more aware of how public discourses or cultural scripts shape their private behavior toward and ways of thinking, feeling, be-lieving about students, their families, and communities and about what should go on in the classroom. The I-Poem and Mask have been discussed earlier in this chapter. The other two assignments, *Cultural Narratives* and *Imaging Whiteness,* are discussed in Lea (2004) and Lea and Sims (2008), respectively.

2. **The Culture Shock:** This assignment is designed to help student-teachers address the stereotypes and anxieties they hold with respect to social and cultural groups about which they have had little and/or negative contact. Student-teachers seek out and experience culture shock in a "safe" situation, with a group of people about whom they hold deficit assumptions. They learn how to navigate their own culture shock. They apply what they

have learned from their own experience to developing ways of helping students who are not part of the mainstream school culture to navigate culture shock in the classroom. They consider how to develop a classroom climate that meets all of their students' needs. (Igoa, 1995)

3. **The Funds of Knowledge:** This assignment is designed to help candidates cross cultural borders, recognize the rich cultural resources that exist in cultural communities that they hitherto saw in deficit terms. Through local schools or other relationships, students identify families from ethnic and socio-economic class backgrounds about whom they have little knowledge or hold deficit assumptions. They ask permission of these families to interview them in their homes as a ways of learning more about their strong cultural knowledge and networks. They then identify the cultural resources located in the homes and communities and list them as the bases for rich, inviting, cultural responsive learning plans. (Moll et al., 1992)

4. **Multicultural Teaching Strategies:** This assignment is designed to help candidates *begin* to develop critical and culturally relevant learning plans that teach students about social justice, equity, and caring, and meet students' needs by incorporating critical multicultural teaching strategies and building on students' "funds of knowledge."

While my students have found all of the assignments important to the development of their critical consciousness, the Culture Shock is the assignment that students cited as having first jolted them out of the discursive water they have been swimming in. The assignment involves students going by themselves into a community about which they honestly recognize that they have deficit and/or stereotypical cognitive and emotional assumptions. They spend about four hours in this environment, identify their emotions and assumptions, and write about these responses to the experience. The goal of the assignment is for students to experience and observe their reactions to the discomforting feelings of disorientation to a cultural world that is strange to them (i.e., many of the familiar cultural markers have moved or are absent). It is an experience familiar to many of their students as they enter the school world colonized by whiteness.

This activity is based on two widely recognized premises: (1) Culture shock is endemic— If we are to move in an unsegregated world, we cannot inoculate ourselves against it. We can, however, improve our recovery mechanisms, minimize discomfort, and maximize our understandings of the unfamiliar cultural world; and (2) Our not-OK feelings, once recognized, have a tendency to dissipate if not disappear all together (Neves, 1998).

One of my students reflected on her culture shock experience as follows:

For my culture shock exercise, I wanted to go somewhere where I would experience a culture that I have had little to no contact with. I decided to go to a Korean church in Santa Rosa. I was surprised to find that before I even went to the church, I expected the Korean people to be shy, quiet, and driven (a stereotype that I have obviously collected from society over the years). After doing this assignment, I realized just how much I have been led astray by society's perception of Koreans and I learned that this ethnic group of people can actually be very lively, outgoing, talkative, and friendly. When I returned home, I began to think of previous encounters I have had with Koreans. I realized that there have actually been many opportunities in which I could have embraced the Korean culture but I had chosen not to simply because they were different and I didn't have to engage with them if I chose not to. This is a sad realization, but it is very true. Little did I realize, I would learn a very similar lesson when conducting my Funds-of-Knowledge activity.

However, public education in the United States does not generally offer students a curriculum that allows students to experience and recover from culture shock, leading to critical consciousness, social justice activism, and hope. I include in the notion of "curriculum" more than is usually understood by the student-teachers who enter my *multicultural pedagogy, educational foundations,* and *social studies methods* courses. Curriculum is an "ongoing, if complicated, conversation" (Pinar, 2004, 188). It is co-constructed, whether the parties are aware of it or not, by teacher and students within school and classroom power relations and cultural norms and values. From a critical multicultural perspective, textbooks and scripted assignments are always interpreted through the discourses/cultural scripts that the teacher and students bring into the classroom. These discourses shape, for example, which reading texts are used or, in an age of mandated texts, *how* they are used. The emergent curriculum, even in a scripted classroom, has the potential to be a site of empowerment, as described by McLaren (2003):

> Schools should provide students with a language of criticism and a language of hope. The languages should be used in order to prepare students to conceptualize systematically the relationships among their private dreams and desires and the collective dreams of a larger social order. New generations of students must be capable of analyzing the social and material conditions in which dreams are given birth, and are realized, diminished, or destroyed. More importantly, students need to be able to recognize which dreams and which dreamers are dangerous to the larger society, and why this is the case. Schools need to foster collective dreaming, a dreaming that speaks to the creation of social justice for all groups, and the eventual elimination of classism, racism, sexism, and homophobia. This can occur only if schools are able and committed to help students analyze the ways in which their subjectivities have been ideologically formed within the exploitative forces and relations of globalized, transnational capitalism. (pp. 178–179)

I agree with McLaren's conception of what schools should provide our students. However, it is more often these days the imposition of a one-sided conservative, back-to-basics narrative that sees the classroom as a tool to prepare students for future economic roles in low-skilled jobs and service industries. It is more than 2000 years since Plato described the ideal social system in *Republic* (Rouse, 1956), yet the notion that such a system naturally consists of a hierarchy is alive and well. Many, if not most, of the teachers I encounter, who have been socialized within a society in which the hegemony of whiteness touches us all, still continue to categorize their students' reading and math levels as "high," "middle," and "low." This categorization is not unlike the classifications Payne (1995) uses in her book—"poverty," "middle class," and "wealth"—which she associated with reductive stereotypes.

Many teachers demonstrate no critical awareness of the potential consequences of the labels high, middle, and low on their own expectations of their students (and on their students' expectation of themselves if they recognize, as they often do, what these labels mean). In Platonic metaphors, most teachers apparently still see students as belonging to groups made of differentially valued metals. They use official classifications of students as unproblematic—English language learners, special education, at-risk, for example—and their pedagogy derives from these classifications.

We are loathe to live in the state of cognitive dissonance that accompanies the process of change (Festinger, 1957). It is not easy to come to different views about the nature of students, people, school, and society than those of our significant others. Such a departure would lead to open conflict with those with whom we crave harmony, company, and support. So we avoid deep personal change. Those among us who have been socialized at an early age into believing that race is a material condition that ranks us hierarchically in society, usually continue to believe in this distortion of reality as we experience it as common sense. The alternative view was, at its inception, that race was a myth whose authors concealed their intentions, perhaps even from themselves, to legitimize slavery, indentureship, and colonialism. They managed to encode this myth in law and public policy and persuade the public of its veracity and common sense. Some of my students have a hard time taking this latter interpretation seriously. They have been raised on a diet of patriotism, saluting the flag in their infancy, spoon fed at least one line from U.S. President Abraham Lincoln's Gettysburg Address of 1863 in which he succinctly explained that "all men are created equal" (Lincoln, 1863). It is hard to unmask the hegemonic nature of what seems like the normal and natural foundation of their lives.

However, as humans and, thus, cultural beings, we are potentially dynamic and open to change. With awareness of our tendency to follow the hegemonic tide down river, we can thrust out towards a tributary and change the direction of our practice. Like the vast majority of students in schools in the United States, my youngest daughter had her own version of what was normal and natural. At age five, she saw the film *Jaws* on television, fell in love with sharks, and dreamed of saving them from human predators. At age fourteen, closely guarding her dream of becoming a marine biologist, she attended the reception for new high school students at our local ethnically diverse, working-class public school in northern California. During the reception, she was approached by a white male counselor, who asked her what she wanted to become when she left school. My daughter told him about her dream of becoming a marine biologist. The counselor was clearly impressed. He asked her where she was thinking of going to school. "UC Santa Cruz," my daughter replied. The counselor was less impressed. He told her to try California State University, Humboldt, or even better to begin her university career at the local junior college.

As an associate professor at a California State University (CSU), I have enormous respect for the public higher education system that the CSU represents, as I do for the California community college system. In spite of the current shortsighted budget proposal that many of us who work in the CSU and Community College systems are currently challenging, these higher education systems have played an important historical role in offering students, whose K-12 experiences were not educationally empowering, the opportunity to pursue higher education. The cuts would disproportionately impact low-income students and students of color.

However, if my child chose to dream of going to a university that was harder to enter— one of the universities that made up the University of California (UC) system—I would not have this counselor, a person who had no knowledge of my child, dampen her dreams. I was standing behind my daughter, and edged forward. My daughter sensed my presence and said to the counselor, "This is my mother." The counselor looked at me and then turned back to my daughter. Momentarily he said, "Maybe you can get into a UC."

The significance of this story is lost unless the reader is aware that my daughter's father is African American. She is a child of African, Cherokee, and European (multiple ethnicities) descent. The counselor took one look at my coloring and features and categorized me as someone whose presence in my daughter's life would give her a better chance of going to a

UC. He may have been unaware of his racist assumptions, but, over time, this man could have exerted considerable negative influence over my daughter if my own whiteness had not interceded—unspoken—and reframed the lens through which he saw my daughter. How many students of color in the United States can draw on unearned white privilege to disrupt the nightmare of racism and whiteness that they all too often encounter in public school in the United States?

My youngest daughter went through high school six years ago. She was very successful in terms of her schooling and was able to fulfill her dream of going to UC Santa Cruz. She is now pursuing a Masters degree at a California State University. However, in my view, my daughter's *education* in her public high school had more to do with the critical and creative spaces that she and her friends—who called themselves "the AP chicas"—constructed within the confines of their schooling than with the official school curriculum. Early on in their high school careers, these seven friends, from African American, Mexican American, Chicano, European American, Japanese American, Indian American, and African backgrounds, developed an understanding that if they were going to be able to navigate the contradictory cultures of school, they would need to do so as a collective. There was strength in their numbers. They could avoid the potential tension that existed because of their friendships with the students in "honors" classes who had decided not to participate fully in what they perceived to be the irrelevant curriculum of school (Kohl, 1991). They did not dream of higher education, perhaps because of what Claude Steele terms "stereotype threat." According to Steele, "when a person's social identity is attached to a negative stereotype, that person will tend to underperform in a manner consistent with the stereotype" (Steele, 2004). Responding to the ubiquitous racist and classist stereotypes, which abounded in my daughter's school, these students did not aspire to enroll in the few AP classes available at the school that would help them get into a UC. To survive in these contradictory waters, the girls decided to study together, hang out together on weekends, and support each other when some of their "friends" called them names for working hard to get the grades that would allow them access to a UC. These seven girls, from diverse ethnic backgrounds, all fulfilled their UC dreams.

Conclusion

As my daughter's stories illustrate, below the surface of change in the United States, whiteness is still playing a role in propping up the hierarchical edifice of capitalism (McLaren, 2005). While we do see some change in the color of the faces of those in the passageways of the mainstream, the underlying socio-economic structures remain intact. Indeed, there is an increasing concentration of wealth in the hands of the few and increasing poverty for the many.

According to Anyon (2005),

> a full 38% of American children are identified as poor—27 million who lived in families with income up to 200% of the official poverty line. These children live in poverty as well—although official statistics do not designate them as such. . .This revised measure reveals a national scandal (which) is that the majority of Black and Latino children still suffer poverty. . .a full 57% of African American, 64 % of Latino children, and 34% of White children were poor in the U.S. in 2001. (Lu, 2003, p. 2)

A few token people of color and women make it to the top of the hierarchy, a greater number make it into the mainstream, and a man of mixed-race descent, Barack Obama, has been chosen by the Democratic voters to run for the presidency of the United States—although not without facing a highly racialized campaign manipulating many of the nation's hegemonic race, socio-economic, and gender commonsense discourses (Dowd, 2008). Yet, people of color and women are still more likely to find themselves at the bottom of the socio-economic scale. This is how race and socio-economic class are interwoven—people of color are still disproportionately poor and experience the consequences of poverty.

Yet, formal education offers us the space in which to unmask the hegemony of whiteness and empower critical and creative multicultural practice. It is not neutral. In the last book he wrote before his death, Paulo Freire, the well-known Brazilian educator wrote: "Nobody can be in the world, with the world, and with others in a neutral manner" (Freire, 2004, p. 60). Freire sees human beings as "a presence in the world." This presence involves taking risks; "education also involves risk and change." Our purpose is not to adapt to the world, but to transform it. Freire also notes that when we feel we have to adapt to the world, we should see this as a temporary phase on the road toward intervening and transforming the world. This is because "being in the world" means recognizing our responsibilities and commitments toward the other human beings in it (Farahmandpur, 2006).

Although the forces of history shape our past and present, we can change the course of history and in the process make history. As Freire puts it, "The future does not make us, we make ourselves in the struggle to make it" (2004, p. 34). We can break away from the chains of history passed down to us from previous generations and make our own history. In other words, while we as human beings are conditioned by history, we can, like Freire, refuse to accept that we are determined by it. For us, as for Freire, history can be possibility.

At the end of the semester, I tell my student-teachers to continue to critically read the official texts they are asked to use in their classrooms and to learn to critically read their world. I ask them to embrace a *Pedagogy of Indignation* as well as a *Pedagogy of Hope* (Freire, 1994). I ask them to look closely at themselves every day to recognize how they contribute to both reproducing and changing the inequities they see around them. I ask them to take whatever risks they can to challenge the existing oppressions and injustices in the world. At the same time, I encourage them, where possible, to stand in solidarity with others in a space that promises the possibility of action in the service of greater humanity and social justice.

By the end of a semester in my Multicultural Pedagogy class, a majority of my white, middle-class students wrote reflections that indicated the effect that some of their experiences in the class had on their ability to unmask whiteness—institutional, cultural and in themselves:

> Throughout this semester I have learned many things about myself that I never thought I would have to examine, I have been forced into seemingly uncomfortable situations in order to get a view from the other side, I have learned to think critically about my culture/ background, my ethnicity, my religion, and other values I hold, and most importantly I have learned to be open and accepting of other opinions put forth by my peers. This process has been both familiar, and at times unfamiliar in its workings. All my life I have tried to convince myself that I am not one to judge, or base my thinking about people off of stereotypes, but in making my way through the course of this class I have discovered that most of these stereotypes I encounter are unconscious. In other words, I have no idea that I am even using judgments in any of my thought processes! I have been able to see the prejudgments I make unconsciously on a regular basis and change my thought processes so that I am able to avoid making stereotypes before learning more about an individual. *(White female student)*

In this chapter, I have shared some small but, I believe, significant and hopeful steps in the form of critical and creative classroom practice in teacher education college classrooms towards unmasking whiteness.

Note

A very significant event has just overtaken this chapter. Yesterday, the United States elected its first Black president, Barack Obama, a reality many of us did not believe possible in our lifetimes. Listening and participating last night, via the television, to the joy of so many African Americans, from ordinary citizens to Civil Rights leaders like Jesse Jackson and John Lewis, the enormity of what had happened swept over me. At the time of writing, 52% of the population has voted for Obama, a number that includes 60% of the white vote, and an overwhelming number of voters under twenty five. The demographic map of Obama's victory looks much more like the United States than that of his opponent. I heard accolades from Kenya, the country from which his father hailed, from Japan, from England and the European Union. Only the president of Russia seemed to offer a less than positive response.

I cried tears of joy for the potential empowerment Obama's election offered my own children, who, like the president elect, were born of a white mother and Black father. Someone "like them" had achieved the highest office in the land. I cried tears of joy that my two-year-old grandbaby, also descended in part from enslaved Africans, would grow up knowing that one drop of African blood would no longer, de jure or de facto, determine what one could achieve in the United States. I cried tears of joy for all of the children who pass through our schools for whom Obama's success might be motivational in their own journeys. I saw the joy of people of color and white allies, at home and abroad, celebrating the possibility of a new future. All of them had hoped and worked long and hard for this day.

I also saw many people whose interest in electing Obama had more to do with his proposed solutions to the economy in crisis than his ethnic background. They chose Obama for the "content of his character"—his policies at a time of economic crisis at home and war abroad—rather than "the color of his skin." Journalists were asking if Obama's election signaled the end of racism. In his concession speech, John McCain said, "I have always believed that America offers opportunity to all who have the industry and will to achieve it."

And herein lies the concern of Bonilla-Silva (2006) and others, a concern I share, with respect to "the new racism" in the United States. We *did* witness last evening a revolution of American values and ideas, but those who voted for Obama constituted barely more than half the electorate. We *have* witnessed a transformation of American politics. However, the rhetoric from the liberal media never once addressed the enormous cultural and structural inequities, represented in law and public and educational policy, that will not be dissipated by this election. Obama's election does not mean that the playing field of United States society is suddenly equitable. The public sphere has not suddenly become an unbiased, objective space in which all comers compete fairly for resources. Structural and cultural racism, classism, the hegemony of whiteness, and other interlocking oppressions continue to shape our lives.

On the other hand, hegemonic forces are already "spinning" this election into a cloth it cannot possibly become. Manning Marable, interviewed by Amy Goodman on the radio/television show, *Democracy Now*, clearly described the reality. African American expectations cannot be realized by the election of one man. The apparatus of American society was not designed to liberate Black people. Indeed, Obama in his acceptance speech warned against outrageous expectations and described a difficult road ahead that requires much work. The majority of the electorate may have moved beyond personal racism in electing Obama, but institutional and cultural racism still colonize the public arena, including school. Our unconscious hegemonic assumptions are, in large measure, still associated with whiteness.

To work towards dismantling hegemony we must feel comfortable in our dissent. Yet, in his concession speech, John McCain also said that there was no reason now why anyone should not cherish his or her citizenship of the United States. In my view, this was a warning to those of us who would continue to critique the socio-economic and political structure of the United States and the way those in power are able to manipulate the public media, education, and other cultural tools to reproduce their power. It was a continuation of the Bush Administration's McCarthyesque warning against dissent after the events of 9/11—a discourse that characterized the McCain campaign. In many parts of the country and in many schools, it will continue to be hard to voice a challenge to the "common sense" (Kumashiro, 2008) hegemonic view that the United States is a meritocracy. It will continue to be difficult to convince people that many corporate and governmental policymakers and administrators see students as "human resources," rather than human beings, competing for existing jobs under a system of "equal opportunity" (Spring, 2007). Some amongst us who are managing to live quality lives will continue to see poor people, who are disproportionately of color, as deficient in some way if they do not make it out of poverty. Moreover, arguments legitimizing the hurdles that punctuate this hierarchical social system and make access to higher education, highly paid jobs, and professional work difficult will continue to be made. Some will use Obama's election as evidence that these hurdles are not so high and that anyone can surmount them with determination and effort.

So, while we must take heart and energy from Obama's victory for the work ahead, we must recognize that whiteness, racism, classism, sexism, homophobia, ableism, and other interlocking oppressions still exist in the light of day in the United States. These realities will have to be brought to the willing consciousness of a critical mass of the people and then systematically dismantled. As Dr. Robert Franklin, president of Morehouse College in Atlanta, overjoyed as he was with the result, said after the election: "Race continues to be an issue but we have bounded forward in an extraordinary way." We have forward momentum that we can harness to continue to interrogate and challenge the whiteness that so many of us embody to a greater of lesser degree. We will need to engage in a vigilant praxis to make sure that we interrupt the whiteness that will otherwise continue to play out in the everyday details of our private and public lives, including school. We will have to work on all fronts to reframe and transform the socio-economic infrastructure that supports the socio-economic, cultural and political inequities that now characterize the landscape of the United States.

Those who are concerned about hegemony as whiteness acknowledge this reality and see this election as a platform from which we should launch an even greater effort to institute critical multicultural education in our schools. Much work is needed to unmask whiteness in the teacher education college classroom and beyond, and engage in critical and creative practice. Indeed, we must work together to bring about greater social justice and caring in our professional and interpersonal lives.

References

Anyon, J. (2005). *Radical possibilities: Public policy, urban education, and a new social movement.* New York: Routledge.

Ball, S. (1990). *Foucault and education.* New York: Routledge.

Berliner, D. & Nichols, S. L. (2007, March 12). High-stakes testing is putting the nation at risk. *Education Week.*

Boggs, C. (1976). *Gramsci's Marxism.* London: Pluto Press.

Bonilla-Silva, E. (2006). *Racism without racists: Color-blind racism and the persistence of racial inequality in the United States.* Lanham, MI: Rowman & Littlefield.

Bourdieu, P. (1993). *Language and symbolic power.* Cambridge, MA: Polity Press.

Bowles & Gintis (1976). *Schooling in capitalist America: Educational reform and the contradictions of economic life.* New York: Routledge.

Dowd, M. (2008, March 2). A wake-up call for Hillary. *The New York Times.* Retrieved May 20, 2008: http://www.nytimes.com/2008/03/02/opinion/02dowd.html?scp=6&sq=Michelle+Obama%2C+Patriotism&st=nyt

During, S. (1993). *Cultural studies: A critical introduction.* New York: Routledge.

Dyer, R. (1988). White. *Screen,* 29 (4).

Emery, K. & Ohanian, S. (2004). *Why is corporate America bashing our public schools?* Portsmouth, NH: Heinemann.

Epstein, K. K. (2006). *A different view of urban schools: Civil rights, critical race theory, and unexplored realities.* New York: Peter Lang.

FairTest (2008, January 25). "Child Left Behind" After six years: an escalating track record of failure. Retrieved April 11, 2008 from the FairTest website: http://www.fairtest.org/NCLB-After-Six-Years

Farahmandpur, F. (2006, January 11). Freire, Paulo. (2004). *Pedagogy of Indignation.* Boulder, CO: Paradigm Publishers. Retrieved May 20, 2008 from The Education Review: A Journal of Book Reviews website: http://edrev.asu.edu/reviews/rev454.htm

Festinger, L. A. (1957). *A theory of cognitive dissonance.* Evanston, IL: Ron Peterson.

Freire, P. (1993/1970). *Pedagogy of the oppressed.* New York: Continuum.

Freire, P. (1994). *Pedagogy of hope: Reliving pedagogy of the oppressed.* New York: Continuum.

Freire, P. (2004). *Pedagogy of indignation.* Boulder, CO: Paradigm Publishers.

Giddens, A. (1997). *Sociology.* 3rd ed. Cambridge: Polity Press.

Grossberg, L. (1994). Introduction: Bringin' it all back home: Pedagogy and cultural studies. In H. A. Giroux & P. McLaren (Eds.), *Between borders: Pedagogy and the politics of cultural studies.* New York: Routledge.

Hall, S. (1993). Negotiating Caribbean Identities. *Walter Rodney Memorial Lecture.* Centre for Caribbean Studies, University of Warwick.

Ignatiev, N., & Garvey, J. (1996). *Race traitor.* New York: Routledge.

Igoa, C. (1995). *The inner world of the immigrant child.* Mahwah, NJ: Lawrence Erlbaum Associates.

King, J. (1991). Dysconscious racism: Ideology, identity, and the miseducation of teachers. *Journal of Negro Education,* 60 (2), 1–14.

Kohl, H. (1991). *I won't learn from you!* Minneapolis, MN: Milkweed Editions.

Kumashiro, K. (2008). *The seduction of common sense: How the right has framed the debate on America's schools.* New York: Teachers College Press.

Ladson-Billings, G. (1994). *The Dreamkeepers: Successful teachers of African American children.* San Francisco: Jossey-Bass.

Lea, V. (2004, March/April). The reflective cultural portfolio: Identifying public scripts in the private voices of white student-teachers. *Journal of Teacher Education,* 55 (2), 116–127.

Lea, V., & Helfand, J. (2004). *Identifying race and transforming whiteness in the classroom.* New York: Peter Lang.

Lea, V., & Sims, E. J. (2008). *Undoing whiteness in the classroom: Critical educultural teaching approaches for social justice activism.* New York: Peter Lang.

Leary, J. D. (2008). Post traumatic slave syndrome: America's legacy of enduring injury and healing. Retrieved May 23, 2008: http://www.joyleary.com/store.html

Lincoln, A. (1863). http://showcase.netins.net/web/creative/lincoln/speeches/gettysburg.htm.

Loewen, J. (1995). *Lies my teacher told me: Everything your high school history textbook got wrong.* New York: The New Press.

Lu, H. H. (2003). *Low-income children in the United States.* National Center for Children in Poverty. New York: Columbia University, Mailman School of Public Health.

Mansell, W. (2007). *Education by numbers: The tyranny of testing.* London: Politico's Publishing.

Maxwell, K. E. (2004). Deconstructing whiteness: Discovering the water. In V. Lea & J. Helfand (Eds.), *Identifying race and transforming whiteness in the classroom.* New York: Peter Lang.

McIntosh, P. (1989, July/August). White privilege: Unpacking the invisible knapsack. *Peace and Freedom.*

McLaren, P. (2003). Critical pedagogy: A look at the major concepts. In A. Darder, M. Baltodano, & R. Torres, R. (Eds.), *The critical pedagogy reader.* New York: RoutledgeFalmer.

McLaren, P. (2005). *Capitalists and conquerors: A critical pedagogy against empire.* Lanham, MD: Rowman & Littlefield.

Moll, L. C., Amanti, C., Neff, D., Gonzales, N. (1992, Spring), Funds of knowledge for teachers: Using a qualitative approach to connect homes and classrooms. *Theory into Practice,* XXXI (2).

Neves, A. (1998). *Multicultural education and the social studies syllabus.* Sonoma State University, CA.

Nieto, S. & Bode, P. (2007). *Affirming diversity: The sociopolitical context of multicultural education.* New York: Allyn & Bacon.

Ogbu, J. (1995). Cultural problems in minority education: Their interpretations and consequences—Part one: Theoretical background. *The Urban Review,* 27 (3).

Payne, R. (1995). *A framework for understanding poverty.* Highlands, TX: aha! Process.

Payne, R. K. (2006, January). Personal communication.

Pinar, W. F. (2004). *What is curriculum theory?* Mahwah, NJ: Lawrence Erlbaum Associates.

Pollick, M. (2008). Hidden curriculum. Retrieved May 23, 2008: http://hiddencurriculum.pnn.com/5726-the-front-page

Pytel, B. (2007, March 16). NCLB: It's all about the test. Good teaching vs. test scores. Retrieved April 11, 2008 from Suite 101 website: http://educationalissues.suite101.com/blog.cfm/nclb_its_all_about_the_test

Rabinow, P. (Ed.) (1984). *The Foucault reader.* New York: Pantheon books.

Roediger, D. R. (1991). *The wages of whiteness: Race and the making of the American working class.* London: Verso.

Rouse, W. H. D. (1956). *Great dialogues of Plato,* translation. Denver, CO: Mentor Books.

Ryan, W. (1971). *Blaming the victim.* New York: Vintage.

Sleeter, C. E. (2004, May). *Critical multicultural curriculum and the standards movement.* Paper presented at the meeting of the California Council on Teacher Education, San Jose, CA.

Spring, J. (2007). *American education.* New York: McGraw-Hill.

Spring, J. (2008). *The American school: From the puritans to No Child Left Behind.* New York: McGraw Hill.

Steele, C. (2004, September 24). Steele Discusses "Stereotype Threat." Retrieved April 11, 2008 from *College Street Journal,* Mount Holyoke College website: http://www.mtholyoke.edu/offices/comm/csj/092404/steele.shtml.

Steinberg, S., & Kincheloe, J. (Eds.) (2007). *19 urban questions: Teaching in the city.* New York: Peter Lang.

Sumara, D. J., and Davis, B. (1998). Unskinning curriculum. In W. F. Pinar (Ed). *Curriculum: Toward new identities.* New York: Garland Publishing.

Thomas, W. I. (1923). *The unadjusted girl.* Boston: Little, Brown, and Co.

Valenzuela, A. (1999). *Subtractive schooling: U.S. Mexican youth and the politics of caring.* Albany, NY: State University of New York.

Zinn, H., & Stefoff, R. (2007). *A young people's history of the United States: Vol. I & II.* Seven Stories Press.

Five

Teaching Outside Whiteness

Judy Helfand

My path to teaching in the Humanities department at a community college began with my anti-racism work in my community, specifically with a workshop I taught on understanding whiteness. Invited to expand on that workshop and to deliver it as a one-time course in the American Multicultural Studies department at Sonoma State University, I accepted and so enjoyed the experience that I decided to obtain a masters degree in order to continue teaching at the college level. My graduate program in cultural studies and American studies culminated in my thesis, "Entering Whiteness with Conscious Intent in Post-Secondary Classrooms." In the years since, I have put many of the theories I explored in the thesis into practice. Reflecting on my practice, I have experimented with my teaching methods and revisited my theories. At conferences and on professional-development days in my own institution, I have offered these evolving theories and practical techniques to my peers. I have talked at times of making whiteness visible and of transforming or subverting whiteness. In thinking about this chapter, I decided that what I am doing is attempting to teach "outside" whiteness, to engage my students in ways of thinking, relating, and constructing knowledge in the classroom that do not support whiteness and that, in fact, model alternatives to the behaviors, norms, ideologies, and values that constitute whiteness. In speaking of whiteness, I define it as a system, a constellation of knowledge, ideologies, norms, values, identities, and behaviors that maintains a race and class hierarchy in which white people disproportionately control power and resources. Within the group of white people, a small, elite minority controls most of the group's power and resources.

It may be useful and appropriate to study whiteness in many college classes, and I do bring it in as a topic for examination in my American Cultures classes. However, my purpose in this chapter is to describe a pedagogical approach and practical teaching techniques that might be applied in any classroom on any topic. My interest is in the hidden underground roots feeding an educational system that trains students to fit into and unconsciously support an inequitable system of white supremacy. In this chapter, I explore how we have learned to think and construct knowledge within the Western tradition, analyzing the physical structure of the classroom, asking whose voices are encouraged and silenced, valuing spirit and emotion, and considering the power of epistemology. The techniques described here often help students to begin questioning long-held beliefs, to become more interested in their relationship to the world around them, to take a more proactive stance in regard to course content in all their classes, and to actively engage with confusion and complexity as necessary aspects of real learning.

Making Pedagogy Visible

Attempting to teach outside whiteness implies using a teaching approach that is likely unfamiliar and uncomfortable for my students—a new experience. I want the class to be interested in and engaged with the classroom experience, so I begin, usually on the second day, by introducing the term *pedagogy* and talking about how teachers study different ways of teaching. I then say a little more about why it is important for them to think about how I teach and how they learn. For example, in American Cultures, I mention my desire to make the dominant culture visible. Schools are among the primary institutions for socialization and enculturation into the dominant culture. Since we often don't think about or analyze what is most familiar, when we do, we can learn about underlying values and norms that in everyday life are invisible. In my World Humanities classes, I may talk about how different cultures have different ways of teaching and differing expectations of how students learn. Mentioning pedagogy is a lead-in to an activity in which we will physically rearrange the seating.

Rows and Circles

After the brief explanation of pedagogy, I ask the students what they expect to find in a typical classroom when they walk through the door. Students easily answer, desks in rows facing front. What defines "front"? The front is where the teacher is, where the whiteboards and projection screens are. Another item found in front is a podium or lectern. One student described a podium as where the teacher "dictates" from. He accompanied this with a wagging finger, emulating dictating. Students usually list a clock among items found in a classroom. After eliciting as many answers as possible regarding the physical makeup of a typical classroom, I ask the students what the physical arrangement implies about how they are *taught*. They quickly reply that information comes from the teacher, who is in the front; that there is little discussion or interaction among the students; and that the information is presented as the only information allowed. The teacher, standing up front, is literally above everyone else, and the implication is that she is superior in knowledge, too. The rows of desks imply that the class will be structured, even linear. After collecting and summarizing their responses, I then ask them to think about what this all says about how they *learn*. One student said he felt he was expected to come to class at a certain hour and turn on his brain, absorb information for the period, and then turn it off. Students often say that the classroom arrangement implies that only the teacher has anything to contribute to learning, especially since they cannot see each other and anything they say feels directed to the teacher. Sometimes a student will remark that she feels she has to accept everything as truth, that there is no room for opinion or different points of view. Others may comment that there are only visual or aural ways of learning, by which they usually mean they have to take in the information either by listening or by viewing what's on the whiteboard. They mention that learning is individual, in the sense that they are separated from each other by the seating arrangements. There is no place for hands-on learning or learning outside the classroom, such as in the community or from each other.

What if we reorganized the classroom to sit in a circle? What does that imply about teaching and learning? Students immediately mention discussion: in a circle they can talk with each other and have conversations. Someone always notes that in a circle, it is possible to see body language and facial expressions, getting feedback for their statements. They can get to know each other. A circle implies that they will learn from each other, that everyone has a chance to contribute. I mention that in a circle, as the teacher, I am also learning. Of course, I still have responsibilities: to plan the lessons; bring in resources, information, and analysis; and facilitate and manage classroom activities. I will present material, ask questions, critique papers and, in many ways, use my knowledge and experience to help them on their own learning journeys. Still, when I join the circle, I open myself to hearing their stories, increasing my understanding of experiences outside my own and learning from my students when they make connections or observations regarding class readings and activities. For example, in talking about *Material World: A Global Family Portrait* (a text used in World Humanities), a student describes how in a picture representing a U.S. family, the parents sit in separate recliners and their children on dining chairs, while in most of the other pictures of families around the world, people are closer, often crowded together on a single couch, something I had never noticed.

After the discussion, I ask the class to rearrange themselves into a circle. Once everyone is reseated, I show a couple of overheads to make evident the pedagogical aspects of what just happened. The first overhead states that the physical design of a traditional U.S. classroom encourages an authoritarian teacher/student relationship with teacher as "expert"; separation of teacher from students and students from each other; and an expectation that objectivity is desired and possible (students have not usually mentioned objectivity on their own). I then show another overhead which presents the information on using a circle, most of which the students have just provided, in an organized manner. This overhead states that a circle interrupts the traditional classroom expectations. First, it is counter-authoritarian: all voices matter. Both students and the teacher possess the learning and experiences crucial to a shared process of constructing knowledge. No single focus is occupied by the teacher, and everyone in the circle is learning. Second, a circle works against separation. Everyone is visible; sitting in a circle feels like being part of a group; the teacher is not removed from the class of students. Finally, a circle encourages acknowledgment of subjectivity. Removal of formal seating in rows reduces barriers to conversation; visible differences are noticed, and it is easier to engage emotion and spirit along with intellect.

Circles in Practice

In my classroom, we begin nearly every class session sitting in a circle. After a few days, the students usually begin rearranging the desks as soon as they walk in. If they don't, I remind them. In rooms with long tables and separate chairs, it is not always easy. Sometimes the room is so small that parts of the circle have to be two deep. Extra chairs may have to be stacked up in a corner. "Anyone in this class doesn't need to go to the gym," I joke. Some rooms have fixed seating so only small groups can form. At the end of the class (unless you have another class following), the desks and chairs must be put back. Students often complain about having to rearrange the furniture, but I don't let that stop me. Using a circle also complicates using the board or projecting onto a screen; some students have to rearrange their seats in order to see. But this makes it easier to break into small groups. The physical arrangement is fluid; chairs and desks are pushed around according to the needs of the moment. Students get up and down, seldom remaining in one seat throughout the class period. I sit at various places in the circle and enjoy being next to and with my students. One year, I had a class that complained every single day for the entire semester. One day, near the end of the semester, I said, "OK. Let's leave the desks in rows today." Within minutes, they were complaining that they couldn't see each other; it didn't seem like class, and they didn't like it! We made a circle.

In their mid-semester self-evaluations, students write about what is or is not working for them, and in their final class evaluations, I receive many comments on the circle, nearly all of which are positive. "I like how we sit in a circle and everyone is facing each other and it is like a team meeting." "Being in a circle really does make a difference." "I've really enjoyed the structure of the class. At first I wasn't too excited about the idea of being in a large circle for the class period. But I've come to like being able to see everyone's response and reaction to something that was said. I also think that it makes the classmates feel equal to one another, which makes it more comfortable to speak in front of each other." One critique was "though moving the chairs into a circle for discussion makes it so everyone is equal, I believe that sometimes it makes people uncomfortable. Students aren't used to having all eyes on them in this way." As my experience in using a circle grows, I have become more convinced of its benefits. However, it is important to create a context for the circle and to make sure the students understand it as a pedagogical approach, not simply a whim on my part.

Validating Change Through Academic Writing

In the next class, after we've changed the seating arrangement, I continue the discussion of pedagogy, using a reading or a presentation to reinforce the ideas that were brought up previously and to validate what may be unfamiliar teaching methods. For example, in American Cultures, I use an excerpt from *Transforming Knowledge* (Minnich, 1990). Placing students in small groups, I ask them to first read Minnich paragraph by paragraph, preferably out loud, stopping after each section to discuss what it means. What is the author saying? They quickly realize that, although they are all reading the same words, they don't all assign the same meaning to the passage. Even before they begin to discuss their own responses to Minnich's writing, they have a discussion about meaning. The excerpt describes Minnich's experience of student reaction to a change in the academic canon, the way in which philosophy courses that draw on women writers are seen as being about women more than about philosophy and how women who are philosophers never get to be identified as just "philosophers"; they are always "women philosophers." Minnich's name appears as E. Minnich, so the students don't know her gender when they begin reading. In one class, a student said that he had unconsciously assumed that the writer was a white man and upon learning her gender immediately began thinking of Minnich as a "female philosopher," affirming her argument. The excerpt continues with a discussion of the impossibility of separating mind and psyche; how emotions play out when classroom norms are violated (through the introduction of women into the curriculum, for example); and how those who are accustomed to being the focus—privileged white men and women—often become defensive and angry when asked to listen to the voices of other than privileged Western men.

This short excerpt (less than two pages of the original text) introduces many of the pedagogical issues I want to make visible to my students. In doing this, I believe I am violating classroom norms because the students are being asked to critically examine how they learn and how I teach. In the context of an American Cultures class, this is the starting point for examining culture, in particular the dominant culture of whiteness we inhabit in the United States. When we reconvene as a group, I ask the students why they think I asked them to read this particular work. "Because we're going to be reading women and minorities" is usually the first answer, along with "so we think about who is not in the curriculum." Most classes also mention multiple perspectives, both in terms of who is speaking and in regard to multiple interpretations, as they noted among themselves in reading Minnich as a group. Students more easily talk about gender than race. For example, they discuss the inclusion of women in the curriculum in their classes but not that of people of color. I often have to bring up the mind/psyche split and the discomfort caused when norms are violated. After exploring why I asked them to read the selection, I let each group bring to the class a particular issue they found interesting and a discussion question. This opens the door to a wide-ranging dialog. I find it especially exciting when students reflect on their own process in reading Minnich, and I talk about that in the discussion. More commonly, students veer off, wondering if sexism is as prevalent now as it was in 1989 (when the book was written), or question some of Minnich's assertions, for example, "Do people who are left out of the curriculum really not notice?" I keep bringing it back to the pedagogical issues, questioning them about their own learning experiences. When class ends, they are usually still deeply involved in the conversation and often walk out of the room talking with each other—a great beginning.

In all my classes throughout the semester, I refer to pedagogical, methodological, and epistemological issues in an ongoing effort to make visible to my students the often unquestioned or unnoticed assumptions and educational norms that are integral to the white supremacist system we inhabit. The activities and readings vary, depending on course content. For example, in World Humanities, I begin with a consideration of methodology, using theory from *Decolonizing Methodologies* (Smith, 1999). I include this and several other readings in class readers to investigate these topics (as described later in this chapter).

Storytelling and Multiple Voices

After our discussions of teaching and learning, most students are clear on the need for multiple perspectives in learning about a given topic. With history, literature, television, radio, and other means of conveying information or entertainment, we can ask "Who's speaking?" For example, history is usually told from a dominant, white perspective, and history texts often provide an airbrushed, "glamour shot" of American history, leaving out social resistance, the contributions of people of color, the struggles of the working classes, the impact of race on immigrant experience, and much more. Mainstream media pump out racist messages and misinformation, excluding the voices of communities of color, the working class, and other marginalized groups, as it creates an idealized, consumerist vision of the white middle class and what "success" looks like. Only by bringing in voices from underrepresented and marginalized groups can we begin to have the multiple perspectives required to construct knowledge. I tell my students that my responsibility, as a teacher, is to make sure we notice whose voices are missing and to bring in those voices through readings, guest speakers, art, film, and music. I emphasize that it is only through *active* efforts to attend events, read books, watch movies, listen to music, and view artwork outside the mainstream that we will experience the multiple authentic voices of the people in the United States or of folks from different cultures around the world. This point is especially important to my white, middle-class students because race and class segregation leave white people, in particular, dependent on mainstream media for the stories of people from different racial and social groups, resulting in misperceptions that thwart cross-cultural communication and fortify racial stereotypes.

As a way of reinforcing the need for multiple voices and perspectives, and to encourage the conscious engagement of spirit and emotion along with intellect, I introduce the concept of storytelling in my classes. I like to talk of telling stories because of the informality and also because it reminds students that each person speaks from a particular place or "social location," which we explore through writing and class activities. We have one structured storytelling activity. Otherwise, I simply reiterate the need for all their stories in constructing knowledge. By mid-semester, students often write favorably of multiple voices, including their own, as a component of their learning.

For example, one student writes, "I like how we share personal experiences to get a feeling of the world in which we are living." Another student writes, "I like to listen to the discussions we have as a class and the arguments. I like taking in different points of view and determining which one I relate to most. Being able to respond to questions freely and listening to responses to my answers gives me a great feedback." Yet another student writes, "One of the things that I like best about the class is the feeling of openness that the class gives. I feel like everyone is given a fair opportunity to share their thoughts and feelings on the topic of the day without being criticized and this in turn opens the doors for even more in depth and heartfelt discussions." One student realizes he is learning about American cultures in learning about his classmates.

> I am really interested in learning more about the people in our classroom as opposed to people in books or stories. Whether its classmates, guest speakers or just an outside opinion, I really think it is more valuable as a student to learn first-hand instead of on paper. While reading on paper is still good at explaining issues, when you hear things firsthand, you are more engaged and want to learn more.

Storytelling takes the focus off the teacher as the source of all information in the classroom and gives the students the responsibility for constructing knowledge from the rich resources offered by their peers and in the readings.

Limitations

Changing the physical arrangement of the room and encouraging students to tell their own stories begins the process of disrupting whiteness by providing students with the opportunity to listen to each other's stories and reflect on their own experiences and worldviews. However, some questions need to be asked. First, do all participants enter the dialog equipped with the same capacity for reflection? This question leads to the realm of cognitive development, and I do not discuss it here. Another question is *how* do participants construct knowledge from their own experiences and the multiple voices and perspectives brought into the classroom? This question raises issues of social power. Some participants may have developed different ways of knowing than those most honored and employed by theorists and educators working within, and expressing the values of, dominant communities. For example, in researching women's ways of knowing, Belenky and Stanton (2000) describe two modes of approaching the construction of knowledge through reflective discourse—the separate and the connected modes. Using the separate approach, those engaged in dialog take a doubting stance, questioning various positions and looking for arguments against what differs from one's own beliefs. Connected knowers, who are women more often than men, look for reasons to believe another's arguments, trying to enter another's perspective. Within a structure based on separated ways of knowing—arguably a typical college seminar—connected knowers would not have the same power and influence as separated knowers. Also interested in *how* we know, Collins in *Black Feminist Thought* (Collins, 2000), develops a theory of black feminist epistemology and describes how the many ways in which black women produce knowledge are discredited in academia. Her work makes clear that issues of power are central to using reflective discourse to construct knowledge.

In a dialog, the group must attend to the ways in which internalized structures of domination are played out in the expectations of what is appropriate to the dialog, in who is seen as having the most valuable contributions, and in how knowledge is validated. These are important questions because, where one person views the discourse community as validating all the members' contributions and offering everyone an equal opportunity to contribute to the dialog, some members may not share this perception. For example, after one small-group activity in which students explored social location, each group reported back to the class on similarities and differences in the group members' stories. When one student noted that they all grew up in white suburban neighborhoods, another student, the only person of color in the group, slowly shook his head. I asked him if he disagreed with the report, and he answered that he grew up in a multicultural urban setting. The other student then amended her comment, "Well, everyone but [student's name] grew up in white suburbia." First the student of color was invisible and then dismissed.

Using Critical Theory to Address Issues of Power

In introducing storytelling, I point out that our own experiences reflect our position within structures of power. This is a message I continue to deliver, explaining that one reason it is so important to hear others' stories is that they can help us understand our own social location and relationship to the world around us. But those structures of power create barriers to hearing from each other. The voices of difference must be heard and knowledge constructed from the mix of experiences—a process complicated by the very inequalities the group seeks to understand and challenge. The teacher must draw attention to issues of racism and sexism, for example, and place them within a historical and cultural context.

The word "critical" is widely used in academic writing, and "critical reflection" is given an important pedagogical role by many theorists. Coming from the Frankfurt school, its original meaning, "critical had to do with examining power relations. To be critical, reflection must be engaged with a power analysis of a situation or context within which learning is occurring." Among educators who have written on addressing issues of power in the classroom, I find Brookfield (2000) to be especially helpful. Brookfield focuses on a process he calls "ideology critique" as necessary to critical reflection. This process seems especially suited to transforming whiteness in the classroom. Ideology critique is the process by which people come to recognize how uncritically accepted and unjust dominant ideologies are embedded in everyday situations and practices. Brookfield uses the example of capitalism, describing how ideology critique can help students explore how capitalism, as a major ideology of the West, shapes belief systems and assumptions that maintain economic and political inequality. What seems to us to be natural ways of understanding our experiences are actually internalized dimensions of ideology. Ideology "is not to be understood as pertaining only to our beliefs about social and economic systems, but as something that frames our moral reasoning, interpersonal relations, and our ways of knowing, experiencing, and judging what is real and true" (Brookfield, 2000, p. 129).

About three-quarters of the way through the semester, I introduce the term *hegemony* to provide a theoretical construct to contain many of the classroom practices I've been encouraging all semester. In three short statements on an overhead projector, I summarize the ideas they have already heard and explored: social groups struggle in many different ways to win the consent of other groups and achieve ascendancy in thought and practice over them. The dominant group projects its way of seeing social reality so successfully that it becomes common sense. Certain cultural forms predominate over others. With a fourth statement, I ask them to take the next step toward understanding: power is maintained not only through domination, but also ideologically, through the voluntary consent of those dominated. I tell them that *hegemony* describes the process whereby ideas, structures, and actions come to be seen by a majority of people as wholly natural, preordained, and working for their own good when, in fact, they are constructed and transmitted by powerful minority interests to protect the status quo that serves these interests so well. When I ask for examples, someone usually ties in whiteness.

Intersecting Privileges and Oppressions

Taking a critically reflective stance in the classroom would mean that the teacher and students undertake the process of identifying and critiquing the submerged power dynamics within the room, including the role of the teacher. The dialog would not begin with an assumption that "we are all free from the distortions of power and influence." Instead, participants would acknowledge the many axes of difference and related inequities. Based on that, they would commit to actively engage with each other to reduce the barriers to communication that result from those differences and invite the passionate learning that can occur when differences are honored and interrogated. In writing about the relationship of power to knowledge, Córdova (1998) states that

> it is not sufficient to speak of identities of race, class, and gender, but we must also speak of identities toward power. To what extent does any one of us identify with the forces of domination and participate in relations that reinforce that domination and the exploitation that goes with it. (p. 19)

In introducing myself on the first day of class, I try to position myself subjectively. By this, I mean that I state that I am a middle-class white woman.[1] I talk about what these social locations have to do with my qualifications to teach the class, the limitations imposed, and the advantages accrued. In particular, I believe that I must speak of myself as white in a class where I am expected to teach about people of color. As educators, we must continue to question how we bring our practice of whiteness, even as we attempt to overcome it. We need to point out the normativeness of whiteness and begin to deconstruct it. White educators also need to acknowledge that a white educator automatically provides an advantage to the white students who enter the classroom with initial feelings of comfort—what Maureen Reddy (1998) calls "white bonding."

About one-third of the way into the semester in American Cultures, I devote a class period to an experiential activity that provides an opportunity for students to explore the multiple privileges and oppressions they experience daily and to gain deeper understanding of their own position in the many interrelated oppressive systems we all inhabit. The activity is framed by a presentation on identity, eliciting from the students the various "labels" they may attach to themselves. Differences in how we identify do not have to produce social, economic, or cultural difference, I explain, but often categories with which we classify difference (race and gender, for example) are social constructions. They might not exist as categories if they did not support systems that maintain and produce inequality and injustice. I also introduce the notion of intersecting oppressions by describing how within a given person, all the various identities interact with each other. In some categories, one may be targeted for oppression and in others, experience privilege.

With this theoretical frame in place, we move the desks to clear a large space (or go to a different room if that is impossible). Students then line up on one side of the room, facing the opposite wall. I read statements about identity and experience, and the students cross to the other side of the room if the statement I am reading applies to them. For example, "Cross to the other side of the room if you identify as African American or black," or "Cross to the other side of the room if neither of your parents attended college." After each category I say, "Notice who is standing with you. Notice who is not." Apart from my reading the categories, the activity is conducted in silence. (Also, I tell the students that they do not have to cross the room if a statement applies to them.) After I've completed reading the categories, students have an opportunity to debrief in small groups and then, in a more structured way, to speak out about the experience and say more about their identities. This activity serves several purposes. It makes visible the diversities within the room. It also makes evident which voices are missing from the classroom. It often shows students that they are not alone in their experiences. It makes it possible for students to "give voice" to who they are without having to talk. It also brings attention to the systemic power imbalances in which we are all enmeshed. In critiquing the class, students often write about this activity. For example, a young man with Mexican immigrant parents wrote

> This exercise has affected me positively, and made me see the world as though I am not alone even in the hardest of experiences. I now question my previous belief that I was the only one to have parents who failed to graduate college or why I never told anyone outside my circle of friends. . . . I think that the American culture has taught us to hide negative aspects of our lives and only talk about the positive; a great phrase comes to mind. It is the one of how easy it is in the U.S. and how anyone can make millions

here in the "the land of opportunity." My parents were extremely lucky to have found people that would help them succeed in life, yet I know for every one person that makes it hundreds do not.

A young white man wrote:

> This activity definitely changed my way of seeing and experiencing the world. Now when I see someone I see a good chance of them being involved in a targeted group, or of any of these bad experiences have happened to them. I thought I was the norm, with nothing that really targets me in my life, but I guess I was wrong. It seems the norm is that 90% of the people have or had events in their life that includes them in a target group(s), while I'm involved in so few. It was definitely eye opening.

"Both/And" Thinking

Crucial to using multiple voices and perspectives to construct knowledge is the ability to use "both/and" thinking. I talk with my students about the tendency in Western thought to use either/or thinking where something is, for example, either black or white, good or bad, true or false. Further, the binaries inherent in either/or often come with prejudgments where one side of the binary is seen as better than or superior to the other. Without going deeply into the concept, I encourage students to try on both/and thinking. For example, a student may make a statement based on her own experience. Another student may talk of a different experience in a similar situation. Instead of feeling like the second statement invalidates the first, that if one is true, the other false, I suggest that in comparing and contrasting the two statements, we can ask questions or form ideas about how both statements can be true, reflecting two individual experiences. What is the point of seeking diverse viewpoints and stories if we simply dismiss them because they don't agree with what we've already heard, thought, or experienced ourselves? A student wrote at mid-semester:

> I am not going to lie by saying I am a changed man because I am not. I feel many of the same feeling that I did before I started this class. The thing I have learned is to accept differences between us, and although people have different opinions, it's important to hear them to be fully educated about a topic. In the past I really didn't listen to different opinions because I just thought they were crazy.

In the United States, debating is often regarded as the best way to explore an issue, akin to the separate-mode approach to knowing described earlier. Debating results in two "sides" where the struggle is to "prove" oneself "right." Using storytelling and both/and thinking requires a deeper exploration of various viewpoints and the creation of new knowledge through the interaction of a group. I have found that such an approach often cuts through the defensiveness that arises when a student's viewpoint is challenged. I have also found that remembering the importance of both/and thinking forces me to carefully word my own responses to students who say something reflective of mainstream opinions, for example, racial stereotypes, that I immediately want to "disprove." Teaching myself not to contradict and instead to make a statement that reflects my experience and feelings is an ongoing effort, but the more I practice, the more I find my students opening themselves up to the scary process of considering new ideas.

Silence

While students are largely appreciative of classroom discussion, some notice that not everyone is talking. In her evaluation, one student wrote: What is not working for me is my desire to hear others' perspectives and thoughts about certain subjects. Some of the students speak up during class discussions, but I would like to hear more ideas and thoughts coming from different individuals. I enjoy listening to my peers and noticing the difference and similarities between each other and what each of us believes.

Critical theory demonstrates that those constructing knowledge through dialog and reflection must interrogate difference in relation to structures of domination and hegemonic ideologies. Yet, within the classroom, can dialog and reflection break through the barriers that result from those very structures and ideologies, which are being experienced in the moment by the educator and students in the room? In *Teaching to Transgress*, bell hooks (1994) describes these barriers as silencing mechanisms in which some voices are devalued or excluded, even within a classroom where the stated aim is to bring to voice marginalized people. Many scholars of color have described this silencing.

> One of the most empowering things we [working-class Chicanas] can do is articulate the mechanisms of silencing: the discourse of silencing, the discourse against giving voice, the discourse against resistance. We are told, for example, that we are direct and confrontational, that we are *difficult*, that we are *irrational, too emotional—too angry*. (Córdova, 1998, p. 38)

Language

One of the mechanisms of silencing is language itself. Why is only "standard" English used in the classroom? In her article "Teaching New Worlds/New Words," hooks (1994) draws attention to the fact that standard English can only express in a certain way, either mirroring or addressing the dominant reality. What would it be like for American-born, middle-class white students in an academic setting to hear a language they haven't mastered, such as black vernacular? Reflecting on the experience could lead to insights regarding both their own position in the dominant culture and ways in which others are marginalized. In writing about the need for African American epistemology in educational theory, Beverly Gordon (Gordon, 1990) refers to Hazel Carby's work: "Carby argues that language provides a shared context through which different groups express their specific group interests and that the terrain of language is a terrain of power relations" (p. 97).

I address the issue of language in my American Cultures class by including selections on language in the class reader. In addition to the hooks article, I include Asa Hilliard (2002), "Language, Culture, and the Assessment of African-American Children." Many students choose to write about a short article by a soon-to-be mother in which she reflects that choosing a baby name that is reflective of her culture may expose her child to increased discrimination (Kashef, 2003). I often create small-group activities where they can explore differences in their own language use depending on the community—school, family, friends, and so on. Using spoken word on CD not only brings in voices and stories of those not present in the classroom but also provides the actual language. The compilation DVD *Race Is the Place* (Telles & Tejada-Flores, 2005) brings those voices to life on the screen. I chose *The Medicine of Memory* (Murguía, 2002) as a class text in part because of the attention to language and the use of Spanish in the text. In introducing the book, I ask students not to pass over the Spanish they can't figure out but to ask another student or a teacher for a translation, emphasizing that there are many who can do so. In World Humanities, I bring students' attention to the privileged place of English worldwide and also point out how much we miss out on in not being able to read or understand the native languages of the countries we study, thereby being limited to either translations or the words of more educated members of the culture. I make an effort to show films from the countries we study so the students can hear, for example, Wolof, Arabic, or Kyrgyz spoken. I project Web sites in unfamiliar languages or use maps with local names and alphabets (Cyrillic or Chinese).

Socioeconomic Class

Socioeconomic class also creates barriers in the classroom. Silence and deference are valued in educational institutions. Loudness, anger, and emotional outbursts are unacceptable and usually associated with the lower classes. "Professors cannot empower students to embrace diversities of experience, standpoint, behavior, or style if our training has disempowered us, socialized us to cope effectively with only a single mode of interaction based on middle-class values" (hooks, 1994, p. 187). It is difficult to create a classroom where everyone takes up their responsibility to contribute and also respects and listens to others when the institution itself is designed to enforce and continue dominant cultural knowledge and values. For example, hooks argues, "Most progressive instructors are more comfortable striving to challenge class biases through the material studied than they are with interrogating how class biases shape conduct in the classroom and transforming their pedagogical practice" (p. 187).

In my introduction to socioeconomic class, I use an activity developed by Chris Cullinan.[2] Students divide into small groups, and I give each group a large sheet of paper from a flip pad and several colored markers. Their assignment is to name the socioeconomic classes and list the markers that enable you to determine which class a person belongs to. This often becomes one of the noisiest, most playful activities as students attempt to sort out the confusing mix of their own lived experiences, media images they've been exposed to, and cultural myths. I believe that using large paper and markers, providing limited direction, and encouraging playful interaction helps break down barriers of "appropriate" classroom behavior to enable students to share on a potentially explosive topic. Cullinan's curriculum on socioeconomic class is an excellent example of ideology critique. Her activities also address issues of silence.

Learning from Silence

When I ask students from diverse races and ethnicities the question, "when are you white?" students of color often answer "in school," thus acknowledging the degree to which the dominant culture requires them to conform in order to obtain an education. In attempting to transform whiteness in the classroom, I try to be aware of the ways in which middle-class white language, values, and practices are privileged, thereby excluding or devaluing the voices that would speak from a different location. I ask students to consider how their peers may be silenced in classroom discussion through readings such as "What's Wrong with a Little Fantasy? Storytelling from the (Still) Ivory Tower," Miranda (2002), I hope that students who are being silenced may feel acknowledged, or even risk speaking, after reading of others in a similar situation.

Yet, even with an understanding of how students are silenced—or choose not to speak—and all the best intentions and efforts for addressing the problem, it may not be possible to create a classroom environment where all students' voices can be heard. In her final class evaluation, one of my students writes about why she doesn't feel comfortable speaking in the class. It seems to her to be because there is "not a unity within the class. I do enjoy the class, but I feel safer staying quieter in this class." After teaching a class on media and anti-racist pedagogies, Elizabeth Ellsworth (Ellsworth, 1989) reflected on the different types of silences and the reasons students may have for not speaking out. She discussed how students must balance the need for safety with the need for visibility that speech gives. Pedagogies based in the need for dialog "must come to grips with issues of trust, risk, and the operations of fear and desire around such issues of identity and politics in the classroom. . ." (p. 313). She goes on to list some of the reasons students did not speak or did not speak authentically:

> fear of being misunderstood and/or disclosing too much and becoming too vulnerable; memories of bad experiences in other contexts of speaking out; resentment that other oppressions (sexism, hetero-sexism, classism, anti-Semitism) were being marginalized in the name of addressing racism—and guilt for feeling such resentment; confusion about levels of trust and commitment surrounding those who were allies to another group's struggles; resentment by some students of color for feeling that they were expected to do "more" and once again take the burden of doing the pedagogic work of educating White students/professor about the consequences of White middle-class privilege; and resentment by students for feeling that they had to prove they were not the enemy. (p. 316)

Such a list invites us to think about Trinh T. Minh-ha's (1990) suggestion that opposing voice and silence may in itself be problematic. Silence may not be exclusively an absence but may have many faces: "Silence as the will not to say or a will to unsay and as a language of its own has barely been explored" (p. 373).

It is important to stress that even as each student's complex relationships with other students, the teacher, the educational institute, the home culture and its cultural institutions, the dominant culture and its cultural institutions, and the student's own history and multiple identities can be problematic for creating a dialog, the urgency of performing this task in the interests of social justice is emphatically affirmed. "Realizing that there are partial narratives that some social groups or cultures have and others can never know, but that are necessary to human survival, is a condition to embrace and use as an opportunity to build a social and educational interdependency that recognizes differences as "'different strengths' and as 'forces of change'" (Ellsworth, 1989, p. 319).

Challenging the Primacy of Intellect

From the very first class, I assert my belief that to accomplish our learning goals, we will need to engage not only the mind, or intellect, but the emotions and spirit. I tell my students that traditional U.S. classrooms center and value intellect, but in this classroom we will recognize the contributions of heart and spirit, especially when considering new ideas that make us uncomfortable. I tell them that the class is participatory, and they will be expected to share their own experiences and knowledge to help us all learn. I repeat these themes often, for example, in talking about the circle and in the discussion on pedagogy. In introducing storytelling, I say that storytelling not only allows us to hear many different voices, it is also conducive to a learning that engages the emotions and spirit, and that the spiritual and emotional content of stories is necessary to transformational learning. Various chapters in the readers bring the students' attention to the role of emotion and spirit in constructing knowledge.

For centuries, Western methods for constructing and validating knowledge have largely honored reason as abstract thought, and devalued or ignored the role of emotions or the spiritual. In her African-centered critique of European cultural thought and behavior, Marimba Ani (1994) argues that this primacy of reason is based on a worldview first articulated by Plato, that confines the mysterious and unknowable—the spiritual—to a phenomenal world, while placing more value in the abstract world of pure truth (created through intellect) than in the material world—which also contains the spiritual. This characteristic of Western thought is often referred to in shorthand as the mind/body split. Unfortunately, this shorthand allows us to forget about spirit—not surprising within a system of thought based on a de-spiritualized universe (Ani, 1994; Córdova, 1998; Dei, Hall, & Rosenberg, 2000; Jensen, 2000; Mindell, 1995; Palmer, 2002). Ani's theory helps explain why the bodily, emotional, and spiritual knowledges are of interest to theorists exploring the limitations of the intellect.

Acknowledging and Affirming Emotion

I am suggesting that the values, beliefs, and behaviors that make up whiteness have emerged from and support the valuation of reason/intellect as superior to other ways of knowing. Using pedagogies that reintegrate the body, emotions, and spirit with intellect promises a deep understanding and possible interruption of whiteness. In fact, this notion circles back to the observations of hooks, Collins, and Ellsworth, in which failure to acknowledge passion, pain, and desire as sources of knowledge interfered with dialog, leaving some student voices unheard or devalued.

Ellsworth bases her work in a theory of multiple oppressions, recognizing that one individual can experience both dominance and oppression depending on context. Using myself as an example, one moment I may be protesting heterosexism from my position as a lesbian and the next, hearing how I silenced another lesbian through my unthinking act of entitlement as a white woman. My status as Jewish, middle-aged, middle-class, and able-bodied affects how I experience both situations. Working from a similar understanding, Dei (2000) states,

> To articulate an integrative approach to multiple oppressions, social difference and the pursuit of politics requires an alternative epistemology which provides a more holistic rendering of events, including the embodiment of spiritual knowing and human emotions as "legitimate and intelligible" knowledge. This "new epistemology" will be an affirmation of the connections between spirituality, collectivity consciousness and sociopolitical agency. (para. 39)

Not only can emotions be a source of knowledge, but studies show that affective learning is often deeply involved in transformative learning: ". . .it is quite clear that affective learning plays a primary role in fostering of critical reflection. Furthermore, it is our very emotions and feelings that not only provide the impetus for us to critically reflect, but often provide the gist of which to reflect deeply" (Taylor, 2000, p. 305). Only through the feeling, emotion, imagination, and intuition occurring around human interactions can participants create connections that enable them to fully hear and make sense of the mix of their shared experiences and reflections. By including in the reader a description of a "pedagogy of discomfort" (Boler & Zembylas, 2003), I provide students with a theoretical context for what they may experience in class.

To engage in critical inquiry often means asking students to radically reevaluate their worldviews. This process can incur feelings of anger, grief, disappointment, and resistance. . . . In short, this pedagogy of discomfort requires not only cognitive but emotional labor. (p. 111)

Spiritual Knowing

Balanced ways of knowing include spiritual and emotional knowing. My interest in spirituality as a pedagogical concern has nothing to do with the other-worldliness often associated with religion in Western contexts. Spirituality is about connection and mystery, encompassing ". . .sensitivity, the art of listening to the world at large and within one, from the hegemony of a conditioned 'me' constantly interfering in the process; the ability to relate to others and to act, without any pre-defined plan or ulterior motives; and the perennial qualities of love, compassion and goodness which are under constant assault in economized societies" (M. Rahnema, 1995, "Participation." In *Development Dictionary: A Guide to Knowledge as Power,* as quoted by Dei, 2000, para. 39). Notice that for Rahnema, the cultural, political, and economic world cannot be split off from the spiritual one. Writing on holistic education, Miller (1999) says something similar,

It makes no sense to have spirituality without democracy, without social justice, without the healing of hatred and racial and class oppression, without sustainable and nourishing relationship to the biosphere. Alongside our spiritual nature, the social and cultural reality that we inhabit is a tremendously important part of our identity and we have to address it directly. (para. 29)

As with emotion as a necessary aspect of learning, I provide a selection in the reader to affirm the importance of spirit in constructing knowledge. The last article in the World Humanities reader is "Forest Dwellers" from *Strangely Like War* (Jensen and Draffan, 2003). My American Cultures class ends the semester with "Healing Sueños for Academia" (Lara, 2002), in which the author describes her near-destruction from physical ailments and the stress she feels as a woman of color in academia, where she internalized the lesson "to 'succeed,' develop your reason, conceal your emotions, fragment your mind from your body" (p. 434). Many students speak or write that they can relate to the essay, which ends with a beautiful prayer we read out loud in class (p. 437):

May these words heal the de-spiritualization of the academy
May these words heal the de-politicization of the spiritual
May these words heal the de-erotization of the body, mind, and spirit
May these words heal our separation from ourselves, each other, and the visible and invisible world
May these words "transfix us with love" so together we will soar.
    —In Lak Ech

Epistemology

Recalling that the definition of whiteness includes knowledge, ideologies, norms and values that support a racial and socioeconomic hierarchy, I see that efforts to teach outside whiteness must include efforts that not only identify evident and expressed knowledge, ideologies, norms, and values, but also uncover the often unexpressed and unnoticed underpinnings that construct and maintain them. The underpinnings that often appear as "universal" principles are culturally specific; the "objective" reality they purportedly reflect is actually a particular worldview. Asking questions about how we have learned to think and construct knowledge within a Western paradigm leads us to explore how we are shaped by our culture. Questions about thought and knowledge guide us deeper to where we can theorize about the forces shaping our history or identity. In turn, such theories enable us to also strategize ways of interrupting the transmission and maintenance of whiteness: ". . .the effort to find out why and how our thinking carries the past within it is part of an on-going philosophical critique essential to freedom, and to democracy" (Minnich, 1990, p. 29).

Critiquing Objectivity

In calling attention to the presence of emotion and spirit during learning, I also ask students to consider rationality and objectivity. Understanding the ways emotion, spirit, rationality, and objectivity are valued in learning requires unraveling an entwined system. For example, students point to the teacher in front of a traditional classroom as a dispassionate conveyer of truth. He is "objective." If we break into a circle, objectivity is disrupted, in part by the visual evidence of emotion on faces and in part by the spirited dialog that grows out of the new arrangement. In their writing, students also confront their familiarity with the academic demand for objectivity when I ask them to respond to our readings with their emotions.

Students are usually familiar with ways of constructing knowledge that are based in positivism, like the scientific method, which holds that the knower, in constructing the knowledge, can objectively observe phenomena. The knower is separated from what is being observed and thus uninfluenced by his or her own beliefs, feelings, and life experience; and further, there is but one reality and through proper observation it can be known. Through the discussion and use of storytelling and frequent reminders of how we see the world through the lens of our own experiences, I challenge students to think about objectivity and the consequences of using rationality as the foundation of knowledge, something most often accepted without question. If we cannot separate our own subjectivity from our observations, what does this mean for the knowledge constructed over the past centuries that rests at the center of U.S. education? Students may begin to see that what is accepted as "knowledge" reflects the interests and attitudes of a small minority of white men. James Banks (1995) notes, "Hegemonic knowledge that promotes the interests of powerful, elite groups often obscures its value premises by masquerading as totally objective" (p. 15). He suggests that "an examination of the historical development of race can help students understand how the subjective characteristics of the knower, as well as the objective reality, influence the knowledge the knower constructs, deconstructs, and reconstructs" (p. 24). Not only must we help students to understand that ideas about race, for example, are socially constructed, but lead an exploration into the way in which these ideas are formed, expressed, and validated.

Critiques of objectivity may turn to subjectivity as its opposite, suggesting that all points of view are equally valid, being but a reflection of how individuals with differing identities experience the world differently. Scholars of color, in particular, have critiqued much postmodern theory for reducing all knowledge claims to but one point of view among many. Arguing for the need to counter hegemonic meaning from a liberatory standpoint, Teresa Córdova (1998) asks, "Is it a coincidence that truth has been declared dead as scholars of color, building on 500 years of resistance, are 'speaking truth to power'?" (p. 29). Other critiques of objectivity focus on the separation of subject and object, arguing that this split obscures the relationship between them, and it is in their relationship that knowledge is constructed (Banks, 1995; Heshusius, 1994). This seems to me a particularly interesting area to explore in examining whiteness. For one thing, it addresses the need for dialog between people from different social groups. It also provides an opportunity to address the ways in which Western thought, in contrast to many indigenous cultures, has de-spiritualized the world. For example, most people raised in dominant culture in the United States would never think of asking a plant to share its healing properties, would not commune with the plant. Any knowledge about that plant would come from examining it as an object.

Ways of Knowing

Posing alternative ways of knowing and exploring why they typically are not valued by U.S. educational institutions, helps reveal the underlying concepts that support whiteness. The point is not to reject or devalue what we uncover, but to bring it to awareness so we can consider how what was previously unnoticed shapes what we consciously experience. Patricia Hill Collins (2000) argues for the study of epistemology: "Far from being the apolitical study of truth, epistemology points to the ways in which power relations shape who is believed and why" (p. 252). As an introduction to World Humanities, I talk about Linda Smith's *Decolonizing Methodologies* (1999). I use her analysis of colonialism and imperialism and illustrate the concepts with the political cartoons collected in *The Forbidden Book* (Ignacio, Cruz, Emmanuel, & Torbio, 2004) from the Philippine-American War, where the images and content underline Smith's theoretical framework with an emotional punch. I want my students to always ask, "who is speaking," to try and make visible the ideologies that frame how they view other cultures, and to recognize that finding "unauthorized" voices from outside the U.S. mainstream requires effort—an effort I make clear throughout the semester in my own efforts to find materials for the class. In learning about other cultures, we cannot simply accept what experts from within our own culture have to say about those "Others," nor can we discount what we find from sources that don't "feel" like proper academic works.

The essays mentioned earlier that I include in my American Cultures reader to make my students aware of the role of emotion and spirit in learning, also address many epistemological issues, such as objectivity, mind/body split, dualism, and questions concerning how we construct knowledge. In World Humanities, I include reader selections from *Indigenous Knowledges in Global Contexts* (Dei, Hall, & Rosenberg, 2000) that describe African philosophical thought and compare traditional African knowledge systems with Western ones. I want my students to think deeply about many taken-for-granted ideas about what counts as "knowledge" and the place of value held by reason in the Western tradition. Western notions of knowledge and reason have been used in the interests of white supremacy over hundreds of years, and continue to be used today. White supremacist thought and culture continue to shift and morph as required to co-opt or devalue new ideas that threaten the ideologies, norms, and values maintaining the race and class hierarchy we live within. For example, consider the recent history of the term *multiculturalism*, which as Minnich (1990) states has been robbed of any radical meaning:

> "Mind," "reason," "knowledge" have been comprehended by particular people in particular ways that variously reflect, reinforce, question, or transcend the deeply felt reality of the articulated hierarchy of power. There is something to lose in any change in what we take to be knowledge, just as there is some-

thing to gain: power is at stake here, including the most basic power of all, the power to define what and who is real, what and who is valuable, what and who *matters*. (Minnich, 1990, p. 173)

Is It Working?

> I believe all classes should consist mainly of lectures and quizzes every now and then since that is how students learn. Truly, I was excited to learn plenty in this class and was disappointed and slightly annoyed that this class consisted only of sitting in circles—it makes me feel like a little kid when we do it every day.

While this statement from one of my students is unusual in its absolute rejection of my pedagogy and beliefs about learning, in every class one or two students let me know that they long for more structure, quizzes, PowerPoint presentations, and lectures with notes on the board. At first, I was shocked. I had never liked classes like that myself. Then I realized that I was violating classroom norms, turning students loose from the moorings of the known and comfortable and asking them to question twelve-plus years of educational experiences. Sometimes I worry that I should deliver more prepared, formal lectures, but I also receive reinforcement for my teaching methods. Many of my students describe initial dismay and later appreciation:

> I was, at first, skeptical of the class structure. In the beginning of the semester I felt more lecturing would provide me more information; however, I am learning a great deal and am beginning to understand your methods. (I am a biology major and so was somewhat turned off by the relaxed learning style.)

One young woman met with me in the second week to discuss her concern that because she was such a structured person, she feared she might not be able to do well in the class where what was "right" was not always clearly defined. She later thrived in the course, doing her own research to explore issues raised in the classroom. In fact, she organized a presentation on modern-day slavery and human trafficking that "rocked" the class. By the end of the semester, she asked if I knew of other instructors who employed similar teaching methods. Another student wrote, "I think the way that you let the class teach everyone is a different style of teaching. I like how we don't have to conform to the typical ways of a usual class environment." She then questioned whether these methods would work with other subjects, which makes me acknowledge that my teaching experiences lie mostly within the humanities.

The most affirming statements are from students who value different ways of knowing; the ones I believe hold the possibility of undermining whiteness. I see hope in their comments.

> I learned that there is a way to gain unquantifiable knowledge from a class.

> This class is working for me because we don't have to conform to standards and can be outspoken individuals in a class of open ideas and very opinionated and headstrong people, which I appreciate very much. I don't think we have studied much of the American cultures, but more each other and how we have grown up in America. *I guess this is our own learning experience and is just as valuable as an actual lesson.* [emphasis added] I like free thinking and ideas expressed in an environment that is healthy and we can fell supported in, which I do very much.

> This is one of the great things about group discussions: learning that we *don't* all think alike!

I tend to answer to the grade in most classes and this class has brought me away from that. I'm speaking my mind without regard to "pleasing" the teacher and it feels good and honest.

The most important thing for me that I have learned would be how to understand material and look deeper into it. I used to just skim the surface. This class has really made me take another look.

The above [conclusion of a response paper] is an opinion of mine, which I have formed by thinking about what we have studied. Many people disagree with it, but no matter if it is right or wrong, the good thing is the fact I have been introduced to thinking about such issues [race].

I placed these student quotes last to ground my theory, reflected back through student experience. I would like those of you reading this chapter to feel inspired to use these ideas in your own teaching and learning. The practical techniques are manifestations of theory I've evolved to suit my temperament and subject matter. My students, with their enthusiasm, boredom, insight, contrariness, sureness, confusion, and simple being, keep me questioning and experimenting. Teaching outside whiteness cannot be a static process. It can be a rewarding one. Most of my students want to live in a world of harmony and peace, where skin color doesn't affect your chances of fulfilling your dreams. I think that many of them leave my classes having taken at least one small step toward making that world a reality. One of my students put it best:

At first I thought this class was going to be really hard and confusing but I've come to learn that with an open mind and heart it is not hard and actually very important to see and hear other "worlds."

Notes

1. I sometimes identify myself as a lesbian in my first-day introduction. More commonly I wait until it comes up naturally in the class. I am not sure why I am unsure of when to come out: this is an ongoing question for me.
2. Chris Cullinan, Ph.D., offers workshops on "Adding Class to the Mix: Preparations, Methods and Cautions for Including Socio-Economic Class in Teaching and Learning About Diversity and Discrimination." She can be reached at University of Oregon, crisc@hr.uoregon.edu

References

Ani, M. (1994). *Yurugu: An African-Centered Critique of European Thought and Cultural Behavior.* Trenton: Africa World Press, Inc.

Banks, J. A. (1995). The Historical Reconstruction of Knowledge About Race: Implications for Transformative Teaching. *Educational Researcher, 24*(2), 15–25.

Belenky, M. F. & Stanton, A. V. (2000). Inequality, Development, and Connected Knowing. In J. Mezirow & Associates (Eds.), *Learning as Transformation: Critical Perspectives on a Theory in Progress* (pp. 71–102). San Francisco: Jossey-Bass.

Boler, M. & Zembylas, M. (2003). Discomforting Truths: The Emotional Terrain of Understanding Difference. In P. P. Trifonas (Ed.), *Pedagogies of Difference: Rethinking Education for Social Change* (pp. 110–133). New York: RoutledgeFalmer.

Brookfield, S. (2000). Transformative Learning as Ideology Critique. In J. Mezirow & Associates (Eds.), *Learning as Transformation: Critical Perspectives on a Theory in Progress* (pp. 125–148). San Francisco: Jossey-Bass

Collins, P. H. (2000). *Black Feminist Thought: Knowledge, Consciousness, and the Politics of Empowerment* (2nd ed.). New York: Routledge.

Córdova, T. (1998) Power and Knowledge: Colonialism in the Academy. In C. Trujillo, (Ed.), *Living Chicana Theory* (pp. 17–45). Berkeley: Third Woman Press.

Dei, G. J. S. (2000). Recasting Anti-Racism and the Axis of Difference: Beyond the Question of Theory. *Race, Gender & Class, 7*(2), 38–57.

Dei, G. J. S., Hall, B. L., & Rosenberg, D. G. (Eds.). (2000). *Indigenous Knowledges in Global Contexts: Multiple Readings of Our World.* Toronto: University of Toronto Press.

Ellsworth, E. (1989). Why Doesn't This Feel Empowering? Working Through the Repressive Myths of Critical Pedagogy. *Harvard Educational Review, 59*(3), 297–324.

Gordon, B. M. (1990). The Necessity of African-American Epistemology for Educational Theory and Practice. *Journal of Education, 172*(3), 88–106.

Heshusius, L. (1994). Freeing Ourselves from Objectivity: Managing Subjectivity or Turning Toward a Participatory Mode of Consciousness? *Educational Researcher, 23*(3), 15–22.

Hilliard, A. G. (2002). Language, Culture, and the Assessment of African-American Children. In L. Delpit & J. K. Dowdy (Eds.), *The Skin That We Speak: Thoughts on Language and Culture in the Classroom* (pp. 87–105). New York: The New Press.

hooks, b. (1994). *Teaching to Transgress: Education as the Practice of Freedom.* New York: Routledge.

Ignacio, A., Cruz, E. d. l., Emmanuel, J., & Torbio, H. (2004). *The Forbidden Book: The Philippine-American War in Political Cartoons.* San Francisco: T'Boli Publishing.

Jensen, D. (2000). Where the Buffalo Go: How Science Ignores the Living World (An Interview with Vine Deloria). *The Sun,* July (295).

Jensen, D., & Draffan, G. (2003). *Strangely Like War: The Global Assault on Forests.* White River Junction, VT: Chelsea Green Publishing.

Kashef, Z. (2003). This Person Doesn't Sound White. *ColorLines,* Fall 2003, 77–79.

Lara, I. (2002). Healing Sueños for Academia. In G. E. Anzaldúa & A. Keating (Eds.), *This Bridge We Call Home: Radical Visions for Transformation.* New York: Routledge.

Miller, R. (1999). Holistic Education and the Emerging Culture. Retrieved February 7, 2002, from http://global-circle.net/rmiller.htm.

Mindell, A. (1995). *Sitting in the Fire: Large Group Transformation Using Conflict and Diversity.* Portland, OR: Lao Tse Press.

Minh-ha, T. T. (1990). Not you/Like You: Post-Colonial Women and the Interlocking Questions of Identity and Difference. In G. Anzaldúa (Ed.), *Making Face, Making Soul/ Haciendo Caras: Creative and Critical Perspectives by Women of Color* (pp. 371–375). San Francisco: Aunt Lute Foundation Books.

Minnich, E. K. (1990). *Transforming Knowledge.* Philadelphia: Temple University Press.

Miranda, D. A. (2002). What's Wrong with a Little Fantasy? Storytelling from the (Still) Ivory Tower. In G. E. Anzaldúa & A. Keating (Eds.), *This Bridge We Call Home: Radical Visions for Transformation.* New York: Routledge.

Murguía, A. (2002). *The Medicine of Memory: A Mexican Clan in California.* Austin, TX: University of Texas Press.

Palmer, P. (2002).The Grace of Great Things: Recovering the Sacred in Knowing, Teaching, and Learning. Retrieved January 28, 2002.

Reddy, M. T. (1998). Invisibility/Hypervisibility: The paradox of normative whiteness. *Transformations, 9*(2), 55–67.

Smith, L. T. (1999). *Decolonizing Methodologies: Research and Indigenous Peoples.* London: Zed Books.

Taylor, E. (2000). Analyzing Research on Transformative Learning Theory. In J. Mezirow & Associates (Eds.), *Learning as Transformation: Critical Perspectives on a Theory in Progress* (pp. 285–328). San Francisco: Jossey-Bass

Telles, R., & Tejada-Flores, R. (Writer) (2005). *Race Is the Place* [DVD]. In R. Telles & R. Tejada-Flores (Producer). U.S.A.: Paradigm Productions.

Six

(Still) Making Whiteness Visible
Implications for (Teacher) Education

Nelson M. Rodriguez

Working with predominantly white, middle-class, pre-service student-teachers around the issue of racism, in particular white racism and white privilege, can be frustrating, disheartening, and tiresome, on the one hand; it can be meaningful, positive and hopeful, on the other. Yet, whatever the emotion attached to this project, examining white privilege and racism with white pre-service student-teachers is a necessity. This necessity arises out of several important social-psychological conditions.

First, although public school demographics nationally show a major increase in the number of students of color, still the majority of public classroom teachers, over 80%, are white. This fact raises important questions, especially around so-called multicultural education. For instance, without an awareness of systemic white racism and white privilege, in what *direction* will white teachers *perform* their antiracist education? Will they see racism, for example, as a "person of color problem" and thereby experience their response only in terms of what they can do to "help" that person? This important yet limited approach to antiracist education can perpetuate white racism in educational and societal settings by not enabling white teachers to understand their own complicity in the problem. Indeed, by only examining racism as something that is a "problem" for people of color, coupled with only seeing one's antiracist (approach to) education in the form of helping the Other, this way of thinking and acting "allows white people to remove themselves from complicity in the problem while thinking that they are doing something about it" (Derman-Sparks & Brunson-Phillips, 1997, p. 16).

The necessity of examining white privilege and racism with white students also stems from a lack of discursive exposure to a more comprehensive understanding of racism and the reasons for its persistence. That is, white students typically have a limited sense of what racism *means*. This lack of knowledge is in large measure the result of a limited range of available discourses in our society for white folks to think through a broader understanding of racism. Indeed, white students often tend to think of racism only as racial prejudice, thereby not confronting systemic white racism and white privilege. One implicit suggestion, then, of this chapter is to urge teacher educators to provide a critical pedagogy that challenges the way most (white) students have arrived at their understanding of the concept of racism.

Finally, the necessity of examining white privilege with white students has to do with the issue of "loss of one's humanity." That is, many whites have not been taught to see their privilege, to understand its significance both personally and socially. To be sure, quite the opposite is the case: They have been carefully taught not to see it. As Peggy McIntosh noted two decades ago in her essay, "White Privilege and Male Privilege: A Personal Account of Coming to See Correspondences through Work in Women's Studies": "As a white person, I realized I had been taught about racism as something which puts others at a disadvantage, but had not been taught one of its corollary aspects, white privilege, which puts me at an advantage" (1997, p. 291). Although McIntosh made this latter statement back in 1990, I would argue that, for the majority of white students, their lack of awareness of and thinking through about white privilege still very much hold true today. The result of this lack of awareness, then, provides fertile ground unfortunately for white students to lose their humanity in their white privilege, that is, to lose sight of the fact that white privilege is typically had at the expense of subaltern racial groups. Cultivating a critical consciousness around white privilege, then, is a responsibility that we educators must "impose" on our students if we want them to become aware of the privileges of the white skin and how they might use such privileges not only for the betterment of people of color but also to prevent themselves from losing their moral consciousness to the abyss of white racism.

This important concern with addressing white privilege with white students raises several important questions that have been debated within the field of critical white studies. These include: Do white students think much about their whiteness? If they do, how do they understand it? For example, do they "see" and construct their white identity around the idea that whiteness is now under attack? Indeed, as Charles Gallagher (1994, p. 168) asks, is it accurate that "whiteness is no longer invisible or transparent as a racial category because it is in crisis?" Other important questions include: For white students who do think about their whiteness, is this understanding "situational and fleeting, or is it more akin to a dull constant pain?" (Gallagher, 1994, p. 166) Do white students ever think about their whiteness in terms of white privilege? Or, is it more the case that white students see racism as "unfortunate" but not something in which they are implicated? What about those students who rarely, if ever, think about their whiteness in any aspect?

Based on my personal experiences and critical work with white pre-service student-teachers that draws its data from interviews, researcher-facilitated group discussions, and content analysis of students' responses to several texts, this chapter seeks to informally "test" (i.e., theoretically explore) the erosion of the white-invisibility thesis put forward by sociologist Charles A. Gallagher (1994) in his essay titled, "White Reconstruction in the University," a seminal and continuously, cited essay in the literature on critical white studies.

An examination of white identity formation among a group of white students at a large urban university, Gallagher's essay is significant on a number of registers, not the least of which is his assertion that whiteness is no longer invisible to white students. Gallagher's "dis-

cursive disruption" to the "invisibility thesis" so pervasive (still) in the field of critical whiteness studies today has positively pushed the conversation in this academic area in a new and
healthy direction. In much of the literature, whiteness as an *invisible* racial marker or norm has
become the typical approach to talking about and analyzing whiteness. As Mike Hill (1998)
remarks: "The fact that the 'invisibility thesis' is evoked and remarked on these days with such
regularity, indeed, itself so visible an hypothesis as to appear unimpeachable, would seem once
again to return whiteness to the ordinary" (p. 230). Because of its centrality in the field, let me
take a few moments to discuss the pervasive "invisibility thesis" within critical white studies.

Although it might appear that the examination of whiteness is a recent undertaking, it
should be noted at the outset that the study of whiteness is nothing new. As an object of
study, whiteness has been undergoing scrutiny for centuries. As an example, historian David
Roediger, who, arguably, is a pioneer in contemporary critical white studies, has exhumed a
past tradition of thinking and writing by blacks about whites in his edited publication (1998)
titled, *Black on White: Black Writers on What It Means to Be White*. So, if the study of whiteness is
not new, what, then, gives contemporary critical whiteness studies their freshness or originality
or even their importance? The answer lies in the argument that whiteness is a social construction. From the perspective of inquiry and research, to say that whiteness is a social construct
is to want to examine the "social mechanisms that falsely legitimate whiteness as normative or
superior" (Thompson, 1999, n.p.).

Implicit, then, in the argument that whiteness is a social construction is the notion that
whiteness is invisible and, therefore, needs to be interrogated and made problematic. "The
project of whiteness theorists [in other words] is to problematize the normalization of whiteness as racelessness, to make 'visible [that is] what was previously unseen'" (Thompson, 1999,
n.p.). This notion of making whiteness visible at the individual, institutional, and/or cultural
levels has come to be understood within the literature as the "invisibility thesis," and it is this
thesis that still animates, albeit in a variety of forms, the majority of theorizing within the field
of contemporary critical white studies. Indeed, whether one takes a psychological, material-
ist, and/or discursive approach to analyzing whiteness, each paradigm in general is concerned
with marking or making visible the "pervasive non-presence" of whiteness. For example, ma-
terialist approaches to whiteness are often concerned with making visible the "multiple material forms that white privilege may take, especially in such arenas as access to equal education,
housing, bank loans, and police protection" (Thompson, 1999, n.p.).

Interestingly, however, even though the invisibility thesis is the pervasive and dominant
idea circulating within contemporary critical white studies, this thesis itself has been recently
contested. Arguing that whiteness is no longer invisible, some theorists within the field believe
that U.S. society and culture in the late twentieth and early twenty-first centuries are characterized by a widespread and aggressive "new politicization of whiteness," thus rendering "the
explanatory powers of the invisibility thesis simplistic and anachronistic" (Gallagher, 1994, p.
173). While I most certainly agree that whiteness has been politicized in the post-civil rights
era, I am concerned nevertheless with the argument that this politicization has somehow
made whiteness visible, especially to white, pre-service student-teachers and to other students
as well. I will explain my position here in a moment when I turn to a series of narratives I've
garnered while working with white student-teachers. These narratives serve as a particular

structure of explanation that helps give insight into the way such students "think about" their whiteness.

The overriding project, then, within critical whiteness studies has been one of deconstructing whiteness, of making visible the various forms of mechanisms of whiteness, and of showing how whiteness is related to racism. As philosopher of education, Audrey Thompson, notes: "For the most part [the emphasis of critical white studies] is not on whiteness as an announced value but whiteness as a suppressed, invisible privilege" (Thompson, 1999, n.p.). Challenging, then, the regularity of the invisibility thesis, Gallagher has opened up the necessary discursive space for thinking through how we talk about whiteness in the twenty-first century.

Having said that, I'm still somewhat puzzled. I have been working over the past four to five years now with undergraduate pre-service student-teachers, most of whom are white. In particular, I've been teaching courses that take up the issue of "education and cultural diversity," in which most of the students enrolled in these courses identify racially as white. When I first started teaching these courses, I conceptualized them around teaching about the "Other." I have always been committed to having my students encounter so-called difference and always within the framework of analyzing social injustice, and how the institution of schooling might be used to challenge such injustice. Also, because these courses encourage, by their very titles, an examination of a range of diversity issues, in addition to teaching units on racial injustice, especially in relation to African American and Native American struggles for racial justice, I have spent much time in these courses on an examination of gender oppression and homophobia and heterosexism. I have come to believe that these courses are rewarding for students in sensitizing them to the struggles, past and present, many subordinate groups have waged for their own liberation, and how these particular struggles have been linked by their commitment to a broader politics of social justice.

Yet, at the same time, I have come to feel that cultural diversity courses, especially those with a mostly white audience, are lacking in their potential transformative politics if they do not critically take up the issue of whiteness. It was in this context that I came (and have returned) to Gallagher's study, which has helped me to think more deeply about the role of a critical whiteness discourse in the diversity classroom. But what Gallagher was expressing in his essay seemed to be at odds with my experience working with students who seemed not to think much about their whiteness. That is, given that Gallagher's study was conducted at a university located in a large urban center in the Northeast, I wondered, based on my experiences, if his argument that whiteness is no longer invisible would bear out with my white students at colleges located in suburban settings. He seems to suggest that it would. Indeed, Gallagher winds down his essay with the following general claim: "No doubt many whites do not think about their whiteness, but I would argue they are increasingly in the minority" (1994, p. 184).

I do not argue here that Gallagher has got it wrong; in fact, I would assert the opposite. Instead, I want to put into dialogue his arguments about the reasons and significance about how white students "get raced" with informal data that I have garnered from working with white pre-service student-teachers who not only attend a college that is predominately white but also have grown up in predominately white communities. Where do these students stand on the issue of whiteness? What similarities are there between them and white students located in urban centers around the country? What differences exist? By putting in dialogue, then,

Gallagher's arguments with my data, I hope to provide another layer to Gallagher's crucial discursive disruption.

As I mentioned earlier, in his essay, Gallagher discusses the implications of an ethnographic study he conducted with white undergraduate students at an urban university in the Northeast. Based on his study, Gallagher arrives at the argument that, because of contemporary racial politics and the effects of the media, whites increasingly see themselves as white and further, have come to see or make sense of their whiteness as a disadvantage. As Gallagher (1994) explains: "Race matters for these [white] students because they have been weaned on a brand of racial politics and media exposure that has made whiteness visible as a racial category while simultaneously transforming whiteness into a social disadvantage" (p. 166). Gallagher concludes his essay with the argument that, based on seeing their whiteness as a liability, the next generation of white adults just might respond to "the political and cultural mobilization of racially defined minorities" (p. 167) in a reactionary way. How? By "develop[ing] solidarity in their whiteness," thus removing themselves from the project of racial equality and social justice (p. 185).

I want to reiterate that Gallagher's essay is important for a number of reasons. First, from the perspective of internal debates within the field, he has challenged the *regularity* of the invisibility thesis within contemporary critical white studies. In addition, Gallagher's argument that whiteness is being redefined as a liability or disadvantage is absolutely on the mark, and his worry that white students may, as a result, develop solidarity in their whiteness should be taken seriously, especially by educators. My bone of contention, then, with Gallagher's argument is one of *degree*. That is, I am not as convinced as he is that *most* white students today think about their whiteness.

As I mentioned earlier, then, my current work wishes to explore Gallagher's thesis that most white students today think about their whiteness. Locating Gallagher's thesis within the specific context of teacher education, I wish to demonstrate that white pre-service student-teachers do not consider the issue of whiteness and white privilege. Such a defining absence, I argue, raises important concerns for how to conceptualize cultural diversity courses that enable white student-teachers to recognize that "everyone [occupies] a place in the relations of racism" (Frankenberg, 1993, p. 6). This chapter, then, represents one example of my ongoing work of connecting critical white studies to the field of education, and in particular, to teacher education.

Racism, Whiteness, and Education for Critical Consciousness

In her essay, "Transformative Pedagogy and Multiculturalism," bell hooks (1993) discusses the importance of an education for critical consciousness. By such an approach, hooks is arguing for getting students to recognize and change societal inequities and injustices and to use the terrain of the classroom for such thinking and action. In short, hooks is calling for a critical pedagogy. However, when educating for critical consciousness, hooks is sensitive that such critical consciousness-raising is often quite painful for many students. This pain arises in part because of how students experience major paradigm shifts in their thinking as a result of being brought to "criticality." As hooks (1993) notes, "Students have taught me that it is necessary to practice compassion in new learning settings where individuals may be confronting shifts in paradigms that seem to them completely and utterly threatening. I saw for the first time that there can be, and usually is, some degree of pain involved in giving up old ways of thinking and knowing and learning new approaches. I respect that pain. And include recognition of it now when I teach, that is to say [when] I teach about shifting paradigms and talk about the discomfort it can cause" (pp. 95–96).

Recently, I witnessed this pain in my students when we discussed the distinction between racial prejudice and racism. More specifically, I had my students read a chapter titled, "Defining Racism," from Beverly Daniel Tatum's (1997) book, *Why Are All the Black Kids Sitting Together in the Cafeteria?: And Other Conversations about Race*. Drawing on David Wellman's (1993) publication, *Portraits of White Racism*, Tatum draws a distinction between racial prejudice and "racism." Racial prejudice would include thoughts and behaviors that most people would think of as racist. These include racial slurs, violence committed against people of color, and "preconceived judgment and opinion, usually based on limited information" (Tatum, 1997, p. 5). Racism, on the other hand, is defined by Tatum as a system of advantage based on race. To fine-tune this distinction, Tatum goes on to make a distinction between active and passive racism so as to point out that one need not be a hate-monger to be complicit in the spread of racism. The point of exposing students to Tatum's definition of racism was not only to engage them in that paradigm shift to which hooks refers, but also to begin the process of gaining insight into how they think about whiteness. Thus, in this phase of my work, I was concerned with the following question: In what way can students' understanding of the concept of racism shed light on the degree to which they think about their whiteness? This is the question with which I initiated my attempts to understand how and whether my students were thinking critically about whiteness.

As mentioned earlier, under the terms of mainstream U.S. ideology, racism is typically defined as personal prejudice, hatred, or violence committed against people of color. From this perspective, racism, while utterly horrible, is viewed as a person of color's problem and not something that implicates mainstream, liberal white society. Defining racism in this way limits it to be seen as a "fringe ideology" and dissociates it from questions of whiteness and white privilege. I believe that most white, pre-service student-teachers arrive at their cultural diversity classes thinking that racism is only about racial bigotry. To see how my students think about racism and, as a result, what this says about the degree to which they think about their whiteness, I had them grapple with Tatum's definition of racism. Below I introduce the data from this portion of my work.

During interviews and group discussions following their reading of Tatum's definition of racism, most of my students' comments betrayed their lack of understanding of racism as above and beyond racial prejudice. The following statements by three different students were typical of most students' comments. One student, Gretchen, put it succinctly, when she said: "I have always equated 'racism' with 'prejudice' and 'discrimination' and never thought twice about these terms having unique meanings." Another student, Jason, responded to his encounter with Tatum's definition of racism in the following way: "I have always known about racism and knew it still existed, but I never saw it the way I do now. For example, I knew about the Civil Rights movement and their fight for equal rights, I knew about the Klan and the types of behaviors they participated in, and I knew that some people didn't like black people. However, I didn't know about passive racism. I never really thought about the idea I guess." Finally, Nichole expressed her thoughts about racism as a system of advantage as follows: "Before reading this essay I had never thought of myself as racist, because I don't believe any race to be superior to another, but that is not the definition of racism the author uses. [The definition of racism as] a system of advantage based on race sheds new light on an old concept."

These comments reveal just how ingrained the notion of "racism-as-bigotry" is in the minds of these students. Indeed, before coming across Tatum's definition of racism, and being challenged by it, these students (and so many others) had not conceived of racism in ways other than personal prejudice. More important, from the perspective of critically thinking about whiteness, these students had not thought about whiteness in terms of associating it with racism. Some students did make the association between whiteness and racism before reading Tatum; however, their association was not a critical but reactionary one. That is, several students commented that whites are experiencing what they called, "reverse-discrimination," especially in such areas as college admissions and scholarship programs. From this perspective, these students did link racism to whiteness prior to reading Tatum but, as with Gallagher's students, they associated whiteness with disadvantage. To repeat, though, most important to this phase of my work was recognizing that the students' limited understanding of racism prevented them from critically thinking about their whiteness as a system of advantage based on race. Not making the association between racism and whiteness can misdirect how white teachers engage in antiracist education.

To illustrate racism as defined above, Tatum (1997) provides the following concrete example:

> In very concrete terms, it means that if a person of color is the victim of housing discrimination, the apartment that would otherwise have been rented to that person of color is still available for a White person. The White tenant is, knowingly or unknowingly, the beneficiary of racism, a system of advantage based on race. The unsuspecting tenant is not to blame for the prior discrimination, but she benefits from it anyway. (p. 9)

In this example, Tatum powerfully shows that one need not be an active racist to be complicit in the perpetuation of racism, a notion that many of my students had not considered. Indeed, by simply being part of a society that is deeply entrenched in racism, all one has to do to perpetuate it is to go about one's life in a usual fashion. As Tatum highlights:

> For many white people, the image of a racist is a hood-wearing Klan member or a name-calling Archie Bunker figure. These images represent what might be called active racism, blatant, intentional acts of racial bigotry and discrimination. Passive racism is more subtle and can be seen in the collusion of laughter when a racist joke is told, of letting hiring practices go unchallenged, of accepting as appropriate the omissions of people of color from the curriculum, and of avoiding difficult race-related issues. Because racism is so ingrained in the fabric of American institutions, it is easily self-perpetuating. All that is required to maintain it is business as usual. (p. 11)

By defining racism, then, as a system of advantage based on race, students painfully recognize that they can no longer remove themselves from the structures of racism. This causes great angst for before encountering the conceptual distinction between racial prejudice and racism, white students could easily point the finger elsewhere and recognize with assurance "a racist." Indeed, there was some comfort in knowing that what they pointed to they certainly did not see in themselves. However, with this newfound sense of the meaning of racism, white students painfully recognize that their own involvement in keeping racism going is much deeper than they had previously thought. This is both painful and irritating. As one student asked in class soon after thinking through the distinction, "Will this be the definition of racism that we will continue to use all semester?" This comment reflects uneasiness, a painful feeling if you will, in thinking about racism as a system of advantage based on race. Indeed, racism defined in this way is like experiencing an irritating thorn in one's side. There were similar comments that in fact were blunter, as when another student remarked, "I understand this distinction, but it makes me uncomfortable, really uncomfortable." What both of these comments demonstrate, especially the second, is that on a conceptual level, students understand and, to a certain extent, can embrace this distinction. On an emotional or affective level, however, the students were struggling to keep their emotions at bay in knowing not only that they are potentially complicit in the spread of racism but also in knowing that being complicit meant that they, too, were "racists." No longer could the finger be pointed simply in one direction.

Indeed, if understanding that they perpetuate racism in ways unknown to them was painful, it was even more painful to be called a racist within this context. Almost all the students I interviewed and worked with in group-facilitated discussions resisted being called a racist. This label was just too painful and for most students would not be accepted. Many students wondered if another word could be used instead. This is interesting because, again, many of the students understood and could accept the distinction, but would not allow themselves to be called a racist. Many students argued that that was an unfair label to use for whites who unknowingly perpetuate racism. Others argued that using such a word would turn off many whites and thereby undermine one's project in getting whites to join in the quest for racial justice. As one student, Melissa, commented:

> I believe that Tatum's definition of racism is valid, yet I am still not giving it my full support. It definitely would not be accepted by our society as a whole. Again I agree with Tatum that the reason for this rejection is how the definition offends people, especially Whites. Not everyone is fortunate enough to have a detailed discussion of this definition and its implications after reading the article, so they may not be able to truly understand what is being said. Until we discussed this topic, I was one of the offended.

Whether the argument is that using the label "racist" is unfair or that it will turn off whites, both arguments do raise the broader pedagogical problem of how to get across these important but touchy subjects. Indeed, as Melissa made clear, most whites do not have the luxury of being able to "unpack" these issues in an intellectual environment.

Yet, I also wonder if their resistance to being called racist stems from other sources, most notably as a defense mechanism. That is, by resisting the label racism, perhaps students are, to a certain degree, resisting the new definition of racism that they seem to understand and embrace on a conceptual level. Indeed, the word "racist" hovers, constantly reminding students of this newfound definition and most important, of their involvement in the spread of racism. In other words, calling oneself a racist in this context is a constant reminder that racism is a *white* problem. Removing the label racist, to put it another way, is a way to, in some way, distance oneself from being complicit in the spread of racism. A coping mechanism no doubt, but a rather effective one indeed. But perhaps there is a way to turn this around so that students see the importance of keeping the label. In my own pedagogical struggle, I responded to another student as follows:

Perhaps using the word racist might actually be a way to get people to work toward eradicating the system of advantage so that they no longer have to consider themselves racists. From this perspective, calling oneself a racist is done not to make one feel guilty; rather, it is done to keep one outraged about racism as a system of advantage as well as keep one committed to eradicating such a system. Eradicating racism as a system of advantage, in other words, can be the motivation for no longer having to consider oneself a racist.

Whether the pain involved stems from being called a racist or from encountering a definition of racism that one had not previously considered, exposing students to a definition of racism as a system of advantage based on race has raised the consciousness of white students about the meaning and function of racism in the twenty-first century. This critical pedagogy, however, more important to the argument set forth in this chapter, has also illuminated how students understand or think through their whiteness. *Or perhaps it might be more appropriate to say that the distinction the students grappled over revealed how much they do not think in critical terms about their whiteness.* It is to this discussion to which I now turn.

Whiteness, Multicultural Education, and Critical Pedagogy

It would be absurd to argue today that whites have not been affected by identity politics. Indeed, living in the post-civil rights era, whites have some sense of their whiteness. They feel it to a certain extent. With white students, this fact is perhaps most evident in their discussions about affirmative action. As Howard Winant (1997) astutely notes:

> Assaults on these policies, which have been developing since their introduction as tentative and quite limited efforts at racial redistribution, are currently at hysterical levels. These attacks are clearly designed to effect ideological shifts, rather than to shift resources in a meaningful way. They represent whiteness as a disadvantage, something which has few precedents in U. S. racial history. This imaginary white disadvantage—for which there is almost no evidence at the empirical level—has achieved widespread popular credence, and provides the cultural and political "glue" that holds together a wide variety of reactionary racial politics. (p. 42)

It is in the sense that no one escapes their whiteness in the post-civil rights era that I agree with Gallagher when he argues that, generally speaking, white students see their whiteness. But there is an issue of degree that is missing from Gallagher's analysis. While, yes, I would argue that most whites in the post-civil rights era have some sense of their whiteness, I think for many white students, the issue of seeing their whiteness is more a question of *degree,* not fact. That is, for most of my white students, their whiteness is something about which they think very little. From this perspective, the questions as an educator that I'm concerned with are: How do I enable them to (1) think about whiteness, (2) think about it in a *sustained* way, and (3) think about it in a *meaningfully transformative* way? With these three points in mind, I conclude by turning to Howard Winant's (1997) discussion of the concept of "white racial dualism."

Having just begun to establish, through Tatum's work, a critical association between racism and whiteness, the second phase of my critical pedagogy focused on involving the students in a more explicit discussion of whiteness. From the perspective of my work and research, the importance of such an explicit discussion was to once again demonstrate that most white pre-service student-teachers either do not think about whiteness at all or do not think about it in *critical* terms. From the perspective of my students, the value of such an explicit discussion was to have them grapple with a set of critical discourses that would raise their consciousness about social positionality, that is, about how their whiteness positions them at an advantage within the web of racial reality.

Engaging in an explicit discussion of whiteness within the context of multicultural education was important for two reasons. First, such a discussion connected the issues of race and racism *directly* to their lives. Second, such a discussion enabled the students to critique forms of multicultural curricula that take up "cultural difference outside of a historical, power-literate context" (Kincheloe and Steinberg, 1997, p. 18). One of my students, Leanne, had this to say about explicitly discussing whiteness in a cultural diversity course: "I have had another education class at this college, which taught us about multicultural education but there was no mention of the injustices and human suffering which are the result of white supremacy within our country. Nor was there any mention about 'whiteness' and what advantages white people receive due to their race. I realize now that my previous education classes have endorsed 'cultural tourism.'"

Underlying theoretically my explicit discussion of whiteness with my students is a concept known as "white racial dualism," an idea that I borrowed from the work of Howard Winant. Drawing from W.E.B. Du Bois, Winant coined this phrase to describe how identity politics in the post-civil rights era has caused whites to experience a kind of double consciousness. As Winant (1997) explains: "[White racial dualism] is an extension to whites of the Du Boisian idea that in a racist society the 'color line' fractures the self which forces [whites] to see themselves simultaneously from within and without" (p. 40). From the perspective of pedagogy, I find Winant's term to be highly useful. That is, because I believe most white pre-service student-teachers do not think about whiteness, I drew upon Winant's concept of white racial dualism to help guide me in selecting materials that would enable my students to begin the critical work of both seeing their whiteness "from within and without." The question I asked myself was, "How can I create within my pedagogy the conditions for cultivating in a meaningful way the experience of white racial dualism among my students?" Winant's concept led me to several texts including Lee MunWah's (1994) film, *The Color of Fear*, and Peggy McIntosh's essay, "White Privilege and Male Privilege." I will end this chapter with a discussion of the implications of McIntosh's article for cultivating the experience of white racial dualism among white student-teachers. I will also demonstrate how my students' responses to such an experience corroborate my thesis that most white pre-service student-teachers do not think about their whiteness.

Although McIntosh is white, I believe that, because of the critical work she has done on herself in the area of whiteness, her voice represents, to the extent that it can, an outsider's view on whiteness. That is, given that most whites do not think critically about whiteness, McIntosh's voice is outside of how the majority of whites think about whiteness. In this sense, McIntosh is an "outsider-within." Indeed, as Alison Bailey (1998) notes, McIntosh represents a small number of "privilege-cognizant whites who refuse to animate expected whitely scripts, and who are unfaithful to worldviews whites are expected to hold" (p. 27). From this perspective, McIntosh's work enables white pre-service student-teachers to awaken to their whiteness from within by virtue of encountering an "outsider's" critical account of whiteness.

Through work that has been done in women's studies in analyzing how men are often asleep to our systemic male privilege, McIntosh then turns the critical gaze back on herself to analyze how she, as a white woman, is privileged by her whiteness. As McIntosh (1997) notes:

"I think whites are carefully taught not to recognize white privilege, as males are taught not to recognize male privilege. So I have begun to ask what it is like to have white privilege" (p. 291). To critically explore her whiteness, McIntosh creates a forty-six item list of the daily effects of white privilege in her life. For example, one item on her list reads, "I can if I wish arrange to be in the company of people of my race most of the time." In another item, she notes, "I am never asked to speak for all the people of my racial group." Finally, in another example, she explains that, "I can turn on the television or open the front page of the newspaper and see people of my race widely represented."

The strength of this list in awakening in my students a critical sense of their whiteness cannot be overstated. Two students' comments, Sara's and Carrie's, provide insight into the impact an explicit discussion of whiteness can have in moving white pre-service student-teachers to new levels of consciousness. In a response paper to McIntosh's essay, Sara, for example, wrote: "Gender topics have always been discussed in my classes so I am always conscious of how my gender affects how I am treated (good or bad). However, I have never, until reading McIntosh's [essay], really considered how my color affects how I am treated." In Carrie's comment, she responded similarly to the shift in consciousness she experienced as a result of engaging in an explicit and critical discussion of whiteness:

> I enjoyed this article because of the list that she provided of the effects of privilege in her daily life. It really made me open my eyes and see all the advantages I have just by being a white individual. This is something I have never thought of, and even more amazingly something that has never been pointed out to me. Personally, when talking about racism I think about people of color, prejudices, and discrimination. Never did I think of racism as involving whites and even more ironically advantages, which is really sad.

Sara's and Carrie's comments demonstrate not only that the students I worked with were not thinking about whiteness but also confirm the importance of engaging students in a pedagogy of whiteness committed to making whiteness visible in critical ways. From this perspective, these students' narratives help demonstrate the political and social urgency of a critical pedagogy of whiteness as integral to the overall discourse on cultural diversity and teacher education. Still, making whiteness visible continues to be central to such a pedagogy.

References

Bailey, A. (1998). Locating traitorous identities: Toward a view of privilege-cognizant white character. *Hypatia*, 13(3), 27–42.

Derman-Sparks, L. & Brunson-Phillips, C. (1997). *Teaching/learning anti-racism: A developmental approach*. New York: Teachers College Press.

Frankenberg, R. (1993). *White women, race matters: The social construction of whiteness*. Minneapolis: University of Minnesota Press.

Gallagher, C. (1994). White reconstruction in the university. *Socialist Review*, 94(1&2), 165–187.

Hill, M. (1998). Souls undressed: The rise and fall of the new whiteness studies. *The Review of Education/Pedagogy/Cultural Studies*, 20(3), 229–239.

hooks, b. (1993). Transformative pedagogy and multiculturalism. In T. Perry & J. Fraser (Eds.), *Freedom's plow: Teaching in the multicultural classroom*. New York: Routledge.

Kincheloe, J. & Steinberg, S. (1997). *Changing multiculturalism*. Philadelphia: Open University Press.

McIntosh, P. (1997). White privilege and male privilege: A personal account of coming to see correspondences through work in women's studies. In R. Delgado & J. Stefancic (Eds.), *Critical white studies: Looking behind the mirror*. Philadelphia: Temple University Press.

McIntosh, P. (1990). White privilege: Unpacking the invisible knapsack. *Independent School*, 49(2), 31–35.

Roediger, D. (1998). *Black on white: Black writers on what it means to be white.* New York: Schocken Books.

Tatum, B. T. (1997). *Why are all the black kids sitting together in the cafeteria?: And other conversations about race.* New York: Basic Books.

Thompson, A. (1999). Book review of *Off white.* Available: http://coe.asu.edu/edrev/reviews/rev76.thm.

Wellman, D. (1993). *Portraits of white racism.* New York and Cambridge: Cambridge University Press.

Winant, H. (1997). Behind blue eyes: Whiteness and contemporary U.S. racial politics. In M. Fine, L. Weis, L. C. Powell, & L. M. Wong (Eds.), *Off white: Readings on race, power, and society.* New York: Routledge.

Section Three

Race and Ethnicity

Seven

Addressing Diversity
Race, Ethnicity, and Culture in the Classroom

Russell Bishop

A common question asked by practitioners is "Isn't what you described just 'good teaching'?" And, while I do not deny that it is good teaching, I pose a counter question: why does so little of it seem to occur in classrooms populated by African-American students? (Ladson-Billings, 1995, p. 484)

We are dealing, it would seem, not so much with culturally deprived children as with culturally deprived schools. And the task to be accomplished is not to revise, and amend, and repair deficient children, but to alter and transform the atmosphere and operations of the schools to which we commit these children. Only by changing the nature of the educational experience can we change the product. To continue to define the difficulty as inherent in the raw material, the children—is plainly to blame the victim and to acquiesce in the continuation of educational inequality. (Ryan, 1976, pp. 61–62)

The widely accepted educational goals for Maori, established at the first Hui Taumata Matauranga held in 2001, are that Maori ought to be able to live as Maori, actively participate as citizens of the world, and enjoy both good health and high standards of living (Durie, 2001). Together with the government goals of equipping learners with twenty-first century skills and reducing systemic underachievement in education, these goals inform the new 2008–2012 Maori Education Strategy, *Ka Hikitia—Managing for Success* (Ministry of Education, 2007), which has as its main strategic outcome: *Maori students enjoying education success as Maori*. Within this frame, there are four student outcomes for Maori: learning to learn, making a distinctive cultural contribution, contributing to Te Ao Maori, and contributing to Aotearoa/New Zealand and the world.

It is unfortunate that, despite these aspirations, statistical data consistently show the persistence of continuing social, economic, and political disparities within our nation, primarily between the descendents of the European colonisers and the indigenous Maori people. Maori have higher levels of unemployment, are more likely to be employed in low-paying jobs, have much higher levels of incarceration, illness and poverty than the rest of the population and are generally under-represented in the positive social and economic indicators of the society. These disparities are reflected at all levels of the education system.

In comparison to majority culture students (in New Zealand they are primarily of European descent), the overall academic achievement levels of Maori students is low (6.9% of Maori boys and 11.5% of Maori girls achieve university entrance, compared to 28.9% and 39% of their non-Maori counterparts); approximately 50% of Maori students leave school without any qualifications, compared to 21% of non-Maori students; 8% of Maori boys and 13% of Maori girls left school in 2005 with a level 3 qualification compared to 28% and 49% for non-Maori respectively; their retention rate to age 17 is 60% of that of their non-Maori counterparts; their rate of suspension from school is three to five times higher, depending on gender; they are over-represented in special education programmes for behavioral issues; enrol in pre-school programmes in lower proportions than other groups; tend to be over-represented in low-stream education classes; are more likely than other students to be found in vocational curriculum streams; leave school earlier, with fewer formal qualifications (41% Maori boys, 39% Maori girls, cf. 18% and 11% respectively, left school before age sixteen), and enroll in tertiary education in lower proportions.[1]

Despite the choice provided by Maori medium education in New Zealand, decades of educational reforms, policies such as multiculturalism and biculturalism, and models of reform that have emphasised the deficiencies, for example, of homes in terms of literacy resources (Nash, 1993), or, more recently, the neurophilosophy claims about the deficiencies of the brain (Clark, 2006), have resulted in little, if any, shift in these disparities for the large proportion of Maori students attending mainstream schools since they were first statistically identified over forty years ago (Hunn, 1960). These outcomes stand in sharp contrast to the aforementioned goals, and it is suggested that, while these outcomes are most clearly exhibited in secondary schools, the foundations for these problems commence in the primary school years. Indeed, while there are achievement differentials evident on children entering primary school, there are indications (Crooks, Hamilton, & Caygill, 2000; Wylie, Thompson, & Lythe, 1999), that by years four and five, these differentials begin to stand out starkly.

The Need for an Explanatory/Theoretical Framework

Teachers require an explanatory theory of how different ways of managing the classroom and creating activities are related to student outcomes. (Alton-Lee, 2006, p. 618

Just how this situation of educational disparity has arisen has been the subject of much debate over the years. Whatever the case, what is important to the Maori people is that the debate does not just focus on causes but, rather, on solutions. However, even this is not as simple as it might appear. Hattie's (2003a) meta-analyses on the influences on student achievement have led him to conclude that "almost all things we do in the name of education have a positive effect on achievement" (p. 4). However, not all effects are equal.

With this caution in mind, two recent studies (Bishop et al., 2003; Bishop et al., 2007), considered the relative importance of such influences on student achievement as whanau, home and community, classroom relationships and pedagogy, teachers, schools and school systems, students themselves, and a multitude of other contributing and confounding factors on learning and achievement, including external socio-economic contexts and systemic and structural conditions. In both of these studies,[2] we spoke with and listened to Maori students talk about their schooling experiences in secondary schools, and the meanings these experiences in mainstream settings (where over 90% of Maori students participate) had for them and for other young Maori people. Both groups of students, in 2003 and again in 2007, identified the development of a caring and learning relationship between teacher and student as the crucial factor in their being able to effectively engage in education. Importantly, in both cases, students (and their whanau) understood themselves to be powerless to make the changes needed to bring about such relationships where they did not already exist and that it was the teachers who had the power to bring about the necessary changes.

The recent large meta-analyses by Hattie (1999, 2003a, 2003b) and Alton-Lee (2003) support the understandings of these young Maori people and their families by telling us that the most important systemic influence on children's educational achievement is the teacher. This is not to deny that other broad factors, such as the prior learning and experiences that the child brings to school, the socio-economic background of the child's family, the structures and history of the school, and the impoverishment of Maori, socially constructed by the processes of colonisation, are not important; it is just that teacher effectiveness stands out as the most easily alterable from within the school system. It is what transcends influences external to the classroom when the student is at school that is the focus of most of the work that seeks to improve the educational futures of all students. Further, as Hattie suggested, this is the most useful site for the provision of professional learning opportunities for teachers when seeking to change the learning culture in schools and to reduce the persistent disparities in educational achievement. This position is supported by numerous international scholars, including Sidorkin (2002), Fullan (2003), Hargreaves (2005), and Elmore (2007), among others, who advocate that changing classroom practices and modifying school structures to accommodate and support these changes are the most likely strategies to improve student performance.

Using Smith's (1997) terms, it is clear that these somewhat 'culturalist' approaches stand in contrast to the more 'structuralist' notions of Nash (1993), Chapple, Jeffries and Walker (1997), and Thrupp (2001, 2007), among others, who advocate a social stratification (low social class, low socio-economic status and resource/cultural deprivation) argument that being poor or poorly resourced inevitably leads to poor educational achievement. Much research in this area looks at the associations between variables such as socio-economic status, ethnicity and other family attributes, and the resulting achievement in ways that suggest that such variables predetermine, or at least strongly influence, achievement outcomes. Anyon (1997, cited in Thrupp, 2001), speaks for this group when she states that:

> Unfortunately educational "small victories" such as restructuring of a school or the introduction of a new pedagogical technique, no matter how satisfying to the individuals involved, without the long-range strategy to eradicate underlying causes of poverty and racial isolation, cannot add up to large victories in our inner cities with effects that are sustainable over time. (p. 20)

Nonetheless, both sets of arguments pose problems for educational practitioners in their search for improvement. The culturalist arguments tend to ignore or downplay the impact of structural impediments on student achievement, whereas the structuralist positions tend to promote the argument that teachers do not have agency in their practice in that there appears to be little that teachers can achieve in the face of overwhelming structural impediments, such as 'school mix' and structural poverty.

Whilst often seen in opposition to each other, both the culturalist and the structuralist or contextualist arguments provide necessary, but not sufficient, conditions for educational reform; the former downplaying external considerations, the latter downplaying internal relationships and interactions, along with teacher agency. Culturalists quite rightly point to the need for pedagogy reform and changes to the school culture as being necessary, but they tend to ignore the lived reality of Maori people—what Ballard (2007) identified as the "racialised social context" of current New Zealand society—and promote a 'universalist' approach or "pedagogy for all" such as Australia's quality education movement, with its focus on providing quality education for all as a means of addressing the increasing diversity and disparity in the schooling population. Structuralists, while quite rightly identifying that children who do not do well in school come from cultural groups not respected by the majority (Ballard, 2007) and that social inequality affects both individuals and schools, tend to forget that schools have long 'called the shots' over what constitutes learning, how relationships between home and schools will be established, and the type of interactions that will take place both between the home and the school and within the classroom itself. However, neither group of theorists has an adequate means of identifying how power differentials are played out in classrooms on a day-to-day basis and the part that teachers, school leaders, and policy makers may play (albeit unwittingly) in the perpetuation of power imbalances and educational disparities. Ironically, Maori students and their families are only too aware of how their power imbalances are played out (Bishop & Berryman, 2006). As Alton-Lee (2003) and Timperley et al. (2007), along with G. Smith (1997) and other Kaupapa Maori theorists in New Zealand and Freire (1997), McLaren (2003), Kincheloe and Steinberg (1997), and Valencia (1997) elsewhere, emphasise, the product of long-term power imbalances needs to be examined by educators at all levels, both in terms of their own cultural assumptions and in a consideration of how they themselves might be participating in the systematic marginalisation of their students. Smith (1997) warns that neither culturalist nor structuralist analyses can satisfactorily account for Maori language, knowledge, and cultural aspirations as major components of existing and developing educational interventions for Maori. For Smith (1997), what is needed is a model that locates culture[3] at the centre of educational reform in the face of deeper structural limitations, in the same manner as that practiced by the Kaupapa Maori educational initiatives of Kohanga Reo and Kura Kaupapa Maori. To Smith (1997), these later institutions have developed "our forms of resistance and transformative praxis which engage both culturalist and structuralist concerns" (p. 222). Therefore, this understanding, developed in Maori medium schooling, offers the English medium sector a model that addresses both the concerns and limitations of the culturalist and structuralist positions, yet also includes a means whereby educators at all levels of the education system can critically reflect upon the part they might play in the wider power plays that mediate Maori participation in the benefits that education has to offer.

Harker (2007) demonstrates such positioning when reconsidering the large data sets of the Smithfield (1994) studies and the Progress at School (1991) studies. He concludes that:

> It is clear from the data presented here that any uni-causal explanation based on socio-economic circumstances is inadequate to explain ethnic differences, thus supporting the caution expressed in Biddulph's BES (Biddulph et al, 2003). The most likely explanation would seem to lie in the interaction between

school environments and the values, attitudes, motivations that underpin the school "culture" and the culture of the home and community environments and the values, attitudes and motivations on which they are based. (p. 17)

Harker goes on to suggest that:

While it is important (even necessary) for the family and community culture of the students to be understood and supported by schools, it is also important (even necessary) for the culture of the school to be understood and supported by families and communities. (p. 17)

Harker (2007) is promoting an analysis that is not based on either a 'schools/teachers barrier' culturalist argument or a 'home/society barrier' structuralist argument. He is, in fact, identifying the discursive shift that has been taking place in New Zealand's educational theorising recently when he suggests moving from positioning oneself within either a structuralist or a culturalist mode of explanation towards drawing from more interactive, relational discourses. In this latter mode, as Harker suggests, we are able to see that the arguments about whether "schools make the difference," or "it is down to the family" are really not useful arguments. It is more a function of the interactions between these two sets of players that offers us explanations of variation in achievement and more importantly, provide us with solutions to problems of educational disparities.

Such a relational theory is put forward in Bishop (2007) and Bishop et al. (2007), where Maori aspirations for self-determination are placed at the centre of the theoretical frame. Self-determination in Durie's (1995) terms "captures a sense of Maori ownership and active control over the future" (p. 16). Nevertheless, despite the fact that self-determination means having the right to determine one's own destiny, to define what that destiny will be, and to define and pursue means of attaining it, there is a clear understanding among Maori people that this autonomy is relative, not absolute, that it is self-determination *in relation to others*. As such, Maori calls for self-determination are often misunderstood by non-Maori people. It is not a call for separatism or non-interference, nor is it a call for non-Maori people to stand back and leave Maori alone, in effect to relinquish all responsibility for the ongoing relationship between the peoples of New Zealand. Rather, it is a call for all those involved in education in New Zealand to reposition themselves in relation to the emerging aspirations of Maori people for an autonomous voice and successful participation in mainstream society (Bishop, 1994; Smith, 1997; Durie, 1998). In other words, the Kaupapa Maori position seeks to operationalise Maori people's aspirations to restructure power relationships to the point where partners can be autonomous and interact from this position rather than from one of subordination or dominance; and this should take place at all levels of education.

Young (2004), explains that indigenous peoples' aspirations for self-determination are relational, acknowledge interdependence, and "are better understood as a quest for an institutional context of non-domination" (p. 187). That is, being self-determining is possible if the relations among peoples and individuals are non-dominating. To ensure non-domination, "their relations must be regulated both by the institutions in which they all participate and by ongoing negotiations among them" (Young, 2004, p. 177). Therefore, the implications of this position are that educational institutions and classrooms should be structured and conducted in such a way as to seek to mediate these potential tensions by actively minimizing domination, co-ordinating actions, resolving conflicts, and negotiating relationships. In Young's terms, this is an education where power is shared between self-determining individuals within non-dominating relations of interdependence.

Discursive (Re)Positioning in the Classroom

To illustrate how useful it is to theorise from a relational rather than a culturalist or structuralist discourse, we can examine the problem as it was presented to us by many teachers in our 2001 and 2005/6 interviews (Bishop et al., 2003, 2007) about why they, with the best intentions in the world, were frustrated in their attempts to reach Maori learners. From a relational positioning, Bruner (1996) offers a solution by identifying that when teaching occurs, progress is decided upon and practices modified as "a direct reflection of the beliefs and assumptions the teacher holds about the learner" (p. 47). This means that ". . .our interactions with others are deeply affected by our everyday intuitive theorizing about how other minds work" (p. 45). In other words, our actions as teachers, parents, or whoever we are at that particular time are driven by the mental images or understandings that we have of other people. For example, if we think that other people have deficiencies, then our actions will tend to follow this thinking, and the relationships and interactions we have with such people will tend to be negative and unproductive. That is, despite our having good intentions, if we lead the students with whom we interact to believe that we think they are deficient, they will respond negatively. We were told time and again by many of the interview participants in 2001 (Bishop & Berryman, 2006) and again in 2007 (Bishop et al., 2007), that negative, deficit thinking on the part of teachers was fundamental to the development of negative relations and interactions with students, resulting in frustration and anger for all concerned. In 2001, the students, their whānau, the principals, and the teachers gave us numerous examples of the negative aspects of such thinking, the resultant problematic and resistant behaviors, and the frustrating consequences for both students and teachers. The teachers spoke of their frustration and anger; the students spoke about negative relations being an assault on their identity as Maori people and their basic need to be accepted. They told us that they aspired to learn but said that negative actions by teachers precluded them from participating in what the school had to offer.

Such understandings have major implications, both for teachers hoping to be agentic in their classrooms and for educational reformers. Elbaz (1981, 1983) explains that understanding the relationship between teachers' theories of practice about learners and learning is fundamental to teachers being agentic. The principles teachers hold dear and the practices they employ develop from the images they hold of others. To Foucault (1972), the images that teachers create when describing their experiences are expressed in the metaphors that are part of the language of educational discourse. That is, teachers draw from a variety of discourses to make sense of the experiences they have relating to and interacting with Maori students.

Therefore, rather than being anything inherent or even biological within the students or even the teachers, it was the discourses teachers drew upon to explain their experiences that kept them frustrated and isolated. It was not their attitudes or personalities. It was what Foucault termed their "positioning within discourse." That is, we are not *of* the explanations; rather, by drawing on particular discourses to explain and make sense of our experiences, we position ourselves within these discourses and act accordingly in our classrooms. The discourses already exist; they have been developing throughout our history, often in conflict with each other in terms of their power differentials, and, importantly for our desire to be agentic, in terms of their practical importance. Some discourses hold solutions to problems, others don't.

The crucial implication from this analysis is that the discursive positions teachers take are the key to their ability to make a difference for Maori students. Therefore, prior to in-class type professional development to promote new quality teaching classroom practices, as culturalist theorists promote, teachers need to be provided with learning opportunities where they can critically evaluate where they discursively position themselves when constructing their own images, principles, and practices in relation to Maori students. Such an activity is necessary so that they can critically reflect upon the part they might play in the wider power plays that mediate Maori participation in the benefits that education has to offer. As we identified in 2001 when we commenced Te Kotahitanga[4] in secondary schools, the most teachers we spoke to at that time were positioned in discourses that limited their agency and efficacy. In particular, the discourses were those suggesting that the deficiencies posed by students, families, schools, the education system, and society create situations and problems that are far beyond the power of teachers to address in the classroom. The learning opportunities offered to teachers in the professional development programme needed to provide them with an opportunity to undertake what Davies called *discursive repositioning*, which means they need to be offered an opportunity to draw explanations and subsequent practices from alternative discourses that offer solutions instead of reinforcing problems and barriers. This approach is supported by Mazarno et al. (1995), who have identified that most educational innovations do not address the "existing framework of perceptions and beliefs, or paradigm, as part of the change process—an ontological approach" (p. 162), but rather assume "that innovation is assimilated into existing beliefs and perceptions" (p. 162). They go on to suggest the reforms more likely to succeed are those that are fundamentally ontological in nature, providing participants with an "experience of their paradigms as constructed realities, and an experience of consciousness other than the 'I' embedded in their paradigms" (p. 162). Or as Sleeter (2005) suggests,

> [i]t is true that low expectations for students of color and students from poverty communities, buttressed by taken-for-granted acceptance of the deficit ideology, have been a rampant and persistent problem for a long time. . . therefore, empowering teachers without addressing the deficit ideology may well aggravate the problem. (p. 2)

According to Burr (1995, p. 146), we are able to reposition ourselves from one discourse to another because, while we are partly the product of discourse, we have agency that allows us to draw from other discourses to change the way we see and make sense of the world. We are free agents and we have agency; what is crucial to understand is that some of those discourses limit our power to activate our agency.

In Te Kotahitanga (Bishop et al., 2003, 2007), we use narratives of the experiences (Bishop & Berryman, 2006) of all the people most closely involved with the education of Maori students, including the young people themselves, to provide teachers with the opportunity to reflect upon the experiences of others involved in similar circumstances to themselves, including perhaps for the first time, the students. Sharing these vicarious experiences of schooling enables teachers to reflect upon their own understandings of Maori children's experiences, the nature of knowledge production, and upon their own theorizing/explanation and practice about these experiences and their likely impact upon Maori student achievement. We are seeking to provide teachers with the opportunity to critically reflect upon their own discursive positioning and its implications for their agency and for the Maori students' learning. Where necessary, teachers are able to discursively reposition themselves from discourses that limit their agency to those where they can be agentic.

As we began to implement what became Te Kotahitanga, we also learned that positive classroom relationships and interactions were built upon positive, non-deficit thinking by teachers about students and their families. This thinking viewed the students as having many experiences that were relevant and fundamental to classroom interactions. This agentic thinking by teachers means that they see themselves as being able to solve problems that come their way; they have recourse to skills and knowledge that can help all their students to achieve, no matter what. We learned that this positive thinking was fundamental to the creation of classroom learning contexts where young Maori people are able to be Maori; where Maori students' humor was acceptable, where students could care for and learn with each other, where being different was acceptable, and where the power of the Maori students' own self-determination was fundamental to classroom relations and interactions. Indeed, it was the interdependence of self-determining participants in the classroom that created vibrant learning contexts which were, in turn, characterized by the growth and development of quality learning relations and interactions and increased student attendance, engagement, and achievement, both in school and national-based measures (see Bishop et al., 2007; Timperley et al., 2007).

Of course, discursive repositioning, while a necessary condition for educational reform, is not sufficient to bring about that reform. However, in theorising from within a relational discourse that addresses the limitations of both the culturalist position (limited consideration of the impact of power differentials within the classroom, school, and society) and the structuralist position (limited consideration of the agency of teachers, school leaders, and policy makers), all levels of education can develop a model that promotes effective and sustainable educational reform drawn from a relational discourse.

Conclusion

The Maori students we spoke to in 2001, 2005, and 2007 (Bishop & Berryman, 2006; Bishop et al., 2007), spoke at length about the importance of whakawhānaungatanga and whānaungatanga, that is, the process of establishing relationships and the quality of the relationships that are established for their engagement with learning and eventual achievement. Similarly, the teachers who positioned themselves within the relational discourse in 2001 and 2005 emphasised the importance of relationships at all levels of the project: within the classroom, between facilitators and themselves, and also between themselves and their management, parents, and community members.

Sidorkin (2002) suggests that these people offer something very valuable to the theorising about educational reform in mainstream education. In making his case for the primacy of a pedagogy of relations, he cites Margonis, who calls for "adopting an ontological attitude towards educational relationships" (p. 86). He explains that Margonis "suggests that relationships ontologically precede the intrinsic motivation for learning and should therefore be placed at the center of educational theory" (p. 870), meaning that establishing relations is a central part of reform activities. We need to be critical of theories positioned within the discourses of individual or cultural deficiencies that assign blame to individual students' lack of motivation, character defects, or their home's lack of scholastic preparation or support. Of course, assigning blame to individuals because of their membership in a particular group is simply unacceptable, as it is racist, sexist, or ageist. Like Deschenes et al. (2001), we also need to be critical of simply re-assigning blame to the schools or to the education system at a structural or systemic level. These latter theories identify that schools are too rigid to cater to ethnic, racial, or cultural diversity and/or that students fail because their cultural backgrounds are too different from the culture of the school. What is significant about these theories is that they assign blame outside the location where the solutions for classroom teachers lie. In doing so, they still leave teacher-student interactions and relationships of power outside the equation and focus on blaming others or, worse still, blame themselves for educational problems.

It is clear from what the students told us in 2001 and again in 2004 and 2005, that the quality of the relationships that are established in classrooms affects their attendance, learning, and achievement. This finding means that, while we cannot ignore the impact of structural impediments, such as socially constructed impoverishment, we cannot allow this analysis to disempower teachers from action. Teacher action is central to educational reform, for, as Elmore (2007) attests, the key to change is *teacher action supported by responsive structural reform*. Hattie (2003a) and Alton-Lee (2003) are clear that it is teachers who have the potential to change the educational outcomes of Maori students. So too are Phillips, McNaughton, and MacDonald (2001), who, in a study that indicated how Maori and Pasifika new-entrant students' reading scores could be improved by addressing teachers' expectations of their learning, found that "low rates of progress in literacy are neither inevitable nor unchangeable in low decile schools. Educators working in these environments can help bring children up to speed—to expected levels of achievement" (p. 10).

The model provided here suggests a means of building on these groundbreaking studies, for it is in the classroom that change begins with the discursive (re)positioning of teachers within a relational discourse. It is, then, the development of support for the range of necessary structural transformations that will bring about the reduction in the socially constructed impediments to Maori fully participating in the benefits that New Zealand society and economy have to offer.

Notes

1. I am very grateful to David Hood for this analysis of the recent statistics.
2. In Bishop et al., 2003, we reported on the initial study of Maori secondary school students' schooling experiences, the narratives of which appear in Bishop and Berryman (2006). The second study, Bishop et al., 2007, reported on the experiences of Maori secondary school students in the classrooms of teachers who had been identified as effective implementers of the Te Kotahitanga Effective Teaching Profile by students, project facilitators, principals and data from formal observations in their classrooms.
3. Unfortunately culture is a much abused term and appears to be used in two ways in this chapter. However, both uses are covered by the definition of culture promoted by Quest Rapuara (1992) but different emphasis is given to usage of the term in this chapter. The first refers there to the sense-meaning making systems of a group of people and the second is the more descriptive notion of the culture of a school.

4. Te Kotahitanga is a New Zealand Ministry of Education funded research and professional development project that seeks to improve the educational achievement of Maori students in English-medium mainstream secondary schools. www.tekotahitanga.com

References

Alton-Lee, A. (2003). *Quality teaching for diverse students in schooling: Best evidence synthesis.* Wellington, New Zealand: Ministry of Education.

Alton-Lee, A. (2006). How teaching influences learning: Implications for educational researchers, teachers, teacher educators and policy makers. *Teaching and Teacher Education* (22), 612–626.

Ballard, K. (2007). *Education and imagination: Strategies for social justice.* The Herbison Lecture presented to the NZARE, University of Canterbury, Christchurch, New Zealand.

Bishop, R. (1994). Initiating empowering research. *New Zealand Journal of Educational Studies.* 29(2) 175-188.

Bishop, R. (2005). Freeing ourselves from neocolonial domination in research: A Kaupapa Māori approach to creating knowledge. In N. Denzin & Y. Lincoln (Eds.). *The Sage handbook of qualitative research* (3rd ed.) (pp. 109–138). Thousand Oaks, California: Sage.

Bishop, R. (2007). Lessons from Te Kotahitanga for teacher education. In L. F. Detretchin & C. J. Craig (Eds.). *International research on the impact of accountability systems* (pp. 225–239). Lanham, Maryland: Rowman & Littlefield Education.

Bishop, R., & Berryman, M. (2006). *Culture speaks: Cultural relationships and classroom learning.* Wellington, New Zealand: Huia Publishers.

Bishop, R., Berryman, M., Cavanagh, T., & Teddy, L. (2007). *Te Kotahitanga phase 3 Whanaungatanga: Establishing a culturally responsive pedagogy of relations in mainstream secondary classrooms.* Wellington, New Zealand: Ministry of Education.

Bishop, R., Berryman, M., Tiakiwai, S., & Richardson, C. (2003). *Te Kotahitanga: The experiences of year 9 and 10 Maori students in mainstream classrooms.* Wellington, New Zealand: Ministry of Education.

Bruner, J. (1996). *The culture of education.* Cambridge, Massachusetts: Harvard University Press.

Burr, V. (1995). *An introduction to social constructionism.* London: Routledge.

Chapple, S., Jeffries, R., & Walker, R. (1997). *Maori participation and performance in education. A literature review and research programme.* Report for the Ministry of Education, Wellington, New Zealand.

Clark, J. (2006). Commentary: The gap between the highest and lowest school achievers: Philosophical arguments for downplaying teacher expectation theory. *New Zealand Journal of Education Studies,* 41(2), 367–381.

Crooks, T., Hamilton, K., & Caygill, R. (2000). New Zealand's national education monitoring project: Maori student achievement, 1995–2000 [Electronic Version]. Retrieved May 9, 2007 from http://nemp.otago.ac.nz/i_probe.htm.

Deschenes, S., Tyack, D., & Cuban, L. (2001). Mismatch: Historical perspectives on schools and students who don't fit them. *Teachers College Record,* 103(4), 525–547.

Durie, M. (1995). Tino Rangatiratanga: Self Determination. *He Pukenga Korero,* 1(1), 44–53.

Durie, M. (1998). *Te Mana, Te Kawanatanga: The politics of Maori self-determination.* Auckland: Oxford University Press.

Durie, M. (2001). *A framework for considering Maori educational achievement.* Paper presented at the Hui Taumata Matauranga, Turangi/Taupo.

Elbaz, F. (1981). The teachers "practical knowledge": Report of a case study. *Curriculum Inquiry,* 11, 43–71.

Elbaz, F. (1983). *Teacher thinking: A study of practical knowledge.* New York: Nichols.

Elmore, R. F. (2007). Professional networks and school improvement. *The School Administrator,* 64(4), 20–24.

Foucault, M. (1972). *The archaeology of knowledge.* New York: Pantheon.

Freire, P. (1997). *Pedagogy of the heart.* New York: Continuum.

Fullan, M. (1993). *Change forces: Probing the depths of educational reform.* London: Falmer Press.

Fullan, M. (2003). *The moral imperative of school leadership.* Thousand Oaks, California: Corwin Press.

Fullan M. (2005). *Leadership and sustainability: System thinkers in action.* Thousand Oaks, California: Corwin Press.

Hargreaves, A. (2005). *Sustainable leadership seminar workbook.* Brisbane: ACEL.

Harker, R. (2007). *Ethnicity and school achievement in New Zealand: Some data to supplement the Biddulph et al. (2003) Best evidence synthesis: Secondary analysis of the progress at school and Smithfield datasets for the iterative best evidence synthesis programme.* Wellington, New Zealand: Ministry of Education.

Hattie, J. (1999). *Influences on student learning.* Inaugural Lecture, University of Auckland, Auckland, NZ: www.staff.auckland.ac.nz/j.hattie.

Hattie, J. (2003a). Teachers make a difference: What is the research evidence? Paper presented at the Australian council for educational research annual conference.

Hattie, J. (2003b). New Zealand education snapshot: with specific reference to the yrs 1–13. Paper presented at the Knowledge Wave 2003 The Leadership Forum, Auckland.

Hunn, J.K. (1960). *Report on the Department of Maori Affairs*. Wellington, New Zealand: Government Print.

Kincheloe, J., & Steinberg, S. (1997). *Changing multiculturalism*. Buckingham, Philadelphia: Open University Press.

Ladson-Billings, G. (1995). Toward a theory of culturally relevant pedagogy. *American Educational Research Journal*, 32(3), 465–491.

Marzano, R., Zaffron, S., Zraik, L., Robbins, S., & Yoon, L. (1995). A new paradigm for educational change. *Education*, 116(2), 162–173.

McLaren, P. (2003). *Life in schools: An introduction to critical pedagogy in the foundations of education* (4th ed.). Boston, Massachusetts: Pearson Education.

Ministry of Education. (2007). *Ka Hikitia—Managing for Success*. Wellington, New Zealand: Ministry of Education.

Nash, R. (1993). *Succeeding generations: Family resources and access to education in New Zealand*. Auckland, New Zealand: Oxford University Press.

Phillips, G., McNaughton, S., & MacDonald, S. (2001). *Picking up the pace: Effective literacy interventions for accelerated progress over the transition into decile 1 schools*. Wellington, New Zealand: Ministry of Education.

Ryan, W. (1976). *Blaming the victim*. New York: Vintage Books.

Sidorkin, A. M. (2002). *Learning relations*. New York: Peter Lang.

Sleeter. (2005). *Un-standardizing Curriculum: Multicultural teaching in the standards-based classroom*. New York: Teachers College Press.

Smith, G. H. (1997). *Kaupapa Maori as transformative praxis*. Unpublished doctoral thesis, University of Auckland, Auckland, New Zealand.

Thrupp, M. (2001). Sociological and political concerns about school effectiveness research: Time for a new research agenda, *School Effectiveness and School Improvement*, 12(1), 7–40.

Thrupp, M. (2007), "Education's 'inconvenient truth': persistent middle class advantage," an inaugural professorial lecture, School of Education, University of Waikato, Hamilton, March 2.

Timperley, H., Wilson, A., Barrar, H., & Fung, I. (2007). *Teacher professional learning and development: Best evidence synthesis iteration*. Wellington, New Zealand: Ministry of Education.

Valencia, R. R. (Ed.). (1997). *The evolution of deficit thinking*. London: Falmer.

Wylie, C., Thompson, J., & Lythe, C. (1999). *Competent children at 8: Families, early education, and schools*. Wellington, New Zealand: New Zealand Council of Educational Research.

Young, I. M. (2004). Two concepts of self-determination. In S. May, T. Modood, & J. Squires (Eds.). *Ethnicity, Nationalism and Minority Rights* (pp. 176–198). Cambridge: Cambridge University Press.

Eight

Minorities vs. Minority Groups
How Language Defines, Defiles and Denigrates for Life

R. Deborah Davis

Language that we, as social scientists, researchers and policy makers create and use in our studies of society, its institutions, its populations, economic and social behavior, becomes codified and used to categorize, stigmatize, denigrate and separate its citizens over time. Those of us who conduct research, teach and write, need to take responsibility for that which is stated and unstated, and the ways in which we describe, subscribe, and relegate groups and individuals to categories—either majority or minority. Looking back over the last century there has been an apparent shift in the way terms are used to categorize, label, define, defile and denigrate people of color, specifically African American individuals.

I will discuss the prevalence of the terms "minority" and "minorities" and their use as nouns to describe/label specific individuals in recent years, versus the original use as adjectives describing nouns as in such phrases as, minority group, minority experiences, minority languages; or as a category or group as ethnic minority(ies), mathematical minority, language minorities. At issue are the instances where we hear these terms now being used to ascribe a person's identity as in "As *a minority*, he/she is. . .."or "He is *a minority*," "a *minority* teacher" or "a *minority* neighborhood" or "a *minority* school."

We notice that even the *Webster's New World Dictionary* definition of minority has evolved from the 1950s' version: "3. a racial, religious, ethnic or political group smaller than and differing from the larger, controlling group in a community, nation, etc." into a more covert (politically correct) definition in *Webster's Universal College Dictionary*, 2001 edition: "3. Also called minority group, a group differing, esp. in race, religion, or ethnic background from the majority of a population." As far back as I can remember, in the black community, "*minority*" has always meant "less than" or "inferior." Majority is more of anything. Minority is less than everything. History does, however, also record instances where minority group members outnumber the majority group members—counties in Mississippi where blacks outnumber whites, South Africa under apartheid, India, where a small number of British ruled hundreds of millions of Indians. "Yet we frequently refer to situations clearly meaning a pattern of relationship, the distribution of power, and not numbers." (Simpson & Yinger, 1972, p.11). These terms are indeed arbitrary since we understand that the term *minority* in the American parlance assumes that a *majority* exists.

Early Understandings of Minority Groups

The usage of the term minority to describe groups of people has a historical legacy of hundreds of years. In the twentieth century the United Nations Subcommission on Prevention and Protection of Minorities codified the term thus: Minorities are ". . .those non-dominant groups in a population which possess and wish to preserve stable ethnic, religious or linguistic traditions or characteristics markedly different from those of the rest of the population." (United Nations Subcommission, 1952). I contend that African Americans do not fit this definition. As a group, they have never advocated the preservation of any one ethnic, religious or linguistic tradition or particular characteristics since their ancestors were brought to the Americas in chains for the sole purpose of servitude and were stripped of their native languages and cultures. African Americans, as a group, have not been trying to be separate but have consistently striven for equal citizenship rights, human rights enjoyed by others as descendants of the builders of this nation.

David W. Hicks (1981), in *Minorities: A Teacher's Resource Book for the Multi-ethnic Curriculum* gives us one perspective:

> Most societies today are multi-ethnic in nature—that is to say they are made up of differing, although sometimes overlapping, cultural backgrounds and expectations. In the United States for example one needs to consider, amongst several other groups, the role of Native Americans (Indians), Chicanos (Mexican Americans) and Asian Americans in society. Similarly in the UK diverse cultural backgrounds are manifested in the presence of Indian, Chinese, Cypriot and Black communities to name a few. (p. 1)

It is interesting to notice that, in his broader discussion of minority group experience, Hicks (1981), in describing groups in the U.K., European and U.S. societies, did not mention the African American (Negro) given that they do not fit the full description of an ethnic minority group.

Wirth (1945), in "The Problem of Minority Groups" gives a more specific description of U.S. society and its minority group status:

> We may define a minority group as a group of people who, because of their physical or cultural characteristics, are singled out from others in the society in which they live for differential and unequal treatment, and who therefore regard themselves as objects of collective discrimination. The existence of a *minority* in a society implies the existence of a corresponding dominant group enjoying higher social status and greater privileges. Minority status carries with it the exclusion from full participation in the life of the society. Though not necessarily an alien group the *minority* is treated and regards *itself as a people* apart. (pp. 347–8). (italics added)

Wirth's (1945) use of the italicized terms, in each case, is referring to the group status not an individual identity. Wirth (1945) also explained the four classic types of objectives sought by minority groups in the U.S.:

1. Pluralistic: desiring peaceful existence side by side with the majority and other minorities;
2. Assimilationist: desiring absorption into the larger society and treatment simply as individuals;
3. Secessionist: seeks both cultural and political independence, e.g., Garveyite movement for a separate nation or Black Muslim separatist tendencies;
4. Militant: goes beyond the desire for equality to a desire for domination—the total reversal of statuses, e.g., the Black Power Movement of the 1960s.

As our history will attest, small groups of African Americans have tried objectives 3 and 4; however in neither case was this movement by consensus or majority of the group. This early discussion of minority groups in the U.S. gives us a sense of the use of the minority group language at a time before the movement for Civil Rights. African American consensus was that of a pluralistic existence, which was, in fact, demonstrated by the Civil Rights Movement in coalition with supporters from the mainstream, all of whom desired a more pluralistic society.

Simpson & Yinger (1972) give us a different view of the relationship: "From the perspective of the individual minority-group member, his status is characterized primarily by its categorical nature; he cannot resign or escape by merit." (p. 12). The individual Negro has come to understand that society views him/her through the lens of Jim Crow propaganda. Simpson & Yinger (1972) continue, "Many Negroes are Assimilationist, desirous of full participation in American society thinking of themselves as sharing the common culture. Some take a pluralistic position, however; still others are secessionist or militant." (p. 14). Each minority group can best be studied in terms of a sequence of profiles, indicating the changing times and circumstances. Their definition of "minority group" is a group of people that can be distinguished by physical or social characteristics different from the characteristics of the majority, those with greatest power and highest status (p. 16). The supposed unassimilability of the Negro and other racial groups, based on phenotype (Native Americans, Asians Americans) in the United States, adds a dimension that must be taken into account in any analysis of the American situation. (p. 17).

Considering that the discussion of minority group issues is a global one with a history that goes at least as far back as the 15th century, Richardson (1977) posits four areas to consider when mapping the issues for majority/minority discussions: Values, Problems, Background, and Action. I will refer to this *Map of Issues* to explore the phenomenon of majority/minority language. These four areas in question give rise to more questions we need to investigate to understand the complexity of the language we use in our research and writing and most importantly that which gets transferred into everyday speech.

Values

From birth we develop our *Personal Values* from our cultural and ethnic backgrounds and being socialized for *"The Good Society."* The pervasiveness of majority/minority experience in the U..S. has created a climate of prejudice that envelopes our daily interactions. Simpson and Yinger (1972) posited three factors that need to be considered if we are to understand how such a climate gets created: First consider the prejudiced people, their socialization and what they think of themselves and their needs as individuals. Second, consider the institutions and structure of society, the power arrangements and historical patterns. Third, consider the cultural attitudes that have been passed down from generation to generation as folklore and family tradition. These values are not only passed on by families and community but also by our institutions of education and the people in them and the ever-changing modes of media we have experienced in our lives.

Problems

As I see it, we live in a climate of prejudice, conscious and unconscious. Our use of language to segment society can be viewed as three major areas: *Identity, Prejudice,* and *Oppression.* The research community has, in an effort to understand different, and differences between, majority/minority groups in the U.S., studied and reported on this phenomenon, creating terms to describe the groups' situations—segregated, displaced, disadvantaged, underrepresented, at-risk—as well as using the terms "minority" and "minority group." Over time these terms have come into the normal parlance in discussing urban, Native American, black (African American and Caribbean American, Latino/a) and poor children. Although complex, children's identities can be affected by this language. Consider the young black male who says "*As a minority* they don't expect me to succeed" or, the president of a black Student Union who says in his speech "*As minorities* we need a voice on this campus." Imagine an internal interpretation that goes like this: "As an inferior person they don't expect me to succeed" or " Because we are inferior, we need a voice on this campus." This is subliminal, psychological rhetoric speaking "as an inferior person or group" rather than a prideful statement of a positive identity, ethnicity or nationality (such as saying persons of color, African American, Chicano or Korean). We often hear children referring to "living in a minority neighborhood" (an inferior neighborhood), "shopping at a minority business" (an inferior business) when despondently talking about their situations. They have been conditioned by our language to think "less than" and "inferior" and accept it as an identity.

Background

Because no problem can be understood without background knowledge, let us investigate language usage before and after the 1960s. In mapping language usage over time, we see that it relates to the *"Hearts and Minds"* of the people, their socialization, *Structures and Institutions* and, "the whole field of communication in its broadest sense involving both formal and informal education and various channels of the media" (Hicks, p. 5). In the United States, aside from "the Negro, the Indian, and the Oriental, who constitute our leading racial minorities" (Wirth, 1945) the population consists of European immigrant groups and their descendants and such religious minorities as Catholics, Jews, and Mormons in a predominantly Protestant country. Wirth (1945) describes the historical situation as such:

> There is little doubt but that the Negro in the United States has become the principal shock absorber of the anti-minority sentiment of the dominant whites. The Negro in this country has been so clearly our leading minority that in comparison with his status the ethnic minorities have occupied a relatively dominant position. Indeed the attitude of the ethnic minorities toward the Negro differs little from the attitude of the long-established white Protestant settlers. Where there are several distinct minorities in a country the dominant group can allow itself the luxury of treating some of them generously and can

at the same time entrench itself and secure its own dominance by playing one minority against another. (p. 353)

Our histories and primary documents, the laws and court records bear witness to the conflicts between the groups (Chinese, Irish, African Americans, Jews, Chicanos) in competition for jobs and housing regulated by White Anglo-Saxon Protestants.

Action

The action we take at both governmental and non-governmental levels, whether one-on-one, in small or large groups, whether verbal, written or non-verbal, is the determinant of what harm or good can be done. Wirth (1945) cautioned us on the objective deprivation that our words and actions can inflict:

> These deprivations circumscribe the individual's freedom of choice and self-development. The members of minority groups are held in lower esteem and may even be objects of contempt, hatred, ridicule and violence. They are generally socially isolated and frequently spatially segregated. Their subordinate position becomes manifest in their unequal access to educational opportunities and in their restricted scope of occupational and professional advancement. They are not as free as other members of society to join the voluntary associations that express their interests. They suffer from more than the ordinary amount of social and economic insecurity. Even as concerns public policy, they are frequently singled out for special treatment; their property rights may be restricted; they may not enjoy the equal protection of the laws; they may be excluded from public office. (p. 348)

They Are "Minoritized"

Minority groups in the U.S., and their members concomitantly experience subjective deprivation with the objective deprivation from the feelings they internalize about their situation. This internalization—the feelings that affect identity and self-esteem—is no less important but rather more important to the health and vitality of a group and a person in a group. Again, I go to Wirth (1945) for an early summary of *internalized oppression*:

> One cannot long discriminate against people without generating in them a sense of isolation and of persecution and without giving them a conception of themselves as more different from others than in fact they are. Whether, as a result of this differential treatment, the minority (group) comes to suffer from a sense of its own inferiority or develops a feeling that it is unjustly treated—which may lead to a rebellious attitude—depends in part upon the length of time that its status has existed and in part upon the total social setting in which the differential treatment operates. Where a caste system has existed over many generations and is sanctioned by religious and other sentiments, the attitude of resignation is likely to be dominant over the spirit of rebellion. But in a secular society where class rather than caste pervades the stratification of people, and where the tradition of minority status is of recent origin, minorities (groups), driven by a sense of frustration and unjustified subordination, are likely to refuse to accept their status and their deprivation without some effort to improve their lot. (pp. 348–9).

It seems that soon after the Civil Rights Movement, when laws had been changed and things were perceived to be on a more "equal" footing, we begin to see analyses of this new society. Makielski (1973) in his overview of what he termed the "beleaguered minorities," presents a snapshot of blacks and their attempt to fit in:

The "beleaguered minorities" in American society consist of those who feel themselves to be surrounded by a hostile environment, who have a long history of being subjected to discrimination and deprivation, and who are relatively powerless in making any change in their condition. As minorities, (in a group) they feel themselves to be alone, even though other minorities (groups) have existed in this country for a long time. In that they sense that they are beleaguered, they are "new." The "old minorities," the ethnic groupings composed of Jews, Italians, Irish, Germans, Slavs, or Scandinavians, have previously faced hostility, prejudice, and maltreatment. As a consequence, it is always tempting to compare the old minorities with the new, arguing that a society that has fairly comfortably accommodated one minority (group) will eventually in the same way make room for another. (p. 4).

It had been relatively easy to subsume the Irish and the Jews, the Polish, the Russians, etc., once they left their culture and language behind. As white people they could melt into the societal pot by speaking and acting like the whites in power. They were accepted with the help of the GI Bill (1944) and the Federal Housing Act (1968) into the suburban middle class. Researchers ceased referring to white ethnic groups as minority groups. On the other hand, people of color are continually referred to as minorities. They were prohibited by laws, ordinances, redlining and societal attitudes from obtaining better employment, housing, and quality of life. African Americans, Hispanics/Latino/as, Native Americans and Asians continue to be minoritized.

The term minority continues to be used in the evaluative way, to describe and discuss persons and groups of African American, Native American, Asian and Latino/a descent. People of color who obtained the education, jobs, and economic status to be middle class were still not able to shed the evaluative term "minority" as an individual or as a group. Oliver C. Cox, looking at the dynamics of the intersection of caste, class and race, posited a theory of exploitation to help make sense of the unassimilated existence of blacks (people of color) in U.S. society. The exploitation theory explains how racism can stigmatize a group as inferior so that the exploitation of that group can be justified (Cox, 1948; Hunter and Abraham, 1987; Wilhelm, 1980 as cited in Schaefer, 1993, p. 43). "The caste approach of racial subordination sees race and social class as closely related, because blacks and other non-whites are destined by the social structure to occupy a castelike position." (Schaefer, 1993, p. 43). Gordon Allport substantiates that the exploitation theory correctly points a finger at one of the factors in prejudice, that is, the rationalized self-interest of the upper classes (1979, pp. 205–206).

Undoing the Degradation

As researchers, policy makers, teachers, parents, guardians and caregivers, we must first realize that this language denigrates the human spirit. It is "hurtful language." We must consider that the effects of the constant usage in articles and in reports continue to support the use of these terms in reflections, in discussions, in conversations by reinforcing the internalization, giving rise to the self-identification as the examples have shown. We must take responsibility for the power we have, the power of the pen, the power of the press, the power of domination. I do not suggest that it will be easy or immediate, but it can be undone as systematically as it has been done, by conscientious, committed action.

I am suggesting that each one of us think about how we use our voice. When we write an article about black/African American and Latino/a, Native American children be clear, be specific. Use the ethnic terms for the group; use the names the groups use for themselves. In this way we allow group members to retain or regain pride in their roots—re-remember their history and heroes. It is relatively simple to effect as indicated in the following example:

> Every generation except for this one has achieved a higher educational level than its parents. And as grim as these statistics are, they are far worse for ~~minorities~~ *people of color*. Population increases are driven largely by population growth among ~~Hispanics, and other minorities~~ *Latinos/as, African Americans, biracial Americans* and immigrants *to America*. This is the work force of the future. (Flores, et al., 2008, p. 16) (Italics are the substituted terms.)

References

Allport, G. (1979. *The Nature of Prejudice*, 25th Anniversary Edition. Reading, MA: Addison-Wesley.

Cox, Oliver C.(1948). *Caste, Class, and Race: A Study in Social Dynamics*. New York: Modern Reader Paperbacks.

Flores, R., et al. It's About Access. *Diverse Issues in Higher Education*, v. 25, no. 10 (June 26, 2008), p. 16.

Hicks, David W. (1981) *Minorities: A Teacher's Resource Book for the Multi-ethnic Curriculum*. London: Heinemann Educational Books Ltd.

Hunter, Herbert M., and Abraham, Sameer Y. Eds. (1987). *Race Class, and World Systems: The Sociology of Oliver C. Cox*. New York: Monthly Review Press.

Makielski, S. J. (1973). *Beleaguered Minorities: Cultural Politics in America*. San Francisco: W. H. Freeman.

Richardson, R. (1977). Studying World Society. *New Era*, 58 (6), pp. 175–84.

Santa Barbara County Board of Education. (1972). *The Emerging Minorities in America: A Resource Guide for Teachers*. Santa Barbara, CA: ABC-Clio Press.

Schaefer, Richard T. (1993). *Racial & Ethnic Groups*, 5th Edition. New York: Harper Collins College Publishers.

Simpson, G. E. and Yinger, J. M. (1972). *Racial and Cultural Minorities: An Analysis of Prejudice and Discrimination*, 4th Edition. New York: Harper & Row.

United Nations Subcommission on Prevention and Protection of Minorities. (1952). *Yearbook of Human Rights for 1950*. New York: United Nations.

Wilhelm, Sidney M. (1980). Can Marxism Explain America's Racism? *Social Problems* 28 (December), pp. 98–112.

Wirth, L. (1945). The Problem of Minority Groups in Linton, R. (ed.), *The Sciences of Man in World Crisis*. New York: Columbia University Press.

Nine

Putting Multiethnic Students on the Radar
A Case for Greater Consideration of Our Multiethnic Students

Erica Mohan

Celebrities and politicians like Tiger Woods and Barack Obama have increased the prominence of multiethnicity in both the media and the public consciousness. Scholars and authors such as Arboleda (1998), Basu (2006), Camper (1994), Krebs (1999), Renn (2004), Root (1992, 1996), Schwartz (1998), Wardle (1996, 1998, 2000), Wilson (1987), and Zack (1993, 1995), to name but a few, have contributed to the substantial increase in the research and literature related to multiethnicity. With the help of organizations like iPride and the Interracial Family Circle, multiethnic families can, in at least some parts of North America, connect in a supportive community. Resources and information related to multiethnicity are now readily available via websites such as those hosted by MAVIN, the Mixed Heritage Center, and the Association of MultiEthnic Americans. And, thanks to programs like iPride's Multiethnic Education Program, educators can benefit from resources, training, and support as they strive to be responsive to, and supportive of, the educational experiences of their multiethnic students. It is fair to say then, that in manifold ways and myriad settings, multiethnicity is finally receiving long overdue attention.

Why then, we may wonder, did a student tell me in a recent interview that "multiethnic students aren't even on the school's radar"? Indeed, in the course of interviews conducted with twenty-six self-identified multiethnic high school and university students, the same sentiment was repeated multiple times and never contradicted: Multiethnicity is a topic that is rarely discussed in schools, addressed by school activities, or covered in the curriculum. But why is this true? And does it matter?

Despite growing awareness of the multiethnic population and their experiences, multiethnic students remain neglected in schools. Moreover, many schools are complicit in the reinforcement of racial and ethnic categories that confine multiethnic identities. As argued here, schools must end this habitual neglect of their multiethnic students and begin to deconstruct and challenge rigid and limited conceptions of race and ethnicity. My central purpose here is to advocate for policies, practices, and curricula in schools that are more sensitive and responsive to the identities and experiences of their multiethnic students. In short, I hope to help put multiethnic students on schools' radars.

I begin with a clarification of terminology, followed by examples of some of the ways in which multiethnic students are neglected in schools. I then set forth six arguments for the consideration of multiethnic students in school policies, practices, and curricula and for more meaningful engagement with the topic of multiethnicity. This is not a "how to" chapter with specific instructions, curriculum suggestions, and activities for educators convinced of the need for greater sensitivity to the identities and experiences of their multiethnic students. For these, one might turn to, for example, Wardle (1996, 1998, 2000), Schwartz (1998), or iPride's Multiethnic Education Program. Nevertheless, I conclude with three more general, yet critically important, suggestions for educators to keep in mind as they develop specific ways to be more inclusive and supportive of their multiethnic students.

To support my arguments, I draw on findings from twenty-six semi-structured interviews conducted with twenty-one high school students from California and five university students from British Columbia. All interviewed students *self-identified* as multiethnic. The interviews with high school students explored the influence of K–12 school policies, practices, social structures, and patterns of behavior on the perceptions of students in relation to questions of self, learning, and belonging. Those interviews with university students focused more generally on their identity construction processes. It is beyond the scope of this chapter to fully examine the unique experiences and identities of interviewed students. Rather, distilled from the data are representative responses and examples related specifically to school policies, practices, and curriculum.

Terminology

Throughout this chapter, I use the term multiethnic instead of multiracial, mixed race, biracial, mixed origin, mixed ethnicity, children of mixed parentage, of blended background, and a variety of other possible terms. I do this more out of ease of use than the belief that multiethnic is the most suitable term. All of these terms are problematic and reinforce the misconception that there exist biologically defined pure races and discrete ethnicities. I am convinced that race is a socially constructed and essentialist categorization and when used should be read as having inverted commas. Nevertheless, despite the dangers of invoking it, race is a categorization with wide-ranging personal, social, political, and economic consequences, and its use should not be replaced by a colorblind stance that ignores persistent and systemic racism and racial inequality. While some prefer a definition of multiethnic to include only children of parents representing two or more races, I expand this definition to include children of parents who may be racially similar, but who represent different ethnicities. Under this conception, the child of a Chinese mother and a Japanese father is considered multiethnic, as is the child of an Afro-Caribbean mother and an African father.

The decision to define multiethnicity in this way is not based on an inaccurate conflation of race and ethnicity or the impact they have on the lives of individuals, but a desire to blur the boundary erected between them. In fact, as Hall, cited in Gunaratnam, argues, this boundary is already blurred.

> Biological racism privileges markers like skin colour, but those signifiers have always been used, by discursive extension, to connote social and cultural differences. . . . The biological referent is therefore never wholly absent from discourses of ethnicity, though it is more indirect. The more "ethnicity" matters, the more its characteristics are represented as relatively fixed, inherent within a group, transmitted from generation to generation, not just by culture and education, but by biological inheritance, stabilized above all by kinship and endogamous marriage rules that ensure that the ethnic group remains genetically, and therefore culturally "pure." (Hall, 2000, in Gunaratnam, 2003, p. 4)

Thus, to differentiate between race and ethnicity would be to miss the significant "interrelations between the two 'registers' of biology and culture in processes of giving 'race' and ethnicity meaning and bringing them to life in the social world" (Gunaratnam, 2003, p. 5).

The Habitual Neglect of Multiethnic Students

During the interviews with students, I heard frequent examples of the ways in which multiethnic students are unintentionally marginalized and ignored in schools, excluded from diversity related lessons and activities, and made to feel as though they must choose between their multiple heritages. Take, for example, the forms still used for standardized tests and applications for many schools and universities, in which students are asked to identify their racial heritage. Nearly every student interviewed recalled these questions and their sense of uncertainty when asked to "pick one racial identification." Other students discussed activities in which they were asked to bring food, make a doll, or give a presentation that represents their heritage, and their uncertainty about which heritage to select for representation. As one student stated, schools "do a lot of ethnic stuff, but I never really connect with it I guess, because I never really know which ethnicity I should be proud of, really." Another student recounted an activity that took place during her school's International Day in which signs representing various racial and ethnic groups (i.e., black, white, Native, Asian, Middle Eastern, Latino) were placed around the gym and students were asked to stand by the sign that represents them. Quite obviously, the need to pick one sign to stand under presents multiethnic students with an awkward decision. Additionally, a similar activity was recalled by two students from two different schools in which a large circle was drawn on the ground and students were asked to step into the circle "if they are not white." Whereas one student (of Chinese and white heritage) chose to enter the circle briefly and then step back out, the other student (of Iranian and white heritage) decided to straddle the circle. Finally, in describing her school's annual Diversity Week, during which students enjoy international food and ethnic dance performances, one student stated that "[the organizers] really try and push different races, except we ignore the fact, obviously, of mixed races, and they really don't, you know, cover the whole broad spectrum of race."

Those activities and practices listed above tend to fall outside of the "formal" curriculum of schools, and particularly secondary schools. Yet, according to students, there is also a notable absence of multiethnicity in the official school curriculum. In fact, aside from references to the sexual exploitation that took place between slaves and their owners during American History lessons, all but three students were unable to think of a time in which multiethnicity was meaningfully discussed in the classroom. At the same time, every single interviewed high school student expressed interest in having multiethnicity added to the curriculum and discussed in class.

Why Educators Must Address Multiethnicity

I set out below six arguments for greater consideration of multiethnic students' experiences and the inclusion of multiethnicity in the curriculum. Other justifications exist, but I have tried to assemble those that transcend differences in school location, size, and student population. As we will see, the six arguments presented here overlap, build on, and support one another. Additionally, several of them are based not solely on the benefits to be gained by multiethnic students but by all students.

Authentic Inclusivity

U.S. Census Bureau estimates from July 2006 indicate that nearly one-quarter of the California population is, in the Bureau's terms, multiracial. Similar estimates were reported for states including Delaware, Florida, Illinois, New Jersey, New York, North Carolina, and Oklahoma, and an estimated one-third of the populations of Alabama, Georgia, Louisiana, Maryland, Mississippi, and South Carolina identify as multiracial (Stuckey, 2008). Given that the Census counts only those who identify with more than one racial group, these numbers do not reflect those who identify with multiple ethnicities, individuals who would likely cause these numbers to be considerably higher. Although already significant, these numbers should be even more compelling for educators when we consider the distribution of multiethnic individuals by age. According to a report based on findings from the 2000 Census, "People who reported more than one race were more likely to be under age 18 than those reporting only one race. . . .Of the 6.8 million people in the Two or more races population [category], 42% were under 18" (Jones & Smith, 2001, p. 9). Based on these numbers, we can assert confidently that a large percentage of the students in our schools are multiethnic, and logic dictates that their numbers will increase with time. This being the case, perhaps the most obvious argument for the consideration of multiethnic students in schools is that *they are already there.*

According to Shields, "a good school is an inclusive community—not one that is homogenous and expects people to 'fit in,' but one that is created from the diverse contributions and abilities of its members" (2005, p. 77). Using similar language, Zirkel states that "an empowering school culture is one in which all students feel welcomed and valued and in which all are seen as contributing members of the community," and that creating such a culture "requires ensuring that a school is equally warm and welcoming for all students" (2008, p. 1163). Yet, as we saw, many multiethnic students report, for example, not being able to accurately self-identify on school forms, feeling pressure to pick one heritage with which to identify, to participate in diversity related activities, and not feeling reflected in the curriculum. As long as these are the experiences of multiethnic students, we cannot reasonably claim to provide an inclusive education or empowering learning environments that acknowledge, honor, and build on all our students' identities and experiences.

Supporting Multiethnic Identity Construction

Many theorists have put forward a conception of multiethnic identity construction as a process fraught with difficulty and confusion. According to Wardle, as a result of the emphasis

North American society places on racial and ethnic identity, multiethnic individuals "often feel disloyal and confused; they have a sense of not knowing where they belong" (1998, p. 8). Poston (1990) and Kich (1992) both proposed models of multiethnic identity construction in which individuals pass through developmental stages. In both of these models, full appreciation and acceptance of one's multiethnic identity are preceded by a period of confusion, guilt, conflict, and/or dissonance about one's identity. Most arguments for paying greater attention to the experiences of multiethnic students are based on such models of multiethnic identity construction. The logic of such arguments is quite clear: In order to help multiethnic students develop a healthy identity and high self-esteem, schools must make efforts to include issues related to multiethnicity in the curriculum, devise activities that do not marginalize multiethnic students or contribute to their feelings of confusion or needing to choose one heritage with which to identify, and raise awareness of the multiethnic experience among all students.

My intention here is not to fully explore models and understandings of multiethnic identity construction. Nevertheless, it is worth pointing out that, based on interview findings, I question the extent to which deficit models of identity construction capture the experiences of multiethnic individuals. Indeed, most interviewed students appeared confident and comfortable in their sense of identity. However, even if one disputes the accuracy and applicability of deficit models, this does not obviate the need for schools to support the identity construction process of their multiethnic students. Based on an analysis of findings from more than a dozen studies, Zirkel points out that "a strong, positive racial or ethnic identity is associated with higher levels of academic performance. . . higher educational aspirations. . . [and] greater academic self confidence. . ." (2008, pp. 1151–1152). Thus, even if the multiethnic identity construction process poses no additional challenges as compared to that of "mono-ethnic" students, we can make a strong argument for practices and curricula that support this process.

Mitigating the Testing and Evaluation of Multiethnic Identities

More than twenty years ago, Wilson argued that the pervasive notion that multiethnic individuals must choose a single race with which to identify stems from the "rigid racial boundaries imposed by our society. . . [making it] impossible to maintain a dual allegiance to both racial groups" (1987, p. 7). The key idea here is that rigid racial boundaries, and I would add ethnic boundaries, are *imposed* on multiethnic individuals. This being the case, not surprisingly, the majority of interviewed students discussed their experiences of being tested for their cultural legitimacy when asserting multiple racial or ethnic identities. This testing, referred to by one student as being subjected to the "invisible measuring stick," often takes the form of questions regarding one's home language, involvement in cultural and religious activities, travel history, and cultural knowledge. Although some students attributed these questions to benign curiosity, in general, students did not discuss this experience as a positive one. As one student said, when tested, you are made to feel as though there are "requirements that you're not meeting."

I think we can safely assume that having one's cultural legitimacy persistently tested, questioned, and challenged does not support the development of a strong sense of belonging, high self-esteem, a healthy identity, and feelings of confidence in defining and asserting that identity. Indeed, whether stemming from benign curiosity, fear of the dissolution of familiar racial and ethnic boundaries, or a more insidious desire to marginalize multiethnic individuals, the questioning of one's identity is unlikely to support, and just as likely to hinder, a healthy identity construction process. Moreover, even if this testing and questioning have no apparent impact on one's sense of identity, the experience is, as one student stated, "just so annoying." My argument here, of course, is that no one should be subjected to this experience, and therefore, simply on the ground of teaching students about the inappropriateness of such questioning, we can argue for the inclusion of multiethnicity in the curriculum. Furthermore, as discussed next, if students learn to challenge anything, it should not be individual identities, but those categories that confine them.

Challenging Racial and Ethnic Categories

The testing and questioning of their identities to which multiethnic individuals are often subjected can reasonably be seen as a by-product of rigid and essentialist stereotypes of what it means to be a certain race or ethnicity. Thus, one way to support the identity construction of multiethnic students is to challenge and deconstruct racial and ethnic categories and the boundaries erected between them. And just as it is important to attend to the identity construction of all students, every student should learn about the complexities of race and ethnicity, the limitations of these concepts, and the ways in which they have been constructed and employed to categorize, segregate, and oppress. In other words, we do a disservice to all students when we reify rigid racial and ethnic categories according to which groups of people can be classified, ignoring the complex, controversial, and socially constructed nature of both race and ethnicity.

The task of educators then, is not just to avoid the reinforcement of narrow, rigid, and essentialist understandings of race and ethnicity but to actively contest, challenge, and deconstruct such understandings. Although there are many ways in which this can be accomplished, one effective approach is through the study of multiethnicity. By examining the experiences of those who refuse to be confined by racial and ethnic categories, and who defy the best efforts of those who seek to defend the boundaries between them, we can begin to unravel these insidious constructs.

At this point, the critical reader might be wondering if, by drawing attention to those who transcend traditional racial and ethnic categories, we run the risk of reifying such categories by sending the message that there exist "pure" racial and ethnic groups. While this is a legitimate concern, it is unwarranted when an examination of multiethnicity is the very tool used to explore the limitations and complexities of racial and ethnic categories. All students stand to benefit from the study of multiethnicity, provided it is used as a launching point into more meaningful, authentic, and critical engagement with race and ethnicity.

In the Name of Historical Accuracy

As discussed above, most students interviewed recalled the inclusion of multiethnicity in the curriculum only, if at all, during lessons on slavery in which reference was made to the sexual exploitation of slaves and the resulting so-called mulatto population. And while most students may recognize Tiger Woods, Paula Abdul, Barack Obama, and Halle Berry as prominent multiethnic figures, how many know that the year 2000 was the first time that multiethnic Americans had the option of indicating multiple racial identifications on the national Census? How many know that Frederick Douglass, most often learned about during Black History Month, at times identified as multiethnic?[1] How many students know of the landmark United States Supreme Court case *Loving v. Virginia* in which, just forty years ago, the Court ruled that anti-miscegenation laws are unconstitutional? How many students are aware of the history of the "one-drop" rule in the United States and the ways in which, as a result of this rule, multiethnic individuals were inaccurately labeled? Learning about the historical and contemporary experiences of multiethnic individuals is an integral component of an inclusive, anti-oppressive, and historically accurate education that does not shy away from the atrocities of our past such as the creation of the myth of the "tragic mulatto," the prohibition of interracial marriage, and the systematic marginalization of multiethnic individuals because of the threat they pose to meticulously constructed racial hierarchies.

Students Are Asking for It

My final argument for greater consideration of the experiences of multiethnic students and the inclusion of multiethnicity in the curriculum can be stated quite simply: Students are asking for it. As previously mentioned, every single high school student interviewed felt that the introduction of multiethnicity to the curriculum would be an important and/or interesting addition. Most students argued for this change in terms of their own experiences and what it would mean to them, although many also pointed out the importance of such lessons for all students. As one student explained, "I think it would be important for people to learn about [multiethnicity], because it can kind of give students a different outlook on things, and they wouldn't really be close minded about certain things."

As student engagement, or a lack thereof, continues to be a cause of concern for practicing educators and educational researchers, when students are so clearly interested in a topic, and when this topic has merited the attention of so many others outside of education, surely its introduction to the curriculum is warranted.

Recommendations

As stated, this isn't a "how to" chapter intended to provide specific instructions, activities, and curricula related to multiethnicity. However, I provide here three general suggestions that I believe are of the utmost importance for educators to keep in mind as they explore ways to be inclusive and supportive of their multiethnic students. As before, there is some overlap here as the suggestions support and build on each other.

Avoid Colorblindness

Through the examination of multiethnicity, we begin to see the limitations of conventional understandings of race and ethnicity. However, arguing for the exploration of these limitations, as well as the disruption of narrow and essentialist understandings of race and ethnicity, is not a call to adopt a colorblind approach that fails to acknowledge the very real material, social, and political inequalities that result from racial and ethnic discrimination. A colorblind approach, which is often invoked as a means to avoid discrimination and to ensure that all students are treated "equally," precludes meaningful engagement with race and ethnicity, and therefore, the opportunity to deconstruct and challenge them. Arbitrary and unsound as racial and ethnic categories might be, to ignore them is not to deconstruct them.

Increased and More Meaningful Engagement with Race and Ethnicity

When asked what recommendations they would offer to educators concerned about making their schools more inclusive and supportive of multiethnic students, interviewed students almost unanimously suggested the inclusion of multiethnicity in the curriculum, along with more meaningful engagement with the topics of race and ethnicity in general. In fact, despite their recognition that race and ethnicity are often considered "taboo" and "uncomfortable" topics, students unequivocally suggested that race and ethnicity be discussed more in schools. The more complex ways in which racial and ethnic categories, as well as stereotypes, influence not just interviewed students' multiethnic identities but their experiences and relationships, perhaps account for their generally shared desire for such conversations. Nevertheless, regardless of what this desire stems from, the fact that nearly all interviewed students provided the same suggestion for schools should not be ignored.

How, then, do interviewed students typically learn about race and ethnicity? During the interviews, I heard numerous stories of Chinese New Year's celebrations, Cinco de Mayo parties, art projects related to race and ethnicity, Multicultural Assemblies in which students from various heritages are invited to perform "ethnic" dances representative of their heritages (e.g., Bhangra, Salsa, and Tinikling), Diversity Weeks with booths for different countries, and, above all else, the presence of food during activities related to racial and ethnic diversity. In fairness, several students discussed particular courses in which race and ethnicity were engaged with in more meaningful ways, but the criticism that schools reduce diversity to food, fashion, and fun or dress, dance, and diet is generally applicable to the experiences of interviewed students. Moreover, several students critiqued the superficiality of such activities with one going so far as to say that they are "empty" and "a joke."

Certainly schools alone are not responsible for the reinforcement and perpetuation of limited, essentialist, and rigid conceptions of race and ethnicity, but we should not ignore the unfortunate tendency of multicultural and antiracist education—two of the most prevalent approaches to teaching students about race and ethnicity—to do just that.[2] As Gosine points out, both models, despite their good intentions, "encourage people to think in terms of discrete, bounded collectivities that possess recognizable sets of attributes that distinguish one group from another" (2002, p. 96). Multicultural and antiracist education constitute critically important components of schooling in our increasingly diverse society. However, their propensity to essentialize racial and ethnic groups and bolster limited understandings of race and ethnicity presents a double-edged sword for multiethnic students.

My recommendation here is twofold: schools should temper their tendency to essentialize racial and ethnic groups in superficial and patronizing ways, and schools should actively and earnestly engage in more meaningful explorations and deconstructions of race and ethnicity. As with many of the arguments for the inclusion of multiethnicity in the curriculum, these recommendations are made with *all* students in mind. Building on my first recommendation, that educators avoid adopting a colorblind approach, my suggestion here is for more meaningful, less essentializing engagement with race and ethnicity in schools, one necessary component of which, of course, is the study of multiethnicity.

Appropriate and Meaningful Inclusion

I hope that by now I have set forth a convincing argument for the need to pay greater attention to the experiences of multiethnic students and to introduce multiethnicity as a topic of study in schools. My final task here, then, is to ensure that any actions to these ends are undertaken appropriately, earnestly, and with sincerity.

Despite their shared recognition of the neglect of multiethnic students in schools, students' responses to this neglect vary significantly. As we saw in the example of students being asked to step into a circle if they are not white, one student stepped in and out of the circle, while another student straddled it. As another example, on forms in which students are asked to pick only a single racial identification, some students choose just one, other students ignore the instructions and check more than one box, and several students indicate that, when given the option, they select "other." Likewise, some students expressed a strong multiethnic identity, while others identify more with one of their heritages. These differences signal the lack of a single multiethnic experience or identity according to which students can be grouped. Or as my white-Indian friend put it, "What do I have in common with Tiger Woods?"

What this indicates is the inappropriateness of uncritically inserting a multiethnic category into an otherwise unchanged approach to teaching students about race and ethnicity. Such an uncritical insertion is another way of masking differences that do indeed make a difference. The idea here is to deconstruct and challenge divisive identity categories, not construct new ones; to move away from the essentializing tendencies of many school activities and curricula, not essentialize yet another group. Indeed, many students were quick to recognize the impossibility of having a multiethnic booth with representative food and artifacts on Diversity Day or a multiethnic dance at the Multicultural Assembly. Thus, we can see the inappropriateness of asking one multiethnic student to "speak for" all multiethnic individuals, as if there were some sort of discrete and fixed multiethnic identity or experience. Accordingly, I urge educators not to be satisfied with simply hanging a poster of Halle Berry or any other multiethnic celebrity in the classroom, or with merely providing a novel or two depicting multiethnic families. Likewise, I discourage the gratuitous inclusion of a brief unit on multiethnicity. Rather, multiethnicity should be incorporated into every discussion of race and ethnicity, and such discussions need to take place more frequently. Finally, as noted above, a cursory examination of multiethnicity runs the risk of reifying racial and ethnic categories and strengthening their classificatory power, and therefore, not discussing multiethnicity may be preferable to its superficial treatment. In other words, there is no acceptable easy alternative to the substantive, sincere, and meaningful engagement with multiethnicity and the appropriate inclusion of multiethnic students.

Conclusion

Multiethnicity is a topic notably absent from too much of the literature related to diversity and diversity education (Wardle, 1996). The fact that there is a chapter on multiethnicity in this reader gives me reason to hope that it might finally garner the attention of more educators. Given that the inclusion of multiethnicity has the potential to help us create more authentically inclusive schools, support the identity construction of multiethnic students, mitigate the testing and questioning that multiethnic individuals are too often subjected to, challenge racial and ethnic categories, provide a more historically accurate and inclusive education, and respond to student demand, we should no longer ignore this important topic. If you are convinced of the need for greater consideration of the experiences of multiethnic students and the inclusion of multiethnicity in the curriculum, you will need to seek out information that will allow you to do so appropriately, confidently, and effectively. One way to do this is to familiarize yourself with pertinent literature and organizations such as those cited at the outset of this chapter.

I close here with a brief anecdote. In a recent undergraduate sociology course that I was teaching, a young woman stated that she is half black and half white. Immediately, another student called out "what does that make you, grey?" I wonder how many educators recognize the inappropriateness of such a comment. How many know how to respond? How many feel comfortable responding? How many recognize this comment as an opportunity to discuss multiethnicity and the misconceptions from which such a comment might stem? It is my hope that more educators will soon be among those who do.

Notes

1. See, e.g., "Icons: Making Mixed-Race History" on www.intermix.org.uk
2. I do not mean to imply that multicultural and antiracist education are indistinguishable approaches. Nevertheless, this critique is equally applicable to both. For an overview of the differences between multicultural and antiracist education and an explanation of the theories underpinning each, see Dei and Calliste (2000).

References

Arboleda, T. (1998). *In the shadow of race: Growing up as a multiethnic, multicultural, and "multiracial" American*. Mahwah, NJ: Lawrence Erlbaum Publishers.

Basu, A. M. (2006). *Negotiating social contexts: Identities of biracial college women*. Charlotte, NC: Information Age Publishing.

Camper, C. (1994). *Miscegenation blues: Voices of mixed race women*. Toronto, ON: Sister Vision Press.

Dei, G. J. S. & Calliste, A. (Eds.). (2000). *Power, knowledge and anti-racism education: A critical reader*. Halifax, NS: Fernwood Publishing.

Gosine, K. (2002). Essentialism versus complexity: Conceptions of racial identity construction in educational scholarship. *Canadian Journal of Education, 27*(1), 81–99.

Gunaratnam, Y. (2003). *Researching race and ethnicity: Methods, knowledge and power*. Thousand Oaks, CA: Sage Publications.

Hall, S. (2000). Conclusion: The multi-cultural question. In B. Hesse (Ed.), *Un/Settled multiculturalisms: Diasporas, entanglements, transruptions* (pp. 209–241). London: Zed Books.

Intermix. (2008). Icons: Making mixed-race history. Retrieved June 10, 2008, from http://www.intermix.org.uk/icons/index.asp

Jones, N. & Smith, A. (2001). The two or more races population: 2000 (Report). Washington, DC: US Census Bureau.

Kich, G. K. (1992). The developmental process of asserting a biracial, bicultural identity. In M. P. P. Root (Ed.), *Racially mixed people in America* (pp. 304–317). Newbury Park, CA: Sage Publications.

Krebs, N. (1999). *Edgewalkers: Defusing cultural boundaries on the new frontier*. Liberty Corner, NJ: New Horizon Press.

Poston, W. S. C. (1990). The biracial identity development model: A needed addition. *Journal of Counseling and Development, 69*(2), 152–155.

Renn, K. A. (2004). *Mixed race students in college: The ecology of race, identity, and community on campus*. Albany, NY: State University of New York Press.

Root, M. P. P. (Ed.). (1992). *Racially mixed people in America*. Newbury Park, CA: Sage Publications.

Root, M. P. P. (Ed.). (1996). *The multiracial experience: Racial borders as the new frontier*. Thousand Oaks, CA: Sage Publications.

Schwartz, W. (1998). The schooling of multiracial students. *ERIC Clearing House on Urban Education Digest*, (No. 138). ERIC Document Reproduction Service No. 425249.

Shields, C. M. (2005). What is a good school? In W. Hare & J. P. Portelli (Eds.), *Key questions for educators* (pp. 77–79). Halifax, NS: Edphil Books.

Stuckey, M. (2008). Multiracial Americans surge in number, voice. Retrieved May 28, 2008, from http://www.msnbc.msn.com/id/24542138/

Wardle, F. (1996). Multicultural education. In M. P. P. Root (Ed.), *The multiracial experience: Racial borders as the new frontier* (pp. 380–391). Thousand Oaks, CA: Sage Publications.

Wardle, F. (1998). Meeting the needs of multiracial and multiethnic children in early childhood settings. *Early Childhood Education Journal, 26*(1), 7–11.

Wardle, F. (2000). Children of mixed race—No longer invisible. *Educational Leadership, 57*(4), 68–71.

Wilson, A. (1987). *Mixed race children: A study of identity.* London: Allen & Unwin.

Zack, N. (1993). *Race and mixed race.* Philadelphia: Temple University Press.

Zack, N. (1995). *American mixed race: The culture of microdiversity.* Lanham, MD: Rowman & Littlefield.

Zirkel, S. (2008). The influence of multicultural educational practices on student outcomes and intergroup relations. *Teachers College Record, 110*(6), 1147–1181.

Ten

The Banality of Colonialism
Encountering Artifacts of Genocide and White Supremacy in Vancouver Today

Timothy J. Stanley

This chapter was written on the traditional territory of the Algonquin people, and presented at a conference 5,000 kilometers away on the traditional territory of the Musqueum
people. Although the Musqueum and Algonquin peoples inhabited these territories for hundreds, and possibly thousands, of years longer than people calling themselves Canadian, apart
from acknowledgments of this kind, this history is largely unmarked in everyday life. This
absence from representation is very much the point of this chapter.

The post-modern cities that most people living in Canada today inhabit are products of
colonialism.[1] This colonialism is not merely a remnant from a now-distant past but involves
on-going acts of cultural reproduction, efforts at fixing meaning, selective remembering, and
deliberately engineered forgetting. As a result, people are surrounded by artifacts of the histories of colonialism, but these artifacts are rendered invisible, common sense, and a part of
taken-for-granted discursive formations, that in some instances are quite literally set in concrete.[2]

Among other things, this means that we are daily in contact with ghosts. Not ghosts of
the ectoplasmic kind, but with countless unseen hands and minds that have quite literally
cemented their meanings into the fabric of our day-to-day lives. The colonialism that created
these spaces was a multifaceted project. It involved the efforts of a group of people of European and, in the last 200 years, especially British origins, who entered the territory and forcibly
took control of it and its inhabitants. At the same time, in a localized version of what Edward
W. Said has called *Orientalism*,[3] these re-settlers remade the cultural landscape of the territory,
imposing their disciplinary practices and ways of knowing on the territory and its inhabitants,
effectively steamrollering the systems of cultural representation and the meanings already in
place. While doing all of this, they simultaneously took steps to ensure that no other group's

meanings could become dominant, often through the expediency of excluding any others who might themselves become dominant from entering the territory. Having done all of this, they erased the memory of having done so, by presenting their occupation of the territory as natural, proper and just, and above all, something to be taken for granted. Knowledge of what was done may be culturally available, but it is not what circulates in popular culture. Colonialism, as a result, is not merely a historical phenomenon in the sense of being something of a now distant past but continues as processes of cultural production through which power legitimizes itself by silencing the memory of its own unilateral construction, at the same time that it seeks to fix and re-fix meaning.[4] Thus, the very artificiality of the cultural production of urban space like modern day Vancouver, British Columbia, is rendered natural, matter of fact, seemingly an act of nature, simply the way the world is and has always been. This presents an enormous challenge, not only to anti-colonial pedagogies, but anti-colonial politics. It seems vital to find ways of disrupting this apparent naturalism, of making visible its constructed nature, of rendering, as Stuart Hall puts it, certain acts of representation uninhabitable.[5]

Although I now live in Ottawa, I focus on Vancouver because it is the city that I lived in for the longest time in my adult life, and because I am an historian of British Columbia, rather than of Ontario. However, it is important to note that with minor adaptations, I can make parallel arguments for any city in the Americas.

This chapter is an effort to draw together three of my related interests. For close to thirty years now, my central project has been to understand the dynamics of racisms, with a view to being better able to effect anti-racism education. Throughout this period, I have been struck by two things. The first is a matter well documented in the literature on anti-racism, the invisibility of racist privilege to those who daily enjoy its benefits, a reality that exists in stark contrast to the evident awareness of this on the part of those who daily are disadvantaged by racisms.[6] This leads me to the question of what hides this privilege and how. The second thing that has struck me is the recurring denial of racism in Canada on the part of the privileged. Racism in Canada is almost always represented in public discourse as a problem existing somewhere else—in fact, as something that is anywhere other than where the people representing it are.[7] When I lived in Vancouver, I heard all the time about the terrible problems of racism that exist in Ontario. Now that I live in Ottawa, Ontario, I hear how terrible it is in Vancouver. If people do admit that racism can be found in Ottawa, they do not admit that it is at the University—well, perhaps at Carleton University, but certainly not at the University of Ottawa. And so the denial goes.

My formation as a historian, semi-literate in Chinese, has led to a second interest in the history of anti-Chinese racism in British Columbia and a book-length argument about racist state formation in British Columbia.[8] Simply put, racism was organized into the British Columbian and Canadian state systems, at the moments of their invention. For example, the second act of the legislature of the new Province of British Columbia took the right to vote away from First Nations people and people of "Chinese race."[9] However, one would be hard pressed to find a university-level survey of Canadian history textbook, let alone a public school textbook approved by a provincial Ministry of Education, that mentions that the ideal of white minority rule founded the territory of British Columbia. That is inconsistent with notions of history, as nationalized by citizenship education. Certainly my engagements with students around histories of racisms have shown that they are continually shocked to discover that their perceived understandings of Canada as the peaceable, multicultural, kinder-gentler America, is a myth. Here I note that even when they are aware of specific discriminatory acts or events, they rarely are able to draw out their larger significance.

My historical interests have led me to consider the role of nationalist narratives in fostering racisms.[10] People from China are often represented as newcomers to the territory that became British Columbia, rather than as people who have been in it as long as any non-First Nations others. Indeed, since the first permanent re-settlers in this territory were a group of Cantonese carpenters and shipwrights brought there by the English sea captain John Meares in 1790, Cantonese has been spoken in this territory longer, if less continuously, than English has. The absence of the histories of the Chinese, and other racialized and excluded groups from common representation led to my third interest: what the social psychologist James Wertsch correctly calls collective remembering. In his important study of the reconstitution of public memory in the former Soviet Union, Wertsch argues that collective remembering is a form of mediated memory and that every society has technologies of memory, such as school textbooks or public monuments, and that these devices mediate our remembering. We remember certain things as we engage with these technologies. As such, collective remembering is not individual memory writ large, but rather a process anchored in technologies that mark what is to be remembered and how.[11] While Wertsch focuses on school knowledge, other scholars have extended this to consider other technologies—public monuments, street names, the Internet, television, newspapers, and the like.[12]

Important for my purposes is a parallel argument developed by Michael Billig, another social psychologist. Billig argues that inhabitants of contemporary, successful nation states are continually reminded of what Benedict Anderson called "nationness."[13] What interests Billig are the flags that mark national belonging, those that fly unheralded in the background, more so than those waved by campaigning politicians or rabid nationalists. For Billig, the deixis of nationalist representation is particularly important. These are the small pointing words—the "the's," "we's," and "ours" that mark membership in the imagined community of the nation. As his study of newspapers in Britain shows, residents of modern nation states are continually bombarded with representations that re-inscribe nation-ness on their bodies, everything from the eliding of specific titles in taken-for-granted phrases like "the Prime Minster" to weather reports that focus on the "the nation" rather than of those places from which the local weather comes. Thus, residents of successful nation states are constantly exposed to the idea that everyone and everything is organized into a nation. Although the answer to the question "what is one's nationality" might be in dispute, the fact that one has a nationality is not. The ubiquitousness of this flagging of national belonging makes nation-ness seem natural, ancient, and an impossible thing to live without. (All of this despite the fact that most of the nation states in the world have come into existence in my lifetime.) But as Billig suggests, and the rapid collapse of the nationalisms of the former Soviet Union shows, national belonging is actually very fragile. Nations and nation-ness are relatively new phenomena on the scale of human history.[14] The point of this for my discussion is that if there are flags and pointing words that remind us of nationalized identities, there are also flags, pointing words, and banal representations that remind us of other identities, including the silencing of histories of colonialism even as we lead our lives on its artifacts.

With all this in mind, I want to draw attention to six artifacts of colonialism that are encountered in the City of Vancouver everyday. To emphasize the banality of these encounters, I organize the encounters that follow by means of an imagined bus ride from the campus of the University of British Columbia (UBC) to Vancouver's Chinatown. As a result, my method is a kind of virtual ethnography. It has been some time since I have actually ridden this bus, but I supplement my own faulty memory with information gleaned from the web. And while I focus on six artifacts, I could also discuss many more, as each stop in the journey is a kind of "wiki stub" that could be expanded into papers and books of great length. Although each of these artifacts is gendered, I focus here principally on how they are racialized and nationalized.

I begin by looking for the sign for Bay 13 for the Number 4 Powell Bus.[15] Finding this requires multiple acts of reading, possible inquiries with passers-by. While I speak French and could also at least ask for directions in Mandarin Chinese, English is the most likely language to use that would solicit a response. It is certainly the language in which the signs for the bus are written. This casual use of English is the first artifact of colonialism that I wish to draw attention to. English is the contemporary world's *lingua franca*, the language of international business, the most commonly learned second or third language, if not the most commonly spoken first language. The fact that English is the dominant language here at the beginning of my journey is supported by more than the frequency with which it is spoken. It is supported in the multiple signs that festoon the area. Somewhere in Vancouver, even on the UBC campus, there are signs in other languages, in Chinese or in Punjabi, or Italian, but these are exceptions. Yet, it is only within the last 100 years that English has become sufficiently dominant to wipe from the map the original Halkomelem that was spoken for thousands of years at the place that I begin my journey. A measure of the extent to which these original languages have been erased from collective remembering is the inability of university students to name the local languages that were spoken for thousands of years on the territories now dominated by English, even when this English dominance is a relatively recent thing in the sweep of human history. For several years now, I have surveyed the students that I teach, ranging from first year undergraduates to students in interdisciplinary Ph.D. seminars, but mainly graduate students in education who have at least two university degrees and teacher education students with at least one, as to whether they can name the language that was spoken on the territory of the University of Ottawa for thousands of years. Few have been able to correctly answer. And indeed, in the day-to-day world that they encounter, there is very little that urges them to come to know this answer, as it is English that is represented 99 times out of 100. So too here at UBC while I look for my bus. While the University does have a First Nations Languages program and offers credit course in Musqueum Salish, its public spaces are marked by a language that comes from half the world away.

But the dominance of English on this territory is itself the product of a history of domination and exclusion. While it is true that people from England who spoke English, as well as their counterparts from what is today Ontario, Quebec, and the Maritimes, most of whom also spoke English, began their colonization of this territory, and hence its linguistic conversion, in the middle of the nineteenth century, English did not become the dominant language until the late nineteenth century. During the early nineteenth century, the fur traders who came to this area were just as likely to speak French or Hawaiian or Gaelic as they were English.[16] English was the language of the colonizing officialdom, or the Royal Navy gunboats that forced the occupation of the territory, and the most commonly used written language. Chinook was the *Lingua franca* of the Pacific Northwest Coast. This was a jargon or trade language that originated out of the languages of several First Nations on the Coast, to which English, French, and Cantonese words were added. Chinook was the language of work on the West Coast throughout the nineteenth century, and remained so in places like the fishing canneries until after the Second World War.[17] Its use documents a reality in which no one language group dominated, and in which multicultural and multiracial workforces needed a shared means of communication.

The linguistic complexity of British Columbia was such that, until well into the twentieth century, Chinook remained such an officially important language that there were official Chinook–English court interpreters. One of these, Won Alexander Cumyow, was born at Fort Harrison in 1861, the son of Hakka-speaking parents who had come from China. Cumyow, the first racialized Chinese person to be born in what is today Canada, grew up fluent in Chinook as well as Hakka, several Cantonese dialects, and English. In the twentieth century, he was the Vancouver Police Department's official Chinese, Chinook, and English translator.[18]

More than anything else, the technology that established English as the dominant language was compulsory, government-controlled schooling. In Ontario, where the government-controlled free, universal, and compulsory schooling was invented, English was legislated as the language of instruction, directly attacking French and Gaelic speakers, among others. In British Columbia, it was the Indian Residential Schools, made compulsory in 1920, that ensured the destruction of First Nations people's bodies, their cultural practices, and their languages. That children in these schools were beaten if they spoke in languages other than English was not an accident or a side effect of well-intentioned ignorance. It was a purposive matter of government policy.[19]

Therefore, if English is dominant in the territory today, it is because its dominance was produced. Indigenous languages were simply steamrollered out of view, and out of use, by government policy. As English became the only language that counted, the only language of instruction in government-controlled schools, the only language of the legislature, and the official language of the courts and the government system, other languages also present were marginalized and came to be seen as alien or foreign languages. The dominance of English tends to have a naturalizing effect, naturalizing the presence of English speakers, while those who speak other languages are represented as themselves, foreign or alien. For example, in the mid-1990s, some residents of Richmond, BC, were upset when the Aberdeen Shopping Mall, a mall catering to expatriate Chinese people, circulated a Chinese-only advertising flyer. Chinese, in its spoken form, has been present in BC since 1790, as long as English has, and has been present continuously in spoken and written forms since 1856. Speakers of Chinese might be tolerated, but the dominance of signs in English tends to position speakers of English as belonging in the territory.

As I search for my bus (Bay number 13 is at a separate turn-around circle than most of the other 14 buses that service UBC it seems), none of this occurs to me. I worry about things like, will I be too late, do I have the correct change, and is this the right bus for me? As I get on the bus, surrounded by advertisements in English, I look out at the University, noting the buildings that seem to have sprung up in odd places (along with the larger bus loop), since I was last here. The sheer size of the campus is impressive. The entire University of Ottawa campus, which has 35,000 students compared to UBC's 44,000, could fit into the part of campus that holds the Faculty of Arts and the Library. Over 50,000 people use this campus every day. Indeed, the University is the largest employer in the Lower Mainland of British Columbia, more a town in its own right, with its own police and fire services, than it is an institution. In this respect, the university models its origins as a Medieval European institution in which individual faculties are fiefdoms and departments squirearchies. For those who visit the campus every day, the presence of a medieval European institution at the end of Point Grey, is a taken-for-granted matter of everyday life, a place where one goes to work or school or to visit. Aspects of the campus may be more contested—is it green enough, is the parking accessible, is there enough money for programs as well as building—but the fact of it is not.

This brings me to the second artifact of colonialism: the taken-for-granted presence of European cultural artifacts on this territory. How the European cultural institution of the University came to be located on the West Coast of what is today Canada is very much a matter of a history of colonialization by people of European, and principally British, origins. The cultural and political transformation of the territory on which the University is located, was effected in the first instance through the use of military force (gunboats), carefully constructed economic hegemony (starting with the late eighteenth century sea otter trade), and the invention of apartheid (a matter associated in most people's minds with South Africa and Zimbabwe/former Rhodesia).[20] The University began as an extension of the Royal Institution for the Advancement of Learning, which was established by a charter from the English monarch in 1801.[21] The Royal Institution became the University of McGill College with another Royal Charter in 1821. It bore the name McGill, because the fur baron, James McGill, bequeathed the land for the university on condition that one of its colleges would be named after him.[22] How this land, originally belonging to the Hochelaga people came to be McGill's, and how he was able to amass a fortune off of the backs of First Nations trappers and Quebecois workers, is another story that I will not look at here. Because of its Royal Charter, McGill could offer extension programs in places far from Montreal. Other institutions, such as the University of Toronto or Queen's University may have wanted to do likewise, but they were limited by provincial incorporations.

Yet in fact, the creation of UBC was quite literally an act of white supremacy, and the political supremacy of racialized white men in particular. The university was established in 1908 by an act of the British Columbia legislature.[23] Although racialized white women would get the right to vote nine years later, at the time of this act only racialized white men could belong to the legislature. This was not, however, because they were the only men in the territory. British Columbia had been created as a Canadian province in 1871. At the time, the population consisted of approximately 8,500 "whites," 4,500 "Chinese," and at least 50,000 "Indians," as well as several hundred Africans and "Kanackers" or Pacific Islanders.[24] In fact, I estimate that because of the gender imbalances within these populations, the Chinese may have been the majority of non-First Nations men in the territory. They were certainly the majority in certain districts like Cariboo. So-called Chinese voted in the first provincial election, but along with First Nations people, they had the right to vote taken away in the second act of the newly elected provincial legislature, a right only returned in 1947. Because at the time, the provincial franchise also determined the federal one,, it also meant that they lost the right to vote federally. When in 1885 John Alexander MacDonald established a separate federal franchise in the Dominion Franchise Act, a piece of legislation he called his "greatest achievement," he made sure that all those of "Chinese race" were barred from voting federally, along with "all aborigines [sic] of North America" living west of the Ontario border (it appears that some of those living east voted Tory). When challenged by opposition members who argued that the Chinese were as good British subjects as he, MacDonald justified the disenfranchisement of the Chinese on the grounds that they were alien, and that if allowed to vote they would elect Chinese representatives who would then legislate with Chinese sensibilities, which would lead to the interbreeding of Chinese and non-Chinese. He told the House of Commons that if the Chinese came to Canada, "the Aryan character of the future of British America should be destroyed."[25] White supremacy was further enacted when the legislature put aside the unceded lands of the Musqueum people as a reserve for the university, reorganized later as the University Endowment Lands.[26]

The white supremacist origins of UBC, and indeed of other dominant cultural institutions in the Lower Mainland of British Columbia, go unmarked in everyday discourse, since white supremacy is taken for granted, the norm. What seems unusual is the challenge of these institutions by other institutions. Change is the arrival of people who are not racialized as white. What goes unmarked is how those racialized as white came to be those with privileged access to existing institutions and how it is that medieval European institutions are taken for granted in a territory in ways in which other institutions are not.

As I ride the bus past the University Endowment lands, the edge of Pacific Spirit Park, and the contested University golf course, recently ceded by the Provincial Government to the Musqueum as part of the settlement of their land claim, an act greeted with significant outcry from the descendants of the original colonizers who seek to re-colonize the territory one more time, I come to the intersection of West 10th Avenue and Blanca, and the beginnings of my engagement with the third artifact of colonialism that I would like to discuss, the giant grid pattern upon which the city is laid out. Cast in concrete and pavement, marked by surrounding property-lines, fences, hedges, and differentiated surface preparations, this grid is encountered almost as if it were an artifact of nature, even though it was created by the hands of unseen workers and unseen engineers, all in accord with the standards and specifications set by unseen planners and city councils and their bylaws. In many instances, the grid was created by people who are now long dead, as municipal infrastructures in much of Canada are one hundred years old and more.

This grid pattern of city streets running as far as possible east and west and north and south was also an import. It was first introduced into the area by the Royal Engineers when they laid out the City of New Westminster in 1862.[27] It, too, was a technology of colonialism, a way of visibly mapping order and disciplined ways of knowing by bulldozing the giant first-growth forest—its very act of creation an act of power, power over nature and power over the people whose land this was. More important than the technologies of axes and saws that allowed the primal forest to be cut down, was a technology of government.

The division of the Lower Mainland into a grid first appears, suddenly and terribly, in a matter of a few short months during 1858. At the beginning of 1858, this territory was indisputably the territory of the Musqueum, Squamish, and Burrard peoples, by the end of the year, they had been shunted aside onto reserves, and the surrounding land was carved up into rectangular parcels and offered for sale or pre-emption to non-First Nations people. Colonialism used the most naked of acts of power to achieve this. First, what is often represented as a process of "settlement," was in fact a process of rapid depopulation. As was the case with other moments of European contact with indigenous people, the British Columbia coast saw a 95% population decline of its indigenous peoples within three generations. The 1862 smallpox epidemic was the most devastating example for many groups, although the Musqueum may have survived its worst effects because many were vaccinated by government officials and missionaries.[28] Still, they had earlier seen their numbers plummet through disease, starting in 1858, with the disruption of their traditional lands and resources. The main technology that achieved this, that established the sovereign power of the British crown, was the naval gunboat. This was the most advanced, organized, and disciplined military technology of the nineteenth century. Gunboats had been used against coastal peoples, their villages, and canoes for the previous ten years. The use of gunboats and the disciplinary practices associated with them, were all matters in which Royal Naval officers were well schooled by the middle of the nineteenth century.[29] In 1858, the Musqueum did not need to have the gunboats used against them to appreciate their power, and the gunboat was anchored at the mouth of the Fraser River in their traditional territory. Instead, they believed the officials who said that the land they wanted and used would be protected and put aside for them. But they did not have access to the new disciplinary regime of property, of English common law, of watchmen and bailiff, and government commissioners and governors, so they were steamrollered.[30]

It was the Royal Engineers, under Colonel Moody, who engraved these new relations into the landscape. The Engineers surveyed the Lower Mainland, starting in the summer of 1858, as well as constructing a capital and potential bastion at New Westminster, on the heights overlooking one of the narrow points of the Fraser River. By 1881, when the first systematic census was taken, the Lower Mainland was a grid of pre-empted and purchased properties, and the Musqueum and other First Peoples were relegated to small reserves, smaller even than the government had promised. Reserves deliberately calculated at twenty acres per adult male, when the colonizers calculated one hundred and sixty acres per European male.

As the distinguished historical geographer Cole Harris writes, the land system of which this grid pattern was an integral measure "was a disciplinary appendage of the anatomy of power. Battles had not been necessary; shows of force and a few summary executions did much to establish the new realities." What he describes as "the brutal application, episodic and public application of sovereign power established its authority, and fear bred compliance. This enabled the application of other disciplinary processes, what Foucault called biopower, something especially evident in the land system:

> It introduced exclusions that established where people could and could not go, and backed these exclusions with a decentred system of surveillance. Suddenly there were survey lines and fences on the land. There were owners who could identify trespassers, tell them to get off, and know that their commands would be backed, if need be by the full apparatus of the state. [First Nations] people suddenly found that they could not go where they had; there were too many watchmen (property owners) backed by too much power.[31]

Significantly, the new regime of property was something that was also reserved for those who were racialized whites. The Land Ordinance of 1866 of the newly united colonies of Vancouver Island and British Columbia barred "Aborigines of this Colony or the Territories neighbouring thereto" from pre-empting land without the consent of the governor.[32] This policy was reaffirmed by the Land Ordinance of 1870, which extended to provision of "any of the Aborigines of this Continent."[33] By 1875, only one First Nations person had pre-empted land.[34] After Confederation, these acts were reaffirmed. The Land Ordinance Amendment Act of 1873 required pre-empters or their agents to establish a "bona-fide" residence on the land, but added, "Provided no such agent shall be an Indian or a Chinaman." Thus, by the mid-1870s a racist pattern of land ownership had emerged in British Columbia. First Nations were relegated to reserves which were owned on their behalf by the federal government. First Nations, and those racialized as Chinese, were barred from pre-empting land in practice and in law, although in theory they could buy land from others who had pre-empted it if they had the capital. But poverty, coupled with the reluctance of others to sell to them, effectively blocked this route to land ownership for First Nations people. After establishment of the federal regime of Indian affairs in 1876, such activities would have been subject to the approval of the Indian agent. The unfettered right to property was in the hands of English-speaking Europeans, of racialized whites. Speaking of the resulting apartheiding of British Columbia, Cole Harris observed, "racism was built into the landscape of settlement."[35]

As the bus turns down West 4th Avenue, I come to a neighborhood where I used to live. Here the streets running north-south bear names such as Collingwood, Trafalgar, Blenheim, and Waterloo. This brings me to the fourth everyday artifact of colonialism that I would like to discuss, the names of places, streets, and mountains. Having the power to cement particular relations of property into the land itself, colonialism also renamed the territory, its landmarks, and points of reference. These names again express the cultural power of the Metropolis, as streets are named after British war heroes and British military victories (as a French friend once pointed out, there are no Trafalgar Squares in Paris). They also celebrate and re-enact the dominance of men. Hence Collingwood, named after Admiral Cuthbert Collingwood, was Nelson's deputy commander at Trafalgar. Blenheim was the site of the Battle of Bleinheim, in which the Duke of Marlborough defeated the armies of Louis the XIV in 1706. A grateful government gave him a palace, and called it Blenheim Palace, the place where Winston Churchill was later born. So if these names express the power of the British metropolis, they do so by eliding the names that had been applied to these territories for thousands of years previously. As I ride the bus, I see the two striking rock formations of the North Shore, I note that "the Sisters" have come to be called "the Lions," because they are reminiscent of the stone lions beloved by British imperialists.

But other names, everyday names, selectively remember and erase the histories of racism, of genocide, and colonization. The other university across town is named after the rapist Simon Fraser, as are streets and a river. The Nlaka'pamux remembers him for the rape of a 16-year-old girl.[36] Consider the most banal of names, the name for the province, "British Columbia." The territory was originally slated to be named "Columbia" (after the River), but was changed at the suggestion of Queen Victoria to "British Columbia," when word came that anti-Spanish revolutionaries in South America were going to call their territory, "Columbia." The river is named after a U.S. ship of the same name, which is in turn, named after Christopher Columbus.[37] Columbus may have been the discoverer of the new world for Europe, but he was also the engineer of the genocide of the Arawak people. He was the one who ordered that their hands be cut off when they did not bring him the gold he wanted, although we now know there was no gold on their islands. In effect, names like this remember the past from the perspectives of the descendents of those who engineered these genocides. Consider how European streets and regions would be named had the Nazis won the Second World War and completed the Holocaust. This is, in many ways, no different. Other architects of genocide are also commemorated. After Collingwood and Waterloo and Blenheim comes Trutch, named after Joseph William Trutch, the first Lieutenant Governor of British Columbia. Trutch was the architect and chief negotiator of the terms of union under which British Columbia entered the Canadian confederation. Trutch was also the chief commissioner of lands for the colonial government of British Columbia, and responsible for the colonial land ordinances that barred racialized First Nations people from pre-empting land. More than anyone else, he was the architect of the reserve lands policy that meant that First Nations starved. In 1867, Trutch wrote, "The Indians really have no right to the lands they claim, nor are they of any actual value to them; and I cannot see why they should either retain these lands to the prejudice of the general interests of the Colony or be allowed to make a market of them either to Government or to individuals."[38] Under his instructions, large reserves laid out earlier were broken up, and new, much smaller reserves established. Indeed, where officials were putting aside 160-acre lots for Europeans of pre-emption, they were laying out tiny reserves, sometimes of no more than a few acres, for First Nations families. Trutch, apparently with no sense of irony, negotiated that the federal government, which would be responsible for "Indians," would pursue "a policy as liberal as that hitherto pursued by the British Columbia Government."[39]

These names mark relations of colonialism on an on-going basis, in which the colonizers are celebrated, their descendents made to feel at home and familiar, while the colonized are excluded, their names and their meanings remembered separately, privately, not in mass everyday circulation.[40] The people on whose territory these artifacts are constructed have also been removed from the land and its memory. The streets referred to above are located in a neighborhood called Kitsilano. The area is named after August Jack Khatsahlano or Xats'alanexw of the Skxwúmesh (Squamish) people. He lived in the village of Snaug, located to the east of present-day Kitsilano beach, on the land upon which the north end of the Burrard Street Bridge is located. This village was one of the oldest and most stable human habitations in the Burrard inlet. It had long been used as a base for people using the fishing weirs located on the sandbars that are today's Granville Island. This village was established as a reserve in 1870, but in 1913, the inhabitants were bribed to move elsewhere. As reserve lands, it was under the jurisdiction of the federal government, which is why Granville Island continues to be federal land today. Jean Barman has described the act of moving people from this reserve, noting it involved anything but due process. Over the preceding decade the newcomers to the area had come to covet this land which was close to the urban center of the young city, just as their counterparts in Victoria coveted the land of the Lekwungen (Songhees) people in Victoria's inner harbor. The Lekwungen were relocated in 1911, when the male heads of household were offered $10,000 each and new land in Esquimault. To ensure that they actually moved, the money was deposited in a bank account in the name of each head of household, but the accounts were only transferred to them after they had moved. Meanwhile, the provincial government decided to act on the Kitsilano Reserve. It offered payments of $11,500 to the heads of household but made no offer of land, apparently on the assumption that they would move into the other Squamish communities. The federal government had meanwhile established its own reserve commission and was reported to be offering $50,000. The heads of household refused. Provincial officials, including the Attorney General (and future premier), William J. Bowser, brought intense pressure to bear, threatening that they would get nothing once the federal commissioners left, also reportedly threatening the use of police to drive them out. After the heads of household capitulated, the community was moved holus bolus on April 18, 1913. Attorney General Bowser celebrated with a press conference at which he claimed "this 'eyesore to the citizens of Vancouver for many years and hindrance to the development of the city' would now make "as much profit as possible for the entire province,'" and later noted that "this very valuable property ... should net us a million dollars profit."[41] Similar events took place in Stanley Park where, a decade later, city officials sought to remark the territory with totem poles, having removed the people who had lived there since time immemorial. The result is that today in the city, the Musqueum, Squamish, and Burrard peoples who claim its territory appear to be strangers, when in fact their histories on the territory are hundreds and thousands of years longer than those whose meanings dominate.

The absence of the people who lived in the territory that became Vancouver from time immemorial reflects a history of ethnic cleansing that is not commemorated in the official sites of memory of the city. Other areas of the city mark other histories. As the bus reaches my destination in Chinatown, I am reminded that the city had long been organized along racialized lines. While the historic boundaries between racialized spaces may have broken down to some extent, the fact the city has a Chinatown is an artifact, not of the ethnic preferences and the close-knitted nature of those who are ethnically Chinese, but rather of a history of ethnic cleansing, now forgotten on this territory. As the bus goes down Pender Street, it passes the location of the former Canton Alley, now occupied by an industrial building. I catch a glimpse of the plaque in the neighboring Shanghai Alley. This plaque remembers Canton Alley as similar to Shanghai Alley, marked by "restaurants, stores, a theatre and several tenements."[42] It does not mention the heavy iron gate that stood at the entrance to Canton Alley for at least twenty years, a heavy iron gate suspended like a portcullis, held up by a rope, and next to the rope, a knife, so that it could be cut quickly. In the event of what? A pogrom.

Vancouver's Chinatown was the product of racist violence. Throughout the last half of the nineteenth and the first quarter of the twentieth centuries, racist violence shaped the resettlement in British Columbia of those racialized as Chinese. Violence was a concern as early as the 1858 gold rush, when racialized Chinese miners had to work sites previously mined by Europeans for fear that if they worked richer sites, their claims would be jumped, and they themselves might be murdered. As the miners too well knew, this is what had happened in California.[43] While it may be that the level of popular anti-Chinese violence never reached the intensity found in the United States,[44] popular violence, coupled with the lack of interest and/or the powerlessness of Canadian government officials to protect them, forced people from Guangdong to band together for their own protection. Popular violence subsequently closed entire areas of the province to racialized Chinese people, effectively making some few areas "Chinese," while preserving the rest for racialized Europeans. During the 1910s and 1920s, *The Chinese Times*, a Chinese-language daily newspaper published in Vancouver, continually reported on which districts were safe for racialized Chinese people and which ones were not, where people were being assaulted, or what anti-Asian speeches had been given and where. These incidents often went unreported in the English-language press.[45]

In this context, the only apparent place of safety was Chinatown. Vancouver's Chinatown began at its present location in the aftermath of the anti-Chinese riots of 1887. In January and February of 1887, mobs drove racialized Chinese workers out of town. These workers had been brought in under contract to clear the Brighouse estate. Mobs of racialized whites forcibly ejected racialized Chinese from the newly created city. Racialized Chinese were only able to return the city after its charter had been suspended and special constables appointed. Even then, they were unable to resettle in places valued by Anglo-Europeans and could only establish their habitations in the tidal mudflats at the northern end of False Creek.[46]

Popular violence was etched into the patterns of resettlement. Indeed, the historical geographer, David Chuen-yan Lai, noted that "[r]acism, hatred, and violence had resulted in residential segregation."[47] He noted that often "voluntary segregation resulted in the birth of a Chinatown, which was a kind of self-defense measure used by the Chinese to avoid open discrimination and hostility. They confined themselves, whenever possible, to the boundaries of Chinatowns, where they felt safe and secure."[48] David T. H. Lee, the original scholar of Chinese Canadian history, noted that in turn-of-the-century Vancouver and Victoria, racialized Chinese were subject to such random violence on the street that "they normally would not dare go outside Chinatown."[49] According to Kay Anderson, Vancouver's Chinatown came into existence under the tacit license of provincial officials, following the riots of 1887. In essence, provincial officials agreed to protect the Chinese, provided that they remained within the confines of Chinatown.[50] At the same time, Chinatown became the area of "maximum entitlement" for racialized Chinese as far as most whites were concerned. Attempts to move out of the area were resisted through a variety of practices, ranging from restrictive real estate covenants, to out and out hostility.[51]

The role of Chinatown as a sanctuary was particularly apparent following the 1907 Vancouver riot. On the evening of September 7, a white supremacist mob rampaged through Chinatown and the neighboring Japanese quarter. The riot followed a rally sponsored by the Asiatic Exclusion League and was supported by all fifty-seven of the city's white-only trade unions, by leading politicians of various stripes including the mayor as well as leading Protestant clergy, and attended by at least one-tenth of the city's population. The mob rampaged through Chinatown, breaking windows and assaulting anyone they could find.[52]

The Vancouver merchant Chang Toy's immediate response to the riot was two-fold. First, he sent his two youngest to stay with two prominent Anglo-European businessmen.[53] This seemingly odd response makes sense only if Chang was expecting a pogrom. As a Chinese patriarch, his first and principal consideration was always the preservation of his *jia* or household. By sending two of his sons to safety, he was ensuring the survival of his *jia* no matter what. The fact that two prominent Anglo-European businessmen were willing to receive them suggests that his fears of a pogrom were shared by others. Chang's fears were solidly based, as ethnic cleansings had taken place up and down the Pacific Coast, including between 1898 and 1906, in the Slocan Valley, in Atlin, Salmo, and Penticton.[54]

Chang's second response was to proceed with his partner, Shum Moon, who was also president of the Vancouver Chinese Benevolent Association at the time, to the local gun merchants McLennan and McFeely. They purchased the firm's stock of revolvers to distribute to their fellow merchants.[55] It appears that several merchants also bought guns, as is evident by the bills they submitted to the William Lyon Mackenzie King Commission that settled the damages.[56] However, the Vancouver riot continued to have an effect on the inhabitants of Vancouver. In the late 1910s/early 1920s, as Sing Lim recalled in his memoir, and the 1924 Survey of Race Relations confirmed, the residents of Canton Alley in Vancouver maintained an iron gate over the entrance to the alley that could be dropped at a moment's notice, in the event of another disturbance.[57] If there is a Chinatown in Vancouver, it is because the rest of the city was a white town, and racist violence and legislated discrimination maintained it as such for seventy years. Curiously, this is something that the city's Heritage Department does not remember on its walking tour of Chinatown.

As I get off the bus in front of the Chinese Cultural Centre, I note that Chinatown continues to have a racializing effect. It helps to maintain the assumption that all people of Chinese origins are the same. In effect, it homogenizes them as a single group. In fact, at the time of the 1907 riot, the people of Chinatown did not have a common spoken language, but spoke as their first languages several different, mutually unintelligible dialects of Cantonese, as well as Hakka and English. The existence of Chinatown also leads to an assumption that all those of Chinese origins and who live in the city, are connected to it and through it to each other. In fact, the vast majority of people of Chinese origins, 80% of the over 1,000,000 people who self-identified as Chinese in the 2001 census, are first generation immigrants from Hong Kong, Mainland China other than Guangdong, Taiwan, and Singapore.[58] These are people whose personal histories have little connection to traditional Chinatowns.

Everywhere that I turn in Vancouver, I encounter artifacts of the histories of colonialism and racism that made this city—its infrastructure, its material arrangement, its symbolic representations, its significations, and its texts and sites of memory. The city itself is a giant artifact of colonialism, a European cultural institution in its own right. The city also is continually re-colonized, as dominating meanings naturalize the Anglo-European occupation of the territory, as the most banal of markings celebrate and silence genocide and ethnic cleansings, and as racialized logics get organized into the fabric of the city's neighborhoods and people's lives.

There may be other ways of remembering, available within this city and elsewhere, as indeed this chapter documents, but these other ways are not the texts that circulate, that are popular, that get widely reproduced, or that get commemorated in sites of memory.

What, then, should or can critical educators do with this? Part of me wants to suggest a campaign for renaming these sites of memory, to replace the names that celebrate genocidaires and rapists with names that celebrate others more worthy of commemoration. But as Stuart Hall reminds us, it is not enough to replace the bad representations with good ones. We need to pull the bad ones apart, to make them uninhabitable.[59]

Perhaps here another idea could help; one that comes from China, rather than Europe. The ancient Chinese philosophers also confronted a world of conflict and chaos. They advanced several solutions to the problems of their times, solutions that laid the basis for Chinese intellectual tradition. One of these ideas is something that they called the Rectification of Names or *zheng ming*. Confucius argued that disorder resulted when authorities took on roles that were not proper to them. The solution was to rectify their functions to correspond to their titles, or as he put it in the patriarchal terms of his era, "Let the ruler be ruler, the minister minister, the father father and the son son."[60] According to the logic of this position, chaos ensues when "tyrants" and "usurpers" call themselves "kings." The solution was to rectify names to accord with realities, to call tyrants "tyrants" and not "kings." Perhaps this is what we need to do in engaging the taken-for-grantedness of colonized material and symbolic spaces. We need to re-mark them, naming them for what they are. In the end, this might create space for other actions, for a politics of anti-colonialism.

Most important, I think, is to return to the other meaning that Michael Billig associated with banal nationalisms. The constant marking of the nation state, of its membership and existence, according to Billig, is not only banal in the sense of being common or ordinary. It is also banal in the same sense with which Hannah Arendt spoke of the banality of evil. Writing about the trial of Adolf Eichmann, the principal architect of the Holocaust, she noted that Eichmann was a clerk with no imagination. Evil, she wrote, was no longer radically different from ourselves; it was common, ordinary, banal.[61] So, too, is colonialism.

Notes

1. Although this chapter focuses on urban spaces, it applies equally well to suburban and rural spaces. The constructed nature of landscape is such that even wilderness is artificially constructed (by decisions not to develop it).

2. Here I am reminded that discourse is not merely symbolic representations but is also its material effects and consequences. The construction provided by Stuart Hall, "The Work of Representation," pp. 13–74 in Stuart Hall (ed.), *Representation: Cultural Representations and Signifying Practices* (London, Thousand Oaks, CA, and New Delhi: Sage, 1997) is particularly useful here. See also Stuart Hall, "The West and the Rest: Discourse and Power," in Stuart Hall, David Held, Don Hubert, and Kenneth Thompson (eds.), *Modernity: An Introduction to Modern Societies* (Cambridge: Blackwell, 1996), pp. 185–227.

3. Edward W. Said, *Orientalism* (New York: Vintage Books, 1979).

4. On the significance of colonialism in contemporary culture, see Edward W. Said, *Culture and Imperialism* (New York: Alfred A. Knopf, 1993) and Derek Gregory, *The Colonial Present: Afghanistan, Palestine, Iraq* (Malden, MA: Blackwell, 2004). On Colonialism as a producer of self-serving knowledge, see Bernard S. Cohn, *Colonialism and Its Forms of Knowledge: The British in India* (Princeton: Princeton University Press, 1996).

5. See Sut Jhally (dir.), *Representation and the Media* [video recording] (Northampton, MA: Media Education Foundation, 1997).

6. See, for example, Phil Cohen, "'It's Racism What Dunn It': Hidden Narratives in Theories of Racism," in James Donald and Ali Rattansi (eds.), *Race, Culture and Difference* (London: Sage, 1992); Leslie G. Roman, "White Is a Color!: White Defensiveness, Postmodernism and Anti-racist Pedagogy," pp. 279–378 in Cameron McCarthy and Warren Chrichlow (eds.), *Race, Identity, and Representation in Education* (New York: Routledge, 1993); Michelle Fine, L. Weis, L. Powell-Pruitt, and A. Burns (eds.), *Off White: Readings on Power, Privilege, and Resistance* (New York: Routledge, 2004); Paul R. Carr and Darren E. Lund (eds.), *The Great White North?: Exploring Whiteness, Privilege, and Identity in Education* (Rotterdam, The Netherlands: Sense, 2007). The classic statement of this is Peggy McIntosh, "White Privilege: Unpacking the Invisible Knapsack," *Independent School*, 49, 2 (Winter 1990): 31–34. See the response of Zeus Leonardo, "The Color of Supremacy: Beyond the Discourse of 'White Privilege.'" *Journal of Educational Philosophy and Theory*, 36, 2 (2004): 137–152.

7. See, for example, Himani Bannerji, *The Dark Side of the Nation: Essays on Multiculturalism, Nationalism and Gender* (Toronto: Canadian Scholars' Press, 2000) and Camille A. Nelson and Charmaine A. Nelson, *Racism, Eh?: A Critical Inter-disciplinary Anthology of Race and Racism in Canada* (Concord, ON: Captus Press, 2004).

8. Timothy J. Stanley, "Striking for Educational Equality: Antiracism, White Supremacy and the Making of Chinese Canadians," Ms.

9. The legislation, first enacted in 1872, was disallowed by the lieutenant governor on the grounds that it interfered in the federal jurisdiction over Indian Affairs. Following the advice of the federal minister of justice that this was not so, substantially the same legislation was passed in 1875. See "An Act to Make Better Provision for the Qualification and Registration of Voters," 1875 in *Statutes of the Province of British Columbia, 1875* (Victoria: Richard Wolfenden, Government Printer, 1875), 18.

10. See Timothy J. Stanley, "Whose Public? Whose Memory? Racisms, Grand Narratives and Canadian History," pp. 31–49 in Ruth W. Sandwell (ed.), *To the Past: History Education, Public Memory, and Citizenship in Canada* (Toronto: University of Toronto Press, 2006).

11. James V. Wertsch, *Voices of Collective Remembering* (Cambridge and New York: Cambridge University Press, 2002).

12. For a useful conceptualization, see Brian Osborne, "Landscapes, Memory, Monuments, and Commemoration: Putting IdentiTy in Its Place," *Canadian Ethnic Studies* (2001): 39–77. For an ethnographic study, see Elizabeth Furniss, *The Burden of History: Colonialisms and the Frontier Myth in a Rural Canadian Community* (Vancouver: UBC Press, 1999). For other explorations, see also David Lowenthal, *The Past Is a Foreign Country* (Cambridge: Cambridge University Press, 1985); Eric Hobsbawm and Terence Ranger (eds.), *The Invention of Tradition* (Cambridge and New York: Cambridge University Press, 1983); Jon Holzman, "The World Is Dead and Cooking's Killed It: Food and the Gender of Memory in Samburu, Northern Kenya," *Food and Foodways,* 14 (2006): 175–200 and H. V. Nelles, *The Art of Nation-Building: Pageantry and Spectacle at Quebec's Tercentenary* (Toronto: University of Toronto Press, 1999).

13. Benedict Anderson, *Imagined Communities: Reflections on the Origin and Spread of Nationalism* (London: Verso, 1983).

14. Michael Billig, *Banal Nationalism* (London and Thousand Oaks, CA: Sage, 1995).

15. See the map of UBC loop. BC Transit, http://www.translink.bc.ca/files/maps/stn_exch_maps/ubcloop.pdf (May 23, 2008).

16. For an introduction to the diversity of fur trade and early colonial society, see Jean Barman, *The West beyond the West: A History of British Columbia* (Vancouver: UBC Press, 1991).

17. Ibid., 169–170.

18. See Maleanie Harbattle, "Won Alexander Cumyow: An Inventory of His Fonds in Rare Books and Special Collections, the Library of the University of British Columbia (2002)," http://www.library.ubc.ca/spcoll/AZ/PDF/C/Cumyow_Won_Alexander.pdf (November 5, 2006).

19. Mary-Ellen Kelm, *Colonizing Bodies: Aboriginal Health and Healing in British Columbia, 1900–50* (Vancouver: UBC Press, 1998); John S. Milloy, *A National Crime: The Canadian Government and the Residential School System, 1879 to 1986* (Winnipeg: University of Manitoba Press, 1999).

20. Key works on this process include, Robin Fisher, *Contact and Conflict: Indian-European Relations in British Columbia, 1774–1890* (Vancouver: UBC Press, 1977); Barry Gough, *Gunboat Frontier: British Maritime Authority and Northwest Coast Indians, 1846–90* (Vancouver: UBC Press, 1984); Paul Tennant, *Aboriginal Peoples and Politics: The Indian Land Question in British Columbia, 1849–1989* (Vancouver: UBC Press, 1990); R. Cole Harris, *The Resettlement of British Columbia: Essays on Colonialism and Geographical Change* (Vancouver: UBC Press, 1997); Daniel W. Clayton, *Islands of Truth: The Imperial Fashioning of Vancouver Island* (Vancouver: UBC Press, 2000); Adele Perry, *On the Edge of Empire: Gender, Race, and the Making of British Columbia, 1849–1871* (Toronto: University of Toronto Press, 2001); R. Cole Harris, *Making Native Space: Colonialism, Resistance, and Reserves in British Columbia* (Vancouver: UBC Press, 2002); John Lutz (ed.), *Myth and Memory: Stories of Indigenous-European Contact* (Vancouver: UBC Press, 2007). For views from First Nations perspectives, see Joanne Drake-Terry, *The Same as Yesterday: The Lillooet Chronicle the Theft of Their Lands and Resources* (Lillooet, BC: Lillooet Tribal Council, 1989); Gisday Wa and Delgan Uukw, *The Spirit in the Land: Statements of the Gitksan and Wet'suwet'en Hereditary Chiefs in the Supreme Court of British Columbia, 1987–1990* (Gabriola, BC: Reflections, 1992) and Keith Thor Carlson (ed.), *A Stó:lo-coast Salish Historical Atlas* (Vancouver: Douglas & McIntyre; Seattle, WA: University of Washington Press; Chilliwack, BC: Stó:lo Heritage Trust, 2001).

21. "A Brief History of the University of British Columbia," UBC Archives, http://www.library.ubc.ca/archives/hist_ubc.html (May 23, 2008).

22. See "History" at "About McGill," http://www.mcgill.ca/about/history/ (May 23, 2008); see also "The Royal Charter of McGill University," http://www.mcgill.ca/secretariat/charter-statutes/royal/ (May 23, 2008).

23. "A Brief History of the University of British Columbia," UBC Archives, http://www.library.ubc.ca/archives/hist_ubc.html (May 23, 2008).

24. *Census of Canada, 1665 to 1871* (Ottawa: I. B. Taylor, 1876), 4: 376–377. These were the "Blue Book" estimates. I. E., estimates compiled by local magistrates and other officials.

25. Ibid., 1589. Opposition members argued that the Chinese were good "British" subjects in their own right.

26. "A Brief History of the University of British Columbia," UBC Archives, http://www.library.ubc.ca/archives/hist_ubc.html (May 23, 2008).

27. See Cole Harris, "The Making of the Lower Mainland," 68–102 in Harris, *Resettlement of British Columbia*. See especially p. 82.

28. Ibid., 90. Earlier plagues in the late eighteenth and early nineteenth centuries probably had already reduced the population by half.

29. See Gough, *Gunboat Frontier*.

30. Here I follow Harris, "The Making of the Lower Mainland."

31. Ibid., 101.

32. See "An Ordinance to Further Define the Law Regulating the Acquisition of Land in British Columbia (Pre-emption Ordinance, 1866)" in *Ordinances Passed by the Legislative Council of British Columbia, during the Session from January to April, 1866* (New Westminster: Government Printing Office [1866]) , Early Canadiana Online, CIHM no, 9_03445_3.

33. See "An Ordinance to Amend and Consolidate the Laws Affecting Crown Lands in British Columbia (Land Ordinance, 1870)," p. 2, clause III in *Ordinances Passed by the Legislative Council of British Columbia, during the Session from 15th February to 23rd April, 1870* (Victoria: Government Printing Office [1870]), Early Canadiana Online, CIHM no, 9_03445_7.

34. Fisher, *Contact and Conflict*, 165.

35. Harris, *Resettlement of British Columbia*, 102.

36. Wendy Wickwire, "To See Ourselves as the Other's Other: Nlaka'pamux Contact Narratives," *Canadian Historical Review*, 75 (1), 1994, pp. 1–20.

37. See "Provinces and Territories—The Origins of Their Names," Mapping Services, Natural Resources Canada, http://geonames.nrcan.gc.ca/education/prov_e.php#pe (May 23, 2008).

38. Cited in Fisher, *Contact and Conflict*, p. 164. See also Robin Fisher, "Joseph Trutch and Indian Land Policy," *BC Studies*, 12 (Winter 1971–72): 3–10. On reserve policy see Cole Harris, *Making Native Space: Colonialism, Resistance, and Reserves in British Columbia* (Vancouver: UBC Press, 2002) and Paul Tennat, *Aboriginal Peoples and Politics: The Indian Land Question in British Columbia, 1849–1989* (Vancouver: UBC Press, 1990).

39. This is from item 13 in the terms. See "British Columbia Terms of Union," http://www.solon.org/Constitutions/Canada/English/bctu.html (July 1, 2008).

40. For an example of the ways in which territories are differently named and remembered in First Nations perspective, see Carlson, *Stó:lo Coast Salish Historical Atlas*.

41. Jean Barman, "Erasing Indigenous Indigeneity in Vancouver," *BC Studies*, 155 (Autumn) 2007, Pro-Quest database (May 23, 2008).

42. See "Walking Tour: Chinatown," Heritage Conservation Program, City of Vancouver, http://www.city.vancouver.bc.ca/commsvcs/planning/heritage/walks/w_ch2.htm (May 23, 2008).

43. See Harry Con, Ronald J. Con, Graham Johnson, Edgar Wickberg, William E. Willmott, and Edgar Wickberg (eds.), *From China to Canada: A History of the Chinese Communities of Canada*, Generations Series (Toronto: Mc-Clelland and Stewart, 1982), 16, 42ff.

44. For a recent study of the history of ethnic cleansing involving racialized Chinese in the United States, see Jean Pfaelzer, *Driven Out: The Forgotten War against Chinese Americans* (New York: Random House, 2007). American scholars have long been aware of anti-Chinese violence and its consequences. For example, Stan Steiner some years ago argued that racialized Chinese people found it safer to travel from place to place in the American West by dressing up as Native Americans. See Stan Steiner, *Fusang: The Chinese Who Built America* (New York: Harper & Row, 1979). On the myth of Canada as peaceable kingdom, see Judy M. Torrance, *Public Violence in Canada, 1867–1982* (Kingston, ON: McGill-Queen's University Press, 1986).

45. Indeed in many ways *The Chinese Times* is the most complete source on anti-Chinese discourse during this era. See Chinese Canadian Research Collection, BOX 4: CHINESE TIMES—Chronological Research Index (Original Notes and Typed Copy) (1914–1931), UBC Archives, Vancouver.

46. The most complete discussion is provided by Kay J. Anderson, *Vancouver's Chinatown: Racial Discourse in Canada, 1875–1980* (Montréal: McGill-Queen's University Press, 1991), pp. 64–71. See also, Wickberg, *From China to Canada*, 62–63; Patricia E. Roy, *A White Man's Province: British Columbia Politicians and Chinese and Japanese Immigrants, 1858–1914* (Vancouver: UBC Press, 1989), 72–73; David Chuen-yan Lai, *Chinatowns: Towns within Cities in Canada* (Vancouver: UBC Press, 1988),79–81.

47. Lai, *Chinatowns*, 34.

48. Ibid., 35. In this respect the formation of the Chinatown in Cumberland was an exception, as this was on land in a one company town set aside by the employer.

49. David T. H. Lee [Li Donghai], *Jianada Huaqiao shi* [A History of the Overseas Chinese in Canada] (Taipei: Zhonghua Da Dian Bianying Hui, 1967), 356. Despite having created the conditions that ensured their spatial segregation, white supremacist discourse represented residential segregation as the product, not of racist exclusion, but of the racial characteristics and preferences of "the Chinese" themselves. The process of creating Chinatown as a "race" characteristic has been thoroughly documented in the case of Vancouver's Chinatown by Kay Anderson. For a discussion of "Chinatown" as a construction of white racism, see Anderson, "'East' as 'West': Place, State and the Institutionalization of Myth in Vancouver's Chinatown, 1880–1980" (Unpublished Ph.D. thesis, UBC, 1986). See also, Kay J. Anderson, "Cultural Hegemony and the Race-Definition Process in Chinatown, Vancouver: 1880–1980," *Environment and Planning D: Society and Space*, 6, 2 (June 1988): 127–149.

50. Anderson, "'East' as 'West,'" 107–111.
51. Ibid., 127–246.
52. See the account in W. Peter Ward, *White Canada Forever: Popular Attitudes and Public Policy Toward Orientals in British Columbia* (Montreal: McGill-Queen's University Press, 1978).
53. Timothy J. Stanley, "Chang Toy," *Dictionary of Canadian Biography*, 15 (1921–1930). Toronto: University of Toronto Press, 2005).
54. Ward, *White Canada Forever*, 64.
55. Ibid.
56. Canada. Royal Commission to Investigate Losses by the Chinese Population of Vancouver, British Columbia, on the Occasion of the Riots in That City in September, 1907, William Lyon Mackenzie King Commissioner, *Report by W. L. Mackenzie King, C. M. G., Deputy Minister of Labour, Commissioner Appointed to Investigate into the Losses Sustained by the Chinese Population of Vancouver, B. C. on the Occasion of the Riots in That City in September, 1907* (Ottawa: S. E. Dawson, 1908), 12. Early Canadiana Online. http://www.canadiana.org/ECO/PageView?id=2a590874c384adf9&display=9_08045+0016 (May 6, 2008). King dismissed the purchases of guns as "unnecessary."
57. On Canton Alley, see Sing Lim, *West Coast Chinese Boy* (Montreal: Tundra Press, 1979), 14. See also "Interview with Mrs. Quong (March 12, 1924)," Survey on Race Relations, 15–22, Interviews, Regional. British Columbia, Hoover Institution Archives Box 15. OFFICE FILE, 1914–1927. http://collections.stanford.edu/pdf/10100000000015_0022.pdf (Accessed: August 4, 2006).
58. See Tina Chui, Kelly Tran, and John Flanders, "Chinese Canadians: Enriching the Cultural Mosaic," *Canadian Social Trends* (Spring 2005): 24–32.
59. Jhally, *Representation and the Media*.
60. Confucius, *Analects*, XII, 11.
61. Hannah Arendt, *Eichmann in Jerusalem: A Report on the Banality of Evil* (New York: Penguin Books, 1977).

Eleven

Young Children and Story
The Path to Transformative Action

Elizabeth P. Quintero

Diversity is much easier talked about than done. High-powered thinkers and consultants spend huge amounts of time and money dwelling on the cultural and sociological intricacies of diversity issues, so that we may better understand them. Ultimately, those of us in educational contexts and communities want to get better at "doing diversity." We know from more than twenty years of research and trial and error in practice that "celebrating" diversity is not the way to facilitate social justice.

I am a teacher/scholar who has spent many years working in classrooms with young children from a wide range of cultural, linguistic, and social class backgrounds, from birth to third grade. I've spent years more recently in teacher education, supporting and working with student teachers who are becoming activists, critical teachers in programs for young children and their families. Throughout the past couple of decades, I've also been fortunate to have worked with immigrant and refugee families in the context of critical, multilingual literacy programs, and have realized that young children (and their families) are the real teachers about diversity. Through their stories—the ones they invent, the ones that are read to them, the ones they act out—children "do" diversity while engaging in play, literacy activities, and learning. They achieve transformative action when given opportunity and encouragement.

Critical literacy, an aspect of critical theory, addresses issues in an integrated and participatory way. Critical theory emphasizes participation through personal histories, sharing of multiple ways of knowing, and transformative action. This chapter will address young children and their teachers using critical literacy and multicultural children's literature, and child-created books to cross boundaries and interact with different constructs within diversity.

Realizing that this stance about children and diversity could easily been seen as social romanticism, I must insist and reiterate what I have seen during my years of working with children and families. I have seen circumstances in which philosophies and teaching provide opportunities for small, but tangible, steps toward educators' learning to really use and build upon learners' past experiences and sources of knowledge. . .even young children—especially young children.

For example, in Faith Ringgold's *Tar Beach* (1996) and *Aunt Harriet's Underground Railroad in the Sky* (1995), the character, Cassie, uses her imagination and her stories to overcome oppression and limitations. Children, through their play, especially when immersed in an environment of literature and art, can provide us with voices and perspectives of possibility. For example, a student teacher who was just beginning to study the ways that critical literacy can be exemplified by young children, wrote in a reflective journal assignment:

> I observed a child (about four years old) and his father riding the subway together. The train was very crowded and there was only enough room for the child to sit down, so the father stood in front of him. He put the child in the seat and gave him some paper and pen to draw. The child looked around for a while and then finally began drawing. The father asked the child what he was drawing and he said he was drawing the father riding the subway. The father replied, "But I'm standing, not sitting down." The child then said, "Not on this train, the train in my drawing has seats for everyone to sit down." (Quintero, 2008)

This child has used some very important critical literacy through his imagination and his art.

Children's literature author, Lunge-Larsen (1999), reminds us of the importance of literature in children's lives in the introduction to one of her children's literature books:

> Children, like the heroes and heroines in these stories (folk tales) perceive their lives to be constantly threatened. Will I lose a tooth? Will I be invited to play? Will I learn to read? By living a life immersed in great stories and themes, children will see that they have the resources needed to solve life's struggles. And, while listening to these stories, children can rest for a while in a world that mirrors their own, full of magic and the possibility of greatness that lies within the human heart. (p. 11)

When learners (children, youth, or adults) talk, dramatize through pretend play, and write about their personal stories, topics becomes layered with the complex issues that must be discussed and addressed in education.

I and my teaching colleagues support students' multiple histories and recognize ways that multiple knowledge sources, identities, and language forms can contribute to the formation of new relationships and meanings. As a community of scholars in a wide variety of classrooms, we respect the learners' backgrounds, plan carefully for their current experiences in school, and prepare them for the future challenges of standardized testing, competitive learning programs, and a variety of future journeys. Our work uses critical literacy as a framework. We define critical literacy as a *process of constructing and critically using language (oral and written) as a means of expression, interpretation, and/or transformation of our lives and the lives of those around us.*

Early childhood educators advocate for programs of high quality that respect families' cultural and linguistic histories, the holistic learning of young children that includes supportive environments for imagination, play, and building of friendships. We believe that teachers must be activist facilitators who provide materials and human interactions that expose children to the arts, social sciences, and physical sciences. We have discovered that the theoretical structure of critical literacy and the magic of multicultural children's literature, including poetry and drama, provide for the children, in the course of their living their lives, to delve in to the various content areas of study, but also the complex topics related to diversity.

Because of the changing needs of families and the persistence of Western intellectual, psychological, and cultural perspectives, changes must continue to be made. Family child-rearing practices must be supported and built upon to enhance social, emotional, cognitive, and physical development. A problem-posing curriculum, based on critical theory and critical literacy, and emphasizing the family and its cultural story and multicultural children's literature, encourages collaboration and enhances multidirectional participatory learning. In other words, in this context, learning not only is transmitted from teacher to students, but teachers learn from students, and students from each other. We must ". . . search for intelligence where one has previously seen only deficiency" (Kincheloe, 2000, p. 81).

The teacher education students I work with participate in a variety of problem-posing, critical literacy activities in teacher education courses before they begin planning and implementing similar activities for the children with which they work. The autobiographical narrative and qualitative research begins at the outset of their participation and continues throughout the use of problem-posing critical literacy with young learners in their classrooms.

Speaking of different ways story enriches young children's learning, author Tim Tingle, Choctaw storyteller and author, tells us about his use of different forms of story as he creates children's literature. He points out that, even in this day of electronic communication, Native Americans live in a world that often accepts the spoken word as the authority. He says, "Even today, many Choctaws are likely to trust a story told to them by another Choctaw, more than anything they read on the printed page" (Tingle, 2006, p. 38). His children's book, *Crossing Bok Chitto*, is what he calls an Indian book, written by Indian voices, and painted by an Indian artist. The story was passed down the Indian, way, told and retold by elders. Tingle (2006) says in his author's commentary about the book,

> in this new format—of language and painting, this book-way of telling—is for both the Indian and non-Indian. We Indians need to continue recounting our past, and from this book, non-Indians might realize the sweet and secret fire that drives the Indian heart. (p. 39)

Teacher Education Students Recalling Personal Story

Teacher education students in my research reflected on their own experiences of critical literacy in their own families and communities. The autobiographical opportunities inherent in problem-posing critical literacy methodology encouraged students to tie their personal family stories to the learning situation of students learning English for the first time when they come to school.

> As a child I was not encouraged to cultivate my home languages of Spanish and Italian in school. So, at home I would refuse to speak anything other than English because I felt that was the "right way," because that is what everyone else in school spoke. As a result, similar to what the article stated, I lost the ability to communicate well with my extended family. Sadly, I am unable to converse with my grandmother who speaks only Italian. (Quintero, in press)

Another student whose parents came to the United States from Colombia when she was a baby wrote about her early literacy experience:

My own memories of literacy were enjoyable. I remember heading to the library almost every week with my older sister and my mother. I would check out as many books as I could. Before I could read, my sister read to me. . . I remember my sister really wanted me to learn to read before I entered kindergarten because I never went to preschool.

My parents were happy that I was just as interested in books as I was in watching television. My father encouraged me to read more books because he felt (and still feels) that television does not educate people. . . Early on, I learned that if we could not afford a whole library of books, the library was available for our use. To this day, I still pick up some books to read for fun, even though I have no time to read them. My family helped me love to read. (Quintero, in press)

Critical Literacy and Problem-Posing with Young Children

Problem-posing teaching, using children's literature, nourishes an integrated curriculum that supports young children's meaningful learning. This method encourages integrated learning that is both developmentally and culturally meaningful through interacting with story, reading literature, and participating in related learning activities. The problem-posing method was developed by Paulo Freire (1973) and critical pedagogists with roots going back to the Frankfurt School of Critical Theory in the 1920s, and was initially intended for use with adult literacy students. The method leads students of any age or experience or ability level to base new learning on personal experience in a way that encourages critical reflection. All activities focus on active participation.

Simply defined, the problem-posing method is comprised of several components: Listening, Dialogue, and Action. Participants listen to each other's stories, discuss issues of power that shaped their identities, and present ways in which action, or transformation, can take place in their own lives. These discussions ultimately lead to students' creating a complex form of autobiographical narrative. This combined use of literature and the arts pushes participants to use their autobiography as a means of understanding how their learning was not "neutral," and that the relationship between schools and families must be a move toward a more well-defined conception of culture that reflects our pluralistic, multicultural society (Willis, 1995).

When university students are initially doubtful about using this method with young children and about children "doing" critical literacy, I bring in *Amazing Grace* to help me demonstrate. I first ask the adult students to imagine themselves as a character in one of their favorite stories or as a painting or other work of art. I ask them to think about: What do you look like visually? Where are you? What are you doing? What is going on around you? Are you saying anything? Draw a sketch or write a self-portrait beginning with "I am. . ." and include as much detail as you can about what you imagined.

Then I ask them to write about a situation in which someone said they couldn't do something they really wanted to do. Did they take the advice? Why or why not?

Then I read the story, *Amazing Grace,* by Mary Hoffman. The story is about Grace who loves stories, whether she hears them, reads them, or makes them up. She uses her imagination and acts the stories out, always giving herself the most exciting parts. So when her teacher announces a classroom production of *Peter Pan,* Grace wants to play the lead. One classmate says she can't because she's a girl and another says she can't because she's black. When Grace relates this to her mother and grandmother, they tell her she can be anything she wants to, if she puts her mind to it. Inspired by her family's support, her own indomitable spirit, and an excursion to a weekend ballet starring a lovely Trinidadian dancer, Grace shines during the class audition, leaving no doubt in anyone's mind as to who will play Peter Pan.

The university students discuss what happened in the story and how the story of Grace relates to what they wrote previously about their own stories. Then we discuss how Grace's actions are examples of critical literacy and transformative action.

Second Grade Story and *A Boy Called Slow*

A student teacher planned and implemented a lesson with a group of second graders at the beginning of the school year, the time at which it is important to establish community in the classroom. She asked the children to sit in a semicircle for the Listening and Dialogue sections to give the message that it was a learner-centered environment. The story is historical and it is also connected to personal history, multiple sources of knowledge, and transformative action.

She asked the children to think of a symbol (a visual of some sort) that has a special meaning for them. She asked that they draw a sketch of it (on their white board or a clipboard) and write a few lines about the meaning it has, and then to write about any knowledge they have about the origins of their own names.

She proceeded to read *A Boy Called Slow: The True Story of Sitting Bull* by Joseph Bruchac (1994) to the group.

The student teacher asked if anyone knew this story. What, if anything, had they heard about American Indian naming ceremonies and traditions? She then asked, "Who chose the names of the babies in your family? How were the names chosen? Did you have any ceremony attached to the naming? What about nicknames? How did they come about? In what ways did any of your naming stories have any similarities with this story?"

The student teacher asked the children to think about inventing a name for themselves and to write a short paragraph about their thinking for choosing the names they did. The children were given the task of thinking of a way to present the meaning behind their names and express this to a partner. Then the pair was asked to develop an artistic way to present this for a class mural.

The class was then asked to read *If Your Name Was Changed at Ellis Island* by Ellen Levine (1993). The book is a historical explanation of Ellis Island, who came there and why, and some of the procedures and policies that immigrants were exposed to when they arrived.

The teacher reflected that this activity gave students the opportunity to learn about American Indians, themselves, and each other. This was intended to encourage student talk, build community, and consider the meaning of the story.

The student teacher reflected about her problem-posing with multicultural children's literature. She said:

> When children take literature to heart, they establish a strong, meaningful connection with that poem or story or verse or whichever type of literature it may be. The content within this piece of literature is relevant to the child's life and s/he may very well carry this idea, moral, or significance with her for the rest of her life. I feel that an artifact can evoke the same intense feelings of devotion, admiration or importance that literature can.
>
> We can introduce a child to a hundred books or a hundred artifacts and never get a response from that child. Sometimes adults need to refrain from dictating their opinions, and let children explore among themselves, their attitudes and their strengths and skills. Much focus is on the knowledge that children portray through their writing and other communicative intents. Most children are eager to write because it helps them to convey their feelings and emotions.

The student teacher reflected on her extended problem-posing work with children about this topic so important to her own learning and living. She wrote:

> We can see the creation of new realities through the magical power of story, art and imagination. When children are exposed to historical information that relates to their own sense of place, families, and communities, they learn. There are many ways that students' ability to translate history into observation requires students to use a language that is not literal, that employs metaphor, illusion, and innuendo; and through story students recognize that problems can have multiple solutions, questions can have multiple answers.

Kindergarten Story and Folk Tales from Around the World

Another teacher education student was studying the issues of critical literacy through fairy tales from different cultures. She decided to try a lesson with kindergarteners using the Brothers Grimm *Little Red Riding Hood* (2004), and a storybook of *Lon Po Po* (Young, 1989) a Chinese interpretation of the Red Riding Hood story.

She began by telling a story about herself. She said, "When I was younger, my brother used to tell me you could dig a hole to China. I later found out he was lying." She asked the children if anyone had ever told them something that isn't true and listened to their answers. She then asked if there was ever a time that they had to protect themselves from a dangerous situation. She listened to them describe the situations.

She then asked them to listen to the stories *Little Red Riding Hood* and *Lon Po Po*. She explained the origin of each tale, and marked the countries on the world map.

Using a Venn diagram, she asked the children to compare and contrast the book *Lon Po Po* with the tale of *Little Red Riding Hood*. As the children discussed the comparisons, she wrote the characteristics on the diagram. When the elements of the story were the same, they were noted in the overlapping part of the diagram.

After this, she asked the children to describe aspects of both stories that they especially liked. Then, the children had two activities to choose from:

1. In groups of three or four children, they were asked to have a discussion of what each child would tell his or her mother when she returned from her visit. Short skits were used to share the ideas with the class.
2. The other choice was to create an interpretation of *Little Red Riding Hood*. By using costumes and props provided, they were to create a new version and perform for the class.

For action outside the classroom, the children were asked to interview family or community friends about a story that they remembered from their childhoods that may or may not have been true. The families were asked how they found out whether or not the information was true. The children reported their results the following week in class.

After the lesson, the student teacher reflected upon the structure of choice she'd used for the purpose of critical literacy.

> I agree with Freire when he says that students' participation in the curriculum is important in achieving democracy and development. My cooperating teacher exemplifies this in her classroom. Although certain periods of the day are defined in terms such as Word Study or Writing Workshop, the children

have choice time when they can choose which work to do. She feels that allowing them to participate in choosing the activities they do helps them to be more interested in the material, learn decision making, and helps them to be more productive. I see the children excited about, and learning from, what they do throughout the day and I believe it is because they are taking part in choosing and creating these activities. They are also confident to bring in critical facts about their stories even if their information is different from other students.

Transformative Action by Preschool Children and Their Teachers

A group of Pre-K student teachers, working with three- to five-year-olds (many of whom are Spanish-speaking English Learners) in Southern California, and studying in a university class focusing on young children's learning and multilingual language acquisition and English language development in the classroom, created groundbreaking learning situations. These experienced student teachers engaged in critical literacy work that supports children's play, fantasy, and learning through story. They worked on the difficult but effective task of creating participatory curriculum that leads to learners' transformative actions. Embedded in the few examples here are illustrations of the teachers' transformative action as well as the young children's transformative action.

One student teacher working with three- and four-year-olds explained, "It all began with Book 20 from Ada and Campoy's (2003) *Authors in the Classroom*. This is the activity called How It Is and How It Could Be" (Quintero, in press). The activity encourages teachers to think first about something that one would like to change or make a difference in and then encourages us to use this idea as a beginning or a catalyst for making change on a personal level. Then, the authors of the book, and we in the class, worked on transferring this idea to our work with children.

This particular student teacher thought about her membership in the Union of Concerned Scientists that lobbies for environmental issues. She wanted to do something that deals with being proactive in preventing water pollution. So she planned a thematic lesson that centered on their class pet fish and its water conditions. She and the children did observations, dictation, oral discussions, writings, drawings, and finger plays. She used visuals, activities to demonstrate how we could make a change in how we care for and conserve our water sources.

They practiced conserving water when washing their hands and picked up trash on their playground. Over the course of three weeks, the children were given a variety of activities and opportunities in English and Spanish with a great deal of consideration given to the conversational and contextual learning surrounding the clean water theme.

Finally, using a digital camera to take pictures of the pet fish and his water, both clean and unclean, and by group dictation, the student teacher and her class created a class book in English and Spanish that told the story of Jack the fish. The book documented the original clean water Jack had, how his water became dirty (unintentionally), how they cleaned the water, and then quickly learned to use dip sticks to check the water for safety for Jack. The book then addressed the "bigger problem" of dirty water and pollution in our communities, oceans, and world.

> We can test our water and even add special drops to clean our water. But remember that even clean looking water can still be dirty. The water cycle cannot clean all of the Earth's water so we have to help keep our oceans, lakes and rivers clean. (Quintero, in press)

The last page of the book is a list of brainstorming ideas that the preschool children came up with that showed that they understood the small steps (and big responsibility) each person has in preventing pollution. The student teacher explained,

> During my group instruction and throughout the implementation of the clean water theme, there was always a balance of English and English Learner students. While I do not have a bilingual program (officially) at work in my classroom, students do receive much of their instruction during the day in both Spanish and English. I provide the students' instruction in fluent Spanish with the use of Spanish speaking parents or my Americorp assistant. Otherwise, I incorporate as much Spanish as I can speak during the day. I read books in Spanish and encourage the students to speak in whatever language that is most comfortable for them.

She goes on to explain:

> I work in a preschool classroom on an elementary school campus with a population of 90% Latino children. My personal goals are to further incorporate optimizing language input that is comprehensible, interesting, and of sufficient quantity, as well as providing opportunities for output, to use languages other than English (Spanish, in my case) 50 % to 90 % of the time, and to create a bilingual environment where development of the native language is encouraged. All children deserve to become bilingual and biliterate without the legislation prohibiting this fundamental right to a fair and adequate education.
>
> By implementing lessons based on a theme, I was able to facilitate content learning. I began with a preview in their native language, a continuation in the target language (English), and then a review in the primary language again. I provided opportunities for language development, interaction with print-rich materials such as books, dictation, children's drawings, maps. We practiced expressive language skills via open discussions.
>
> Culturally, many of the children live with other families in small, one-bedroom apartments; most of the apartments do not have a community swimming pool. When we discussed uses of water, I found that most of the children would describe the small, round plastic pools as their swimming pool. Also some of the children were able to describe trips to the beach. Some children described a small patio of plants and chairs, while others do have a front yard and a backyard. This was an awesome conversation for me and the children had a lot to say. I think that they all got the idea that the places that they live are all very similar and maybe they even connected with a sense of community.
>
> Through the means of my clean water theme, I focused on giving the three-year-olds as much instruction in Spanish as possible. My focus shifted from what I needed them to do (speak English), to trying to meet their needs of gaining a better foundation in their primary language.

Further reflecting on her own transformative action she said,

> I did take Spanish courses at the Community College and here at the university. I am just beginning to grasp the language, and even though I have a long way to go, I can effectively communicate with Spanish speakers. Not having those skills the first year I taught was difficult, and I was focused on my own learning of a second language. This gave me insight into what the children were experiencing, and I connected with them on that level.
>
> My future hopes on a large scale are to continue to try and learn Spanish by taking Spanish classes at the university, create bilingual and biliteracy activities, while strengthening my skills as an early childhood teacher. I know that I will continue to cultivate the ideologies of cross-cultural awareness among students, parents, and co-workers in my future work with bilingual children. Last but not least, I myself will defend the rights of all children and their right to an above standard education.

Another student teacher planned a book-making project with her preschoolers and their families. She explained:

> I wanted this to be a project that included children and their families so I asked children and parents to contribute a song, a poem, or a nursery rhyme that was special to their family in some way. I asked them

to try to think of something the parents had grown up with, a favorite tradition, or something they would like to share with their child.

She added:

> I wanted to do a project that promotes literacy and encourages multilingual language use among our families and children. I wanted to include parents, grandparents, aunts, uncles, and siblings so that I would receive contributions from many different languages and cultures. I wanted this to be a project that included children and their families, so I also asked that everyone who contributed do some kind of picture or art work with their child to put in the book.
>
> I received many different forms of literacy. I received songs that families sing but had never written down. I received poems that they had recited from childhood memories. I received poems and nursery rhymes that they picked out of books, and I received pictures the family members and children drew, interpreting their contributions.

Just a few of the examples of family contributions to the book are as follows:

> Seb's[1] mother brought in a counting song from her native country of Romania. Seb spends a lot of time with his grandparents and they sing this song to him quite frequently. His mother informed me that Seb loves the song, and I should ask him to sing it for me. I had no idea that Seb even spoke Romanian! During circle time, we shared the song with the other children raising their hands wanting to sing songs, most of course were in English, but we had one boy sing a song in Spanish and a girl who sang in Farsi.
>
> One little four-year-old boy who was with us in circle time went home and told his mom that he needed her to bring a song to me for the book, and it needed to be in Danish. So she translated a song for me and brought it in the next day with a picture that her son drew. She really didn't understand why she was bringing in the song, but her son was so adamant that she did as he requested. I was, of course, ecstatic. She later conveyed that the process of picking a song with Andy and trying to translate it into English was a lot of fun. Many of the words don't translate directly into English and they laughed and laughed over the translation.
>
> Luis and Julio's family is from Mexico. Luis attended our school when he was younger, and Julio is in our pre-k room. Both boys speak Spanish and English, and their parents are diligently working on their own English skills. The boys' mother explained to the boys what I wanted for my book, and both boys wanted to pick out songs for the book. They picked out songs from a book they had that contained both the Spanish and English translations of the songs. Luis and Julio drew pictures for me while their mother made dinner; their mother informs me that this has become a nightly ritual for them ever since. She makes dinner and both boys sit and draw pictures and discuss which ones we might use in the books. She also reports that when they read a story or poem that they particularly like, they want to bring it in and share it with me. When I showed the boys the book with their pictures included in it, I thought Julio was going to jump out of his skin, his face lit up and he squealed, "Looook Ms. J, it's meeee, it's my picture!"

The Fat Boy and Transformative Action

Finally, in our university class, as we were discussing transformative action, a student teacher reported a crisis in her preschool class. A four-year-old girl came running over to the student teacher. She was visibly upset, her face tense and fists clenched. "The fat boy took the truck from me!" Within seconds, the boy, dragging the truck, rushed over to where they were talking, and through his sobs, began trying to explain. The student teacher asked, "What happened?" (She reported being a little surprised that *he* was so upset because he did have the coveted truck.) The boy stammered, "She c..ca...called me... The Fat Boy!" The student teacher turned to the girl and asked, "Is that what you called him?" "Yes," she said. "Why?" "I don't know his name."

The student teacher focused on both children and asked, "What do you think we could do about this?" The girl immediately said, "Make a book." "Yes?" the teacher wasn't sure what she was planning. "Yes, we'll take pictures of everybody and put names on the pictures."

So, the girl and boy together set off with the class digital camera and took pictures of each child in the class. The teacher printed the photos and then the bookmakers asked each child to write her/his name under their picture. Then, after a trip to the processing shop to laminate the pages and bind the book, the class had a book so no one had to use derogatory names for children because they didn't know their real names.

Wouldn't it be nice if adults could learn from these young ones?

Note

1. Names have been changed to protect privacy.

References

Ada, Alma Flor, & Campoy, F. Isabel. (2003). *Authors in the classroom: A transformative education process.* New York: Allyn & Bacon.

Bruchac, J. (1998). *A boy called Slow: The true story of Sitting Bull.* New York: Scott Foresman.

Freire, P. (1973). *Education for critical consciousness.* New York: Seabury.

Grimm, J., & Grimm, W. (2004). *The annotated Brothers Grimm.* New York: W. W. Norton.

Kincheloe, J. (2000). Certifying the damage: Mainstream educational psychology and the oppression of children. In Soto, Lourdes D. (Ed.) *The politics of early childhood education*, pp. 75–84. New York: Peter Lang.

Levine, E. (1993). *If your name was changed at Ellis Island.* New York: Scholastic.

Lunge-Larsen, L. (1999). *The troll with no heart in his body and other tales of trolls from Norway.* Boston: Houghton Mifflin

Quintero, Elizabeth P. (in press). *Critical literacy in early childhood education: Artful story and the integrated curriculum* New York: Peter Lang.

Ringgold, F. (1995) *Aunt Harriet's underground railroad in the sky.* New York: Crown.

Ringgold, F. (1996). *Tar beach.* New York: Dragonfly Books.

Tingle, T. (2006). *Crossing Bok Chitto: A Choctaw tale of friendship and freedom.* El Paso, TX: Cinco Puntos Press.

Willis, A. (1995). Reading the world of school literacy: Contextualizing the experience of a young African American male. *Harvard Educational Review*, 65 (1), 30–49.

Wong Fillmore, L. (1991). Second language learning in children: A model of language learning in social context. In E. Bialystok (Ed.) *Language processing by bilingual children.* Cambridge: Cambridge University Press.

Young, E. (1989). *Lon Po Po.* New York: Philomel.

Section Four

Sexuality and Gender

Twelve

Creating Schools That Value Sexual Diversity

Elizabeth J. Meyer

Sexuality. It's a hot topic, sure to spark controversy in any school community. Most teachers and administrators avoid the issue at all costs. Many parents also tend to avoid the issue. This absence of adult support leaves many young people without guidance and accurate information about relationships, physical development, sexual health, and important aspects of their identities. It also creates a hostile school environment for students who do not conform to its heterosexual social hierarchies. There can be a wide variety of reasons for this non-conformity: clothes, hairstyle, body size, makeup and accessories (too much, not enough, the "wrong" kind), and extra-curricular interests. These behaviors are often connected to perceptions of a student's masculinity, femininity, or sexual orientation and often results in a student being excluded and/or targeted for bullying and harassment (California Safe Schools Coalition, 2004; Kosciw & Diaz, 2006; Meyer, 2006).

One of the most important things to remember when talking about sexuality is that everybody has one. Heterosexual, bisexual, gay, lesbian, queer, and asexual are some of the descriptors used for talking about sexuality and sexual diversity. Although some may argue that the absence of sexual attraction, or asexuality, is not a sexuality, there are advocacy groups and researchers who recognize it as a category of identity and orientation (see www.asexuality.org). A person's sexuality and associated sexual identity intersect and interact with other identities we may have, such as gender, ethnic, class, dis/ability, racial,[1] and linguistic. These various identities are important to all discussions and educational initiatives that address diversity.

This chapter will discuss important factors related to sexual diversity in schools. The first section will define sexual diversity and several related terms that are important for education professionals to understand. The second section will give a brief history of the stigma around sexualities in Western cultures and how this has been reflected in educational institutions. The third section will explore contemporary youth sexualities and some of the various identities embraced by youth today. The fourth section will provide an overview of some of the legal issues that are important to be aware of when talking about sexuality in schools. The last section will conclude with specific recommendations for teachers, counselors, and administrators on how to make their schools more inclusive and supportive of all forms of sexual diversity.

What Is "Sexual Diversity"?

Sexual diversity is a term that is used to refer to the wide variety of sexual identities and orientations that exist in modern society. It can also be used to describe the wide variety of sexual behaviors that humans choose to engage in, but that is not the focus of this chapter. Since this chapter is written for the current or future professional educator, it will focus on the everyday issues that are already present in schools. As many multicultural educators have argued, it can be unhealthy and alienating to ignore parts of our identities when we enter a school or a classroom (Delpit, 1993; Nieto, 1999; Paley, 1979). These identities, particularly in terms of gender and sexuality, are influenced by deeply embedded orientations. The distinctions between identity, orientation, and behavior are important to make, since most controversies surrounding school efforts to be more supportive of sexual diversity result from opponents' mistakenly believing that explicit details on sexual behavior will be taught and discussed. This is generally not true. With the exception of some officially approved sexuality education programs, most initiatives on sexual diversity specifically address issues related to identity and orientation—not sexual behavior. Topics such as respect, physical and emotional safety, friendships, family dynamics, and the harmful impact of inaccurate myths, stereotypes, and discriminatory attitudes and behaviors are the main focus. There are four important terms that must be carefully explained to help educators understand the various elements related to sexual diversity: sexuality, sexual orientation, sexual behavior, and sexual identity.

Sexuality is a term that has different meanings depending on the context in which it is used. As mentioned, every person has a sexuality, which is often used to describe a range of internal identities and external behaviors. Many individuals struggle with their sexuality during and after puberty. However, individuals who are pan-/omni-/bi- or homosexual may experience more stress and anxiety during this time as a result of the lack of adult role models and accessible information and support (Cass, 1979; Troiden, 1988). As a result, these students may be more aware of their sexualities. They may also experience social exclusion or discrimination as a result of the way their tendencies, predispositions, and desires (orientation) impact their sense of themselves (identity) and their interactions with others (behavior) (Blumenfeld, 1994; Savin-Williams, 1990). Each of these terms is explained in more detail.

Sexual orientation describes whom we are sexually attracted to and is generally determined at a very young age. The following are the four main categories of sexual orientation:

1. Asexuals—not sexually attracted to anyone
2. Pan-/omni-/bisexuals—attracted to some members of all/both sexes to varying degrees[2]
3. Heterosexuals—primarily attracted to some members of a different sex
4. Homosexuals—primarily attracted to some persons of the same sex

Scholars disagree on whether sexual orientation is determined by biology, including genes and hormones, or sociology, that is, mostly influenced by upbringing and environment. However, most researchers acknowledge that it is the result of an interaction of the two (Lipkin, 1999, pp. 25–28). Regardless of which factor exerts a larger force on one's sexual orientation, there is general agreement that sexual orientation is decided early in a child's life and cannot be changed. For example, one study found that gay, lesbian, and bisexual (GLB) youth report first becoming aware of their sexual orientation at age ten (D'Augelli & Hershberger, 1993); another reported that gay adolescents report becoming aware of a distinct feeling of "being different" between the ages of five and seven (Leo & Yoakum, 1992). Although some medical professionals and religious groups claim to be able to change a person's sexual orientation from homosexual to heterosexual, most professional organizations, including The American Academy of Pediatrics, The American Counseling Association, The American Psychiatric Association, The American Psychological Association, and The National Association of Social Workers do not endorse any type of counseling that is a form of "reparative therapy" (Frankfurt et al., 1999). Since there is widespread professional agreement that one's sexual orientation cannot be changed through counseling or religion, those who fear that the homosexual agenda in schools is to "recruit" or "convert" impressionable students may find some comfort in this information.

Sexual behavior is the term used to describe the types of sexual activities in which an individual actually engages. People may engage in a wide array of sexual behaviors, depending on what arouses them physically and emotionally. The sex of one's partner does not limit the types of sexual behaviors one can engage in. One can find as much diversity of sexual behaviors within a group of heterosexuals as among bisexuals and homosexuals. For example, in the late 1940s and early 1950s, Alfred Kinsey and his colleagues conducted a series of interviews with men and women about their sexual desires and behaviors. In this study, they found that the participants engaged in many types of sexual behaviors, regardless of the sex of their partners. He also noted that approximately 37 % of adult males and 19 % of adult females have had some same-sex erotic experience. In his report, he noted that this reported number was most likely artificially low due to reluctance of participants to report same-sex behaviors (Kinsey, Pomeroy, & Martin, 1948, p. 623; Kinsey, Pomeroy, Martin, & Gebhard, 1953, p. 453).

Sexual behavior is generally informed by one's sexual orientation but not always. Since behavior can be chosen, people may choose to engage in certain behaviors and not others. These can also be influenced by one's culture, social group, and romantic partners. It is not uncommon for people who feel attracted to members of the same sex to engage in heterosexual relationships to avoid the stigma and isolation from friends if they were to "come out" as gay or lesbian, nor is it uncommon for heterosexuals to engage in some same-sex behaviors. Orientation influences our behavior, it does not dictate it. However, when orientation and behavior are in conflict, it is difficult for an individual to develop a cohesive sexual identity, and a healthy sense of self (Cass, 1984; Troiden, 1988).

Sexual identity is how a person chooses to describe him or herself. One's identity can be formed around many aspects of self, including race, culture, religion, language, family, career, and physical or mental dis/ability. The identity-formation process can be long and complex, and many theories exist that use stage-models to describe this process for individuals in Western cultures, including the works of Sigmund Freud, Erik Erikson, and Jean Piaget. More recently, scholars have developed theories of identity development that seek to explain the shared experiences of youth who identify as gay, lesbian, queer, or same-sex attracted (Cass, 1979, 1984; Dube & Savin-Williams, 1999; Kumashiro, 2001; Troiden, 1988). Although these theories explain some of the commonalities individuals may experience, it is important to acknowledge that this process is shaped and influenced by factors such as friends, school, class, race, ethnicity, religion, and gender identity and expression (Rowen & Malcolm, 2002; Waldner-Haugrud & Magruder, 1996). Some of the more widely recognized sexual identities embraced by contemporary youth are discussed at greater length later in this chapter.

Unlearning the Stigmas Attached to Sexual Diversity

Historically, Western cultures have constructed homosexuality as an illness, a deviance, and a sin. This negative bias was created through psychological research, religious ideologies, and the political and financial privileging of heterosexual, monogamous family structures by the state through marriage; this bias has been disrupted and challenged by gay rights activists in movements that gained momentum in the 1960s and 1970s. Many authors have examined the social, historical, and political forces that have worked together to construct the idea of the homosexual and then demonize it (Bem, 1993; Foucault, 1980; Jagose, 1996; Sears, 1998; Weeks, 1985).

Heterosexism, compulsory heterosexuality (Rich, 1978/1993), the heterosexual matrix (Butler, 1990), and gender polarization (Bem, 1993) are all different terms that seek to explain the social construction of opposite-sex attraction and sexual behavior as dominant and "normal." The concept of homosexuality, and subsequently heterosexuality, is just over a century old (Jagose, 1996, p. 17). The resulting prejudice against those who deviate from the heterosexual social script has been carefully developed by institutional heterosexism through organized religion, medicine, sexology, psychiatry, and psychology (Bem, 1993, p. 81). Sandra Bem explains how the cultural lens of *gender polarization* works to reinforce heterosexuality by serving two major functions.

> First, it defines mutually exclusive scripts for being male and female. Second, it defines any person or *behavior* that deviates from these scripts as problematic. . . taken together, the effect of these two processes is to construct and naturalize a gender-polarizing link between the sex of one's body and the character of one's psyche and one's sexuality. (81)

These powerful social discourses are generated through various institutions, including schools.

Educational structures wield extraordinary ideological power because of their role in teaching what the culture deems important and valuable to future generations. Ministries of Education, textbook publishers, and teachers determine what lessons are passed on to students and whose knowledge or "truth" is valued (Apple, 1990, 2000). Subsequently, schools are important sites that contribute to the normalization of heterosexual behavior. In Richard Friend's article, "Choices Not Closets," he exposes two processes through which such lessons are passed on in schools: systematic inclusion and systematic exclusion. Systematic inclusion is the way in which negative or false information about homosexuality is introduced into schools as a pathology or deviant behavior. Systematic exclusion is "the process whereby positive role models, messages, and images about lesbian, gay and bisexual people are publicly silenced in schools" (Friend, 1993, p. 215). Ironically, schools make efforts to de-sexualize the experience of students while they simultaneously and subtly, yet clearly, affirm heterosexual behaviors and punish those who appear to deviate from them. Epstein and Johnson explain,

> Schools go to great lengths to forbid expressions of sexuality by both children and teachers. This can be seen in a range of rules, particularly those about self-presentation. On the other hand, and perhaps in consequence, expressions of sexuality provide a major currency and resource in the everyday exchanges of school life. Second, the forms in which sexuality is present in schools and the terms on which sexual identities are produced are heavily determined by power relations between teachers and taught, the dynamics of control and resistance. (1998, p. 108)

These acts of surveillance are rooted in Foucault's (1975) concept of the panopticon—an all-seeing, yet completely invisible, source of power and control. This type of surveillance and control is particularly effective, because we all unknowingly contribute to it, unless we actively work to make it visible by questioning and challenging it. This is one of the most powerful ways that schools reinforce heterosexism. Through the surveillance and policing of bodies and language, school structures mandate hyper-heterosexuality using the curriculum and extra-curricular activities.

The heterosexism of the curriculum is invisible to many due to its unquestioned dominance in schools and communities. Some examples include the exclusive study of heterosexual romantic literature, the presentation of the 'nuclear' heterosexual two-parent family as the norm and ideal, and the teaching of only the reproductive aspects of sex or abstinence-only sex education. Other forms of relationships and the concept of desire, or *eros,* are completely omitted from the official curriculum (Britzman, 2000; Fine, 1993; Pinar, 1998). Extra-curricular functions that also teach this compulsory heterosexuality include Valentine's Day gift exchanges, kissing booths at school fairs, and prom rituals that include highly gendered formal attire (tuxedos and gowns) and the election of a "king" and a "queen." This prom ritual has begun to be subverted by alternative proms often organized by gay-straight alliances or community youth groups. At these events, there may be two kings (a male king and female "drag king"), and two queens (a female queen and a male "drag queen").

Art Lipkin's (1999) groundbreaking work, *Understanding Homosexuality, Changing Schools,* provides in-depth accounts of the discrimination experienced by gay, lesbian, and bisexual educators, as well as the painful and enduring stories of students who were emotionally and physically harassed for their perceived or actual non-heterosexual, non-gender conforming performance of identity. In other words, schools are not safe for "guys who aren't as masculine as other guys" or "girls who aren't as feminine as other girls" (California Safe Schools Coalition, 2004). Although the people in control of the school do not directly harass and inflict harm on the non-conforming students (in most cases), it is their lack of effective intervention in cases of homophobic and sexual harassment (California Safe Schools Coalition, 2004; Harris Interactive, 2001; Kosciw & Diaz, 2006; NMHA, 2002) that, along with the invisible scripts that are reinforced by the school through surveillance and discipline, sends the message that these identities are not valued or welcomed.

Heterosexism and its more overt partner, homophobia, are clearly linked to cultural gender boundaries and are informed by sexism and misogyny (Francis & Skelton, 2001; Friend, 1993; Meyer, 2006; Mills, 2004). Misogyny is the hatred or devaluing of all that is female or 'feminine.' For example, the most effective challenge to any boy's masculinity is to call him 'gay,' 'homo,' 'fag,' or 'queer' (Epstein & Johnson, 1998; Mac an Ghaill, 1995; Martino & Pal-lotta-Chiarolli, 2003). What is being challenged is his masculinity—his gender code—but it is being done by accusing him of being gay, which is equated with being 'feminine.' Girls are subject to similar kinds of policing (Brown, 2003; Duncan, 2004), but research shows that it is much more prevalent among male students (Harris Interactive, 2001; California Safe Schools Coalition, 2004). The harmful harassment and violence that result from the policing of hetero-sexual masculinity and femininity is why some activists and educators are pushing for a de-construction of gender codes and de-labeling of sexual orientations. As long as we continue to live within the narrow boundaries of language and behavior, the hierarchical binaries of male-female and straight-gay remain unchallenged. This work of dismantling socially invented categories is necessary to create educational spaces that liberate and create opportunities, as opposed to limiting and closing down the diversity of human experiences. We must move towards understanding identities and experiences as falling on a continuum of gender expres-sions and sexual orientations. Fortunately, many youth are leading the way in exploring diverse sexual identities that break away from the traditional binary of gay and straight and the notion that one's identity is permanent and fixed.

Understanding Diverse Sexual Identities

In conversations about sexual diversity, the realities and experiences of heterosexual-identi-fied, or straight, individuals are often ignored. This is a common error in diversity work where the focus is on the marginalized 'other' rather than on understanding the perspective and ex-periences of those in the dominant group. It is important to discuss heterosexuality, especially in terms of heterosexual privilege and how it works to make some people's relationships and experiences more valued than others. One valuable pedagogical tool available to help students explore heterosexual privilege is, "The Heterosexual Questionnaire." This activity was created by Martin Rochlin, Ph.D., in 1977 and has been adapted for use in anti-homophobia training around the world. Sample questions from this activity include the following:

1. What do you think caused your heterosexuality?
2. When and how did you first decide you were heterosexual?
3. Is it possible that your heterosexuality is just a phase you may grow out of?
4. If heterosexuality is normal, why are so many mental patients heterosexual?
5. The great majority of child molesters are heterosexual males. Do you consider it safe to expose your children to heterosexual teachers?
6. Would you want your children to be heterosexual, knowing the problems they would face, such as heartbreak, disease, and divorce? (Advocates for Youth, 2005)

These questions are intended to stimulate the reader to reflect on social assumptions about heterosexuality and the related stereotypes and stigmas attached to homosexuality. Although there can be controversy if this tool is not used in the proper context or if the conversations are not well facilitated (Rasmussen, Mitchell, & Harwood, 2007), it often leads to a greater awareness on the part of heterosexuals with regards to how heterosexism and heterosexual privilege function.

The terms 'gay' and 'lesbian' are preferred when speaking about people who identify as homosexual. Although the term 'homosexual' is widely used in the medical and psychological professional communities, it has a very specific history and meaning. When using the term homosexual, these professional organizations generally refer to individuals who engage exclusively in same-sex sexual behaviors. This does not necessarily mean that these individuals choose to *identify* as gay or lesbian. The term 'gay' came into wider use to describe men who engage in homosexual relationships during the gay liberation movement that erupted after the famous police raid at The Stonewall Inn on June 27, 1969, in New York City (Jagose, 1996). Although the word 'gay' can also be used to describe women, many women prefer the term 'lesbian.' This word also has a political history attached to the women's liberation movement of the 1960s and 70s, and is often associated with the concept of lesbian-feminists. Some of these activists considered themselves separatists and chose to live and work independently from men (Jagose, 1996). It is no mistake that these terms both gained wider use during this era of important political changes. The concept of identity politics asserted that "coming out" and publicly identifying as gay or lesbian was an important step towards achieving public visibility, reducing negative stereotypes, and securing greater social equality (Weeks, 1985). Because of the historical specificity and cultural stereotypes that have grown up around these terms, many individuals who engage in same-sex behaviors and relationships may choose to use different words to identify themselves.

For people who do not identify as heterosexual, the terms gay and lesbian are not the only ones they may identify with. Many adolescents and young adults prefer terms such as: bi-curious, fluid, hetero- or homo-flexible, open, omni- or pan-sexual, polyamorous, questioning, or queer (Driver, 2007, pp. 42–43; Meyer, 2008). Although the meaning of "queer" changed over the years from "odd or strange" to an insult for gays and lesbians, it is now being reclaimed as a powerful political term by some members of the gay, lesbian, bisexual, and transgender community (Jagose, 1996; Meyer, 2007a). Although there is much debate over the use and meaning of the term "queer" within the LGBTQ community, when used as a source of pride and with a sense of inclusivity, "queer" can be a very empowering term. Some also argue that queer is an exclusively white identifier, whereas Ian Barnard, in his book *Queer Race*, explains that "queer theory already has a racial politics," and that "particular racializations are and can be queer,. . . [and] queerness can be racialized" (Barnard, 2004, pp. 6, 18). As Driver explains in her book *Queer Girls and Popular Culture*, "queer as a strategically chosen term works against the foreclosure of desires and the imposition of controlling assumptions; it is deployed by girls as a way of enabling possibilities rather than guaranteeing identity or knowledge about identity" (Driver, 2007, p. 43). Even with this postmodern re-appropriation of 'queer,' if it is used to insult and exclude, it still has the power to deeply wound. Even with all these emerging identities, there are many individuals who reject static labels, choosing not to identify their sexuality in any way. This demonstrates a move away from the identity politics of the gay and lesbian rights movement and the tendency for young people to create new identities and communities that more authentically represent their experiences.

The identity categories transgender, transsexual, and two-spirit are often included in conversations of sexual diversity. This is usually because the trans- and two-spirit communities have been active contributors to equality projects taken on by the gay, lesbian, and bisexual community. In the acronym GLBT, the "T" may represent one, two, or all three of these groups. I have chosen to include them here to clarify the links these communities have to the topic of sexual diversity. It is important to understand that transgender, two-spirit, and transsexual people have strong ties to the gay, lesbian, and bisexual community because of shared experiences, discrimination, and exclusion from mainstream culture that are connected to their public challenging of traditional sex and gender role expectations of dress and behavior. However, their experiences are not tied directly to their sexual orientation; rather, they are connected to their gender identity and expression. There is not sufficient room in this chapter to explore these concepts fully, but I have included a brief definition of each of these terms below.

The word transgender entered the English language in the 1980s from the transsexual and transvestite communities (Cromwell, 1997, p. 134) to describe individuals whose gender identity is different from the sex that they were assigned at birth. There are many myths and misconceptions about transgender individuals, and there are as many masculinities and femininities (gender expressions) within the transgender community as there are in non-trans men and women. Some transgender people strongly embrace traditional notions of gender and proudly live as highly feminine or highly masculine people. Other transgender people choose to challenge and disrupt the categories of masculinity and femininity, embracing varying degrees of each (Bornstein, 1998; Feinberg, 1998; Wilchins, 2004). The word transgender is often used as an umbrella term to describe a wide variety of people who challenge traditional notions of sex and gender, including transsexuals, two-spirited people, cross-dressers, and individuals who identify as genderqueer (Nestle, Howell, & Wilchins, 2002).

Transsexuals are individuals who were born as genetic females (XX) or genetic males (XY) and developed the associated physical traits of their genetic sex. However, transsexual people have a gender identity, or an internal sense of themselves, that does not align with their physical characteristics. This conflict between physical and psychological traits has been termed gender dysphoria by the medical profession. Transsexuals are usually assigned the clinical label "gender identity disorder" (GID) from the Diagnostic and Statistical Manual of Mental Disorders (DSM IV) of the American Psychiatric Association, although activists have been trying to get this condition removed from the DSM. As the lead character in the film *Transamerica* so eloquently argued, "If it can be fixed with plastic surgery, is it really a mental disorder?" (Tucker, 2005). Transsexual men and women choose to undergo a series of medical treatments to realign their physical characteristics with their internal identity. These treatments generally include hormone injections and surgery (GIRES, 2006b, p. 29). According to some research, only 23 % of children who experience tension between their assigned sex at birth (and thus, their gender of rearing), and their own gender identity, are transsexuals who choose to undergo physical transformations (GIRES, 2006a). Some won't have surgery and hormone treatments because of the expense and challenge in securing approval, and others may not because they are uncomfortable with the risks and limitations of surgery, and still others are happy with their bodies as they are.

Two-spirit or two-spirited are terms used to describe people who are alternatively gendered and are members of Native American (also known as Amerindian, First Nations, Inuit, and Métis) communities. It replaces the earlier term, "berdache," used by anthropologists who studied these cultures (Lang, 1997, p. 100). Early anthropologists often misunderstood the spiritual element of the two-spirited individual and described it as a form of institutionalized male homosexuality. As more recent authors have pointed out, becoming a "berdache" was related more to occupational preferences and social roles than to sexual behavior (p. 101). The term two-spirit is an attempt to create an English-language term to describe a cultural concept of gender that is different from, but refers to, the male/female Western binary. Although the concept of two-spirit emerges from many traditional aboriginal cultures, these communities have been subject to Western colonizing influences and now share many of the heterosexist and homophobic beliefs created by Western European ideologies.

All of these identity categories are complicated and formed over an individual's lifetime. Although some people argue that it is inappropriate to discuss sexuality with younger children, their lives are also impacted by sexual diversity. In addition to their own developing sense of themselves, they are shaped by the lives of the adults around them. Many educators who work in early childhood and elementary education believe that discussions of sexual diversity have no place in their schools. However, most families in Western cultures are based on relationships created out of romantic love, thus children's home lives and family structures tend to reflect the sexualities of their parents and caregivers. Recent studies on the experiences of children of gay and lesbian parents indicate that they experience increased harassment at school, and their parents were often excluded from school life (Kosciw & Diaz, 2008; Ray & Gregory, 2001). For these reasons it is important for educators to address diverse family structures and to include sexual diversity when addressing diversity issues with students of all ages. *It's Elementary: Talking About Gay Issues in School* is an excellent film that provides models of how to do this appropriately and effectively with younger students (Chasnoff, 1996). In addition to developing a better understanding of sexual diversity and how it impacts individual lives, it is important for educators to be aware of the various legal issues involved that relate to the topic of sexual diversity in schools.

Sexual Diversity and the Law

U.S.A. There are currently no federal protections that explicitly protect gay, lesbian, and bisexual (glb) people from discrimination in the United States. However, sexual minorities are entitled to the same protection as any other identifiable group. Consequently, a variety of courts across the country have begun holding school districts accountable for violating the rights of students who are being harassed or who have requested the right to form extra-curricular groups that address their needs and interests. The main existing legal protections that are relevant in these cases include: Equal Protection, Title IX, state non-discrimination laws, and The Equal Access Act.

The Equal Protection Clause of the Fourteenth Amendment guarantees equal application of a law to all people in the United States (Macgillivray, 2007). An equal protection claim requires the student to show that school officials (1) did not fairly and consistently apply policies when dealing with the student, (2) were deliberately indifferent to the student's complaints, or (3) that the student was treated in a manner that is clearly unreasonable. The first example of this argument being successfully applied to a case of homophobic harassment in schools was in the case *Nabozny v. Podlesny* in Wisconsin. In this case, Jamie Nabozny was subjected to violent and persistent anti-gay harassment over several years in his school. As a result of this harassment, he had been hospitalized, dropped out of school, and attempted suicide (Lipkin, 1999). The federal appeals court for that region of the United States, the Seventh Circuit, decided in favor of the student. In their decision, the judges wrote that ". . .we are unable to garner any rational basis for permitting one student to assault another based on the victim's sexual orientation. . ." and the school district settled with Nabozny for $900,000 (Bochenek & Brown, 2001). More recently in a case in California, *Flores v. Morgan Hill* (2003), the court found sufficient evidence of deliberate indifference to the ongoing sexual orientation harassment of six students in this California School District, which resulted in a $1,100,000 settlement with the students (ACLU, 2004), and the requirement that the school district implement a training and education program for its administrators, faculty, and students (Dignan, 2004).

Title IX is another federal protection that exists to address issues of homophobic harassment in schools. It provides statutory protection for student-on-student sexual harassment under the following conditions: (1) school personnel have actual knowledge of the harassment, (2) school officials demonstrate deliberate indifference or take actions that are clearly unreasonable, and (3) the harassment is so severe, pervasive, and objectively offensive that it can be said to deprive the victim(s) of access to the educational opportunities or benefits provided by the school (*Davis v. Monroe*, 1999). Several cases have successfully made the argument that Title IX protects students from peer sexual orientation harassment. For example, a California Federal District Court concluded,

> the Court finds no material difference between the instance in which a female student is subject to unwelcome sexual comments and advances due to her harasser's perception that she is a sex object, and the instance in which a male student is insulted and abused due to his harasser's perception that he is a homosexual, and therefore a subject of prey. In both instances, the conduct is a heinous response to the harasser's perception of the victim's sexuality, and is not distinguishable to this court. (*Ray v. Antioch Unified School District*, 2006)

In 2000, two important cases were decided that applied Title IX to incidences of homophobic harassment: *Ray v. Antioch Unified School District* (2000), and *Montgomery v. Independent School District* (2000). In both of these cases, separate courts decided that schools could be held liable under Title IX for acting with "deliberate indifference" towards students who have reported persistent and severe homophobic harassment at school. These decisions established important precedents for the cases that followed.

A few years later, a Kansas federal district court considered that the gender stereotyping and related anti-gay harassment of a student who did not identify as gay was actionable under Title IX (*Theno v. Tonganoxie*, 2005). The court wrote that "the plaintiff was harassed because he failed to satisfy his peers' stereotyped expectations for his gender because the primary objective of plaintiff's harassers appears to have been to disparage his perceived lack of masculinity." Therefore, they concluded that the harassment of Dylan Theno was so "severe, pervasive, and objectively offensive that it effectively denied (him) an education in the Tonganoxie school district" (*Theno v. Tonganoxie*, 2005*)*. The district settled with Dylan for a total of $440,000 (Trowbridge, 2005).

One case had a very different outcome. In *Doe v. Bellefonte Area School District* (2004), the court decided for the school district. It determined that campus administrators took Doe's complaints seriously, instituted a series of steps in response to complaints, and escalated punishment when necessary. Therefore, the district was not deliberately indifferent to the harassment of Doe. In addition to federal protections that exist, some states have non-discrimination laws that can offer students some relief.

State non-discrimination laws that protect individuals based on sexual orientation, and/or gender identity, only exist in twenty states and the District of Columbia[3] (National Gay and Lesbian Task Force, 2007). However, according to a study published in 2006, only nine states (California, Connecticut, Maine, Massachusetts, Minnesota, New Jersey, Vermont, Washington, and Wisconsin) and the District of Columbia have statutes specifically protecting students in schools from discrimination on the basis of sexual orientation and/or gender identity (Kosciw & Diaz, 2006). Students in these states experienced significantly lower rates of verbal harassment than their peers. Since this report, several states (including Nebraska, Iowa, Kentucky, and Wyoming) legislatures have at least considered bills either expanding or limiting the rights of sexual-minority students (Buchanan, 2006). There are also seven states that have legislation that prohibit the positive portrayal of homosexuality (Alabama, Arizona, Mississippi, Oklahoma, South Carolina, Texas, and Utah), and students in these states reported being verbally harassed at a higher frequency than students from states without such legislation (47.6% versus 37.2%) (Kosciw & Diaz, 2006, p. 86).

A recent case in New Jersey extended the protections offered by state anti-discrimination laws to cover students in schools. As a result of the case brought by a student who had suffered persistent homophobic harassment, *L.W. v. Toms River Regional Schools Board of Education* (2007), the New Jersey Supreme Court decided that schools may be held liable under the Law Against Discrimination for permitting student-on-student bias-based harassment (American Civil Liberties Union-New Jersey, 2007). This decision established state-wide protections for students in New Jersey.

The Equal Access Act (EAA) is another legal protection that is being used successfully to advance education around sexual diversity in schools through extra-curricular diversity clubs. Peer support groups, commonly known as gay-straight alliances (GSAs), have become increasingly common in schools (Cloud, 2005; Fischer & Kosciw, 2006). Very little research is available on the efficacy of GSAs, but Fischer and Kosciw (2006) found that the presence of a GSA directly predicted greater school belonging, and indirectly predicted greater academic achievement for sexual-minority youth. Also Szlacha (2003) found in her evaluation of the Massachusetts Safe Schools Program that the presence of a GSA is the aspect "most strongly associated with positive sexual diversity climates" (73). This finding makes intuitive sense when considering the importance of supportive heterosexual peers to a positive experience for sexual-minority youth. However, GSAs are not always met with open-mindedness from students, teachers, administrators, parents, community members, and school boards. Since the late 1990s, there have been several cases of schools trying to exclude these groups from meeting on schools grounds. Courts have consistently found that school districts have violated the EAA when banning GSA groups from meeting. *Straights and Gays for Equity v. Osseo Area Schools* (2006) and *White County High School Peers in Diverse Education v. White County School District* (2006) serve as two recent examples. Due to the time and courage put forth by the students who work to initiate these GSAs, there are now over 3,000 such groups in schools, and at least one in every state in the United States (Macgillivray, 2007). Whereas students in the United States have had to search for various forms of protection against discrimination based on sexual orientation, Canada has clearly worded provincial and federal human rights codes that offer such protections.

CANADA The current progressive political climate in Canada was achieved through a long and slow process of legislative reform that culminated in the adoption of the *Canadian Charter of Rights and Freedoms*. This important document was entrenched into the Canadian constitution by the Constitution Act in 1982 (Watkinson, 1999, p. 22). As part of the supreme law of Canada, this document superseded all existing laws, and for the first time the rights of all persons to be treated equally were given constitutional status. Although public education is governed by provincial statutes, all publicly funded institutions must abide by the spirit and letter of the *Charter* (Watkinson, 1999). This new constitution guaranteed protections for many historically marginalized groups. Sexual orientation, however, was not initially included as a protected class for equality rights under section 15 of the *Canadian Charter of Rights and Freedoms*. The original language of this section reads as follows:

> Every individual is equal before and under the law and has the right to the equal protection and equal benefit of the law without discrimination and, in particular, without discrimination based on race, national or ethnic origin, colour, religion, sex, age or mental or physical disability. (*Canadian Charter of Rights and Freedoms (s. 15)*, 1982)

Although the federal government wasn't willing to explicitly include the phrase, "sexual orientation" in the *Charter,* other provinces had already established human rights codes that included this language. In 1977, the Province of Quebec led the way in the equality movement for sexual minorities by adding "sexual orientation" to its *Charter of Human Rights and Freedoms*. Ontario followed suit nine years later. These were the first legal protections that clearly included sexual orientation as a protected class (Hurley, 2005). Although equality rights supported by the *Charter* were enforced starting in 1985, sexual minorities were not recognized as a protected class until thirteen years later, following a unanimous decision of the Supreme Court of Canada in the landmark case of *Egan v. Canada* (1995). Although this case was not about discrimination in schools, it addressed the issue of access to public services. The ruling provided that discrimination based on sexual orientation was prohibited by s. 15 of the *Charter,* and the justices observed: "*Sexual orientation is a deeply personal characteristic that is either unchangeable or changeable only at unacceptable personal costs, and so falls within the ambit of s. 15 protection as being analogous to the enumerated grounds*" (*Egan v. Canada, 1995, para. 5*).

This case established the precedent to include sexual orientation as a protected class and had "sexual orientation" read into the *Charter*. Every Canadian was guaranteed equal protection from discrimination based on sexual orientation. Although some provinces were slow to add the term "sexual orientation" to their individual human rights codes, this protection was federally guaranteed as a result of this important ruling.

Since the Supreme Court's 1995 decision in *Egan v. Canada,* various cases have tested the interpretation and application of the equality rights extended in that case. In the first case in an educational institution after Egan was decided (*Vriend v. Alberta*, 1998), a university employee was fired from his position as a lab coordinator, solely because of his homosexuality. He initially brought forward a human rights complaint; however, it was dismissed because the province of Alberta did not have sexual orientation listed as a protected class in its human rights legislation. In this case, the Supreme Court stated that not protecting individuals from discrimination based on sexual orientation was an "unjustified violation of s. 15 of the *Canadian Charter of Rights and Freedoms*," and ordered that the words "sexual orientation" be read into provincial human rights codes as a prohibited ground of discrimination (*Vriend v. Alberta*, 1998, p. 2).

The next test came in May 2001 when the Supreme Court of Canada heard a case from Trinity Western University (TWU), a private, religious institution filed against the British Columbia College of Teachers (BCCT). In this instance, the B.C. professional teachers' organization had responded to a request from TWU to be fully responsible for its teacher training program, which it shared with Simon Fraser University. Trinity Western University wanted more autonomy in the program in order to reflect its Christian worldview. The BCCT chose not to accredit this institution because it believed the institution was discriminating on the basis of sexual orientation in its demands on its students. Trinity Western University required its students to sign a statement that asserted they would "refrain from practices that are biblically condemned," including homosexuality *(Trinity Western University v. British Columbia College of Teachers,* 2001, para. 4)

In its decision, the British Columbia Supreme Court found in favor of TWU, stating that teachers could hold "sexist, racist or homophobic beliefs" (para. 36). However, the Court also made the following distinction:

> Acting on those beliefs, however, is a very different matter. If a teacher in the public school system engages in discriminatory conduct, that teacher can be subject to disciplinary proceedings. Discriminatory conduct by a public school teacher when on duty should always be subject to disciplinary proceedings [and] disciplinary measures can still be taken when discriminatory off-duty conduct poisons the school environment. (*Trinity Western University v. British Columbia College of Teachers,* 2001, at para. 37)

Although this majority opinion sided with TWU and allowed them to continue mandating anti-gay beliefs in their future teachers, the judges made the important distinction between discriminatory behaviors and beliefs, which is common in cases regarding religious freedom. The decision clearly states that teachers may not discriminate overtly against their students but does not address the issue of the subtle and persistent homophobic behaviors that homophobic attitudes engender and the impact they have on a classroom or school community.

This position was reinforced in the case of a teacher who was suspended for making public statements that were understood as anti-gay in nature. In February 2004, a B.C. teacher, Chris Kempling, was suspended for one month for "conduct unbecoming" a teacher because he had published articles that were considered to be defaming of homosexuals in a local newspaper (*Kempling v. British Columbia College of Teachers,* 2004, para.1). The Christian teacher appealed this decision to the B.C. Supreme Court, but the court held that the BCCT was within its jurisdiction to suspend him. The court's rationale for its decision was based on the "wrongful public linking of his professional position to the off-duty expression of personally held discriminatory views in order to lend credibility to those views" (*Kempling v. British Columbia College of Teachers,* 2004, para. 2). These cases have established a clear responsibility on the part of schools in Canada to create learning environments that are free from discrimination. The final case discussed here demonstrates what happened when a school failed to provide such an environment.

Azmi Jubran, a student in Vancouver, was repeatedly called 'gay,' 'faggot,' and 'homo' by his peers in secondary school. In addition to these verbal taunts, he was spit upon, shoved in class and the hallways, and even had his shirt burned. Jubran and his parents made repeated complaints to the school, and, after receiving no satisfactory response, they filed a human rights complaint in November 1996. In April 2002, the Human Rights Tribunal of British Columbia found that the school board in Vancouver had contravened the *Human Rights Code*, "by failing to provide a learning environment free of discriminatory harassment" (*School District No. 44 v. Jubran*, 2005, para. 2). This was an important decision because it affirmed the school's responsibility to protect students from discriminatory behavior and to respond effectively and consistently to incidents of homophobic harassment. After a series of appeals, the fate of this case was decided on October 20, 2005, when the Supreme Court refused to hear a final appeal, and effectively upheld the lower court's decision. This was an important decision. The court acknowledged that the school had made some effort to discipline the students who had targeted Jubran individually but said that it had not done enough. The court stated that the school needed to have communicated its code of conduct to students and provided teachers with resources and training on how to deal with homophobia (CLE Staff, 2005; Meyer, 2007b). This case sent a clear message to educators that they must mobilize multiple resources and be proactive when addressing issues of school climate and student safety that relate directly to human rights protections.

As the above listed cases demonstrate, there are legal precedents that exist to protect students from discriminatory behavior in schools. However, many school boards and educators are ignorant of their legal responsibilities and fail to effectively implement policies, programs, and curricular materials that support full inclusion of sexual diversity in school communities.

Creating Schools That Value Sexual Diversity

While overt acts of discrimination are difficult for schools to ignore, daily acts of covert discrimination persist and impact students' lives in ways that many teachers and administrators fail to acknowledge. When bias against an identifiable social group is present throughout an institution, the entire school is implicated, and the culture must shift. In order to transform ignorance of, and intolerance for, forms of sexual diversity, all stakeholders in the community must be involved in the process: students, families, teachers, administrators, and school board personnel. The tone must be set by the leadership, but everyone must be engaged in changing the culture of the institution. In order to better identify what steps can be taken at each level, recommendations are provided for the following: administrators and school boards, teachers and support staff, students, parents, and community members.

ADMINISTRATORS AND SCHOOL BOARDS At the school leadership level, important changes must be made in three areas to set the tone for a positive and supportive school environment. These are policy, education, and resources and support. Without the institutional support provided by the following examples, the isolated efforts of overworked teachers, frustrated parents, and targeted young people will only have a small, short-term impact on the experiences of the students in the school community. In order to have a larger, more lasting effect on the school culture, systemic changes must be made.

Policy: When drafting policies that address issues of bullying and harassment in schools, a whole-school policy that includes clear, definite guidelines on actions against bullying, including response protocols and implementation strategies, is essential (Arora, 1994; Cartwright, 1995; Sharp & Smith, 1991; Whitney & Smith, 1993). Language must also be clear, consistent, and include specific protections against harassment, violence, and discrimination based on sexual orientation and gender identity or expression (Goldstein, Collins, & Halder, 2005).

Education: A policy will not be effective unless those expected to enforce it are made aware of their obligations and community members are informed of the changes. Examples of such efforts include discussing the new policy in staff meetings; inviting a law expert to present a workshop on the definitions of harassment and the school's duty to prevent it; creating study circles with the staff to examine the new policy and discuss implementation strategies; publishing information in school newsletters; and distributing brochures, including information about the new policy.

Resources and support: The school district needs to allocate resources: time, money, and materials to ensure that these shifts in school climate can occur. Instead of hiring a one-time speaker, some school boards have created full-time positions in order to ensure that the expertise and knowledge will be readily available to support the efforts being made in individual schools. In the state of Massachusetts (Perrotti & Westheimer, 2001) and on the Toronto District School Board, several positions were created that were integral to the success of their programs, such as human-sexuality program workers, equity-department instructional leaders, and student-program workers (Goldstein et al., 2005). The institutional support offered by these various initiatives gives credibility and value to the daily efforts of individuals on the front line.

TEACHERS AND SUPPORT STAFF Teachers and support staff, such as bus drivers, cafeteria personnel, and lunchroom monitors, have the greatest opportunity to observe and intervene in incidents of discrimination and harassment in schools. Teachers and support staff can focus development in the following areas: understanding of school policies, sharing and practicing intervention tools for incidents of discrimination and harassment, and finding and using appropriate curricular materials and programs that are inclusive of sexual diversity. These expectations mean that teachers and support staff will need to attend workshops and courses, and take some responsibility for their own professional development, in addition to participating in the educational opportunities provided by the school administration. There are many resources available for these pursuits, some of which are listed in the reference list at the end of this chapter. Examples of curricular interventions that can address some of the underlying issues of homophobia and heterosexism include the following:

1. A campaign against name-calling that includes education about what words mean, and why certain insults are inappropriate and discriminatory.
2. Curricular inclusion of contributions by gays, lesbians, bisexuals, and transgendered people to history, art, science, literature, politics, and sports.
3. Providing inclusive and diverse information about sex, gender, and sexual orientation in biology, health, and sexual education classes.
4. Conducting critical media literacy activities that analyze gender stereotypes and heterosexism in popular culture.

Although teachers and support staff have a significant impact on the school climate, without the participation of the student body, a true shift in culture and behavior cannot take place.

STUDENTS Students make up the largest percentage of a school community and are the trend-setters for what is valued in school. Without the support and investment of student leaders, there will continue to be student-only spaces where incidents of discrimination and harassment take place, such as locker areas, washrooms, and areas on playgrounds and athletics fields. Schools that successfully engage student leaders, such as athletics team captains, student council members, peer mediators and others, can have a much broader and deeper impact on the lives of all students in school. Ways that this can be done include conducting summer leadership retreats, student discussion groups, or weekend workshops that educate students about sexual diversity, and solicit their help and support in challenging homophobia, heterosexism, and other forms of bias in the school. In addition to engaging prominent students in the school population, all students should be informed of the school's policies on harassment and discrimination by posting a code of conduct in each classroom, having students sign a behavior contract, and/or by having home-room discussions about the policy, what it means, and how it might affect them.

FAMILIES AND COMMUNITY MEMBERS Finally, no school community is complete without the input and influence of families and community members. The parents' association and other community groups should be invited and encouraged to become actively involved in developing the school policy and educational strategies. By developing these partnerships early on, schools can anticipate any resistance or potential backlash, and work through these issues before they grow into negative publicity for the school. To be a supportive and inclusive school, it is important to reach out to same-sex parented families to let them know that their input and involvement is welcomed. Gay and lesbian parents may stay closeted or separate from the school community if they are not given any positive indicators that their family is valued and will be included in that community. Most families are deeply invested in the education and development of their children and therefore should be included in such initiatives. Although there may be some resistance to addressing sexual diversity, schools can create a lasting network that will potentially expand their efforts to reduce such bias in the community at large by building strong ties with parent groups and other community organizations,

Sexual diversity is all around us, although it is often invisible and silenced. Schools cannot make the controversies surrounding sexual diversity disappear by ignoring them. In many of the legal cases mentioned earlier, ignoring the issues exacerbated and escalated the problems. As educators who are responsible for supporting and teaching the next generation, it is our responsibility to create schools and classrooms that value and teach about the diversity that is already present in our communities. Teachers and administrators also have the legal obligation to create safe learning environments that are equitable and free of discrimination. By unlearning the harmful messages from old stereotypes and misinformation, educators have the potential to create and teach more contemporary messages of equality, inclusiveness, and diversity.

Notes

1. The use of the term "racial" here is in the critical multicultural sense of acknowledging the social constructedness of race while simultaneously addressing the very real impacts of racism in society. See (Kincheloe & Steinberg, 1997, pp. 215–216) for more on this.
2. There is not sufficient space in this chapter to explore the notion that there more than two sexes. For more information on this assertion please see (Fausto-Sterling, 2000).

3.   Minnesota (1993); Rhode Island (1995, 2001); New Mexico (2003); California (1992, 2003); District of Columbia (1997, 2005); Illinois (2005); Maine (2005); Hawaii (1991, 2005, 2006); New Jersey (1992, 2006); Washington (2006); Iowa (2007); Oregon (2007); Vermont (1992, 2007); Colorado (2007); Wisconsin (1982); Massachusetts (1989); Connecticut (1991); New Hampshire (1997); Nevada (1999); Maryland (2001); New York (2002).

References

ACLU. (2004). *Settlement fact sheet: Flores v. Morgan Hill Unified School District.* Retrieved March 28, 2006, from www.aclu.org

Advocates for Youth. (2005). The heterosexual questionnaire. Retrieved March 2, 2008, from http://www.advocatesforyouth.org/lessonplans/heterosexual2.htm

American Civil Liberties Union-New Jersey. (2007). Victory for gay and other students who face harassment. Retrieved October 10, 2007, from http://www.aclu-nj.org/pressroom/victoryforgayandotherstude.htm

Apple, M. (1990). *Ideology and the curriculum.* New York: Routledge.

Apple, M. (2000). *Official knowledge: Democratic education in a conservative age* (2nd ed.). New York: Routledge.

Arora, C. M. J. (1994). Is there any point in trying to reduce bullying in secondary schools? A two year follow-up of a whole-school anti-bullying policy in one school. *Educational Psychology in Practice, 10*(3), 155–162.

Barnard, I. (2004). *Queer race: Cultural interventions in the racial politics of queer theory.* New York: Peter Lang.

Bem, S. (1993). *The lenses of gender: Transforming the debate on sexual inequality.* New Haven: Yale University Press.

Blumenfeld, W. (1994). Science, sexual orientation, and identity: An overview. Unpublished research paper. Gay, Lesbian, and Straight Education Network.

Bochenek, M., & Brown, A. W. (2001). *Hatred in the hallways: Violence and discrimination against lesbian, gay, bisexual, and transgender students in U.S. schools.* Human Rights Watch.

Bornstein, K. (1998). *My gender workbook.* New York: Routledge.

Britzman, D. (2000). Precocious education. In S. Talburt & S. Steinberg (Eds.), *Thinking queer: Sexuality, culture, and education* (pp. 33–60). New York: Peter Lang.

Brown, L. M. (2003). *Girlfighting: Betrayal and rejection among girls.* New York: New York University Press.

Buchanan, W. (2006, April 1). Bills nationwide address gays in schools [Electronic Version]. *SFGate.* Retrieved April 12, 2006 from www.sfgate.com.

Butler, J. (1990). *Gender trouble.* New York: RoutledgeFalmer.

California Safe Schools Coalition. (2004). *Consequences of harassment based on actual or perceived sexual orientation and gender non-conformity and steps for making schools safer.* Davis: University of California.

The Canadian Charter of Rights and Freedoms (s. 15). Part I of the Constitution Act c. 11 (1982).

Cartwright, N. (1995). Combating bullying in a secondary school in the United Kingdom. *Journal for a Just and Caring Education, 1*(3), 345–353.

Cass, V. (1979). Homosexual identity formation: A theoretical model. *Journal of Homosexuality, 4*, 219–235.

Cass, V. (1984). Homosexual identity formation: Testing a theoretical model. *Journal of Sex Research, 20*, 143–167.

Chasnoff, D. (Writer) (1996). *It's elementary: Talking about gay issues in school.* H. S. Cohen & D. Chasnoff (Producer). USA: Ground Spark.

CLE Staff. (2005). BCCA: North Vancouver school board liable for homophobic harassment of student. [Electronic Version]. *Stay current: The continuing legal education society of British Columbia, April 8.* Retrieved April 9, 2005 from www.cle.bc.ca/CLE.

Cloud, J. (2005). The battle over gay teens. *Time, October 10.*

Cromwell, J. (1997). Traditions of gender diversity and sexualities: A female-to-male transgendered perspective. In S.-E. Jacobs, W. Thomas, & S. Lang (Eds.), *Two-spirit people: Native American gender identity, sexuality, and spirituality* (pp. 119–142). Chicago, IL: University of Illinois Press.

D'Augelli, A. R., & Hershberger, S. L. (1993). Lesbian, gay, and bisexual youth in community settings: Personal challenges and mental health problems. *American Journal of Community Psychology, 21*, 421–448.

Delpit, L. (1993). The silenced dialogue: Power and pedagogy in educating other people's children. In L. Weis & M. Fine (Eds.), *Beyond silenced voices: Class, race, and gender in United States schools* (pp. 119–139). Albany, NY: SUNY Press.

Dignan, J. (2004, January 8). Important victory for gay students *Gaycitynews.com* Retrieved October 15, 2007, from http://www.gaycitynews.com/site/index.cfm?newsid=17008546&BRD=2729&PAG=461&dept_id=568864&rfi=8

Doe v. Bellefonte Area School District (3rd Cir U. S. App. 2004).

Driver, S. (2007). *Queer girls and popular culture: Reading, resisting, and creating media.* New York: Peter Lang.

Dube, E., & Savin-Williams, R. (1999). Sexual identity development among ethnic sexual-minority male youths. *Developmental Psychology, 35*(6), 1389–1398.

Duncan, N. (2004). It's important to be nice, but it's nicer to be important: Girls, popularity and sexual competition. *Sex Education, 4*(2), 137–152.

Egan v. Canada (2 S.C.R. 513 1995).

Epstein, D., & Johnson, R. (1998). *Schooling sexualities.* Buckingham: Open University Press.

Fausto-Sterling, A. (2000). *Sexing the body: Gender politics and the construction of sexuality.* New York: Basic Books.

Feinberg, L. (1998). Allow me to introduce myself. In *Transliberation: Beyond pink or blue.* Boston: Beacon Press.

Fine, M. (1993). Sexuality, schooling, and adolescent females: The missing discourse of desire. In L. Weis & M. Fine (Eds.), *Beyond silenced voices: Class, race, and gender in United States schools* (pp. 75–99). Albany, NY: SUNY Press.

Fischer, S. and Kosciw, J. (2006, April 6). The importance of gay-straight alliances: Associations with teacher and staff response to homophobia. Paper presented at the annual meeting of the American Educational Research Association. San Francisco, CA.

Flores v. Morgan Hill Unified School District, No. 02-15128 (9th Cir. 2003).

Foucault, M. (1975). *Surveiller et Punir: Naissance de la Prison.* Paris: Gallimard.

Foucault, M. (1980). *The history of sexuality, Volume I: An introduction.* New York: Random House.

Francis, B., & Skelton, C. (2001). Men teachers and the construction of heterosexual masculinity in the classroom. *Sex Education, 1*(1), 9–21.

Frankfurt, K. et al. (1999). *Just the facts about sexual orientation and youth: A primer for principals, educators, and school personnel.* New York: GLSEN, National Education Association, American Psychological Association, American Federation of Teachers, the National Association of School Psychologists, and the National Association of Social Workers.

Friend, R. (1993). Choices, not closets: Heterosexism and homophobia in schools. In L. Weis & M. Fine (Eds.), *Beyond silenced voices: Class, race, and gender in United States schools* (pp. 209–235). Albany: SUNY Press.

GIRES. (2006a). Atypical gender identity development—A review. *International Journal of Transgenderism, 9*(1), 29–44.

GIRES. (2006b). *Gender dysphoria.* Surrey, UK: Gender Identity Research and Education Society.

Goldstein, T., Collins, A., & Halder, M. (2005). *Challenging homophobia and heterosexism in elementary and high schools: A research report to the Toronto district school board.* Toronto: Ontario Institute for Studies in Education of the University of Toronto.

Harris Interactive. (2001). *Hostile hallways: Bullying, teasing, and sexual harassment in school.* Washington, DC: American Association of University Women Educational Foundation.

Hurley, M. C. (2005). *Sexual orientation and legal rights* (Current Issue Review No. 92-1E). Ottawa: Library of Parliament.

Jagose, A. (1996). *Queer theory: An introduction.* New York: New York University Press.

Kempling v. British Columbia College of Teachers (B.C.D. Civ. 2004).

Kincheloe, J., & Steinberg, S. (1997). *Changing multiculturalism.* Buckingham, UK & Philadelphia, PA: Open University Press.

Kinsey, A., Pomeroy, W., & Martin, C. (1948). *Sexual behavior in the human male.* Philadelphia, PA: W.B. Saunders.

Kinsey, A., Pomeroy, W., Martin, C., & Gebhard, P. (1953). *Sexual behavior in the human female.* Philadelphia, PA: W.B. Saunders.

Kosciw, J., & Diaz, E. (2006). *The 2005 national school climate survey: The experiences of lesbian, gay, bisexual and transgender youth in our nation's schools.* New York: Gay, Lesbian, and Straight Education Network.

Kosciw, J., & Diaz, E. (2008). *Involved, invisible, ignored: The experiences of lesbian, gay, bisexual and transgender parents and their children in our nation's K–12 schools.* New York: GLSEN.

Kumashiro, K. K. (Ed.). (2001). *Troubling intersections of race and sexuality: Queer students of color and anti-oppressive education.* Lanham, MD: Rowman & Littlefield.

L.W. v. Toms River Regional Schools Board of Education, A-111-05. (New Jersey Supreme Court 189 N.J. 381, 915 A.2d 535 2007).

Lang, S. (1997). Various kinds of two-spirit people: Gender variance and homosexuality in Native American communities. In S.-E. Jacobs, W. Thomas, & S. Lang (Eds.), *Two-spirit people: Native American gender identity, sexuality, and spirituality* (pp. 100–118). Chicago, IL: University of Illinois Press.

Leo, T., & Yoakum, J. (1992). Creating a safer school environment for lesbian and gay students. *Journal of School Health* (September 1992), 37–41.

Lipkin, A. (1999). *Understanding homosexuality, changing schools.* Boulder, CO: Westview Press.

Mac an Ghaill, M. (1995). *The making of men: Masculinities, Sexualities, and Schooling.* Philadelphia: Open University Press.

Macgillivray, I. K. (2007). *Gay-straight alliances: A handbook for students, educators, and parents.* New York: Harrington Park Press.

Martino, W., & Pallotta-Chiarolli, M. (2003). *So what's a boy? Addressing issues of masculinity and schooling.* Buckingham: Open University Press.

Meyer, E. (2006). Gendered harassment in North America: School-based interventions for reducing homophobia and heterosexism. In C. Mitchell & F. Leach (Eds.), *Combating gender violence in and around schools* (pp. 43–50). UK: Trentham Books.

Meyer, E. (2007a). "But I'm not gay": What straight teachers need to know about queer theory. In N. Rodriguez & W. F. Pinar (Eds.), *Queering straight teachers* (pp. 1–17). New York: Peter Lang.

Meyer, E. (2007b). Lessons from *Jubran*: Reducing school board liability in cases of peer harassment. *Proceedings of the 17th Annual Conference of the Canadian Association for the Practical Study of Law in Education,* Vol. 1, pp. 561–576.

Meyer, E. (2008). Lesbians in popular culture. In C. Mitchell & J. Reid-Walsh (Eds.), *Girl culture: An encyclopaedia* (Vol. 2, pp. 392–394). Westport, CT: Greenwood Press.

Mills, M. (2004). Male teachers, homophobia, misogyny and teacher education. *Teaching Education, 15*(1), 27–39.

Montgomery v. Independent School District No. 709, 109 F. Supp. 2d 1081, 1092 (D. Minn. 2000) 2000.

Nabozny v. Podlesny, et al. (7th Cir. (Wis.) 1996).

National Gay and Lesbian Task Force. (2007, September 17). State nondiscrimination laws in the U.S. Retrieved January 3, 2008, from http://www.thetaskforce.org/downloads/reports/issue_maps/non_discrimination_09_07.pdf

Nestle, J., Howell, C., & Wilchins, R. (2002). *Gender queer: Voices from beyond the sexual binary.* New York: Alyson Books.

Nieto, S. (1999). *The light in their eyes: Creating multicultural learning communities.* New York: Teachers College Press.

NMHA. (2002). *"What does gay mean?" Teen survey executive summary.* National Mental Health Association.

Paley, V. (1979). *White teacher.* Cambridge, MA: Harvard University Press.

Perrotti, J., & Westheimer, K. (2001). *When the drama club is not enough: Lessons from the safe schools program for gay and lesbian students.* Boston: Beacon Press.

Pinar, W. F. (1998). Understanding curriculum as gender text: Notes on reproduction, resistance, and male-male relations. In William F. Pinar and Mary Aswell Doll (Eds.), *Queer theory in education.* Mahwah, NJ: Lawrence Erlbaum.

Rasmussen, M. L., Mitchell, J., & Harwood, V. (2007). The queer story of "the heterosexual questionnaire." In N. Rodriguez & W. F. Pinar (Eds.), *Queering straight teachers: Discourse and identity in education* (pp. 95–112). New York: Peter Lang.

Ray, V., & Gregory, R. (2001). School experiences of the children of lesbian and gay parents. *Family Matters, 59,* 28–34.

Rich, A. (1978/1993). Compulsory heterosexuality and lesbian existence. In H. Abelove, D. Halperin, & M. A. Barale (Eds.), *The lesbian and gay studies reader* (pp. 227–254). New York: Routledge.

Rowen, C. J., & Malcolm, J. P. (2002). Correlates of internalized homophobia and homosexual identity formation in a sample of gay men. *Journal of Homosexuality, 43*(2), 77–92.

Savin-Williams, R. (1990). *Gay and lesbian youth: Expressions of identity.* New York: Hemisphere.

School District No. 44 (North Vancouver) v. Jubran, 2005 BCCA 201 (BCSC 6 2005).

Sears, J. T. (1998). A generational and theoretical analysis of culture and male (homo)sexuality. In W. F. Pinar (Ed.), *Queer theory in education* (pp. 73–105). Mahwah, NJ: Lawrence Erlbaum.

Sharp, S., & Smith, P. K. (1991). Bullying in UK schools: The DES Sheffield bullying project. *Early Child Development and Care, 77,* 47–55.

Szlacha, L. (2003). Safer sexual diversity climates: Lessons learned from an evaluation of Massachusetts safe schools program for gay and lesbian students. *American Journal of Medicine.* 110(1), 58–88.

Straights and Gays for Equity (SAGE) v. Osseo Area Schools District No. 279. (8th Cir. 2006).

Theno v. Tonganoxie Unified School Dist. No. 464 (2005 WL 3434016 [D. Kan. 2005]).

Trinity Western University v. British Columbia College of Teachers (S.C.R. 772, 2001).

Troiden, R. R. (1988). The formation of homosexual identities. *Journal of Homosexuality, 17*(1/2), 43–74.

Trowbridge, C. (2005, December 29). Former student, district settle lawsuit [Electronic Version]. *The Tonganoxie Mirror.* Retrieved March 16, 2006 from www.tonganoxiemirror.com

Tucker, D. (Writer). (2005). *Transamerica* [film]. USA: Belladonna Productions.

Vriend v. Alberta (1 S.C.R. 493 1998).

Waldner-Haugrud, L. & Magruder, B. (1996). Homosexual identity expression among lesbian and gay adolescents: An analysis of perceived structural associations. *Youth and Society, 27*(3), 313–333.

Watkinson, A. (1999). *Education, student rights and the charter*. Saskatoon, SK: Purich.

Weeks, J. (1985). *Sexuality and its discontents*. New York: Routledge.

White County High School Peers in Diverse Education v. White County School District (Civil Action No. 2:06-CV-29-WCO (N. D. Georgia, Gainesville Division). 2006).

Whitney, I., & Smith, P. K. (1993). A survey of the nature and extent of bullying in junior/middle and secondary schools. *Educational Research, 35*(1), 3–25.

Wilchins, R. A. (2004). Time for gender rights. *GLQ: A Journal of Lesbian and Gay Studies, 10*(2), 265–267.

Thirteen

(Dis)Embedding Gender Diversity in the Preservice Classroom

sj Miller

What is gender? Why is it important to understand how gender affects classroom flow? What does gender look like in classroom discourse? How do we locate it in and outside of the classroom? What do we draw upon to help conceptualize understandings of gender? How can we prepare our students to remain open to accepting a socially constructed continuum about gender over space and time and in emerging contexts? Even more important, why are such questions about gender necessary? Such questions are timely tipping points for students to discuss as they consider their own positions about their views on the diversity of gender. In this narrative, I explore myriad ways that my undergraduate preservice English students and I have both theoretically and empirically unpacked gender in the classroom and in the context of their teaching lives. Some discussion will focus on describing how students have wrestled with gender in and outside of the classroom space and illuminate how they have been challenged to renegotiate their views about the gender continuum.

What Is Gender?

There are two longstanding arguments about gender. One view holds that gender is something one just *is* such as secondary sex characteristics; the other view portrays gender as something one *has* such as how one is socially positioned as subject. In the first view of gender, one's (biological) sex affects what one does, because of biological characteristics, which include chromosomes, genes, anatomy, gonads, hormones, and so on, and which is typically socially reinforced through a heterosexual model (Wittig, 1983). In the latter argument, feminist research reveals that gender is the social construction of roles, behaviors, and attributes that is considered by the general public to be "appropriate" for one's sex and which is assigned at birth, typically as female or male (Butler, 1990) or as androgyny. In this school of thought, gender roles vary among cultures and along time continuums. de Beauvoir (1973) argues that if gender is constructed, that one becomes a gender and thereby has agency in one's social development as it intersects with culture. She also questions the former argument that the body is not a contested site, that it is quite passive, and already has predetermined social norms attached to it. Irigaray (1985) argues that gender, as social phenomenon, is connected to patriarchy and binds women's bodies to men's control. In other words, women are made or "othered" in men's eyes and so is their sex(uality). Both gender and sex have therefore been socially reproduced to reinforce hegemonic dominance and heteronormativity and to further procreation.

Today, there is a widening divide between notions of gender and sex in society. However, in spite of the gap, teachers often reinforce gender normativity in the classroom. As we educate ourselves on shifting gender norms, we can relocate ourselves as subjects in multiple contexts, and be better equipped to unveil and utilize the shifting discourse. de Beauvoir (1973) argues that the female body should be a site of freedom and a tool of empowerment, and that it is not essentialized. This is highly complex and conflated by a history of male ownership of women through law and religion, and social, economic, and cultural practices. In fact, this institutionalized history, has infused itself into social and cultural practices and by proxy, schooling. Fortunately, the rising waves of feminism and research have sought to place women on equal footing with men both socially and culturally and have been careful not to perpetuate the predated dynamics of subjugating one gender to the other.

Although several theories on gender have been fundamental in shaping dominant perspectives on gender, this discussion is premised on Butler's (1990) notion that gender is performance, which is an outgrowth of prior feminist theories on gender. Butler suggests that the given identity of the individual is illuminated by the gender that one performs. Butler says, "gender is an identity tenuously constituted in time, instituted in an exterior space through a *stylized repetition of acts*" [*sic*] (p. 140). She goes on to suggest that gender is a "surface signification" and that gender "is created through sustained social performances" (p. 141). Butler essentially argues that the individual is a subject, capable of action—not an object to be constructed. Such reasoning infers that people have agency in how they invite and embody an identity. Building from this premise then, by inviting discussion about gender in classrooms, we can begin to see how any identity can take on various gender-performed roles.

An identity is how the core self is illuminated in a given space such as "teacher," "mechanic," "dancer," or "coach." When one leaves one space for another, an identity may be less illuminated in a new space, but it is nonetheless part of what that person performs. Gee (1996) suggests that identities are dialogical and relational, constructed in relation to power and discourse. He also says that individuals have multiple and even hybrid identities, which are intercontextually malleable and consequently ever-changing and readily influenced by space and time. An identity then is something one comes to embody and own as s/he self-defines different aspects of the self and comes into different contexts in space and time (Gee, 1996). An identity is illuminated based on the relationship the individual has within and to the various contexts or social spaces. Social spaces are impacted by political (power) and social ideologies (Foucault 1980, 1986; Lefebvre 1991) and are thereby never totally neutral. Foucault (1986) and Bourdieu (1980) suggest that the effects of power construct identities and that the embodiment of identities is vulnerable as a result of power. Social spaces become central to understanding an identity in terms of "race, ethnicity, social class or gender. . . those identifications shape engagements in spatial tactics of power and in everyday social, cultural and literate practices" (McCarthey & Moje, 2002, pp. 234–235). Because social spaces are defined in relationship to society, such as a school, café, or bar, identities are highlighted by those social spaces and by the way their identities have been defined in relationship to society. Selves therefore are illuminated by their identities within specific social spaces and yet can be excluded when their identities are not defined by their relationship to that space. Identity can therefore either be stabilized, or affirmed in a given social space, or destabilized when a social space excludes or is unwelcoming of a particular identity. As individuals change and merge with other social spaces, their identities can become hybrids layered with a multitude of subjectivities. Preservice teacher identity co-construction as seen through this premise is thereby sociospatial (Leander, 2002) and teacher identities are discoursed.

Understanding that individuals are subjects within a larger matrix of life is also important in unpacking how gender is performed. Therefore preservice teachers should begin to understand how to co-opt their identities to help them see that they are subjects, capable of acting on and transforming their students' lives, not objects to be constructed. By rupturing the notion that teachers are objects, we shift the status of teachers from subservient clones into transformational agents.

Danielewicz (2001) says that teacher education programs should foster teacher

> identity development to the highest degree possible. In helping preservice teachers recognize their own identity co-constructions, they become more informed about their own subjectivities that can empower them to challenge being co-opted by hegemonic-based discourse and thinking. Recognizing that their own teacher identities are situated within a complex networked matrix of spacetime relationships can help them negotiate their identity co-constructions and help them relocate to spaces that stabilize and affirm their teacher identities. (Miller, 2007b, p.18)

A teacher with agency is a teacher who is better able to challenge the body/mind split.

The body/mind split is important in understanding agency. The dualism of the mind/body split can render a preservice teacher helpless if the individual does not understand the sociopolitical implications of the separation. If a teacher blindly accepts particular curriculum or ideas without completing background research, s/he may be sabotaging her/his agency. Some sociopolitical teaching ideologies are constructed in such a way that teachers may not understand how they divide body from mind and thus, separate one from her/his power to be fully embodied and have agency. If a teacher teaches from this place, s/he passes on the binary of perpetuating status quo ideology that often displaces personal agency. Such thinking sustains dominant culture and binary categorization—meaning that the answer falls into concrete, fixed categories such as black or white, good or evil, just or unjust.

On the other hand, the empowerment that can arise from the teacher as a whole being, not as object, can lead teachers to be conscientious about their power in constructing their own, as well as students,' identities in the classroom. The importance of such empowerment shifts the binary dynamics and power structures within hegemony and helps individuals become nonbinary agents capable of acting on and transforming the worlds in which they live. On this Bhabha (1994) admonishes us not to simulate the discourse of dominant culture because it reinforces status quo constructs. Nonbinary thinking can liberate and open doors to new possibilities that over time may lead to subvert traditional paradigms once used to keep people silenced and marginalized (Freire, 1970). When we teach preservice teachers to co-opt their own identities, we can liberate them from binary and dominant perceptions that may have once had their time and place in education but which are now antiquated. Rose (1993) advocates for transcending binary constructs and believes that a politics of "difference and identity built on the opening of new spaces" relocates us to a place where counterhegemonic principles can lead to a liberal democracy (Soja, 1996, p. 111). Such a politics lifts us out of binary identifiers and relocates us to a space where ideas can "co-exist concurrently and in contradiction" (Rose, 1993, quoting deLauretis (1987), as in Soja, 1996, p. 112). Teacher education has the power to greatly challenge and subvert dominant paradigms through each of the constituents impacted.

As we move toward nonbinary understandings of gender, it is important to familiarize ourselves with emerging terminology. As we move into the classrooms where we teach, we are likely to meet students who are typically more familiar with these terms than we are because the space and time that youth are living in are more pluralistic. If we hope to support students to adapt to changing times, we can begin to expand our discourse (and our teaching) around gender. Some common ways today that individuals self-identify with regard to gender can be categorized but not essentialized into ag/aggressive, agendered, androgyne/ androgynous, Berdache, bigendered, gender-diverse, genderqueer, intergender, pangender, transandrogyny, transgender, transsexual, and two-spirited (see Appendix A for explanation of terms). Each of these gender categories has sublanguages of its own that are relegated to each of its own cultures. Two other terms are important to define when referring to these emergent gender categories: *gender identity* and *gender expression*. *Gender identity* is one's personal sense of his or her correct gender, which may be reflected as gender expression and *gender expression* is one's choice and/or manipulation of gender cues. Gender expression may or may not be congruent with or influenced by a person's biological sex. If we are to have a true pluralistic understanding about gender, we must begin to inform ourselves about the emerging politics and discourse so we can inform our own students with current and accurate information that will prepare them for real world understandings.

Unfortunately, currently there are only two genders—male and female—that have equal protection under the law. We have gradually seen transgender-identified people receiving more basic human rights than in times past but it is far from equivalent to those who claim to be in the male/female binary. Miller (2007c) writes:

> The transgender movement seeks to have equal protection for transgender people that prohibits discrimination based on "gender identity or expression" and ensures that all transgender and gender nonconforming people are protected by law. This includes jobs, housing, health care, hate crimes legislation, legislative language, antidiscrimination bills, foster care and adoption, marriage, bathrooms, changing birth certificates to reflect the chosen gender, students in school, and being visible in the mainstream eye.[1] (p. 182)

Another way the transgender movement has gained more visibility is through media portrayals, some of which are accurate, some of which are poor. We see these current transgender characters on TV: Alexis Meade on "Ugly Betty," Max on the "L Word," Carmelita on "Dirty Sexy Money," Zarf on "All My Children," Alexis Arquette on "The Surreal Life," and Ava Moore on "Nip/Tuck." In film, we have seen Tina Washington in *The World's Fastest Indian;* Bree in *Transamerica;* Asanee Suwan in *Beautiful Boxer;* Roy in *Norma;* Hedwig in *Hedwig and the Angry Inch; Paris is Burning;* Lola in *Kinky Boots;* several characters in *The Adventures of*

Priscilla, Queen of the Desert; Noxeema, Vida, and Chi-Chi in *To Wong Foo, Thanks for Everything, Julie Newmar;* Robert Eads in *Southern Comfort;* Brandon Teena in *Boys Don't Cry;* Hank in *The Adventures of Sebastian Cole;* Ludovic in *Ma Vie En Rose;* Dil in *The Crying Game;* Gwen in *A Girl Like Me: The Gwen Araujo Story;* Patrick in *Breakfast on Pluto;* and Luis Molina in *Kiss of the Spider Woman.*

The transgender movement for some has been a way to claim a space or a territory that is connected to the mainstream population but which has its own cultural cues. Common pronouns embraced by some transgender people are "zhe," "hir," and "per" that correlate to he, her, and person. Such as "zhe is going to the bathroom" or "what is hir name?" or "who is that per?" Such a claiming of space means that we must be mindful about speaking in ways that privileges one gender over the other. We have a social and moral responsibility to ask our students what pronouns we should use, what name they want to be called, and if there is anything that we should be made aware of about their gender identity.

Gender Politics in the Classroom

Conjecturing that when we speak about gender in the classroom most students are oblivious to how binary views of gender affect students or their participation because gender is normalized. In fact, criticism is likely to be more about preferential treatment based on gender or appearance. It is not likely that students during this space and time are critical that their teachers are not using inchoate language about gender. However, once we become conscious of change, it is very difficult to go back into binary definitions. As preservice teachers become schooled in emerging gender definitions, the more change can be effected.

Teachers have a social and moral responsibility to update themselves on emerging sociopolitical issues and how they impact the classroom. Likewise, if a teacher lacks particular knowledge and gender performance, s/he may inadvertently marginalize or even destabilize a student who does not fit into the binary. In fact,

> Some students may be hesitant to disclose until they feel safe enough, but unless teachers demonstrate through discourse and behavior that they are an ally, students are likely to assume that they cannot open up. Along similar lines, we must also be concerned about fostering competitions in classrooms albeit they may appear fun; they reinforce power dynamics and binary roles and beliefs about gender. This means eliminating activities and categories of boys versus girls. It means that we are sensitive with our language all the time and we are deliberate in our actions when designing lessons so we do not marginalize nor reinforce sexism on any level. (Miller, 2007c, p. 183)

Although schools are set up to maintain the status quo (the binary) and to reproduce students who then support the principles under any given democracy, every student deserves a fair and equal education regardless of ethnicity, national origin, national language, appearance, social class, ability, gender, sexual orientation, or gender identity. The consequences, however, may be that if a teacher does not affirm student differences (varying identities) the student may shut down, not complete work, feel separate from the classroom, or be hurt, or in the worst case scenario, attempt or complete a suicide. Teachers can therefore interrupt the cycle of student reproduction (Apple, 2002) as they begin to lead by example and invite social change into the classroom space.

When we begin to discuss gender with our students, there are myriad ways to approach it. Broadening the scope of how our students use gendered discourse must be a deliberate act, and we must therefore also consider our curricular choices, pedagogical stances, and actions so as to reflect the emerging language. Gender is but one aspect within a long continuum of challenging the binary and can and ought to be taught along with ethnicity, national origin, national language, appearance, social class, ability, or sexual orientation. The more inclusive we can be in our teaching, the greater likelihood that it can have a positive efficacy in the lives of students.

The following examples for preservice teachers can be useful in working with their own classroom students.

1. When we speak we must be sure that we explain that all genders should have equal opportunity and that none is privileged over others, although laws are not yet completely equitable or inclusive for all transgender people let alone any of the others. By saying all genders, we mean male, female, transgender, and the other previously referenced genders. The way we also speak about gender, gender identity, and gender expression should be nonbinary because while there are commonly regarded definitions, beliefs, and meanings for gender, there is also a continuum that allows for people to fall outside of what we commonly perceive as binary. As we stay open to a nonbinary understanding of gender, we challenge ourselves to reflect on the changes that occur in our language use every day.

2. Be sure the pedagogy you employ is inclusive, nonbinary, and multidimensional. Examples of such pedagogy include equity pedagogy, critical pedagogy, critical hip-hop pedagogy, liberatory pedagogy, engaging pedagogy, feminist pedagogy, queer pedagogy, and transformative pedagogy.

3. Select texts from all cultures that challenge gender norms and gender identity/expression (see Appendix B).

4. Carefully consider the texts you use and how gender is written about, portrayed, or discussed. Ask questions of your students about texts such as: How is gender portrayed in the text? Describe any variations of gender. What is the gender of the author? How is gender challenged? Affirmed? What do we learn that is new about gender from the text?

5. Use gender-inclusive language in all communications with students, parents, school administrators, and peers. Talk about the broader issues of gender bias, sex-role stereotyping, and discrimination and work to promote gender equity.

6. Create a class library that has a diverse range of texts that embrace differences of culture, class, ethnicity, gender, ability, weight, religion, national origin, sexual orientation, size, gender identity, and gender expression.

7. Place only gender-inclusive posters/placards in the classroom or do not place any at all.

Not all students will be open or receptive to these activities so it is important to assess your classroom students and school environment prior to engaging your students in these gender challenges. In some cases, you may have to solicit parental or principal approval. On the other hand, some students may be ready for this challenge, so you will have to decide how to incorporate these activities based on your assessment. The following are several ways to open discussions about gender.

Activities to use with classroom students (should be modified to suit grade level):

- Discuss new terms about gender and invite discussion and debate.
- Ask students to provide examples of nonbinary portraits of gender in the media.
- Invite discussion and debate about gender norms.
- Ask students to describe where and how they first developed their concept of their own gender identities. Why did they believe that to be true? Who told them? How were those beliefs socialized?
- Ask students to describe how they express their gender. Is that binary/nonbinary?
- Ask students at what age they began to challenge what they learned about themselves? What made them reconsider those beliefs?
- Discuss gender as performance versus gender as fixed.
- Reflect on if there was there ever a time where they thought their answers did not fit the images society had ingrained into them? How did they respond?
- Research former laws related to gender and have them look for bias. Reflect on current change.
- Review antidiscrimination laws.
- Research Title IX, its past, and its future.
- Research which states have nondiscrimination laws and understand how nondiscrimination policies work by state.
- Research which states have laws that privilege homosexuals and transgender people.
- Research which states discriminate against homosexuals and transgender people.
- Research which state laws exclude homosexuals and transgender people.
- Have a critical discourse analysis of a TV show or film on gendered language use.
- Have a discourse analysis of students' use of gendered language.
- Interview people in the local community who challenge the gender binary.
- Invite guest speakers who challenge the gender binary.
- Rewrite a scene or passage from a film (see Appendix B) or text (poem, play, or short story) and shift the use of gendered language so it affirms the characters.
- Deconstruct how mainstream ads reinforce the gender binary.
- Examine what kinds of TV commercials and TV shows are on at particular times and how that sustains the gender binary.
- Examine different genres of musical lyrics and how they affirm or contest the gender binary. (There are hundreds of musical performers who identify outside of the gender binary, see Appendix C.)
- Review clips in the media about how female politicians are compared to male politicians.
- Examine random pay scales in various professions and look for gender equity.
- Review the history of all human rights and all of the major social movements (civil rights, gay/lesbian/bisexual/transgender/two-spirited, women, second-language speakers, bilingual, immigrants, Asian Americans, Native Americans, Latina/o Americans,

veterans, war dissenters, disabled, students with disabilities or special needs, and any other nondominant groups).

- Review the "isms" and unpack how prejudice and oppression manifest in students' lives (see chapter 7, Miller, 2007c).
- Talk about what it means to be an ally and how students can become allies for others.

The following activities may be more risky, so first consider discussions with the principal, other teachers, and parents/guardians.

- Challenge students to dress outside of the gender norm (gender expression) for a class period or if successful and it is safe, for an entire school day.
- Invite your students to design a nonbinary gender day for the school with speakers, panelists, and poetry.
- Invite students to attend lectures of community presentations at local universities or colleges to expose them to different perspectives about gender

Keep in mind that students may be quite resistant to challenging the ways that they understand gender so try to be patient, not preachy, and continue to provide opportunities for them to engage in experiences that challenge the binary. Whether or not they agree with the nonbinary idea is not essential; it is more important to expose students to the inevitable changes that are emerging in the world.

It is also important to understand, for both your students as well as yourselves, the consequences of not addressing or challenging the gender binary. By introducing a different way of talking about gender, we can challenge some of the forms of gender oppression that exist. Our students will be better prepared for handling sexism, sexual harassment, bullying, self-injury, or even hate crimes. Sexism is the systemic oppression of individuals that privileges one gender over the other, and in the United States that is typically men over women (Miller, 2007c, p. 182). Generally stemming from a history of institutional policies and social values defined by men, this system operates to the advantage of men, and more often white men, and to the disadvantage of women. It is vital that we develop a social consciousness with our students around gender bias issues so as not to perpetuate oppressive gender-based hierarchies that are deeply entrenched in society. As we deepen awareness about gender oppression, we ultimately shift gender dynamics in dominant culture and may thwart attacks on individuals who fall outside of the gender binary.

Wrestling with the Gender Binary Inside and Outside the Classroom

This section draws upon empirical examples from my teaching of preservice teachers and illuminates how they have each been challenged to renegotiate their views about the gender continuum. When I consider how to design my syllabus during a particular semester, I take into account what is happening in my students' communities, the nation, and the world at large. I try to choose texts and design lessons that best reflect my students' cultures and values for that particular class or select texts about areas in which we need to enhance our understanding of humanity. When selecting texts, I ask myself what voices I need to have echoed back to my students. The answer often resides in the class itself. As I come to know my students through the dialogic (Freire, 1970) and understand their issues and home lives, I become more informed so I can select authors who resonate with them and their own stories. I often teach works by authors of color and select authors who have been marginalized by dominant society. I also deliberately select texts that have characters or story lines that point to prejudice and that can help point to deeper sociopolitical issues (see examples in chapter 7, Miller, 2007c).

From day one, I raise examples that help students understand how power, privilege, and oppression have been institutionalized and through examples, essentially conduct a historical analysis of groups and individuals that that have been disenfranchised in hegemony. This scaffolding process fosters a larger context for understanding oppression and aptly prepares us to understand how gender is one form among many kinds of institutional oppression. The pedagogy I embrace, employ, and embody is a combination of liberatory and transformative mixed with the theory of critical literacy.

A liberatory pedagogy is one that seeks to educate students to act on and transform their worlds through acts of cognition first, and action second (Freire, 1970). Freire suggests that when we adopt a liberatory pedagogy, two distinct changes will occur: "when the oppressed unveil the world of oppression and through the praxis commit themselves to its transformation," and "in which the reality of oppression has already been transformed, this pedagogy ceases to belong to the oppressed and becomes a pedagogy of all the people in the process of permanent liberation" (p. 54). In so doing, we help free the oppressed from the oppressor, which then activates the oppressed to become agents capable of acting on and transforming their worlds; thus, we emancipate the oppressed. Although our students are not oppressed per se, they certainly are embedded within a matrix that sustains a hegemonic power and that reinforces particular social values and morals. A liberatory pedagogy prepares them to think critically about their worlds and gives them the tools to be informed citizens so that when they need to act, they know how.

Lewinson et al. (2002) suggest that the field of critical literacy is defined by "disrupting the commonplace, interrogating multiple view points, focusing on sociopolitical issues and taking action and promoting social justice" through texts (p. 3). Therefore, critical literacy can be a vehicle through which identity is negotiated as texts bump up against the self. Since critical literacy is "political practice influenced by social, cultural and historical factors"(Barton & Hamilton, 2000; Street, 1995, as in Hagood, 2002, p. 249) and is "committed foremost to the 'alleviation of human suffering and [to] the formation of a more just world through the critique of existing social and political problems and the posing of alternatives'" (Hagood, 2002, p. 249), texts taught through a poststructuralist lens can be a way to help youth negotiate and affirm their identities as they make meaning of the world in which they live. A poststructuralist reading of texts can be a powerful way to assist youth in holding onto their authentic selves while it teaches them to interact with the world so they may act on it in a fashion that does not perpetuate hegemony or the status quo. Youth, with an affirmed authentic self, can seek to transform the world through a subjective self that does not ascribe to the construction that the school system seeks to impose upon them. Consequently, the world/environment becomes vulnerable to a new subjectivity as it transacts with authentic selves, free of construction.

Hagood (2002) contends that critical literacy should assist students in developing an understanding of how texts "produce particular formations of self" (p. 248). Texts are situated within certain social and cultural groups. For all purposes, texts are imbued by larger sociopolitical issues of power that are associated in cultural and social groups. Texts reflect the changes in society, such as in how power may change within particular ethnicities, classes, and/or social patterns. In other words, as perceptions of ethnicities change, and as they may each gain access to positions of power and authority, texts reflect those changes. Our identities are impacted by their transactions with those texts, and when the texts shift along with the changes in society, so too do our identities shift. This means that from a poststructuralist perspective identities are constantly in flux.

An experience of one of my former undergraduate students, Matt, has stayed with me now for a couple of years. It emerged from a unit in an undergraduate humanities literature course in which I was teaching *Herland*, by Charlotte Perkins Gilman. Keep in mind that my students had been schooled in gender-inclusive language so they were quite ready for this activity. The background to the story is as follows. I was teaching a unit about gender normative behavior and doing an activity called the "Gender Box" (see www.glsen.org for more details). Essentially, the words *male* and *female* are placed next to each other in a box that looks like this:

Male	Female
•Breadwinner	•Soft, caring
•Hard working	•Stays home
•Unemotional	•Raises children
•Sports nut	•Committed
•Uncommitted	•Emotional
•Player	•Less educated
•Rugged	•Manipulative

Next, students are asked for words that describe typical gender behaviors or roles played by each. Typically this is quite lively and students tend to challenge each other. Once the box is full, start to have a conversation about what happens to people who don't fit into these behaviors or roles. Generally students spout negative epithets such as "dyke," "fag," "butch," "queer," etc. Then, discuss how the binary has reinforced these negative perceptions and the consequences that may befall anyone who does not fit into the binary. Next, tell students that sometimes we fall within both sides of the box and we transcend gender norms and sometimes we don't fit on either side of the box and we transcend gender norms.

After participating in this activity, Matt raised his hand and said, "Dr. Miller, I have always identified as a male, but now that I see this box, I don't fit into stereotypical categories of male. Therefore, I must be transgendered." I stopped and looked at him and didn't know what to say. After contemplating a supportive answer, I said, "Matt, you can identify however you want."

A preservice student named Samantha I taught in a methods course had an eye-opening experience in the middle school classroom where she was teaching. I had taught a unit in methods on the possible negative effects of bullying on students if left unattended, such as cutting, self-injury, acting out, depression, attempted suicide or successful suicide, risky behavior, and drug use. We examined statistics that revealed which groups of students were at particularly high risk for bullying (see chapter 3, Miller, 2007a). Prior to this students had, once again, been schooled with emerging terminology about gender.

Samantha decided to teach Tolan's *Plague Year*, a story about Molly and Barn who were harassed for their appearances, physical traits, and personalities. Samantha had to be cautious about what to talk about and bring up because she was teaching with a conservative cooperating teacher and was concerned about redress. She put bullying into a larger context that described why some people are bullied while also carefully introducing some of the emerging terms in Appendix A. At the time she taught this, she was very pleased with the outcome because students took it very seriously and even conducted a whole-school survey on who is bullied and for what reasons. Results were published in the school paper. Unbeknownst to her at the time she was teaching, a young woman who identified as male and who did not fit into the binary was ingesting Samantha's teaching. Two years after she left Samantha's course, she ran into her in the local supermarket. The conversation went something like this:

> Girl: "Hi Ms. L. Nice to see you."
> Sam: "Great to see you too. How are you doing?"
> Girl: "Remember the unit you taught on bullying, well it has given me courage to be who I am."
> Sam: "I am very pleased for you—that is so cool."
> Girl: "Yeah, in fact, I started a gay/straight alliance at the high school."
> Sam: "No way, that's fantastic."

We may not always know the impact we are making in students' lives but we must find the courage in ourselves to open new doors for students to walk through as they struggle to find their sense of place in the world. Samantha, seemed to have a stronger sense of self and even if she has no support in her life, she will always know that a person of credibility validated her sense of belonging. What more can we hope for?

What I realized from both Matt's and Samantha's experiences is that in broadening their awareness about gender norms, depending on where students are in their cognitive, moral, emotional, and psychological development, they will begin to be challenged by or challenge others about gendered offensives. Such awareness can diversify human experience and lead us to places that are still emerging during this and other spaces and times.

(Dis)Embedding Gender: Moving Between Spaces

In our commitment to grow as individuals, we must also stay actively involved in the areas of our lives that can enhance our classroom practice. This could mean staying active by watching all kinds of media, going to popular culture events, attending presentations and lectures, traveling, putting ourselves in situations that challenge our thinking, taking more courses, reading as much as we can (see Appendix D), and conducting research. Not only will we be better informed but so too will the students whom we teach. I still have students who write me and teach me about new terms and ways they self-define, and I look forward to those letters and e-mails as a way to apply change in my own teaching life. Though it may not always be easy to teach about topics that may make us uncomfortable, if we don't, we are cheating our students out of being informed about the emerging contexts during any space and time.

Appendix A: Terms

Ag / Aggressive*: used to describe a female-bodied and identified person who prefers presenting as masculine. This term is most commonly used in urban communities of color.

Agendered*: person who is internally ungendered or does not have a felt sense of gender identity.

Androgyne/Androgynous*: person appearing and/or identifying as neither man nor woman, presenting as either mixed or gender neutral.

Berdache*: used to refer to a third-gender person (woman-living-man). The term berdache is generally rejected as inappropriate and offensive by Native peoples because it is a term that was assigned by European settlers to differently gendered Native peoples. Appropriate terms vary by tribe and include one-spirit, two-spirit, and wintke.

Bigendered*: person whose gender identity is a combination of male/man and female/woman.

Gender: expressions of masculinity, femininity, or androgyny in words, persons, organisms, or characteristics.

Gender Diverse*: person who either by nature or by choice does not conform to gender-based expectations of society (e.g., transgender, transsexual, intersex, genderqueer, cross-dresser, etc.). Also referred to as gender variant because it does not imply a standard normativity.

Genderqueer*: gender diverse person whose gender identity is neither male nor female, is between or beyond genders, or is some combination of genders. This identity is usually related to or in reaction to the social construction of gender, gender stereotypes, and the gender binary system.

Intergender*: person whose gender identity is between genders or a combination of genders.

Pangender*: person whose gender identity comprises all or many gender expressions.

Sex: medical term designating a certain combination of gonads, chromosomes, external gender organs, secondary sex characteristics, and hormonal balances. Because usually subdivided into male and female, this category does not recognize the existence of intersex bodies.

Transandrogyny*: gender diverse gender expression that does not have a prominent masculine or feminine component.

Transgender: person who lives as a member of a gender other than that expected based on anatomical sex. Sexual orientation varies and is not dependent on gender identity. A transgender person may or may not be pre- or post-operative; if s/he is, the individual is likely to refer to him/herself as transsexual. This has become an umbrella term for nonconforming gender identity and expression. Often associated with this term is FTM/F2M (female to male) and MTF/M2F (male to female).

Transsexual*: person who identifies psychologically as a gender/sex other than the one to which they were assigned at birth. Transsexuals often wish to transform their bodies hormonally and surgically to match their inner sense of gender/sex.

Two-Spirited*: Native persons who have attributes of both genders, have distinct gender and social roles in their tribes, and are often involved with mystical rituals (shamans). Their dress is usually a mixture of male and female articles and they are seen as a separate or third gender. The term *two-spirit* is usually considered specific to the Zuni tribe. Similar identity labels vary by tribe and include *one-spirit* and *wintke*.

*terms from *Trans and sexuality terminologies* (Green and Peterson (2004)).

Appendix B: Young Adult Literature

(texts and films taken from pp. 43–44 of Miller, 2007a, *Unpacking the Loaded Teacher Matrix*)

Middle School Texts

Including gay/lesbian/bisexual/transgender themes:
Alice Alone, Phyllis Reynolds Naylor
Alice on the Outside, Phyllis Reynolds Naylor
The Eagle Kite, Paula Fox
I Feel a Little Jumpy around You: A Book of Her Poems & His Poems Collected in Pairs, Naomi Shihab
     Nye and Paul B. Janeczko
From the Notebooks of Melanin Sun, Jacqueline Woodson
The House You Pass on the Way, Jacqueline Woodson
Risky Friends, Julie A. Peters
The Misfits, James Howe
The Skull of Truth, Bruce Coville and Gary A. Lippincott

High School Texts

Heterosexual (*made into a film):
Boys Lie, John Neufeld
Lucky, Alice Sebold
Out of Control, Shannon McKenna

Shattering Glass, Gail Giles
*Speak,** Laurie Halse Anderson
*To Kill a Mockingbird,** Harper Lee
Unexpected Development, Marlene Perez

Gay/bisexual themes:
Alt Ed, Catherine Atkins
Am I Blue? Marion Dane Bauer and Beck Underwood
The Drowning of Stephan Jones, Bette Greene
Geography Club, Brent Hartinger
The Perks of Being a Wallflower, Stephen Chbosky
Rainbow High, Alex Sanchez
Rainbow Boys, Alex Sanchez
Shattering Glass, Gail Giles
Simon Says, Elaine Marie Alphin
What Happened to Lani Garver?, Carol Plum-Ucci

Lesbian/bisexual themes:
Am I Blue? Marion Dane Bauer and Beck Underwood
Annie on My Mind, Nancy Garden
Color Purple, Alice Walker
Empress of the World, Sara Ryan
Keeping You a Secret, Julie Anne Peters
Kissing Kate, Lauren Myracle
Name Me Nobody, Lois-Ann Yamanaka
Out of the Shadows, Sue Hines

Transgender themes:
Define "Normal," Julie Anne Peters
The Flip Side, Andrew Matthews
Luna, Julie Anne Peters
My Heartbeat, Garret Freymann-Weyr
Standing Naked on the Roof, Francess Lantz
Written on the Body, Jeanette Winterson

Films

We encourage you to have discussions with your cooperating teacher, clinical supervisor, university instructor, and administrator if you intend to use any of these films. Some of these films are better suited for the methods classroom.

A Girl Like Me, Billy Elliot, Boys Don't Cry, Beautiful Thing, But I'm a Cheerleader, Camp, Confronting Date Rape: The Girl's Room, Date Violence: A Young Woman's Guide, It's So Elementary, This Boy's Life, Ma Vie En Rose, Normal, School Ties, Speak, You Ought to Know: Teens Talk about Dating and Abuse

Appendix C: Bands with Gender-Fluid People

The Cliks
Rolling Stones
REM
New York Dolls
All the Pretty Horses
Scissor Sisters
Girl Friday
David Bowie
Grace Jones
Lipstick Conspiracy
Lisa Jackson & Girl Friday
Katastrophe
Peecocks
Storm Florez
Pepperspray
Veronica Klaus
Angel Wayward
Georgie Jessup
Harisu
Bambi Lake
Bitesize
Gurlfriendz
Transisters
Angela Motter
Peter Outerbridge
Imperial Drag

Appendix D: More Resources about Gender and Sex Issues

Binnie, J. (2004). *The globalization of sexuality*. Thousand Oaks, CA: Sage.
Bohjalian, C. (2000). *Trans-sister radio*. New York: Random House.
Bornstein, K. (1995). *Gender outlaw*. New York: Vintage.
Browning, F. (1994). *The culture of desire*. New York: Random House.
Eugenides, J. (2002). *Middlesex*. New York: Picador.
Feinberg, L. (1993). *Stone butch blues*. Ithaca: Firebrand.
Foucault, M. (1991). *History of sexuality, Vol. 1*. New York: Vintage.
Halberstam, J. (1998). *Female masculinity*. Durham: Duke University Press.
Hennessey, Rosemary. (2000). *Profit and pleasure: Sexual identities in late capitalism*. New York: Routledge.
Lorde, A. (1983). *Zami: A new spelling of my name*. Trumansburg: Cross Press.
Moraga, C., & Anzaldua, G. (1981). *This bridge called my back: Writings by radical women of color*. New York: Kitchen Table/Women of Color Press.

Rubin, G. (1998). Thinking sex: Notes for a radical theory of the politics of sexuality. In P.M. Nardi & B. Schneider (Eds.), *Social perspectives in gay and lesbian studies*. New York: Routledge.

Russo, V. (1987). *The celluloid closet: Homosexuality in the movies*. New York: Harper & Row.

Sedgwick, E.K. (1991). *Epistemology of the closet*. Berkeley: University of California Press.

Seidman, S. (1997). *Difference troubles: Queering social theory and sexual politics*. Cambridge: Cambridge University Press.

Signorile, M. (1997). *Life outside*. New York: HarperCollins.

Signorile, M. (1993). *Queer in America*. New York: Doubleday.

Sullivan, A. (1996). *Virtually normal*. New York: Random House.

Sullivan, N. (2003). *Critical introduction to queer theory*. New York: New York University Press.

Warner, M. (2000). *The trouble with normal: Sex, politics, and the ethics of queer life*. Cambridge, MA: Harvard University Press.

Wittig, M. (1992). *The straight mind and other essays*. Boston: Beacon Press.

Woolf, V. (1928). *Orlando*. New York: Penguin

Note

1. For more information on transgender rights and current laws see the ACLU, http://www.aclu.org/getequal/trans.html; the Human Rights Campaign, http://www.hrc.org/index.html; the Transgender Law and Policy Institute, http://www.transgenderlaw.org/; the National Gay and Lesbian Task Force (NGLTF), http://www.thetaskforce.org/ourprojects/tcrp/; and http://www.mappingourrights.org for current rulings on discrimination by state.

References

Apple, M. (2002). *Official knowledge*. New York: Routledge.

Barton, D., & Hamilton, M. (2000). Literacy practices. In D. Barton, M. Hamilton, & R. Ivanic (Eds.), *Situated literacies: Reading and writing in context* (pp. 7–15). New York: Routledge.

Bhabha, H. A. (1994). *The location of culture*. New York: Routledge.

Bourdieu, P. (1980). *The logic of practice*. Stanford: Stanford University Press.

Butler, J. (1990). *Gender trouble: Feminism and the subversion of identity*. New York: Routledge.

Danielewicz, J. (2001). *Teaching selves: Identity, pedagogy and teacher education*. Albany: State University of New York Press.

de Beauvoir, S. (1973). *The second sex*. (Trans. E.M. Parshley). New York: Vintage Books.

deLauretis, T. (1987). *Technologies of gender: Essays on theory, film and fiction*. London: Macmillan.

Foucault, M. (1980). *Power-knowledge: Selected interviews and other writings, 1972–1977*. New York: Pantheon.

Foucault, M. (1986). Of other spaces (J. Miskowiec, Trans.). *Diacritics, 16*(1), 22–27.

Freire, P. (1970). *Pedagogy of the oppressed*. New York: Continuum.

Gee, J.P. (1996). *Social linguistics and literacies: Ideology in discourses* (2nd ed.). New York: Falmer Press.

Gilman, C.P. (1979). *Herland*. New York: Pantheon.

Green, E., & Peterson, E. (2004). *Trans and sexuality terminologies*. Retrieved January 8, 2008 from http://www.trans-academics.org.

Hagood, M. (2002). Critical literacy for whom? *Reading Research and Instruction, 41*, 247–266.

Irigaray, L. (1985). *The sex which is not one*. (Trans C. Porter & C. Brooke). Ithaca: Cornell University Press.

Leander, K. (2002). Locating Latanya: The situated production of identity artifacts in classroom interaction. *Research in the Teaching of English, 37*, 198–250.

Lefebvre, H. (1991). *The production of space*. Oxford: Blackwell.

Lewinson, M., Flint, A.S., & Van Sluys, K. (2002). Taking on critical literacy: The journey of newcomers and novices. *Language Arts, 79*(5), 382–392.

McCarthey, S., & Moje, E. (2002). Identity matters. *Reading Research Quarterly, 37*(2), 228–238.

Miller, s. (2007a). The loaded matrix in classroom and school environments. In sj. Miller & L. Norris, *Unpacking the loaded teacher matrix: Negotiating space and time between university and secondary English classrooms* (pp. 33–83). New York: Peter Lang.

Miller, s. (2007b). The loaded matrix: Theoretical and practical framework. In sj. Miller & L. Norris, *Unpacking the loaded teacher matrix: Negotiating space and time between university and secondary English classrooms* (pp. 11–31). New York: Peter Lang.

Miller, s. (2007c). Social justice and sociocultural issues as part of the loaded matrix. In sj. Miller & L. Norris, *Unpacking the loaded teacher matrix: Negotiating space and time between university and secondary English classrooms* (pp. 157–203). New York: Peter Lang.

Rose, G. (1993). *Feminism and geography: The limits of geographical knowledge.* Cambridge: Polity Press.

Soja, E. W. (1996). *Thirdspace: Journeys to Los Angeles and other real-and-imagined places.* Malden: Blackwell.

Street, B.V. (1995). *Social literacies: Critical approaches to literacy in development, ethnography, and education.* London: Longman.

Tolan, S. (1991). *Plague year.* New York: Random House.

Witting, M. (1983). The point of view: Universal of particular? *Feminist Issues, 3*(2), pp. 63–69.

Fourteen

Eating Cake
The Paradox of Sexuality as a Counter-Diversity Discourse

Gerald Walton

> . . . And you knew who you were then. Girls were girls and men were men.
> Mister, we could use a man like Herbert Hoover again.
> People seemed to be content. Fifty dollars paid the rent.
> Freaks were in a circus tent. Those were the days.
> Hair was short and skirts were long. Kate Smith really sold a song.
> I don't know just what went wrong. Those Were The Days.
> —Theme song to the 1970s American sitcom *All in the Family*, by Lee Adams and Charles Strouse

In this chapter, I take the reader through a conceptual and political journey. I first untangle the concepts "sex" and "gender," terms that are certainly not new but are nevertheless intertwined in ways that are problematic for understanding a third concept, sexuality. Teasing apart these concepts, I then explore how homosexuality, being socially forbidden, is at once shrouded from public view and the object by which gays and lesbians are interrogated through widespread attitudes and hate-generated campaigns. I explore ways in which language shapes perceptions of, and attitudes towards, gays and lesbians in society, including schools. Finally, I argue that assimilationist approaches to gay and lesbian social justice maintain double standards where privilege is accorded to straight people at the expense of gay and lesbian ones.

Sexuality

In the mid-1990s, I took a social theory course. One day in class, a student mentioned the difficulties she experienced because of the reactions of people whenever she used the pronoun "her" to describe her partner, rather than the more expected "him." The next day, the professor expressed surprise that people would talk about such a personal aspect of their lives with strangers in a public venue like a university classroom. Had she referred to a male partner, it is doubtful that the professor would have felt perplexed; it seems ridiculous to even suggest the possibility. But his feelings and words are evidence of a double standard that had not occurred to him to analyze. I did not have the words to express it then, but I would now describe such a double standard as a *strategy of containment* that privileges straight people but reduces gay and lesbian people to "sexualities."

Such strategies, largely unexamined and typically unintentional, are recurring patterns in social interactions. Inside schools, sexuality predominantly refers to heterosexual experiences, sexual mechanics, and related biological and medical issues that are mostly confined within "sex education" curricula. Such realms of discussion do not limit straight students to mere sexuality. Other dimensions of straight identities flourish throughout schools, as they do in wider society. Most students are straight. Most students have straight parents, brothers, sisters, and other relatives. Heterosexual public displays of affection are commonplace in schools and elsewhere. Most people do not give such straight visibility a second thought.

However, gay and lesbian students are typically denied such commonplace visibility and social validation. Homophobia, which I refer to as attitudes, expressions, and behaviours against gay and lesbian people, is a response to gay and lesbian visibility. It is seen explicitly through verbal and physical expressions and implicitly through exclusion, ignorance, and strategies of containment. Overtly homophobic people are preoccupied with the sexual dimension of being gay or lesbian. Perhaps not surprisingly, social realms such as schools are sites where heterosexuality is positioned as the default category of sexuality and thus normalized. For most people, heterosexuality need not be theorized or even acknowledged. It just somehow *is*. In finding ways of acknowledging and supporting other modes of sexuality, I suggest that the very word sexuality is a discourse that confounds, rather than facilitates, the building of inclusive environments in schooling for students who are not heterosexual and/or whose families include those who are not heterosexual.

I also argue that terms like "sexuality," "sex," and "gender" are not self-evident, even if they are used routinely in common lexicon. Sex and gender, in particular, are mostly used interchangeably. It is widely assumed that male equals boy or man, female equals girl or woman, and all are presumed to be heterosexual unless evidence suggests, or proclamations state, otherwise. Such connections may indeed accurately describe many people. Many, perhaps even most, people identify as heterosexual (including some who behave otherwise) and generally conform to dominant gender norms. Yet, this should not deter the asking of such basic, exploratory questions as, how has it come to be that humans are organized and categorized in these particular sexual and gendered ways? How are some categories privileged through social processes such as schooling, while others are marginalized, even vilified? Rather than presuming that we all know what these terms mean and taking it for granted that people are socially organized in these ways "just because," I would instead propose that these notions have become a rather jumbled mess of meanings, assumptions, and normative expectations. In short, they are linguistic devices that shape, and in turn are shaped by, normative conventions that are exclusive rather than inclusive. Such is the very nature of categories. Some are in. Others are out.

Ticking the Appropriate Box

Next, then, I would like to unravel the jumble. In the undergraduate courses on diversity in education that I teach, I have found it useful as a crucial first step to identify the patterns of assumptions, such as that sex is interchangeable with gender. Illuminating such patterns helps students to identify how schooling perpetuates the dominant perspectives on sexuality and the social practices related to it, to the detriment of all students but to some more than others. Untangling the strands serves three functions: It provides a platform from which to discuss how language itself replicates dynamics of inclusion and exclusion. It illuminates how those who do not fit the norms of heterosexuality might be "normalized" in schools and in society. And, it indicates strategies that would foster and validate human diversity, itself a problematic term, in ways other than the more usual ones of race, ethnicity, religion, and culture.

In addition to the social theory course mentioned earlier, I also took a course for my undergraduate degree called, Sociology of Human Sexuality. The professor, Dr. Aaron Devor, began by writing three words on the board, namely, sex, gender, and sexuality. He asked us, the students, for our thoughts on what these terms mean. Are they the same? Are they different? How are they similar? How are they dissimilar? Judging from the blank or confused looks on most of our faces, it was evident that many of us had not stopped to consider what these terms might actually mean or to tease our assumptions apart. Aren't sex and gender self-evident, many of us wondered. If a person is a boy, then he is male. Isn't he? If someone is a girl, then she is female. Isn't she?

Not necessarily. As Devor (1997) and Bornstein (1998, 1994) each point out, sex and gender, as concepts that shape and organize people's lives, are not that simple, even if the normative link between sex and gender applies to most people. Devor describes a series of assumptions that he calls the "dominant gender schema" that shape our collective perceptions—and thus our notions of "reality"—about sex and gender. Sex, according to Devor, is widely assumed to be an "intrinsic biological characteristic" (p. 71). Usually there are two and only two categories of sex, namely, male or female. For most people in society, filling out a form to identify ourselves as either male or female is a simple and unproblematic step that most of us do not have to think about. Tick! It's done.

The sexes, as Devor (1997) describes them, are "presumed. . . to be biologically determined properties which members of society simply recognize on the basis of scientific evidence" (p. 72). Such evidence relies on visual inspection of genitalia at birth. When people are born with ambiguous genitalia, known as intersexed people, it is widely considered by medical practitioners to be an abnormality, as opposed to a variation, for which surgery might be employed as a corrective mechanism.

Genders, on the other hand, are social manifestations of sex (Devor, 1997). As the expression goes, sex is between the legs; gender is between the ears. Males are thus also boys or men; females are also girls or women. In the usual forms of North American socialization, boys should be interested in rough-and-tumble play, trucks, and superheroes and should choose blue or green as favorite colours rather than, say, pink. Girls, by contrast, should enjoy dolls and playing house and should fantasize about marrying the man of their dreams. Her future wedding day is widely promoted as the most important day of her life, after which she will live happily ever after.

While it can be claimed that such descriptions are stereotypes that, at best, only crudely describe the polarities of gender in society (boy/man and girl/woman), it is also the case that particular media perpetuate such stereotypes and generate massive profits from doing so. The documentary *Mickey Mouse Monopoly: Disney, Childhood, and Corporate Power* (Sun, 2001), for instance, makes the claim that Disney cartoons depict male heroes as aggressive, muscular, white, and dominating, while female heroines are gentle, subordinate to males, white (Pocahontas and Mulan notwithstanding), skinny, and pretty by North American, media-influenced standards. The Disney Corporation has enormous social influence around the world. More generally, Leistyna and Alper (2007) assert that

> elite private interests have worked diligently to monopolize the means of production and distribution of information and ideas so as to be able to more effectively circulate, legitimate, and reproduce a vision of the world that suits their needs; a world where profit trumps people at every turn (p. 54).

A problem is that the two-sexes–two-genders model does not capture the wide diversity of sexual or gendered expressions and identities that are evident throughout human history (Devor, 2007; Carroll, 2005; Lovaas, 2005). Further, such categories are imposed upon everyone in society (everyone in contemporary Western societies, at least) through assumptions about what is "normal" and "natural." As impositions, these categories are hegemonic, a concept that McLaren (2007) describes as

> the maintenance of domination not by the sheer exercise of force *but primarily through consensual social practices, social forms, and social structures produced in specific sites such as the church, the state, the school, the mass media, the political system, and the family.* (p. 203, italics in original)

Through repetition, gender certainly seems that way for most people, and many identify themselves in gendered ways (boy/man; girl/woman) quite comfortably. Contrary to the usual notion that gender describes what people inherently *are*, Butler (1990) argues that gender is what people *do*. According to Butler, people learn to present themselves to the world as either boys/men or girls/women. She refers to such presentations, which have been normalized and rendered invisible through repetition, as gender performativity. When boys and girls do not "perform" gender in socially acceptable ways, they are usually shamed into changing their behaviour, or as Butler might put it, their performance. Her analysis provides an avenue for thinking about gender beyond the limited range of the two categories that are assigned at birth—only one per person, please—based on visual categorization of sex.

Having only two boxes to tick (male or female) implies that we must all be one or the other (we cannot be both or neither) and that anything other than one or the other is contrary to the gendered social order and, furthermore, will not even be acknowledged or considered. Having only two genders that are attributed to sexual categories (boys and men for males; girls and women for females) also does not represent the wide variation of gendered interests, expressions, and identities (Bornstein, 1994; Wilchins, 2002). Instead, discourse, as it is employed in daily interactions, constructs normalcy. By discourse, I am referring to habituated patterns of speech and talk that shape our collective and individual senses of reality. Sex and gender, specifically the two-sex, two-gender model, are thus dominant discourses in contemporary society.

Such discourses shape ideas about how people "should" be. "Should" suggests that hegemonic notions of sex and gender are ideological (Devor, 2007). Drawing again from McLaren (2007), he describes ideology as *the production and representation of ideas, values, and beliefs and the manner in which they are expressed and lived out by both individuals and groups.* Simply put, ideology refers to the production of sense and meaning. It can be described as a way of viewing the world, a complex of ideas, various types of social practices, rituals, and representations *that we tend to accept as natural and as common sense.* (p. 205, italics in original)

Those who present themselves (who *perform*, as Butler would put it) in society as normal by conventional standards will usually be accepted by similar others; those who do not fit into the usual normative expectations of what it means to be a girl or woman, boy or man are typically ostracized. For everyone, gendered expectations are imposed and limit the ways in which people, as gendered beings, can express themselves in society due to the implicit (and sometimes explicit) threat of rejection, ridicule, and violence towards those who do not conform.

Many students have experienced these harsh realities firsthand in their schools. An unidentified young man in Cambridge, Nova Scotia, for instance, bore the brunt of homophobic bullying in 2008 when he wore a pink golf shirt to school (Canadian Broadcasting Corporation, 2007). Whether or not he was gay is publicly unknown and misses the point, in any case. Significantly, he (perhaps unintentionally) broke the rules of gender, one of which is that pink is a girl's colour. One might say that he publicly, if unwittingly, challenged gender ideology. Some men, such as Donald Trump and Canadian hockey commentator Don Cherry, may be able to get away with wearing pink and avoid social censure of their manhoods, but only if their masculine prowess is solidified in other ways, such as through the power of wealth and aggressive gender performance.

The bullied young man in Cambridge presumably had no such counter performances that would render wearing pink a non-issue. The price he paid for merely wearing pink, a colour supposedly off-limits to boys and men, was being targeted with violence by some of his peers. Not just generic violence, but violence with a particular characterization specifically employed for maximum impact, namely, homophobic violence. Fortunately, two other boys from his school, David Shepherd and Travis Price, launched a campaign to challenge such violence and bullying. According to news coverage, David and Travis bought several dozen pink shirts at local thrift stores and distributed them throughout their school. Their actions launched a "wear pink" anti-bullying campaign that spread quickly throughout Canada and elsewhere on the wings of Internet communications. February 27, 2008, became Wear Pink Day.

Unfortunately, other bullied students have not received similar support from their peers or teachers and administrators. Azmi Jubran, a former student in the North Vancouver School District, and David Knight, a former student in a school near Burlington, Ontario, each survived their grade schooling in spite of ongoing and malicious bullying, some of which was on-line and anonymous. Both of these two young men were victims of verbal and physical violence. Not just generic violence, but violence of a specific kind, namely homophobic harassment that questioned their gender status as men. Neither received support from their peers, teachers, or administrators, unlike the student from Cambridge. Both eventually employed legal mechanisms by filing human rights complaints to enact change within their schools and school districts, simply because school administrators would not enact such change.

These cases provide evidence that gender, especially among boys and men, is a site of significant personal vulnerability. Being called "sissy," "fag," "gay," "homo," or "queer" is a powerful assault on boys and young men, attacking them where they are most vulnerable, namely, their gender identity. To state it clearly, homophobia is gendered violence (Meyer,

2006) rather than sexualized violence. Masculine bravado masks the vulnerability of gender identity (Katz, 2006).

Gendered violence and bullying tend to manifest differently for boys than for girls. With boys, homophobia characterizes the typical slurs of choice. With girls, notions of "the bad girl," along with attacks on body image (Simmons, 2002), are powerful affronts. "Bitch," "whore," "fat," and "ugly" are like knives that shred at emotions and sever confidence. David Knight's sister, Katherine, targeted for merely being David's sister, was routinely called a "slut, whore, bitch, and dirty" (Malarek, 2002). In the case of either boys or girls, men or women, such violence is gender-based (Meyer, 2006) and supports the view that gender is not "natural," but instead is socially constructed and continually policed and regulated by peers, among others, in daily interactions, attitudes, values, and norms. As Goffman claimed in 1963, those who are identified and vilified as deviant or different serve to normalize others. Similarly, Eribon (2004) succinctly observes that, "a society defines itself by what it excludes" (p. 77).

The brief overview of the ways in which gender is presumed to connect with sex and in which both dimensions organize society encompass what might be called Gender 101. Through admittedly crude brushstrokes, I have argued that sexual and gendered categories are hegemonic, ideological, and constructed through socialization, social interactions, and expectations and norms about gendered behaviours. With Macedo (2007), Steinberg (2004), and Giroux (2004), I would add media influences to the list. I have found that untangling the strands of, and challenging the usual assumptions about, sex and gender leaves many students blankly staring into space. For some, I shattered, or at least vigorously shook, the paradigm of the two-sex, two-gender model and the investment that they had unwittingly made in it. I attempted to disrupt the taken-for-granted assumption that people are naturally either male or female and boy/man or girl/woman, respectively. In the classes that I teach, I sometimes consider leaving students to sort out the intricacies of sex and gender on their own, resisting the temptation to add more complexity to what, for many people, appears quite simple. But doing so would result in omitting a third vital construct that intersects gender and sex. When I add the notion of sexuality to the discussion, some students look even more perplexed.

Containing Sexuality

Sexuality is a third strand that is woven throughout the complexities of sex and gender, adding to the human tapestry. As with sex and gender, sexuality is specified as categories, usually heterosexual and homosexual, sometimes bisexual, occasionally, asexual. These supposedly discrete categories represent (with the exception of the latter) the grouping of attractions, desires, fantasies, and behaviours that constitute sexuality. However, it would be misleading to suggest that such indicators are linear and necessarily result in any particular sexuality. Consider, for instance, the ways in which identity intersects the constellation of factors that form sexuality. Many who identify themselves as heterosexual (also known as straight) fantasize about having sexual experiences with a member of their own sex. Personals ads are replete with ads from people who describe themselves as "straight but curious." AIDS organizations have launched campaigns to reach not only gay and bisexual men but also "men who have sex with men," MSM for short, but who do not identify as homosexual, gay, bisexual, or queer. These examples indicate that actual sexuality (fantasies, desires, behaviours) is often not congruent with identity.

An added complication is that private identity is often not the same as public identity. Some people present themselves in the world as straight and may be married to a heterosexual partner but have sex with members of their own sex when opportunities arise. Famous examples of such "closet cases" include Rock Hudson and, more recently, Ted Haggard, a televangelist in the United States whose homosexuality was exposed to the world in 2006, who also had routinely proclaimed to millions of people that hell and damnation await gay and lesbian people who refuse to turn away from their sin. A mere three weeks after his downfall from the pulpit, Haggard claimed to have been completely healed of his homosexuality. In my view, that which is not disease cannot be healed (Walton, 2005).

Homophobia, whether from the pulpit of hypocritical Christians such as Ted Haggard or from students in schools, hinges upon the assumption that being gay or lesbian is only about sexuality, and not mere sexuality, but an inferior version of the heterosexual norm. For instance, many straight people proclaim that gays and lesbians should not "flaunt" their sexuality in public. Yet, it is not only heterosexual homophobes who focus unduly on sexuality in relation to gays and lesbians. It is not uncommon for gay and lesbian people themselves to say that their sexuality is "none of anyone's business." Thus, such people have internalized their own oppression and have accepted the dominant ideology of sexuality.

As a former Christian and recovered "ex-gay,"[1] I can attest to the usual rhetoric among fundamentalist and evangelical Christians that gay "lifestyles" spread immorality, disease, and moral corruption and that young people should be protected from such potential harm. The term "lifestyle" is used by other people in less vitriolic ways, yet the result, perhaps unintentional, is that being gay or lesbian is unwittingly conceptualized only as sexual behaviour. To make a point that should be obvious to everyone but clearly is not, there is no such thing as a homosexual lifestyle. Gays and lesbians lead a variety of lifestyles, as do heterosexual people. There is no such singular lifestyle that is inherently and necessarily connected to being gay or lesbian. The persistence of such ideas is rooted in homophobia (because lifestyle speech in this context is usually condemning in tone) and heterosexism (because it presumes that being heterosexual is not also a lifestyle and thus does not need to be justified or explained). Homogenization of gays and lesbians through sexuality discourse is deployed in the service of oppression.

Heterosexual or straight people do not have to face such reductionist accusations. I use the word reductionist to convey how it is that sexuality in the context of gay and lesbian people confines their identities to genitally focused pleasures, precluding other dimensions of individual identity, such as family, relationships, and community. For example, when, in 1997, the Surrey School Board banned three picture books for children that depicted families with two moms or two dads, supporters routinely made claims that children should not be exposed to such ideas, as though being gay or lesbian were a disease of sexual and mental deviance.

Such a misinformed connection has a grim history. Only in 1969 was homosexuality decriminalized in Canada under the leadership of Pierre Elliott Trudeau. Only in 1973 was homosexuality removed as a category of mental illness from the *Diagnostic and Statistical Manual of Mental Disorders* (DSM), the bible of the American Psychiatric Association. It is not that teachers must necessarily endorse sexuality, identity, diversity, and family plurality or change their values and beliefs to be more politically correct, as so many of them, along with legions of parents, seem to fear. Rather, teachers have legal responsibilities in public schools in accordance with the *Canadian Charter of Rights and Freedoms*, to not discriminate against students on the basis of gender, sexual orientation, or family composition.

Outside the realm of criminal law and psychiatry, traces of similar claims about the presumed inferiority of gay and lesbian people persist today. Some heterosexual people (or, at least, some people who claim to be heterosexual) cry out that kids should be "protected" from gay and lesbian lifestyles. Some gay and lesbian people insist that it is "nobody's business what I do in my bedroom." Of course, such claims are true in the sense that actual sex is typically performed in private. However, how is it the case that publicly acknowledging gay and lesbian relationships, for example by holding hands in public or getting married, is "flaunting" one's homosexuality? Why are not similar accusations made when straight people engage in public displays of affection or proclaim their partnership through rites (rights) such as marriage? The fact is that heterosexual people have particular rights in society, enshrined in law in most countries of the world, that are denied to gay and lesbian people. Such rights are concretely *special* rights. In Canada, the right to marry became democratized when wording in the Marriage Act was changed from "a man and a woman" to "two persons" in 2005. The irony is that gays and lesbians are usually the ones accused of demanding special rights not accorded to straight people when, in fact, such changes in law reflect equal—not exclusive—access to legal recognition. A glaring double standard also exists where most straight people claim public space without recognizing it as unearned privilege.

The point I want to illuminate here is that language, as discourse, shapes people's perceptions and realities. Simply put, being gay and lesbian involves many dimensions of life other than sexuality. In schools across the country, it is taken for granted that students will form heterosexual relationships and demonstrate them in schools through such behaviour as holding hands. It is never questioned that parents may come to the school as a couple on parent-teacher interview days. It never sparks controversy when heterosexual couples dance together at school dances. Books that depict straight couples are never banned for that reason alone. Straight teachers who happen to mention their opposite-sex wives, husbands, or partners never have to consider whether or not their colleagues will morally judge them on the basis of their partnership. Such taken-for-granted assumptions are both heterosexist (the assumption that all people are, or should be, heterosexual: Unks, 1995; Herek, 1992) and heteronormative (the practices that position heterosexuality as the unquestioned norm: Yep, 2005). Combined, such assumptions and practices form what Adrienne Rich (1980) famously described as "compulsory heterosexuality."

Gay and lesbian students, parents, and teachers do not have the same privileges in schools as do straight ones. In schools and communities across the country, reductionist discourses such as "sexuality" confine being gay or lesbian to a singular dimension, negating other dimensions such as family, identity, and community. Such discourses are what I call strategies of containment. In 2002, a twelfth-grade student by the name of Marc Hall was assailed by negative attitudes rooted in reductionist discourses about sexuality. In small-town Ontario, he attended a Catholic public school that refused to allow him and his then boyfriend to attend the high school prom (Smith, 2002). He was not requesting special rights but simply wanted to participate in school activities on par with his straight peers. The school authorities said no. Marc took legal action, and an Ontario superior court eventually ruled in his favour. The chair of the school board was quoted in the *Globe and Mail* as saying that "homosexual romantic activity" contravenes Catholic values about sexuality (Oziewicz, 2002). Yet, aspects of love, relationship, and family—all strongly endorsed by a broad range of Christian faiths including Catholicism—are routinely ignored in discourse that is focused upon, even preoccupied with, mere sexuality. Further, such judgments preclude the notion that identity does not necessarily equal sexual activity. Can students identify as straight without having had heterosexual sex? Certainly. Yet, for gay and lesbian people, age notwithstanding, the assumption is that one is gay or lesbian because one has had homosexual sex.

Reductionism as a strategy of containment is evident in reactions to proposed changes to curriculum. In addition to parents who rallied in support of the Surrey School Board book ban in 1997, the Catholic Civil Rights League in 2007 lobbied school boards throughout British Columbia to guarantee that parents would be able to pull their children out of instruction that some parents might find "objectionable" (Steffenhagen, 2007). Their lobbying efforts were in reaction to a proposed course called Social Justice 12 that covered "isms" in society, such as ableism, consumerism, cultural imperialism, heterosexism, racism, and sexism. Some groups and parents interpret such courses as undermining parental authority over what their children learn, even though the course is an elective. Apart from the issue of why some parents feel entitled to proclaim what other people's children may and may not learn, it is significant also to note how such arguments are framed through reductionist discourse.

In yet another instance, a play that took place in a school in the North Vancouver School District featured kisses between a straight couple and one between a lesbian couple. In response to parental objections, the lesbian kiss was cut from the play but not the straight kiss. Tellingly, depictions of domestic violence and rape were neither cut nor even commented upon (Gatchalian, 2004). Gay and lesbian people are widely perceived and depicted as only sexual beings, divorcing them from other realities of their lives and identities, such as family, relationships, and communities. Such strategies of containment will continue to have political and social influence, even if fueled by bigotry, in countries such as Canada and the United States, which purport to be beacons of freedom and democracy.

Having Our Cake

In my analysis of sexuality as a discourse, I do not mean, nor do I want the reader to get the impression, that I am positioning an anti-sexuality argument. I am not suggesting that gays and lesbians need to adhere to respectable standards to win the approval of the heterosexual majority, particularly parents, teachers, politicians, and others in positions of power. I am not advocating that being good gays and lesbians is a necessary strategy for winning the approval of young men who would otherwise cruise the streets in small groups looking for "faggots" to bash. I am not advancing an assimilationist perspective that gays and lesbians are the same as straights (with only one teeny-tiny difference of which straights need not be afraid), a perspective employed to defuse demonization. I am not suggesting that teachers have to "teach children about homosexuality," which is the typical response to curriculum that recognizes gay and lesbian issues and histories. Such claims are misguided, though politically powerful, rhetoric that underlies fear and hostility. Finally, I am not pitting gays and lesbians against each other through constructions of morality, dividing them into two camps, one representing those who claim to be upstanding, moral citizens with houses, white picket fences, and "2.5 children" and the other being those who reject marriage both as a personal choice and as a political strategy, and who eschew compulsory *till death do us part* monogamy.

Instead, I am suggesting that the ways in which sexuality is employed and deployed in campaigns against social justice reduce whole human beings to dehumanized sexualities. In other words, gays and lesbians are depicted as uni-dimensional. Reductionism is a strategy for legitimizing violence. Aaron Webster was kicked and stomped to death by a group of four men in Vancouver in 2001. Twenty-two-year-old student Matthew Shepard was tortured and beaten to death by two young men in 1998. Two gay men were murdered within days of each other in Halifax in 2007 (Moore, 2007). In 2008, openly gay, fifteen-year-old Lawrence King was shot to death by a fellow student in Oxnard, California, for wearing makeup and jewelry. The list goes on (see, for instance, Janoff, 2005; and http://www.gayamericanheroes.net/).

Less violently, the identities of gay and lesbian children, their families and relationships as well as of children who have two moms, two dads, or gay siblings or relatives are not acknowledged or supported in schools in discussions about (hetero)sexuality. Sexuality is, of course, a significant issue and a key aspect of childhood, adolescence, and beyond. However, it should not preclude other aspects of people's lives. Doing so is precisely the strategy of choice that perpetuates harmful stereotypes and facilitates bigotry in society and in schools, much to the pleasure of those who think of gay and lesbian people as sick, perverted, disgusting, or immoral. An advertisement by *Focus on the Family Canada*, a conservative Christian organization, was launched in 2005 in response to the menacing spectre of so-called gay marriage in Canada. The ad presumptuously claimed, "We believe in Mom and Dad. We believe in marriage," as though gays and lesbians do not and, more specifically, cannot have the same beliefs because, by implication, being gay or lesbian is only about sexuality. Gays and lesbians apparently do not have families or moms or dads. Straight people apparently never divorce, and straight parents and their straight children are never estranged from each other.

It is doubtful that organizations such as *Focus on the Family Canada* would openly advocate actual violence against gays and lesbians. Yet, at the same time, spokespeople of *Focus on the Family Canada* have not launched campaigns that counter vitriol of an overtly hate-mongering nature. For instance, Fred Phelps, reverend of the Westboro Baptist Church in Topeka, Kansas, proclaims that "God hates fags" and "fag enablers" (see godhatesfags.com) as though positioning himself as God's right-hand man. Violence is similarly advocated in a news article that was printed in the *Vancouver Sun* in 2004. In bold, highlighted text, a nineteen-year-old American soldier stationed in Iraq promoted the killing of "faggots and bastards" as a tactical necessity to win the war (Harnden, 2004). The *Vancouver Sun* did not comment on his casual bigotry and thus implied through silence that such killing is insignificant. If people who spew homophobic bigotry can ignore other aspects of gay and lesbian lives, such as family, friends, community, relationships, then verbal or physical assault is justified and becomes that much easier. Dehumanization is the nature of bigotry, channeled by reductionist discourse.

Regardless, gays and lesbians should be able to have their cake and eat it too, as most straight people do, obliviously. By this, I mean that forging public representations of gay and lesbian families, communities, and relationships need not be done while also denying actual sexuality. With straight people, gays and lesbians should not have to hide their sexuality identities in public spaces, eclipsed by wholesome images of family and community.

Focus on the Family and other examples of Archie Bunker–style bigotry support a "girls were girls and men were men" perception of the gendered world that enshrines the dominant gender schema (Devor, 2007) and normalizes heterosexuality and straight couples and families while demonizing other sexuality identities and ways of performing gender. In spite of such romanticized and sanitized versions of North American life, those were the days that never actually were.

Note

1. So-called "ex-gay" ministries are programs of evangelical Christianity that perpetuate, and reap profits from, the persistent notion that being gay is morally depraved but curable through the love of Christ. These programs proliferated throughout North America in the 1980s and continue to be promoted by right-wing Christian organizations today.

References

Bornstein, K. (1994). *Gender outlaw: On men, women, and the rest of us.* New York: Routledge.

———. (1998). *My gender workbook: How to become a real man, a real woman, the real you, or something else entirely.* New York: Routledge.

Butler, J. (1990). *Gender trouble: Feminism and the subversion of identity.* New York: Routledge.

Canadian Broadcasting Corporation. (2007, September 19). *Bullied student tickled pink by schoolmates' T-shirt campaign.* http://www.cbc.ca/canada/nova-scotia/story/2007/09/18/pink-tshirts-students.html Accessed 2008, March 8.

Carroll, L. (2005). Gender identity. In James T. Sears (Ed.), *Youth, education, and sexualities: An international encyclopedia* (pp. 358–361). Westport, CT: Greenwood.

Devor, A. H. (1997). *FTM: Female-to-male transsexuals in society.* Bloomington, IN: Indiana University.

———. (2007). http://web.uvic.ca/~ahdevor/HowMany/HowMany.html

Eribon, D. (2004). *Insult and the making of the gay self* (Michael Lucey, Trans.) Durham, NC: Duke University.

Gatchalian, C. E. (2004, April 15). School censors same-sex kiss: Handsworth play takes out kiss, but leaves in rape. *Xtra! West,* p. 17.

Giroux, H. A. (2004). Are Disney movies good for your kids? In Shirley R. Steinberg and Joe L. Kincheloe (Eds.), *Kinderculture: The corporate construction of childhood* (pp. 164–180). Boulder, CO: Westview.

Goffman, E. (1963). *Stigma: Notes on the management of spoiled identity.* Englewood Cliffs, NJ: Prentice-Hall.

Harnden, T. (2004, November 6). US assault on Fallujah will 'finish the job': Scores of wounded and 'angels' are anticipated. *Vancouver Sun,* p. A16.

Herek, G. (1992). The social context of hate crimes: Notes on cultural heterosexism. In Gregory Herek and Kevin T. Berrill (Eds.), *Hate crimes: Confronting violence against lesbians and gay men* (pp. 89–104). Newbury Park, CA: Sage.

Katz, J. (2006). *The macho paradox: Why some men hurt women and how all men can help.* Naperville, IL: Sourcebooks.

Janoff, D. (2005). *Pink blood: Homophobic violence in Canada.* Toronto, ON: University of Toronto.

Leistyna, P. and Alper, L. (2007). Critical media literacy for the twenty-first century: Taking our entertainment seriously. In Donaldo Macedo and Shirley Steinberg (Eds.), *Media literacy: A reader* (pp. 54–78). New York: Peter Lang.

Lovaas, K. (2005). Gender roles. In James T. Sears (Ed.), *Youth, education, and sexualities: An international encyclopedia* (pp. 364–369). Westport, CT: Greenwood.

Macedo, D. (2007). Deconstructing the corporate media/government nexus. In Donaldo Macedo and Shirley Steinberg (Eds.), *Media literacy: A reader* (pp. xvii–xxxii). New York: Peter Lang.

Malarek, V. (2002, June 3). Ontario teens suing school board over bullying. *Globe and Mail,* p. A4.

McLaren, P. (2007). *Life in schools: An introduction to critical pedagogy in the foundations of education,* 5th ed. Boston, MA: Pearson.

Meyer, E. (2006). Gendered harassment in North America: School-based interventions for reducing homophobia and heterosexism. In C. Mitchell and F. Leach (Eds.), *Combating gender violence in and around schools* (pp. 43-50). Basingstoke Hants, UK: Trentham Books.

Moore, O. (2007, May 15). Gay cruising areas on alert after killings: Halifax homosexual community in shock after two men found dead in similar circumstances. *Globe and Mail,* p. A3.

Oziewicz, E. (2002, May 11). Supreme Court challenge looms: Catholic school board to take case to trial after judge overturns ban on gay prom date. *Globe and Mail*, p. A10.

Rich, A. (1980). *Blood, bread, and poetry.* New York: W. W. Norton.

Simmons, R. (2002). *Odd girl out: The hidden culture of aggression in girls.* New York: Harcourt.

Smith, G. (2002, May 11). Gay teen wins prom fight. *Globe and Mail*, pp. A1, A10.

Steffenhagen, J. (2007, January 8). Schools warned on 'values': Catholic civil rights group seeks guarantee that parents can pull children over 'objectionable' material. *Vancouver Sun*, pp. A1, A4. [Corren]

Steinberg, S. R. (2004). The bitch who has everything. In Shirley R. Steinberg and Joe L. Kincheloe (Eds.), *Kinderculture: The corporate construction of childhood* (pp. 150–163). Boulder, CO: Westview.

Sun, Chyng (Producer). (2001). *Mickey Mouse monopoly: Disney, childhood, and corporate power* [Motion Picture]. Northampton, MA: Media Education Foundation.

Unks, G. (1995). Thinking about the gay teen. In Gerald Unks (Ed.), The gay teen: Educational practice and theory for lesbian, gay, and bisexual adolescents (pp. 3–12). New York: Routledge.

Walton, G. (2005). Reparative therapy. In James T. Sears (Ed.), *Youth, education, and sexualities: An international encyclopedia* (pp. 710–712). Westport, CT: Greenwood.

Wilchins, R. (2002). It's your gender, stupid! In Joan Nestle, Clare Howell, and Riki Wilchins (Eds.), *Genderqueer: Voices from beyond the sexual binary* (pp. 23–32). Los Angeles, CA: Alyson.

Yep, G. A. (2005). Heteronormativity. In James T. Sears (Ed.), *Youth, education, and sexualities: An international encyclopedia* (pp. 395–398). Westport, CT: Greenwood.

Fifteen

Untangling 'Gender Diversity'
Genderism and Its Discontents (i.e., Everyone)

Liz Airton

This reader is about diversity in its many manifestations. This chapter is supposed to present one of these manifestations—gender diversity—in an accessible and introductory way, making connections to education and the sorts of things that teachers need to know about gender. Expectations probably vary regarding the contents of a chapter loosely titled 'gender diversity.' You may be anticipating an extended definition of terms that you have heard before, such as transsexual or intersex. You could also be expecting less common terms, such as genderqueer, butch, femme, or trans. Although such expectations will be satisfied to a limited extent, the story told here about gender does not offer a touristic account of lives lived with particular difficulty, due to rigid norms of sex and gender.[1] Presumably, this chapter could also be a review of literature on gender or 'sex differences' in education; familiar themes there include alleged sex differences in particular cognitive capacities or learner characteristics on the one hand (innate), and on the other, student experiences or outcomes on the basis of their treatment as a member of 'one or the other sex' (learned). Expectations along these lines will not find a home here because the concept of 'sex difference' is undone by even one exception in a particular context (i.e., what do we do with a girl who is really good at math but surrounded by recuperative sex-differentiated measures which tell her that she is different or even gender-deviant?). Most studies of sex differences in educational outcomes do not even define the terms sex, gender, boy, girl, male, female, etc., assuming that the meanings we attach to these words are universal and universally understood. Instead of dabbling in objectification or the construction of absolutes, this chapter addresses the ways in which *we all* come to understand ourselves in the wake of receiving a particular grammatical tag—pronoun—upon our messy entrance into the world. Our course is plotted there and then, and addressing someone with the wrong pronoun is an occasion for immediate correction and even apology. I consider 'gender' to be everything which follows this initial act of naming and which is done to, by, and 'for' us to ensure that we are always given that pronoun whenever pronouns are required.

Throughout this chapter I use sex, gender and sexuality differently than most in that the meaning of these terms does not rely on the presence of certain ways of being for their explanation. For starters, your *sex* is determined by the degree to which your body and its morphology (physical appearance) perceptibly fit with prevailing ideas of what bodies should look like (we normally call these male and female sex characteristics). Although sex affects chromosomes (XX, XY, XO, XXY, etc.), hormone levels (but not presence—we all have androgen, estrogen and testosterone) and physical characteristics (e.g., internal structures, genitalia, hair, body shape, voice, etc.), your birth or assigned sex was named (or not) based on a quick visual survey of your external genitalia and its being named in turn as looking enough (or not) like a penis or a vagina.[2] Your *gender* is an evolving relationship negotiated among your lived experience, your context and your feelings about your body. Many people situate their gender within the categories of masculine or feminine and find common ground with many countless others who do the same. Some of these people also find themselves represented on TV and in other forms of media as long as they have and are recognizable as having a male or female sex, respectively. Finally, your *sexuality* is your choice of, or orientation towards, a desired sexual or affectional object. Everyone has sexual preferences (including the preference to not have sex) and an orientation (or none). Many people situate their sexuality inside heterosexual behaviors, customs and representations while countless others do not. Although sex, gender and sexuality are conceptually separate in order to prevent our ideas about one from determining how we necessarily live the others, they do interact potently with each other as central components of our relationship with ourselves and the world around us. This chapter is concerned primarily with gender, although sex enters into the discussion in many places.

Judith Butler (2004), a foundational gender theorist whose name you will see in many places throughout this chapter, similarly talks about gender as "a practice of improvisation within a scene of constraint" (p. 1). In other words, our gender is a facet of ourselves that is individually negotiated but never outside of our participation in the social world. As limitless as the names we are given, our unique ways of thinking about ourselves as gendered people are somehow constrained in accordance with the shape of our external genitalia: male *or* female. The discussion of 'gender diversity' which follows, then, is less about what gender *is* and more about what gender *does* and how we tend to recognize 'gender' only in certain limited ways. I hope that, after reading this chapter, its implications follow you as you begin (or continue) to teach.

The Trouble with 'Gender Diversity' as Concept

When I was a little girl I was stunningly beautiful. I looked like Judy Garland at her best. I was two crazy parents and one long undefended border shy of Jon Benet Ramsey. I had beautiful curly long brown hair always in real ribbons, big dark eyes, rosy cheeks and bright red lips through some biological miracle. Maybe they just put the red on for the portrait session at The Bay in 1986. But I doubt it. I didn't need any aesthetic prostheses because I was perfect. My solo portrait hung on the wall in The Bay photo studio for a while and on the wall in the upstairs hallway until my parents sold our house a few summers ago. The hair, the hallmark of the photograph, disappeared two years later after I had endured over five hundred hours of sitting on the kitchen table after my bath, braving the loud noise and heat of the blow-dryer, having my hair pulled this way and that with the curly brush, trying to concentrate on the story I was reading while all of this was going on. Amazingly, that hair disappeared when I asked it to and I ended up with horizontal hockey hair instead, short but with earflaps. Two years after that it was variably mushroomed or squashed under a Florida Marlins baseball cap. I have never figured out if I was a born genderqueer or just a strong utilitarian.

Before discussing gender further, it is important to convey my understanding of the term 'diversity.' As you will see, my idea of diversity is important to understand why this chapter will *not* be rooted in the expectations I described. 'Diversity' is a concept inextricably linked with difference and generally understood to mean the presence of a multitude of differences. The most basic implication of 'diversity' as a concept is that distinct categories exist that we can reach into in order to pull enough different things or people together to make a 'diverse' group. For example, in order to say that a group of people is ethnically diverse, we must have prior understandings of 'ethnicity' in which particular ethnicities can be said to be categorically different from each other. Thinking about diversity in this categorical way requires that the categories are delimited (i.e., they begin and end) and static (i.e., unchanging). If we can't definitively say that a particular 'ethnicity' is different from others it becomes very tricky to claim that what we are seeing is a group representing more than one ethnicity. We would have instead a group of individuals who, like everyone, just happen to be from somewhere. The same can be said about race, class, ability, sexuality and many other levels on which people and groups are said to differ categorically from each other.

When we consider what gender means as a delimited and static characteristic that can be ascribed to people or groups, another central implication of 'diversity' is revealed: diversity is unfailingly linked to the visual, or to what is visually signified.[3] We are all familiar with photographic or other pictorial representations of 'diversity' wherein identifiably different people hold hands in a circle or stand together in an amiable clump. A simple internet image search will turn up dozens of examples. If the image is drawn, skin tones on the otherwise identical people illustrated will probably vary from whitish (the colour of the paper underneath) to yellowish to reddish to brownish to deep brownish. If we are looking at a photograph, differences in skin colour will be less extreme but still very self-evident. In both cases, the essentializing subordination of ethnicity to colour (and arguably, race) is in full swing. No one will wear a salwar kameez, but a yarmulke might be found on someone (with no accompanying peyes to indicate orthodoxy).[4] If we are fortunate, in our example there might be someone of a particular skin colour (probably white) in a self-propelled wheelchair, representing disabled people as a whole. Older people may be represented unless we are seeing a happily diverse corporate world. In this case, not only might any hand-holding disappear, but so would the older people. Larger ('fat') people will most certainly not exist. Little people[5] will be in absentia, as will exceptionally tall people. Bald or balding people might show up somewhere but, seeing as baldness is a normal characteristic of many older—patriarchal—male subjects, this is no aberration. Class positionality is invisible. 'Bad teeth' are only a bad memory in a sea of gleaming smiles. People of an array of sexualities are present, to be sure, but we can only assume that this is the case from what we do not see. Finally, women and men must be present in equal number to symbolize not only diversity, but also parity and, by extension, equality.

This hypothetical image is not based on a statistical average or content analysis of hundreds of drawings and photographs. It is an illustrative amalgam of similar images which I have been subjected to throughout my life as a targeted consumer of mainstream Canadian and, through the magic of digital media, American culture. As a second-generation Canadian, I have been fortunate to see myself represented in images of diverse, multicultural utopia to a limited (but still very privileged) extent. I am white, of 'average' size, and able-bodied (but temporarily so, as are most of us), but I am not readily identifiable as either male or female and am therefore guilty of 'looking like' asexuality. (Heterosexuality is the invisible and presumed norm; I do not look like nor pass as heterosexual.) In fact, each of the facets of people and groups visually represented in our phantom image (race, ethnicity, ability, age, size, class, sexuality, gender) are woefully incomplete in terms of the full spectrum of human differences. One might argue that any representation of diversity, visual or otherwise, contains within it what is *absent* as well as what is *present*.

Butler (1991) makes the following comment about identity categories which can be extended to the naming of a group as 'diverse':

> To claim that this is what I *am* [or what 'this is'] is to suggest a provisional totalization of this "I." But if the I can so determine itself, then that which it excludes in order to make that determination remains constitutive of the determination itself. In other words, such a statement presupposes that the "I" exceeds its determination, and even produces that very excess in and by the act which seeks to exhaust the semantic field of that "I." In the act which would disclose the true and full content of that "I," a certain radical *concealment* is thereby produced. (p. 15; original emphasis)

Following Butler, the act of determining that *any* image is what diversity *is,* is an admission that the determination itself is impossible. In other words, the trouble with any representation of 'diversity' begins at the totalization of diversity in the act of representation; when visually represented, 'diversity' comes to be a symbol not of difference but of whatever is contained in the image itself. If the image is one of a particular context (e.g., a staged corporate photograph showcasing visible differences among employees as a non-issue), 'diversity' signifies the smattering of ages, colours, abilities, etc., distributed among the identifiably male-masculine and female-feminine people depicted. 'Diversity' is therefore dishonest in its connotation of 'many,' applying itself to only *some* visual categories of difference. However, 'diversity' never ceases to represent *what is not there* as the very terms of its inscription—i.e., what has to be done in order to say that 'this is diversity'—to contain other things which are *not* admissible as possibilities for what *is*. Arguably, then, the delimited and static categories of human difference contained within are implicitly said to be the only possibilities of *being* human.

So if diversity is not, in fact, the representation of many things but of only some, what is gender diversity? As we have seen, the act of definition in its many forms (visual, textual, etc.) necessarily contains and creates the things which cannot be contained in the definition. If we say categorically that a man is someone with a penis and testicles, we could spark a debate regarding the many men who might have a penis and no testicles (and vice versa), or who have neither but who have been raised as men (or not) and who are read as men (or not) on a daily basis. Although this might lead us to conclude that representing a truly 'gender-diverse' group of people, containing every kind of man, is impossible, such a conclusion is unlikely. This is due to the pervasive—and I would say false—*certainty* about gender which characterizes the social world (i.e., we say with certainty that men are men and that's that).

Returning to our phantom image, a representation of diversity is *inconceivable* which contains all ethnicities, all abilities, all ages, all sizes, all classes, and all sexualities—let alone their infinite intersections. Each of these identities has multiple expressions although they are often reduced to a bare centre-margin formula (i.e., white/non-white, differently abled, etc.) which serves to reinforce the power of the dominant group (e.g., 'non-whites' instead of people of colour—the latter does not require that whiteness be referenced in order to signify a race or ethnicity). These politics of language play out in systemic relations of domination, violence and colonialism throughout the world. I can say with confidence that it would not be very hard to convince someone of the impossibility of an exhaustive representation of diversity (e.g., an image or list which contains every single ethnicity in existence, etc.). However, it would be quite difficult to convince someone that an exhaustive representation of *gender* is impossible because gender is largely thought of as a binary containing only two options: male *or* female. The saturation of 'gender diversity' is commonly presumed to be reached when we see/have an equal number of identifiably male and female people. Besides, who else would we have to see in order to say that a representation of people is *gender-diverse?*

The question should not be 'what else is there to represent?' but 'what does the act of representation *do?*' If we cast about looking for 'other genders' to include alongside male-masculine and female-feminine, we are doomed to fail as our new larger field of identities will still contain what they *do not* represent. An example in the arena of sexuality is this weighty acronym (among many) employed by some queer organizations—GLBTTIQQ, standing for gay, lesbian, bisexual,[6] transgender, transsexual,[7] intersex,[8] queer and questioning.[9] There is the obvious difficulty of continually adding to this laundry list of identities and then, when viewed from the perspective of those excluded from the list (e.g., genderqueers, butches, femmes, asexuals, polyamourists, pomosexuals, etc.), there is injustice and exclusion. The question 'what else?' will invariably lead back to 'what isn't?'

What the act of representation *does* in every instance of 'diversity' is associate the contents of a representation with what is positive or with what is 'good.' People smile in these images. Diversity itself carries an entirely positive or progressive connotation and is rarely, if ever, spoken of as a 'bad thing' to do or be. Moving on from diversity now, almost every representation of human beings offered in language or image contains only people who are men and/or women, masculine and/or feminine. What is truly problematic—and in many cases life-threatening—about this *gender binary* is the denial of the existence of other or different ways of being which logically follows. Beyond the 'good' and the 'bad' in questions of representation lies the very possibility of being, at all. What does one do when one does not exist?

Gender Is Not Only About Its Others

When I was a pre-adolescent boy I looked the same as I do now but smaller and rounder. I was a chubby and athletic boy who was just like other boys until someone said my name out loud. When that happened time would slow down to a standstill. I would see them stop and turn around, size me up, notice the barely perceptible swells underneath my t-shirt, the same brand and colour as theirs, realizing that they hadn't even named them before because chubby boys had those. But now I was named and so was my body, with its shy yet persistent beginnings of breasts. And now they were staring, and then they realized that they were staring at a girl's breasts. The boys who didn't know me, whose soccer game I joined, who had chosen me as a teammate over other boys who stood still clinging to the chain-link fence, would take a good long look at me and find that things were wrong and look away. No one would pass the ball to me ever again if another boy was open, even if I was bigger, faster, or sharper. It was game over for me or I could be the goalie, if I wanted to stick around. I had been spotted, and now I would have to start over somewhere else. That's what I did, but never quietly. I would stroll up to the captain of the moment, make eye contact, ask to play, play well, become the captain, become a girl again suddenly and then lose what I had worked so hard to get.

When I use the word 'exist,' it is important to note that I am not suggesting that there are no people who are seen or who identify as other than gender-normatively male/masculine or female/feminine. You are probably aware that such people do exist, and many are especially prolific.[10] Instead, 'existence' here means what is commonly *shown* to exist or to be real. There are two ways to interpret the idea of 'not existing' in terms of gendered representation. First, you might assume that I am talking about the people we do not see and who, by extension, can be said to not formally exist or to be unrecognizable. For instance, if an extraterrestrial was observing various forms of human popular culture as part of a fact-finding mission about what humans are and do, they would likely float away with the impression that all human beings are either *this* way or *that* way when this is not actually the case. One can immediately see how 'not existing' is an uncomfortable and untenable position in which to find one's self. As Butler (2004) reminds us,

> The human is recognized differentially depending on its race, the legibility of that race, its morphology [physical characteristics], the recognizability of that morphology, its sex, the perceptual verifiability of that sex, its ethnicity, the categorical understanding of that ethnicity. Certain humans are recognized as less than human, and that form of qualified recognition does not lead to a viable life. Certain humans are not recognized at all, and that leads to yet another order of unlivable (sic) life. (p. 2)

As we have seen with the example of ethnicity, the essence of being recognized (or represented) as someone who is 'x' is a readily accessible 'x' category to which that someone could belong. Having one's identity wrongly attributed to a particular category based on certain visual cues is problematic, and in many ways, unliveable.[11] However, without being visually recognizable as a member of any sex or gender category one is denied the possibility of having any sex or gender at all. Being someone who does not exist—who is unrecognizable to most people—is challenging and uncertain in a world where most people are assumed to be 'one or the other.'

S. Bear Bergman (2006) is a butch[12] who writes on the perils, pleasures and nuances of being what I term an Other of sex and gender:

> at the supermarket and the airport, on the street and anywhere else I go, I am not in control of my identity. I am being identified by others and living with the results. I'm lucky, and also skilled. I have good theater training and a good understanding of gender. If I really care to, I can get people to see me as whatever gender I want. But that's if I'm willing to perform a recognizable identity, a recognizable gender. Young Professional Woman. Dutiful Granddaughter. Nice Young Man. Whatever. These are genders that the heteronormative world recognizes, and when I dress for them and pitch my voice appropriately for them, and hold my head and my hands just right and stand and sit and walk with care and attention to them, I can get recognition as something known. (p. 20)

Bear and many others like hirself[13] risk a great deal when every instance of being 'seen' while picking up the mail or buying a litre of milk necessarily unhinges someone else's ideas about gender. However—and this brings us to the second interpretation of 'not existing'—the same limited mechanisms of seeing, knowing and naming which turn Bear and others into occasions for stares, laughs or acts of violence (this point will be discussed in detail) are the causes of systemic sexism against women, girls and female-identified people in general. In North America sexist discrimination is at the root of inequities such as higher rates of poverty for women, lower wages than men for similar work, higher reported cases of sexual violence toward women, the unequal distribution of non-economic labour, etc. Butler (2004) links many intersecting forms of oppression and inequity, noting that "phobic violence against bodies is part of what joins antihomophobic, antiracist, feminist, trans, and intersex activism" (p. 9). This is not to say that these struggles are always happily joined. As we are often reminded, the same structures of domination which pervade society as a whole are alive and well in many marginal contexts:

> Transgender failed me in so many ways throughout college and continues to do so in its mainstream incarnations. Despite the fact that transgender identities seemed to explain so well how I felt genderwise, I steered clear of the students who identified with transgender masculinities like FTM or genderqueer, who cut their hair, changed their names, grew stubble, and took a college van to the True Spirit[14] conference every year, all without worrying about where they were going to get the money to fund all these actions that were seen as central to their identities. I just couldn't relate to them and sometimes even feared them. I questioned the wisdom of some of the same white kids I knew to be racist fucks taking on masculine privilege and using their transgendered otherness to shield themselves from being called out on actions that were racist, classist, or misogynistic. (Dacumos, 2006, pp. 27–28)

Although oppressive divisions exist which sometimes preclude the alignment of the struggles Butler describes, their adherents are united through the hurt caused by having a body that is marked or not marked and named or not named in certain ways. A particular body could display evidence in a given time or place of not being the 'correct' colour, sex, size or shape (etc.) and similar measures would be taken on an individual (self-surveillance, modification of one's body or self-presentation), social (violence, harassment, coercion), psychological (confinement in institutions, forced psychological treatment), biomedical (eugenics, non-consensual surgery or hormonal therapy) or legal (legislated denial of self-determination or self-identification) level to make that body be(come) correct or disappear altogether from view. This theme underscores every instance of racism, sexism, homophobia, and *genderism*.

Genderism is a term which is only seldom used in discussions of sex or gender but which has a long and variegated history.[15] Hill (2002) used the term as one part of a three-fold framework for thinking about anti-trans (transgender and transsexual) attitudes in society:

> Genderism is an ideology that reinforces the negative evaluation of gender non-conformity or an incongruence between sex and gender. It is a cultural belief that perpetuates negative judgments of people who do not present as a stereotypical man or woman. Those who are genderist believe that people who do not conform to sociocultural expectations of gender are pathological. Similar to heterosexism,[16] we propose that genderism is both a source of social oppression and psychological shame, such that it can be imposed on a person, but also that a person may internalize these beliefs. (Hill & Willoughby, 2005, p. 534)

Hill and Willoughby (2005) also give an account of the other two parts of Hill's (2002) framework, *transphobia* and *gender-bashing*. Genderism is the ideology necessary for transphobia, which is

> an emotional disgust toward individuals who do not conform to society's gender expectations. Similar to homophobia, the fear or aversion to homosexuals, transphobia involves the feeling of revulsion to masculine women, feminine men, cross-dressers, transgenderists,[17] and/or transsexuals. Specifically, transphobia manifests itself in the fear that personal acquaintances may be trans or disgust upon encountering a trans person. (Hill & Willoughby, 2005, p. 534)

Thirdly, gender-bashing is defined as "the assault and/or harassment of persons who do not conform to gender norms" (ibid.). This three-fold explanation of the exclusion of gender non-conforming people[18] is useful because it describes a societal attitude which *can* lead to fear or hatred and that *sometimes* leads to violence and harm. We do not have to wait for the fear, hatred, violence or harm to occur in order to say that injustice or discrimination has happened to someone on the basis of their gender identity or expression. Hill's definition of genderism also has an internalized component which could lead to people changing or shaping the way they are in order to satisfy the stringent requirements of genderist ideology. Although this could lead us to thinking about genderism as infecting the lives of everyone engaged in the social world, however, Hill and others (e.g., Beckwith, 1994; Browne, 2004; Lombardi, 2007; etc.) use genderism, transphobia and gender-bashing only to refer to violence done to the Others of sex and gender, i.e., those who are not perceived to be gender-normative or who live outside of or (differently within) the sex of their birth.

Hill and Willoughby (2005) have a very good reason for requiring the presence of the Others of sex and gender in order to claim that genderism, transphobia, or gender-bashing have occurred; they are researchers in psychology and deploy Hill's (2002) framework to conduct various psychometric stress tests on transgender and transsexual people who have experienced any or all of these. The exclusive definition of these phenomena as affecting transgender and transsexual people makes sense for their study, but they do not stop there. As we have seen, Hill and Willoughby include references to "masculine women, feminine men" (p. 534) as people who could be subjected to genderism. However, this brings us back to the problem of representation and identity categories. For instance, we might ask whether masculine women are (look, act?) masculine all the time or even if these masculine women self-identify in this way or even as 'women' at all. Depending on the answers to these questions, we might be unable to apply a definition of genderism or transphobia to the fear or dislike of a female-bodied, female-identified person (usually referred to as a woman) who is unidentifiable as feminine only on a particular day. It could be Halloween, or this person could be sporting an oversized winter parka, a short hair cut, snowmobile boots and a pair of aviator sunglasses. If this person encounters unease or discomfort in her dealings with others who perceive her as ambiguously gendered (masculine?) prior to her removal of the parka or the sunglasses, genderism has reared its ugly head.

It is no accident that clothing stores are divided into clearly marked sections for male and female shoppers, and we would absolutely be able to tell what section we find ourselves in regardless of whether we see the sign. This certainly poses problems for people like S. Bear Bergman and others, but the story goes much farther than that. The person in our example, being female-bodied and female-identified, has endured a lifetime of socialization which would probably have led her on most other days to wear clothing that would render her completely and totally *recognizable* as female. Because of the reality of gender binary socialization, then, genderism *not only* "reinforces the negative evaluation of gender *non*-conformity or an *in*congruence between sex and gender" (ibid.; emphasis mine). Genderism is more pervasively manifested as the fearful *anticipation* of non-conformity and any incongruence between biological sex, and the way these are lived and expressed through gender. In this way, genderism does not only characterize instances of injustice against gender non-conforming people; genderism shapes and scaffolds the ways in which everyone—whether trans, non-trans, gender non-conforming, gender-conforming, us, them, you or me—is socialized to be of *one 'recognizable' gender*, however this is locally understood.

Doing, Practicing and Performing: Three Theoretical Models of Gender

When I was a brand new teenage girl I was in hell. I didn't understand what was going on. Having been on a diet for a while I was a size ten in tapered jeans and an extra large in humongous hoodless sweatshirts. I had three polo neck t-shirts in which I would only feel comfortable, and these would see me through the next three years. I wore big chunky man glasses and I had shoulder-length ruler cut brown hair. And I played someone's mother in Fiddler on the Roof. *I spent the time between my scenes skateboarding on the basketball court in my apron, kerchief and old lady make-up. That was my proudest moment. For three weeks everything seemed to come together. I acquired an Australian boyfriend who wrote pathologically depressing poetry and wore English Leather cologne. He was older than me by two years. He told me he loved me while ending a phone conversation in which he confessed that he suffered from chronic depression. I dumped him in a cafe two days later in case he was ever so depressed down the road that he threatened to commit suicide 'if I left him.' He asked if he could keep my gum wrapper as a souvenir. I said sure. It all went downhill from there.*

As we have seen, it is relatively safe to say that our understanding of our own gender and the gender of others revolves around what is visible on the body or in one's behavior. When we see someone we take in their physical characteristics, hairstyle, mannerisms, affect, speech patterns, clothing, accessories and other cues which combine to point us in one of only two directions in our appraisal of their 'gender': male or female. This is not to say that we drag out a checklist and pencil every time we pass someone on the street; as West and Zimmerman (1987) point out, "it is precisely when we have a special reason to doubt that the issue of applying rigorous criteria arises" (p. 133). Simply put, we *must* know what that person *is* and we will exhaust our semantic field of possibilities until we are able to determine the answer. I was once approached in a Montreal mall by a man who asked me for the time in French. When I answered him, he asked me again as though he had not heard; I obliged, but he asked a third time, now in English. The man then inquired if I was male or female and, very irritated at having my goodwill taken advantage of just so someone could ascertain the quality of my voice, I told him it was none of his business. He exclaimed, "Oh—you're female!" and when I refused to verify this he followed me and asked another bystander for his opinion of my gender. I do not fault the curiosity itself—I myself watch people in this way, but usually to find Others like me—but I was extremely offended by his disingenuousness and threatening persistence. Presumably, this man had watched me very closely and been unable to figure me out. He just *had* to ask.

I have deliberately resisted an extended theoretical discussion of gender until now because I believe it is more important to first understand genderism as a force of social coercion before getting into the causal mechanisms of gender. However, it is important to understand where gender comes from and, although there is no one account which can be said to tell 'the truth' about gender, West and Zimmerman (1987), Paechter (2002, 2003) and Butler (1999) all provide ways to think about gender which do not simply follow from 'common sense' ideas about girls and boys. It is important to be wary of common sense in all its forms, as what is 'common' is likely to be what is *dominant and normative,* dressed up in the language of the everyday. Many different theories have evolved to explain how or why acts of 'seeing' and naming lead to the categorization of ourselves and others within a very narrowly and contextually-defined field of possibilities. This process of seeing and categorizing is integral to gender, a term understood within the field of gender studies today not as a naturalized fixture of male or female people as we have seen, but as an activity in which everyone participates for the sake of defining one's own identity with or against others' and providing a similar point of reference for everyone else. At the level of the everyday, gender is a localized and highly particular set of practices (Paechter, 2002, 2003) in which everyone engages "at the risk of gender assessment" (West & Zimmerman, 1987, p. 136) and in the interests of being found accountable (ibid.) as a successful approximation of what is locally agreed upon as being outwardly male *or* female. What gender theories try to do is provide an account of gender as something which ought to be closely examined and whose presence ought not to be merely catalogued or assumed in a given context.

In one of the most widely-cited arguments for considering gender as other than a reified biological determinant of male or female behavior, West and Zimmerman (1987) describe gender as "a routine, methodical, and recurring accomplishment" where *doing* gender "involves a complex of socially guided perceptual, interactional, and micropolitical activities that cast particular pursuits as expressions of masculine and feminine 'natures'" (p. 126). They locate gender as a socially contextualized *activity* consisting of three separate components—sex, sex category and gender—and the mechanisms whereby each of these is *done*. According to West and Zimmerman, 'sex' is a "determination made through the application of socially agreed upon biological criteria for classifying persons as females or males" (p. 127) where criteria could be chromosomes, hormones and/or genital morphology. Placement in a 'sex category' is "established and sustained by the socially required identificatory displays [i.e., clothing, accessories, hair style, etc.] that proclaim one's membership in one or the other category" (ibid.). Opposed to sex category—the visual attributes which are used to infer one's sex—is 'gender,' "the activity of managing situated conduct in light of normative conceptions of attitudes and activities appropriate for one's sex category" (ibid.). In other words, behavioral attributes such as mannerisms, gestures, intonation, pitch, facial expressions, humour and gait are all components of one's gender which are read against one's physically signified membership in a given sex category. Sex category in turn references one's biological sex.

Another way to think about and theorize gender is offered by Paechter (2002, 2003), who writes about masculinities and femininities as localized communities of practice to which infants are nominated depending on their genital sex categorization at birth. Infants named as either male or female are proposed as candidates for membership in one or the other corresponding community of masculinity or femininity practice:

> Such an understanding would imply that children and young people would learn what it is to be masculine or feminine (in various forms and ways in various circumstances) through legitimate peripheral participation in these communities of practice, while simultaneously taking part, as full participants, in their own child and adolescent masculinities and femininities. (Paechter, 2002, p. 70)

Throughout a child's life their status as a legitimate peripheral member of a local community of adult masculinity or femininity practice will be heavily guided by full members (adults) of the community who engage the child in masculine or feminine activities and encourage the development of masculine or feminine behaviors/preferences *or*, and I would argue, more commonly, dissuade the child from showing interest in oppositional masculine or feminine things. Membership in the adult community is gained not just through being masculine, for example, but through the display of certain masculine-typed behaviors specific to the *local* community. Community membership is therefore central to one's identity as masculine or feminine, male or female: "[identity] is defined not just internally by the individual but externally by the group's inclusive or exclusive attitude to that individual" on the basis of the individual's "level of conformity to a whole constellation of practices, some more central to group identity than others" (p. 74). In other words, it's not just about claiming an identity; you have to be seen as that identity (or as a legitimate peripheral participant) by others who are already accepted as members of the community to whom the identity belongs.

What counts as practice and the function fulfilled by practice within these communities is "not fixed, but fluid; the practices of a particular community are constantly being shifted, renegotiated and reinvented" (2002, p. 71). Members must maintain their connection to the community and be involved in shared practice in order to be continually aware and apprised of shifts in practices. Engaging in otherwise heterogeneous and arbitrarily linked practices is a source of coherence for a community of masculinity or femininity practice, and you must demonstrate knowledge of why this combination of practices 'makes sense' to the community in order to achieve full membership. Paechter also states that "joining a community of practice involves entering not only its internal configuration but also its relationship with the rest of the world" (p. 73). Boundaries which separate members from Others and outsiders are intensely policed. Stamped out and/or punished with expulsion are behaviors associated with the 'other' sex as well as those found among communities of similarly gendered yet distinct practice: "for example, middle class [...men] define their own forms of masculinity partly through rejection of the macho" (ibid.). Most importantly for my argument in this chapter, practice is seen to be localized even though "wider gender regimes are built out of and related to localised regimes" (ibid.). The "local" might not be defined geographically as this pertains to practice; geography, ancestry and the internet are all 'localizing' elements which form these communities.

Whereas West and Zimmerman (1987) give us a relatively simple idea of what 'doing gender' means in everyday social life which is largely confined to *one* kind of maleness or femaleness, Paechter describes gendering as being a highly deliberate process which is sprung from biological sex but effectively amounts to *multiple* communities that create specific ways of being masculine or feminine.[19] Paechter also shows us how identities are multiple and intersecting, i.e., one is not only white, gay, masculine, middle-class and urban but one is a white gay masculine middle-class urban subject. Hers is an exponential and not arithmetical understanding of identity which "brings to the forefront the possibility (indeed near-inevitability) of multiple membership and therefore of multiple forms of identity" (Paechter, 2002, p. 74) such as those based in race, ethnicity, class, geographic origin, linguistic background, religious or cultural affiliation, or sexuality. Despite the positive attributes of both theories, however, West and Zimmerman (1987) and Paechter (2003) rely on the Others of sex and gender in order to give substance to their claims that gender is a universal activity. West and Zimmerman discuss the life history of a transsexual woman in order to explain sex, sex category and gender only to turn around and reference—as a credible source on trans experience—possibly the most widely derided and inflammatory transphobic publication in existence: Janice Raymond's (1979, 1994) *The transsexual empire: The making of the she-male.* Noted transgender writer and theorist Patrick Califia (2003) gives a précis of Raymond's anti-trans politics:

> Hounding transsexuals out of the lesbian-feminist community has been Raymond's raison d'être. She is much more than simply a feminist theorist with an axe to grind about transsexuals. She is also an anti-transsexual crusader who has worked hard to make it more difficult for transsexuals to obtain sex

> reassignment. This career bears an interesting stylistic resemblance to Anita Bryant's 'Save Our Children' antigay crusade in Florida in the late seventies, but unlike Bryant, Raymond hasn't given up campaigning. (p. 92)

Clearly, it is an act of betrayal to deploy a trans life as an exemplary application of one's theory, and then casually offer the words of a virulently transphobic person as an informed perspective on the lives of trans people.[20] Whereas this example from West and Zimmerman (1987) represents the farthest edge of the perils of using the Others of sex and gender as examples, Paechter (2003) hesitantly deploys intersex lives in order to discuss the power-knowledge implications of her theory of communities of masculinity and femininity practice. She states that "I am aware of the ethical issues arising from writing, as a non-intersex person, about those people who are intersex. I would not wish to silence their voices nor would I wish to use their experiences "merely to illustrate the social construction of binary sexes." In discussing what happens to intersex babies and their parents, I hope to remain mindful of these issues" (p. 546). Despite this noble caveat, Paechter still uses 'the intersex example' to show how the ways in which we know and recognize bodies as potentially legitimate peripheral members of communities of masculinity or femininity practice (i.e., men or women, respectively) are constructed by multiple forms of power. In contrast to these theories, Butler (1999) provides a way of thinking about gender which deconstructs the very idea that there *even exist* people who are not Others; we are all only, always, *performing*.

Butler's (1999) theory of gender revolves around the notion of performativity. As you will see, what Butler suggests about gender is related to her observations on identity categories:

> Acts, gestures, and desire produce the effect of an internal core or substance, but produce this *on the surface* of the body, through the play of signifying absences that suggest, but never reveal, the organizing principle of identity as a cause. Such acts, gestures, enactments, generally construed *are performative* in the sense that the essence or identity that they otherwise purport to express are *fabrications* manufactured and sustained through corporeal signs and other discursive means. That the gendered body is performative suggests that it has no ontological status [i.e., being or existence] apart from the various acts which constitute its reality. (p. 173; original emphasis)

Butler adds another level to theories which say that gender is socially constituted and grounded in biological sex or its naming; instead, she maintains that when we gender a body (e.g., by labelling it as male, female, masculine or feminine) we are not referencing *anything* other than the various signs we have decoded to ascertain the gender of that body. Instead of saying that hair style, clothing, voice pitch, mannerisms, etc. refer to some real grounding (most often thought of as biological sex), these performative gestures only refer to themselves. Bodies are real and bodies have organs, but *gendered bodies* are only the mechanisms that make them. Therefore, gender is performative because it is only ever a performance in and of itself; it is not a performance of something else.

Butler discusses the cultural phenomenon of drag or stylized gender impersonation in order to take her notion of performativity even farther. In the interests of clarity this passage is worth quoting at length:

> The performance of drag plays upon the distinction between the anatomy of the performer and the gender that is being performed. But we are actually in the presence of three contingent dimensions of significant corporeality: anatomical sex, gender identity, and gender performance. If the anatomy of the performer is already distinct from the gender of the performer, and both of those are distinct from the

gender of the performance [i.e., the 'drag' gender is not the performer's everyday gender identity nor anatomical sex], then the performance suggests a dissonance not only between sex and performance, but sex and gender, and gender and performance. . . . *In imitating gender, drag implicitly reveals the imitative structure of gender itself—as well as its contingency.* Indeed, part of the pleasure, the giddiness of the performance is in the recognition of a radical contingency in the relation between sex and gender in the face of cultural configurations of causal unities that are regularly assumed to be natural and necessary. (p. 175; original emphasis)

By showing that there is no logical follow-through of sex and gender, Butler also shows us that any gender can be imitated by anyone of any gender identity or anatomical sex; this is what she means when she says that gender is contingent, as opposed to static and unchanging. Because gender can be imitated in this way, we have to concede that gender is always and only an imitation. The same gestures (i.e., hair, clothing, make-up, mannerisms, etc.) performed by people who we see as very different (e.g., women and drag queens) are *in fact both imitations* of the same thing. But if we can't say that certain people (and not others) who perform a certain gendered gesturing are doing it *for real*, then "gender parody reveals that the original identity after which gender fashions itself is an imitation without an origin" (ibid.). Thinking about gender as performativity, then, brings us to the conclusion that gender as we conceive of it is not the property of a particular anatomical sex or even a gender category; it is "a personal/cultural history of received meanings subject to a set of imitative practices which refer laterally to other imitations and which, jointly, construct the illusion of a primary and interior gendered self" (p. 176). No one can be 'Other' to something which has no origin. As such, Butler gives us a framework for thinking about gender that necessarily implicates every one of us in performance and imitation, whether we appear to be or no.

It can be difficult to imagine what these theories look like when enacted on a daily basis, but it is useful to think of how we are at all times doing and performing gender even when we get undressed and open our mouths to sneeze. It is also useful to recognize features of our childhood and adolescence to be efforts (of the adults around us and ourselves) to prepare us right so that we could (or not) become members of adult communities of masculinity or femininity practice and be recognized (or not) as legitimate peripheral members throughout our childhoods. Many of us will have sought out other communities and later engaged in similar processes of legitimate peripheral participation for which we were never groomed as children or youth. Many more of us will have remained in the communities to which we were assigned to at birth, doing our very best to approximate the features required for full membership. By recognizing that gender is performative we open ourselves up to the possibility that what we see in the behavior of others does not have to be related to our ideas of their body and what would logically follow from that sex/gender combination. When we become so open, we are less likely to expect that the children and youth we teach will demonstrate this congruency or conversely, that they ought to one hundred percent of the time in order to be normal (read: gender-normative and heterosexual).

As teachers, you are *in loco parentis* in the lives of children and youth who are simultaneously gendered and being groomed for future participation in communities of gender practice. Their gender is continually performed and (re)created by themselves but with the direct involvement of their parents and the surrounding community. What happens at school might be the instantiation of gender norms that are impossible for a child or youth to approximate without creating the conditions for unlivability. On the other hand, we might also instantiate gender norms that are dangerously at odds with a child's legitimate peripheral participation in a particular community. For these reasons, anti-genderism is not a crusade against gender itself. Instead, anti-genderist classroom practice requires that we are aware of what we bring with us when we talk to a student about their past, present, or future preferences, surroundings, or possibilities (cf. Mayo, 2006; McDonough, 2007).

Now We Have to Worry About Everyone: Gender Goes to School

When I was an eighteen-year-old university queer I was in heaven. Like my new friends, I took up smoking. I lived in an all-girls university dormitory where I could smoke in my room. I was frightened of clothing and took to wearing formless cotton pants with backpack snap closures in primary colours and shades of magenta or grey. Swathed in my yellow massive pants in my basement room with my Camels (this is Canada, remember—if I was going to smoke then by golly I was going to do it right) and my guitar, I wrote an entire album of torch songs about girls. Seeing as I had decided I was queer and looked the part, I'd been roped into the Women's Union where I was fast learning about menstrual activism and how to make things called "handles" (pieces of printer paper cut four ways with political messages on them). I dated everyone and I nursed a perpetually broken heart which sounded superb onstage at benefit shows for campus groups. After one break-up I decided my heart was so broken that I went shopping, somehow ending up in the men's section of a store which sold Dickies (men's pseudo-work clothing and hallmark of youthful butch fashion). I had never seriously entered the men's section before but occupied the grey area of formless things in between. I inexplicably purchased some jeans, some wool sweaters and some Doc Martens. I never wore my candy raver shapeless pants again. Soon after I returned for a blue Dickie jacket. My white, middle-class butch 'I' was born in a store in the heart of the main consumer stroll in Montreal. I still wear the Dickie jacket today, proudly faded with time.

It is very easy to slip into the realm of common sense when thinking about boys and girls as learners and social actors in schools. You have read over and over again in this chapter that gender is most often perceived commonsensically as a 'natural' dualism of male and female in keeping with biological modes of reproduction. In practice, however, many culturally ascribed 'gendered' behaviors and expectations can be traced back to ideas about reproductive roles. For example, discourses of gestation, childbirth and child-rearing all contain references to the 'innate' nurturing capacity of women. This is justified on the basis of women being habitual carriers and primary points of attachment for newborn infants and the children they grow to be. The fact that not all women are or desire to be mothers somehow has no bearing on the supposed 'innateness' of female (and feminine) nurturance. We justify various toy selections for female-assigned children based on the perceived need to draw out and nourish their nurturing and care-centered 'female-ness.'[21] Needless to say, male-assigned children are given toys and are engaged with in such a way so as to cultivate the 'opposite' behaviors to nurturance and emotionalism. This process leads to the prevalence of a binaristic (two-fold and oppositional) way for conceptualizing gender that only offers male-masculine or female-feminine boxes to tick off and live within. Through infinite individualized processes we try to somehow stuff ourselves into either one although we are usually only aware of the struggles of people who find these boxes completely and utterly unliveable.

When gender is only thought of as a *gender binary*, oppositional characterizations of male and female fill many blanks. If a particular trait is associated with femaleness (e.g., emotionalism, the capacity for nurturing, etc.) its absence or opposite is associated rather arbitrarily with maleness (e.g., stoicism, an inferior capacity for nurturing, etc.). What is missing from many conversations about gender is the critical consideration of whether—in having different expectations and prescribing different clothing, activities and toys based on children's genital morphology—we are drawing out traits which are already there or implanting ones we wish to see so that we can claim children as 'successful' boys or girls. In many ways, we require these successfully and completely gendered people as the outcomes of pedagogies designed to guide young humans along the path of 'normal development' toward what we think of as well-adjusted maturity. Because of this, teachers are unofficial arbiters of what counts as normal or aberrant in the gender department. This means that you will be on the front lines in the identification of what ought to be addressed through various pedagogical or other interventions. What 'ought to be addressed' is code for what is different and, in this case, what is wrong.

These considerations are indisputably related to questions of teacher agency and responsibility. Consider, for example, the response of a teacher who witnesses a child involved in atypically gendered play that, in the particular local context *of that school*, i.e., not necessarily in the child's other context(s), is considered to be inappropriate for a child of their assigned sex. If a teacher intervenes in the play behavior, we cannot assume, as is often the case, that this intervention is based on nothing and no one; there is a particular context for every action and the teacher is always accountable to a wide variety of actors. We cannot look to the law or to policy as justification or grounding for such intervention or non-intervention, as the case may be. As a non-legislated area, the freedom to express and live our gender as we wish is not protected like that of sexual orientation in Canada, for example. A teacher might well be called to justify their *inaction* if parents later discover that their child was behaving 'inappropriately' as per their particular beliefs and stipulations about gender.

In a changing climate of parental rights and school accountability, gender expression is effectively a grey area which allows for the perpetuation of localized or highly personal standards of exactly what children should or ought to be or do or, ultimately, become. When faced with an issue of gender non-conformity, particularly in a young child, teachers are apt to adopt a mantle or mandate of gender socialization particularly as this pertains to naming a behavior or characteristic as a *problem* or an *issue* to be 'dealt with' in some way. Several research studies have been undertaken which point to the myriad ways in which the gender binary is naturalized and simultaneously assumed to be natural in the classroom practices of teachers. The following studies are presented with an eye to critically considering how gender and genderism operate and their implications for the identities and lived experiences of students.

In a quantitative investigation of student teachers' approaches to categorizing student behaviors as serious or worthy of intervention, Kokkinos et al. (2004) found that student teachers—when compared with experienced teachers—were more apt to label certain behaviors (e.g., crying) and character traits (e.g., suspicious, sensitive, cowardly) as 'serious' in boys whereas behaviors labelled 'serious' in girls included profane language, rudeness, restlessness, distrust and disobedience. Kokkinos et al. (2004) offer this observation on the rigidity of gendered expectations among preservice teachers: "Because non-stereotypic behaviors may violate preservice teacher expectations they may be considered more salient and attract attention" (p. 118). In other words, the authors concluded that behaviors which differ from preservice teachers' gendered *expectations* of students would likely stand out to them as more meaningful. The implications bear directly on responses to student behavior which may or may not be viewed as especially 'problematic' outside of the teacher's own context and socially located understanding of gender. Norms of student behavior and development are also heavily raced and classed (see Artiles et al., 2002; Oakes et al., 1997, etc.) in accordance with dominant (read:

white, middle-class, gender-normative, etc.) conceptions of what it means to be a 'normally' developing and well-behaved student. To name and address a child's behavior as 'serious' is to assert that a shift toward some ideal type is necessary to de-escalate the deviance. Most importantly, we must bear in mind that Kokkinos et al. showed a predilection among *student teachers* to resort to the gender binary in the absence of a more fully-developed professional knowledge base. We need to be skeptical when thinking about where these knowledges about gender and child development come from which are applied to actual, individual children from a wide variety of backgrounds.

When children are already being named as having developmental or other exceptionalities, genderism can bear even more heavily on processes of naming. This is probably because children who are already named as exceptional in some way are more likely to stand out in the teacher's consciousness, particularly if the teacher is required to track that child's progress in a more detailed or involved manner. In the case of children diagnosed with Attention-Deficit Hyperactivity Disorder (ADHD), Lloyd and Norris (1999) have noted that "research into ADHD tends to involve only boys. Some discussion of gender differences relies on social context-based explanations for the differences despite earlier assertions of an individualistic, biologically-based account" (p. 514). Showing the wide reach of this conflict, Lloyd and Norris cite a practical guide for teachers and a medical study (Cooper & Ideus, 1996; Swanson et al., 1998), both of which offer fluctuating social and biological (and yet gender binary-based) explanations for the disproportionately high rate of boys diagnosed with ADHD. Lloyd and Norris (1999) conclude their discussion with the following cautionary note: "The gender issue points again to the importance of the promotion of an understanding of the social context which challenges the notions that culture is irrelevant in understanding children's behavior and that you can transfer a 'syndrome' from one culture to another, and expect to find an identical incidence and response" (p. 514). The trouble is that a 3:1 to 9:1 ratio of boys to girls with ADHD (Swanson et al., 1998) makes sense according to genderist ideologies that place increased activity firmly in the 'boy camp.' Now what does this have to do with teachers?

In keeping with the gendered patterns of ADHD diagnosis, Jackson and King (2004) conducted a quantitative study of elementary teachers' perceptions of student behaviors to find out whether teachers were being influenced by the perceived gender of a child in their labeling of ADHD or Oppositional Defiant Disorder (ODD).[22] Teachers were shown video footage of boys and girls coached to display a particular set of inattentive and hyperactive or oppositional behaviors in keeping with clinical guidelines for diagnosing ADHD and ODD, respectively. Jackson and King found that

> the boy actor exhibiting oppositional behavior received teacher ratings of hyperactivity and inattention that were roughly half of those elicited by his portrayal of ADHD itself. The girl actor portraying ADHD generated oppositional defiant ratings that were roughly two thirds of those elicited from her performance as a child with ODD. (p. 215)

The implications of this study are fairly clear. Boys who consistently defy teacher authority in keeping with diagnoses of ODD are more likely to be seen as being hyperactive, whereas girls who display hyperactive behaviors in keeping with ADHD are more likely to be seen as pathologically defiant. Jackson and King sum up these findings, stating that "these teacher rating tendencies could contribute to higher diagnostic rates of ADHD among boys and ODD among girls" (ibid.). Each of these diagnoses can potentially lead to a completely different 'treatment' pathway. If teachers are so influenced by genderist conceptions of student behavior, it can be argued that a child given a medical diagnosis and pharmaceutical behavioral remedy is perhaps so targeted due to being seen as one particular gender and not another. This is especially troubling when we recall how teachers are the vanguard of child development as well as gatekeepers of services for children with learning and behavioral difficulties.

Beyond thinking about the naming of serious behavior or diagnostic patterns, genderism in its extreme form allows for transphobic harassment and violence to be perpetrated against all students whether on the level of the ideological or interpersonal. The message here is that the way we make judgments and assumptions with regard to gender is directly tied to real physical and emotional harm. Although some studies (e.g., Kimmel, 2003; Klein & Chancer, 2000) have demonstrated concrete links between masculinity and violence, still others (e.g., GLSEN, 1999, 2003, 2005) have uncovered systemic harassment, assault and violence against students on the basis of their lack of conformity to *any* localized gender norm (see Messerschmidt, 2004 for a detailed discussion of gender-based violence in the lives of youth). Responding to this challenge on an individual level requires more than an understanding of what gender is and does. We have to fight the notion that genderism is something which only happens to students (and teachers) who are not gender normative. Part of this process is coming to understand ourselves as people who benefit from genderism in ways that others who are oppressed by genderism do not.

Going Forward: Thinking in Terms of Privilege and Oppression

When I was a genderqueer butch with grad school preoccupations, I was trying to figure out how I was supposed to work on such a weird identity while reading books which screamed how no one's identity is ever 'finished.' I had had the same haircut for two years and it finally started to make sense. It was my castle, sticking up perfectly straight and stiff in a dignified aerodynamic fin crowning the top of my head. I had a tattoo of my own design which symbolized my distrust of gender and this contrasted pretty badly with my need to feel like I had a real, tried and tested gender identity which would stand up as stiff as my hair. Whenever I or my hairdresser would move cities I would become morose at the thought of negotiating anew the price (I don't pay the women's price for a men's haircut, thank you very much), the style (don't touch my wee little sideburns) and the finished product (if it doesn't stand up straight I will die, I swear). My wardrobe consisted of jeans and crisp button down men's shirts in stately stripes and solids which I fetishized in their drycleaner plastic, once a month. I bought a fedora at a trendy downtown store and wore it every single day. When I began to get stared at menacingly on the bus and in the street on a daily basis, I realized that I was now doing 'this' too well to be safely dismissed anymore as young or going through a phase. I looked too dangerously comfortable to be anything other than a 'real' butch, whatever that means. It seems I found my realness in others' discomfort with me and I smile back as widely as I can.

One theme in particular has underscored the above discussions of 'gender diversity,' genderism, gender theory and the place of gender in education, namely that we cannot make implicit or explicit assumptions about people on the basis of what we see—or do not see—on their bodies. The theories of West and Zimmerman (1987), Paechter (2002, 2003), and Butler (1999) to which you have been introduced here offer various ways to think about gender which apply to all bodies and not only the ones which are obviously discontinuous with their assigned sex and/or localized gender norms. Although I hold that genderism—the fearful anticipation of gender non-conformity which structures gender binary socialization processes—applies to everyone, genderism is also a socially stratifying system of privilege and oppression which gives things to some people and denies them to others based on one's adherence to highly localized rules of signification. What this means is that, in a particular context, some people have *gender-normative* privilege which they enjoy as a consequence of correctly and seamlessly approximating what it means to be that gender in that place and time. Other people experience *gender non-normative* oppression when they are unable or choose not to approximate these norms. What this means is that, to the extent that heterosexism privileges heterosexuality (people and practices) as the correct or universal sexuality, genderism privileges the gender-normative.

People who are gender-normative exist in an economy of comparison wherein their normativity requires other people who are *non-normative* in order to define itself. However, as Butler would have it, gender-normativity cannot be said to belong to any one anatomical sex or gender identity. Despite the fact that most people are read as gender-normative and receive gender-normative privilege, there exist instances in the lives of *every single person* when they will be gender non-normative. Perhaps this is because the gender landscape has shifted (i.e., they now find themselves in a different context wherein unfamiliar gender norms prevail) or perhaps they made a small mistake (e.g., got dressed too early in the day for a cross-gender role in a school play; see Moffatt, 1994). Thinking back through our lives and locating these moments wherein we have been oppressed—or unexpectedly privileged—by genderism is key to enacting a more conscious and equitable pedagogy. I encourage you to take this on.

Acknowledgments

Special thanks to Dr. Laila Parsons and the members of the Women's Studies graduate seminar at McGill University in 2008. Your questions, comments and insights were invaluable in the preparation of this chapter and the development of my overall approach to writing and teaching about gender. For these and many other things, I am grateful.

Notes

1. Whereas many theories of gender deploy the lives of intersex (see note 8 below) and trans people (see note 7 below) to illustrate 'gender diversity' or the social construction of gender (i.e., "look—there are people who are not male or female!"), these theories often exclude the fact that most intersex and trans people happily identify and live as male or female. Claiming these lives as radically Other or as somehow outside of gender norms is imperialism (Namaste, 2005), theoreticism (the privileging of theory over experience) and representational violence. For more information see Hale (2006) and Koyama (2003) on objectifying trans and intersex people, respectively.
2. See *Sexing the body: Gender politics and the construction of sexuality* by Anne Fausto-Sterling (2000) for an in-depth discussion of how sex characteristics are socially constructed in accordance with prevailing ideas of *gender*.
3. Signification is the process of socially located meaning-making wherein the signifier or sign (e.g., clothed exterior) contains and expresses the signified (e.g., one's gender, age, class, ethnicity, etc.). The relationship between the signifier and the signified is termed 'signification.'
4. Salwar kameez is a two-piece garment common to the Indian subcontinent and South Asian diaspora communities all over the world. A yarmulke is a small round head-covering often worn by observant Jewish men and boys. Peyes are locks of hair grown on the sides of the forehead and usually curled in front of or behind the ears; these are worn by Hasidic Jewish men and boys as well as male members of some other strictly observant Jewish sects.
5. 'Little people' is a term preferred by many people with achondroplasia or other forms of 'dwarfism.'
6. Gay usually refers to men who are romantically, sexually, and affectively attracted to and who desire relationships with other men. Lesbian usually refers to women who desire the above with other women. 'Gay' is often used as an umbrella term to include gays and lesbians, e.g., the gay community. Bisexual is a term used for people who desire the above with men or women. Like all identity categories, it is important to note that the use of these terms changes across places and times. Not all men who have sex with men identify as 'gay' or

bisexual, and not all women who have sex with women identify as lesbian or bisexual. Claiming gay or lesbian, in particular, as an identity in many cases involves asserting your affinity with the forms and structures of gay or lesbian community. The anthologies edited by Mattilda, a.k.a Matt Bernstein Sycamore (2004, 2006), contain many examples of authors who take exception to these communities but who still identify as other than heterosexual or heteronormative.

7. Transsexual refers to people who identify with a sex other than that which they were assigned as birth and who may seek out gender-confirming surgical, hormonal or other medical treatment in order to transition to their sex of identity (there are, of course, transsexuals who do not seek out surgery, and many transsexuals choose to have some surgeries or medical procedures and not others). Namaste (2000) describes the material realities of transsexuals as being qualitatively different from those of transgender people. Transgender is a term whose meaning is not always clear. It is used as an umbrella term for transsexual people, transgender people, and those who do not identify tidily (or at all) as male or female. However, the umbrella use of transgender has been strongly criticized by Namaste (2005) for obscuring the fact that most transsexual people do in fact identify as male or female and do so quite happily, often without identifying as trans at all. When applied to individuals, transgender or trans are mostly used by people whose gender identities or presentations defy the gender binary or culturally ascribed standards of masculinity and femininity, maleness and femaleness. Terms such as transman, transwoman, FTM (female-to-male) and MTF (male-to-female) as identities are most often used by trans people who clearly identify with being trans as well as with a particular gender, i.e., not just as 'male or 'female.'

8. Intersex is a term which is applied to people whose bodies differ physically, hormonally, or chromosomally from what we commonly understand to be 'male' or 'female.' Intersex lives are often (but not always) characterized by horrific and non-consensual genital surgeries (often called mutilations), and other procedures performed throughout infancy, childhood, and early adolescence that aim to 'correct' or 'normalize' genitalia termed 'ambiguous.' Widely condemned, such practices are associated with less genital sensitivity, less sexual function (as self-defined) and, in some cases, incontinence. This is done in the interests of creating an external genitalia which will 'pass' for a penis or vagina in socially naked situations. Koyama (n.d.) notes that there are many problems with including the 'I' in GLBT acronyms and organizations since "people with intersex conditions generally do not organize around the 'identity' or 'pride' of being intersex; 'intersex' is a useful word to address political and human rights issues, but there is yet to be an intersex 'community' or 'culture' the way we can talk about LGBT communities (although this may change in the future). In other words, adding the 'I' does not necessarily make the organization appear more welcoming to intersex people. For many people, 'intersex' is just a condition, or history, or site of horrifying violation that they do not wish to revisit" (n.p.). For more information on intersex issues see www.ipdx.org (Intersex Initiative Portland) and www.isna.org (Intersex Society of North America).

9. Queer is a term used to refer to individuals (e.g., "I'm queer" or "I'm a queer woman," etc.) as well as groups and communities (e.g., the queer community, the Queer Studies Special Interest Group of the American Education Research Association, etc.). When used for an individual, the adjectival form is used (i.e., "he's queer" as opposed to "he's a queer"). A person who identifies as queer has an identity or orientation which is other than heterosexual. Some—by no means all—queer people identify as queer in order to indicate greater fluidity than is perceived to exist in the categories gay, lesbian or bisexual. Nevertheless, the phrase 'queer community' usually refers to the constituency of society which is non-heterosexual, whether represented by community organizations or no. Questioning is not so much an identity as a term appended to organizational acronyms in order to indicate that people who are unsure of their sexual orientation or gender identity are welcome. People who are questioning are just that—they are in the process of negotiating their identity or orientation. Some people hold that everyone is always 'in process' and therefore the term 'questioning' is redundant.

10. The following books (and many others) are mostly available in libraries and contain a multitude of ways to trouble how we usually think about gender: *Gender Outlaw: On Men, Women and the Rest of Us* and *My Gender Workbook* by Kate Bornstein (1994; 1998); *Butch Is a Noun* by S. Bear Bergman (2006); *The Persistent Desire: A Butch-Femme Reader* edited by Joan Nestle (1992); *Nobody Passes: Rejecting the Rules of Gender and Conformity* edited by Mattilda a.k.a. Matt Bernstein Sycamore (2006); *Brazen Femme: Queering Femininity* edited by Chloë Brushwood Rose and Anna Camilleri (2002); and *Transgender Warriors: Making History from Joan of Arc to Dennis Rodman* by Leslie Feinberg (1996). It is important to note that a majority of the editors and authors of/within these and other widely read texts which deconstruct gender (and sexuality) from an experiential standpoint are white. In addition to many of the above, several authors (e.g., Ferguson, 2004; Han, 2008; Lee, 1996; Mattilda a.k.a Matt Bernstein Sycamore, 2004, 2006; Morgan, 1996; Namaste, 2000, 2005; Nast, 2002, etc.) explicitly address the intersections of race, ethnicity, gender and sexuality, seeking to account for the disproportionality of whiteness in queer and genderqueer representations.

11. Here I am making particular reference to the femme-identified queer and/or genderqueer people who are read as gender-normative and heterosexual on a daily basis. In many ways, being perceptibly verifiable as gender non-normative or as queer (these often go hand in hand in the realm of the visual) is a great privilege in certain contexts. With regard to gender there are many other kinds of folks who are automatically lumped into a normative or other category against their will and identification, such as trans people who identify as trans but are only read as men or women (and by default, of course, heterosexual), etc.

12. A butch is a person who is usually queer, female-bodied (i.e., assigned female at birth) and masculine-identified. Butches are usually associated with femmes—queer, female-bodied, and feminine-identified people—although butches and femmes come in all shapes and sizes (and genders) and certainly cannot be said to always exist in butch-femme couples or communities. Butch-femme as a label originally referred to 1950s butches—female-identified (for the most part) or female-bodied and very masculine, usually working class women—who were in or who desired relationships with female-identified and feminine women called femmes. Butch-femme relationships were/are stylized and highly-gendered in terms of both private and public behavior. Heavily raced and classed, historical butch-femme communities were actively harassed and persecuted by police in most North American cities prior to *and* after the Stonewall riots of 1969 (see Carter, 2004) which sparked rights-based campaigns by other non-heterosexual communities. Butch-femme couples were also heavily derided by the budding lesbian-feminist movement and dismissed as copies of oppressively and traditionally gendered heterosexual relationships. Butler (1991) provides an excellent critique of this view. For more information on the history and culture of butch-femme communities and individuals, see Nestle (1987; 1992), Kennedy and Davis (1994), and Faderman (1991). It is important to note that, although the adjectives butch and femme are in wide usage among queer communities to denote certain gendered behaviors, people, etc., the noun forms of these words tend to refer to people who identify with the historical legacy of butch-femme. These identities are very much alive today.

13. *Hir* is a gender-neutral pronoun commonly used in place of him/her and his/hers. *Hirself* is used in place of her/himself and *ze* is similarly used in place of she or he. Examples of their use can be found most notably in Bergman (2006) and Feinberg (1993).

14. The True Spirit conference is organized yearly in the Washington DC area by American Boyz (AmBoyz), an organization which supports female-to-male transgender and transsexual people and their families.

15. The legendary sociologist Erving Goffman (1977) is credited with the first use of the term 'genderism' although he used it to mean "a sex-class [male or female] linked individual behavioral practice" (p. 305) or behavior ascribed to male-masculine or female-feminine people and not—as I use the term—a societal attitude towards people based on their gender identity or expression. Keat (1983) first distinguished between sexism and 'genderism' as attitudes, defining the latter as the "unjustified assumption of the superiority of gender specific characteristics" (qtd. in Sherman, 1984, p. 321). Sherman (1984) used the term to call for the reconstitution of the philosophy of education, particularly as this applies to the way emotions are understood in aesthetics education. Given that sex and gender are usually considered to be separate entities (biological and sociocultural, respectively), Beckwith (1994) championed the use of genderism in psychological research in place of sexism when describing the experiences of some transgender and transsexual people. As with terms such as racism and homophobia, genderism seems to have slipped into the context of common usage, i.e., does not require citation. Beckwith does not reference Keat nor Goffman and neither does Onken (1998), who names genderism as "the structural-cultural judgment that it is right and natural to divide people into two and only two mutually exclusive sexes" (p. 17). Browne (2004) goes so far as to claim that genderism is a "*new term* [...] to describe the hostile readings of gender ambiguous bodies" (p. 332; emphasis mine). Lombardi has a history of publication on trans people and public health (e.g., Lombardi, 2007; Lombardi et al., 2001; Lombardi & van Servellen, 2000; Reback & Lombardi, 2001; etc.) and defines the term genderism as "the ideology that people's physical sex and psychological, social, and legal genders are linked and binary, and that anything different from this condition is abnormal" (p. 639). Surprisingly, the term has been largely left out of broader discussions of sex, gender, privilege and oppression in the social sciences and humanities. I use Hill (2002) and Hill and Willoughby (2005) for my discussion of genderism as their framework is the most complex.

16. Heterosexism is the pervasive and systemic belief in the innateness, superiority and universality of heterosexuality. An example of heterosexism is asking a woman if she 'has a boyfriend' instead of a partner. Heterosexism is the underlying ideology which allows for instances of homophobia and gay-bashing to take place.

17. Transgenderist is another less common and less widely preferred term for a trans or transgendered person.

18. I must point out here that many transgender and transsexual people *are* gender-conforming and often in ways that far outstrip the efforts of people who live as the sex into which they were born and who are seen as having a 'birthright' to membership in that sex category.

19. I would argue that, in subsequent formulations of the communities of practice theory with regard to gender, 'masculinity and femininity practice' could be replaced with 'gender practice,' i.e., communities of *gender* practice, in order to reference that there exist communities in which gender is not necessarily lived in strict accordance with this gender binary. Such a shift in terminology would also make room for the existence of certain marginal communities of gender practice that are often entered into during adulthood (e.g., genderqueer, butch, femme, etc.).

20. West and Zimmerman (1987) quote Raymond in order to illustrate that "although no one coerces transsexuals into hormone therapy, electrolysis, or surgery, the alternatives available to them are undeniably constrained" (p. 145). They follow this up with a quote from *The Transsexual Menace* (1979, 1994): "When the transsexual experts maintain that they use transsexual procedures with people who ask for them, and who prove that they can 'pass,' they obscure the social reality. Given patriarchy's prescription that one must be *either* masculine or feminine, free choice is conditioned [ref: Raymond, 1979, p. 135, italics added]" (West & Zimmerman, 1987, p. 145). This quote gives West and Zimmerman license to assert that "The physical reconstruction of sex criteria pays ultimate tribute to the 'essentialness' or our sexual natures—as women *or* men" (ibid.). There are numerous flaws here, with Raymond and West and Zimmerman's accounts (see Califia, 2003 for a detailed overview and deconstruction of Raymond's many anti-trans arguments). First, many transsexuals *are* coerced into undergoing certain medical procedures by health care professionals and/or restrictive legal frameworks (see Namaste, 2000, 2005). Second, implying that the existence of the *gender* binary prevents people from freely choosing to live and be read as another *sex* is completely nonsensical. Third, transsexuals' desire to pursue gender-confirming surgery does not "pay ultimate tribute to the 'essentialness' of our sexual natures" (West & Zimmerman, 1987, p. 145), but instead disrupts our ideas about essential sexual natures by showing that these do not logically follow from our assigned biological sex. Had West and Zimmerman cited writings by (or consulted) trans people themselves instead of their chief detractor the authors likely would have reached conclusions which actually reflected some transsexuals' lived experience.

21. For an accessible discussion of the literature on gender role socialization and play preferences in early childhood see Raag and Rackliff (1998).

22. The American Academy of Child and Adolescent Psychiatry describes ODD as follows: "In children with Oppositional Defiant Disorder (ODD), there is an ongoing pattern of uncooperative, defiant, and hostile behavior toward authority figures that seriously interferes with the youngster's day to day functioning. Symptoms of ODD may include: frequent temper tantrums; excessive arguing with adults; active defiance and refusal to comply with adult requests and rules; deliberate attempts to annoy or upset people; blaming others for his or her mistakes or misbehavior; often being touchy or easily annoyed by others; frequent anger and resentment; mean and hateful talking when upset; [and/or] seeking revenge. The symptoms are usually seen in multiple settings, but may be more noticeable at home or at school. Five to fifteen percent of all school-age children have ODD. The causes of ODD are unknown, but many parents report that their child with ODD was more rigid and demanding than the child's siblings from an early age. Biological and environmental factors may have a role" (AACAP, 1999, ¶ 2).

References

American Academy of Child and Adolescent Psychiatry [AACAP]. (1999). Facts for families No. 72: Children with Oppositional Defiant Disorder. Retrieved February 2, 2008 from http://www.aacap.org/cs/root/facts_for_families/children_with_oppositional_defiant_disorder.

Artiles, A.J., Harry, B., Reschly, D.J., & Chinn, P.C. (2002). Over-identification of students of color in special education: A critical overview. *Multicultural Perspectives, 4*(1), 3–10.

Beckwith, J.B. (1994). Terminology and social relevance in psychological research on gender. *Social Behavior and Personality, 22*(4), 329–336.

Bergman, S. Bear. (2006). *Butch is a noun.* San Francisco: Suspect Thoughts Press.

Bornstein, Kate. (1998). *My gender workbook.* New York: Routledge.

Bornstein, Kate. (1994). *Gender outlaw: On men, women and the rest of us.* New York: Routledge.

Browne, Kath. (2004). Genderism and the bathroom problem: (Re)materialising sexed sites, (re)creating sexed bodies. *Gender, Place & Culture: A Journal of Feminist Geography, 11*(3), 331–346.

Brushwood Rose, Chloë, & Camilleri, Anna (Eds.). (2002). *Brazen femme: Queering femininity.* Vancouver, BC: Arsenal Pulp Press.

Butler, Judith. (1991). Imitation and gender insubordination. In Diana Fuss (Ed.), *Inside/out: Lesbian theories, gay theories* (pp. 13–32). New York: Routledge.

Butler, Judith. (1999). *Gender trouble: Feminism and the subversion of identity* (2nd ed.). New York: Routledge.

Butler, Judith. (2004). *Undoing gender*. New York: Routledge.

Califia, Patrick. (2003). The backlash: Transphobia in feminism. In *Sex changes: Transgender politics* (2nd ed.) (pp. 86–119). San Francisco, CA: Cleis Press.

Carter, David. (2004). *Stonewall: The riots that sparked the gay revolution*. New York: St. Martin's Press.

Cooper, P., & Ideus, K. (1996). *Attention deficit disorder: A practical guide for teachers*. London: David Fulton.

Dacumos, Nico. (2006). All mixed up with no place to go: Inhabiting mixed consciousness on the margins. In Mattilda a.k.a Matt Bernstein Sycamore (Ed.), *Nobody passes: Rejecting the rules of gender and conformity* (pp. 20–37). Emeryville, CA: Seal Press.

Faderman, Lillian. (1991). *Odd girls and twilight lovers: A history of lesbian life in twentieth-century America*. New York: Penguin.

Fausto-Sterling, Anne. (2000). *Sexing the body: Gender politics and the construction of sexuality*. New York: Basic Books.

Feinberg, Leslie. (1993). *Stone butch blues*. Ann Arbor, MI: Firebrand.

Feinberg, Leslie. (1996). *Transgender warriors: Making history from Joan of Arc to Dennis Rodman*. Boston: Beacon Press.

Ferguson, Roderick A. (2004). *Aberrations in Black: Toward a queer of color critique*. Minneapolis: University of Minnesota Press.

GLSEN (Gay, Lesbian and Straight Education Network). (1999). *GLSEN's national school climate survey: Lesbian, gay, bisexual and transgender students and their experiences in school*. Retrieved September 12, 2006 from: http://www.glsen.org.

GLSEN (Gay, Lesbian and Straight Education Network). (2003). *GLSEN's national school climate survey: Lesbian, gay, bisexual and transgender students and their experiences in school*. Retrieved September 12, 2006 from: http://www.glsen.org.

GLSEN (Gay, Lesbian and Straight Education Network). (2005). *From Teasing to Torment: School Climate in America— A survey of students and teachers*. New York: GLSEN. Retrieved September 12, 2006 from: http://www.glsen.org.

Goffman, Erving. (1977). The arrangement between the sexes. *Theory & Society, 4*(3), 301–331.

Hale, Jacob. (2006). *Suggested rules for non-transsexuals writing about transsexuals, transsexuality, transsexualism, or trans _____*. Retrieved February 2, 2008 from http://sandystone.com/hale.rules.html.

Han, Chong-suk. (2008). No fats, femmes, or Asians: The utility of critical race theory in examining the role of gay stock stories in the marginalization of gay Asian men. *Contemporary Justice Review, 11*(1), 11–22.

Hill, Darryl B. (2002). Genderism, transphobia, and gender bashing: A framework for interpreting anti-transgender violence. In Barbara C. Wallace & Robert T. Carter (Eds.), *Understanding and dealing with violence: A multicultural approach* (pp. 113–136). Thousand Oaks, CA: Sage.

Hill, Darryl B., & Willoughby, Brian L.B. (2005). The development and validation of the genderism and transphobia scale. *Sex Roles, 53*(7/8), 531–544.

Jackson, David A., & King, Alan R. (2004). Gender differences in the effects of oppositional behavior on teacher ratings of ADHD symptoms [Abstract]. *Journal of Abnormal Child Psychology, 32*(2), 215–224.

Keat, R. (1983). Masculinity in philosophy. *Radical Philosophy, 34*, 15–20.

Kennedy, Elizabeth, & Davis, Madeleine. (1994). *Boots of leather, slippers of gold: The history of a lesbian community*. New York: Penguin.

Kimmel, M. (2003). Adolescent masculinity, homophobia, and violence. *American Behavioral Scientist, 46*(10), 1439–1458.

Klein, J., & Chancer, L.S. (2000). Masculinity matters: the omission of gender from high-profile school violence cases. In S.U. Spina (ed.), *Smoke and Mirrors: The Hidden Content of Violence in Schools and Society*. Lanham, MD: Rowman & Littlefield.

Kokkinos, Constantinos M., Panayiotou, Georgia, & Davazoglou, Aggeliki M. (2004). Perceived seriousness of pupils' undesirable behaviors: The student teachers' perspective. *Educational Psychology, 24*(1), 109–120.

Koyama, Emi. (2003). Suggested guidelines for non-intersex individuals writing about intersexuality and intersex people. In Emi Koyama (Ed.), *Introduction to intersex activism: A guide for allies* (pp. 15–16). Portland, OR: Intersex Initiative Portland. Retrieved February 2, 2008 from http://www.intersexinitiative.org/publications/pdf/intersex-activism2.pdf.

Koyama, Emi. (n.d.). Adding the 'I': Does intersex belong in the LGBT movement? Retrieved April 24, 2008 from http://www.intersexinitiative.org/articles/lgbti.html.

Lee, JeeYeun. (1996). Why Suzie Wong is not a lesbian: Asian and Asian American lesbian and bisexual women and femme/butch gender identities. In Brett Beemyn & Mickey Eliason (Eds.), *Queer studies: A lesbian, gay, bisexual and transgender anthology* (pp. 115–132). New York: NYU Press.

Lloyd, Gwynedd, & Norris, Claire. (1999). Including ADHD? *Disability & Society, 14*(4), 505–517.

Lombardi, E.L. (2007). Public health and trans-people: Barriers, to care and strategies to improve treatment. In Ilan H. Meyer & Mary E. Northridge (Eds.), *The health of sexual minorities: Public health perspectives on lesbian, gay, bisexual and transgender populations* (pp. 638–652). New York: Springer.

Lombardi, E.L., & van Servellen, G. (2000). Building culturally sensitive substance use prevention and treatment programs for transgendered populations. *Journal of Substance Abuse Treatment, 19,* 291–296.

Lombardi, E.L., Wilchins, R.A., Priesing, D., & Malouf, D. (2001). Gender violence: Transgender experiences with violence and discrimination. *Journal of Homosexuality, 42*(1), 89–101.

Mattilda a.k.a Matt Bernstein Sycamore (Ed.). (2004). *That's revolting! Queer strategies for resisting assimilation.* Brooklyn, NY: Soft Skull Press.

Mattilda a.k.a Matt Bernstein Sycamore (Ed.). (2006). *Nobody passes: Rejecting the rules of gender and conformity.* Emeryville, CA: Seal Press.

Mayo, Cris. (2006). Pushing the limits of liberalism: Queerness, children, and the future. *Educational Theory, 56*(4), 469–487.

McDonough, Kevin. (2007). The 'futures' of queer children and the common school ideal. *Journal of Philosophy of Education, 41*(4), 795–810.

Messerschmidt, James W. (2004). *Flesh and blood: Adolescent gender diversity and violence.* New York: Rowman & Littlefield.

Moffatt, Tracey. (1994). *The wizard of Oz, 1956* [Photograph]. The Tate Museum, London. Retrieved April 25, 2008, from http://www.tate.org.uk/servlet/ViewWork?cgroupid=999999961&workid=26285&searchid=12451

Morgan, Tracy D. (1996). Pages of whiteness: Race, physique magazines, and the emergence of public gay cultures. In Brett Beemyn & Mickey Eliason (Eds.), *Queer studies: A lesbian, gay, bisexual and transgender anthology* (pp. 280–297). New York: NYU Press.

Namaste, Viviane K. (2000). *Invisible lives: The erasure of transsexual and transgendered people.* Chicago: University of Chicago Press.

Namaste, Viviane K. (2005). *Sex change, social change: Reflections on identity, institutions and imperialism.* Toronto, ON: Women's Press.

Nast, Heidi J. (2002). Queer patriarchies, queer racisms. *Antipode: A radical journal of geography, 34*(5), 874–909.

Nestle, Joan. (1987). *A restricted country.* Ithaca, NY: Firebrand.

Nestle, Joan (Ed.). (1992). *The persistent desire: A butch-femme reader.* New York: Alyson.

Oakes, J., Wells, A.S., Jones, M., & Datnow, A. (1997). Detracking: The social construction of ability, cultural politics, and resistance to reform. *Teachers College Record, 98*(3), 482–510.

Onken, Steven J. (1998). Conceptualizing violence against gay, lesbian, bisexual, intersexual, and transgender people. *Journal of Gay and Lesbian Social Services, 8*(3), 5–24.

Paechter, Carrie. (2002). Masculinities and femininities as communities of practice. *Women's Studies International Forum, 26*(1), 69–77.

Paechter, Carrie. (2003). Learning masculinities and femininities: Power/knowledge and legitimate peripheral participation. *Women's Studies International Forum, 26*(6), 541–552.

Raag, Tarja, & Rackliff, Christine L. (1998). Preschoolers' awareness of social expectations of gender: Relationships to toy choices. *Sex Roles, 38*(9–10), 685–700.

Raymond, Janice. (1979). *The transsexual empire: The making of the she-male.* Boston: Beacon Press. Second edition (1994) published by New York: Teachers College Press.

Reback, Cathy J., & Lombardi, Emilia L. (2001). HIV risk behaviors of male-to-female transgenders in a community-based harm reduction program. In Walter O. Bockting & Sheila Kirk (Eds.), *Transgender and HIV: Risks, prevention, and care* (pp. 59–68). Philadelphia, PA: Haworth Press.

Sherman, Ann L. (1984). Genderism and the reconstitution of philosophy of education. *Educational Theory, 34*(4), 321–325.

Swanson, J.M., Sergeant, J.A., Taylor, E., Sonuga Barke, E.J., Jenson, P.S., & Cantwell, D.P. (1998). Attention deficit disorder and hyperkinetic disorder. *The Lancet, 351,* 429–433.

West, Candace, & Zimmerman, Don H. (1987). Doing gender. *Gender & Society, 1*(2), 125–151.

Sixteen

Uncovering Truth
In Search of a "BMSALA" (Black Male Same
Affection Loving Academician)

C.P. Gause

The historical evolution of the gender identity of African American males presents many problems for analysts due, in large part, to the poor quality and paucity of data that survived due to slavery. It is clear, nevertheless, that at the level of values, attitudes, and behaviors, distinct characteristics of African American males can be discerned. Utilizing critical spirituality, black masculinity, collaborative activism, and issues around integration, I explore the following questions: What does it mean to be male and black in America? What informs the construction of black masculinity in our society? How visible and/or invisible is sexuality, particularly black sexuality from diversity discourses? The construction of race is the precursor to understanding what it means to be black and male in America; however it is the intersectionality of race, class, and gender that informs the totality of our being. To be a black male or an African American male in America is inextricably tied to the history of servitude, slavery, and sex within and between the races in our society; however, it is more important to question why (homo) sexuality is conveniently left out of slave narratives and why this continues to reify issues of oppression when educators enter a discourse centered within diversity and multiculturalism as it relates to the African American community (Gause, 2008).

Previous research shows that while many elements within the values, attitudes, and behaviors of white and black males are shared, the total configuration differs in terms of quantity, quality, and relationship to each other. While this can be partially attributed to the legacy of African culture, more significant causal factors derive from the dialectic of development of African American slavery and its Jim Crow aftermath, and, more recently, the social dynamics of black urban life (Booker, 1997). Of singular importance in this regard, is the evolving male role as African American males themselves perceive it, against the role for them perceived by the larger, white society.

Based on the sociocultural dynamics of definitions of male and female, gender may have little to do with an individual's actual biological sex or sexual orientation (Case, 1995; Eskridge, 2000; Franke, 1995; Miller, 1995; Somerville, 2000; Terry, 1999; Valdes, 1995; Yoshino, 2002). "Gender is an ongoing, life-long series of evolving performances. Sex is chromosomal" (Lugg, 2007, p. 120). Regarding masculinity, Chafetz (1974) presents in descriptive terms seven areas of masculinity:

1. Physical: virile, athletic, strong, brave. Unconcerned about appearance and aging.
2. Functional: breadwinner, provider for family as much as mate.
3. Sexual: sexually aggressive, experienced. Single status acceptable.
4. Emotional: unemotional, stoic, *boys don't cry.*
5. Intellectual: logical, intellectual, rational, objective, practical.
6. Interpersonal: leader, dominating, disciplinarian, independent, free, individualistic, demanding.
7. Other personal characteristics: success-oriented, ambitious, aggressive, proud, egotistical, moral, trustworthy, decisive, competitive, uninhibited, adventurous. (pp. 35–36)

Those scholars who pinpoint the black male dilemma as deriving basically from the gap existing between the ideal male gender role for the overall American society and the actual ability of black males to realize it miss the mark. Throughout American history, black males were not, in fact, expected to be able to fulfill the ideal male gender role. Indeed, it was made abundantly clear that severe repercussions would follow if they made serious and persistent efforts to do so. Exercising power, at the economic, political, social, and cultural level, was not only not expected it was fervently opposed. Indeed, this was the source for innumerable violent conflicts, notably lynching, pogram-like invasions of the African American communities, and lesser forms of repression (Booker, 1997).

Black males and females of every period were quite aware of these iron ceilings placed on their advancement and of the restrictions that bound their every movement. For this reason, these barriers were regarded as a fact of black life, a clearly observable injustice, and this premise was embodied in the historically molded gender role values that emerged within African America. Thus, notions of the proper methods to respond to systematic injustice were and are an integral element of the evolving African American masculinity (Weatherspoon, 1998).

The dialectic of development for white males was historically linked to the underdevelopment of African American males. Slavery, Reconstruction, Jim Crow, and other forms of exploitation served to transfer resources from blacks to whites. While there are some parallels between the social construction of white masculinity and that of blacks, it is notable that in almost every instance of, for example, war, technological change, or migratory movement, the lived experiences, perceptions, and the responses of black and white males to these challenges were distinct. In particular, the African American male experience with war has left a significant imprint on their masculinity, attitudes, and behavior.

Black Male Images: Tools of Liberation or Consumption

The international face of the United States of America is African American and male. The explosion of rap music, hip hop culture, and professional sports has turned the black male image into a marketing icon designed to sell by any means necessary (Magubane, 2002). The popularity of reggae, jazz, and rap music in places like Bosnia, China, and New Zealand testify to the global rise of the cultures of the black diaspora. During the days of American apartheid, representations of blackness was nearly absent in American popular culture. Black characters, with the exception of the occasional maid or butler, were rarely seen in television shows and movies. In less than four decades African Americans have gone from being invisible in popular culture to being dominant. Douglas Keller (1995) in his book *Media Culture* speaks to the significance of media culture in our society:

> Our current local, national, and global situations are articulated through the texts of media culture, which is itself a contested terrain, one which competing social groups attempt to use to promote their agendas and ideologies, and which itself reproduces conflicting political discourses, often in a contradictory manner. Not just news and information, but entertainment and fiction articulate the conflicts, fears, hopes, and dreams of individuals and groups confronting a turbulent and uncertain world. The concrete struggles of each society are played out in the texts of media culture, especially in the commercial media of the culture industries which produce texts that must resonate with people's concerns if they are to be popular and profitable. Culture has never been more important and never before have we had such a need for serious scrutiny of contemporary culture. (p. 20)

The marketing and commodification of celebrities, particularly black celebrities and their images, are so important to advertising in this digital age, one of the distinguishing features of late-capitalist culture has been the fusing of American culture's latent and persisting desire for blackness with consumerist desire.

The political disturbances and cultural re-articulations of the black male image as presented by the media require a critique that moves beyond the hypersexualized heterosexual menace to society. In *Scripting the Black Masculine Body: Identity, Discourse, and the Racial Politics in Popular Media*, Ronald L. Jackson II asserts, "With the emergence of new media transducing racialized information from multiple popular cultural constituencies and mass-mediated news sources, and through the steady climb of hate group prosyletization via the Internet, Black bodies are being socially reconstituted and redefined on a daily basis" (p. 5). While the varied images of super athlete, gangster, and ghetto superstar travel across different fields of electronic representation and social discourse, there are multiple representations of black gender identity that are absent from mediated discourses. Black heterosexual masculinity is used in policy debates, in television news, and popular film representations to link the signs of patriotism, whiteness, family, nation, and individual responsibility.

Gender is fluid and not a static concept. Our human behaviors and their interpretation by those who witness them speak to how gender is constructed, enacted, performed, and contextualized. To be male or female means a pattern of behaviors must be engaged in and read for the production of gender. Masculinity and black masculinity are not a compilation of life styles, although popular culture seeks to construct black masculinity from a pattern of consumption. Black masculinity is constituted and constructed in relation to other gender identities. These constructions are based on how those relations interface with social structures. Gender and masculinity are performed based on the circumstances and people that surround us and how we view the way in which we are viewed. Commercial hip-hop and its construction of black masculinity create environments that nurture aggressive behaviors we see portrayed in music videos and hear in the lyrics of many heavily circulated songs. The action of these heavy rotations serves as a vehicle to continue the construction of black masculinity in popular space as a way to reify negative constructed identities.

Rux (2003) utilizing an interpretation of Fanon's (1986) dream reality/dream identity, speaks to the social construction of gender. Rux (2003) asserts African Americans, the oppressed, continue to live in the dream of identity, the dream that (in reality) the oppressed are, in fact, Negro, colored, black, minority, Afro or African American, Hispanic, oriental, dykes, bitches, hos, niggaz. All are accepted as real identities. The acceptance of these identities further compels a performance of these identities, whether compliant or rebellious. Juan Williams in his work *Enough: The Phony Leaders, Dead-End Movements, and Culture of Failure That Are Undermining Black America—and What We Can Do About It,* offers this. In March 2006, the *New York Times* reported on its front page that a "huge pool of poorly educated black men are becoming ever more disconnected from mainstreamed society and to a far greater degree than comparable white or Hispanic men'" (p. 23).

For oppressed black males in America, a systematically oppressed and depressed group, they must no longer accept nor perform these identities. Discursively located outside of the margins, representations of African American males who are contributing legally to the American economy by serving as power brokers in Fortune 500 companies, rearing children in same gender multiracial households, and providing financial, cultural, human, and social resources to their communities do not serve as the symbolic basis for fueling and sustaining panics about crime, the nuclear family, and middle-class security while displacing attention from the economy, racism, sexism, and homophobia (Gause, 2008. Contemporary expressions of black masculinity work symbolically in a number of directions at once; these expressions challenge and disturb racial and class constructions of blackness; they also rewrite and destroy the patriarchal and heterosexual basis of masculine privilege (and domination) based on gender and sexuality. The contemporary images and expressions of black masculinity I offer work to disturb dominant white representations of black masculinity. These images also stand in conflict with definitions and images of masculinity within blackness. This is found most notably in constructions of black masculinity produced by the middle-class wing of the echo boomers (children of baby boomers) and those produced more recently by black men who negotiate and navigate gender/transgressing sexualities/identities. So how did we end up in this situation?

In her insightful book, *We Real Cool: Black Men and Masculinity*, bell hooks writes:

> Without implying that black women and men lived in gender utopia, I am suggesting that black sex roles, and particularly the role of men, have been more complex and problematized in black life than is believed. This was especially the case when all black people lived in segregated neighborhoods. Racial integration has had a profound impact on black gender roles. It has helped to promote a climate wherein most black women and men accept sexist notions of gender roles. Unfortunately, many changes have occurred in the way black people think about gender, yet the shift from one standpoint to another has not been fully documented. For example: To what extent did the Civil Rights Movement, with its definition of freedom as having equal opportunity with whites, sanctioned looking at white gender roles as a norm black people should imitate? Why has there been so little positive interest shown in the alternative lifestyles of black men? In every segregated black community in the United States there are adult black men married, unmarried, gay, straight, living in households where they do not assert patriarchal domination and yet live fulfilled lives, where they are not sitting around worried about castration. Again it must be emphasized that the black men who are most worried about castration and emasculation are those who have completely absorbed white-supremacist patriarchal definitions of masculinity. (pp. 9–10)

The current construction/representation of the black male brings together the dominant institutions of (white) masculine power and authority—the criminal justice system, the police, and the news media—to protect (white) Americans from harm. Working this heavily surveyed and heavily illuminated public arena, the figure of the menacing black male is the object of adolescent intrigue, fascination, and commodification. By drawing on deeply felt moral panics about crime, violence, gangs, and drugs, numerous black entertainers, namely athletes and rap artists, have rewritten the historic tropes of black masculinity from provider and protector to pusher and pimp. This corrosive nihilistic construction of maleness reifies notions of (hyper) sexuality, insensitivity, and criminality, which serve as the new tropes of fascination and fear for the dominant culture.

The cultural effects of these images are as complex as they are troubling. The complex cluster of self-representations embodied in images of the black male as rap artist, athlete, and movie star is complicit in racist depictions of black males as incompetent, oversexed, and un-civil—ultimately a perceived threat to middle class notions of white womanhood, family, and patriotism. Self-representations of black male youth who construct their identities based on these media images rely on definitions of manhood that are deeply dependent on traditional notions of heterosexuality, authenticity, and sexism. Black heterosexual male youth who employ these representations see themselves as soldiers in a war for their own place in American society. These soldiers believe in doing battle they must threaten and challenge the white man's (liberal and conservative) conceptions of public civility, private morality, and individual responsibility. Through this performative act of black masculinity these youth become casualties of their own war.

Writing about the plight of the black male in the 2006 *Black Enterprise* essay "Can Young Black Men Be Saved?" Matthew Scott describes the condition of black males in America: "The statistics have reached near pandemic proportions. Several reports released at the start of 2006 highlighted a litany of corrosive trends: 50% of all black males drop out of high school; 72% of black male high school dropouts were unemployed in 2004; and by the time they reach their mid-30s, 60% of black male high school dropouts had spent some time in jail." I often ask the very same question: can young black men be saved?

Black Identity and Masculinity: Politics of the Academy

Students who enter the learning space I facilitate come seeking answers on how to educate different cultural and linguistic populations; however, most of them have a hard time receiving the messenger as well as the message. Having spent many years living in various cities in the United States and visiting many abroad, I find that living and working in the South is a very unique and different experience. I have served as a principal in very rural South Carolina and I now teach at the college level in Greensboro, the third largest city in North Carolina. Teaching in the academy is a place of privilege and one that I enjoy immensely; however, it does come with its own set of challenges. I am the only African American male faculty member in my department and for the past three years I have been the only African American male faculty member in the entire school of education. So when I think of democratic education and the purpose of public schools, my own academic identity situated within the context of carrying the weight of race and gender on my back informs my role as an educator and public intellectual. Understanding the environment that I inhabit I also realize my black male identity is formed out of those who were enslaved by individuals who framed this country's democratic experiment and institutions of higher learning (Gause, 2008).

> The paradox of teaching for social justice in higher education—which comprises revered institutions grounded in patriarchal, Anglocentric norms—challenges any faculty member striving to use critical, liberatory pedagogies. Faculty members of color doing this work, however, must confront a second paradox: that of being disproportionately oppressed, devalued, and scrutinized by the same structures, institutions, and social norms that we work within, critique, resist, and encourage others to defy. (Cooper and Gause, 2007, p. 201)

As an African American male academician many of the critical perspectives regarding the intersections of race, class, and gender affront the white southern Christian values my students hold near and dear. The expectation is for me to operate out of false civility and behave as if these values should not be critiqued and/or interrogated, but honored and celebrated regardless of how they assault the plurality of values students bring into public schools daily. Coupled with my being a faculty member of color, regardless of credentials, ideological orientation, and instructional style my students at times implicitly and explicitly challenge my professorial authority, scholarship, intellect, and political agenda (Gause, 2008). After speaking truth to power in many of our dialogic encounters I have often heard students call me "the angry black man" or "Dr. Thug." I find it interesting that they construct my passion for the subject and fiery delivery style as a place of subjugation. Given the atrocities occurring in public education in our nation today we should all be angered to action and express moral outrage. Shields (2004) suggests,

> Educators, policymakers, and indeed, the general public are increasingly aware that despite numerous well-intentioned restructuring, reform, and curricular efforts, many children who are in some way different from the previously dominant and traditionally most successful White, middle-class children are not achieving school success. (p. 111)

In order to transform schools we must hold our students accountable. We do this by shifting them from a traditionalist view of education and democracy to one that is radical and transformative. We can do this by promoting environments that require students to engage in independent thinking, motivate them to take ownership of their learning process, and by providing opportunities for rigorous intellectual study and committed activism that moves beyond arriving at the "right" answers. This requires critical change in teaching PreK-20 and the courage to lead.

> In forging a democratic discourse on progress in American education, the most immediate and pragmatic response among progressive educational leaders may well be a politics of individual and collective resistance to the "machines" of urban schooling, including "high stakes" testing. As I have long argued, teachers represent a potentially powerful counter hegemonic power bloc in democratic educational renewal and there is much good, progressive work to be done in teachers' unions and professional organizations. At some point, however, progressives also must move beyond critique and resistance toward the forging of a countermovement for progress in America, linked to a new commonsense discourse on the renewal of public education and public life. (Carlson and Gause, 2007, p. 23)

I consider myself a charismatic activist educator with radical consciousness who strives to make a difference in our humanity; however, being the only African American male in the professoriate in the school of education at the University of North Carolina-Greensboro, who at the time of this writinghas just received tenure. I constantly struggle with not allowing myself nor the multiple identities I navigate to become co-opted. bell hooks in *We Real Cool: Black Men and Masculinity* asserts, "Individual charismatic black male leaders with radical consciousness often become so enamored of their unique status as the black man who is different that they fail to share the good news with other black men. Or they allow themselves to be co-opted—seduced by the promise of greater monetary rewards and access to mainstream power that are the payoffs for pushing a less radical message" (p. xvii). This at times can be difficult, particularly if you really are the only one. I believe it is virtually impossible to integrate our schools, churches, civic groups, businesses, leadership ranks of our society, and professions until students from underrepresented groups become high achievers. Many African American educators have espoused those beliefs and spoke to the lack by various communities in encouraging our young people to become high achievers. Teachers must set high expectations and empower our young people to develop the resources to engage in inquiry that is critical and dynamic.

The purpose of writing this chapter is to push academic and public discourse around issues of visible and invisible diversity, particularly within the constructs of sexuality. This work is important because I have had to negotiate the intersections of the multiple identities I enact while remaining silent during moments of witnessing injustices in professional arenas. I use the term *enact* because I believe we perform our identities given the situations and circumstances that occur in our daily lives. I was struggling with writing a journal article regarding sexual identities and educational leadership and realized how I was subconsciously avoiding utilizing any of the GLBTIQQ (gay, lesbian, bisexual, transgendered, intersexual, queer, and questioning) language in the article. As I interrogated my own position as the author of the text, I closeted myself from how I viewed myself as a *same affection loving* black man in the academy.

I utilize the term *same affection loving* to speak to the spiritual attractions I have for individuals devoid of the performance of a sex act. My attraction to someone begins with a spiritual connection. The affection of soul connection speaks to my desire for another human being and because this is soul-practice, the body they inhabit has little meaning in terms of establishing a relationship. Their physical appearance, cognitive abilities, and social/cultural capital are not the first thing I experience when introduced. Through the spiritual realm of our existence my desires are awakened and my senses are aroused for the individual. The current terms for expressing alternative gendered identities is too limiting for how I construct my own sexual identity. I am first attracted to an individual spiritually then intellectually; therefore, the person can be housed in a biologically male or female body. I offer you this personal definition because it is mine and also to problematize how we recognize gender and sexual identities in this society. I will further explain the notion of *same affection loving* in a future piece of scholarship. I realize the reason I was closeting myself in my own scholarship was because of fear. Parker Palmer in his work, *The Courage to Teach: Exploring the Inner Landscape of a Teacher's Life,* explores this notion of fear. He asserts, "Fear is what distances us from our colleagues, our students, our subjects, ourselves. Fear shuts down those "experiments with truth" that allow us to weave a wider web of connectedness—and thus shuts down our capacity to teach as well" (p. 36).

I was fearful of professing to be who I saw myself to be because being the "other" in our society is a badge of hatred and shame. Living an alternative-gendered identity in America when one can clearly see that I am an African American male is difficult at its best in the academy, but quite problematic in everyday African American communities. How could I speak truth to power as an African American male who is partnered with another African American male when homophobia still continues to be the norm in black communities and institutions particularly in the South? When you have individuals questioning whether Barack Obama is authentically black and electable as the first black president of the United States or Hillary Clinton as the first female president of the United States, for me being a *same affection loving* black man teaching aspiring educational leaders to engage in transformational leadership at a major southern university, pretenured is unfathomable. It takes courage to lead and navigate the multiple identities I perform given the cultural resistance inherent in southern communities. The poem I am writing is a journey of self-reflection.

From the perspective of the academy, I am a relatively young tenureed faculty member of color who holds doctoral and other advanced degrees from tier-one research institutions. I was mentored by highly distinguished educational scholars who were from diverse ethnic and gendered identities. I have various experiences leading public, private, and nonprofit organizations. I teach research and evaluate K-12 schools situated in a range of political, geographical, and cultural contexts. The additional elements of my identities are African American, male, *same affection loving*, Christian, northerner, southerner, and midwesterner, and my praxis is rooted in collaborative activism, social justice, political struggle, and resistance. Parker Palmer (1998) in his work, *The Courage to Teach: Exploring the Inner Landscape of a Teacher's Life,* explores this notion of courage. He asserts, "The courage to teach is the courage to keep one's heart open in those very moments when the heart is asked to hold more than it is able so that teacher and students and subject can be woven into the fabric of community that learning, and living, require" (p. 11).

The codifying of the experiences of African American educators is very limited in first-person narrative form. Their "stories" and their "voices" are virtually silent in educational discourses. African American educators of course are not nonexistent; however, their lives, contributions, and experiences in educating youth from their own personal account are quite limited. "Research on teachers; though extensive, has generally failed to include the experiences of African American teachers" (Foster, 1990, p. 123). The stories of people's lives are communicated through the use of narratives.

Personal narratives of the *Brown* ruling and its impact on African American educators are very limited in academic discourse. In 1954, only .001 percent of black students attended majority white schools. As a result of the decision the number of African Americans attending majority white schools increased significantly. From the late 1960s through 1988, almost 43.5% of southern black students attended majority white schools, however, at the expense of black educators. Chesley and Lyons (2004) posit one of the first negative impacts for African Americans stemming from desegregation was the dismissal and demotion of black principals and teachers. I add that *all* black high schools were also casualties in the integration experiment. Booker T. Washington High School in Columbia, South Carolina, my mother's alma mater, is one notable example. Rosenwald and Ochberg (1992) eloquently speak to the importance of personal stories and their role in identity construction, "personal stories are not merely a way of telling someone (or oneself) about one's life; they are a means by which identities may be fashioned" (p. 1). Bruner (1990) argues that narratives are the natural mode in which human beings make sense of lives in time. "People do not deal with the world event by event or with text sentence by sentence. They frame events and sentences in larger structures" (as cited in Polkinghorne, 1997, p. 12).

My critical reflection became even more critical of my role as researcher, educator, African American male, and all of the other multiple identities that construct "me." I realize the struggle in which we are all a part began on the "backs of our ancestors." Knowing this has created in me a desire to rise up against injustice wherever it may be and this was my purpose. The African American educators and the "street educators" wanted their stories to be told and I happened to be the conduit so this text had to be written. Because of the nature of this work and how academic texts are viewed by general audiences and how texts for general readership are viewed by academics, I have to code-switch. The following text is designed to be written as a journal article, however, I don't believe there is an academic journal that would publish this, therefore, I include it here as a representation of the way I negotiate my identities as I navigate the sociocultural politics of my profession even in the academy. In a sense for me it is a form of protest and resistance. Scholarship, especially research in educational leadership, is often evaluated and assessed through white heteronormative dimensions.

CP! Academically Speaking—The Lost Journal Article

A discourse regarding the intersections of black masculinity, queerness, and educational leadership is quite limited in academic scholarship. This project moves beyond the questioning of masculinities to advance a project that interrogates the bestial, hypersexualized, endangered imagery of African American males within the public sphere. I further platform this chapter by interrogating my role as a school administrator in the late 1990s juxtaposed to my current position as educational leadership faculty in a major university in the southeastern part of the United States who seeks to co-construct democratic learning communities with current practitioners.

When RuPaul arrived on the music scene in 1993 as an African American "brotha" turned drag queen with the hit single "Supermodel," the American mainstream music scene was blindsided. The song lauded the beauty of the international models of the fashion industry and how they worked the runway bringing the designer clothes on their bodies to life. The tag line of the song, "you better work" was gay slang for "do your stuff and do it well." "Supermodel" peaked at #45 on the Billboard Hot 100, which was regarded as an unlikely accomplishment for the drag entertainer. It found the most success on the U.S. Billboard Hot Dance Music/Club Play where it peaked at #2.

How could a 6'3" pecan tan 200-pound black male in on a blond wig, sequin gown, and makeup capture the American music scene? Boy George, Culture Club's androgynous front man, did in the early 1980s but he was white and could sing by some standards. His androgynous costumes spoke to the fusion of the 80s punk scene with queer exploration. No other African American male except for Sylvester, a transgendered songstress of the 1970s and '80s, made an attempt to display their sexuality in the public sphere by utilizing mediated imagery. Sylvester was a big disco star with several hits but did not achieve the level of success RuPaul experienced. With MTV RuPaul was able to move gay camp female impersonation from the stages of gay clubs in cities across the United States into mainstream popular culture. RuPaul hosted MTV's Spring Break, made various appearances at many of the entertainment industry's awards shows, and played major concert venues throughout the country. RuPaul became so popular he even had his own talk show sponsored by MTV.

RuPaul was most popular with young white kids from the suburbs (Magubane, 2002). This was not to say that he did not have any African American fans; however, his following consisted of white club kids. Just like hip hop is purchased and consumed more by young white males than any other demographic in the United States. I experienced the RuPaul craze of the 1990s and was reminded of my dance club experiences when one of my life-long friends saw a copy of *Keeping the Promise: Essays on Leadership, Democracy and Education* (Carlson & Gause, 2007) and decided to call me. We talked about life and work and he wanted to know if I was still single. I told him of course because the right person has yet to come along and win my heart. He stated, "C. P., I saw the book. Honey, they aren't ready for you, you better work!" I laughed for a moment and then I began to realize some of the difficulties I experienced as a *same affection loving* tenure-track faculty member of color in a majority minority research-intensive university located in the southeastern part of the United States. Before ending our call, we vowed to remain in touch and to continue on our paths of liberation. Given the media representations of African American and Latino males in this country I could only think about the line Oprah Winfrey delivered as Sophia in the movie the *Color Purple*; "all my life I had to fight."

Fighting the Fight

This work, unlike the work of the sex-role reformers in the 1970s, is not a push for androgyny in schools or our communities, although I do see a need for change. However, the sex-role reformers of the 1970s "underestimated the complexity of masculinities and femininities, [and] put too much emphasis on attitudes and not enough on material inequalities and issues of power" (Connell, 1992, p. 205). This work strives to "trouble" the inherent power of the construction of race, gender, and sexuality, particularly as enacted and performed in schools (Butler, 1990; Foucault, 1979). My experience with public schools and the way they silence anything outside of the dominant culture provides me the space to speak to these issues as a scholar, practitioner, and student. As I journeyed through K-12 education, first as a student, then as a professional, I thought often of my race and position as a black male; particularly as a black male educator who negotiated multiple public spheres. It was not until I began my doctoral studies that I began to interrogate my sexuality and the ways in which I viewed gender. I did give some thought to sexual orientation and the ways in which it was constructed by dominating discourses, but I didn't fit those little boxes. My phrase, *same affection loving* was how I described myself: a form of spiritual lovingness where sexual performance was de-centered. It was my way of *queering*. To others this was a form of passing, sexual passing, which shares the same connotation of racial passing. If I am light enough, no one can see my blackness and therefore, I am white. If I am *queer* enough no one can see my gayness, which in the African American community is a sign of weakness, therefore, I am perceived to be straight. According to Heasley (2005), The hegemonic heteromasculine is represented culturally in the icons of religion, sports, historical figures, economic and political leaders, and the entertainment industry; however, in these arenas, males are presumed to be straight and hold stereotypically masculine beliefs, attitudes, and values unless and until they present themselves as other. (p. 310)

Within the black church, by some considered to be the most homophobic institution of the black public sphere, gayness and queerness are often perceived in stereotypical forms: the flamboyant preacher, the faggot choir director, and the sissified musician. Many members of the black church community have come to embrace the talents of the homosexual in our churches, but we refuse to acknowledge their life partners, their openness regarding how they sexually identify, as well as their leadership capabilities. I doubt in we will ever witness openly queer pastors, bishops, or national leaders of any traditional mainstream black religious denominations or spiritual organizations. This speaks to the prejudices and homophobia present in the black community. We are committed to sexist thinking but we scream racism when other groups remain committed to racist thinking. According to hooks (2004), "Allegiance to sexist thinking about the nature of leadership creates a blind spot that effectively prevents masses of black people from making use of theories and practices of liberation when they are offered by women" (p. xvi). I concur with hooks; however, I would argue the allegiance to sexist thinking becomes greater when such theories and practices of liberation are offered by nonheterosexist black males. Lemelle and Battle (2004) assert

> Stigma associated with homophobia and homosexuality helps us to understand that in everyday and face-to-face interactions, black masculinity is unique in the management of identity. For one thing, black masculinity is a stigmatized status. This means that gay black males' identities are spoiled on tripartite dimensions: as black males, as gay black males and as mortified gay black males who have internalized civil and health experiences of discrimination. (p. 48)

I experience this "oneness" in terms of my position at the university. Although colleagues within my department and the School of Education have been extremely supportive, I am speaking to the challenges of being "the only one." According to Stanley (2007) African Americans, Native Americans, Asian Americans, and Latinas/Latinos, in particular, constitute between 20% and 25% of the U.S. population. However, they represent 13.4% of the faculty at degree-granting institutions of higher education (Internal Citation omitted, p. 1). I am the first and only African American male faculty member in the history of my department and currently I am the only African American male faculty member within the School of Education. I am very open and pragmatic regarding gender identity, equity, and full representation of those who are considered "the other." There are white male faculty members who are indeed allies and who demonstrate queer masculinity. Heasley (2005) defines queer masculinity. He posits, "Many straight men experience and demonstrate "queer masculinity," ways of being masculine outside hetero-normative constructions of masculinity that disrupt, or have the potential to disrupt, traditional images of the hegemonic heterosexual masculine" (p. 310). I am thankful for those men and women who challenge what it means to be a scholar and colleague in my department and within the School of Education at the University of North Carolina at Greensboro. Even though they are few and far between, I forever remain hopeful.

Uncovering Truth: I Am Who I Am

As a former school teacher, principal, and administrator I was not open regarding my sexual identity for risk of repercussions. I taught in the South during the mid-1990s and being *same affection loving* was for white boys. The sociocultural and political dynamics of sexual orientation was one of liberation and the good life. Circuit parties, Fire Island, and P-Town were subversive and the media represented them as such. I became a school administrator during the mid-to-late '90s and was able to witness how gay culture was being commodified by the mass media and industry. However, I was not represented in *Advocate* or *Out* magazines. The media communicated to me that I was threatening, aggressive, and intimidating (Gause, 2008. I did not see anyone on the fashion runway in America that I could identify with, but I did hear many students, black and white, explore the use of the words "gay" and "fag" in the classroom, on the playground, and in the cafeteria. I was horrified by the open expression and use of these terms by kids who did not know the sociocultural and political meanings of these terms. This was not appropriate and it could not be tolerated.

This language was not acceptable. The faculty and staff of our K-8 school, under my direction began a character program that communicated democratic and community values to our students. I did not tolerate bullying of any kind; however, I never had conversations with those students who were questioning their identities. I did bring in a community liaison who had a program that spoke to puberty and abstinence, but I stayed away from those issues. I needed to for fear of being perceived as "one of them." This label would have been death to a career that I worked so hard to achieve, and to me who I was and what I did in the privacy of my home was my own business.

As a professor in higher education whose pedagogical framework is rooted in equity, social justice, and anti-oppressive education (Carlson & Gause, 2007). I have often utilized the aforementioned scenario with my students to discuss the intersections of race, class, gender, and power. I was not pragmatic or genuine while a teacher and administrator in sharing my narrative as a black queer male. An interesting point is that there were teachers and students who knew that I was queer. The reality is that I did not want to ever be in a situation where I would have to "out" myself. I also knew that I was an outsider within that community (I lived 70 miles away) and I did not want my sexuality viewed as a deficit regarding my leadership abilities especially if I made a decision that was not popular.

In conclusion, where does this leave me? I have spent this week teaching a class of aspiring and practicing administrators "notions of resistance," within the context of "Spirit." I am frustrated with the whole dialogue surrounding shallow visceral murmurings of "this is how I think it should be," which always translates into "why do we have to talk about diversity and sex?" What must we do as educators to utilize these "discords of resistance" to create a melodic musing of harmony, peace, and justice to bring the invisible to the visible and the hidden into plain sight. Most aspiring educators are surprised when I discuss sexuality and that by hiding who I was as an administrator, I was not advocating for students who articulated their sexuality and positionality far from what is accepted in our schools and mainstream society (Gause, 2008). There are some educators in my courses who have "come out" and discussed their multiple identities; however, it has always been after my openness and the emphasis on creating engaging and affirming learning spaces.

As a transformative educator, I believe my activism is essential to my pedagogy and my role as an educational leader. As an African American, I believe my activism is connected to the post–civil rights revolution, and the diverse ways in which I engage school administrators regarding this activism helps them to "see" diversity beyond skin color. Therefore, transformative educators, particularly African Americans, who view themselves from social locations that include alternative gendered identities must (1) engage in a discourse of leadership for social justice, (2) deconstruct the "grand" narratives reified by the "media," by telling their stories, and certainly (3) create a "space" through rupture, that will situate educational leadership within the context of the prophetic spirituality (West, 1993, Dantley, 2003), which is such a part of the African American experience.

My American dream is not shattered by the "unscripted reality" that exists within the fabric of my being or the faceless identity the media has created. We are yet African American males whose lives of love, unless we forget, are interwoven with the intersections of *our* race, class, gender, and political selves. Our *same affection loving* orientation disrupts, or better, ruptures the very institutions that we have constructed to liberate our oppressed identities: our family, our schools, and our churches. This love for our created selves, or the lack thereof, is situated in institutionalized oppressive practices that are enacted by how we interpret the text of the scribes who recorded the logos. We must not forget, the very Creator in which we believe created each of us within a "divine image of love," and that image must be transformed into the love of the self. Who are we then? Who is it that transverses our presence and creates our invisibility? Is it I? Maybe you? No. It is all of us, the mighty, who refuse to remain oppressed. We breathe life into the lifeless and speak for those who refuse to speak. Only then will we overcome our silence, and transgress from the borders of the margins to allow our passion to become our activism—there lies the visibility of our invisibility.

References

Booker, C. (1997). Historical overview of the African-American male. *African-American Research*, 2 (1–5).

Bruner, J. (1990). *Acts of Meaning*. Cambridge MA: Harvard University Press.

Butler, J. (1990). *Gender trouble: Feminism and the subversion of identity*. New York: Routledge

Carlson, D., & Gause, C. P. (2007). *Keeping the promise: Essays on leadership, democracy, and education*. New York: Peter Lang.

Case, M. A. C. (1995). Disaggregating gender from sex and sexual orientation: The effeminate man in the law and feminist jurisprudence. *Yale Law Journal*, 105: 1–105.

Chafetz, J. S. (1974). *Masculine/feminine or human?: An overview of the sociology of sex roles*. Itasca, Illinois F. E Peacock Publishers.

Chesley, J. and Lyons, J. E. (2004). Fifty years after *Brown*: The benefits and tradeoffs for African American educators and students. *The Journal of Negro Education*, 73, 298-313.

Connell, R.W (1992). "A Very Straight Gay: Masculinity, Homosexual Experience, and the Dynamics of Gender" *American Sociological Review*. Vol.57 Dec.

Cooper, C., & Gause, C. P. (2007). "Who's afraid of the big bad wolf?" Facing identity politics and resistance when teaching for social justice. In Carlson, D. & Gause, C. P. (Eds.). *Keeping the promise: Essays on leadership, democracy, and education*. New York: Peter Lang.

Dantley, M. (2003). Principled, pragmatic, and purposive leadership: Reimagining educational leadership through prophetic spirituality. *Journal of School Leadership, 13* (2), 181–198.

Eskridge, Jr. W. N. (2000). No Promo Homo: The sedimentation of antigay discourse and the channeling effect of judicial review. *New York University Law Review*, 75: 1327–1411.

Fanon, F. (1986). *Black Skin, White Masks*. London, UK: Pluto Press

Foster, M. (1990). The politics of race: Through the eyes of African American teachers. *Journal of Education*, 172(3), 123-141.

Foucault, M. (1979). *Discipline and Punish: The birth of the prison*. Trans. Alan Sheridan. New York: Vintage.

Franke, K. M. (1995). The central mistake of sex discrimination law: The disaggregation of sex from gender. *University of Pennsylvania Law Review*, 144: 1–99.

Freire, P. (1970). *Pedagogy of the oppressed*. New York: Continuum

Gause, C. P. (2002 September). Who am I? No, I'm not just another Black face: Article presented at the Commonwealth Conference on Educational Administration and Management bi-annual conference, Sweden.

Gause, C. P. (2008). *Integration matters: Navigating identity, culture and resistance*. New York: Peter Lang.

Giroux, Henry A. (1988). *Schooling and the struggle for public life*. Minneapolis: University of Minnesota Press.

Giroux, H. A. (2000). *Impure acts: The practical politics of cultural studies.* New York: Routledge.

Giroux, H. A. (2001). *Stealing innocence: Youth, corporate power, and the politics of culture.* New York: Palgrave.

Guy-Sheftall, B., & Cole, J. B. (2003). *Gender talk: The struggle for women's equality in African American communities.* One/World Ballentine.

Hale-Benson, J. (1982). *Black children: Their roots, culture, and learning styles.* Baltimore: Johns Hopkins University Press.

Harper, P. B. (1996). *Are we not men: Masculine anxiety and the problem of African-American identity?* New York: Oxford University Press.

Harris, S. M. (1995). Psychosocial development and Black male masculinity: Implications for counseling economically disadvantaged African American male adolescents. *Journal of Counseling and Development,* 73 (3), 279–287.

Havinghurst, R. J. (1976). The relative importance of social class and ethnicity in human development. *Human Development,* 19, 56–64.

Heasley, R. (2005). Queer masculinities of straight men: A topology. *Men and masculinities,* 7 (3): 310–320.

hooks, b. (2004). *We real cool: Black men and masculinity.* New York. Routledge.

Hopkins, R. (1997). *Educating black males: Critical lessons in schooling, community, and power.* Albany, NY: State University of New York Press.

Hutchinson, E. (1996).*The assassination of the black male image.* New York: Touchstone Press.

Jackson, R. L. (2006). *Scripting the black masculine body: identity, discourse, and racial politics in popular media.* New York: State University of New York Press-Albany.

Kellner, D. (1995). *Media culture: Cultural studies, identity and politics between the modern and the postmodern.* London: Routledge

Koschoreck, J. W. (2003). Easing the violence: Trangressing heteronormativity in educational administration. *Journal of School Leadership. 13* (1) pp. 27–50.

Ladson-Billings, G. (1994). *The dreamkeepers: Successful teachers of African American children.* San Francisco: Jossey-Bass.

Lather, P. (1993). Fertile obsession: Validity after poststructuralism. *Sociological Quarterly, 34* (4), 673–693.

Lemelle, A & Battle, J. (2004). Black masculinity matters in attitudes towards gay males. *Journal of Homosexuality.* Vol. 47 (1), 39-51.

Lindsey, R., Robins, K. N., & Terrell, R. (1999). *Cultural proficiency: A manual for school leaders.* Thousand Oaks, CA: Corwin Press.

Lugg, C. A. (2007). Sissies, faggots, lezzies, and dykes: Gender, sexual orientation, and a new politics of education? In Carlson, D. & Gause, C.P. (Eds.). *Keeping the promise: Essays on leadership, democracy, and education.* New York: Peter Lang.

Madhubuti, H. R. (1990). Black men: Obsolete, single, dangerous? In *The Afrikan American family in transition: Essays in discovery, solution, and hope.* Chicago: Third World Press.

Magubane, Z. (2002). Black skins, black masks or "The return of the white negro": Race, masculinity, and the public personas of Dennis Rodman and RuPaul. *Men and Masculinities,* 4 (3): 233–257.

Majors, R., & Billson, J. (1992). *Cool pose. The dilemmas of black manhood in America.* New York: Simon & Schuster.

McBride, D. A. (1998). Can the queen speak?: Race essentialism, sexuality and the problem of authority. *Callaloo* 21: 363–379.

McCarthy, C., & Crichlow, W. (1993). *Race Identity and representation in education.* New York: Routledge.

McWhorter, J. (2000). *Losing the race.* New York: The Free Press.

Miller, N. (1995). *Out of the past: Gay and lesbian history from 1869 to the present.* New York Vintage Press.

Neisser, U. (Ed.). (1982). *Memory observed.* New York: W. H. Freeman.

Palmer, P. (1998). *The Courage to Teach: Exploring the Inner Landscape of a Teacher's life.* San Francisco, California: Jossey-Bass.

Polkinghorne, D.E. (1997). Reporting qualitative research as practice. In W. Tierney & Y. Lincoln(Eds.), *Representation and the text: Re-naming the narrative voice* (pp. 3–22). Albany: SUNY Press.

Prideaux, G. (1991). Applying learning principles to the development of health services managers. *Journal of Health Administration Education,* 9 (2), 215–251.

Quantz, R. A. (2003). The Puzzlemasters: Performing the mundane, searching for intellect, and living in the belly of the corporation. *Review of Education, Pedagogy, and Cultural Studies,* 25: 95–137.

Rose, T. (1994). *Black Noise: Rap music and black culture in contemporary America.* Hanover: University Press of New England.

Rosenwald, G.C., & Ochberg, R. L. (1992). Introduction: Life stories, cultural politics, and self-understanding. In G.C. Rosenwald & R. L. Ochberg (Eds.), *Storied lives: The cultural politics of self-understanding* (pp. 1–18). New Haven: Yale University Press.

Rux, Carl Hancock (2003). Eminem—The new white Negro. In Greg Tate (Ed.) *Everything but the burden—What white people are taking from black culture*. New York: Harlem Moon Broadway Books, pp. 15–37.

Sears, J. T. (1991). *Growing up gay in the South: Race, gender, and journeys of the spirit*. New York: Haworth Press.

Shields, C. M. (2004). Dialogic leadership for social justice: Overcoming pathologies of silence. *Educational Administration Quarterly*. 40(1), 109–132.

Stanley, C. A. (2007). When counter narratives meet master narratives in the journal editorial-review process. *Educational Researcher*. 36 (1): 14–24.

Somerville, S. B. (2002). Queer fiction of race: Introduction. *MFS Modern Fiction Studies*, 48 (4): 787–794.

_____. (2000). *Queering the color line: Race and the invention of homosexuality in American culture*. Durham, NC: Duke University Press.

Tenni, C., Smyth, A., & Boucher, C. (March 2003). The researcher as autobiographer: Analysing data written about oneself. *Qualitative Reporter*, 8 (1), 1–12. (http://www.nova.edu/ssss/QR/QR8-1/tenni.html) accessed August 28, 2003.

Terry, J. (1999). *An American obsession: Science, medicine, and homosexuality in modern society*. Chicago: University of Chicago Press.

Valdes, F. (1995). Queers, sissies, dykes, and tomboys: Deconstructing the conflation of "sex," "gender," and "sexual orientation" in Euro-American law and society. *California Law Review*, 3–377.

Watkins, W. H. (1993). Black curriculum orientations: A preliminary inquiry. *Harvard Educational Review*, 63 (3), 321–338.

Weatherspoon, F. D. (1998). *African-American males and the law: Cases and materials*. New York: University Press of America.

Weis, L. (1988). *Class, race, and gender in American education*. Albany, NY: State University of New York Press.

West, C. (1993). *Race matters*. New York: Vintage Press.

White, J., & Cones, J. (1999). *Black man emerging*. New York. W. H. Freeman.

Williams, J. (2006). *Enough: The phony leaders, dead-end movements, and culture of failure that are undermining Black America—and what we can do about it*. New York: Three Rivers Press.

Woodson, C. G. (1933). *The mis-education of the negro*. Washington, DC: Associated Press.

Yoshino, K. (2002). Covering. *Yale Law Journal*, 111: 769–939.

Section Five

Social and Economic Class

Seventeen

Schooling and Social Class

J. Grinberg, J. Price, F. Naiditch[1]

Many educators, whether beginning or experienced teachers, often look at parental income and other issues of poverty or wealth as a way to explain student success or failure. While economic factors play a role in the educational process, the ways in which social class is a cultural, social, and historical system are often overlooked. When we develop curriculum or pedagogy for students in school, we might view school subjects in relation to the cultural experiences of students. How is it that students from middle and upper middle class homes tend to continue on to college and professional careers, while students from working class or poor families do not? We rarely ask whose class interests this curriculum and pedagogy serve. And many teachers might see some students having less or more social class culture than themselves as though one form or class culture is better than another. Whatever questions we might pose, a reality persists in American schools whereby students from working class homes continue to have educational experiences that oftentimes result in them getting pushed out or dropping out of schools.

Social class has been explained traditionally by discussing access to opportunity, resources, and educational experiences. This process is often explained at the level of school systems, procedures, organization, laws, and policies. In addition, social class is also explained as an examination of the beliefs, values, and norms that pervade schools and the larger society, as well as the processes in and out of school that produce school experiences. When we use the term *social class*, we acknowledge that social class is dynamically shaped by other systems of marginalization and privilege, such as race, ethnicity, language, and gender. However, given that other chapters in this volume focus on these other forms of difference, we focus on social class as a system that shapes and organizes social life in ways that provide some groups with more advantages than others and which are sanctioned also through the experience of schooling.

In this chapter we explore the relationship between social class and schooling in the United States.[2] We argue that schools have not become an equalizer. We explain how this happens. We also argue that teachers who are committed to advancing social justice can contribute to alter these processes when, in solidarity with students and local communities, they foster a critical pedagogy.

We begin with a historical account of the promise of schools in the United States as social institutions that are shaped by participants in and out of the education system. This is followed by a discussion of the ideologies that help sustain the false promise of equal opportunities as well as what social class means as a cultural and social phenomenon. We conclude with some ideas and actions that might address the persistence of social class inequalities.

The Common School: The Great Equalizer

The right to attend school in the United States is not written into the Unites States constitution. Rather, the creation of the public school system emerged in the nineteenth century in an effort to provide educational opportunity to citizens. At this time, there was a vast difference between the education received by wealthy and poor students. While Jefferson argued that some form of schooling was important to the survival of democracy in the United States, his proposals were elitist and sexist, and their expensive and centralized characteristics led to their rejection. Thus, in the 1820s Horace Mann's interest and advocacy for the solidification and standardization of education led to his recognition as one of the central figures in the establishment and expansion of America's public school systems.

By the 1820s, Massachusetts was debating the quality and the expansion of its school systems. Horace Mann advocated for the creation of a state board of education and became its first secretary. In his role as secretary of the board, he took it upon himself to visit schools all over the state in both large and small communities and was extremely meticulous in reporting what he observed. From these visits, he noted that most buildings were in disrepair, materials were not appropriate, some teachers were poorly educated themselves, pupils' attendance was irregular, significant numbers of schools were one-room schools, and the teachers were in charge of cleaning and maintaining the building. Many schools were unable to function for a long period of time. In numerous places, pupils spent hours reciting passages from books that oftentimes they brought from home. Horace Mann's concern was that differential access to knowledge would create different levels of education among the population. It is important to note that the educational conditions that Mann noted stood in marked contrast to the private school education that many middle class and wealthy pupils received. In sum, students across Massachusetts experienced education very differently. In an effort to improve the quality of education, a number of reforms were proposed and, after much debate, were later approved.

In Horace Mann's reports, he advocated for significant forms of standardization across all schools. The proposals included standardization in the physical space allotted to a classroom, particular kinds of furniture considered important to learning, and of course, the use of certain materials. In addition, he also advocated for the standardization of the curriculum and methods of teaching.

A considerable challenge that Mann and his supporters faced was ensuring continued financial support for these schools. Hence the idea was put forth that these common schools would be supported with taxes paid by local communities. The schools were common schools because all children from all backgrounds would attend them. They would be free of charge. Irrespective of the students' backgrounds, they would have the right to an education offered by the community and the state and an opportunity to be successful. Such an idea was met with opposition, particularly from middle class families. Those who owned property were the ones who paid taxes, and often they were able to afford private education for their children. What arguments then could Mann and his supporters use to convince property owners to pay taxes directed for supporting the education of other children?

For democracy to succeed, schools were needed that would be common to all and free of charge. Such schools would be standardized in many ways thereby ensuring that every student, regardless of their family background, their social class, or their religion, would have an opportunity to be successful. As Mann himself put it:

> If one class possesses all of the wealth and the education, while the residue of society is ignorant and poor... the latter in fact and in truth, will be the servile dependents and subjects of the former. (Mann, 1848/1891, p. 251)

In the Jeffersonian tradition, Mann advocated for the opportunity of access to education and for the opportunity to maximize students' achievements according to their skill, effort, and intelligence. Thus, if given equal opportunities to all, students' success depended on their own dedication. In this way, communities would have a sense of involvement in efforts to establish and develop a system of schools in which everyone could be successful.

Furthermore, Horace Mann saw schools as an opportunity to rebuild the sense of community and to advance the formation of the American nation. The common school was seen as a public good, which meant that the whole community and the whole nation are not only invested in its success but will benefit from it. An educated citizenry means learning a high sense of responsibility, participation, character, and accountability. Furthermore, a good education would teach citizens to pay taxes, obey the laws, and participate in public affairs.

Taxpayers would agree to support such a system because schools and education simultaneously served both the individual and the community. Schools could provide a sense of a shared past, present, and future. Besides this sense of nationhood created by the movement to create free public education, schools were also viewed as a place to educate future workers. The standardization measures that were introduced meant, on one level, that students within a community received the same education; on another level, schools would be a place to discipline and control students through the kinds of basic knowledge they accessed but also through the behaviors, morals, and senses of duty that were instilled in the classroom and school life. The concepts also embraced the hope that a solid public education would allow U.S. society to prevent the kind of social unrest that was taking place in Europe where abhorrent labor conditions, exploitation of workers, and dramatic differences between the rich and poor prevailed. The system of public common schools that provide equal opportunity to all would not only prevent such antagonisms but would also enable all to escape poverty:

> Education, then beyond all other devices of human origin, is the great equalizer of the conditions of men—the balance wheel of the social machinery. . . . It does better than to disarm the poor of their hostility toward the rich; it prevents being poor. (Mann, 1848/1891, p. 251))

Mann was also instrumental in establishing the first normal schools in America. These normal schools were institutions that prepared teachers for American schools. Such institutions already had been successful in places such as France and Prussia. The idea of these schools was that by normalizing the preparation of teachers, a certain level of uniformity could be accomplished in curricular and pedagogical terms. At the same time, there would be a minimal level of competency expected by normal school graduates. Horace Mann's writings were read not only in Massachusetts and America but also all over the world.[3]

Thus far, we have explained the historic roots of the public school system in the United States. We have highlighted reformers' goals of providing access to education in communities. However, as noted earlier, a critical component of the quest to build the common school was to facilitate a commitment to building a nation. This was enabled through the identification of national symbols such as the flag, the representation of heroic individuals and events that are common to all, and the development of a common ideology. Hence schools also served as a socializing institution in that they promoted certain values, norms, and beliefs over others. In establishing a common curriculum, and standardized use of space and time, students' education entailed not only learning facts, skills, or knowledge but also learning about particular norms, values, morals, and rules of social life. A common belief was that a school system would enable students to improve themselves and achieve and attain social mobility, thereby enhancing the individual's status in relation to that of the family they were born into, gaining access to better things, better material resources, and more access to cultural goods. This notion of meritocracy saw education, and hence schools, becoming the unifying center of hope through an ideology that rests on the expectation that individual effort will be compensated.

The Myths of Meritocracy and the Classless Society

The belief that we are all equal and that there are no socioeconomic dividers in America is a myth that clearly denies class markers that are so strongly apparent in American life and American institutions evidenced in hierarchies, social prestige, pay scales, educational levels and degrees, and the distinction between public and private schools just to name a few. As W. Lloyd Warner (1993) has already pointed out,

> We are proud of those facts of American life that fit the pattern we are taught but somehow we are often ashamed of those equally important social facts which demonstrate the presence of social class. Consequently, we tend to deny them, or worse, denounce them and by doing so we tend to deny their existence and magically make them disappear from consciousness. (p. 11)

America has been divided along the lines of class, race, and ethnicity from the outset and the attempts to cross those lines have almost always resulted in conflict and social tension (Zinn, 2005). Historically, there is a divide between what America is and what it wants to be or what it believes it is. It may be because of this belief or wishful thinking for a classless society that it is expected that teachers and educators ignore or neglect class markers and differences in their classrooms in order to achieve equity and equality.[4] This is not the route we believe needs to be taken. In fact, we believe the exact opposite effort will promote a more equitable educational system.

Since colonial times, social class distinctions have been reproduced the same way they were brought to America by the Europeans. Nationally celebrated and widely recognized

American historical landmarks like the American Revolution, the Declaration of Independence, and even the U.S. Constitution bluntly ignore the role of ethnic groups other than white Europeans. Moreover, there is no acknowledgment of slavery, poverty, or any other element that would even hint at a discriminatory or class-based society.

America, however, has not only reproduced class differences; it has also widened the gap between them in pure economic terms.[5] The concentration of wealth and the consequent difference between the haves and have-nots are two major factors that have contributed to the establishment and development of a class system in America (Kerbo, 2008). In addition, America is considered to have the widest class stratification in the "free world" (Cohen, 1998). A class system also implies that there are social and political benefits for those at the top and social and political consequences for those at the bottom. A society, particularly a capitalistic one, depends greatly on social stratification in order to function.

The myth that America is a classless society is accentuated by another myth, that of meritocracy. Americans like to believe that they are all equally capable of achieving financial success and that wealth is a reflection of a person's merit. The belief is that people who succeed due to their effort and hard work deserve corresponding financial and social benefits. In other words, the myth of meritocracy is closely related to that of the American dream: America is the land of opportunity and those who work hard will enjoy and profit from these opportunities.

This idea of a promised land of opportunities is what makes people believe that, even if one recognizes America as a stratified society with extremely marked social classes, there is always the possibility (and the opportunity) of social mobility. Upward mobility is seen as a result of economic prosperity, as more income is assumed to inevitably lead to a better position in society. Social and economic mobility are usually studied together as one is seen as closely related to or dependent on the other, and they are both closely related to income (Lipset & Bendix, 1959). In fact, mobility in the economic ladder has always been thought of as a promise that underscores the American dream (Leonhardt, 2005).

Considering that many still see opportunity as a key element in the analysis of social mobility and financial success, it should come as no surprise that education is usually mentioned in the same breath with opportunity. The idea is that the more educated one is, the better the opportunities that one has. Education is often considered to be at the heart of the social class equation because for a society that values and rewards knowledge and associates it with power, education takes a vital role: it is seen as a determinant factor of future social and economic success.

This is the understanding that permeates the notion of schooling in America. By offering and promoting universal education, schools are seen as the great equalizer. This belief was born out of the common schools movement and leads us to believe that we are working toward the societal goal of equality, equity, access, and opportunity. It is common knowledge that social and economic factors affect and even determine student outcomes and that there is indeed a great achievement gap in the U.S. educational system. In this scenario, it is expected that schools will serve the ultimate purpose of overcoming the social and economic causes of low achievement. People who expect schools to offer solutions and to be the place where economic differences will not matter, though, tend to neglect the fact that in order for learning to occur and for learners to achieve academically, minimum conditions must be present to promote learning. Schools cannot be made responsible for larger social issues that affect certain underprivileged communities. As Rothstein (2008) puts it,

> Closing or substantially narrowing achievement gaps requires combining school improvement with reforms that narrow the vast socioeconomic inequalities in the United States. Without such a combination, demands (like those of No Child Left Behind) that schools fully close achievement gaps not only will remain unfulfilled, but also will cause us to foolishly and unfairly condemn our schools and teachers. (p. 2)

Rothstein goes on to say that "our first obligation should be to analyze social problems accurately; only then can we design effective solutions" (p. 2). Part of the solution may be with the schools and they can definitely serve as a mediator in this dialogue between the larger society and the different communities that they serve. However, educators should not be the only ones to advocate for reform, and in any case, school reform could only occur if accompanied by socioeconomic reform.

In identifying two common myths of a classless society and meritocracy we have shown a way by which education and schooling influence the social class divisions that have prevailed in the United States. We now turn to a discussion of the relationship between social class and schools. In this discussion we show how social class is more than economic wealth, including elements such as the form and nature of educational experience, as well as other social and cultural factors.

Understanding Social Class and School

According to a study published in the *New York Times* in 2005, there are four traditional factors that contribute to determining a person's socioeconomic standing in society: occupation, education, income, and wealth.[6] It stands to reason why these four elements would be used to define or predict one's social class, but one needs to understand that they are intrinsically dependent on each other and should be analyzed together for a broader understanding of class. Moreover, these elements perhaps focus on measurable indicators that overshadow other subtle and important factors such as representations of certain knowledge and culture and the ways in which teachers value and embrace students' cultural resources in their teaching. It is not so easy to pinpoint all the elements that determine social class, though. A student from a middle class background might be working his or her way through college by working at a job in the fast food service industry. Does having this job make the person working class? Or does the person remain middle class because of the way they speak, or what they know, or how they spend their free time?

Looking at social class and using income as a way to understand social class location might be limiting on some levels. Might we also want to think about access to material and cultural resources as a way of thinking about social class location? Factors such as income or wealth, which can be statistically calculated, need to be considered along with other factors such as cultural and educational experience and the geographical area in which one resides. All of these elements contribute to the United States as a stratified society with class distinctions that are economically, culturally, and socially marked.

If we turn to the institution of school and view it as a social institution that is historically shaped by the desires and interests of particular social and cultural groups, we begin to see that there are great variations in how and what students experience at school. For instance, the ways in which we participate in school has an impact on educational achievement. Hence, even the kind of education that a student experiences is shaped by the policies and practices that favor certain ways of being and knowing while these same policies and practices, also in pedagogical terms, silence or marginalize other students. Hence how students, teachers and administrators participate in the school system and promote certain values, beliefs, and ideas over others becomes integral to the process of schooling. As teachers, we are often caught up in focusing on the individual needs of students, and developing curriculum and pedagogical experiences that enhance students' understanding of the world. Yet, how we teach, what we teach, and where we teach is not culturally neutral. How knowledge is structured, how students learn, and what students learn reflect a process that allows some groups to organize social life to their own advantage.[7]

Further adding to an understanding of these processes, the educational system is considered the central institution controlling the allocation of status and privilege in contemporary societies (Bourdieu, 1994; Bourdieu & Passeron, 1977; Bourdieu & Hacquant, 1992). Schools represent the primary institutional setting for the production, transmission, and accumulation of various forms of cultural capital that Bourdieu defined as "cultural goods," that is, schemas of appreciation and understanding internalized by individuals through socialization.[8] Bourdieu argues that education actually contributes to the maintenance of a nonegalitarian social system by allowing inherited cultural differences to shape academic achievement and occupational attainment. Historically in the United States, education has become the institution most responsible for the transmission of social inequality, cultural resources, and educational credentials. Furthermore, educational practices, the mechanisms for selection, admission, and cognitive or academic classifications, are controlled by individuals and groups who perpetuate their own positions of privilege and power. Therefore, we argue that constantly and consistently we as teachers have to ask what Freire (1970, 1998) suggested: In favor of whom were these practices fostered and who participates in decision making and who does not? (Grinberg et al., 1994).

While reports provided by the National Assessment of Educational Progress show how the analysis of some quantifiable variables such as students' gender, race/ethnicity, whether students had a disability, if students were English language learners, if there is a computer in the home, eligibility for free/reduced-price school lunch, participation in the Title I program, number of books in the home, and number of absences from school illuminate the significant differences of access and services, these data are not enough to help us understand why differences in achievement have been a constant for so many decades. Once again, Bourdieu and his colleagues provide us with a theoretical tool: such status quo benefits social class reproduction through schooling because it has been misrecognized as a result of ignoring economic and political interests that manifest through taken-for-granted practices such as classifying students by ability, type of need, and other ways by which schools construct students' categories. As Grinberg and Saavedra (2000) explain,

> Because educators believe these classifications to be academic, they use them as legitimate labels without full awareness of their social and ideological consequences. Through socialization, these labels and classifications have been incorporated as a practice of instruments that agents [educators] employ practically

without conscious reflection. However, these academic judgments are also social judgments that ratify and reproduce social class distinctions. (p. 430)

Some examples of these classifications were documented in the classic work done by Oakes (1985) on the practice of tracking students by academic levels for the purpose of tailoring content and instruction to more homogenous groups of students. Her studies describe the perpetuation of distinctive curricular and pedagogical differences in terms of access to knowledge and the opportunities to develop critical thinking and understanding of subject matter, including higher expectations for the groups of students classified as better or stronger. Coincidently, higher track classes often consisted of white affluent students while lower tracks mostly consisted of minority students from more underprivileged groups with all of the tracks within the same comprehensive high schools. The important points here are not only the inequality of experiences but also the use of academic classifications as neutral categories.

Another example of classification of students is that of the ethnography of a high school science class in a Midwest community with a significant number of Mexican American children of immigrants working in a neighboring meat-packing factory conducted by Richardson and Roberta Vann (2007). This study describes how a class of English language learners (a category) is instructed about how to dissect pigs because the expectation is that this would benefit their skills to secure jobs in the local factory. A further discussion of this study (Calabrese-Burton, Grinberg, & Richardson, 2007) determines that

> [B]eyond the clear difference in terms of social class, cultural capital, and classroom resources, the way in which teachers teach and the knowledge of the subject matter can make an extraordinary difference in how students build themselves as "young scientists," in an identity sense, as well as in consequence, how do they immerse in the disciplinary discourse which will enable them actually to engage at some point in a critique of whose science, for what purpose, under which conditions, and for the benefit of whom, as could have been the missed opportunity by Linda [teacher] when students inquired as from where are the pigs coming. (p. 62)

Thus, the curriculum and pedagogy sanctioned by academic distinctions one more time close opportunities to choice. The expectation of the common schools of the nineteenth century that education will serve to provide opportunity and equalize does not occur for the students in this science class. It begs the question, again, of the purpose of such curricula and pedagogies. Kincheloe (2008a) expands on these topics, "Poor people, individuals from Diasporas from the most economically depressed parts of the world, and residents of the 'developing countries' are positioned on these hierarchies as less intelligent, less civilized, and more barbaric than upper–middle class, white, Christian, and often male Westerners" (p. 3). Furthermore, while discussing the relationship of public schools with local communities, Grinberg et al. (2005) assert that

> Many schools in the USA are institutions that are geographically in the community, but culturally and socially removed from them. . . these schools are "divorced" from the local community; they are "foreign" institutions "planted" in a location,. . . schools deliver the same package of activities with no interest in knowing if this is relevant for the students. They operate with what Freire (1970) called the "banking model," since it imposes an interpretation of the world assuming a passive recipient role on the student, while it marginalizes further the local ways of knowing, the local meanings, and the local needs as defined by the locals.

Discussing these relationships vis-à-vis culture and school categories, Nieto (2000) provides examples of what she calls "cultural discontinuities" such as the difference in the concepts of being smart or intelligent. While in American culture intelligence is a birth quality, for Latinos intelligence is learned and needs networks of support as those provided by family, friends, and communities. Again, Grinberg et al. (2005 discuss this issue: "The school, often, represents a break with the values, behaviors, beliefs, and ways of knowing of Latina/o students, thus creating a cultural rupture between the dominant institution and the dominated, but not necessarily passive and domesticated clients" (p. 228).

These arguments then help us expand our understanding of social class and help us see the role of cultural resources as integral to our understanding of social class and social class in schools. Understanding patterns of hierarchy, domination, and oppression is integral to understanding social class. But social class categories of students are not fixed unitary categories. Within each category such as working class, middle class, or upper middle class, there is a range of experiences, and some of these experiences indeed overlap across groups. However, we use each of these categories essentially as a heuristic device to highlight a range of experiences.

Connell et al. (1982) argue that in order to understand social class, we also need to look at the ways in which people live their lives, the kinds of options they have and use, and the kinds of priorities they place for themselves. They argue that it is what people "*do* with their resources and their relationships that is central" (p. 33). Bearing these points in mind, we might want to think about social class categories through considering the *kind* of work a student and/or their parents do, how they spend their recreation time, the kinds of schools they go to, and their experiences across all aspects of schooling.

Integral to discussions about opportunity, power relations, and the role of the culture and structure of institutions such as school in the making of social class is an understanding of the various social class groups that exist in the United States. A debate about the formation of social class gained heightened significance in the 1980s with the provocative contribution of William Julius Wilson's *The Truly Disadvantaged* (1987). This work highlighted the significance of an "underclass" as a distinct, historically marginalized group. Wilson eloquently made a case for the existence of an "underclass" in the United States as a way of understanding contemporary U.S. poverty. He provided a structural explanation as the cause of concentrated poverty, increased joblessness, and social isolation in urban black communities. He argues that such a group includes "individuals who lack training and skills and either experience long-term employment or are not members of the labor force, who are engaged in street crime and other forms of aberrant behavior, and families that experience long-term spells of poverty and/or welfare dependency" (p. 41). While Wilson later recommends the abandonment of the term, his contributions provoked fierce debate. For example, Dill (1989) suggests that his proposal failed in a large measure to demonstrate that the ghetto communities are a logical outgrowth of the U.S. economic system. In the same vein, authors from Katz's (1993) volume *The "Underclass" Debate* object to the word *underclass* as inappropriate in capturing the historical conditions such as poverty or homelessness. Instead, they argue that the notion of underclass should rather be viewed as a metaphor of social transformation. Through the discussion, the authors from Katz's volume show the complicated shifting relations among historical issues such as family, ecology, institutions, culture, and policy and their interaction with race and gender. The contributing authors make the case against reifying concepts of poverty, underclass, race, culture, and family as fixed entities and rather present them as "history, which is to say as relational, shifting in meaning and content, to be interpreted in terms of time and place" (Katz, 1993, p. 23).

From these debates about underclass, and current contributions from social theorists about the relevance of social class, there is clearly an important lens through which to understand social circumstances. For example, Apple (1993) argues that

> Just because class is called now (through what I think is a misreading of history) a "grand narrative," one that takes a reductive form, this doesn't mean that class has gone away... Too often the idea that class analysis was "reductive" has meant that people feel free to ignore it. This is disastrous theoretically and politically. To purge class does a disservice to the women and men whose shoulders we all stand on, not just to their theory but even more importantly to their lived struggles. (p. 25)

Apple's point is significant in considering Price's (2000) study of six young African American men from different social class backgrounds. He shows how differing access to material and cultural resources significantly influenced how the young men saw the world and the opportunities and barriers they encountered as they went to school that cannot be explained solely through a single lens of gender or race.

In sum, the concept of social class must include a wide range of factors. As we examine the relationship between schools and social class in students' lives, we need to look beyond factors such as income, wealth, educational opportunity, or other structural factors; we also need to consider various cultural processes within school.

Explaining Social Class Inequalities

Determining how to address the reality that students from different social class backgrounds are afforded different opportunities has been a topic of discussion since the inception of the public school system. Imbued with the belief that the system is meritocratic and that we live in a classless society, educational success or failure is thereby viewed as the product of individual effort. But historians, educators, and policymakers alike are continually alarmed by the fact that the educational experiences of students tend to reflect their social class location, and that social location in a large measure tends to influence the kinds of educational experiences and opportunities afforded middle-class, working class, and economically poor students.

Hence, there have been numerous policies and practices developed to ensure the provision of educational opportunities and experiences that meet the needs and potentials of *all* Americans. In the midst of the Civil Rights Movement, an important debate emerged, spearheaded by the Coleman Report (Coleman et al., 1966). This report claimed that family background was a determinant of school failure and success more than any other factor. In other words, schools could not influence or change the scripts of social, political, and economic marginalization that large sections of the population experienced. Respected sociologists Karabel and Halsey (1977) challenge Coleman's findings and suggest that "schools at least reinforce the inferior position of disadvantaged children with respect to educational opportunity" (p. 21). And other scholars such as Jencks et al. (1972) suggest that schools are "marginal institutions" in their quest for a more egalitarian society and the economy, not schools or families, may be the most central sphere that needs consideration. These arguments continue to place blame on a particular aspect of society, be it school itself, the economy, the family, and even the individual.

Most studies, however, did not consider the dynamic institutional and cultural connections between schools, the economy, and families. In the late 1980s, scholars began to reexamine the multiple variations and historical situations of families through a frame of interlocking structures of race, class, and gender (see Collins, 1990; Stack & Burton, 1994). In other words, most studies did not explain how the institutions of school and family interacted and influenced each other, nor how the connections and contrasting experiences of the day-to-day experiences of economically marginal families interacted with schooling.

Connell et al. (1982) provide an important contribution toward our understanding of the relationship between school and family and how processes within school and the family interact with one another. In their study of the relationships between school, family, and social class in Australia, they provide insights about how social class and social division are "made." These authors challenge the functional explanations developed to explain the relationship of family background to school achievement. Through a lens of material and cultural experiences of teachers, students, and parents, they examine the relationship between school and the family and consider each of these groups' current and past relationships with schools. They argue that

> The family is what its members do, a constantly continuing and changing practice, and as children go to and through school, that practice is reorganized around schooling. For its part the organization of the school varies with the kind of families in its catchment and the nature of their collective practices. (p. 78)

Connell et al. went "beyond the assumption" that family and school are independent spheres that contain separate processes. They argue that schools and families interact in ways that influence how each comes into being and continues to emerge, and that the social class experiences of parents and teachers played a significant role in how they viewed each other. Connell et al.'s (1982) and Lareau's (1990) explorations of the dynamic connection between school and family seem important in attempting to understand the relationship among social class, school, and society. These writers move beyond debates that "blamed" one institution or the other and instead try to explain how the relationships between family and school come to exist. Connell et al. and Lareau suggest that school experiences are influenced and constructed through orientations toward school produced by family members of the school students.

Conclusion: Possibilities and Hope

In the prior sections we discuss the expectation that common schools will disable poverty, the definition of social class, and its relationships to education. We turn now to the half-full glass: what hopes and possibilities a teacher has if she or he is interested in changing complex patters of practice in schools. As Goldfarb (1998) argues, educational institutions are important places to start, sustain, and advance social justice practices. Goldfarb and Grinberg (2002) define social justice as "The exercise of altering these [unjust] arrangements by actively engaging in reclaiming, appropriating, sustaining and advancing inherent human rights of equity, equality, and fairness in social, economic, educational, and personal dimensions, among other forms of relationships" (p. 162).

In this view, families, caregivers, children, youth, and others in local communities where public schools operate, in solidarity and partnership with teachers, have to assert their own destinies, challenging dependency on institutions and agents that classify their children and youth and define needs for them under the guise of academic expertise but that perpetuate their social class status. Otherwise these inequities persist intergenerationally. This is possible because, as Ross (1991) argues, a cycle of social reproduction occurs, which she called the "Bourdieu effect." Based on the work of Ranciere (1991), she explains this effect in the following terms: "They are excluded because they don't know why they are excluded; and they don't know why they are excluded because they are excluded" (pp. xi–xii).

A teacher interested in social justice has to question existing practices and reform proposals not to be more efficient at doing more of the same but with the purpose of imagining and constructing new pedagogical and curricular possibilities, both formal and informal (Grinberg, 2000): "Everyday decisions about what to teach, how to teach, and to whom to teach what, are inherently political acts. These decisions can open or close opportunities, and cannot be made 'neutrally' since neutrality works in favor of the status quo" (p. 3). Therefore in order to start, a committed teacher could ask: Who are and what is the participation of children, care-givers, parents, teachers, and the community in the direction of schools, in their curriculum and practices? Who am I as a teacher and who do I serve by the pedagogies I foster? Furthermore,

> Since empowerment is not provided by the agency[9] of an institution, but by the social agency of the participants. . . the role of the teacher is, therefore, that of facilitating the opportunity for empowerment rather than "delivering" it, because such delivery will perpetuate dependency. This way, the institutional power is used to create mechanisms and spaces for democratic processes. (Goldfarb & Grinberg, 2002)

In order to enable and sustain teachers committed to social justice, educators have to engage in solidarity practices by forming partnerships among themselves and with the students and communities where their work is to be done in democratic and participatory ways.[10] Goldfarb and Grinberg (2002) argue that "This potential transformation of power arrangements creates spaces to practice social justice since it is generated through popular participation in a democratic process in order to serve the needs and expectations of the community as defined by its members. . . defining their interests and in deciding about the use of resources for meeting their own needs, in their own terms" (p. 161).

To conclude this chapter, we argue that a teacher committed to social justice must be a critical pedagogue, which Kincheloe (2008b) explains eloquently,

> [F]irst and foremost critical pedagogy is a way of living. . . . I would argue that learning to become a critical educator involves becoming someone who lives the transformative concepts associated with the tradition. In the immediacy of interpersonal relationships, classroom interactions with students, the ways we deal with those below us in status hierarchies, and the ways we act against oppression in the world, we live our critical pedagogy. (p. 2)

Notes

1. Jaime Grinberg, Ph.D., is professor of educational foundations and co-director of Jewish American studies. Jeremy Price, Ph.D., is professor and department chair of educational foundations. Fernando Naiditch, Ph.D., is an assistant professor of curriculum and teaching. All of them teach at Montclair State University.
2. We utilize U.S. and America to refer to the United States of America as a political modern nation state. We regret however that "America" is so engrained in common speech that it ignores the many other American nations and countries that are within and outside of the United States.

3. For example, the Argentine president Domingo Faustino Sarmiento, credited with the development of a public school system in Argentina, and very influential in the creation of normal schools in Chile and Argentina,
not only studied Mann's reports and visited U.S. schools in the mid-nineteenth century but recruited some U.S.
educators to assist with his plans.
4. Equity in education concerns itself with the individual as well as with the group and focuses on justice, while
equality focuses on standardization. Often equity has been explained as fair and impartial access to education
regardless of economic or social status. Therefore, it is not about having access to equal resources, but about
having access to needed resources in order to provide such justice.
5. For instance, in 1999 a *New York Times* article pointed out that in the United States there was a huge inequality in distribution of wealth: "The wealthiest 2.7 million have as much to spend as the poorest 100 million"
(see *New York Times*, September 5, 1999, p. 14, which used Congressional Budget Office data analyzed by the
Center on Budget and Policy Priorities). This tendency has been aggravated in the last decade.
6. Reference: Class Matters: A *New York Times* Special Report http://www.nytimes.com/pages/national/class/
index.html
7. For detailed discussions of this issue in pedagogical terms refer to the work in "critical pedagogy." See, for
instance, Freire, 1970, 1998; or Kincheloe, 2004.
8. *Cultural capital* refers to cultural "instruments for the appropriation of symbolic wealth socially designated as
worthy of being sought and possessed" (Bourdieu, 1977, p. 488).
9. *Agency* in social settings such as schools is defined as a "person's ability to shape and control their own lives,
freeing self from the oppression of power" (Kincheloe, 2004, p. 42).
10. We find useful Anderson's (1998) suggestion for understanding the discourse of "participation" by answering
the following questions "Who participates? Participation in which spheres? What conditions and processes
should be present locally?" (p. 587). The answers to these questions may illuminate how authentic this participation is in terms of the extent interested groups and individuals can have a say over decisions that have an
impact on their interests.

References

Anderson, G. (1998). Toward authentic participation: Deconstructing the discourses of participatory reforms in
education. *American Educational Research Journal, 35* (94), 535–570.
Apple, M. W. (1993). *Official Knowledge—Democratic education in a conservative age.* New York: Routledge.
Bourdieu, P. (1977). Cultural reproduction and social reproduction. In J. Karabel & A. Halsey (Eds.), *Power and ideol-
ogy in education* (pp. 487–511). New York: Oxford University Press.
Bourdieu, P. (1994). *The social structures of the economy.* Cambridge: Polity Press.
Bourdieu, P., & Hacquant, L. (1992). *An invitation to reflexive sociology.* Chicago: University of Chicago Press.
Bourdieu, P., & Passeron, J. C. (1977). *Reproduction in education, society and culture.* Beverly Hills, CA: Sage.
Calabrese-Burton, A., Grinberg, J., & Richardson, K. (2007). On pigs and packers. *Cultural Studies of Science Educa-
tion, 2* (1), 61–71.
Class Matters: A New York Times Special Report. (2005). Times Books. http://www.nytimes.com/pages/nation-
al/class/index.html Retrieved on May 15, 2008.
Cohen, M. N. (1998). *Culture of intolerance: Chauvinism, class, and racism in the United States.* New Haven: Yale University
Press.
Coleman, J. S. et al. (1966). *Equality of educational opportunity.* Washington, DC: U.S. Government Printing office.
Collins, P. H. (1990). *Black feminist thought—Knowledge, consciousness, and the politics of empowerment.* Boston: Unwin Hy-
man.
Collins, R. (1979). *The credential society.* New York: Academic Press.
Connell, R., Ashenden, D., Kessler, G. and Dowset, G. (1982). *Making the difference: Schools, Families, and Social Divi-
sions.* Sydney: Allen & Unwin.
Dill, B. T. (1989). Comments on William J. Wilson's *The Truly Disadvantaged*: A limited proposal for social reform.
Journal of Sociology and Social Welfare, 16 (4), 69–75.
Freire, P. (1970). *Pedagogy of the oppressed.* New York: Seabury Press.
Freire, P. (1998). *Pedagogy of freedom: Ethics, democracy, and civic courage.* Lanham, MD: Rowman & Littlefield.
Gilbert, D. (1998). *The American class structure in an age of growing inequality.* London: Pine Forge Press.
Goldfarb, K. (1998). Creating sanctuaries for Latino immigrant families: A case for the schools. *Journal for a Just and
Caring Education, 4* (4), 454–466.
Goldfarb, K., & Grinberg, J. (2002). Leadership for social justice: Authentic participation in the case of a commu-
nity center in Caracas, Venezuela. *Journal of School Leadership, 12* (March), 157–173.

Grinberg, J. (2000). Desafios y posibilidades para el futuro de la educacion: El papel del docente lider (Challenges and possibilities for the future of education: The role of the practitioner-leader). EDUFORUM, http://www.utdt.edu/eduforum/ensayo4.htm. (Web Publication).

Grinberg, J., Goldfarb, K., & Martusewicz, R. (1994). The legacy of Paulo Freire to democratic education. *Democracy and Education, 8* (4), 44–45.

Grinberg, J., Goldfarb, K., & Saavedra, E. (2005). Con coraje y con pasion: The schooling of Latinas/os and their teachers' education. In P. Pedraza & Rivera (Eds.), *Latino education: An agenda for community action research: A volume of the national Latino/a education research and policy projects* (pp. 227–254). Mahwah, NJ: Lawrence Erlbaum.

Grinberg, J. & Saavedra, E. (2000). The constitution of bilingual/ESL education as a disciplinary practice: Genealogical explorations. *Review of Educational Research, 70* (4), 419–441.

Jencks, C. et al. (1972). *Inequality*. New York: Harper and Row.

Karabel, J., & Halsey, A. H. (1977). Educational research: A review and interpretation. In J. Karabel & A. H. Halsey (Eds.), *Power and ideology in education* (pp. 1–85). New York: Oxford University Press.

Katz, M. B. (1993). (Ed). *The "underclass" debate*. Princeton: Princeton University Press.

Kerbo, H. R. (2008). *Social stratification and inequality* (7th edition). New York: McGraw-Hill.

Kincheloe, J. (2004). *Critical pedagogy*. New York: Peter Lang.

Kincheloe, J. (2008a). Critical pedagogy and the knowledge wars of the twenty-first century. *International Journal of Critical Pedagogy, 1* (1).

Kincheloe, J. (2008b). An introduction to IJCP. *International Journal of Critical Pedagogy, 1* (1-10).

Lareau, A. (1990). *Unequal childhoods: Class, race, and family life*. Berkeley, CA: University of California Press.

Leonhardt, D. (2005). *A closer look at income mobility. New York Times*. May 14, 2005.

Lipset, S. M., & Bendix, R. (1959). *Social mobility in industrial society*. Berkeley: University of California Press.

Mann, H. (1848/1891). Twelfth annual report. In *Annual reports of the secretary of the board of education of Massachusetts for the years 1845–1848*. Boston: Lee and Shepard.

Nieto, S. (2000). *Affirming diversity: The sociopolitical context of multicultural education*. New York: Teachers College Press.

Oakes, J. (1985). *Keeping track: How schools structure inequality*. New Haven, CT: Yale University Press.

Price, J. N. (2000). *Against the odds: The meaning of school and relationships in the lives of six young African-American men*. Stamford, CT: Ablex/Greenwood.

Ranciere, J. (1991). *The ignorant schoolmaster: Five lessons in intellectual emancipation*. Palo Alto, CA: Stanford University Press.

Richardson, Bruna K., & Roberta Vann, R. (2007). On pigs and packers: Radically contextualizing a practice of science with Mexican immigrant students. *Cultural Studies of Science Education, 2* (1), 19–59.

Ross, K. (1991). Translator's introduction. In J. Ranciere (1991). *The ignorant schoolmaster: Five lessons in intellectual emancipation* (pp. vi–xxxiii). Palo Alto, CA: Stanford University Press.

Rothstein, R. (2008). Whose problem is poverty? *Educational Leadership*, 65 (7), pp. 8–13.

Stack, C. B., & Burton, L. B. (1994). Kinscripts: Reflections on family, generation and culture. In E. N. Glenn, G. Chang, & L. R. Forcey (Eds.), *Mothering—Ideology, experience, and agency* (pp. 33–44). New York: Routledge.

Warner, W. L. (1993). *What social class is in America: The American dream and social class*. New York: Irvington.

Wilson, W. J. (1987). *The truly disadvantaged. The inner city, the underclass and public policy*. Chicago: University of Chicago Press.

Zinn, H. (2005). *People's history of the United States: 1492 to present*. New York: Harper Perennial Modern Classics.

Eighteen

An Introduction to Social Class and the Division of Labor

Curry Stephenson Malott

If it is our intent to properly introduce a study of social class, it would be wise to begin by asking a simple question: what *is* social class? At its most basic level, social class can be understood as a hierarchical grouping of people based on similar economic and occupational characteristics that gives way to the collective experience of social rank and caste, such as lower/working class and upper/ruling class, and the manifest relationships between and within such strata. Associated with the notion of class, and especially with caste, is the idea that they are determined by governments or a noble authority that loosely determine, by birthright, what occupations are available to what groups. As this chapter has been conscripted to focus on North America, the next question that begs asking is, does social class exist in this region?

Because occupation is not judicially determined by birthright in the United States, Mexico, or Canada, it is commonly argued that the differences in wealth and power that exist in those countries are not the result of social class but, rather, are indicative of the division of labor that roughly represents the natural distribution of intelligence and drive. *Socioeconomic difference* is therefore no more or less important to human diversity than is eye color or body type, that is, it is one of many *neutral* differences, which are entitled to universal respect and dignity. Class difference is therefore not something to be resisted but *tolerated*. Within this paradigm, the concept of social class, unsurprisingly, is rarely discussed.

There are others who argue that the unequal relationship between what we might call bosses and workers is not the natural outcome of genetically determined endowments and deficiencies but is the result of a long legacy of coercion, brutality, and manipulation that manifests itself in highly concentrated accumulations of wealth and power. These are as nearly deterministic as birthright in reproducing the class structure and social relations that more generally affirm the central role that class plays in a capitalist society. Within this paradigm, the concept of social class is most fundamentally represented in the relationship between the vast majority that is divested from the means of production and therefore possesses only their labor to sell as a commodity, and the few who hold in their hands the productive apparatus, land, resources, and the vast fortunes they have accumulated by purchasing the labor of the landless multitudes at a price far below its value. In short, this antagonistic relationship between social classes represents the heart of what capitalism *is*.

From this perspective, as long as social class exists, that is, as long as there are two antagonistically related groups—workers and bosses, rich and poor, or oppressed and oppressor—there will not be consensus on what explains the basic structures of society because what is good for one group tends not to be beneficial to the other. For example, the idea that social class does not explain the inequality rampant in capitalist societies but is the result of natural selection is good for the beneficiaries of market mechanisms. At the same time, the notion that the violent class relations are at the core of capitalist society has provided much fuel against capitalism. In short, the class struggle of capitalism is represented in the "fact" that higher wages are good for workers because they increase their standard of living but hurt the bosses by encroaching on margins/profits.

From here, a smart place of departure might be to observe a few pieces of evidence regarding the structure of the world today. A look at the data suggests that there exists a relatively small wealthy sector of the population; at the same time, there is a much larger group who are incredibly poor and impoverished and who, as a result, suffer great hardship and sorrow. The data also suggest that there is an in-between or middle-class group that has experienced a steady period of decline, thereby swelling the ranks of the poor and pissed off. Let's take a few examples from the global context, quoted from Malott (2008, p. 140).

- Every day, more than thirty thousand children throughout the world die of easily preventable starvation-related diseases because, in a capitalist market-driven system, food is a source of profit, not nutrition.
- The richest few hundred people have a combined net worth that exceeds that of nearly half of the world's population.
- Twenty percent of the people in the most developed countries consume eighty-six percent of the world's commodities and services.

How do we account for these differences and inequalities? The remainder of this chapter examines different approaches to these class-based issues.

***

It is worth restating, at the risk of unnecessary repetition, that social class and related concepts have, in Western political discourse, traditionally been articulated along an antagonistically related continuum. On one end, there is the idea that the existence of social class is evidence of a natural evolution of human society; it is increasingly necessary as civilization becomes more complex and advanced. On the other end of the spectrum, it tends to be argued that the existence of social class is the result of the appropriation of a naturally occurring division of labor and is therefore conceived of as an unequal relationship that has been continuously and rather violently forced upon humanity. These two positions do not merely represent *both sides*, as it were, each possessing equal weight and therefore existing independently, unaware of or unaffected by the other. In the material that follows I demonstrate the intimate relationship between these competing perspectives on social class, one hegemonic and therefore endowed with the power of the capitalist-state (that is, supporting the interests of the rich and powerful) and the other, counter-hegemonic and, as a result, historically marginalized by the dominant society (that is, representing the interests and concerns of the vast majority).

In the process of outlining this dialectical discourse, we have demonstrated the complex and contradictory nature of the concrete context, thereby underscoring both the conceptual limitations and benefits of the hegemonic/counter-hegemonic dichotomy just laid out. After these forays, I turn to a discussion of critical pedagogy, drawing on a number of epistemological and ontological perspectives, including an indigenous conception of human sociability that transcends hegemonic, and contributes to counter-hegemonic, Western ideas and understandings of social class. We begin the following discussion in Europe because it was the European model of class society that was reproduced around the world through the process of colonization; in most regions, such as North America, it continues to serve as the dominant paradigm.

Competing Conceptions of Social Class

Among the many scholars who have engaged in the in-depth study of the innermost workings of Europe's model of class society, that is, capitalism, Karl Marx has proven to be the most influential, resilient, relevant, and responded to (both positively and negatively). One of the most widely read documents of all time, the *Manifesto of the Communist Party* (1848/1978), by Karl Marx and Frederick Engels, has touched, in one way or another, every major revolution around the world, making its conceptualization of social class particularly important for the study at hand.

By the end of the manifesto's first sentence—a relatively short one—Marx and Engels have clearly broken with the idealistic romanticism of bourgeois scholarship by firmly situating their analysis of class within an historical dialectic of antagonistic, competing interests, noting that "the history of all hitherto existing society is the history of class struggles" (p. 473), which, taken to its logical conclusion, underscores the tenuousness of the present moment. The duo continue, linearly and temporally, from a European-centered perspective, naming what they understand to be stages of the conflicting interests that define human social development, beginning with ancient Rome, which transitioned into the Middle Ages, and finally giving way to the modern bourgeois era: "freeman and slave, patrician and plebeian, lord and serf, guild-master and journeyman, in a word, oppressor and oppressed, stood in constant opposition to one another, carried on an uninterrupted, now hidden, now open fight, a fight that each time ended, either in a revolutionary reconstitution of society at large, or in the common ruin of the contending classes" (Marx & Engels, 1848/1978, pp. 473–474). In short, Marx and Engels argue that human society tends not to stand still; it is always in a stage of development. In making their case that the relations of production under capitalism will eventually be torn asunder, Marx and Engels document the process by which Europe's (concentrating on France, England, and Germany) bourgeois capitalist class emerged "from the ruins of feudal society" (p. 474), playing "a most revolutionary part" (pp. 474–475) in that transformation.

The massive amounts of wealth extracted from the Americas by European powers led Marx and Engels to the conclusion that "the discovery of America," as they called it, was one of the primary driving forces behind "the increase in the means of exchange and in commodities generally" and therefore was the "revolutionary element in the tottering feudal society, a rapid development" (p. 474). The argument is that small-scale feudal arrangements were not equipped to organize the large armies of labor necessary for transforming the massive amounts of raw materials imported from the Americas that were needed to meet the exploding European demand for commodities, which was fueled by the influx of unprecedented resources. What is more, unlike Europe's nobility, whose power stemmed from their possession of land, the emerging bourgeoisie, without land, gained their advantage through the accumulation of capital stemming from the mercantile role they played in the extraction of American and African wealth. Summarizing the bourgeoisie's transformation from the oppressed to the oppressors, Marx and Engels unveil their most feared and celebrated prediction—that the bourgeoisie who are still in power, like all oppressors before them, too will fall.

> The bourgeoisie, wherever it has got the upper hand, has put an end to all feudal. . .relations. It has pitilessly torn asunder the motley feudal ties that bound man to his "natural superiors," and has left remaining no other nexus between man and man than naked self-interest, than callous "cash payment. . ." It has resolved personal worth into exchange value, and in place of the numberless indefeasible chartered freedoms, has set up that single, unconscionable freedom—Free Trade. . .The weapons with which the bourgeoisie felled feudalism to the ground are now turned against the bourgeoisie itself. . .The bourgeoisie forged the weapons that [will] bring death to itself; it has also called into existence the men who are to wield those weapons—the modern working class. . . (pp. 475–478)

While the broad strokes painted in the *Manifesto of the Communist Party* are useful for beginning to understand why Marx's dialectical materialism continues to be both feared and exalted, we must turn to his more elaborated work on the division of labor to transition into the perspectives of his critics, which continue to hold political sway in the contemporary context of global capitalism. In one of his major classic works, *Capital: Volume 1*, Marx's (1867/1967) discussion of primitive accumulation as part of the historical development of the capitalization of humanity, which began in England roughly a decade before Columbus set foot in present-day Haiti, is useful here in understanding Europe's engagement in the Americas, in particular, and global affairs in general. Because of the light it sheds on the discussion that follows, a sizable excerpt taken from *Capital: Volume 1* is presented here:

> The so-called primitive accumulation. . .is nothing else than the historical process of divorcing the producer from the means of production. It appears as primitive, because it forms the pre-historic stage of capital and of the mode of production corresponding with it.
>
> The economic structure of capitalistic society has grown out of the economic structure of feudal society. The dissolution of the latter set free the elements of the former.
>
> The immediate producer, the labourer, could only dispose of his own person after he had ceased to be attached to the soil and ceased to be the slave, serf, or bondman of another. To become a free seller of labour-power, who carries his commodity wherever he finds a market, he must further have escaped from the regime of the guilds, their rules for apprentices and journeymen, and the impediments of their labour regulations. Hence, the historical movement which changes the producers into wage-workers, appears, on the one hand, as their emancipation from serfdom and from the fetters of the guilds, and this side alone exists for the bourgeois historians. But, on the other hand, these new freedmen became sellers of themselves only after they had been robbed of all their own means of production, and of all the guarantees of existence afforded by the old feudal arrangements. And the history of this, their expropriation, is written in the annals of mankind in letters of blood and fire. . ..

> The starting point of the development that gave rise to the wage labourer as well as to the capitalist was the servitude of the labourer. The advance consisted in a change of form of this servitude, in the transformation of feudal exploitation into capitalist exploitation. . ..
>
> The expropriation of the agricultural producer, of the peasant, from the soil, is the basis of the whole process. The history of this expropriation, in different countries, assumes different aspects, and runs through its various phases in different orders of succession, and at different periods. (pp. 714–716)

From Marx's work we can begin to gain an understanding of how the entire process of value production through the capital-labor class relation, from primitive accumulation to petrol-chemical industrialism, is a form of class struggle initiated by the bourgeoisie against the feudal lords, some of the last remnants of Europe's Dark Ages. Ultimately, it has been the vast majority of humanity, disconnected from the soil and therefore from their indigenous culture, who have suffered from centuries of bourgeoisie pathology. In his examination of the historical development of class relations, Marx points to the division of labor as offering a place of origin.

That is, Marx argues that during the early stages of human development, the division of labor was a naturally occurring by-product of age- and sex-based physical differences. We would add that it is also the result of the non-hierarchical creative diversity/multiple intelligences unique to human consciousness as well as to the unpredictable nature of complex events, such as the establishment of purposeful economic systems. Within the division of labor, according to this perspective, reside the most basic structural roots of organized society. Commenting on the division of labor Marx (1867/1987) notes,

> Within a family, and after further development within a tribe, there springs up naturally a division of labor, caused by differences of sex and age, a division that is consequently based on a purely physiological foundation, which division enlarges its materials by the expansion of the community, by the increase of population, and more especially, by the conflicts of different tribes, and the subjugation of one tribe by another. (p. 351)

The issue of one tribe subjugating another will be taken up later. For now, I would like to focus on the context in which Marx situates this naturally occurring division of labor. Marx (1867/1967) hones in on the place-specific nature of tribal communities, commenting that "different communities find different means of production and different means of subsistence in their natural environment" (p. 351). In other words, the development of technology is informed by the specific characteristics of physical place or geography, such as climate, terrain, availability of arable land, game, waterways, and distance and accessibility to other human communities, and so on. As a result, human societies have developed vastly different technologies based on geography, which constitutes the original source of commodities, that is, products produced in one context and consumed in another. For example, civilizations that emerged close to large bodies of water have tended to create ship-building technology, whereas communities whose traditional lands are covered with ice, such as in the Arctic, have developed technologies more conducive to efficiently navigating the snow, such as sleds and snow shoes.

In the following analysis, Marx begins to break, however slightly, from his Eurocentric, linear analysis, acknowledging the persistence of ancient communities in the "modern" era. As an example, Marx points out that "those small and extremely ancient Indian communities, some of which have continued down to this day, are based on possession in common of the land. . .and on an unalterable division of labor" (p. 357). However, "each individual artificer" operates independently, "without recognizing any authority over him" (p. 358). Marx attributes this independence, in part, to the fact that within these arrangements products are produced for direct use by the community and therefore do not take the form of commodities and therefore avoid the associated value-generating process. As a result, the alienating division of labor engendered by the exchange of commodities is also avoided. Marx defines commodities as products consumed by others rather than by the people who produced them, and those who produce under capitalism are not independent craftsmen but are externally commanded.

Marx (1867/1967) quickly returns to Europe and goes on to argue that the guilds, which more or less labored independently, resisted the bourgeoisie's commodification of production and therefore ". . .repelled every encroachment by the capital of merchants, the only form of free capital with which they came into contact" (p. 358). Marx notes that the guild organization, by institutionalizing stages of production as specialized trades separate from one another, such as the cattle-breeder, the tanner, and the shoemaker, for example, created the material conditions for manufacture but "excluded division of labor in the workshop," and, as a result, "there was wanting the principal basis of manufacture, the separation of the labourer from his means of production, and the conversion of these means into capital" (p. 359). Marx stresses that the process of value production is unique to capitalism and is therefore a "special creation of the capitalist mode of production alone" (p. 359), and therefore not an original or natural aspect of the division of labor. Driving this point home, Marx critiques the "peculiar division" of manufacture, which "attacks the individual at the very roots of his life" giving way to "industrial pathology" (p. 363). Because of the forcefulness and accuracy of much of Marx's work, many proponents of capitalism have been forced to attempt to refute the idea that capitalism is a form of pathology and that the capitalist relations of production, between what we might crudely call bosses and workers, is negative or harmful for those who rely on a wage to survive, that is, to the vast majority of humanity. What follows is a brief summary of some of Emile Durkheim's pro-capitalist arguments.

***

The widely influential French sociologist Emile Durkheim is considered to be one of the fathers of sociology and anthropology. Throughout the late 1800s, Durkheim challenged much of Marx's analysis, setting out to demonstrate that the deep inequality between social classes that drew much attention from critics like Marx—a central aspect of the Industrial Revolution that began in England—was a natural product of the development of human societies; it should therefore not be resisted but encouraged by means of such sorting mechanisms as schools. Essentially, Durkheim (1893/2000) argues that humanity (those relegated to the status of worker) would be wise to divest itself of any illusions of maintaining an independent existence. Instead, "equip yourself to fulfill usefully a specific function" (p. 39) because society requires it; that is, we need to bend ourselves to fit within the system that exists, to submit ourselves to the labor it requires. What Durkheim suggests is that the bourgeoisie, rather than a ruling class that embodies its own negation, represents the end of history and therefore the manifestation of the final and most advanced stage of human social evolution.

However, Durkheim could not ignore the class antagonism highlighted by Marx, which was due, in part, to the intensity of the class struggle of his time and the recent memory of the workers' Paris Commune of 1871. Acknowledging the human need not to be made a slave or to be externally controlled, while maintaining his belief that inequality serves a necessary function in advanced societies, Durkheim notes that "moral life, like that of body and mind, responds to different needs which may even be contradictory. Thus it is natural for it to be made up in part of opposing elements" (p. 39). In effect, Durkheim tells us that progress has a price—a price that tends to cause distress within the individual—but that is the nature of the universe, and it is not wise to challenge laws of nature. Building the foundation for this "functionalist" approach to sociology, Durkheim (1893/2000) in his dissertation theorizes:

> We can no longer be under any illusion about the trends in modern industry. It involves increasingly powerful mechanisms, large-scale groupings of power and capital, and consequently an extreme division of labor...This evolution occurs spontaneously and unthinkingly. Those economists who study its causes and evaluate its results, far from condemning such diversification or attacking it, proclaim its necessity. They perceive in it the higher law of human societies and the condition for progress. (pp. 37–38)

Again, Durkheim does not stop here; he reaches ever deeper into the grandiose, going on to argue that the division of labor does not just occur within the realm of economics but can be identified in every aspect of life, and in all forms of life, which renders it a "biological phenomenon" and, therefore, a law of nature. By claiming that capitalism happened "spontaneously" and "unthinkingly," Durkheim effectively rewrites history, erasing the long struggle against a commodification of humanity that was anything but spontaneous or without thought. Essentially, Durkheim takes Marx's idea of the naturalness of the division of labor, divests it of its independent and communal nature, and replaces it with the notion that inequality and subservience to power are necessary manifestations of the advanced development of the division of labor. This basic formula has roots in Platonic epistemology, where intelligence is viewed as naturally and unevenly distributed, and continues to exist in the contemporary hegemonic discourses of the ruling elite. Not only does Durkheim support the idea of a naturally occurring hierarchical conception of class within societies, but he ranks civilizations/nations on a similar scale. Essentially, Durkheim argues that there is a tendency among societies that demonstrates that as they grow larger, the division of labor grows more specialized and entrenched, and, as a result, they become more advanced. However, confronted with the existence of larger non-white nations, Durkheim argues that there are exceptions to this rule, which seems to stem from his belief in racial hierarchy. Consider that

> the Jewish nation, before the conquest, was probably more voluminous than the Roman city of the fourth century; yet it was of a lower species. China and Russia are much more populous than the most civilized nations of Europe. Consequently, among these same peoples the division of labor did not develop in proportion to the social volume. This is because the growth in volume is not necessarily a mark of superiority if the density does not grow at the same time and in the same proportion... If therefore the largest of them only reproduces societies of a very inferior type, the segmentary structure will remain very pronounced, and in consequence the social organization will be little advanced. An aggregate of clans, even if immense, ranks below the smallest society that is organized, since the latter has already gone through those stages of evolution below which the aggregate has remained. (p. 49)

Durkheim's implied white supremacy was not his own invention nor was the idea that there was a natural hierarchy among the Europeans represented within the division of labor new to him. However, it is beyond the scope of this chapter to trace the origins of those ideas. What follows, rather, is an analysis of how hegemonic conceptions of the division of labor have influenced a policy in the United States that is situated in a more contemporary context, from Lippmann to Friedman. Beginning with Lippmann, we investigate how the idea of a natural hierarchy represented in the existence of rankable social classes informed his ideas and practice concerning both domestic and foreign affairs.

Propaganda and Capitalism in the United States

Walter Lippmann was a highly influential architect of this discursive model and contributed significantly to its implementation, a point to which the world-renowned scholar/activist Noam Chomsky (1999) has consistently given much attention. For more than fifty years, Lippmann was perhaps the most respected political journalist in the United States, "winning the attention of national political leaders from the era of Woodrow Wilson through that of Lyndon B. Johnson" (Wilentz, 2008, p. vii). However, within the Western tradition of hegemonic philosophy and practice, Lippmann's ideas tended to fall on the liberal end of a distorted continuum. That is, while he believed that it was the paternalistic responsibility of a democratic government made up of those endowed with a naturally superior intelligence to mold "the will of the people," this must be carried out without the conscious manipulation of propaganda. Opposed to what he believed to be the crude tactics of McCarthyism and the Red Scare, Lippmann was concerned with purifying "the rivers of opinion that fed public opinion" (Steel, 2008, p. xv).

Like Durkheim before him, Lippmann discounted the ideals of democracy (such as the notion that the will of the people does not need to be externally commanded) as "illusion," referring to them in *Public Opinion* (1922) as "the original dogma of democracy." Lippmann biographer Ronald Steel (2008), in his foreword to the recently re-issued *Liberty and the News* (1920/2008), reasons that

> the horrors of World War I had shattered his optimism about human nature. His propaganda work, reinforced by the repressive activities of the government's propaganda bureau, the Committee on Public Information, had made him realize how easily public opinion could be molded. He had always believed that a free press was the cornerstone of democracy. He still believed that, but with a new qualification. (pp. xii–xiii)

That qualification was his assertion that democracy itself is an unachievable ideal. Contributing to his belief in the inferior intelligence of the general public was his engagement with the emerging field of psychology, which reinforced his beliefs about the nature of human perception that rendered most people unfit to participate in the democratic process. For example, in *The Phantom Public* (1927) Lippmann argues that, "man's reflexes are, as the psychologists say, conditioned. And, therefore, he responds quite readily to a glass egg, a decoy duck, a stuffed shirt, or a political platform" (p. 30). Lippmann was clearly informed by the idea that the public is limited; it perceives the world only as it has been trained to. As a result, there tends to be a great gap between what the public believes about the world and the actual world. According to Lippmann (1927), not only is the public inherently limited in its sense of perception, but in its desire to know: "the citizen gives but a little of his time to public affairs, has but a casual interest in facts and but a poor appetite for theory" (pp. 24–25).

Summarizing his position, Lippmann (1927) concludes that it is false to ". . .assume that either the voters are inherently competent to direct the course of affairs or that they are making progress toward such an ideal. I think it is a false ideal. I do not mean an undesirable ideal. I mean an unattainable ideal. . ." (pp. 38–39). Lippmann therefore viewed education no more suitable to the achievement of democratic ideals than any other false sense of hope. As it turns out then, the United States, which has long presented itself as *the* world's leading proponent of democracy, has a history of being influenced by thinkers who believe in hierarchy and supremacy and who therefore view the theoretical context of democracy as not representative of the concrete context of human nature and thus an unwise goal to pursue.

Of course, men like Lippmann, armed with superior capabilities, do not suffer from the afflictions of inadequacy. From this perspective, the division of labor is largely based on naturally occurring, unequal capabilities of men that render some more fit than others to lead and design the social structure, while the most useful function for the vast majority resides in their physical ability to follow direction and to labor—as passive spectators rather than active participants. The responsibility of those most fit to lead, the responsible or capable men, is therefore to regiment the public mind as an army regiments its troops. This is the boss's moral and paternalistic "commitment," as Lippmann (1943) referred to it. Not only was Lippmann's conception of class based on the assumption of a natural hierarchy, but, paradoxically, on a moral relativism as well. This stands in stark contrast to Marx's privileging of democratic relations over the unjust relationship between labor and capital, that is, between the oppressed and their oppressors. In making this case—a case that is ultimately against democracy—Lippmann (1927) proclaims, "it requires intense partisanship and much self-deception to argue that some sort of peculiar righteousness adheres to. . .the employers' against the wage-earners,' the creditors' against the debtors,' or the other way around" (p. 34).

The peculiar nature of Lippmann's political relativism is further brought to the fore in his discourse on U.S. foreign policy where he draws on the notion of "justice" as it pertains to the use of force. Lippmann's analysis in *U.S. Foreign Policy* (1943), seems, in many ways, to be a direct response to the arguments presented in the highly publicized *War Is a Racket* (1935/2003) by anti-war activist and World War I veteran, Brigadier General Smedley D. Butler. Summarizing his position on war, Butler (1935/2003) comments:

> War is a racket. It always has been. It is possibly the oldest, easily the most profitable, surely the most vicious. It is the only one international in scope. It is the only one in which the profits are reckoned in dollars and the losses in lives. (p. 23)

Reflecting on the United States' involvement in the First World War, Butler (1935/2003) notes that, "we forgot, or shunted aside, the advice of the Father of our country. We forgot Washington's warning about 'entangling alliances'" (p. 26). In *U.S. Foreign Policy: Shield of the Republic*, published eight years after *War Is a Racket*, Lippmann (1943) invests a significant amount of time making an argument against the pacifism alluded to in *War Is a Racket*, without, however, referring directly to Butler or his work. Like Butler, Lippmann too draws on the legacy of General George Washington but draws almost opposite conclusions. Consistent with his usual style, Lippmann (1943) paints a picture of the benevolent leader whose responsibility it is to protect the national interest—the interests of the rich—which *he* must have the military capacity to do. Otherwise, through his vulnerability, he is inviting his enemy's provocation and therefore irresponsibly putting those who rely on his paternalistic protection at unnecessary risk.

> Washington did not say that the nation should or could renounce war, and seek only peace. . . For he knew that the national "interest, guided by justice" might bring the Republic into conflict with other nations. Since he knew that the conflict might be irreconcilable by negotiation and compromise, his primary concern was to make sure that the national interest was wisely and adequately supported with armaments, suitable frontiers, and the appropriate alliances. (Lippmann, 1943, p. 51)

Lippmann's reasoning here is simple enough: an empire, such as the United States, will not survive without room to grow and the muscle needed to protect its "interests," that is, the interests of the rich or responsible men, which include the subjugation of the local population and the extraction and concentration of wealth. The essence of his argumentation lies in the same age-old paternalistic guardianship and moral relativism that allows questions of justice to be freed from issues of domination and subjugation. In making his argument Lippmann cites the Monroe Doctrine of 1823 as evidence of the United States' "commitment" to extend its "protection. . .to the whole of the Western hemisphere" and that "at the risk of war, the United States would thereafter resist the creation of new European empires in this hemisphere" (p. 16). Monroe's doctrine has come to be interpreted as "professing a unilateral US 'right' to circumscribe the sovereignty of all other nations in the hemisphere" (Churchill, 2002, p. 335) influencing its aggressive dealings with indigenous sovereigns within its boundaries and those within its hemisphere such as Cuba and Jamaica and all other Latin American and Caribbean nations (Malott, 2008; Cole-Malott & Malott, 2008).

The context in which Lippmann situates U.S. foreign policy provides a useful lens for understanding the nation's current policies, such as those concerning, not only Cuba, but global issues. After all, it is the responsibility of the more capable men to make decisions for less capable men, and any illusions concerning democratic principles only restricts the natural development of the division of labor worldwide. As we will see below, Milton Friedman (1962/2002) picks up on this line of reasoning, arguing that restrictions on the extraction and accumulation of wealth and the further entrenchment of class antagonisms only threatens the freedom of "progress," that is, capitalism, and of the men and women pursuing it.

***

Milton Friedman, pro-capital economist extraordinaire, received worldwide recognition in 1976 when he won the Nobel Memorial Prize in Economic Sciences, and he has been touted as the world's most influential economist of the twentieth century. Friedman has drawn the attention of internationally renowned political analyst and activist Noam Chomsky (1999), who referred to him as a "neoliberal guru" while vociferously critiquing his *Capitalism and Freedom* (1962/2002) for hegemonically equating "profit-making" with "the essence of democracy" and saying that "any government that pursues anti-market policies is being anti-democratic, no matter how much informed popular support they might enjoy" (p. 9). Informed by this logic, the primary responsibility of government is therefore to protect private property (Chomsky, 1999). Chomsky (1999) connects Friedman's philosophy to practice.

> Equipped with this perverse understanding of democracy, neoliberals like Friedman had no qualms over the military overthrow of Chile's democratically elected Allende government in 1973, because Allende was interfering with business control of Chilean society. (p. 9)

Friedman leaves little room for misinterpretation regarding his conceptualization of democracy and social class. In many ways it is, as we will see, almost the exact opposite of Marxism, which underscores, in a sense, Marx's continued relevance, the way his work directly and indirectly informs popular democratic movements that challenge basic structures of power and demand a response by the architects of contemporary U.S. public hegemonic discourse and policy. Within his paradigm, Friedman (1962/2002) situates capitalism (defined here as a system of free enterprise) as the central driving force behind human evolution and therefore responsible for the "great advances of civilization," such as Columbus' "seeking a new route to China" (p. 3), a venture that led to the emergence of vast fortunes generated by Europe's colonialist empire building—slavery, genocide/depopulation and repopulation—on a scale so massive, so horrendous and so utterly barbaric as to render comprehending its manifestation as a criminal act carried out by real living, breathing, feeling people almost unimaginable. Friedman, therefore, does not seem too different from his predecessors. That is, describing Columbus' coming to the Americas as one of the great advances in civilization can only be understood as callous and thoroughly Eurocentric, a viewpoint that is always frigidly cold and uncaring.

But, again, Friedman draws on the example of Columbus for the "advances" that have resulted from the "freedom" to pursue private "economic interests" and therefore as evidence to support capitalism. Friedman (1962/2002) goes so far as to argue that free-market "capitalism is a necessary condition for political freedom" (p. 10). Friedman's thesis can be understood as a direct response to the popular support for nationalized economies designed to promote an equal distribution of the wealth generated by the productive apparatus arguing that "collectivist economic planning has. . .interfered with individual freedom" (p. 11). Individual freedom, for Friedman, stems from unregulated market mechanisms that are "stabilized" by a limited government whose function is to "protect our freedom both from the enemies outside our gates and from our fellow citizens: to preserve law and order, to enforce private contracts, and to foster competitive markets" (p. 2). Friedman points to the Soviet Union as an example of what he argues is the coercive tendency of government intervention in economic affairs. It is not surprising that Friedman does not mention the infinitely more democratic and egalitarian nature of Cuba's centrally planned economy compared to the U.S.-supported free-market systems in the Caribbean and Latin America (Malott, 2007).

The "law and order" referred to by Friedman can best be understood as the way in which "the descendents of European colonizers shaped. . .rules to seize title to indigenous lands" (Robertson, 2005, p. ix) and to "enforce" these "private contracts." Similarly, the Monroe Doctrine, touted by Lippmann (1927) as bounded by "law" and "custom," can be understood as extending the United States' "sphere of influence" to the entire western hemisphere. That is, to ensure that the resources and productive capacities of not only this region, but much of the world, would be controlled by U.S. interests. These self-endorsed "commitments" of the United States have been upheld with deadly force, which helps to explain the United States' simultaneously open and hidden war against the Cuban Revolution and Castro's trouble-making in the hemisphere (Chomsky, 1999; Malott, 2007). While the hegemony of U.S. power has seemed all but total, it has not been without critique and resistance from, not only Cuba and Latin America, but also within the United States. At the heart of this counter-hegemony has been the on-going development of critical pedagogies, one of the primary philosophical influences of which can be traced to both Southern and Northern Native America.

Critical Pedagogy and Indigeneity: Democratic Praxis against Social Class

Although he is certainly not the first critical pedagogue, the late Brazilian radical educator Paulo Freire is the practitioner credited with the founding of what we have come to know in North America as *critical pedagogy*. His first book, *Pedagogy of the Oppressed,* published in Brazil in 1967 and in the United States in 1970, is arguably the seed from which North American critical pedagogy in education has sprouted. Freire and other critical theory–trained Latin American critical pedagogues were highly influenced by liberation theologists such as Leonardo Boff (1971/1978) and Leonardo Boff and Clodovis Boff (1987) of Brazil; Peruvian Gustavo Gutiérrez (1973/1988); and world-renowned Archbishop Oscar Romero (1988/2005) of El Salvador, who was assassinated in 1987 after becoming "known across the world as a fearless defender of the poor and suffering," which earned him "the hatred and calumny of powerful persons in his own country" (Brockman, 1988/2005, p. xv). What is common among these leaders is that they all practiced (practice) and developed their theologies with the poorest and most oppressed sectors of their societies, which, wherever indigenous peoples are found, tend to be indigenous peoples. Within these theologies of liberation, we can therefore find the democratic impulse that can be treated, risking romanticization, as a common characteristic among a diverse range of traditional indigenous communities.

Critical pedagogy has always been concerned with challenging the discourse of hierarchy that legitimizes oppression and human suffering as indicative of the natural order of the universe. Rather than viewing intelligence as unequally distributed and the practice of democracy therefore extremely limited, critical pedagogy is based on an armed love and radical faith in people's ability to tend to their own economic and political interests in the spirit of peace and mutuality. In a recent series of interviews with David Barsamian, international activist, Noam Chomsky (2007), describes the characteristics of what he understands to be the praxis of democracy, that is, widespread political participation.

> There can't be widespread structural change unless a very substantial part of the population is deeply committed to it. . . If you are a serious revolutionary, you don't want a coup. You want changes to come from below, from the organized population. (p. 121)

This unyielding democratic impulse of Western-trained, North American critical pedagogy can be largely attributed to the generous philosophical gifts of not only native South Americans, but Native North Americans such as the Haudenosaunee. According to Donald A. Grinde (1992) in "Iroquois Political Theory and the Roots of American Democracy," many of the "founding fathers" of the United States, Benjamin Franklin most notably, rejected the anti-democratic European model, drawing instead on the brilliance of the Iroquois system of shared governance that was designed to ensure democracy and peace by putting power and decision making in the intelligent hands of the people, who were united in a confederation of nations, and not in divine right or the assumed superiority of a ruler. Grinde and others in *Exiled in the Land of the Free* (Lyons & Mohawk, 1992) document, in great detail, the generosity of the Iroquois leaders in assisting Euro-Americans before, during, and after the American Revolution in creating, as the foundation for long-term peace, freedom, liberty and democracy in North America, a unified nation composed of the original thirteen colonies. Putting the American Revolutionary war in a context foreign to traditional social studies instruction,

Grinde (1992) notes that "the first democratic revolution sprang from American unrest because the colonists had partially assimilated the concepts of unity, federalism, and natural rights that existed in American Indian governments" (p. 231). It is abundantly clear that the gift of democracy received by the United States government from the Haudenosaunee has all been but subverted. For examples of the democratic tradition in contemporary times, outside of the Native communities themselves, we have to turn our attention to the highly marginalized critical tradition.

However, we might say that this democratic tradition, which is commonly associated with European critical theory (i.e., Marxism), is an appropriation because the Native American source of these generous gifts tends not to be cited in the contemporary context. For those already engaged in the life-long pursuit of knowledge, this is an easily amendable flaw—requiring of such Western-trained critical theorists/educators an active epistemological and material engagement with Native Studies and indigenous communities the world over (Ewen, 1994; Kincheloe, 2007). We might say that the critical theoretical tradition, rooted in indigenous conceptions of freedom and liberty, represents a rich history of opposition to anti-democratic, authoritarian forms of institutionalized power—private (corporate), federal (state), and religious (clergy/church)—for it is this unjust power that poses the greatest barrier to peace. The example of the Haudenosaunee is indicative of this tradition, which stands in stark contrast to the anti-democratic model perpetuated by Durkheim, Lippmann, Friedman, and the like. What follows is therefore a summary of the origins and fundamentals of Haudenosaunee political thought.

***

According to "Haudenosaunee oral history," millennia before the arrival of Europeans, "Native peoples of the northeast woodlands [including present-day western New York] had reached a crisis" because of the existence of rampant violence and "blood feuds" between "clans and villages" (Sotsisowah, 1978/2005, p. 31). From this atmosphere of terror there emerged a young man with a vision of peace. Because his name is only used during ceremonies, he is commonly referred to as the Peacemaker. This Peacemaker has been credited with being "one of the great political philosophers and organizers in human history" (p. 31). His story begins in the now predominantly Canadian-controlled regions north of Haudenosaunee territory. After failing to persuade his own countrymen, the Huron, to adopt his message of peace, he traveled to the land of "the people of the flint," the Kanien'kehá:ka, or Mohawk, where he sought out the most feared "destroyers of human beings" and "brought to each one his message" (p. 31). The warriors took his message and became his disciples, assisting in its dissemination and perpetuation.

Eventually, these efforts resulted in the peaceful union of five of the Nations in the region, the Oneida, the Onondaga, the Mohawk, the Seneca, and the Cayuga, which stands as one of the first, and therefore one of the oldest, democratic confederacies in human history. Eons later, after the arrival of Europeans, it became Six Nations; this history, however, is beyond the scope of this essay. While these histories are very interesting themselves, what is of particular importance here are the fundamental principles of the Peacemaker's Great Law of Peace.

The "first principle" that the Peacemaker presented was that the world in which we live was created by the "Giver of Life," who did not intend for humans to "abuse one another," as had been the case amongst the Native Americans of the northeast (p. 32). Essentially, the Peacemaker reasoned that "human beings whose minds are healthy always desire peace, and humans have minds that enable them to achieve peaceful resolutions" (p. 32). Towards these ends, "government would be established for purpose of abolishing war and robbery among brothers and to establish peace and quietness. . .by cultivating a spiritually healthy society" (pp. 32–33). Particularly significant was the Peacemaker's conception of peace because it went further than advocating for the absence of war, calling instead for "universal justice." The idea of peace therefore emerged from societies that had established power, reason, and righteousness. Haudenosaunee leader, Sotsisowah, defines these *dispositions*, which, because of the value of "hearing" his voice and considering his perspective, are quoted at length:

> "Righteousness" refers to something akin to the shared ideology of the people using their purest and most unselfish minds. It occurs when the people put their minds and emotions in harmony with the flow of the universe and the intentions of the "Good Mind" or the Great Creator. The principles of righteousness demand that all thoughts of prejudice, privilege, or superiority be swept away, and that recognition be given to the reality that the creation is intended for the benefit of all equally—even the birds, animals, trees, and insects, as well as the humans. The world does not belong to humans. . . Nothing belongs to human beings, not even their labor or their skills, for ambition and ability are also gifts of the creator. (p. 33)

> "Reason" is perceived to be the power of the human mind to make righteous decisions about complicated issues. The Peacemaker began his teachings based on the principle that human beings were given the gift of the power of reason in order that they may settle their differences without the use of force. . .and that force should be resorted to only as defense against the certain use of force. . .and there is an ability within all human beings. . .to grasp and hold strongly to the principles of righteousness. (p. 33)

> The "power" that the Peacemaker spoke of was intended to enable the followers of the law to call upon warring or quarreling parties to lay down their arms and to begin a peaceful settlement of their disputes. . . It was power in all the sense of the word—the power of persuasion and reason, the power of the inherent goodwill of humans, the power of a dedicated and united people, and, when all else failed, the power of force. (p. 34)

Sotsisowah (1978/2005) continues, explaining that the Peacemaker's law, in a sense, "anticipated" the emergence of social classes, and was therefore designed to "eliminate" any arrangements that might resemble the competing interests of class society, especially in the area of property. As a result, it banned the existence of separate territories that had previously caused much jealousy and conflict. Toward these classless ends and therefore through the establishment of a highly complex system of *direct* democracy, the leaders were positioned to be *direct* conduits through which flowed the power and authority of a society held in the hands of the people.

Even though the content that has just been presented is a somewhat incomplete description of Sotsisowah's (1978/2005) summary of the Peacemaker's law, it fulfills the task of highlighting the rich democratic tradition within the Iroquois confederacy. Again, while this framework was conceived by the Peacemaker as a gift to all people, it is especially relevant to those who live in the United States because the creation of the U.S. government was highly influenced by Six-Nations leaders informed by the Peacemaker's Great Law of Peace. Sotsisowah argues, and I would concur, that the law of the Peacemaker, which survives despite tremendous odds, has yet to be fulfilled, rendering its central themes currently relevant because ". . .the possibility remains that the Peacemaker's vision of a world in peace and harmony may yet be realized" (p. 40). Not only is the world at war, but the entrenchment of class antago-nisms only seems to be growing. The Haudenosaunee form of direct democracy against class interests is therefore perhaps more needed now than ever.

Conclusion

Despite the central role that social class plays in determining the conditions of human life in a capitalist society, it is a concept that receives very little attention in the corporate media outlets. On rare occasion when it is introduced, it tends to be treated as the objective state of falling within a particular income bracket and is, therefore, just one of the many ways in which people are diverse, no more or less special than being male or female, short or tall, for example. What is implied is that inequality is the natural state of humanity and that any centrally planned attempt to democratize the distribution of wealth is therefore *un*natural because it limits the individual's freedom to create his or her own economic destiny, allowing the cream to rise to the top, as it were. The entire history of coercion, propaganda, genocide, and conquest that has paved, and continues to pave, the way for class society to exist and the on-going resistance against it tends to be left out of these discussions, almost without exception. Making a similar observation, Chomsky (1993) plainly states that "in the United States you're not allowed to talk about class differences" unless you belong to one of two groups, "the business community, which is rabidly class-conscious" and "high planning sectors of the government" (p. 67).

It is therefore not saying too much that the class perspective found in the work of Dur-kheim, Lippmann, and Friedman has greatly influenced the business press, which tends to be "full of the danger of the masses and their rising power and how we have to defeat them. It's kind of vulgar, inverted Marxism" (Chomsky, 1993, p. 67). What we find is that this self-serv-ing perspective of those who benefit from class-based inequalities, in mainstream, dominant society, is presented as objective reality—as normalized and naturalized. However, because our humanity can be limited, but never completely destroyed, hegemony cannot be complete, and the less it is, the more seriously we take the wisdom of those who counter-hegemonically came before, and those who continue to generously contribute to the critical tradition.

References

Boff, L., & Boff, C. (1987). *Introducing Liberation Theology*. Translated from the Portuguese by Paul Burns. Maryknoll, NY: Orbis.

Boff, L. (1971/1978). *Jesus Christ Liberator*. Maryknoll, NY: Orbis.

Brockman, J. (1988/2005). Preface. In Oscar Romero. *The Violence of Love*. Compiled and translated by James R. Brockman. Maryknoll, NY: Orbis.

Butler, S. (1935/2003). *War Is a Racket*. LA: Feral House.

Chomsky, N. (1993). *The Prosperous Few and the Restless Many*. Interviewed by David Barsamian. Berkeley, CA: Odonian Press.

Chomsky, N. (1999). *Profit over People: Neoliberalism and Global Order*. New York: Seven Stories.

Chomsky, N. (2007). *What We Say Goes: Conversations on U.S. Power in a Changing World*. Interviews with David Barsamian. New York: Metropolitan Books.

Churchill, W. (2002). *Struggle for the Land: Native North American Resistance to Genocide, Ecocide, and Colonization*. San Francisco, CA: City Lights.

Cole-Malott, D. & Malott, C. (2008). Culture, Capitalism and Social Democracy in Jamaica. In Brad Porfilio & Curry Malott (Eds.). *The Destructive Path of Neoliberalism: An International Examination of Education*. New York: Sense.

Durkheim, E. (1893/2000). *The Division of Labor in Society*. In Timmons Robert and Amy Hite (Eds.). *From Moderni-zation to Globalization: Perspectives on Development and Social Change*. New York: Blackwell.

Ewen, A. (Ed.) (1994). *Voices of Indigenous People: Native People Address the United Nations.* Santa Fe, NM: Clear Light.

Friedman, M. (1962/2002). *Capitalism and Freedom.* London: University of Chicago Press.

Freire, P. (1970). *Pedagogy of the Oppressed.* New York: Continuum.

Grinde, D.A. (1992). Iroquois Political Theory and the Roots of American Democracy. In Chief Oren Lyons & John Mohawk (Eds.). *Exiled in the Land of the Free: Democracy, Indian Nations, and the U.S. Constitution.* Santa Fe, NM: Clear Light.

Gutiérrez, G. (1973/1988). *A Theology of Liberation: History, Politics and Salvation.* Maryknoll, NY: Orbis.

Kincheloe, J. (2007). Critical Pedagogy in the Twenty-First Century: Evolution for Survival. In Peter McLaren & Joe Kincheloe (Eds.). *Critical Pedagogy: Where Are We Now?* New York: Peter Lang.

Lippmann, W. (1920/2008). *Liberty and the News.* Oxford: Princeton University Press.

Lippmann, W. (1922). *Public Opinion.* Boston: Little, Brown.

Lippmann, W. (1927). *The Phantom Public: A Sequel to "Public Opinion."* New York: Macmillan.

Lippmann, W. (1943). *U.S. Foreign Policy: Shield of the Republic.* Boston: Little, Brown.

Lyons, O., & Mohawk, J. (1992). *Exiled in the Land of the Free: Democracy, Indian Nations, and the U.S. Constitution.* Santa Fe, NM: Clear Light.

Malott, C. (2007). "Cuban Education in Neo-Liberal Times: Socialist Revolutionaries and State Capitalism." *Journal for Critical Education Policy Studies.* 5(1). [Online] Available at: http://www.jceps.com/?pageID=article&articleID=90.

Malott, C. (2008). *A Call to Action: An Introduction to Education, Philosophy, and Native North America.* New York: Peter Lang.

Marx, K. (1867/1967). *Capital: Volume 1: A Critical Analysis of Capitalist Production.* New York: New World Paperbacks.

Marx, K., & Engels, F. (1848/1978). *Manifesto of the Communist Party.* In Robert Tucker (Ed.). *The Marx-Engels Reader: Second Edition.* New York: Norton.

Robertson, L. (2005). *Conquest by Law: How the Discovery of America Dispossessed Indigenous Peoples of Their Lands.* New York: Oxford University Press.

Romero, O. (1988/2005). *The Violence of Love.* Compiled and translated by James R. Brockman. Maryknoll, NY: Orbis.

Sotsisowah (1978/2005). Thoughts of Peace: The Great Law. In Akwesasne Notes (Ed.). *Basic Call to Consciousness.* Summertown, TN: Native Voices.

Steel, R. (2008). Foreword. In Walter Lippman, *Liberty and the News.* Oxford: Princeton University Press.

Wilentz, S. (2008). General Editor's Introduction. In Walter Lippmann. *Liberty and the News* (1920/2008). Oxford: Princeton University Press.

Section Six

Religion as Diversity

Nineteen

Diversity in Education and the Marginalization of Religion

Spencer Boudreau

At an education conference I recently attended, some of the participants in the sessions introduced their questions or comments by stating that they had an "I wonder" question or comment. Personally, I have had an "I wonder" thought for some time regarding the presence or absence of the phenomenon of religion in multicultural or intercultural courses. I finally examined the syllabi of a number of these courses, and my suspicions were confirmed. The issue of race and minorities was very evident in these courses. Indigenous issues were also very present. Gender, disability, and homophobia were obvious subjects of concern. Not surprisingly, references to the impact of religions on cultures, and vice versa, were either absent or hardly present. Why I am not surprised is the subject of this chapter.

The Media and Religion

To begin, the media has had a sometimes turbulent relationship with religion. There is a pervasive view emanating from the media that religion has a negative, regressive effect on society. This perception was reflected by the cover story of the July 1995 issue of the *American Catholic* magazine, which was entitled: "Why Can't Religion Get Good Press?" The fact that religion gets bad press is not just a perception. Research at the University of Rochester was conducted to analyze what Americans learn about religion from reading the newspapers, and the perception that religion gets bad press was confirmed as a result of their study. It revealed that nearly half of all 314 religion stories in twelve top newspapers, such as the *New York Times,* the *Boston Globe* and the *Washington Post,* were about political, legal, or criminal activities. A majority of stories about Muslims and Catholics were about "bad deeds and criminality" (*Religion in American Newspapers: A Critique and Challenge,* University of Rochester, 2003). Curt Smith, who co-directed the study, observed that "coverage of Catholics and Islam was unbalanced everywhere. . .If you were from another planet, you'd think all Muslims were terrorists and all Catholics were pedophile priests" (Zenith, 2003). Other scholars concur with this analysis, and the Catholic Church appears to get even worse coverage than Islam since it is attacked more viciously, in the American press at least, than any other religion. Philip Jenkins, distinguished professor of history and religious studies at Pennsylvania State University, points this out in his book published by Oxford University Press, *The New Anti-Catholicism: The Last Acceptable Prejudice*. He refers to anti-Catholic rhetoric as the "thinking man's anti-semitism" and the poor reporting generally on the subject of religion.

> [C]overage of religion remains superficial, oscillating back and forth between exposes of religious hypo-crites and fluff pieces on exotic faiths. According to journalist Jeffrey Sharlet, 'Religion, in the broad sense, underlies, controls, permeates at least half the stories in the news, probably a lot more.' Iran, Iraq, and Israel, he notes, are all religion stories. But it's a rare reporter who captures that reality, in part because the average reporter is no more informed about religion than the average American. (Jenkins, pp. 126–127)

Nicholas Kristof, an editorialist for the *New York Times*, wrote an article in which he noted that the media treats religion and politically religious groups, such as evangelical Christians, through the "filter of the Northeast educated elite." In his article, he writes that although he personally disagrees with evangelicals, he acknowledges that "liberal critiques sometimes seem not just filled with outrage at evangelical-backed policies, which is fair, but also have a sneering tone about conservative Christianity itself. Such mockery of religious faith is inexcusable" (Zenith, 2003). This liberal mockery of almost a third of the American population (Pew Research Center, 2008) seems to ignore the fact that there are evangelical Christians who have issues beyond gay marriage and abortion. Evangelical Christians for Human Rights (yes, such an organization exists) have criticized President Bush because he has "failed to deal with poverty at home and abroad and turned a blind eye to torture, ignored climate change, and neglected the human suffering from the war in Iraq" (Evangelicals for Human Rights, n.d.).

If we also take into consideration the recent debate in Quebec regarding the "reasonable accommodation" of immigrants, we have also been witness to religion bashing from different quarters—the uneducated and the highly educated. Lois Sweet notes:

> Ironically, we seem, as a society, to have shifted a full 180 degrees. We've gone from times when religious were often intolerant of the non-religious, or those of a different religion, to today, when it is those who hold religious convictions who are subjected to societal intolerance. (Sweet, 1997, p. 7)

Doug Underwood underlines that the sceptical and empirical mentality of journalists can make them blind to the importance of religion in the lives of many people. He observes: "There appears to be a consensus across religious groups that journalists do not 'get it' when it comes to the portrayal of people of faith and the way they express the spiritual underpinning of their lives" (Underwood, 2002, p. 275).

Charles Taylor is concerned about such a negative image and its consequences. He points out that "our identity is partly shaped by recognition or its absence. . .non-recognition or mis-recognition can inflict harm, can be a form of oppression, imprisoning someone in a false, distorted, and reduced mode of being" (Sweet, 1997, p. 14).

Academia and Religion

A number of distinguished scholars have perceived among academics discomfort with, if not hostility to, religion. Yale professor Stephen Carter, in his book *The Culture of Disbelief: How American Law and Politics Trivialize Religious Devotions,* writes "the message of contemporary culture seems to be that it's perfectly all right to believe that stuff. . .but you really ought to keep it to yourself." Later on, he states,

> Rather than envisioning a public square in which all are welcome, the contemporary liberal philosophers insist on finding a set of conversational rules that require the individual whose religious tradition makes demands on his or her moral conscience to reformulate that conscience—to destroy a vital aspect of the self—in order to gain the right to participate in the dialogue along other citizens and such a requirement is possible only in a liberal world that regards religious knowledge as being of a decidedly inferior sort. (Carter, 1993, p. 229)

Alister McGrath perceives an even more negative view of religion and notes that many academics believe that religion's (in this case Christianity's) ". . .central ideas were ridiculous and untenable; socially it was reactionary and oppressive" and it was time "to break free of its clutches, once and for all" (McGrath, 2004, p. xii). Charles Taylor notes that such individuals envision the dissolution of religion altogether.

> [Many people are] convinced as a matter of fact that religion will gradually disappear and everyone will think as they do. For them, the secular world is one in which we all end up agreeing fundamentally that there's no god, and that agreement is the basis of everything. Taylor adds, "That's an impossible scenario. . . ." (Anderson, 2004, p. 3)

Richard John Neuhaus concurs with these views and states that in "centers of higher learning it is more or less taken for granted that ours is a secular society" (Neuhaus, 1984, p. 103). In addition, Neuhaus points out that there is a notion in academia that everyone should think like the academy, and the academy thinks that "religion is residual, backward, primitive, definitely of the past. . . and an obstacle to the coming of the desired new order" (Neuhaus, 1984, p. 205).

Peter Berger highlights that there is the belief in the inevitable victory of secularism over religion and that "eventually Iranian mullahs, Pentecostal preachers, and Tibetan lamas will all think and act like professors of literature at American universities" (D'Souza, 2007, p. 4). Biologist Kenneth Miller confesses that "a presumption of atheism or agnosticism is universal in academic life. . .The conventions of academic life, almost universally, revolve around the assumption that religious belief is something that people grow out of as they become educated" (p. 37). This is referred to as "convergence pluralism."

> Convergence pluralism expects that in the future everybody will converge on a shared vision of core liberal values and ideals. This form of liberalism has been described as a form of "liberal fundamentalism." Convergence pluralism can be as intolerant an ideology as any religious fundamentalism. (ESCC, 2008, pp. 2–3)

Kenneth Strike agrees and underscores that "we try to privatise religion and to keep religious voices out of the public square. . .Those who use God-talk in the public square need their mouths washed out with liberal soap" (Strike, 2007, p. 694).

Furthermore, not only is there a systematic exclusion of religion from the public square, but the attacks on religious belief appear to be more frequent and virulent:

> many who have not chosen to pursue a religious life are unwilling or unable to understand how such a life can be valuable for anyone. Accordingly, they see no harm in excluding room for religious expression. . . In addition, a new and troubling ideology has been surfacing in recent years. An aggressive comprehensive liberalism despises religion as "toxic" source of conflict, violence, irrationalism, bigotry, and social fragmentation. Severe denunciations of religion and religious belief now have considerable appeal in some sectors of society. (ESCC, 2008, p. 6)

Books like Richard Dawkins' *The God Delusion* and Christopher Hitchens' *God Is Not Great: How Religion Poisons Everything* are examples of academic discourses against religion. Hitchens even goes as far as comparing religion to a virus and a disease that must be purged (Guillen, 2004, p. 36).

This view puzzles people whose meaning and purpose of life is anchored in religious faith.

> Many of the people holding to a religious view, for example, are baffled by the notion that everything religious should be kept private, especially given that the typical person who is truly religious has social, political, and intellectual views that are powerfully shaped by their religious outlook. For the religious person, talking about these social, political, and intellectual views without reference to the religious origins of some of one's viewpoints cannot be done with either integrity or depth. The informal or formal strictures against discussion of these ideas produce a constrained climate in which interaction is inhibited, depth is avoided, and issues are not fully explored. The person with a religious view is bothered by the apparent commitment of the academic world to secularism, or the worldview of naturalism, in a manner that marginalizes other worldviews. (Anderson, 2008, p. 105)

Jürgen Habermas is against this imposition of a single world view.

> The neutrality of the state on questions of world views guarantees the same ethical freedom to every citizen. This is incompatible with the political universalization of a secularist world view. When secularized citizens act in their role as citizens of the state, they must not deny in principle that religious images of the world have the potential to express truth. Nor must they refuse their believing fellow citizens the right to make contributions in a religious language to public debates. (Habermas and Ratzinger, 2006, p. 51)

The Challenge of Religious Illiteracy

If it appears without doubt that religion is such an important, if not essential aspect of culture, then the lack of knowledge about religion should be of serious concern. Denise Bombardier, a well-known Quebec journalist and commentator, wrote an editorial in the newspaper *Le Devoir* entitled, "La perte des repères" (The loss of reference points) that provides a convincing essay about the present state of religious ignorance. This is not a question of understanding one's religion. It is a question of understanding one's history, art, architecture, and literature. She concludes, "Les jeunes actuels, élevés sans un minimum de culture religieuse, sont devenus des handicapés culturels" (Today's youth, raised without a minimum of religious culture, have become culturally handicapped) (Bombardier, 2002). David Carr concurs that ". . . any and all serious (cultural) literacy would seem to require religious literacy" (Carr, 2007, p. 670). Kevin Williams, in reference to French culture, writes, "An understanding of religion is necessary to an informed response to the considerable body of religiously inspired poetry, music and art in French culture and in western culture in general" (Williams, 2007, p. 681). Bernard Shapiro, the former principal of McGill University, has also expressed his concern about this lack of knowledge.

> You can't understand the history of this country or the culture of Western civilization if you don't understand Christianity. It's absolutely criminal to bring anyone up in this culture who doesn't understand what Christianity is and what it stood for. (Sweet, 1997, p. 191)

Shapiro's view seems easy to defend. Without some knowledge of Christianity, it is difficult to see how anyone can appreciate Shakespeare (who has hundreds of biblical quotes in his writings), Milton's *Paradise Lost*, Handel's *Messiah*, and pre-Renaissance and Renaissance paintings—to give just a few examples. The same can be said about the importance of religion in other cultures. I had the privilege to visit and study in India. There can be no doubt about the importance of understanding something about Hinduism in order to comprehend the Indian culture. An understanding of Arab culture necessarily has to include a minimal understanding of Islam. Yet, many continually seem to be unwilling to engage with this essential element of culture. This has been pointed out by Michael Peers in reference to the Canadian context.

> Secularism according to some contributors. . . will bring unity and strength to our country by removing from its life the divisiveness of religion. . . . This kind of thing, I think, would prove to be not only a suppression of the pluralist reality, but also a folly of the worst sort for society. If we think we can achieve unity by the suppression of knowledge of, and respect for, religious diversity, then we will never understand our world. . . .Imagine telling Sikhs and Muslims that their culture is respected in this country but the society has no place for their faith. Faith and culture are intimately connected. (McGrath, 2004, p. 268)

This neglect of the religious dimension of culture has resulted in widespread religious illiteracy. According to Stephen Prothero, the chair of the religion department at Boston University,

> Every year colleges provide bachelor's degrees to students who cannot name the first book of the Bible, who think Jesus parted the Red Sea and Moses agonized in the Garden of Gethsemane, who know nothing about what Islam teaches about war and peace, and who cannot name one salient difference between Hinduism and Buddhism. (Prothero, 2007, p. 139)

When I ask my university students what the expression "the patience of Job" means and refers to, I get blank stares. The fruits of neglecting the importance of religion are ignorance and intolerance. It is referred to as an "unnatural exclusion" by Martin Marty (Marty, 2000, p. 66).

The Need for a Balanced View of Religion

I am not proposing a "kumbaya" version of religion. Anyone who has been a serious student of religions is well aware of the sins of hordes of people who declare themselves adherents of a particular religious tradition. The problem is that all one hears about are the failings of religion. It is perfectly legitimate to present the Marxist or Freudian view of religion, but it would not do justice to the subject (and to education) if only a one-dimensional view is presented. Ronald Anderson, professor of education at the University of Colorado, points to positive aspects of religion.

> In contrast to some stereotypes, religion can be a source of freedom, a basis for positive mental health, the foundation of positive relationships, and can result in (a point based in the results of empirical research) better physical health and longer life. (Anderson, 2004, p. 60)

Religious organizations are involved in a number of sectors in civil society, and a host of volunteers affiliated with these organizations dedicate their time and energy to the poor, the dispossessed, immigrants, the elderly, the sick, and the imprisoned. In my city of Montreal, several church organizations provide food and lodging for the homeless and lobby the government of behalf of the voiceless. The Catholic congregations of sisters in Canada have made the battle against human trafficking their priority. Examples abound elsewhere. Martin Marty refers to the influence of religion in the Civil Rights Movement in the United States.

> Many of the movement's leadership and workers were explicitly inspired by religion. It was not an accident that a key group's name was the Southern *Christian* Leadership Conference and that many of the movement's leaders were called "Reverend"—King, Abernathy, Young, Walker, Shuttlesworth, Bevel, Jackson, and others, twenty-deep. . .They chided and rallied citizens by citing Hebrew Scriptures, the New Testament teachings of Jesus and Paul, and more contemporary religious leaders from Howard Thurman to Gandhi. To deal with the Civil Rights Movement while excluding religion deprives students of the full substance and context of the story. (Marty, 67)

Martin Luther King's struggle for freedom and equality for African Americans was rooted in his Christian faith. In his famous "I've been to the mountaintop" speech on April 3, 1968, the day before he was assassinated, he declared,

> We need all of you. And you know what's beautiful to me, is to see all of these ministers of the Gospel. It's a marvellous picture. Who is it that is supposed to articulate the longings and aspirations of the people more than the preacher?
>   Somehow the preacher must be an Amos, and say, "Let justice roll down like waters and righteousness like a mighty stream." Somehow, the preacher must say with Jesus, "The spirit of the Lord is upon me, because he hath anointed me to deal with the problems of the poor." (AFSCME, n.d.)

However, the religious roots that motivated his struggle were camouflaged by the media, as noted by Richard Neuhaus.

> Those of us who received the grace of working with Martin Luther King, Jr., know how profoundly his life and work were empowered by religious faith. . ..The point at hand has to do with a small but significant event following Dr. King's assassination, April 4, 1968. There was an ecumenical memorial service here in Harlem, with numerous religious, political and cultural dignitaries in attendance. The service was reported on television news that evening. The announcer, standing before St. Charles Borromeo church where the service was held, spoke in solemn tones: "And so today there was a memorial service for the slain civil rights leader, Dr. Martin Luther King, Jr. It was a religious service, and it is fitting that it should be, for, after all, Dr. King was the son of a minister."
>   How explain this astonishing blindness to the religious motive and meaning of Dr. King's ministry? The announcer was speaking out of a habit of mind that was no doubt quite unconscious. The habit of mind is. . . that matters of *public* significance must be sanitized of religious particularity. It regularly occurred that the klieg lights for the television cameras would be turned off during Dr. King's speeches when he dwelt on the religious and moral-philosophical basis of the movement for racial justice. They would be turned on again when the subject touched upon confrontational politics. In a luncheon conversation, Dr. King once remarked, "They aren't interested in the *why* of what we're doing, only in the *what* of what we're doing, and because they don't understand the why they cannot really understand the what" (Neuhaus, 1984, pp. 97–98).

There are many examples in other cultures of religion's positive contribution to justice and peace. Gandhi was a devout Hindu and his doctrine of *ahimsa* (nonviolence) inspired many in their struggle for freedom and equality—including Martin Luther King. In 2007 the secretary general of the United Nations referred to Gandhi as his personal hero and in his speech quoted Gandhi's commitment to non-violence: "Non-violence is the first article of my faith. It is also the last article of my creed" (UN, 2007).

A few years ago, I had lunch with educators from South Africa. They were Marxists so I was curious about what their thoughts were about Archbishop Desmond Tutu. They replied, "Mandela is our liberator, and Tutu is our conscience." Tutu was the key player in the Truth and Reconciliation Commission and, as a result, the truth and reconciliation that emanated from this commission astounded the world. In 1985, Desmond Tutu won the Nobel Peace Prize for his role in ending apartheid in South Africa. The motivation for his struggle was his faith, as noted by a BBC journalist:

> Under his vigorous leadership, the church in South Africa became immersed in the political struggle against apartheid. Mr Tutu constantly told the government of the time that its racist approach defied the will of God and for that reason could not succeed. He has strived to remain outside party politics and always used the Bible as his text, saying God decreed all Africans were equal. (BBC News, 1998)

In India and around the world, the Dalai Lama has led the nonviolent struggle for the survival of the Tibetan culture. Again, his essence and message are grounded in Buddhism. In his speech when accepting the Nobel Peace Prize in 1989, he reiterated this.

> As a Buddhist monk, my concern extends to all members of the human family and, indeed, to all sentient beings who suffer. I believe all suffering is caused by ignorance. People inflict pain on others in the selfish pursuit of their happiness or satisfaction. Yet true happiness comes from a sense of brotherhood and sisterhood. We need to cultivate a universal responsibility for one another and the planet we share. (Dalai Lama home page, 1989)

I could enumerate many other examples of individuals whose positive contribution to the world is grounded wholly, or at least partly, in their religious beliefs. Some individuals' religious connection may even be surprising to some. My colleagues at McGill University who founded the Paulo and Nita Freire International Project for Critical Pedagogy, Joe Kincheloe and Shirley Steinberg, told me that Paulo Freire's home was adorned with crucifixes. Freire came from a devout Catholic home and was influenced by Catholic philosophers like Emmanuel Mounier and Jacques Maritain and by the tenets of liberation theology. It should not be surprising that a figure like the crucified Jesus, who identified himself with the poor, hungry, imprisoned and marginalized, would serve as an inspiration for an apostle of the same people.

Accommodation Pluralism and the Inclusion of Religion

Religion is sometime referred to as "wish fulfillment." Maybe so, but it is here to stay despite the wishes of many. More than a century after Nietzsche declared God dead, no less a scholar than Peter Berger asserts, "Religion has not been declining. On the contrary, in much of the world there has been a veritable explosion of religious faith." He points to "resurgent Islam and dynamic evangelical Protestantism." He notes how the media and intellectuals have ignored this reality.

> The rise of evangelical Protestantism has been less noticed by intellectuals, the media and the general public in Western countries, partly because nowhere is it associated with violence and partly because it more directly challenges the assumptions of established elite opinion: David Martin, a leading British sociologist of religion, has called it a "revolution that was not supposed to happen." (Berger, 2008)

Berger gives other examples.

> The Catholic Church, in trouble in Europe, has been doing well in the Global South. There is a revival of the Orthodox Church in Russia. Orthodox Judaism has been rapidly growing in America and Israel. Both Hinduism and Buddhism have experienced revivals, and the latter has had some success in proselytizing in America and Europe.
>
> Simply put: Modernity is not characterized by the absence of God, but by the presence of many gods—with two exceptions to this picture of a furiously religious world. One is geographical: Western and Central Europe. The causes and present shape of what one may call Eurosecularity constitute one of the most interesting problems in the sociology of contemporary religion. The other exception is perhaps even more relevant to the question of secularization, for it is constituted by an international cultural elite, essentially a globalization of the enlightened intelligentsia of Europe. It is everywhere a minority of the population—but a very influential one. (Berger, 2008)

Having read a number of predictions about the demise of religion, I am reminded of Mark Twain's comment, "Rumors of my death have been greatly exaggerated." As Alister McGrath points out, quoting William S. Bainbridge and Rodney Stark,

> The most illustrious figures in sociology, anthropology and psychology have unanimously expressed confidence that their children—or surely their grandchildren—would live to see the dawn of a new era in which, to paraphrase Freud, the infantile illusions of religion would be outgrown. (McGrath, 2004, p. 189)

McGrath notes that "...they have not been outgrown. If anything, the reverse is true (p. 189). McGrath goes on to quote Robert Fulford, who admits he was "stupid enough" to believe that nationalism and religion "as a force in worldly affairs, were slowly but inevitably fading away" (McGrath, p. 190). In the fall of 2007, a special edition of the *Economist* focused on the subject of politics and religion. A clear consensus gleamed from the articles is that the influence of religion on world politics is on the rise—to the surprise and dismay of secularists.

> How frightening (or inspiring) is this prospect? As our special report explains, the idea that religion has re-emerged in public life is to some extent an illusion. It never really went away—certainly not to the extent that French politicians and American college professors imagined. Its new power is mostly the consequence of two changes. The first is the failure of secular creeds: religion's political comeback started in the 1970s, when faith in government everywhere was crumbling. Second, although some theocracies survive in the Islamic world, religion has returned to the stage as a much more democratic, individualistic affair: a bottom-up marketing success, surprisingly in tune with globalization. Secularism was not as modern as many intellectuals imagined, but pluralism is. (The New Wars of Religion, 2008)

Accommodation pluralism recognizes diversity in all its forms, and is willing to engage and dialogue with a multitude of worldviews and ways of thinking, being and acting (ESCC, 2008, p. 5). This would include, naturally, religious ways of thinking, being, and acting. As David Carr underscores "...exclusion of religious claims from educational consideration on secularist grounds—which are not themselves beyond controversy—could hardly be more acceptable than dismissal of secularist claims on religious grounds..." (Carr, 2007, p. 661). This willingness to recognize and engage with the religious other in all its dimensions seeks the goal of a manner of living together, a modus vivendi, un vivre ensemble that is inclusive and always respectful of the other. The new Ethic and Religious Culture program in Quebec that became compulsory in all Quebec schools in 2008 has three competencies— "reflects on ethical questions, demonstrates an understanding of the phenomenon of religion and engages in dialogue" (Ethics and Religious Culture Elementary, 2007, p. 7). The objective of the program is "the recognition of others and the pursuit of the common good. . ." (p. 7). Despite the criticism of the program from both secular and religious quarters, the relevance of the objective of the program cannot be easily dismissed.

I am proposing that religion not be excluded from the discourse that informs our understanding of all aspects of culture—language, art, music, history, ethics, ethnicity, and philosophy because that is, as Martin Marty pointed out, an "unnatural exclusion." I am also proposing that the view of religion not be one dimensional such as a Freudian or Marxist view, or based on one's personal distaste of matters religious. Religion has not always been only bad and ugly; it has also been good and deserves to be treated fairly in the classroom and public square. Robert Jackson of the University of Warick proposes a pedagogical path when reflecting on religious themes.

> The model encourages a view of religion which acknowledges their complexity, internal diversity, and their varying interactions with culture. It especially emphasises the personal element in religion, seeing religion as part of lived human experience. However, the approach is not relativistic with regard to truth, aiming for a procedural epistemological openness and acknowledging varying and often competing truth claims. (Jackson, 1997, p. 122)

In an open and fair critical view of religion, we will discover an understanding of some aspects of what it means to be human. Abraham Maslow recognizes the need to be inclusive when considering the goals of education.

> The final and unavoidable conclusion is that education—like all our social institutions—must be concerned with its final values, and this in turn is just about the same as speaking of what have been called "spiritual values" or "higher values." These are the principles of choice which help us to answer the age-old "spiritual" (philosophical? religious? humanistic? ethical?) questions: What is the good life? What is the good man? The good woman? What is the good society and my relation to it? What are my obligations to society? What is the best for my children? What is justice? Truth? Virtue? What is my relation to nature, to death, to aging, to pain, to illness? How can I live a zestful, enjoyable, meaningful life?. . . What shall I be loyal to? What must I be ready to die for? (Maslow, 1970, p. 52)

The words of Carr certainly summarize my thoughts on this issue, ". . . we do not have to take the *Mahabharata* or the Old Testament book of Job and other religious texts as literally true in order to appreciate that these works also contain insight and wisdom of enduring human value" (Carr, 2007, p. 667). I wonder if the academy will be willing to mine that wisdom.

References

AFSCME Web site. (n.d.). Retrieved April 6, 2008 from afscme.org/about/1549.cfm
Anderson, Ronald D. (2004). *Religion & Spirituality in the Public School Curriculum*. New York: Peter Lang.
———. (2008). *Religion and Teaching*. New York: Lawrence Erlbaum Associates.
BBC Web site. (1998). Retrieved April 6, 2008 from http://www.news.bbc.co.uk/1/hi/special_report/1998/10/98/truth_and_ reconciliatiio/202503.stm

Berger, P. (2008). Secularization Falsified. *First Things: The Journal of Religious Culture and Public Life,* 23–27.

Bombardier, D. (2002, January 12). La perte des repères. *Le Devoir.* Editorial.

Boudreau, S. (1999). *Catholic Education: The Quebec Experience.* Calgary: Detselig Enterprises.

Carr, D. (2007). Religious Education, Religious Literacy and Common Schooling: A Philosophy and History of Skewed Reflection. *Journal of Philosophy of Education, 4,* 659–673.

Carter, S. (1994). *The Culture of Disbelief: How American Law and Politics Trivializes Religious Devotions.* New York: Anchor Books.

D'Souza, D. (2007). *What's so Great about Christianity.* Washington: Regnery.

Dalai Lama Web site. (1989). Retrieved April 13, 2008 from http://www.dalailama.com

English Speaking Catholic Council (ESCC). (2008). *Reasonable Accommodation and Freedom of Religion in Quebec.* Montreal, Quebec.

Evangelicals for Human Rights Web site. (n.d.). Retrieved April 12, 2008 from http://www.evangelicalsforhumanrights.org/

Guillen. M. (2004). *Can a Smart Person Believe in God?* Nashville: Nelson Books.

Habermas, J. & Ratzinger J. (2006). *The Dialectics of Secularization: On Reason and Religion.* San Francisco: Ignatius Press.

Jackson, R. (1997). *Religious Education: An Interpretive Approach.* London: Hodder and Stoughton.

Jenkins, P. (2003). *The New Anti-Catholicism: The Last Acceptable Prejudice.* New York: Oxford University Press.

Keller, T. (2008). *The Reason for God: Belief in an Age of Skepticism.* New York: Dutton.

Marty, M. (2000). *Education, Religion and the Common Good.* San Francisco: Jossey-Bass.

Maslow, A. (1970). *Religion, Values, and Peak-Experiences.* New York: Penguin Books.

McGrath, A. (2004). *The Twilight of Atheism: The Rise and Fall of Disbelief in the Modern World.* New York: Doubleday.

Neuhaus, R.J. (1984). *The Naked Public Square: Religion and Democracy in America* (2nd ed.). Grand Rapids, MI: William B. Eerdmans.

New Wars of Religion, The. (2008, November 3). *Economist,* 15.

Pew Research Center Web site. (2008). Retrieved March 4, 2008 from http://pewresearch.org/pubs/743/united-states-religion

Prothero, S. (2007). *Religious Literacy: What Every American Needs to Know—and Doesn't.* New York: HarperCollins.

Quebec Education Program Elementary Education. (2008). *Ethics and Religious Culture.* Ministère de l'Éducation, du Loisir et du Sport.

Strike, K. (2007). Common Schools and Uncommon Conversations: Education, Religious Speech and Public Spaces. *Journal of Philosophy of Education, 4,* 693–708.

Sweet, L. (1997). *God in the Classroom: The Controversial Issue of Religion in Canada's Schools.* Toronto: McClelland & Steward.

Taylor, C. (2007). *A Secular Age.* Cambridge, MA: The Belknap Press of Harvard University Press.

Underwood, D. (2002). *From Yahweh to Yahoo: The Religious Roots of the Secular Press.* Champaigne: University of Illinois Press.

United Nations Web site. (2007). Retrieved April 12, 2008 from http://www.un.org/News/Press/docs/2007/sgsm11199.doc.htm

University of Rochester, Education Web site. (2003). Retrieved April 14, 2008 from http://www.rochester.edu/College/REL/graphics/religion_news.ppt

Ward, K. (2004). *The Case for Religion.* Oxford: Oneworld Publications.

Williams, K. (2007) Religious Worldviews and the Common School: The French Dilemma. *Journal of Philosophy of Education, 4,* 675–692.

Zenith Web site. (2003). Retrieved November 9, 2004 from http://www.zenith.org/article-17411?l=english

Twenty

Religion and Diversity in Our Classrooms

Christopher Darius Stonebanks and Melanie Stonebanks

So you're a backbench MP. You see a cuddly early day motion praising a group that sends much-needed Christmas presents to deprived children abroad. Do you sign it? Well, of course you do. Do you check the group out first? Well, probably not.
    —Bartholomew, 2006

For over a decade, teachers, administrators, and parents who work within governing school structures (governing boards, parent association, special interest groups, volunteers, etc.) have been coming to terms with a substantial change in their schools, one that requires them to adopt and advance a viewpoint on religion that is not based in proselytizing or promoting a singular perspective but rather on providing students with the tools to critically and respectfully examine both religious and secular viewpoints. The professional challenge for many teachers is to research, develop, and implement curriculum that may or may not represent their "own beliefs and points of view" (Ministère de l'Éducation, du Loisir et du Sport, 2007, p. 7). Primarily through a personal narrative methodology of our own experiences as students, teachers, teacher educators, and parents, this chapter examines the professional choices teachers make when confronted with, not only the current education laws in Quebec but also with parents and peers who call into question pedagogical decisions regarding religious instruction that would at one time have been considered normal but are now viewed as opposing contemporary academic educational thought on promoting an acceptance of diversity.

Having met when we were in high school, worked in elementary schools since 1992, and married since 1994, we have been discussing the subject of education for quite some time. During this period, we have, on a number of occasions, had the opportunity to accuse each other of being either a naïve optimist or a cynical pessimist. We entered the field for polar opposite reasons: one of us loved her school experience and could not wait to reproduce it; the other suffered through his primary and secondary education with a commitment to changing it. Our perspectives on schools are as different as our cultural and religious roots. Melanie, who loved school, is a multigenerational Canadian of English, Christian, and European descent, who was raised as a Protestant. Christopher, who disliked school, immigrated to Canada with his family at a very young age and is of multiethnic and multireligious roots and was raised to be aware and respectful of these many backgrounds. School, for Melanie, was a safe environment, something to look forward to: her mother laying out new clothes for the first day of school was a joy. School, for Christopher, was a location of disconnect, something to dread: hearing Walt Disney's theme song during the Canadian Broadcasting Corporation's Sunday evening television programming would create a pit in his stomach as it forecast the coming of Monday.

We both love working in schools, or, rather, we love working with our students, but our differing childhood schooling experiences have sparked many arguments between us over the nature and function of schools, and the typical late spring ceremony that transitions students from primary to secondary education has provided many opportunities to have the discussion over and over again. In particular, we have disagreed over the use of Robert Frost's (1915) poem "The Road Not Taken." The Frost poem is a favourite amongst final-year elementary school teachers as an end of the year reading to their students. Challenging young students on their future life journey, there is, of course, a natural suggestion of comparison to the challenger, in this case the teacher, to their own choices as a role model.

When we worked in the same school, our experiences with the Frost poem and the primary school graduation ceremony would generally go something like this:

> For one of us (Melanie), usually standing at the assembly podium, the Frost poem has been a staple of her graduation ceremonies. Hitting the conclusion of the poem, "Two roads diverged in a wood, and I. . .", she takes the moment to insert the dramatic pause and then continues, her eyes brimming with tears, ". . . I took the one less traveled by." At this point, children and parents are genuinely responding to her sincere tears of affection. A moment of composure and the final words, "And that has made all the difference." On cue: students' tears and applause from parents. Sitting with the staff, the other (Christopher), smiles artificially frozen through the speech and inwardly rolling his eyes, claps along with everyone, all the while he sees images of television commercials with celebrities or models holding up Coke or Pepsi cans assuring the consumer that if everyone buys their products, they too are assured of their radical individualism.

The ensuing discussion usually centers on the question, what is the point of the Frost poem? The usual arguments from Melanie would be that we, as educators, are trying to impart to children a notion that they should go out into the world and lead their young lives as individuals, free from imposed doctrine and narrow-mindedness. They should be strong and stand up for what they believe in, choose the right path, and not allow themselves to give into the peer pressure they will undoubtedly encounter in high school, which will ultimately wear them down until they are simply another one of the mindless masses. The typical arguments from Christopher would center on the simple retort: is that really what schools want—individuality and free choice? Are peers really a cause for concern in comparison to the manner in which schools function to ensure conformity in their understandable and rightful desire to be problem free and procedurally smooth in operation? Despite how we may disagree on whether not freedom of choice and individuality is something that is promoted in the formal context of public North American schools, one aspect of schools we can agree on is that few, if any,

North American teachers would argue against the idea that individuality is something to be respected and promoted within the class.

> The Notion that "we are all different" and therefore, "we are all the same" ignores how power operates to determine the difference some differences make. The process and practices by which certain differences are normalized, minimized or ignored is not explored and thus the power of invisibility of dominant groups is assured. (Cavanagh and Harper, 1994, p. 28)

Although we hear teachers say that "all children are treated equally in their classrooms," the sentiment is usually tempered with the impression that diversity, too, is something they value. In relation to education, diversity, and/or multiculturalism, few North American teachers in the twenty-first century would openly advocate "fitting in" for all children and students in their classroom as an overt education priority within the context of discussing their pedagogical philosophies. Teachers will, on the whole, advocate creating inclusive classrooms, where their students are valued individuals who work together as a team. What has become difficult to discern is how individuality intersects with the prevalent model in North American schooling, which, despite the changes it has undergone, has stayed fairly true to its original intent of not only teaching children the basics but teaching socialization to the dominant norms as well. For example, imagine an elementary school early in the school year and an eager young teacher having her or his students placing their hands in different coloured finger paints and then making their hand mark on a big sheet of white paper within the confines of an outlined rainbow. Off in the corner, the kids who have finished early are working on a painting of the planet Earth that will be glued onto the center of the rainbow. The multicoloured piece of artwork is then hung proudly in the hallway next to the classroom door with a banner perhaps exclaiming something with a multi-cultural flair, like, "Our Many Hands Can Colour the World." If a dove is added to the top of the rainbow, we might see text with a somewhat religious flair such as, "This Is Our Promise for a Better World." Certainly, this would be a visual that either of us would be, upon first impression, content to see upon walking into a school. However, a combined thirty years of working in schools have left us, to different degrees, wary of what lies behind such proclamations.

Closing in on the 100-year anniversary of Frost's poem, we wonder if his suggestive road less traveled has been superseded by the reflective Generation-X narrative of the "beaten path" of corporate individualism, which was captured brilliantly in the character of Joanna, a waitress in director Mike Judge's 1999 film *Office Space*. Joanna tries endlessly to navigate with the manager of the franchise restaurant Chotchkie's on her "flair," flair being the buttons Chotchkie employees wear in "sameness" on their uniforms to promote their individual expression of self; their individuality and freedom of choice as dictated by the corporation.

> Chotchkie's Manager: We need to talk about your "flair."
> Joanna: Really? I have fifteen pieces on.
> Chotchkie's Manager: Well, okay, fifteen is the minimum. Okay? Now, so, you know, it's up to you if you want to do the bare minimum. . . or. . . Well, like Brian over there, for example has thirty-seven pieces of flair.
> Joanna: Okay, so you want me to wear more?
> Chotchkie's Manager: Look, we want you to express yourself, Okay? Now if you feel that the bare minimum is enough, then. . . okay. But some people choose to wear more. . . and we encourage that. (*Office Space*, 1999)

When we were asked to write this chapter on religion and diversity, we could not help but connect them with the professional responses of teachers and draw further parallels to our own experiences of working in schools. Nor could we help but connect them with the prevailing notions of respect for diversity and individualism that are touted in North American schools and the realities we see in the same institutions. In short, diversity, as it relates to respecting religious differences, has far too often become one of the pieces of "flair" for teachers. We do not know a single teacher who proudly states he or she is against diversity or the acceptance of individual religious differences among students. Education courses that touch upon these ideas certainly provide pre-service teachers with the framework they need to build upon respect and appreciation for religious, philosophical, spiritual, humanist, and worldview diversity. This foundation allows them to continue with their professional responsibility to grow as teachers. In regard to the specifics of religion, it allows them to challenge their views and understanding and to be transparent and accountable in regard to the curriculum they develop, modify, or reproduce in their classrooms. Far too often, in our opinion, this professional responsibility is met, whether unconsciously or not, in a superficial manner, becoming, in effect, pieces of "I ♥ Diversity" button-flair worn on their teaching uniforms.

Both authors of this chapter started working in schools within Quebec's former Catholic system. The inner-city schools we worked in contained the kind of diverse classrooms that would be the desire of any photographer working for Canada Heritage to promote multiculturalism. While most of our students were Catholic, many were not. Prior to the change from religious to linguistic school boards, we cannot remember any significant in-practice options for moral and/or religious instruction in anything but Catholicism, which was not only part of the formal religious instruction class but was infused into the general curriculum as well. Because religious school boards were legal bodies, we accepted this reality, even though, in many cases, it went against what we had been taught at university about respect for diversity, especially in regard to the areas of culture and religion. Since neither of us was Catholic, we were also aware that we were both fortunate to be employed; at the same time, we were working in a system that had no obligation to reflect our pedagogical perspectives. As the switch from a religious to linguistic make-up of the boards began, parents of newly registered new students could check off the "Catholic," "Protestant," or infamous "other" box (that sometimes took on different wording but still meant Other) creating the possibility of choosing the focus of their child's moral and religious instruction. Still, the schools retained their religious roots, and we understood that change would not occur overnight. We respected that teachers in both Protestant and Catholic school boards who considered themselves to belong to one of these religions and had been trained in their teacher education programs to teach within this context in schools that reflected their own beliefs and way of life would have varying degrees of comfort with the changes that were taking place.

As in any other workplace or profession, we saw varying degrees of adaptation and willingness to try to engage in the changes that were underway. Certainly, there was resistance from some, acceptance from others, and obliviousness from a few. We watched the full spectrum of responses from administrators and teachers, which took conscious, unconscious, and dysconscious forms. Conscious efforts might lead an individual to speak up and object to the changes in a public forum or to embrace the new changes in the curriculum. The actions of the teachers who disagreed were either overt, that is, speaking or writing publicly, or covert, that is, maintaining the status quo in the hope that the changes were a fad that would simply blow over. An unconscious response might come from a teacher who quite honestly did not understand and could not keep up with the pedagogical reforms. The dysconscious response is one that we connect to King's (1991) description of dysconsciousness in which there is exclusion of and disconnect from the Other's pain. In King's analysis of the discrimination associated with dysconscious attitudes toward teaching, she states "dyconscious racism is a form of racism that tacitly accepts dominant White norms and privileges. It is not the absence of consciousness (that is, it is not unconsciousness) but an impaired consciousness or distorted way of thinking about race as compared to, for example, critical consciousness" (p. 135). Such teachers understood the changes being made to curriculum to build toward greater inclusion of differing religious perspectives and the professional demands that were required, yet they made the decision to perpetuate the same schools of thought that they found so much comfort in and to simply ignore the detriment.

> Most of the pre-service teachers I taught at Santa Clara University for 12 years were White. Because most of them accepted the myth that America is a White nation that is *becoming* more diverse, they also believe that their mission as teachers was to help these diverse "others" to be like them. (King, 2000)

For a combined fifteen years, we have been working with pre-service teachers in the English-speaking higher education institutions, in rural, suburban, and urban settings in the Canadian province of Quebec, and, to King's observation, we will add that most of them are, to one degree or another, either observant or secular self-described Christians. They find comfort in their beliefs, values, and customs and, for the most part, see them as a universal viewpoint that others need to be exposed to, taught, and to learn. Reproducing this as a norm in teaching may be conscious and unconscious, but, far more often, in our experience, it is carried out in a dysconscious manner. For Christopher, as a "half and half" (O'Hearn, 1998) immigrant of Iranian-European (Italian-English) descent from a Muslim, Christian and Jewish background, the reality that North American schools reproduce dominant white norms and privileges was a lived experience. For Melanie, as a multi-generation Canadian, from a white, Christian background, the effects of such schooling would only be truly felt when she had multi-cultured children of her own.

Let us be clear: none of our three wonderful children shares the visible "othering" features of their father. Besides comments on how easily they tan, very few North Americans would consider them anything but white. A common joke in our family is that, beneath Christopher's looks, let's say orange on the scale of Homeland Security's terror alert coding, there is a large recessive gene pool. When Christopher wheeled our first child into Melanie's hospital room twelve hours after she was born, we had to check her wristband ID as she opened up her big, beautiful, crystal blue eyes, to make sure he had not taken the wrong child from the nursery. Hand-in-hand walks through shopping malls for Christopher and our children have been mercifully uneventful, as they have never thrown temper tantrums in public spaces, although Christopher secretly worried that the children would discover their "ace-in-the-hole" leverage: thankfully, scenarios of one of the children matter-of-factly stating, "Dad, if you don't want me to wig-out and have Security arrest you for kidnapping, I suggest you buy me this "super-pony-rainbow-airport-funland set" never materialized. Suffice it to say that most teachers, based on visual perceptions, have inaccurately assessed their heritage.

What has received little research or writing in education are the experiences of children of multi-racial/ethnic/religious families in North American schools, how those who work in the field perceive them, and the consequences of those perceptions. For our three children, like many other children in North America, navigating through the public school system has had its ups and downs, but it has been profoundly negative when it comes to the "miseducation of the West" (Kincheloe and Steinberg, 2004) about the Middle East and Islam, as they must silently compare what they are being "taught" about that part of their family. Far too often, what they *know* about their own heritage and people, (the love, kindness, intelligence, and humour, in essence, the humanity), are perspectives that are not accepted in our schools (Stonebanks, 2008). Our children have attended multiple schools and, to be sure, they have had outstanding teachers to whom we are forever grateful. But, we cannot deny that we have, on a number of occasions, pulled our children from schools because of the discriminatory actions, either conscious or dysconcious, of teachers and administrators. (We are very understanding of unconscious actions because naming and examining them can provide opportunities for everyone to grow professionally.) The example we provide, of the prevalent Operation Christmas Child, is one of too many and is forwarded because, if you have been involved in North American schools as a student, teacher, or pre-service teacher, it likely has been a part of your experience, as it was with ours.

Truth be told, for the both of us, our initial introduction to the Operation Christmas Child shoebox campaign was a gentle one. A new, young teacher who brought the project into her classroom as a charity activity for her students made Christopher aware of it. His initial reaction was to smile. He thought that it seemed like a nice exchange between children who may perhaps be of different faiths. It seemed a simple lesson on giving, sharing, and charity; how could anything be wrong with it? For Melanie, it was an activity that her own mother and her daughter participated in together, Grandmother and granddaughter filling a box with of age-appropriate toys and school supplies for needy children in another part of the world. It was a sharing time, and it generated a feeling of goodwill. What a wonderful intergenerational endeavour, or so we believed.

We thought nothing more of this charitable activity until a few years later when our two oldest children were in elementary school. One afternoon during the drive home, our son, answering the daily question, "How was school today? What did you do?" mentioned that everyone had gone to the gym to watch a movie. They had been somewhat confused by the nature of the film but came away with the message that they were to fill two shoeboxes up with gifts because Jesus had told them this is what they should do. As the conversation continued at home that evening, it slowly began to dawn on us that there was more to this charitable activity than met the eye.

The next day at school, Christopher questioned one of the teachers, asking if there had been a mix-up as our children had clearly been registered to receive non-religious education. We felt that this was a responsibility of the home and not the school, especially given the proselytizing nature of the religious education that was still being taught. The teacher replied that the decision had been made for all the children to watch the Operation Christmas Child promotional film since it would not cause any "harm" for any of them to see it. In essence, it was promoted as a cultural exchange. But the idea of showing a video that clearly contained a proselytizing message to a captive audience could do no harm was perceived by Christopher as a bizarre consideration. After all, no one, we were told, was being forced to participate after they saw the video.

One year later, there was a discussion in one of Christopher's university classes in which his students were trying to understand the disconnect between what they were learning about respect for diversity in their studies and what was actually occurring in classrooms. They wondered why, in academia, our schools were being presented as locations of secular education when the actual daily life in schools was suffused with an underlying Christian view of the world. Christopher urged them to provide an example of what they had witnessed, and Operation Christmas Child was brought up as case in point. Christopher's response, based on his superficial understanding of the program, was that the concept of sharing between cultures should not be immediately seen as negative because of its association with religion. One student then raised his hand and said, "I don't think you really understand what Operation Christmas Child does," to which Christopher responded in a spirit of ignorant bliss, "I don't think I want to." The student recounted his own research of the organization and explained that its mission was to use its generous action as a tool for religious conversion.

> Since 1993, this Samaritan's Purse project has shared the Good News of God's love with hurting children through the simplest of gifts—shoe boxes! Filled with school supplies, toys, and personal items that are packed by caring people, these boxes help introduce children to Jesus Christ. Local believers follow up with evangelistic programs, and many precious boys and girls later receive Jesus as their Saviour. (Graham, www.samaritanspurse.org)

On the Samaritan's Purse Web site, Operation Christmas Child traces its roots to a couple who watched a television broadcast about Romanian orphanages and felt the need to do something to help. They organized a convoy of trucks carrying supplies and gifts for the children, and this marked the beginning of the world's largest children's Christmas program. A few years later, in 1993, Franklin Graham, the son of the well-known evangelical minister Billy Graham and international president of Samaritan's Purse, took over this budding charitable endeavour. In the past fifteen years, this outreach program has collected fifty-four million shoeboxes internationally from eleven countries and distributed the gifts to children in 125 countries worldwide (Hamilton-McCharles, 2007). Although the organization's endeavours have been uncritically reviewed by local experts in Quebec, it has received more vigorous scrutiny from professionals abroad. Reverend Fraser, vicar of Putney and lecturer in philosophy at Wadham College, Oxford remarks in his article "The Evangelicals Who Like to Giftwrap Islamophobia" (2003) that "Ironically, it is the story of the good Samaritan that provides one of the most effective put-downs to precisely the sort of Islamophobia displayed by Christian fundamentalists such as Graham." He notes that the simplistic conclusion that is typically drawn from the story is that "we must help those in need." However, he argues, this interpretation completely misses its quite radical point.

> A man is mugged in the Wadi Qelt between Jerusalem and Jericho. Whereas the religious pass by and do nothing, it is the Samaritan who offers care. Those listening to the story would have despised Samaritans. The words "good" and "Samaritan" just didn't go together. Indeed, theirs would have been the General Boykin reaction: that Samaritans worshipped the idol of a false god. Therefore, in casting the Samaritan as the only passer-by with compassion, Jesus is making an all-out assault on the prejudices of his listeners. (. . .) The story of the good Samaritan, in the hands of Franklin Graham, is conscripted as propa-

ganda for the superiority of Christian compassion to the brutal indifference of other religions—almost the opposite of the purpose of the story. (. . .) The truth is quite the reverse. (Fraser, 2003)

Fraser's assessment of the organization's hidden agenda is quite clear, so maybe you are wondering where our concern lies with this, as Melanie puts it, seemingly benevolent charity. It is not with the distributing of gifts to children at Christmastime, nor even with the fact that religious literature is handed out with the shoeboxes. Although we must express that we are disturbed with the statement of religious and spiritual inferiority and demonization that has been made time and again by Franklin Graham and is, thereby, condoned by his organization, we are, however, committed to the right of every person to practice their religion. We have friends and colleagues who are evangelical and wish for us prayers of good fortune and health. We know they do so with an open heart, and we accept them with an open heart as well. Likewise, as adults, we understand the calling and truly appreciate the sentiment of those who clearly see their path as right and who *know* they need to share that message of eternal salvation with us. In their personal lives and places of worship, we offer them nothing but the best of wishes for their endeavours through Operation Christmas Child and their desire to spread their religious vision, just as we have no issue with any other religions or worldviews that want to "educate" others on their beliefs and/or perspectives. Where our issue lies is that this program has found its way into our public school system, and administrators, teachers, and the young children themselves are now acting, whether consciously or not, as missionaries, in effect promoting a religious view of the world that has on more than one occasion denounced those who hold beliefs that differ from their own.

(F)rom the refugee camps we traveled to the subcontinent of India, with its hundreds of millions of people locked in the darkness of Hinduism. . .These people were bound by Satan's power. (Graham, 1997, pp. 138–139)

Graham is also noted to have ". . . caused controversy in the US by branding Islam 'wicked, violent and not of the same god' " (McCurry, 2002). Now let's be very clear on this point, because it has been our experience that in these contexts, misinterpretation often occurs. Although we feel Graham's statements are hateful, if this charity event were being organized in the realm of the evangelical church, whether in a place of worship or a private home, we would not feel compelled to write about it so ardently. However, when a program of this nature is promoted with such resolve in so many public elementary and secondary schools, then we are ethically and morally bound to speak up and try to bring about an awareness of what our legal and professional responsibilities are to the children who have been put in our care.

This is not to say that teachers do not speak out against inappropriate programs that are brought into their school. Pre-service teachers in particular have, on the whole, a strong sense of "social justice" and what should or should not be taught in our schools. However, most have spent very little time considering their own subjectivity concerning these ideas, since teaching tends to attract members of the dominant white, Christian group (King, 2000; Stonebanks, 2008; Meiners, 2002; Cavanagh and Harper, 1994) who are accustomed to their perspectives being the norm. As an example, Christopher provides this "professional dilemma" to his pre-service teachers in his Ethics and Religious Culture class:

You are a principal at a large public elementary school in urban Quebec. The population of the school is approximately 600, and has a significant Muslim and Hindu student body. A teacher comes to you and says that she would like to bring in a charity project called "Eid Bag," which would celebrate the end of Ramadan by giving donations of toys to underprivileged children in South America. In the program, children are given bags and asked to fill them with a 'peaceful' toy, and a suggestion is made that if they also donate $10, the monetary contribution will assist in the costs associated with delivery. The teacher notes that Ramadan is meant to be a time of giving to the less fortunate, and this would be a great opportunity for all the children in the school to participate in a charitable cause. The project gains support in the community and for a number of years, the school receives praise from the local newspaper and school board for its spirit of giving. However, a problem occurs when a parent contacts you with information on "Eid Bag," and she provides information that you had never seen. According to multiple reliable sources including the project's own Web page, a Koran is placed either in or along with each of the bags before it is shipped to children. Moreover, the Eid Bag website explicitly states that the true purpose of giving children these toys is to convert them to Islam. To further compound the issue, the religious leader of Eid Bag has openly made statements that are anti-Semitic, said that aboriginal religious beliefs were evil, and referred to Christians as misguided and lost. The parent herself is Jewish and says she is very upset that such a program is allowed in a public school. She demands to know what process had been implemented within the school that ensures accountability, and what possible effect could come to her children if the school administration and staff support a program that asserts anti-Semitic sentiments. What do you do?

The same dilemma can apply to the multiple groups that are separated in the class and can center on a "Humanist Bag," a "Diwali Bag," or similar others, and are designed to play upon the preconceived ideas and stereotypes that pre-service teachers may bring with them into their education. Whatever the scenario, responses from pre-service teachers are pretty much absolute: the program would be removed from the school, apologies should be made to the parent, and greater measures should be taken to ensure it never happens again. Arguments are also forwarded that public schools should not support a program that clearly does not respect other religions and that the religious leader running the program is engaging in "hate speech." *Accountability, in these contexts, becomes unquestionable.* They see such clarity in these moral dilemmas, have such a strong sense of right and wrong. When the Operation Christmas Child shoebox is then brought out after the first decisions are voiced and the scenario brought forward with the real-world "players" revealed, the responses become confused, absolutes become fuzzy, and what a moment earlier should undeniably be banned, suddenly becomes something worth discussing. *Accountability is superseded by familiarity.* Very few in the field, and we use that term in a purposefully broad way, ever see any real problem with the idea that a teacher, or teachers, would bring into the school a program whose leader says that people who follow specific religions are "wicked," "violent," "bound by Satan's power," in essence, evil. As parents with relatives who are members of these religions targeted by Graham, can or should we, really be expected to believe that a teacher who knowingly brings this into her school will treat our child equitably?

> Schools supporting this massive fund-raising effort for a particular Christian evangelical ministry are failing in their responsibility to respect the dignity of all of their students. I cannot imagine any other religious groups being given permission to enter schools and channel our children's enthusiasm and money to promote their specific beliefs in this manner. . .I strongly encourage school councils—and school boards—to show strong ethical leadership on this issue by taking action to protect the students entrusted to them. Being provided with more complete information on the shoe box program will no doubt lead many parents and teachers to select other, more appropriate charitable activities for their children. (Lund, 1999)

From our experience as educators who grew up in the predominantly white Christian suburbs of Montreal, we know that some responses from teachers will be that Lund's example speaks only to a textbook multicultural context: an inner-city class somewhere else, filled with visible minorities that really only exist in a Hollywood studio with a Michelle Pfeiffer–type actor taking the role of the teacher who brings civility to the uncivilized. This perspective ignores so much of what teacher obligations are in a multi-cultural country such as Canada and sets teaching apart from other "true" professions that function under universal oaths. It should be noted here that Darren Lund, associate professor in the Faculty of Education at the University of Calgary, has made a substantial contribution in fostering professional awareness in this area through his research activities that examine social justice activism in schools and communities. He has pursued issues related to equity and human rights regardless of the backlash he has endured.

Both authors have taken a route in our university teaching that at times has brought about a great deal of anger from our young students and would indeed do the same for veteran teachers already in the field. In our first-year class, Introduction to Teaching, we give our pre-service teachers an article by Jon Bradley entitled, "Some Random Thoughts on Ethical Behavior of Teacher Candidates. Report from the Field" (1998), which clearly affirms that teaching is not a "true" profession and asserts that until teachers adopt a public and accountable ethical regime for their actions, the vocation will continue to be a quasi-profession. Schools and staffs that allow such learning, in opposition to the acceptance of diversity and multi-culturalism into their classrooms, with open arms or an uncritical eye and defend their actions as being educationally sound, are guilty of maintaining this viewpoint. We offer the challenge for proponents (tacit or explicit) of this type of programming, with the idea that a publicly funded school should, in any way, support an organization that is clearly promoting one religion over another, to stand up in a public forum such as the American Educational Research Association and professionally justify what they are exposing their students to. Until such time as they prove that what they are teaching is within the pedagogical framework laid down by our profession and not simply something they believe is "the right thing to do," then they have no professional leg to stand on. We are open to the possibility that we are, within a pedagogical context, wrong. Just as accepted laws existed that sanctioned residential schooling and segregation, our reference to professional stances can be proven wrong by those who believe that programs which place one religion above all others in a public school setting is desirable. Simply put, this dialogue needs to take place in a professional forum—not on the radio, on television, nor in an environment where the "show" is often more important than content.

If charity is truly a necessary component of the school curriculum and not, as Franklin Graham believes and clearly states on his Web site, "a tool for evangelism," then we urge pre-service teachers, teachers, and their students to move away from the prescriptive and engage in the challenge of research. As Kincheloe notes, teachers and their students must join the culture of research if a new level of educational rigor, quality, and professionalism is ever to be achieved (2003, p. 18).

> When teachers put Freire's methods to work in their own classrooms, they teach students the research techniques they have learned. . .to engage students in meta-analytical epistemological analysis (. . .) Developing students as researchers is a pedagogical process where students and teachers work together in the activity known as learning. (Kincheloe and Steinberg, 1998, pp. 16–17)

Like Kincheloe (2003), we have been fortunate throughout our careers to come in contact with some brilliant teachers and pre-service teachers who take it upon themselves to set an example—of lifelong learners, positive and dynamic role models of reflection and independent research that students so desperately need. These are the real educators, who are not resigned to merely reading from a script that was written in the backroom of some publishing house, content to play the part of "blue collar workers, passive recipients of the dictates of the experts" (p. 2). Moreover, they are not the kinds of teachers who passively accept programs in their schools without any kind of accountability or investigation, or who, when exposed to the problematic, simply ignore it.

The following is an excerpt from an e-mail sent to us by a young teacher who is determined to beat out her own path as she navigates the often-bumpy road of teacher researcher. Her storyline goes like this: For the past four years, this keen and globally conscientious student has been participating in the Operation Christmas Child campaign organized by a "Christian group" at her university. She had been led to believe that her charitable donation was making a small difference in a child's life with, as the Pursestring's Web site puts it, no strings attached. As she became aware that there was a possibility she had been misled, she took it upon herself to look more closely into the organization she had been supporting. Further research lead to more questions that she wanted answered, so she met with the Christian club's representative, confident, as she put it, that she or he would be as shocked by her findings as she was:

> I began my meeting with [representative] by expressing my concern about the organization's goals. I informed [him/her] that I had been unaware that for the past 4 years, my shoebox had been tampered with—reopened and stuffed with Christian propaganda in the hope of converting needy children to the Christian faith. I hoped that [s/he] was perhaps unaware of this and expected that [s/he] would be as shocked by this as I was. To my surprise, the situation was quite the opposite. [S/he] was utterly indifferent to the fact that I had been lied to by a member of [her/his] organization. [S/he] then told me that [s/he] thought it was quite obvious that the purpose of OCC was to spread the message of Jesus Christ and that it should come as no surprise that bibles were packaged along with the toys that were sent to children all over the world. I asked why [s/he] would not explicitly state this to begin with. . . because my friends that also had been involved in this project also felt they had been misled. [S/he] continued, explaining that [s/he] thought it was fairly obvious that a mission led by Franklin Graham was a religious one and that the University students that were involved were probably aware that the goal was to touch the lives of children around the world with the love of Jesus Christ. I then asked if [s/he] would not mind putting up a small sign then at [her/his] table saying something along the lines of "Your shoebox will be opened before a child receives it and a Bible along with Christian children's literature will be placed in it." [S/he] did not think this was necessary and added; "I think that if we did that, less people would be inclined to give to the organization." [S/he] admitted that if the students at our university knew of the purpose behind the project they would not want to be involved. Essentially, it was beneficial to [her/him] to conceal the truth.

The frustration felt by this astute and diligent student did not end there. She did what any responsible person would do. She took her concerns to a higher level of authority confident that in their positions of power they would be able to assist her:

> It was quite the awakening for me. I talked to [a religious leader] at our University who was well aware of the organization and although [s/he] did not agree with their policies, [s/he] did not want to cause any trouble. Talking to some of the Education students about all of this, I was surprised by the apathy I encountered. No one seemed to mind that we had an organization on campus that was supporting a man with such despicable views.

It saddens us to read and write about the ambivalence of so many people who have been made aware that this type of program's discriminatory agenda is being championed in our schools. Why do so many educational leaders and teachers feel the need to support and defend this charitable activity? As Reverend Fraser (2003) so plainly explains, "There is, of course, a huge emotional hit in wrapping up a shoebox for a Christmas child." He continues on though to offer some well-needed advice, "But if we are to teach our children properly about giving, we must wean them off the feel-good factor. . .We must get over our fondness for charity and develop a thirst for justice."

Adding insult to injury in our personal experiences, it was not the school, in the professional sense, that was able to come forward and question the ulterior motives of a program that were unsuitable for a public institution. Rather, it was the support of community parents, who were able to look at this organization with a more critical eye than the educators, which led to its removal from the school. It is embarrassing for someone who is part of the profession to recount this, just as it would be for a doctor or a lawyer to have a layperson point out something that a group from their own field didn't even see.

It is crucial for the reader to understand that we do not put this problem out there without trying to find a solution ourselves. If charity, sustainability, and justice are elements that you feel has a place in your curriculum, as we feel it does in ours, then a program needs to be planned that puts students and teachers together to discover what these ideals mean to all the participants and how it can then be implemented in an authentic and meaningful way. Melanie has attempted at various times to help her students raise funds for a cause that they felt was worthy.

In 2003, Melanie worked with an energetic group of eleven- and twelve-year-olds at a dynamic multicultural inner-city school. On returning from the Christmas break (the December break in this school board is formally referred to in this manner), the classroom was filled with discussions on the earthquake that had struck Bam, Iran on December 26th, killing more than 30,000 people and injuring 30,000 as well. The children were gravely concerned with the news that seventy percent of the city had been destroyed, and so many people were in need of help and were suffering. Melanie asked her students what they wanted to do, as she knew her students to be caring and compassionate, as most youngsters are. Together, teacher and students began researching what had occurred, where there was need, and how they could go about offering some form of relief. Her student researchers worked diligently at school and on their own time. Dialogue ensued over whether donations should meet short-term needs or enable long-term sustainability. The students decided, after careful consideration and much more dialogue, that they would raise money for the organization, "Doctors Without Borders." The class held a school-wide penny drive and bake sale and raised $450 for this aid organization. In the end, the program that the school supported was decided on by the students, but the responsibility for the choice made in her classroom rested squarely on the teacher's shoulders, meaning that if a parent or a peer had come forward with information, questions, or concerns, Melanie would have been accountable to them for her actions.

Why have we written this chapter? What are we hoping to gain? Is it to put an end to schools' participating in charity events that assist others? Of course not. Is it to denounce the teaching of religious culture to our students? Most certainly the answer is no. What we are hoping to change is how teachers view themselves and their role in our schools. When our family's educational dilemma began, we received a realistic caution from a colleague who expressed that, in the end, if any change took place that Christopher, given his heritage, would be the one blamed—in an "O'Reilly Factor" war on Christmas kind of way—despite our repeated statement that our questions had nothing to do with schools celebrating the Christmas holiday and everything to do with a public institution promoting one religion as superior to others. It was a warning that was brought up at a local level and ignored by most, save by one higher-level school board administrator. At the end of this year's semester, a pre-service teacher stopped by Christopher's office and, based on a school's staffroom "buzz," asked if he was the professor being vilified for trying to ban Christmas from the schools. Sad but true, this is indeed the risk of taking the road less traveled.

References

Bartholomew, R. (2006, November 1). [Weblog] Samaritan's Purse Controversy in UK Parliament. Bartholomew's Notes on Religion. Retrieved May 26, 2008 from http://blogs.salon.com/0003494/2006/11/01.html

Bradley, Jon G. (1998). "Some Random Thoughts on Ethical Behavior of Teacher Candidates: Report from the Field." *McGill Journal of Education* 33 (2), pp. 299–324.

Cavanagh, Sheila and Harper, Helen. (1994). "Lady Bountiful: The White Woman Teacher in Multicultural Education." *Women's Education/Des Femmes* 11 (2), pp. 27–33.

Fraser, Giles. (2003, November 10). "The Evangelicals Who Like to Giftwrap Islamophobia." *Guardian*. Retrieved May 1, 2008 from http://www.guardian.co.uk/world/2003/nov/10/religion.society

Graham, Franklin. (1997). *Rebel with a Cause*. Nashville, TN: Thomas Nelson.

Hamilton-McCharles, Jennifer. (2007, November 8), "Board Pulls Out of Program (Operation Christmas Child); Organizers Try to Understand Reasoning." *North Bay Nugget*. Retrieved May 1, 2008 from http://www.freerepublic.com/focus/f-news/1923050/posts

Judge, Mike (Director). (1999). *Office Space*. [Film]. USA: Twentieth Century Fox.

Kincheloe, Joe L. (2003). *Teachers as Researchers: Qualitative Inquiry as a Path to Empowerment*. London: RoutledgeFalmer.

Kincheloe, Joe L. and Steinberg, Shirley R. (1998). *Students as Researchers: Creating Classrooms That Matter*. London: RoutledgeFalmer.

———. (2004). *The Miseducation of the West: How Schools and Media Distort Our Understanding of the Islamic World*. Westport, CT: Praeger.

King, J. E. (1991). "Dysconscious Racism: Ideology, Identity, and the Miseducation of Teachers." *Journal of Negro Education* 60 (2, Spring), pp. 133–46.

———. (2000). "White Teachers at the Crossroads." Teaching Tolerance. [www document] Retrieved May 11, 2008 from http://www.tolerance.org/teach/printar.jsp?p=0&ar=174&pi=ttm

Lund, Darren. (1999, November 10) "Samaritan's Purse Should Be More Open about Mission." *Calgary Herald*. Retrieved May 1, 2008 from http://www.pursestrings.ca/strings.htm

McCurry, Patrick. (2002, December 18). "Presents Imperfect." *Guardian*. Retrieved May 1, 2008 from http://society.guardian.co.uk/societyguardian/story/0,861580,00.html

Meiners, E. R. (2002). "Disengaging from the Legacy of Lady Bountiful in Teacher Education Classrooms." *Gender and Education* 14 (1), pp. 85–94.

O'Hearn, C. C. (1998). Half and Half: Writers on Growing up Biracial and Bicultural. New York: Pantheon.

Ministère de l'Éducation, du Loisir et du Sport (2007). "Ethics and Religious Culture; Programme de formation de l'école québécoise : Éducation préscolaire, enseignement primaire," Québec, Gouvernement du Québec.

Stonebanks, Christopher D. (2008). "An Islamic Perspective on Knowledge, Knowing and Methodology." In *Handbook of Critical and Indigenous Methodologies* ed. Denzin, N., Lincoln, Y., and Smith, L. Thousand Oaks, CA: Sage.

"What Is Operation Christmas Child?" (2008) Samaritan's Purse. Retrieved May 1, 2008 from http://www.samaritanspurse.org/OCC_About.asp

Twenty One

Kill Santa
Religious Diversity and the Winter Holiday Problem

Özlem Sensoy

We listen to music, we drink alcoholic beverages in public or private places, we dance and at the end of every year we decorate a tree with balls and tinsel and some lights. This is normally called "Christmas Decorations" or also "Christmas Tree" letting us rejoice in the notion of our national heritage and not necessarily a religious holiday. . .

For the last few years to draw away from religious influences or orientation no "prayer room" is made available for prayer or any other form of incantation. Moreover, in many of our schools no prayer is allowed. We teach more science and less religion.

—Municipality of Hérouxville, Quebec, Canada
Standards, 2007[1]

Introduction

Hérouxville is a small village in the province of Quebec in Canada. Founded in 1904, its population is just under 1400 residents, virtually all of whom are French-speaking, White, and Catholic. By most accounts, no immigrants, people of color, Jews, Sikhs, Muslims, or persons of Indigenous heritage live in Hérouxville. So why might a town that is likely to be near the bottom of any immigrant family's "move-to" wish list be relevant to a discussion of Santa, religious diversity, and the winter holiday problem of schools?

In this chapter I explore the interrelated sets of issues concerning discrimination, oppression, and privilege and the ways in which these issues become manifest when we seek "solutions" to the "problems" of religion in schools, religious celebrations, and holy days. I would like to argue that rather than a being a fringe "jittery bunch" (*Toronto Star*, editorial, 2000), the town council and folk who wrote, supported, published, and distributed the town's standards illustrate a widespread confusion about social issues—and social oppression. How the "Christmas problem" and its solution are conceptualized in most school settings and in broader societal conversations about religion and religious accommodation is rooted in a miseducation about how oppression operates. Hérouxville is emblematic of broad common-sense confusion about two key concepts in equity studies: oppression and privilege. Understanding how social oppression and privilege operate is extremely liberating for at least three reasons: first, it removes the burden of having to identify "bad" people or deeds (such as those who impose their religion on us or who impose their standards on everyone). Second, since the problem is no longer a hunt for bad people or deeds, one gets a new sense of how the winter holiday problem could be conceptualized. And third, having conceptualized it differently, new avenues for addressing the problem can emerge.

In the Beginning

God rest you merry gentlemen let nothing you dismay;
For Jesus Christ, our Saviour was born on Christmas day;
To save us all from Satan's power
When we were gone astray;
—"God Rest You Merry Gentlemen," traditional fifteenth-century English carol

My time as a public school student in the province of British Columbia on the west coast of Canada was not that long ago: I graduated from high school in 1990. Since that time, I have often wondered about the winter holiday problem, where it is located, for whom it is a problem, and what a solution to this problem might look like.

I remember a consistent pattern of activities in the classroom routine between the end of Halloween and the end of the Gregorian calendar year. Hallways decorated with tinsel, rows of construction-paper reindeer, and strumming "Jingle Bell Rock" during music class were accompanied by a media culture that every year had me watching such regimented classics as *White Christmas* (1954) and *The Sound of Music* (1965). The year would conclude with a Christmas pageant during which Heather Goldstein and I lip-synced our way through *God Rest Ye Merry Gentlemen.*

But surely the landscape of winter these days is different. Heather and I were the only kids in my class who did not spend December 24th wondering what goodies a jolly, fat, White man would bring the next morning. Today, with the heightened sensitivity (or a discourse about a heightened sensitivity) to religious diversity in classrooms, December must surely look different.

In my current role as professor of social education, many of my students are involved in schooling, most are K–12 classroom teachers or student teachers. I was confident that Christmas activities in Vancouver—a city where a high percentage of immigrant and other minoritized communities live[2]—would play out differently. So I recently asked my students to reflect on the previous December in their schools and to make a list of all the December activities they had seen in the school. Here's a selection from their lists of goings-on in elementary and secondary schools throughout the lower mainland of Vancouver:

There were activities around dress:

- The staff often dress in red and green.
- Female staff members wear Christmas earrings that look like wreaths.
- Reindeer horns (antlers); many teachers wear these on their heads.

There were activities related to decorating the school:

- Decorations—kindergarten—little Santa Clauses made of cotton balls were put on the walls.
- The classrooms and bulletin boards in the hallways were decorated with garlands and other Christmas-related decorations.
- There was a decorated Christmas tree in the main office, with big presents underneath it.
- The head of PAC (Parent Advisory Council) put a tree in the front hallway and decorated it.

There were activities involving food:

- Lots of Christmas cookies and chocolate kisses in the main office.
- In the home economics class all the lessons revolve around Christmas, like baking Christmas cookies.
- The cafeteria sells Christmas-themed foods, with names like "Rudolph dumplings" for brownies.
- Santa giving out candy canes at lunch and staff run a Christmas breakfast.

There were charity activities, mostly revolving around food banks:

- There was a food bank in the main office and food drives in each class, with competition for which class can collect the most food.
- Our yearly hampers are given during Christmas time to families that are in need. Typically the hampers contain, food, presents, and basic staples such as toothbrushes, toothpaste, etc.
- A World Vision fundraiser.

There were other celebratory contests and activities:

- Contests for which class had the best Christmas-decorated classroom or door.
- Christmas parties in classrooms, each student brings one dish and there's a potluck.
- Advertisements on bulletin boards informing people of the annual Christmas dance (junior high and high school) at which punch and other Christmas treats are served.
- PA system announcements, often including a countdown, for example, "sixteen days left until Christmas" or announcing Christmas-related events in the school.
- Christmas music began playing in the front hallway each morning (I think this began two weeks before the official kickoff to school holidays).
- Snowman-building contest.
- Some classes had gift exchanges.
- PAC opened a store for kids to buy presents for their families and friends. This store was open during school hours and classes could come down and browse as well as purchase gifts and after school.

Then, there was "the concert":

- A sing-a-long where the whole school sang Christmas songs. The song words were even on an overhead for those of us who didn't know the words.
- We had a winter assembly where students showcased their talents and some classes did presentations. Parents were welcome to attend. We had students playing the piano, drums, singing Christmas favorites. At the end, the staff does a spoof on an old Christmas jingle, and everyone gets a kick out of seeing the teachers make fools of themselves.
- Our Christmas event is the winter assembly where students perform, a talent show of sorts. Teachers may choose to do something with their class and present. Christmas is a theme but is not the only theme presented
- A hoedown in the gym; Christmas assembly/concert (drama, live music, videos, speeches).
- We did *Deck the Halls*, a primary winter concert, and a primary and an intermediate carol sing-a-long.
- We alternate, doing a winter concert or a spring concert on alternate years.
- The multicultural club organized a lot of events starting in November, including Diwali and Eid celebrations. The yearbook and student council organized Breakfast with Santa, Hollywood Scene, and the Snowflake Ball, a school dance.

Does any of this sound familiar?

While many of my students highlighted that their schools tended to avoid the word "Christmas," the curriculum, activities, celebrations, food, clothing, and walls remained saturated with Christmas. What this reveals is not heightened *diversity* characterized by a high degree of non-Christian "others" but rather the *endurance* of mainstream normative values. Yet there is increasing grumbling that we ("p.c." multiculturalists) want to kill Santa. After all, as conservative media commentator John Gibson (2005) argues, there is an all-out war against Christians and Christmas: "In schools, any appearance of Christianity is treated like a hazmat crisis" (p. xxiv). We must be careful not to write off Gibson or the town councilors of Hérouxville and take both their claims and the well-meaning folks who try to be inclusive by coding Christmas festivities as a "winter assembly" seriously. There is a deep miseducation about two interrelated concepts that, when clearly understood, can facilitate a clearer—and I believe a different—understanding of the winter holiday "problem" and potentially reveal some new and useful ideas for responding to it.

Understanding Institutionalized Oppression and Privilege

In equity studies, we conceptualize social issues, or *-isms* (racism, classism, and sexism), to be different from discrimination. *Discrimination* refers to the preferential treatment of one/some over another/others, while *-isms* refer to a set of historically based, institutionalized systems of power. Anyone can discriminate. I make discriminatory decisions all the time, such as whether I want Indian or Japanese cuisine for lunch, whether I will buy local organic foods or exotic fare from far-away places, or whether I will choose to read only my native-language newspaper or join a women-only gym. But oppression (or -isms) refers to discrimination *plus* social power. It is a concept that captures the unearned privileges some groups have at the expense of others.

Let me illustrate with an example I often use with students:

Are you left-handed? If so, you may notice the myriad, pervasive ways in which our group (since I am left-handed too) is marginalized in society: classroom desks set up for right-handed people, the shape of scissors, the location of the buttons on carry-on luggage handles, and even the standard way one is taught to strum a guitar. You may never have noticed these things, and perhaps they don't seem too significant to you (even if you are left-handed). It may even be the case that left-handed people discriminately prefer to use "regular" tools, have always just gotten used to doing things the "backwards" way, and so on. And perhaps there are some right-handed folks who, just for fun, like to use left-handed tools just to see how it feels to be a lefty for a while. However, this is always an outcome of choice, for they can always *choose* to go back to being normal and comfortable after they try out the novel new toys.

While both groups can discriminate, have preferences, and may vary in the degree to which they may or may not take offense and demand correction of perceived injustices, it is still the case that only right-handed people benefit—or have unearned *privilege*—just because they were born right-handed into a social world designed with right-handedness as normal. It wouldn't be difficult to see the ways in which some loud and perhaps even radical lefties (and perhaps some guilt-ridden righties) got together to demand all sorts of special accommodations for lefties: special scissors, knives, can openers, perhaps the re-organizing of orchestral seating arrangement. These radical lefties and guilty-righties always seem to be asking for something "special," and the list never seems to end.

Moving on from left-handedness to consider a case with obviously higher stakes, consider how *ableism* operates. As persons who fit a fluid category of "normal" able-bodied-ness, we can go through entire days, weeks, and even months never having to consider the limits of our ability to physically access any social environment. Whether I can get to a certain event, the transportation I'll use to get there, that coffee shop I'll eat in, or when I arrive at my destination, my ability to use the facilities with ease, etc., does not depend on anything but my will to proceed. I could discriminate and choose not to go to locations that do not have proper access for all. But this would be a function of my *choice*, where as for a person with a physical disability, it becomes a limit on their choices. This does not mean that able-bodied folks intend to oppress people with disabilities. Rather, it means the social environment was set up to accommodate us as normal, giving us social privilege, protecting us from ever having to think about life without such "rights."

"But," you may protest, "there are more right-handed than left-handed people, or people *without* disabilities than people *with* disabilities. Obviously we should accommodate the majority." While it is true that biological variance exists among humans, the social rules built around those differences taken to matter are humanly constructed. For example, if you wear glasses, consider where on the spectrum your weak vision moves from being a physical biological reality to being a socially determined disability with particular constraints, restrictions, rules, and beliefs associated with it. Sometimes the privileged groups (men, Whites, the able-bodied) *are* the majority, but this is not the key criterion. For example, women are the majority of the world, as are the poor and working people, and Blacks were the majority under apartheid in South Africa. The key criterion is social power. Thus while biological differences exist, societal rules and structures were socially created by some and imposed upon all, and these past decisions made by those in power (whether the numerical majority or not) have resulted in an accumulation of power, wealth, and social privilege for some at the expense of others.

Discrimination fails to address the issue of social power. Were we to account for power, we would see that there is no such thing as reverse-sexism, or reverse-racism, or any reverse -ism, because -isms are not about individual acts of discrimination. Rather, -isms are about historically-based institutionalized power (the power to make that which is particular to you seem to be what's "normal" for everyone), and institutionalized privilege (to benefit from that "normal" because you happen to belong to the group). Thus returning to a previous example, despite women's numerical majority over men, or any discriminatory feelings they may have held and acted upon, women did not have the social power to grant themselves the right to vote. Only men could actually grant suffrage to women because they held the institutional power to do so.

We are each deeply embedded in social environments (schools, media, the drugstore, toy store, etc.) that teach us about the "normal" expectations, behaviors, and values of members of the dominant social group. Those who have the power to establish what those expectations are, have "privilege." You don't have to *want* privilege to benefit, just as you don't have to *intend* to offend in order to cause offense. Consider how the able-bodied person does not have to intend to oppress those who have different bodies, in order to be a beneficiary of socially constructed privilege. Rather, the closer your values, ideas, language, faith, and body are to what is "normal" in a society, the more privilege you have.

Richard Dyer (1997) writes, "there is no more powerful position than that of being 'just' human" (p. 2), and Michael Kimmel (2003) describes it this way, "To be white, or male, or straight, or middle class is to be simultaneously ubiquitous and invisible. You are everywhere you look, you're the standard against which everyone else is measured" (p. 3). There is something profoundly "normal" in the deployment of social power. Whiteness in mainstream Eurocentric society—this means those who are White, male, and Christian—has the highest degree of privilege and power. This power has now been threatened; it is the war that Gibson (2005) warns about and the councilors of Hérouxville fear. Kincheloe (2006) describes these culture wars as "efforts to 'recover' white supremacy, patriarchy, class privilege, heterosexual 'normality,' Christian dominance, and the European intellectual canon" (p. 221).

Understanding Christian Privilege

Just as the able-bodied are the only recipients of privilege in ableism, men the only recipients of privilege in sexism, and Whites the only recipients of privilege in racism, Christians are the only beneficiaries of privilege in the religious oppression paradigm. Schlosser (2003) defines Christians as those who "believe in (a) Jesus Christ as their Lord and Savior and (b) the teaching of the Old and New Testaments (e.g., belief in the Holy Trinity and the resurrection of Christ)" (p. 45). The largest groups to fall into the category of Christian include Catholics, Protestants and other smaller denominations. Groups that experience oppression on religious grounds include those who practice Buddhism, Hinduism, Judaism, and Islam (Schlosser, 2003). Historically there has been a very close link between Whiteness (not necessarily "Caucasian"-ness) and Christianity. Brodkin-Sachs (2003) makes the point in her discussion of the very narrow construction of white Christianity that "sanctified the notion that real Americans were white, and real whites came from northwest Europe" (p. 118). While Canada and the United States do not share an identical history, they are both nations built upon a history of colonial rule, and a racial legacy of marginalization and scientific racism (see, for instance, Angus McLaren's *Our Own Master Race: The Eugenic Crusade in Canada*, 1990 Toronto: McLelland Stewart). For these reasons, to understand Christian privilege, we must simultaneously be aware of the relationship between Christian privilege and whiteness.

Reflecting on the annual Easter egg roll on the White House lawn, Warren Blumenfeld (2006) examines how Christian privilege is rooted in public schooling.

> Many people (most likely the majority) consider these events played out in Washington, D.C., and in some schools in the United States as normal, appropriate, and joyous seasonal activities. Upon critical reflection, however, others experience them as examples of institutional (governmental and educational) (re)enforcements of dominant Christian standards and what is referred to as 'Christian privilege,' though presented in presumably secularized forms. They represent some of the ways in which the dominant group (in this instance, Christians) reiterates its values and practices while marginalizing and subordinating those who do not adhere to Christian faith traditions. (p. 195)

Blumenfeld is arguing that the normalizing of Christian faith traditions as "normal," as traditions that "we all" should value, uphold, and practice is problematic. There are three levels at which privilege and oppression (as partner concepts) play out: the individual/personal level, cultural/social level, and institutional/structural level (Mullaly, 2002; Blumenfeld, 2006).

The individual/personal level of oppression is closely aligned with discriminatory acts (Blumenfeld, 2006). These can be actions or beliefs, for example, about the inferiority of non-Christian faiths, or the cultural or religious poverty among people in parts of the world that are familiarly identified as the "developing" world. Blumenfeld (2006) describes how, in schooling, this can play out when a student from a marginalized religious community (Sikh, Muslim, Hindu, Jew) is expected to teach the class about his/her tradition. Christian students (wherever they are on the spectrum from orthodox to secular) are never asked to educate others about Christianity. On the contrary, it is a de facto assumption that everyone in the class is familiar with Christian traditions.

The cultural/social level refers to the cultural practices that are normalized by the dominant group. In the case of Christian privilege, Blumenfeld (2006) describes how educational leaders who push to teach creationism or for constitutional amendments banning same-sex marriage are examples of oppression at the cultural/social level. In spaces outside of schooling, we can think about dietary norms and restrictions as just one cultural domain that is a pervasive yet invisible level of privilege in public settings. Another level of Christian cultural norms that permeate public settings, including schools, includes non-denominational prayer or other such rituals that Seifert (2007) argues often stem from Christian practices. All of the items generated by my students in the Christmas-time activities list above are examples of cultural privilege.

At the institutional/structural level, privilege and oppression play out as governmental, educational, and other policies "that explicitly or implicitly privilege and promote some groups while limiting access, excluding, or rendering invisible other groups" (Blumenfeld, 2006, p. 204). Generating a modified "knapsack" inventory of race and gender privileges (McIntosh, 1988), Clark et al. (2002) developed a list of forty-five examples of Christian privilege. Their list includes the following:

It is likely that the state and federal holidays coincide with my religious practices, thereby having little to no impact on my job and/or education.

The central figure of my religion is used at the major point of reference for my calendaring system (i.e., B.C. and A.D., as well as B.C.E., and C.E.)

My religious holidays, having been legally constructed as "secular" can be openly practiced in public institutional settings without a thought given to the violation of the separation of religion and state.

It is important to remember from this tri-level conceptualization that these levels are not discrete but are interconnected. If you are feeling uncomfortable at this point in the chapter, it is likely because you feel that your religion or tradition is under attack (much as the Hérouxville town councilors may have felt). In fact, Blumenfeld (2006) and Schlosser (2003) both describe how simply talking about Christian privilege is a 'sacred taboo' and surfaces deep feelings. Joshi (2006) also points out that despite centuries of religious oppression (well before a post-9/11 world) there has been a masking of religion oppression, often explaining the experience as a race-based one. She asks her students to consider the question, are we a Christian country or a pluralistic society? Each person's response to this will likely shape one's conceptualization—or perhaps *re*-conceptualization of the winter holiday problem.

Conclusion: Reconceptualizing the Winter Holiday Problem

According to Peggy McIntosh (1988), we must reconceptualize our common-sense ideas about "privilege" as being something that everyone must want and to instead more accurately describe the condition of systematic overempowerment of some groups, a "conferred dominance." This shift describes in more useful ways the actual experiences of institutionalized power and privilege and simultaneously allows us to conceptualize the Christmas problem differently.

Returning to the examples of Christmas activities in the school, we can see how the conversation—both the problem and the correction—are relegated to the individual and cultural levels of oppression and privilege, leaving the institutional dimensions untouched. This level of discussion confines our conceptualization of the problem to the cultural activities of some people and the imposition of those on some others. While this alone can be a worthwhile discussion, any solution is positioned as the "special" parking spot, "special" dietary menu, and the "special" accommodation of prayer space.

The conversation we ought to be having is not at this level. What we ought to be talking about is how to make visible the normalcy of the water around us. What is clear from the scholarship on oppression and privilege is that the primary way in which privilege operates is by virtue of its perceived normalcy. Therefore, *making things visible* can be an act of resistance to structures that confer dominance over some members of our community. Another act of resistance is for allies (those who have unearned privilege—men, Whites, heterosexuals, the able-bodied, and Christian allies) to take action. This of course is a different project for each of us, since we are never simply one aspect of our identities (i.e., *only* White). One could be a White woman, or a gay White man, etc., and depending on what other group dynamics are at play, one's work to support the ending of conferred dominance will change. However, what we can all do is be aware that *religious oppression at the structural level is everywhere*. It isn't just in the reindeer, or the special room that Muslim students require for prayer, or the Christmas carols children learn to sing and strum. It is everywhere. Practice seeing it.

As a professor who works with teachers and student-teachers, I notice, as Christmas draws closer every year after Halloween, all the ways in which "coded Christmas" becomes a more sophisticated part of our vocabulary, "happy holidays," let's have a "faculty winter dinner," or our "annual celebration" and "annual food drive." These are examples of the problem conceptualized at the cultural level, as well as the solutions conceptualized at that level. To address oppression at the structural level can seem like an insurmountable task. How can any of us work against the power of the recovery movement that Kincheloe (2006) describes? While we may not be able to overtly influence all (or any) of the institutional structures with we live, it is clear that all of these structures function within a Roddenberry-esque cloaking device. We must work at making visible that which is cloaked. For this reason alone, I appreciate Hérouxville's town standards. They remind us the importance of asking questions about what *else* is going on. For instance, when religion is highlighted, what other elements are backgrounded? When we spotlight how looney "those" townsfolk are, what does it allow us to avoid discussing?

The winter holiday problem is not simply a problem of winter. In order to prepare young people to live in this world in ways that are not imposing and menacing, but kind, compassionate and well informed, we must do more than dilute our faith-based practices (which have deep and historical meanings to us) into nondescript "friendship trees." Rather, young people must become comfortable with discomfort and tension and develop the skills with which to see structurally conferred dominance of some groups over others.

Notes

1. Retrieved from websource http://municipalite.herouxville.qc.ca/Standards.pdf
2. According to the 2006 Census Canada report, 875,300 of the city's total population of 2,097,965 are visible minorities. http://www12.statcan.ca:80/english/census06/data/profiles/community/Details/Page.cfm?B1=All&Code1=933__&Code2=59&Custom=&Data=Count&Geo1=CMA&Geo2=PR&Lang=E&SearchPR=01&SearchText=Vancouver&SearchType=Begins

References

Blumenfeld, W. J. (2006). Christian privilege and the promotion of 'secular' and not-so 'secular' mainline Christianity in public schooling and in the larger society. *Equity & Excellence in Education*, 39, 195–210.

Brodkin-Sachs, K. (2003). How Jews became white. In M.S. Kimmel and A.L. Ferber (Eds.), *Privilege: A reader.* pp. 115–134. Boulder, CO: Westview Press.

Clark, C., Brimhall-Vargas, M., Schlosser, L., & Alimo, C. (2002).It's not just "secret Santa" in December:Addressing educational and workplace climate issues linked to Christian privilege. *Multicultural Education*, 10, 52–57.

Dyer, R. (1997). *White: Essays on race and culture.* New York: Routledge.

Editorial. (2007, Jan 31). Hérouxville bienvenue [electronic version]. *The Toronto Star.* Retrieved May 2, 2008 from http://www.thestar.com/article/176411.

Gibson, J. (2005). *The war on Christmas: How the liberal plot to ban the sacred Christian holiday is worse than you thought.* New York: Sentinel.

Joshi, K. Y. (2006). Guest editor's introduction. *Equity & Excellence in Education*, 39, 177–180.

Kimmel, M. S. (2003). Towards a pedagogy of the oppressor. In M.S. Kimmel and A.L. Ferber (Eds.), *Privilege: A reader.* pp. 1–10. Boulder, CO: Westview Press.

Kincheloe, J. L. (2006). A critical politics of knowledge: Analyzing the role of educational psychology in educational policy. *Policy Futures in Education*, 4 (3), 220–235.

McIntosh, P. (1988). *White privilege and male privilege: A personal account of coming to see correspondences through work in Women's studies.* Wellesley, MA: Wellesley College Center for Research on Women.

Mullaly, R. (2002). *Challenging oppression: A critical social work approach.* Don Mills, ON: Oxford University Press.

Schlosser, L. Z. (2003). Christian privilege: Breaking a sacred taboo. *Journal of Multicultural Counselling and Development*, 31, 44–51.

Seifert, T. (2007). Understanding Christian privilege: Managing the tensions of spiritual plurality. *About Campus*, May-June, 10–17.

Section Seven

Physical Diversity

Twenty-Two

Health and Diversity
What Does It Mean for Inclusion and Social Justice?

Kathleen S. Berry

Although there is no clear line between premodern, modern and postmodern eras, there are marked differences in how people thought of health. The original Latin/Greek meaning, the originating languages for the rise of Western, Eurocentric civilization, used the word healthy to mean the unity of body, mind and spirit. With the modern knack for dismembering that meaning, generally health has come to mean separation into parts; physical health, mental health and emotional health and so on. Problematic to these divisions is how the individual is held responsible for healthy(ness) and blamed for unhealthy(ness) while the hegemonic power and knowledge of institutions ranging from medical, legal and educational professions to workplace, health plans, media and corporations manipulate, develop discourses, policies and practices of surveillance that govern what and who counts as health(y). In addition, the individual's lack of agency over what policies and practices are developed by institutions removes diversity, equity, democratic participation and social justice. Furthermore, the discourses and practices of health, when controlled by institutions and privileged societal homogenization, ignores the diversity of the individual and possible structures available. The responsibility for maintaining responsibility at the individual level actually maintains the hegemonic powers of society and institutions. Finally, leaving institutional and societal power removed from the economic, political, cultural and historical contexts of how health is handled at any level prevents any recognition that change is needed or that transformative action is possible in today's Eurocentric, modernist world.

Diversity in the context of discussions in the postmodern means not just attention to how culturally different worlds are shaped and included in everyday life. Additionally, diversity has come to mean difference as shaped by gender, race, class, age, religion, ethnicity, nationality and the host of other culturally diverse constructions. More importantly, diversity has come to mean the difference within and between culture constructions in terms of knowledge, values, beliefs, and practices. Finally, and most importantly to the troping of health with diversity, is how and why history, politics, economics, societies and institutions have assigned power and privilege to certain discourses and practices regarding who and what counts as health and diversity and excluded or marginalized ontological and epistemological ways of health and diversity.

Modern notions of health also permit organizing the world in a manner where the body is subject to hegemonic practices that control what is meant and treated as health, what and who counts as healthy and who gets to be healthy. While feminists have talked about the personal as political and critical theories politicize the world, the modern discourses and practices of health have stayed within the boundaries and rationality of the individual as responsible for knowing and being healthy. And institutional and societal discourses and practices continue to circulate and maintain the governance of health responsibility at the individual level mainly through corporate hegemony, western medicine and media.

Does troping health with diversity necessarily change the theoretical conditions of knowledge and truth about what healthy means and subsequently what societal and institutional structures and practices are put in place? The postmodern and poststructural theoretical knack for attaching the discourses of diversity to another field, in this case health, doesn't necessarily transform the epistemological or ontological meaning and practices. What is needed is:

1. a problematizing of the modern notions of health studies and practices;
2. a historical and political archeological and genealogical contextualizing of how health became constructed to date and legitimized the homogenizing of current discursive policies and practices;
3. an expansion and blurring of the boundaries of current knowledge about what counts as health and whose health counts;
4. a politizing of the questions and implications of the areas stated in #1 to #3 and finally
5. an articulation of action to transform the field of health studies to create diversity, exclusion, equity, social justice especially in the context of participatory democracies.

Author's Positionality in Discussions of Health

An author's theoretical stance and call for transformative action is always shadowed by her past and present position in the world. I'm no exception. Born into the world where generally I was privileged by a working class genealogy where grandfathers and fathers held two and three jobs to sustain families, housing and food and where grandmothers and mothers held many domestic jobs to maintain that level of subsistence. But that class background also marginalized our history in terms of economic opportunities to experience travel, other classed worlds and people, social and economic mobility and experience time and space differently with leisure activities. It seemed my ancestors and I were always working—labor as compared to say academically intensive work at that.

My educational genealogy is limited. Archeologically, there were few if any ancestors who went beyond grade seven and parents who went beyond high school. I was one of those war babies encouraged to get a university education but, as a female, that meant teaching or nursing. I struggled, however, to enter even teaching because of the societal and institutional abnormalizing and exclusion of a body made different in childhood by the polio virus. And those opportunities for postsecondary education were further limited by struggling parents who had to raise a child with polio without any societal or institutional support such as Medicare. Having to scrape dollars and sell houses just to pay partial aspects of the medical bills, parents couldn't save to accumulate money to send their child to university. All they could do is hope. But hope and attitude don't pay the bills.

So health for me does not lie in an individual body or responsibility. The reduction of my body as disabled created a world of exclusion, homogeneity and constant struggle. Psychologically speaking, society and institutions created an overachiever always trying to prove that I could fit in with mainstream society and learn and work in institutions such as university, business, social work and teaching. Politically speaking, even as an overachiever, society and institutions excluded difference. Although a good student, entry into several school and university programs was limited and in many cases, prohibited. Institutional powers and policies at the time (sixties/seventies) wrote in requirements that defined who got hired or not. Criteria suited abled bodies but discursively and bureaucratically excluded me (and many others) on grounds built on conformity and mainstream ideas. Many times those criteria conveniently changed when the visible difference was spotted and supported by institutional practices and societal attitudes. Although individuals acted in favor of my hiring, exclusion was enacted at the institutional level. To reiterate, diversity about who counts and why was available at the individual level but not at the institutional or societal levels. In other words, health and diversity is a political matter and cannot be reduced to individual or medical responsibility.

Since structures, cultures, policies, language, institutions, society and so forth are built by and for mainstream, dominant knowledge, values and beliefs, these constructed systems create a world that requires innovation and creativity for persons of difference, to manage a world meant for conformity, homogeneity in thought, body and practices. Perseverance and continual struggle might work to move a person forward, access the privileges and opportunities afforded individuals of the patriarchal, middle/upper classed, Eurocentric ancestral, Christian, heterosexual and ablized knowledge and values. These categorical groupings, however, are where I trope health and diversity to culturally constructed worlds such as class, gender, society, institutions and so forth. Each categorical grouping with its specific scientific rationality (as compared, for example, to subjective, local and gendered rationality), objectivity in addition to the discourses and practices, societal and institutional powers have been reduced over time, history, and space (context) by Enlightenment and liberal discourses, leaving structures and practices of health simply created, circulated and maintained by the Westernized medical profession. Although traditional, Eastern and Aboriginal notions of health are penetrating the field of Western health, these areas still are generally questioned and excluded from government policies and societal trust. Not only does this leave the power to govern who counts and what counts as health(y) in the hands of a few practitioners but hegemonically herds the masses into accepting that power with limited to nil opportunities to participate, challenge and transform modern structures and practices of health and healthiness—a loss of diversity so to speak.

Problematizing Modern Health

As a critical pedagogue who uses critical discourses to deconstruct and legitimate my discussions and suggestions, the word and world, in this case health, must be problematized. As we enter the postmodern as a means to challenge the modern, it might appear that dismantling dominant modern institutional, societal structures and practices leads to chaos. However, as chaos theory would have it, in the chaos lies the complexity (diversity). Instead of reducing health to a masterful fulfilling of a need for simplicity, objectivity, and scientific rationality that can be bureaucratically structured, homogeneously administered and politically driven by certain dominant discourses complicit with those of a world constructed and favored mainly by a Western, patriarchal, middle-classed, white raced, colonized, Christian society, the complexity of diversity avoids, perhaps not totally, the current reductionism of modern health. The compatibly constructed institutions and Enlightenment's promises can still be part of the dialogue while constructions of health make the turn to postmodern, poststructural and postcolonial studies that reach for diversity. In so doing, health becomes a rethinking and restructuring of what counts as health and whose health counts.

It appears in modern worlds that the power to construct health has been further reduced and subjected to control, surveillance, governance and defined mainly by the medical profession, government departments of health and corporate profiteers (such as drug companies) including the media. Not only do these institutional powers create the discourse about what gets said and who gets to say what counts as health, they get to structure the institutions and knowledge about the world of health. At the same time as these institutions manipulate the knowledge, they also hegemonically turn the discourse and the practices legitimized by their discourses back on the individual. Discourses and practices structured by modernist's thinking such the Enlightenment, scientific rationality, neo-liberalism, and capitalism only work if individualism is granted the freedom to act. However, these modernist discourses exclude, if not ignore, the diversity of individuals that are not privileged nor belong to these dominant discourses. These hegemonic practices of the power institutions governing health through historical, economic and political processes, while claiming every individual has the right to healthiness, are actually controlling individuals to consent to their power. Not often do we hear or know of the cycle of poor health of the millions of individuals living in conditions of poverty; single mothers struggling to pay bills or get an education so they can buy the food that government agencies claim is necessary for good health; aboriginal populations depending on federal governance and monies that are only possible because of the land resources (oil, minerals, lumber, housing) that created privilege and profit for non-aboriginal ancestry; working class parents faced with layoffs, selling homes to pay medical expenses; people living in metropolis conditions of pollution, long hours of commuting and crowded, expensive living quarters; seniors living on incomes meant for previous times while the dominant institutions of health increase incomes meant to maintain power and privilege and the many more conditions in which health is governed, accessed and privileged by and for the few. And when we do hear from or know about these individuals, somehow they are blamed or made to feel guilty about the conditions of inhumane health, rendered agentless and voiceless—"just too plain tired to fight anymore," as one single mother expressed when government funding was removed from programs for her autistic son. So where's the diversity of healthy conditions and practices for these people?

As a result of the overwhelming power of media discourses, especially TV in most homes, the cult of individualism is hegemonically fed regarding health. Talk shows like Oprah and Dr. Phil and the plethora of others seduce audiences of all ages, mainly female, to be responsible for their personal health and body. Everything from weight issues (overweight discourse to bulimia) to modernist discourses surrounding mental health (mainly encoded in psychological and medical discourses) are presented by these celebrity media-produced missionary-like experts. Little do the audiences seem to realize or question that for each individual rendered healthy through celebrity counselling, these institutionally constructed, privileged self-help saviors are earning millions of corporate dollars from advertisers at the expense of the individuals appearing on and/or watching the show. What constructions of health are being produced in the public domain if media gurus establish the dominant and privileged discourses and practices and maintained by corporate powers? What diversity is there where the dominant few can influence society's knowledge, practices and agency?

A Historical and Political Archeological and Genealogical Contextualizing

If health and diversity is problematized beyond individualism and the body into the realms of society and institutions, then, without a doubt health discourses and practices must be contextualized in the culturally constructed worlds of history, economics, politics, geography, gender, class, race, religion, age, and so forth. It would move health(iness) into the postmodern world and include the diversity requested but eliminated by modern reductionism and scientific rationality. Health(iness) of a culture, of a state, of a nation, of a world cannot be built on individualistic structures and practices. Granted certain national, missionary and celebrity empires would fall if health(iness) were contextualized in the diversity of historically, politically, economically and culturally constructed worlds. For example, if health were contextualized within postcolonial discourses and practices and along the axis of gendered, raced and classed privilege and oppression, the reduction of Euro-colonized populations, including Aboriginal peoples, to conditions of poverty and centuries of Euro-American dependency, would end. It amazes me how in the early twenty-first century, corporate write-offs, missionary advertising, national and celebrity aid to Africa, for example, reproduces the cycle of colonization and dependency on Euro-American privilege including keeping others living in un-healthiness, politically, economically and bodily. Reducing the health(iness) of the Other maintains the privilege of the few even within the structures and practices of nationalism.

A Brief Expansion and Blurring of the Boundaries

To address health and diversity requires an expansion, not a destroying—a blurring, not a muddling of boundaries of current discourses and practices. The point is to recognize the boundaries created by modern Enlightenment and Liberal discourses, how and where they broke with pre-modern practices regarding health as thought about currently. How the creation of scientific rationality and objectivity emerged as modern constructions of individual, societal and institutional health practices are important to understanding what counts as health. For example, what was once thought of as healthy practices, local and in many cases in the hands of matriarchal powers, shifted into Western universalizing health practices created and dominated by practices that connected to the power of patriarchal societies and circulated by European colonization. Thus the exclusion of traditional pre-modern notions removed and/or reduced the diversity of health practices and materials. Pre-modern and culturally different notions of health were seen as subjective, superstition, dangerous and non-legitimized by Western society and institutions. The individual's subjectivity was considered non-valuable yet singularly responsible for ill-health of society and nations. The diversity of a pre-modern and modern mix of health has succumbed to a medical and media, popular culture, digital reduction of health as an individual problem and responsibility.

Today, there are many locations that bear witness to the loss of diversity in modern health. The dominance of media, corporation, government and medical powers in Western culture to define and control health and what counts as health has created very clear boundaries, mainly through a historical process of moving the informal and local practices into the formalized systems created, circulated, maintained and legitimized by certain institutions. To include diversity means to expose and track the hegemonic process of how health came to be moved into these formalized structures and consented to but is also difficult to challenge and change by the masses. Several personal and local neighborhood experiences come to mind that, without those voices, become lost to the neutralization, non-historical, cultural homogenization of current modern societies and institutions. Although socialized medicine has been introduced in Canada in the 1950s, government politicians and medical practitioners still control where and to whom money is given as health care. For example, parents who don't belong to the privileged class, single mothers, elderly persons, rural communities, unemployed persons tend to be marginalized or excluded from the unlimited power of government and medical discourses and practices. The masses, especially those with limited political and economic power, are forced into accepting the boundaries set by modern society and institutions. In order to provide socially just and diverse health care, modern boundaries must be dismantled, challenged and transformed. To do so is an arduous task. Perhaps where to begin is with certain critical questions that examine and dismantle modern discourses, boundaries and practices regarding whose health and what counts as health.

Politicizing the Questions

Recently when I was waiting at the gas station for Charlie to fill my gas tank, several local male citizens who meet daily for a coffee and "a gab session" were exchanging comments and questions about several events and issues. As I listened I realized they were asking the big political questions needed to examine and dismantle the discussions of problematizing, contextualizing and boundaries presented above. When I was driving home to work further on this chapter, I wondered why those questions never reach out beyond the local and into the very institutions that should be concerned and acting on these people's thoughts and concerns. Even more surprising as I reflected on those questions is how interconnected and complex they were and how they related to health and diversity—similar to the game '7 steps to Kevin Bacon.' Each question debated and discussed somehow connected and led to health and diversity, a postmodern condition where nothing is absolute or fixed, constantly shifting in meaning and contexts.

Here's the gist of the conversation.

> H'Kath. How r'ya?
> Fine. You?
> See the paper about the proposed uranium mine near here?
> Yep.
> Wha'ya think? (I bypass the group to pay my bill. They continue)
> Damn government. What the hell are they trying to do to us? Here they go again. No sense of people. Just like the time they gave the Smith's (a private corporation) the go-ahead on the gravel pit even

though they (gov't) knew the problems it causes. I went t' the meetin' in town and they (Smith's) had their big wigs there. The gov't was there, said they'd listen to both sides. (Corporation and locals). We had letters, petitions, documents, facts, a young kid who started an environmental group to remove the causeway spoke up ...

Yea, look at the damage that did to the river just 'cause a few ritzy muckie mucks want an artificial lake to sail their g.. d.. sailboats on ... money talks eh?

At the meeting we told 'm about how cancer rates went up in the area, 13 women on one road died from cancer! 13!, noise and dust polution—killin' the environment, ruinin' our neighborhood, property values went down.... for what? Six months later the gov't approves the pit ... money (Smith's) sure does talk... y'ad think my tax money would go to somethin' better.. Buildin' a hospital for us... jes' christ if we get sick anyway from the pit we still drive for a half hour to the nearest hospital after waiting a half hour for an ambulance ... ... even if they gave us local doctors and clinics Im out sick on the (Lobster) boat...

Joe, we're just fishers an' farmers ... think anyone cares about us?

Geeeeeeze—even my kids haven't a chance ... an hour on an old school bus, and they'll be breathing them uranium fumes all day.. Did ya' sign that petition? Here we go again... what's the use? .....think they'd (gov't) invest in that new technology like solar and wind power, Nova Scotia and PEI (two nearby states) are... where the fuck is our gov't on this?... global warmin' and everythin' ... they say it (uranium mine) will increase the job market around here.. Boost the local economy?... boost the local economy my ass... we'll (locals) do all the digging just to send it to another place to boost their economy while we back here breathing in uranium... coughing our lungs out... dying ... just like them (coal) miners in Springhill... for years unnoticed.. Dying, poor economy... run by a family who got rich off them poor miners' hard labor...money going out of the community to feed some guy's family that sends his kids to private school... you can be damn sure they won't be breathin in fumes like my kids... what's a man to do?...

Within this text lie the questions, knowledge and values of a local community feeling and questioning the power of institutions and how isolated and agentless they feel against those powers. In the links between each question and comment, if dismantled, expanded, and examined, we find contextualizations ready for the application of critical readings. Encoded in the five-minute conversation are examples of knowledge that has power at that moment but gets lost in the everyday routines and requirements of daily life. These men have asked questions about health, all intertwined in the contexts of economics, politics, and history and linked to local, state, corporate and global worlds. If we were to apply questions and challenges to their text, we'd find missing questions about health; questions coming from the culturally constructed difference of a gendered, racialized, classed, secularized, heterosexualized, and anglosized world. These men were white, working class, mainly Catholic, heterosexual and Francophone. Their questions and conversations were perhaps specific to them, lacking an inclusion of difference. Join their questions and thoughts to those of other local people and the range of knowledge and challenges to the boundaries of modern society and institutions would be expanded and blurred. Health and diversity might become a reality.

These questions show the diversity and complexity of health if they were actually acted upon. The struggle is to move these questions into the realms of the dominant powers, to challenge and dismantle their power, to initiate solidarity instead of the hopelessness many of these men expressed. Articulation of action built upon the questions and challenges moves the local into the political, hopelessness into agency, local solidarity into action, local action into power.

Transformative Action

An articulation of action to transform the field of health studies to create diversity, exclusion, equity, social justice especially in the context of participatory democracies is the burden of critical theorists and practitioners. Articulations of action can be pulled from local conversations as presented above combined with academic and institutional discourses such as those of media texts and certainly the new digital technologies. The real struggle is how to move the plethora of questions into the political realm, give them voices and faces and create spaces where action is initiated.

When I arrived home from that gas station, on my email was a request to sign a petition against the uranium mine, another text similar to the gas station's, only in print. Ross and Shelly are local activists, rebel rousers, thank heavens. They are critical theorists in action not just words. Their questions and conversations lead to transformative action; to taking health seriously, to create diversity, to challenging institutional powers, to organizing at the local levels and to hold meetings for participatory democracy. Local heroes that speak to many worlds. Here is a snippet of their text that asks questions and provides knowledge similar to that of the gas station text.

> Subject: Uranium mining in NB
> Please sign for—No mining for Uranium Mining in New Brunswick, NB and forward to every one you know. Thanks
> Did you know that they are planning to open a Uranium Mine in Saint-Antoine? We would be one of five sites. No, well neither did I until my sister told me that she saw the plans at a meeting held in Moncton. Uranium is a Radioactive product. What does that mean? It causes cancer especially leukemia), birth defects and all around hazard to your health. Uranium dust can travel up to 100 miles from the mines. What does that mean for us? We will no longer be able to plant gardens, no more live stock, no more apple orchards, no more fishing and what about our water supply everything will be infected with Uranium dust. If the contract is signed, they have the right to drill a half mile hole in your yard and just leave it open. That means that the Uranium fumes can escape from that hole and really get you good. We need to join together to protect our families, our kids and grand-kids future. If this contract is signed our community will become a ghost town.Our property value will drop to nothing. The mines are not even being done to profit Canada; it is to be ship out of the country. So we get to get sick and die for a foreign country. How nice is that? I ask that you pass this very important e-mail to everyone you know. Write to your MLA, speak to your mayor. Please sign this petition and pass it along.

This is just the beginning of transformative action. These people do this on their own time and money while still carrying on daily lives. There will be meetings and conflicts and a diversity of truths, knowledge and silences. Contradictions will arise both within and between those involved. Non-involvement by many will occur but many will continue to demand action for health reasons—healthy in body, mind and spirit; healthy economically, socially and politically with the inclusion and application of the principles of diversity.

Note

I have not quoted from academic sources in order to retain the power of local and lay voices. However as a critical theorist, many academic references are encoded in this discussion mainly derived from critical feminist and Foucauldian discourse. I accept full responsibility for any misinterpretations of these theories and have used them in spite of the multiple contradictions in those texts alone.

Twenty Three

Tipping the Scales
Disability Studies Asks "How Much Diversity Can You Take?"

David J. Connor and Susan Baglieri

The Relative Absence of Disability in Educational Discourse of Diversity

In contemplating contemporary notions of diversity, issues such as race, ethnicity, gender, social class, nationality, and sexual orientation often come to mind. Civil rights movements foregrounded the struggle of African Americans, women, and homosexuals and gave rise to increased access to all aspects of society. To state the obvious, while some progress has been made, there is still a long way to go. Of great importance is that these markers of identity have grown to affect the ways in which diversity is theorized and taught in teacher preparation programs (Banks, 2001) and integrated into the school curriculums (Brown, 1996). Just as Civil Rights Movements foregrounded race, gender, and sexual orientation, people with disabilities and their allies forged a movement that sought to shift them from society's margins toward its center (Fleischer & Zames, 2001). Why is it, then, as Hamre, Oyler, and Bejoian (2006) ask, that "in many progressive spaces where commitments to social justice are real and enduring, the lives and experiences of people with disabilities are sometimes overlooked?" (p. 91). The reasons are manifold, complex, and worthy of exploration.

Competing agendas for pluralistic curricula in schools—often captured in the umbrella term "multicultural"—have resulted in a paradoxical narrowing of the frames of identity and diversity that may be considered in curriculum reform. While efforts to re-imagine a curriculum that more accurately reflects the histories of women and people of African descent have gained strength, and authentic representation of the issues of GLQBT people has gained tentative ground, attempts to include disability studies have been subject to criticism. Linton, Mello and O'Neill (1995), for example, describe the following criticisms: "scholarship on disability will 'water down' the diversity requirement; its purpose is to increase self-esteem, or capitulate to interest group pressure; it's not valid or rigorous scholarship; it's parochial, and will further atomize the curriculum" (p. 9). They call attention to the paradox of narrowing pluralism, noting that "the criticisms previously heard from proponents of the traditional canon are now being used against the inclusion of disability in curriculum transformation efforts" (p. 9).

A central purpose of this chapter is to address such criticisms and concerns and to provide a theory of practice for positioning disability studies as part of a broader diversity agenda. First, we theorize disability in social, cultural, and historical terms, asserting the usefulness of articulating disability as a category akin to race, gender, and sexual orientation. Second, we advocate the need for critical educators to continue their work in troubling normalizing practices around ability and human worth. Third, we examine the "master script" (Swartz, 1992) or "hidden curriculum" (Apple, 1971) in professional preparation and K–12 school curriculum to reveal what adults, children, and youth, with and without disabilities, typically learn about disabilities. Fourth, we explore ways in which disability can be taught within K–college curriculum. Finally, we emphasize the promise of linking theory to trouble practice about disability, and practice to trouble theory about disability.

Confronting Ableism

First and foremost are the widespread and pervasive beliefs that disability is always a negative human characteristic, a tragedy, a flaw, an abnormality (Stiker, 1999). These entrenched beliefs are fundamentally challenged by the field of disability studies, which reframes disability as a natural human characteristic that falls outside cultural notions of normalcy. The concept of normalcy is rooted within ableist assumptions of how a body should look and act. Ableism— analogous to racism, sexism, heterosexism—is the belief that those with disabilities are inferior to non-disabled people, who are not quite fully human. The subsequent devaluation of disability within society becomes evident in educational policies and practices based upon

> attitudes that uncritically assert that it is better for a child to walk than roll, speak than sign, read print than read Braille, spell independently than use a spell-check, and hang out with nondisabled children rather than with other disabled students. (Hehir, 2005, p. 15)

Simply put, attitudes and ideas about disabled people rise from belief systems constructed by thousands upon thousands of negative associations that we experience throughout our lives. These associations become ascribed to people perceived to be not normal, causing their stigmatization. In his work on stigma, Goffman asserts, "the normal and the stigmatized are not persons but rather perspectives" (1963, p. 138). We believe that disability, like beauty, is in the eye of the beholder, and concur with Davis that "the body is never a single physical thing so much as a series of attitudes toward it" (2002, p. 22; see also Butler, 1993). It can be argued that it is the attitudes toward those deemed abnormal that actively causes their disablement, not their physical or sensory impairment or their perceived lack of cognitive ability or "appropriate" behaviors. Unwillingness to accept people with disabilities in all public places, or perhaps indifference, serves as the biggest barrier to their full participation in society.

Idealized and Defective Citizens

Despite the espoused embrace of diversity within the United States, the notion of an idealized American citizen has remained constant. Almost fifty years ago, in his exploration of stigma in society, Goffman (1963) noted, ". . .in an important sense there is only one complete un-blushing male in America: a young, married, white, urban, northern, heterosexual Protestant father of college education, fully employed, of good complexion, weight, and height, and a recent record in sports" (p. 128). Indeed, almost half a century later, the phrase "all-American boy" conjures up almost the same picture, except that now he would most likely reside in the suburbs. Disability bursts this European-American-male citizen bubble in ways that, arguably, both differ from and overlap with race, gender, and sexual orientation. The notion of an ideal-ized citizen is one to which people aspire. It promises many privileges such as "full" status into normalcy and theoretically guarantees widespread access and acceptance into all domains of society. As noted by Murphy (1995), this rhetoric of perfection is contested by disability,

> The pursuit of the slim, well-muscled body is not only an aesthetic matter, but also a moral imperative. . .It hardly needs saying that the disabled, individually and as a group, contravene all the values of youth, vi-rility, activity, and physical beauty that Americans cherish, however little most individuals may embody them (p. 153).

Clearly, these notions of an idealized, desirable citizen reflected in a perfect, God-like body undergird our culture. But, if people with disabilities do not mirror this desirability, neither do most citizens. Indeed, attempts to approximate an out-of-reach ideal for the overwhelming majority of citizens raises many interesting questions, including about perceived differences in people, competition, the ways in which capitalism organizes individuals, and how power operates. The broad cultural devaluation of people with disabilities, unsurprisingly, results in a widespread denial of social currency, oftentimes discounting those with disabilities from "be-ing in the running" (or mainstream) in schools, as workers, and as mates.

At the same time, people with disabilities are expected *not* to act in certain ways. As Gordon and Rosenblum (2001) point out, "They are not expected to be dominant, active, independent, competitive, adventurous, sexual, self-controlled, healthy, intelligent, attractive, or competent" (p. 14). In brief, they are "denied the attributes valued in the culture" (p. 13). It is assumed that a person cannot be disabled *and* possess power. This point was exemplified by President Franklin D. Roosevelt, a wheelchair user, whose publicity photographs during his entire time in office were manipulated to disguise that fact and *pretend* he was non-disabled (Alter, 2006). This illustrates how the general public perceives physical strength as corresponding to moral and intellectual force. Conversely, a physical impairment is often erroneously associated with a moral and intellectual weakness. Roosevelt was a contradiction. How could one of the most powerful men in the world, the commander and chief of the United States of America, be disabled? Yet, his situation—being competent but vulnerable to ableist perceptions of incom-petence—is commonplace.

The Need for Another Other

Just as disability is "put to the side" in sociology (Gordon & Rosenblum, 2001), in the field of education, it is usually relegated to the medical conceptual framework of special education. Disability is also commonly ignored or downplayed in issues of diversity within education (Anderson & Collins, 1998). However, in her essay, "Disability History: Why We Need An-other 'Other,'" Kudlick (2003) makes a robust argument that disability should be considered "a key defining social category on par with race, class, and gender." In claiming disability as a social experience and rejecting it as a primarily medical diagnosis, the field of disability studies eschews the individual as a unit of analysis. Instead, it focuses on the social systems that construct disability, interactions within and among them, how bodily difference is constructed, and the meaning and value of that difference.

Disability studies provide a conceptualization of disability that allows us to deal squarely with perspective and attitude, which Davis (2002), Goffman (1963), and Butler (1993) suggest are central to the meaning we make about bodies. Disability covers a broad array of impairments and is a highly contextualized experience, rendering it far more fluid than other seemingly "permanent" phenomena. Davis (2002) describes disability as "an amorphous identity with porous boundaries," causing "other identity groups in the United States [to] have had difficulty in incorporating it into their goals" (p. 36). Despite the struggle, however, disability studies "challenge long held perceptions that relegate it [disability] to the unglamorous backwaters primarily of interest to people in rehabilitation, special education, and other applied professional fields" (Kudlick, 2003).

Gordon and Rosenblum (2001) make a strong case that disability shares many characteristics with American constructions of race, gender, and sexual orientation. They consider the way that each status is constructed through unceasing social processes in which people are named, aggregated and disaggregated, dichotomized and stigmatized, and deprived of opportunities to acquire the attributes our culture values. Yet, as Davis notes, there is no section on disability studies or disability per se in the bookstore, nor can the definition of ableism be found in the dictionary (Weise, 2004). In response to the invisibility of disability, Davis (1997) believes that

> studies about disability have not had historically the visibility of studies about race, class, or gender for complex as well as simple reasons. The simple reason is the general pervasiveness of discrimination and prejudice against people with disabilities leading to their marginalization as well as the marginalization of the study of disability (p. 1).

His sentiments are echoed by Linton (1998), who asserts, "The enormous energy society expends keeping people with disabilities sequestered in subordinate positions is matched by the academy's effort to justify isolation and oppression" (p. 3). The larger academy has been slow to embrace the exploration of disability as a field, and special education has clung tenaciously to its positivist research base, emphasizing medical interpretations of disability as disorder, deficit, and dysfunction. Moving beyond, or perhaps ahead of questions of diagnosis and treatment, disability studies ask: What is normal? What is abnormal? What are the meanings of such labels? Who gets to decide? How are labels tied to social standing, power, identity, and access to—or limitations placed on—all aspects of society?

Unraveling Normalcy

Just as the world is racialized, genderized, and sexualized, it is also normalized. In her work *Extraordinary Bodies* (1997), Garland-Thomson asserts that

> disability is a representation, a cultural interpretation of physical transformation or configuration, and a comparison of bodies that structures social relations and institutions. Disability, then, is the attribution of corporeal deviance—not so much a property of bodies as a product of cultural rules about what bodies should be or do (p. 6).

She refers to the non-stigmatized figure in society as a "normate," a synonym for the desirable citizen discussed earlier. Through the thousands of daily acts, chosen to define normalcy, abnormalcy becomes established. Conversely, as abnormalcy becomes reified, it verifies understandings of normalcy. Davis (2002) elaborates:

> Whether we are talking about AIDS, low birth weight babies, special education issues, euthanasia, and the thousand other topics listed in the newspapers every day, the examination, discussion, anatomizing this form of "difference" is nothing less than a desperate attempt by people to consolidate their normalcy (p. 117).

Inflexible school practices such as standardized norms, tracking, age- and grade-appropriate expectations, highly ritualized behaviors and interactions, and a professional obsession with normalcy have led what Baker (2002) refers to as "The Hunt for Disability" in schools. The burgeoning numbers of students labeled learning disabled (LD), emotionally disturbed (ED), behavior disordered (BD), cognitively delayed (CD), attention-deficit disordered (ADD), attention-deficit-hyperactivity disordered (ADHD), oppositional defiant disordered (ODD), or with speech and language deficits (S & L), and so on, testify to the fixation within education to seek, label, and relocate children who are not deemed sufficiently normal in terms of learning, behaving, focusing, speaking, and following instructions. Rather than hunting for labels to name the "deficiencies within" such children and youth, we believe it is more beneficial to contemplate ". . .the ways in that bodies interact with the socially engineered environment and conform to social expectations [and] determine the varying degrees of disability or able-bodiedness, or extra-ordinariness" (Garland-Thomson, 1997, p. 7).

In thinking about how bodies (people) interact with their environment, the medical model of disability that pervades the pseudo scientific discourse of schooling is confronted. Linton (1998) urges that we do not let society off the hook:

> [S]ociety, in agreeing to assign medical meaning to disability, colludes to keep the issue within the purview of the medical establishment, to keep it a personal matter and "treat" the condition and the person with the condition rather than "treating" the social processes and policies that constrict disabled people's lives (p. 11).

The assignment of bodies to disability categories has a long history within schooling practices (Terry & Urla, 1995). However, scholars in disability studies urge us to reject medicalized notions of differences that are characterized as inherent deficits and instead, to be understanding of cognitive, physical, sensory, and behavioral diversity among students. Pathologizing difference can only lead to continued forms of othering and stigmatization. Davis (2002) conveys the value of unraveling the status quo: "Disability studies demands a shift from the ideology of normalcy, from the rule and hegemony of normates, to a vision of the body as changeable, unperfectable, unruly, and untidy" (p. 39).

The Role of Critical Educators

Educators within disability studies seek to challenge the typical presentation of disability in education as sets of clinical/scientific/medical conditions indicating a personal tragedy waiting for treatment, remediation, and restoration to normalcy. Education, particularly Special Education, is often criticized for not recognizing disability as a set of social processes and—

along with being saturated in medical discourse—operating within a legislative paradigm. Ironically, the laws that protect children and youth with disabilities can also paradoxically limit their participation in general schooling (Connor & Ferri, 2007). As Christensen (1996) notes, "...schooling itself is disabling, that its lack of flexibility in accommodating a diverse range of learners creates disabled students" (p. 65). Baker's (2002) observation about the plethora of "soft" disability labels (previously listed) suggests a factory-like educational process of trained professionals technically selecting defective children and sorting them from their standard-issue peers. Yet, Varenne and McDermott provocatively comment, "without schools, [there are] no learning disabilities" (1998, p. 143).

In focusing upon the system rather than the child as the site of responsibility, the prime concern for many scholars and critical special educators in the field of disability studies is the need to combat ableism and to avoid stigmatizing difference, while simultaneously creating access to educational opportunities. As Sapon-Shevin explains, "Educators need to transcend discussions of diversity as a classroom problem and regard it as natural, desirable, and inevitable occurrence that enriches educational experiences for both teachers and students" (2000, p. 34). Educators and scholars who come to disability studies are usually those who have always rejected, or transitioned to outrightly reject the limited conceptualization of disability in the field of education (Gallagher, Heshusius, Iano, & Skrtic, 2004). As a result, we explore many issues, including how teacher preparation programs often unwittingly induct potential educators into harmful ways of thinking about students with disabilities (Brantlinger, 2004); how many educationally based disabilities labels are highly subjective and based on cultural demands (Reid & Valle, 2004); how labeling serves to segregate the population according to disability (Baker, 2002); how the overrepresentation of students of color has been occurring for decades within special education classes (Ferri & Connor, 2006); and the creation of theory, policy, and practice to set a new course for pluralistic education (Gabel, 2005; Danforth & Gabel, 2006).

The continued exclusion of students labeled disabled from the educational opportunities afforded to their non-identified peers is justified through the medicalized conceptual frame of education. In contrast, a disability studies perspective compels us to consider the evaluation of disabled bodies as an exercise of normative power that has served to limit the power and position of students labeled with disabilities in schools. Reductionist methods of teaching and watered-down curricula, characteristic of segregated special education settings, have resulted in inequitable academic opportunity and limited educational gain (Ellis, 1997; Heshusius, 1989). Tomlinson (2004) notes that even in inclusive contexts, students labeled with disabilities are "more likely to encounter curricula focused on drill, seatwork, giving right answers, going over questions, reviewing, and other low-level tasks," as reflective of their placement in "low-group" and "low-track" general education settings (p. 520). It has also been found that students labeled with disabilities often remain both socially and academically segregated in inclusion classrooms (e.g., where labeled students are rejected by peers; where the class temporarily relocates to an inaccessible setting) (Hehir, 2003). He explains that if teachers view students labeled with disabilities as *others*, they may be complicit with, less attentive to, or unaware of the way that students become marginalized through activities and curricula that exclude them from class experiences.

As with other forms of institutionalized oppression, the theory-making that undergirds our exclusionary practices occurs not only at the sites of practice but also in the character of what adults and children learn about disability in society, the workplace, and schools. In addition to movies and media that reify stereotypes and tropes about disability and disabled persons' lives, workplaces and schools seem to more often adopt curricula in service to a medical model. In the next section, we use Swartz's (1992; 1997) idea of master scripting to review past work in disability curriculum.

Examining Disability Curriculum: Master Scripting Ability

Swartz (1992; 2007) describes the master script as classroom practices, pedagogy, and instructional materials that are grounded in particular ideologies of knowledge and performance. "Master scripting," she explains, "silences multiple voices and perspectives, primarily by legitimizing dominant, White, upper-class, male voicings as the 'standard' knowledge students need to know" (Swartz, 1992, p. 341). Other, especially contrary, accounts are either omitted from the master script or brought under control through re-shaping by the dominant voice. For example, Blanchett (2006) points out that Dr. Martin Luther King's tactics and leadership in the Civil Rights Movement are more commonly recognized than those of Malcolm X. As an additional example of master scripting, she notes the characterization of Rosa Parks as a "tired seamstress" (Ladson-Billings, cited in Blanchett, 2006, p. 26), rather than as a woman who engaged in a strategic act of protest. In both cases, social action and leadership are removed from context and reduced to *happenstance*—in the representation of Parks—or *sanitized* to control the discourse surrounding notions of black power, or resistance, "by any means necessary," for example. Master scripting maintains a disempowered characterization of resistors and controls and sanitizes the violence of oppression and counter-movements of equal intensity.

Swartz's (1992, 2007) concept of master scripting with regard to the dominant knowledge made about people of African descent can be applied toward locating the master script of ability. The master script of ability can be discerned in the medical model of disability and its profound impact on knowledge that is made about disabled persons. Master scripting through a medical model characterizes knowledge about extraordinary bodies and minds as most meaningful in binaries of abled/disabled, which privileges the voices of scientists, or doctors and other experts in the helping professions over the desires or experiences of persons with disabilities. Remediation and cure of the individual or attention to compliance with anti-discrimination policies (ostensibly crafted and implemented by an abled, white, male, European-descent majority in government) are made central in the dominant knowledge about disability.

Discerning the Master Script of Ability

In curricula, the most typical location for disability is in special "disability awareness" events, which often take place in conjunction with disability awareness weeks or months. As in other institutional efforts to recognize "special groups" one month at a time, disability awareness takes center stage in states like Indiana and Missouri and in scores of universities and cities across the nation in March. The United States Congress recently designated October as National Disability Employment Awareness Month, and Idaho, North Carolina, and New York also recognize October as a time for "disability history" events. Efforts to create resource lists, interactive Web-based activities, and to generate event ideas are ongoing. Two excellent examples are those provided by the Museum of disABILITY History in Williamsville, NY (http://www.museumofdisability.org), and the EDGE (Education for Disability and Gender Equity), which offers interactive, Web-based activities on multiple topics of disability history and content (http://www.disabilityhistory.org/dwa/edge/curriculum/culture.htm). Both resources adopt "disability history" as their main thrust and seem to reflect the scholarship of disability studies and the disruption of a master script. "Disability awareness," in contrast, more often maintains a medical, colonial master script of ability.

"Disability awareness" events tend to offer activities like charity drives to benefit cure research and one-night-event guest presenters who tell stories of overcoming adversity that are intended to emphasize the potentiality of "normalcy" that lies within disabled experiences. Disability is something to cure or overcome, which exemplifies the superhuman work ethic and *joie de vivre* of those who have "risen above." Wheelchair basketball games and wheelchair races featuring "abled" athletes competing with everyday wheelchair-users provide fun and novelty. For the able-bodied, blindfolding, limb-tying, ear-plugging, and wheelchair-riding are simulation experiences that claim to increase empathy and understanding for disability experiences. Perhaps the Frustration, Anxiety and Tension workshop, known as F.A.T. City (Lavoie, 1989), which presents participants with nonsense words and impossible activities to simulate a learning disability, may be held, or a relatively innocuous depiction of school-based inclusion, such as the Academy Award–winning documentary *Educating Peter* (Wurzberg, 1992) screened.

In "disability awareness," disability curriculum is relegated to special events in the "appropriate" week or month, and the character of the events tends to re-inscribe pity, fear, discomfort, and misunderstanding of disability, particularly for abled participants. Brew-Parrish (1997; 2004), a disabled activist, recalls her daughter's experience of a disability simulation from which students emerged "terrified of their newly created disabilities," and with ideas that "persons with disabilities had horrible lives. A few thought they might be better off dead" (http://www.raggeded gemagazine.com/focus/wrongmessage04.html). A master script of ability is produced when disability is largely presented as an experience of either extreme dysfunction—as abled persons simulate "conditions" with which they have not learned to function—or extreme success, in inspirational stories of over-achievers—the trope of the "supercrip."

Disability awareness fails to capture the richness and complexity of actual lives that are described or claimed as disabled. Skepticism about adding disability to the pantheon of other "Others" who seek pluralistic curricula is well placed if awareness curricula draw critique. In its presentation of non-complicated inspirational personas, offer of novelty spectator events involving abled athletes struggling in wheelchairs, and disingenuous simulations, awareness does, indeed, focus on the parochial and on self-esteem, which, as Brew-Parrish (2004) points out, still misses the mark. The presence of awareness may, in fact, produce more powerful master scripts of ability within various curricula than would be produced in its absence. While the master script of ability can be found within many discourses, in the following section we call attention to three: attention in the workplace; teacher education; and content curricula in the arts and social sciences.

The Workplace

Compliance with Section 504 of the Rehabilitation Act, The Americans with Disabilities Act, and the Individuals with Disabilities Education Act is commonly presented as the rationale for addressing disability in the workplace and in education (Barrett, 1997; Gordon, Lewandowski, & Keiser, 1999; Lissner, 1997; Vogel, Leyser, Wyland, & Brulle, 1999). The struggle for equity in employment and the education of disabled persons emerges as a battle over money and semantics in the courts, with businesses scrambling to meet minimum compliance requirements with policies that actually do very little to improve the lives of disabled persons (Russell, 1998). The dominant discourse of disability read through law and policy, however, appears comprehensive and effectively controls and sanitizes others' accounts of lived, daily struggles that could be presented in workplace curricula (Russell, 1998; O'Brien, 2001).

Teacher Education

In teacher education, a medical model of special education has given rise to a host of dispositions and practices intended to support the inclusion of students with disabilities in general education. Beyond the separation of "special" from "general" education, which reveals that the master script of ability is at work even in our *initial* conceptualization of schooling, the recommendation that teachers learn to modify curriculum for disabled learners is listed among the more important teaching skills recommended for special educators (Vaidya & Zaslavsky, 2000; The National Joint Committee on Learning Disabilities, 1998). On its own, learning to modify curriculum seems like a promising idea to realize equity and pluralism in schools. However, the master script of the medical model imbues the practice of modifying curriculum with contradictory implications.

Teacher education often specifies that inclusive educators be prepared to "modify" and "adapt" general education curricula to meet the needs of students labeled with disabilities. For example, Vaidya and Zaslavsky (2000) assert that teacher education should ". . .help teachers *modify* [emphasis added] curricula, deliver effective instruction, and employ alternative-assessment strategies to meet the needs of diverse learners." (p. 145). The National Joint Committee on Learning Disabilities (1998) also states that general educators must "*modify* [emphasis added] instruction given students' unique learning characteristics." (p. 184). In these examples, *modified* refers to a process of changing from a presumed baseline of curriculum or pedagogy to one created specifically to meet the needs of particular students labeled with disabilities. This perspective constructs education as static, in which difference is extraordinary to a presumed normal course of instruction. The construction of an accessible curriculum as exceptional to a presumed standard reifies a medical model. In other words, conceptualizing curriculum changes as, first, necessitated by disability and, second, as outside of a general course of teaching, we reify a view of particular students as disordered, thus upholding a master script that reinforces the abled/disabled binary.

In each of these contexts—awareness events, workplace compliance, and teacher education—a sanitized view of disability emerges. We overly simplify disability experiences by addressing disability primarily through the courts or through superficial efforts to empathize or adapt. Compliance to policy in the workplace and the ways we imagine best practices in education privilege a medical model of disability, in which government or professional expertise, to recall Swartz's (1992) description, "silences multiple voices and perspectives, primarily by legitimizing dominant, White, upper-class, male voicings as the 'standard' knowledge" (p. 341). The master script of ability in business and school practices can be discerned in ways similar to reading master scripts of race. It should come as little surprise, therefore, that treatment of disability in content-area curriculum in the arts and social sciences emerges in analogous constructions as well.

Content-Area Curricula

Efforts by teachers to incorporate disability-related topics into content-area curriculum have been noted by Connor and Bejoian (2006). They describe, for example, a teacher "who highlights the disability rights movement as a consequence of the Civil Rights Movement," and another who "briefly taught about the impact of the German eugenics movement that forcibly interned citizens who had disabilities and then systematically killed them" (p. 52). Both teaching examples, while admittedly well intended, were positioned as supplemental to the general curriculum in ways that reveal a master script of ability.

Describing the disability rights movement as a mere "consequence" of another movement serves to silence the voices and experiences of disability rights activists, and positions the movement as happenstance. By attaching the experiences of disabled persons to the broader genocide of the Third Reich, we whitewash both the particular impact of eugenic policies on disabled persons and the role that American eugenics played in the actions of Nazi Germany. Linton, Mello, and O'Neill (1995) point out, for example, "the use of the 'lethal chamber' option was supported by leaders in the field of mental retardation in the United States before it was applied in Nazi Germany" (p. 7). Despite best intentions, efforts to include disability in the curriculum reflect a compensatory approach (Swartz, 1992) that serves as a quick but insufficient nod in the direction of including disability diversity.

In another example from social studies content, the story of President Franklin D. Roosevelt is now a commonly incorporated disability topic in the school curriculum. Related to the controversy during the late nineties over whether a statue depicting the president in a wheelchair should be included in his Washington, D.C. memorial, a retrospective of Roosevelt positions him as a premier American figure with a disability (Fleischer & Zames, 2001). As with Rosa Parks, however, the discussion of Roosevelt tends to be removed from the historical context in which he hid his disability from the public. When Roosevelt is described as a president who "happens to have had a disability" or presented as an inspiring example of overcoming adversity, his disability experience is reduced to mere happenstance.

Alter's (2006) biography of Roosevelt, however, re-characterizes the president's disability experience as, not simply an extraordinary feature of his biography, but as a central factor in his humanistic New Deal policies. The potential to provide a fuller context to Roosevelt's life and work is present through an analysis of his abled/disabled identity, presidential policies, and contradictions in historical and modern representation of him as a wheelchair-using polio survivor. However, master scripting produces the more common presentations of Roosevelt as a president who "happens to have had" a disability or who overcame adversity in his presidency, neither of which comprehensively captures the complexity of his life, work, and past and present representations.

As in history, the study of literature is filled with opportunities to address the meaning assigned to the extraordinary bodies of scores of literary characters. Fairy tales, myths, legends, folktales, Shakespearean and classic characters from Beecher Stowe, Steinbeck, and Morrison, to name a few, can all be rich sources for students' exploration of disability in literature (Connor & Bejoian, 2007; Garland-Thomson, 1997; Mitchell & Snyder, 2000). More typically, however, the use of disability in the literary canon serves symbolic purposes. Little time is spent troubling the idea of using disability as metaphor rather than reflecting actual lived experiences (Mitchell & Snyder, 2001). Furthermore, the stereotypes and tropes of disability that are reified in many texts and perpetuated through extraordinary characters—more often villains—are not usually addressed (Shapiro, 1999). In brief, master scripting in the study of literature reveals sterile methods of "neutral" literary analysis that position disability to be useful as metaphor and as an effective literary device for characterization. It incorporates disabilities imagined by non-disabled authors rather than realistic lived experiences of people with disabilities (Kleege, 1999).

Rewriting Master Scripts

Master scripting in ability is similar to master scripting with regard to race. "The debate over the centrality or marginality of race, class, and gender groups in the production of knowledge," Swartz (1992) points out, "is not over the relative importance of historical figures and events, nor is it over the potential impact of the curriculum experience on self-esteem or the modeling of race, gender, and class heroes and heroines" (p. 341). Rather, it relates to the "maintenance or disruption of the Eurocentrically bound 'master script' that public schools currently impart to their students" (p. 341). Achieving a pluralistic approach to curriculum cannot be realized in the mention of a few historical figures who "happen to have disabilities," by reading one book on Helen Keller, or by engaging in non-critical analyses of disability in literature. We also do not suggest that disability becomes centered in ways that marginalize other groups. Rather, we imagine pluralistic curriculum to engage students in sophisticated analyses that examine the master script alongside, and in contrast to, counter-stories. Complexity may be emphasized in the experiences and identities or characterizations of historical and literary figures with regard to multiple markers of group membership and intersections.

In addition, there are important interrelations between master scripting of race and ability that suggest the fruitful expansion of plurality to include disability. Gould (1996) claims the construction of intelligence measures helped to "establish" the superiority of Northern European white men (and their descendents) over virtually all others as scientifically defensible. Despite current espoused values for a "color-blind" strategy for educational practice a century later (Leonardo, 2007), the science of ability continues to justify inequity in education between European Americans and African Americans (and other students of color). As Carrier (1986), Sleeter (1987), and Ferri and Connor (2006) point out, special education emerged primarily to protect racially segregated education and is practiced in ways that continue to disadvantage students of African descent (Blanchett, 2006; Losen & Orfield, 2002). The master scripting of ability interrelates with master scripting of race. The intersections and parallels of master scripts about ability and race, and their dual impact on the knowledge made of disability and race, suggest the fallacy in fears that disability studies "atomizes" an agenda for pluralistic curricula. In teacher education, especially for prospective educators, opportunities must exist to examine the intersections and interactions among traditions of knowledge that act together to justify inequity and misrepresentation of groups of students made marginal through master scripting (Swartz, 2007; Ware, 2006).

Far from parochial, and decidedly not geared to improving self-esteem, disability studies adds a rich element to the ways in which students can learn to "read the world" (Freire, 1970). Disability studies offers numerous lenses for analysis and inquiry to trouble (mis)representation, ongoing marginality, happenstance interpretations of disability, and devaluation of disability experiences. Those who operate within a master script of disability marinated within a medical model, or interpret disability as metaphor or trope, fail to recognize the importance of accounts and experiences of persons with disabilities. Incorporating actual accounts exemplifies Swartz's (2007) process of "re-membering," the approach designed to produce more accurate, contextual representations of people of African descent in curriculum. A process of "putting the members of history back together" (p. 173), re-membering emphasizes representation, critical thinking, and indigenous voice as central components to teaching content about people of who have been othered, as well as in building knowledge about their roles in history. As in the reexamination of race, approaches can be adopted to re-member curriculum for people with disabilities, another important "other" (Kudlick, 2003).

How Can We Teach Disability as Diversity?

When thinking about curriculum, two major issues co-exist: the *content* of the curriculum and *access* to that content. In this section we will focus on the first issue, advocating that disability should be studied in the broadest contexts possible and across all disciplines. James Banks (1994) suggests five dimensions of multicultural education, and we believe they are equally apt when applied to disability: (1) diversity must be integrated into the content, and not an additive approach; (2) the origins and construction of knowledge are openly addressed, including the influence on scholars; (3) a pro-active approach is used to reduce prejudice and help students develop positive attitudes to different groups; (4) equitable pedagogy is employed, encouraging diverse forms of interaction such as cooperative learning; and (5) an empowering school culture and social structure are consciously cultivated. Used together, these dimensions support a transformative approach to education, encouraging plurality in perspectives, and acknowledge the epistemological contributions of formerly marginalized groups. Through the exploration of disability from social and cultural perspectives, we can teach disability as another way of being.

In subsequent sections are some ideas for content *and* strategies to help students engage in materials and discussions. Although we have divided areas into suggestions for elementary, middle, and high school, followed by teacher education, it is our belief that each idea can potentially be modified.

Elementary School

Teaching children to understand and value difference begins in elementary school. Teachers can introduce the notion that differences are often perceived very differently by individuals. Furthermore, the person perceived as different (whether based on race, class, ethnicity, gender, age, or body size) is neither better nor worse than the person beholding. Put disability on the list. Compare how people without disabilities view people with disabilities, and then contrast that with how people with disabilities view themselves—deliberately challenging notions of incompleteness, unhappiness, common *inability*, and overall inferiority.

In general, children's literature has been criticized for inaccurately representing life with a disability, largely portraying "poor little things," and "brave little souls" (Ayala, 1999, p. 103), evoking pity and/or admiration. This phenomenon can be countered by teaching the broad topic of difference in classic books such as *Charlotte's Web* (White, 1952/2004), *Chrysanthemum* (Henkes, 1996), *The Secret Garden* (Burnett, 1909), and the perennial *Rudolph the Red-Nosed Reindeer* (May, 1939). Student-centered discussion can focus on topics such as: How is the character different? What do other characters think of him/her? What happens to character because of his/her difference? How does the character, in turn, respond? What can we learn and appreciate about the idea of difference from knowing the character? Several scholars in education have designed criteria that are useful in evaluating children's stories for accuracy of disability representation (see Blaska, 2004; Worotynec, 2004; Ziegler, 1980). In addition, inclusive education has been responsible for a growth in the direct incorporation of disability teaching into the curriculum (see "Nine Ways to Evaluate Children's Books That Address Disability as Part of Diversity" at http://circleofinclusion.org).

Another way to teach disability is by providing progressive representations of disability in literature. Tiny Tim in Dickens's *A Christmas Carol* (1843/1986) is the poster child of quintessential helpless, passive, sickly, pitiable victimhood. To challenge such "classic" portraits, use contemporary books depicting disabled children as being able to do many things and unable to do some things. Stories such as *Friends in the Park* (Bunnet, 1992), *Lester's Dog* (Hesse, 1993), *The Wonderful Life of a Fly Who Couldn't Fly* (Lozoff, 2002), *Mandy Sue's Day* (Karim, 1994), and the autobiographical *Trouble with School: A Family Story about Learning Disabilities* (Dunn & Dunn, 1993) provide more accurate and realistic representations of disability (Blaska & Lynch, 1998).

Given how much children love cartoons, an analysis of them yields interesting classroom discussions. Inarticulate Elmer Fudd, short-sighted Mr. Magoo, developmentally delayed Dopey the Dwarf, stuttering Porky Pig, and so on, all share the unenviable position of being openly laughed at because of their disability. Students can talk about and critique the connection between comedy and disability—and how laughing at others due to their difference is essentially how prejudice operates and causes hurtful consequences.

In designing a unit called, Teaching about Difference to a Third-Grade Class, one educator used the movie *Babe* (1995) about an unwanted piglet that is bought by a farmer. While the teacher used the film as a vehicle to address the measurement skills required in the traditional curriculum such as weight, length, time, and temperature, she also selected specific themes from the movie to focus on. These themes included welcoming newcomers into the community, nurturing independence, and fostering interdependence. Discussion questions she posed to students included: Why did no one want Babe? Why did others prefer his brothers and sisters? How did Babe fit in with the other animals? In what ways did Babe prove people wrong? What could Babe do that no one else could? How are Babe's experiences like those of children? (Connor & Bejoian, 2006).

Finally, many traditional myths, tales, legends, and fairy stories are ripe for a disability studies reading. What might be said about the "lame boy" in *The Pied Piper of Hamelin*? Hans

Christian Andersen's Tin Soldier with one leg? The socially ostracized Ugly Duckling? What of general themes such as physical ugliness mirroring moral ugliness (ugly stepsisters, wicked witches, pirates, trolls) or physical beauty representing virtue (Sleeping Beauty, Cinderella, princes)? In what ways do these stories all teach messages about what make "good" and "bad" bodies/people?

Middle School

As putdowns by peers are rife in middle school, there is all the more reason to openly discuss the widespread use of disability-related language in our society. Some examples worthy of consideration include "That's retarded," "You're a spaz," "Are you blind?" "He's crazy," "She's nuts," "Schitzo!" "Are you deaf?" and "That idea is so lame." What associations with disability can be found in these expressions? What are the implications of these associations? What do people with disabilities think about non-disabled people using this language? Most importantly, what are some alternative ways of expressing the same meaning without using disability as a "put-down"? (Mairs, 1996)

Keeping with the use and significance of language, students can study the meaning of the words "able" and "disabled." How might they respond when asked what does it mean to be able-bodied? What are able-bodied people "able" to do? While admittedly sounding strange at first, the question prompts thinking how able-bodied people have the luxury of not having to think about this question. Indeed the majority of people do not usually acknowledge their status of having full access to most aspects of the world, feeling part of the mainstream, and not being "invisible." On the other hand, many people with disabilities are prevented from gaining full access to the world, feel excluded from the mainstream, and are constantly made aware of their "disabled" status. What are some barriers (structural? economic? cultural?) preventing disabled people from gaining access to the mainstream, and how have some of these barriers been surmounted in the past (Charlton, 1998; J. Shapiro, 1993)?

Another way of teaching disability is to use books that are written to help students understand themselves. A small but significant body of literature exists which aims to help students understand the ways their own bodies and minds function. Two examples by Mel Levine include *Keeping a Head in School* (1990) and *All Kind of Minds* (1993). The first is a book for adolescents that explains the ways in which the mind works and how humans manage the executive functions of their brains in negotiating the academic and social demands of school. The second describes fictional middle-school students who struggle with attention, organization, memory, behaviors, receptive and expressive use of language, featuring ways students address their own areas of need.

On a different note, the arts offer an excellent venue for discussing disability-related issues. Disability has informed the creative process of many great painters who gave us masterpieces that are appreciated the world over. For example, Andrew Wyeth's *Christina's World* portrays his next-door neighbor, who was unable to walk. Yet, in the painting he purposefully positioned her looking toward a wide-open space, not inhibited by expectations of confinement (Mayer, 2004). Artists who were disabled include Frida Kahlo, arguably the most famous female painter in the world, whose deeply personalized canvases and drawings depict the lifelong physical and emotional effects of surviving a street accident; Matisse and Monet, whose later larger works were influenced by the limitations of their eyesight (Linton, 2004); Van

Gogh who produced vivid, vibrant paintings, of unparalleled intensity, throughout his emotionally turbulent life; and Beauford Delaney's brilliantly colored canvases that are inextricable from his schizophrenia. The artists above are examples of people who could be researched with their disability considered a shaper of their work.

Within social studies, students can learn about the disability rights movement, instrumental in organizing political power from a grass roots level. Access to education, employment, transportation, health care, housing, community integration, and technology has significantly improved the lives of many people with disabilities. The vanguard of these changes consisted of disabled activists who staged demonstrations, sit-ins, and argued determinedly to speak for themselves and be heard. Students can determine in what ways the disability rights movement is similar to, and different from, other movements, as well as describing the breadth and limitations of this movement.

Finally, read-alouds can be a great venue for facilitating discussions about different disabilities (Richardson & Boyle, 1998). For example, *Stuck in Neutral* (Trueman, 2001) is narrated from the point of view of a teenager with multiple disabilities who is unable to speak, who comes to believe that his father is preparing to carry out a "mercy killing" on him. In *Freak the Mighty* (Philbrick,1995), a small, physically fragile child teams up with a large, cognitively delayed adolescent to navigate a world that is openly hostile toward them both, forging strong friendship through mutual respect for each other's differences. Read-alouds can be used to deliberate a variety of relevant issues while also meeting state standards (Kates, 2006).

High School

In the higher grades become, students become increasingly aware of complex concepts. At this age, students are able to contemplate the idea of disability as a minority label. Disability can be explored along with other "markers of identity" that are recognized as signifying minority-group status, such as race, ethnicity, gender, and sexual orientation (Gordon & Rosenblum, 2001). Students can also be asked, when people with disabilities claim kinship as a minority group, in what ways that changes their self-perception, and how others perceive them. They can then explore some of the inequities in society faced by people with disabilities, addressing to what degree disabled people and their allies have addressed these inequalities. What are further ways in which these inequities can be addressed?

The history of people with disabilities can also be taught, whether framed explicitly in a unit, woven throughout an interdisciplinary curriculum, or offered as potential research project. Although people with disabilities have always existed, the cultural understanding of various conditions and impairments have differed within various societies and changed over time (Stiker, 1999). For example, people with disabilities were: accorded special powers in ancient Egypt (people of short stature); believed to be possessed by demons (epilepsy); annihilated in Nazi death camps (developmentally and physically disabled); and were responsible for organizing the Disability Rights movement (Fleischer & Zames, 2001). These fragments offer a glimpse into a fascinating and complex history of human diversity that has yet to be fully realized.

As films can be seen as cultural texts that students learn from, it is worthwhile including critiques of disability representation in movies. The vast majority of films portray people with disabilities in inaccurate and damaging ways, reinforcing stereotypes and circulating misleading information (Darke, 1998; Safran, 1998a; Safran, 1998b). These depictions can be openly challenged. For example, after learning about the real life experiences of blind people, watch the film *Scent of a Woman*. While unquestionably entertaining, Al Pacino's Oscar-winning performance as a lonely, self-loathing, bitter, despondent, socially-rejected man who feels faces to "see" a person (myth), has an incredible sense of smell (myth), and is suicidal (myth), conforms with many misunderstandings of blindness. Students can discuss what is problematic about such pervasive representations. More importantly, students can also clarify that blindness is simply an everyday experience that is "normal" for some people.

Teachers can also use progressive representations of disability in film to dispel myths and undermine stereotypes. Fairly recent movies in which disability is seen as an everyday fact of life, including *The Station Agent* (person of short stature leading a "normal" life), *Finding Nemo* (having a "gimpy" body part is only one aspect of a person), and *Rory O'Shea Was Here* (young adults struggle to choose where they live and with whom). The Farrelly brothers often produce films that are controversial in the disability community and the source of lively debates about stereotypes and the ethics and meanings of representation. One recent film, *The Ringer*, is about a non-disabled man who pretends to have "mental retardation" in an attempt to infiltrate and win the Special Olympics. On another level, popular movies, such as the *Shrek* series, joyfully invert traditional expectations of surface appearances when "monstrous" physical attributes are seen as endearing, simply another way of being, and handsomely chiseled princely looks do not correspond with inner beauty. In his article, "Using Movies to Teach Students about Disabilities," Safran (2000) offers a student-friendly tool to help evaluate positive and negative representations of disability.

Within the language arts classroom, students can analyze representations of disability in classic literature. Most classic texts taught in schools are actually populated with disabled characters, such as Shakespeare's *Richard III* (1600/2004), Melville's *Moby Dick* (1851/2001), Steinbeck's *Of Mice and Men* (1937/1986), Tennessee Williams's *The Glass Menagerie* (1945/1999), Toni Morrison's *Sula* (1973), and August Wilson's *Fences* (1986). However, on closer inspection, the character's disability is often the *defining* trait, and usually serves as a symbol and/or plot device to advance a theme and/or further the action (Mitchell & Snyder, 2000). Examples of this *signification* include: a hunchback as representative of personal evil and inevitable doom; a slow mind unable to comprehend the physical strength of its accompanying body; a wooden leg that fuels a vengeful desire; a limp indicates a stifling, restricted world, resulting in narrowed opportunities for all the family; a mentally ill brother whose war service translates to financial reparation; and a one-legged woman overseeing an unconventional household and all it represents. Unsurprisingly, the characters usually either die or remain in the margins of society. Students can juxtapose this signification with the real experience of disabled people, write alternative endings, or create original portrayals in which a disability is merely part of a character and not a defining characteristic that triggers demise.

Finally, the Center on Human Policy at Syracuse University has an excellent unit and lesson bank of disability-related material, largely focusing on the 6-12 grade curricula (http://www. disabilitystudiesforteachers.org). Unit topics include an introduction to studying disability, Deaf Education, crusader Dorothy Dix, "Freak Shows," Conscientious Objectors of World War II, Deaf Culture and Diversity, Intelligence Testing, Eugenics, and the Social Model of Disability.

Teacher Education

The medical/scientific/psychological model of disability takes a while to become undone in the minds of those unaware of different lenses through which to view disability. All of the strategies and ideas previously listed in this chapter must first become "owned" by the educators before they will use them. Foregrounding the social model/cultural/historical model of disabilities, and including other perspectives (religious, aesthetic, etc.), is a long and complex undertaking that is achieved over a course of studies. World views of teachers and students rarely change overnight.

Fortunately, there are many excellent resources in the form of books and documentary films. Some of the films include *Vital Signs: Crip Culture Talks Back, Liebe Perla, Refrigerator Mothers, The Sound and the Fury, Murderball,* and *When Billy Broke His Head.* What unites these films is their centering of people with disabilities to tell their stories, share their lives, and invite the viewer to see who they are and how they live. In terms of educational films, in addition to ones listed in the middle school section, *Including Samuel* narrates the story of a young boy with multiple disabilities as he attends school with his non-disabled peers.

Once educators have a basic understanding of a disability studies framework, they develop an automatic sense in analyzing all contexts in which they move. For example, when traveling, or entering a building, or using a bathroom in a restaurant or bar, they assess how accessible it is for non-ambulatory peers. In addition, when reading newspapers, novels, or watching movies, characters become framed within a lens of dis/ability, allowing deeper connections to be made behind the initial surface of the text. Subtexts from a century of movies, such as *Freaks, The Sweet Hereafter, Donnie Darko, Elephant Man,* and *Gattaca,* can become unpacked in deeply nuanced ways.

Current events on disability also become points of reference. For example, recently in London, a statue was erected of a heavily pregnant woman with shortened arms due to the drug thalidomide. A controversy ensued, with debate after debate on tastefulness (or lack thereof). However, the debacle did raise fascinating questions about issues raised by juxtaposing a disabled female figure with the fixture of Trafalgar Square, the noticeably disabled war hero, Lord Nelson (who lost an arm in battle). What does this situation say about disability, gender, war, and who belongs where?

This question could be addressed in a self-reflective piece within teacher education. Past research that has examined teachers' experience of learning about and through social models of disability prioritizes discussion of learning in relation to particular course materials or experiences. In surveying research on using disability studies approaches in teacher education classes, Baglieri (in press) notes the value of teacher self-reflection as a device that helps individuals shift their thinking, often from a secure place to an area of uncertainty. Furthermore, she notes how encouraging teachers to contemplate where they are located in terms of intersectional markers of identity in terms of race, class, gender, ethnicity, nationality, and sexual orientation ultimately informs how they then interpret all other people. Examining the processes of reflection that teachers engage in to make meaning of disability and disabled persons' experiences informs the potential of teacher educators to emphasize students' past experiences and knowledge to support their new learning. Providing learners a forum to draw from their background knowledge and/or experience with other cultural and religious groups' concerns regarding identity, equity, and cultural representation is a fruitful way to support teachers' learning of social and cultural models of disability to interrupt a medical model.

Conclusion

We began this work by troubling the frequent absence of disability from typical conceptualizations of diversity. We note that critiques about broadening the "diversity agenda" include fears that scholarship in disability is invalid (pun respectfully intended), that its inclusion further atomizes curriculum, and that the study of disability is geared toward self-esteem. We offer disability studies as a growing field of theory, research, and practice that challenges a master script determined by a medical model of disability. In lieu of this form of damaging reductionism, disability studies confront the normative ideologies and social practices in society, work, and school that perpetuate the continued marginalization of and stigma assigned to "extraordinary" bodies and minds. Examining the meaning made of ability and disability *alongside* others seeking curriculum reform toward pluralism creates opportunities for expanding possibilities within theory, research, and practice. Rather than atomize or "water down" curriculum, the cross-disciplinary and eclectic thinkers who comprise disability studies promise to enrich and support its own and others' work toward equity.

We offered a critique of some disability curricula to acknowledge and better define the problems in selected past practices. These included: awareness days that control and sanitize disability experiences; histories that offer master scripts of ability, rather than incorporate the voice of the "other;" and literary and artistic analyses that fall short of the potential to add another dynamic lens for understanding. We ended, however, with possibility, as we look toward curriculum and practice that can provide learners of all ages and in many settings opportunities to think about disability as diversity, simply another way of being. Because disability does tip the scales of what counts as diversity for many educators, Linda Ware (2001) has asked, "Dare we do disability studies?" Indeed, we urge us all to dare.

References

Alter, J. (2006). *The defining moment: FDR's hundred days and the triumph of hope.* New York: Simon & Schuster.

Anderson, M. L., & Collins, P. H. (Eds.). (1998). *Race, class, and gender: An anthology.* Belmont, CA: Wadsworth.

Apple, M. (1971). The hidden curriculum and the nature of conflict. *Interchange, 2*(4), 27–40.

Ayala, E. C. (1999). "Poor little things" and "brave little souls": The portrayal of individuals with disabilities in children's literature. *Reading Research and Instruction, 39*(1), 103–116.

Baglieri, S. (in press). "I connected": Reflection and biography in teacher learning toward inclusion. *International Journal of Inclusive Education.*

Baker, B. (2002). The hunt for disability: The new eugenics and the normalization of school children. *Teachers College Record, 104*(4), 663–703.

Banks, J. A. (1994). Transforming the mainstream curriculum. *Educational Leadership, 51*(8), 4–8.

Banks, J. A. (2001). *Cultural diversity and education: Foundations, curriculum and teaching.* Boston: Pearson, Allyn & Bacon.

Barrett, B. (1997). Explaining learning disabilities to colleagues: Treatment and accommodation. In B. M. Hodge & J. Preston-Sabin (Eds.), *Accommodations—or just good teaching? Strategies for teaching college students with disabilities* (pp. 2–4). Westport, CT: Praeger.

Blanchett, W. J. (2006). Disproportionate representation of African-American students in special education: Acknowledging the role of White privilege and racism. *Educational Researcher, 35*(6), 24–28.

Blaska, J. K. (2004). Children's literature that includes characters with disabilities or illnesses. *Disability Studies Quarterly, 24*(1). Retrieved October 15, 2006, from www.dsq-sds.org/_articles_html/2004/winter/dsq_w04_blaska.html

Blaska, J. K., & Lynch, E. C. (1998). Is everyone included? Using children's literature to facilitate the understanding of disabilities. *Young Children, 53*(2), 36–38.

Brantlinger, E. (2004). Confounding the needs and confronting the norms: An extension of Reid and Valle's essay. *Journal of Learning Disabilities, 37*(6), 490–499.

Brew-Parrish, V. (1997). The wrong message [Electronic Version]. *Ragged Edge Online, March/April.* Retrieved April 10, 2008 from http://www.raggededgemagazine.com/archive/aware.htm.

Brew-Parrish, V. (2004). The wrong message—Still [Electronic Version]. *Ragged Edge Online.* Retrieved April 10, 2008 from http://www.raggededgemagazine.com/focus/wrongmessage04.html.

Brown, J. E. (1996). *Exploring diversity: Literature themes and activities for grades 4–8.* Portsmouth, NH: Teachers Ideas Press.

Bunnet, R. (1992). *Friends in the park.* Bellingham, WA: Our Kids Press.

Burnett, F. H. (1909). *The secret garden.* New York: Harper Classics.

Butler, J. P. (1993). *Bodies that matter: On the discursive limits of "sex."* New York: Routledge.

Carrier, J. G. (1986). *Learning disability: Social class and the construction of inequality in American education.* New York: Greenwood Press.

Charlton, J. I. (1998). *Nothing about us without us.* Berkeley: University of California Press.

Christensen, C. (1996). Disabled, handicapped or disordered: "What's in a name?" In C. Christensen & F. Rizvi (Eds.), *Disability and the Dilemmas of Educational Justice* (pp. 63–78). Buckingham, PA: Open University Press.

Connor, D. J., & Bejoian, L. (2006). Pigs, pirates, and pills: Using film to teach the social context of disability. *Teaching Exceptional Children, 39*(2), 52–60.

Connor, D. J., & Bejoian, L. (2007). Cripping school curricula: 20 ways to re-teach disability. *Review of Disability Studies, 3*(3), 3–13.

Connor, D.J, & Ferri, B. A. (2007). The conflict within: Resistance to inclusion and other paradoxes within special education. *Disability & Society, 22*(1), 63–77.

Danforth, S. & Gabel, S.L. (Eds.). (2006). *Vital questions for disabilities studies in education.* New York: Peter Lang.

Darke, P. (1998). Understanding cinematic representations of disability. In T. Shakespeare (Ed.), *The disabilities studies reader: Social science perspectives* (pp. 181–197). London: Cassel.

Davis, L. J. (1997). Constructing normalcy. In L. J. Davis (Ed.), *The Disability Studies Reader* (pp. 9–28). New York: Routledge.

Davis, L. J. (2002). *Bending over backwards: Disability, dismodernism, and other difficult positions.* New York: New York University Press.

Dickens, C. (1843/1986). *A Christmas carol.* New York: Bantam Classics.

Dunn, K.B., & Dunn, A. B. (1993). *Trouble with school: A family story about learning disabilities.* Rickville, MD: Woodbine House.

Ellis, E. S. (1997). Watering up the curriculum for adolescents with learning disabilities: Goals of the knowledge dimension. *Remedial and Special Education, 18*(6), 326–346.

Ferri, B. A., & Connor, D. J. (2006). *Reading resistance: Discourses of exclusion in the desegregation and inclusion debates.* New York: Peter Lang.

Fleischer, D. Z., & Zames, F. (2001). *The disability rights movement: From charity to confrontation.* Philadelphia, PA: Temple University Press.

Freire, P. (1970/1997). Pedagogy of the oppressed. In D. J. Flinders & D. J. Thornton (Eds.), *The curriculum studies reader* (pp. 150–158). New York: Routledge.

Gabel, S. L. (Ed.). (2005). *Disability studies in education: Readings in theory and method.* New York: Peter Lang.

Gallagher, D. J., Heshusius, L., Iano, R. P., & Skrtic, T. M. (2004). *Challenging orthodoxy in special education: Dissenting voices.* Denver, CO: Love.

Garland-Thomson, R. (1997). *Extraordinary bodies.* New York: Columbia University Press.

Goffman, E. (1963). *Stigma: Notes on the management of spoiled identity.* New York: Simon & Schuster.

Gordon, B. O., & Rosenblum, K. E. (2001). Bringing disability into the sociological frame: A comparison of disability with race, sex, and sexual orientation statuses. *Disability & Society, 16*(1), 5–19.

Gordon, M., Lewandowski, L., & Keiser, S. (1999). The LD label for relatively well-functioning students: A critical analysis. *Journal of Learning Disabilities, 32*(6), 485–490.

Gould, S. J. (1996). *The Mismeasure of Man.* New York: W.W. Norton and Company.

Hamre, B., Oyler, C., & Bejoian, L. B. (2006). Guest editors' introduction. Narrating disability: pedagogical imperatives. *Equity & Excellence in Education, 39*(2), 91–100.

Hehir, T. (2003). Beyond inclusion. *School Administrator, 60*(3), 36–39.

Hehir, T. (2005). *New directions in special education: Eliminating ableism in policy and practice.* Cambridge, MA: Harvard Education Press.

Henkes, K. (1996). *Chrysanthemum*. New York: Harper.

Heshusius, L. (1989). The Newtonian mechanistic paradigm, special education, and the contours of alternatives: An overview. *Journal of Learning Disabilities, 22*, 402–415.

Hesse, K. (1993). *Lester's dog*. New York: Crown.

Karim, R. (1994). *Mandy Sue's day*. New York: Clarion Books.

Kates, B. (2006). "There's no such thing as normal." Paper presented at the annual meeting of Society for Disability studies, Bethesda, MD.

Kleege, G. (1999). *Sight unseen*. New Haven, CT: Yale University Press.

Kudlick, C. J. (2003). Disability history: Why we need another "other." Retrieved August 22, 2003, from http://www.historycoop.org/journals/ahr/108.3/kudlick.html

Lavoie, R. (Writer) (1989). How difficult can this be? The F.A.T. City workshop. USA: www.ricklavoie.com.

Leonardo, Z. (2007). The war on schools: NCLB, nation creation and the educational construction of whiteness. *Race, ethnicity and education, 10*(3), 261–278.

Levine, M. (1990). *Keeping a head in school*. Cambridge, MA: Educators Publishing Service.

Levine, M. (1993). *All kinds of minds*. Cambridge, MA: Educators Publishing Service.

Linton, S. (1998). *Claiming disability*. New York: New York University Press.

Linton, S. (2004). *What is disability studies?* PMLA 120(2).

Linton, S., Mello, S., & O'Neill, J. (1995). Disability studies: Expanding the parameters of diversity. *Radical Teacher, 47*, 4–10.

Lissner, L. S. (1997). Legal issues concerning all faculty in higher education. In B. M. Hodge & J. Preston-Sabin (Eds.), *Accommodations—or just good teaching? Strategies for teaching college students with disabilities* (pp. 5–22). Westport, CT: Praeger.

Losen, D. J., & Orfield, G. (Eds.). (2002). *Racial inequity in special education*. Boston, MA: Harvard Educational Publishing Group.

Lozoff, B. (2002). *The wonderful life of a fly who couldn't fly*. Charlottesville, VA: Hampton.

May, R. L. (1939) *Rudolph the red-nosed reindeer* song.

Mairs, N. (1996). *Waist-high in the world: A life among the nondisabled*. Boston, MA: Beacon Press.

Mayer, P. (March, 2004) Personal communication.

Melville, H. (1851/2001). *Moby Dick*. New York: Bantam Classics.

Mitchell, D. T., & Snyder, S. L. (2000). *Narrative prosthesis: Disability and the dependencies of discourse*. Ann Arbor: University of Michigan Press.

Morrison, T. (1973). *Sula*. New York: Knopf.

Murphy, R. F. (1995). Encounters: The Body Silent in America. In B. Instad & S. R. White (Eds.), *Disability and cultures* (pp. 140–157). Berkeley: University of California Press.

National Joint Committee on Learning Disabilities. (1998). Learning disabilities: Preservice preparation of general and special education teachers. *Learning Disability Quarterly, 21*(3), 182–186.

O'Brien, R. (2001). *Crippled justice: The history of modern disability policy in the workplace*. Chicago: University of Chicago Press.

Philbrick, P. (1995). *Freak the mighty*. New York: Scholastic.

Reid, D. K., & Valle, J. (2004). The discursive practice of learning disability: Implication for instruction and parent school relations. *Journal of Learning Disabilities, 37*(6), 466–481.

Richardson, J., & Boyle, J. (1998). A read-aloud for discussing disabilities. *Journal of Adolescent & Adult Literacy, 41*(8), 684–686.

Russell, M. (1998). *Beyond ramps: Disability at the end of the social contract*. Monroe, ME: Common Courage Press.

Safran, S. P. (1998a). Disability portrayal in film: Reflecting the past, directing the future. *Exceptional Children, 64*(2), 227–238.

Safran, S. P. (1998b). The first century of disability portrayal in film: An analysis of the literature. *Journal of Special Education, 31*(4), 467–479.

Safran, S. P. (2000). Using movies to teach students about disabilities. *TEACHING Exceptional Children*, 32(3), 44–47.

Sapon-Shevin, M. (2000). Schools fit for all. *Educational Leadership, 58*(4), 34–39.

Shakespeare, W. (1600/2004). *Richard III*. Washington, DC: Folger Library.

Shapiro, A. (1999). *Everybody belongs: Changing negative attitudes toward classmates with disabilities* (Vol. 14). New York: Routledge.

Shapiro, J. P. (1993). *No pity*. New York: Three Rivers Press.

Sleeter, C. E. (1987). Why are there learning disabilities? A critical analysis of the birth of the field in its social context. In T. Popkewitz (Ed.), *The formation of school subjects: The struggle for creating an American institution* (pp. 210–237). London: Falmer Press.

Steinbeck, J. (1937/1986) *Of mice and men.* New York: Penguin.

Stiker, H. J. (1999). *A history of disability.* Ann Arbor, MI: Love.

Swartz, E. (1992). Emancipatory narratives: Rewriting the master script in the school curriculum. *Journal of Negro Education, 61*(3), 341–355.

Swartz, E. (2007). Stepping outside the master script: Re-connecting the history of American education. *Journal of Negro Education, 76*(2), 173–186.

Terry, J., & Urla, J. (Eds.). (1995). *Deviant bodies.* Bloomington: Indiana University Press.

Tomlinson, C. A. (2004). The Mobius effect: Addressing learner variance in schools. *Journal of Learning Disabilities, 37*(6), 516–524.

Trueman, T. (2001). *Stuck in neutral.* New York: HarperCollins.

Vaidya, S. R., & Zaslavsky, H. N. (2000). Teacher education reform effort for inclusion classrooms: Knowledge versus pedagogy. *Education, 121*(1), 145–152.

Varenne, H., & McDermott, R. (1998). *Successful failure.* Boulder, CO: Westview Press.

Vogel, S. A., Leyser, Y., Wyland, S., & Brulle, A. (1999). Students with learning disabilities in higher education: Faculty attitude and practices. *Learning Disabilities Research and Practice, 14*(3), 173–186.

Ware, L. (2001). Writing, identity, and the other: Dare we do Disability Studies? *Journal of Teacher Education, 52*(2), 107–123.

Ware, L. (2006). Urban educators, disability studies and education: Excavation in schools and society. *International Journal of Inclusive Education, 10*(2–3), 149–168.

Weise, J. (2004). "I'll pick you up by your back brace and throw you like a suitcase." *Review of Disability Studies, 1*(1), 29–33.

White, E. B. (1952/2004). *Charlotte's web.* New York: Harper Trophy.

Williams, T. (1945/1999). *The glass menagerie.* New York: New Directions.

Wilson, A. (1986). *Fences.* New York: Plume.

Worotynec, S. Z. (2004). Contrived or inspired: Ability/disability in the children's picture book. *Disability Studies Quarterly, 24*(1). Retrieved October 15, 2006, from www.dsq-sds.org/_articles_html/2004/winter/dsq_w04_worotynec.html

Wurzburg, G. (Writer) (1992). *Educating Peter.* USA: www.directcinema.com.

Ziegler, C. R. (1980). *The image of the physically handicapped in children's literature.* New York: Arno Press.

Twenty Four

The Hegemonic Impulse for Health and Well-Being
A Saga of the Less Well and the Less Worthy

Linda Ware

If I had my way, I would build a lethal chamber as big as Crystal Palace, with a military band playing softly and a cinematograph working brightly; then I'd go out in the back streets and the main streets and bring them in, all the sick, the halt and the maimed; I would lead them gently, and they would smile me a weary thanks, and the band would softly bubble out the 'Hallelujah Chorus.'
　　—The Letters of D.H. Lawrence (1908)

Disability requires adaptation, and we fool ourselves if we believe our buildings and policies will be expected to change more than the individuals who must access them.
　　—D. T. Mitchell, Foreword to *A History of Disability* (1999)

With the launch of each new semester, college campuses across the nation welcome new and returning students amid banners and with celebratory rituals designed to assure students that they have chosen one of America's Best Colleges! Typically, the search for a suitable college, facilitated by the initial browsing of colleges' Web profiles, begins well in advance of a student's senior year of high school. In streaming texts that proclaim a uniquely "exclusive" experience, unlike that offered by any other institution, many college Web sites look remarkably the same, with images of brown, black, Asian, and "other" diverse bodies parading across college Webpages—product-placement style—as if to convey exclusivity as synonymous with diversity. Market-managed mission statements brand colleges today as champions of diversity, social justice, and equity; some even link specific course offerings to ongoing campus-based diversity concerns. Students peruse college Websites in the hunt for the perfect fit, weighing institutional reputations, individual academic interests, extracurricular offerings, and increasingly, on-site recreational facilities, which will provide all the amenities to support personal wellness and a healthy lifestyle. Health, the hegemonic imperative, is conveyed in today's culture by constructs that tap into beauty, intelligence, consciousness, wellness, and even campus safety concerns.[1]

Far fewer students begin their search for postsecondary education informed by the content outlined on the Office of Disability Services (ODS) Web page, which is usually linked to the college administration homepage. These exclusively text-based pages are less engaging as compliance and legal language requirements than the glossy images of fun-seeking students, that fill the screen. Despite diversity/justice/equity campaigns that herald a welcome for all, "the sick, the halt, and the maimed" are conspicuous by their absence in the welcome-back campaigns of many college campuses. What will become more apparent in the discussion of ableism that follows is that the mandate to view disability as pathology is embedded in society is viewed through an exclusively medical lens that has been shaped by the professions and the institutions designated to "deal" with disability. It should come as no surprise that disability falls outside the traditional multicultural concerns of many colleges and universities in North America. Certainly, this is a topic that merits further consideration. However, this chapter has as its focus "visibility" in the example of disability. It considers the unwritten assumption that equates attainment with entitlement for the most able in society, and it challenges the boundary thinking in many institutions of higher education that have yet to recognize the relevance of exploring disability in interaction with different constructs of diversity.

Notes on Ableism and a Nod to Disability Studies

The analysis presented in this chapter necessitates a few brief notes on ableism and something of a nod to disability studies. Disability studies is a burgeoning field in academe that includes area studies scholarship in the humanities, cross-disciplinary scholarship in the social sciences, and recent work emerging in schools of education. In each instance, these interdisciplinary literatures trouble historical interpretations of disability that have been exclusively medicalized, deficit-driven, and bureaucratically managed to produce the socially marginalized individuals we label disabled. At the center of this field of interdisciplinary scholarship are analyses of the social construction of disability and richly layered critiques of ableism that aim to reclaim and reimagine disability as more than a medical/biological event that is rooted in individual pathology lodged.

Ableism is an equally new construct that is prevalent in disability studies academic literature and yet is also very much rooted in contexts both in and out of academe, as evidenced by this chapter. The disability studies scholar, Simi Linton (1998) defined ableism in the context of a "divided society" where privilege and power by non-disabled people operate in both overt and covert ways. Her often-cited book *Claiming Disability, Knowledge and Identity* draws on the work of the feminist theorist Iris Marion Young (1990), who outlined the limits of a conception of justice that fails to seek institutional remedy for the unintended cultural sources of oppression (*Justice and the Politics of Difference*). For Young, parallels between racism, sexism, homophobia, ageism, and ableism turn on recognition of modern society's impulse to denigrate some bodies as "'different,' as the 'Other.' . . in terms of bodily characteristics such as 'ugly, dirty, defiled, impure, contaminated, or sick' " (p. 123). In discussion of the politics of difference, Young recognized the impact of cultural change when "despised" groups seize the means of cultural expression to redefine a positive image of themselves—an argument Linton endorsed in her call for *claiming* disability, identity, and knowledge. Whereas ableism, like racism, sexism, and ageism, is readily grasped in the context of social justice, Lennard J. Davis (2002) warned that in everyday use, ableism should not be reduced to a "trait or habit of thought on the part of certain somatically prejudiced people" (p. 102). Instead, he urged the use of critical literary analysis to ensure a "move away from the 'victim-victimizer' scenario, with which ableism, along with racism, sexism, and other isms, has been saddled and which leaves so little room for agency" (p. 102).

Ableism and Agency

Agency in the case of disability proves complex given the untroubled assumption that disability is synonymous with dependence and lack of attainment, as Nirmala Erevelles (2000) noted in her discussion of the politics of citizenship for persons with severe and/or cognitive disabilities. Similar to Linton, Erevelles borrowed from Young (1990), although she noted the limitations of Young's analysis as it excluded persons viewed by society as (im)material due to cognitive impairment (p. 12). Erevelles explored issues of social justice in the example of individuals who fall outside that which is deemed "normal"—a concept generated by statisticians in the 19th century (see Davis, 1995; Hacking, 1990). Hacking, though, was quick to remind that statistics actually "uses a power as old as Aristotle to bridge the fact/value distinction, whispering in your ear that what is normal is also right" (p. 160).

Among contemporary philosophers engaged by disability studies and discussions on ableism, their scholarship considers issues related to personhood (Anita Silvers, 1995; Silvers & Wasserman, 1998); dependence and caring (Eva Kittay, 1999); autonomy (MacIntyre, 1999); opportunity and justice (Martha Nussbaum, 2006); and philosophical analyses of the just distribution of resources for special education provision in Pre K–12 settings (Lorella Terzi, 2008). Terzi veers from the antifoundational arguments typical of special education and instead draws on many of the foregoing philosophers and John Rawls (2001) to propose a framework for the just distribution of opportunities and effective access to educational equality for all.

Ableism, Agency and Education

Although disability has come to be viewed as the exclusive domain of special education, disability studies scholars are quick to trouble this assumption given the tradition in the social sciences and education that has long fixed individuals with disabilities as objects of study. Disability studies scholars Sharon Snyder and David Mitchell, in their treatment of the cultural locations of disability, contend that among the disciplines most dependent upon narratives of disability in need of "normalization" (special education, physical therapy, occupational therapy, communication disorders, etc.), disability studies represents both a "threat and a saving grace" (2006, p. 189). On this, they offer:

> It represents a threat in the sense of a once silenced object now given the agency to talk back to the professions that would speak its inferiority; a saving grace in that the inclusion of disabled people in any meaningful way suggests fields that are beyond reproach in their humanitarian commitment (p. 189).

Thomas Hehir (2002), the former director of the Office of Special Education Programs and now on the faculty of Harvard, defined ableism as "the devaluation of disability" (1). In his essay "Eliminating Ableism in Education," Hehir cited the "pervasiveness" of the ableist assumptions that come into play in the education of children with disabilities that "not only reinforce prevailing prejudices against disability but may very well contribute to low levels of educational attainment and employment" (ibid). Hehir argued that "ableist assumptions become dysfunctional when the educational and developmental services to disabled children focus inordinately on the characteristics of their disability to the exclusion of all else." (4).

In sponsored research for the New York City (NYC) Department of Education (DOE), Hehir and his colleagues completed a comprehensive review and evaluation of the special education program that included the DOE's oversight of this legally mandated program (2005). Their discussion of the dysfunctional and bloated bureaucracy that has long characterized the NYC DOE underscored an "inordinate reliance on medical model service delivery systems [that] can compromise the interests of children with disabilities" (p. 13). In the final analysis, their report resonates with the insights of Gregg Beratan in discussion of "institutional ableism" (2006). Beratan traced educational policy for disabled children and youth across decades of federally funded initiatives mandated by the Individuals with Disabilities Act (IDEA) and Section 504 of the Rehabilitation Act of 1973 that has, in practice, ensured disparate opportunity for disabled children in public education. Both Hehir and Beratan point to the structures that have been codified by society through legal bureaucratic means and financed by public dollars that undermine educational opportunity for the less able and less well among us. Finally, in complement to Hehir's analysis, the Australian sociologist Fiona Campbell (2008) raised discussion of "internalized ableism" which, like internalized racism, is an "ingrained feature of our landscape, it looks ordinary and natural to persons in the culture" (p. 152).

Disability as a "Symbolic Network"

What becomes apparent in this brief overview of disability studies scholarship is that when we shift to understanding disability as a "symbolic network" of meaning, we find that death, disease, injury, rehabilitation, and cure are de-emphasized and greater emphasis is placed upon disability as a product of social injustice. On this, Tobin Siebers (2008) argued:

> [disability studies] does not treat disease or disability, hoping to cure or avoid them; it studies the social meanings, symbols, and stigmas attached to disability identity and asks how they relate to enforced systems of exclusion and oppression, attacking the widespread belief that having an able body and mind determines whether one is a quality human being.

Disability studies writ large, offer insight into historical, political, and social meanings ascribed to disability and to disabled populations that reveal the workings of power, knowledge, and culture. With this as the background, our attention can turn to an interrogation of systems that have long shaped a form of social oppression unique to people with disabilities. Disability studies offers the opportunity to understand this system of oppression while simultaneously asserting the positive value of the contributions to society by disabled people (Linton, 1998; Siebers, 2008; Snyder & Mitchell, 2006).

The section that follows attempts to contextualize ableism and disability studies situated within the context of burgeoning concerns for temporarily disabled students in postsecondary institutions. The "Case of Cat" offers a composite narrative informed by various data sources that include interdisciplinary disability studies literature; media accounts that inform the public construction of disability and wellness; e-mail discussion specific to the role of disability service provision on college campuses; information posted on college Web sites across the United States and accessed during the 2007–2008 academic year; and excerpts from the "local" experiences of undergraduate students who participated in campus activism in support of disability awareness and access at Graceland (pseudonym), a small liberal arts college in upstate New York during the 2007–2008 academic year.

The Case of Cat

Following a minor accident during her freshman year, Cat sustained an injury that resulted in the acquisition of a temporary mobility disability that would shape the remainder of her undergraduate college experience at Graceland. Self-described as "unpoised," but armed with a set of aluminum crutches, Cat recounted her early efforts as she "crutched" across campus—a term she coined in an effort to spin out her new, albeit temporary identity. Graceland is noted for its exceptional beauty, located at the Western "gateway" to the Finger Lakes region of upstate New York, it is distinguished by gorgeous hills and a nearby gorge. Sloping pathways wind through the campus beneath a canopy of hardy trees whose gnarly roots shape a network of raised seams along the brick and cobblestone paths. Following Cat's injury, this picture-postcard setting became a danger-riddled obstacle course that included a forty-five minute excursion (one way) from the freshman dorms tucked below the base of the "Hill" to her classes atop the "Hill."

With an enrollment of just under 6,500 students, the campus is not expansive. However, the only roadways are those located along the perimeter, near faculty parking lots and student dorms. Not unlike many college students managing a fifteen credit-hour course load, Cat usually filled her backpack to capacity. Now that she was sporting crutches, the weight of the backpack intensified. However, this was a "no choice" scenario: she either crutched all the way back to the dorm at midday to drop off her morning materials and collect her afternoon supplies before crutching back up the Hill, or she would bear up and carry the full load all day. Depending on other daily commitments including labs, college-wide events and extra-curricular activities, Cat planned her day with this in mind. This route became even more treacherous as the winter months covered the paths with snow and ice. Repeated falls and slips resulted in re-injury and extended her use of crutches for months beyond the six weeks her physician initially recommended.

A Trip to ODS

Cat's early attempts to seek support as a temporarily disabled student led her to the Graceland Office of Disability Services (ODS). She searched the ODS Web site where she learned:

> Graceland, in compliance with Section 504 of the Rehabilitation Act, the Americans with Disabilities Act (ADA) of 1990, and related state and federal legislation, is dedicated to providing responsible advocacy, reasonable accommodations, and support services to students with disabilities who present current and proper documentation of disability to the Office of Disability Services. It is the mission of the Office of Disability Services to provide qualified students with disabilities, whether temporary or permanent, equal and comprehensive access to college-wide programs, services, and campus facilities by offering academic support, advisement, and removal of architectural and attitudinal barriers.

And further:

> The Office of Disability Services will proactively provide, at no cost to the student, reasonable accommodations designed to ensure that no qualified student with a disability is denied equal access to, participation in, or benefit of the programs and activities at Graceland.

In sum, ODS maintained, "It is the goal of the Office of Disability Services to maximize student success, self-advocacy, and independence in an accessible academic environment."

Despite this seemingly responsive language, Cat would soon learn that Graceland was similar to many colleges across the United States that had yet to institutionalize support mechanisms for temporarily disabled students. Support turned on a student's "qualification" for entitlement that ultimately turned on the decisions made by one individual. Reasonable accommodation was not provided in Cat's case as her primary needs pertained to *access,* which meant moving from point A to point B across campus. Upon arriving at various campus buildings, access also meant getting inside without having to balance herself on one crutch as she pulled a heavy door towards her and then pivoted in a turn to right herself to enter. Access included temporary transportation on campus via the low-speed Global Electric Motorcars (aka "Gem" cars) used by Graceland to move computer hardware, garbage, recycled materials, and other small loads. In Cat's estimation, the Gem cars could greatly facilitate campus access for students with temporary disabilities. Finally, *access,* at a minimum, meant that Graceland would provide a map that designated accessible routes on campus (i.e., doors with pushbutton entry, elevator designations, non-stair/step pathways, and disabled parking spaces) so as to minimize wasted steps and lost energy. When Cat learned that Graceland had no such map, she created one. Each semester, the map passed from office to office for approval, at the time of her graduation four years later, the map still awaited approval.

Campus Access: A Non-Issue

By the end of her freshman year, Cat had related her concerns to various administrators including the president, the provost, and the dean of students, since Graceland maintained a literal "open door" policy for students and faculty alike. Given the inclement weather that year that sequestered students in their dorms, it was perhaps the image of an "unpoised" Cat propped up on crutches, with her mountaineer's backpack precariously perched on her slight physique, that suggested the seriousness of her concerns. With each visit, she recounted the obstacles she experienced, questioned how permanently disabled students navigated the Graceland campus and how visitors and family members managed on the campus. She volunteered to organize a campus walk-through for the administrators to point out the obstacles, but despite her valiant efforts to raise awareness, she ended her freshman year with a sense of failure. Her repeated efforts to voice her concerns yielded little more than empathetic gestures and a polite nod that preceded the question, *"Have you shared your concerns with ODS?"* At first, the question seemed sincere, but after Cat had heard it again and again, it became an insult: of course she shared her concerns with ODS!

The question also served to remind that all things disability-related were considered the exclusive domain of ODS, and that office held the administrative power to determine the response to issues, and to dismiss what amounted to a non-issue. In Cat's view, this seemed odd (pun intended) as her concerns were tagged as unique and "special," yet they fell outside the general concerns of the campus. Cat soon realized that there were very few disabled students and faculty on the Graceland campus, with the exception of those who, like herself, were temporarily disabled. This reality, against the refrain she heard again and again: "Our campus is just not friendly to people with disabilities," proved increasingly troublesome. It, too, was an odd construction, seeming to suggest that the "campus" was culpable, rather than the individuals who constituted the campus. In Cat's mind, this was contrary to the emphasis on "community" that was repeatedly stressed well past her initial welcome to campus, and one in which the "community" was intended to represent individuals rather than structures, buildings, and policies.

The Administrative Nod to Disability

In the spring semester of her sophomore year, Cat was invited to speak to the Campus Committee on Safety. As she once again recounted her experiences, *sans* any visible markers of disability, she noted the polite attention of students, staff, and faculty who made up the committee, although her concerns did not appear to register as a legitimate "safety" issue. Following her presentation, as if on cue, one of the committee members asked, *"Have you shared your concerns with ODS?"*

Cat would later learn that in the final report to the President, prepared by the Campus Committee on Safety it was noted that when the committee returned the following year (Cat's junior year), her concerns merited further attention. However, no such notification followed until the spring of her senior year. At that time, Cat submitted a letter chronicling four years of concerns specific to access, addressed to the Chancellor of the state system. Soon thereafter,many things quickly fell into place, as we will see.

After Cat's initial injury she grew acutely aware of the difference between architectural and attitudinal barriers. She was drawn to strangers she saw crutching across campus, whom she often pressed for information about their access experiences. She became increasingly aware of the absence of visibly disabled students and visitors on the Graceland campus. This was remarkable given the number of students with visible disabilities that had been part of her public school experiences. Cat wondered about the impact of this exclusion and whether the lack of visibility influenced the non-issue status of her concerns, and she wondered if the administration's nod to disability was visible to anyone else.

The Constitutive Outside

In the disability studies literature, Michel Foucault is often summoned to explain societal responses to excluded people, which many scholars have extended to include discussion specific to disability (Davis, 2002; Mitchell & Snyder, 1997, 2000; Tremain, 2005). Recent scholarship by Tobin Siebers (2008) expanded on the notion of the "constitutive outside" in a treatment that borrows from Foucault's (1984) use of "heterotopias"—places external to all places, even though they may be possible to locate in reality (Foucault, 1984). These spaces assume movement back and forth from the center to the margin such that the center "requires for its very existence the others at the margins, and that in this sense the margin is the true center" (Siebers, 2008: 133). What holds in the example of Cat is how this theoretical notion might be applied to explain the *dis-ease* summoned by her early interactions with Graceland administrators.

Although Cat held only a temporary pass to the land of disability, she nonetheless entered a "heterotopia" by virtue of this "different experience." According to Siebers:

> People with disabilities living on the margin have a different experience. Their experience demonstrates that society is constructed without their access in mind and with little thought of visiting the places left to them (Siebers, p. 133).

In a nuanced discussion of the value of disability experience as "evidence," Siebers draws from various media accounts of marginalized individuals who, on a daily basis, experience the prejudice (somatic or intentional) that accompanies their disability. He cited the case of George Lane, a wheelchair user who was jailed for his refusal to climb up two flights of stairs to a courtroom in Tennessee. Lane was subsequently jailed for contempt, and when he attempted to seek damages, his case was declined on the basis of "states rights." Several legal bouts later, his case made its way to the United States Supreme Court (*Tennessee v. Lane* 2004), and in a surprise decision, Lane won the right to sue the state of Tennessee for damages under Title II of the ADA. The particulars of the case are elaborated upon by Siebers (see especially pp. 120–134). Suffice it to say, the attitudinal "v." architectural issues noted by Cat were revealed in this case as well.

Siebers also cited, for example, the fact that of the 12,487 taxis in New York City, only three are accessible, leaving few options for the many disabled people in need of an accessible cab, whether as residents or visitors. Similarly, in the case of Robert Fine, a native New Yorker who acquired multiple sclerosis and became a wheelchair user and was reluctant to give up his West Village apartment. Instead, Fine opted for a life that was largely restricted to his apartment, taking only occasional trips out when, his friends would carry him down from the second-floor. These are common, "no choice scenarios," faced by disabled people in the example of transportation and housing, and they parallel, in many ways, those experienced by Cat. They reveal the challenges posed by understanding the socially constructed nature of disability experience, which Siebers contends has the "potential both to augment social critique and to advance emancipatory political goals" (p. 122). With allusion to the often-anthologized H. G. Wells short story, *In the Country of the Blind* (1904), Siebers observed:

> In a country of the blind, the architecture, technology, language use and social organization would be other than ours. In a country of the mobility impaired, staircases would be nonexistent, and concepts of distance would not imitate our own. In a country of the deaf, technology would leave the hands free for signing, and there would be no need to shout across a noisy room (p. 122).

Awareness Beyond the Nod

On temporary assignment to the disability "gulag" (Harriet McBryde-Johnson, 2003),Cat was acutely aware of both the social marginalization the disabled experienced on campus and the fact that disability was not among the diversity concerns targeted by Graceland. Like many campuses across the nation, the legally mandated ODS "owned" all disability-related issues on campus. It operated in higher education in much the same way that special education operates in general education: it is highly invested in specialization, exclusivity, and the promulgation of a form of beneficence that would ultimately mark the field as "beyond reproach in their humanitarian commitment" (noted earlier by Snyder & Mitchell, 2006). Thus, there was no collective investment in access and the inclusion of disabled individuals on campus outside the ODS. In much the same way that Graceland, as a structure, not as a collective community, was ultimately faulted for being hostile and unfriendly to the disabled, the onus for including disability beneath the banner of multicultural concerns fell to no one person in particular. Or, as in Cat's case, it did fall to one person in particular, the ODS administrator.

Cat came to this insight slowly as there were no venues on campus to discuss any aspect of disability except those framed by treatment, cure, and correction. The nuances Siebers outlined relative to disability experience rooted to cultural concerns, agency, and value that would advance emancipatory political goals were not part of any social, academic, or administrative conversation at Graceland. As a psychology major, Cat searched the course offerings at Graceland and found only one course that offered a somewhat unique approach to disability, a freshman writing seminar titled, Disability in America, a new offering for 2007–2008 academic year.

Well into her senior year, Cat was less than hopeful about raising awareness beyond the nod. To her surprise, much finally came together in her final semester—albeit fully by coincidence. The section that follows outlines a few coincidences that ultimately served Cat in her efforts to educate Graceland, and for purposes of this chapter, they offer a compelling case of how the hegemonic impulse for health and well-being informs ableism, or more to the point, institutionalized ableism operates at the hands of "somatically prejudiced people" (Davis, 2002, p. 102).

Coincidence One: The Roommate

In the fall of her senior year, Cat's roommate, Gen, sustained a sports-related injury that necessitated the use of crutches. As a senior, Gen was distressed to sitout the season; however, it paled in comparison to the distress of crutching across the campus. With each obstacle Gen encountered, Cat's feelings of *déjà vu* turned into rage as a now "hostile witness" given her knowledge that the real barriers at Graceland were attitudes rather than architecture. When she wrote her letter to the Chancellor of the state system, Cat realized how thorough her documentation was, and she realized the strength of her commitment to educate Graceland about students who are welcomed until they become less well and less worthy of support by the College.

Coincidence Two: The Campus Personal Safety Subcommittee on Access

On the day following acknowledgment of the receipt of her registered letter to the chancellor, Cat's inbox was flooded with responses from the president, vice president, provost, dean of students, various campus directors (i.e., grounds and services, buildings and maintenance), university police, and the faculty member who chaired the subcommittee on campus access and was the newly appointed co-chair of the Campus Personal Safety Committee. By coincidence, this same faculty member taught the writing seminar, Disability in America, and by further coincidence served as the faculty advisor for a newly formed interdisciplinary student organization, Students Educating About/Against Ableism (SEAA). Cat met with this faculty member, who ultimately supported Cat and her campaign to educate Graceland, although it was an undertaking that was far more challenging than either had anticipated:

Prejudices against disability are extremely difficult to overcome because they are built into the environment. Even if one could wave a magic wand and improve everyone's attitudes about disability, the built environment would still remain as a survival of discrimination and an impenetrable barrier to the participation of people with disabilities. For those who doubt the existence of disability discrimination, the built environment should stand as living proof of the social exclusion of the disabled, but attitudes sometimes prove as rigid to change as concrete walls, wooden staircases, and cobblestone walkways (Siebers, 2008, p. 134).

Coincidence Three: A SEAA Change

SEAA had just won temporary approval by Graceland to organize as an officially sanctioned organization. The students modeled SEAA after a similar student organization founded at nearby Syracuse University[2]—although all that the two programs shared was ideology. Syracuse was internationally recognized as being among the most proactive institutions in the support of disability activism. Course offerings and scholarly production by faculty had, for decades, produced the most critical work on disability outside the pathology/problem paradigm. Syracuse was a relatively short distance from Graceland and, thus, bound by similar geographic and architectural obstacles, although efforts to challenge institutionally ableist attitudes were part of an ongoing campus initiative, viewed through a collective lens of shared investment.

Following the first round of the application process, students were notified that SEAA appeared to be a duplication of the student branch of the Council for Exceptional Children (CEC), a professional organization for special educators. Several conversations later, the SEAA students convinced the campus Student Association director that ideologically, SEAA was quite distinct from CEC. The conversation was new to the SA director who was stymied by the notion of an organization that challenged the traditional humanitarian impulse to cure and care. The application was finally approved, with a position statement and a mission outlined as follows:

Position Statement

Disability is more than just a physical, sensory, cognitive, or mental impairment. Disability affects more than just the person who has it. It is the right of every human being to be educated about disability and given the opportunity to discuss the sociocultural aspects associated with it (Syracuse University, original citation). The Graceland community will be enhanced by a broader conceptualization of disability that demands inclusion, equality, and social justice. Inclusion, equality, and social justice as well as accessibility, supported by the law, are just the starting points.

Mission

It is the mission of SEAA to educate the campus and community of Graceland about disability, informed by the value and necessity of interdependency in all human endeavors. SEAA seeks to provide a forum that encourages a closer scrutiny of what can be done to change the stigma associated with disability. These opportunities will include discussions, film series, and community events pertaining to educating about ableism.

Cat was invited to present at the first "official" SEAA meeting—a last-minute invitation that coincided with the previously slated agenda which included a discussion of only two items: Alliance with the Richland Center for Disability Rights (CDR) in nearby Richland, and "Campus Alliances—Where Are They?" As Cat once again recounted her experiences and concerns, it became clear to the SEAA members that Graceland might benefit from activism rather than alliance at this time. Cat would later explain how extremely emotional it was to share her experience with this audience and feeling, for the first time, that it mattered. She was honored rather than dismissed, and noted that "I felt like I had hit a wall, one that SEAA broke down and gave me in its place, hope and courage" (personal correspondence).

In very short order, SEAA organized an action in partnership with CDR and an official campus tour guide in a campaign to raise awareness about ableism. The action was staged as a "regular" campus tour with Chris, the director for advocacy at CDR (a wheelchair user), and five non-disabled Graceland students who wheeled along in chairs on loan from a nearby wheelchair rental. Other students followed on crutches, a mix of both temporarily disabled students (recruited by Cat), and those enacting disability (recruited by SEAA) for this event to create the visibility that was sorely needed at the Graceland. The action would simultaneously serve as the campus walk-through that Cat had, for years, offered to provide for the administration. The Graceland guide worked with Cat in advance of the tour to follow what would be a typical tour that would incorporate a few dead-end barriers similar to those she navigated as a freshman.

In addition, Cat and Gen invited various Graceland administrators, and flyers were posted all over campus the previous day. The Graceland action ultimately included numerous non-disabled allies who joined in the action scheduled at noon—the exact moment when many Graceland students, faculty, and staff would otherwise be scurrying to lunch. A reporter from the campus newspaper and a photographer were assigned to the "campus tour."

Coincidence Four: Oh No! Not a Simulation!

It bears mentioning that disabled people and their activist allies rarely endorse simulation activities as they quickly revert to parody rather than providing perspective on living with disability. Although the SEAA advisor initially discouraged the simulation component of the action, after much discussion, the students decided to choreograph the event as serious theater for the benefit of the Graceland community. One SEAA member, a theater major, scripted different characters in meaningful roles that necessitated the use of mobility devices as more than mere props. Her script was written with the greatest attention to detail to minimize stereotypical constructions and insensitive actions. One student was in character as a recently disabled person, with a bearing of aggressive, non-compliant behavior that could be read in her body language and behind her forbidding, oversized dark sunglasses. Another student positioned himself separately from the crowd, as if planning an escape or adamantly unwilling to fall in line on the mock tour. Others rolled along in pairs, unfazed by the obstacles they encountered and cheerfully greeting the flummoxed students who came their way. Others—working without the benefit of a script—voiced their grievances to the administrators, including the ODS director, who remained visibly annoyed throughout the action. Sweaty and frustrated, the students turned to her with their questions: "Where is the elevator?" "Who has the key to the elevator?" "Why isn't there any signage?" "How would I get into that so-called "accessible" dorm when the doorway is so narrow?" At one point, a student asked why the button on the exit to the library door was broken. In response, the ODS administrator shrugged, "It keeps breaking because non-disabled students use it."

What had once been Cat's private experience at Graceland now became an incredibly public display of institutional disregard for disabled students' needs, voiced by many in the Q&A that followed the "campus tour." Many of the same issues Cat had wondered about earlier were contextualized by the experiences of other students. In addition to the challenges of access, many cited clear instances of prejudice that illustrated Siebers' notation that everyday exclusion can be depicted in "no choice" scenarios. One student explained that when his family wanted to tour the campus prior to his admission, his younger sister could not accompany them because she was a wheelchair user. Another student explained that during graduation, his grandfather was not seated with his family, but had to sit with other disabled people in a "ghetto" designated as "special seating." In an emotional account, a residence assistant (RA) explained that weeks before a wheelchair user arrived for her campus tour and was assigned to the accessible dorm on campus. However, the dorms were inaccessible because the doorways were too narrow to accommodate her chair, and she was forced to sleep in the shared suite. The RA, having witnessed the visitor's difficulties, acknowledged shamefully that she did not report this incident beyond her immediate supervisor. As reported in the student newspaper, *Staff Editorial:* "Due to the lack of options for disabled students, many have been forced to wrestle with the ultimatum: health or education? Nobody should have to even ponder this question" (4.17.08). In addition, the Graceland action was fueled by the student newspaper blog that revealed the need for education at Graceland. Comments reflected a range of reactions, from an obvious lack of information and education to obvious contempt, as indicated by the post: *Why would someone in a wheelchair even come to our campus?*

Conclusion

Until disability is experienced first hand, most students, staff, and faculty move through inaccessible physical spaces on their college campus, unaware of the obstacles posed by heavy doors, circuitous routes to elevators, broken or dented sidewalks, steep topographical inclines/declines, and the many manmade architectural barriers erected in public spaces. Should access or supports be needed in the event of an accident, most disabled individuals soon realize the need for poise and persistence in order to obtain even the most basic entitlements that might ensure continued participation in daily routines. Despite the rhetoric posted on ODS pages promising the "removal of architectural and attitudinal barriers," the reality is that such a job belongs to each of us.

Beyond one's individual experience with disability—experience that will happen to anyone who lives long enough—the need exists to raise awareness about ableism through secondary and postsecondary curriculum. The approach needed is one that promotes understanding through cultural perspectives and disability-related themes throughout the undergraduate and graduate curriculum, in dance programs, athletic programs, women's studies coursework, film, history, music, philosophy and even psychology, and science provided deficiency is not the fundamental starting point. Efforts to promote disability visibility are underway on many college campuses, and similar to Graceland, the efforts will necessitate action that exceeds one individual office or entity charged to address disability through a "services" orientation. As the SEAA position statement noted, disability affects more than just the person who has it. Clearly a broader conceptualization of disability demands inclusion, equality, social justice, and accessibility in the local context, so as to better grasp the spirit of the law applied more broadly. As this chapter reveals, the efforts of non-disabled allies helped to expose limits of the systems and structures designated to meet the compliance requirements for ADA. More importantly, while the students gained a deeper understanding of the disability experience—and were, indeed, much the wiser for it—much remains to be determined by the institution's policies that may unwittingly endorse the hegemonic imperative for health and well-being, while somatically authorizing institutional ableism.

Acknowledgment

The author wishes to acknowledge the noble efforts of the following students: Cat Urban, Gen Bernier, Rachel Coleman-Gridley, Dan Koch, Emma Martin, Chrissy Meyer, Liz Squairs, Jenni Sussel, Anthony Vitale, and Sean Kaplan.

Notes

1. Valerie Harwood offers a critical analysis of the aftermath of the Virginia Tech massacre in 2007, noting how pervasive policies have become in response to the threat from students who may appear less well, as in her discussion of those identified with depression. Her article is forthcoming in *Theory, Culture & Society*.
2. The Beyond Compliance Coordinating Committee at Syracuse University can be accessed at (bccc.syr.edu). Although the committee began under the direction of graduate students, it has served Graceland students well in their efforts to bring attention to issues ofdisability as diversity on college campuses.

References

Baker, B. (1999). Disabling methodologies. *Pedagogy, Culture & Society*, 7 (1), 91–115.

Beratan, G. (2006). Institutionalizing inequity: Ableism, racism and IDEA, *Disability Studies Quarterly*, 26 (2), available on line http//w.w.w.dsq-sd.org/articles.

Boulton, J. T. (1979). *Letters of D. H. Lawrence*. Vol.1. Cambridge, England: Cambridge University Press. This excerpt is from the opening lines of the essay.

Campbell, F. (2008). Exploring internalized ableism using critical race theory. *Disabililty & Society*, 23 (2), 151–162.

Davis, L. J. (1995). *Enforcing normalcy: Disability, deafness, and the body*. New York: Verso.

_____. (1997/2006).*The disability studies reader*. New York: Routledge.

_____. (2002). *Bending over backwards: Disability, dismodernism, and other difficult positions*. New York: New York University Press.

Erevelles, N. (1996).Disability and the dialectics of difference.*Disability and Society*, V 11 (4), 519–537.

_____ (2000). Educating unruly bodies: Critical pedagogy, disability, and the politics of schooling, *Educational Theory*, 50 (1), 25–48.

Foucault, M. (1984). "Des Espacesautres." *Architecture, Movement, Continuite* 5 (October), 46–49.

Hacking, I. (1990). *The taming of chance*. Cambridge, England: Cambridge University Press.

Hehir, T. (2002). Eliminating ableism in education. *Harvard Educational Review*, 72 (1), 1–32.

Johnson, Harriet McBryde.(2003). The disability gulag.*New York Times Magazine*. November 23, 58–64.

Kittay, E. F. (1999). *Love's labor: Essays on women, equality, and dependency*. New York and London: Routledge.

Linton, S. (1998). *Claiming disability, Knowledge and identity*. New York: New York University Press.

MacIntyre, A. (1999). *Dependent, rational animals: Why human beings need the virtues*. Chicago Open Court.

Mitchell, D. T. and Snyder, S.L. (Eds) (1997). *The body and physical difference*. Ann Arbor: University of Michigan Press.

_____. (2000). *Narrative prosthesis: Disability and the dependencies of discourse*. Ann Arbor: University of Michigan Press.

Nussbaum, M. (2006). *Frontiers of justice: Disability, nationality and species membership*. Cambridge & London: Belknap Press of Harvard University Press.

Rawls, J. (2001). *Justice as fairness: A restatement*. Ed. Erin Kelley. Cambridge, MA: Harvard University Press.

Siebers, T. (2008). *Disability theory*. Ann Arbor: University of Michigan Press.

Silvers, A. (1995). Reconciling equality to difference: Caring (f)or justice for people with disabilities. *Hypatia*10 (1), 30–55.

Silvers, A. and Wasserman, D. (1998).*Disability, difference, discrimination*. Lanham, MD: Rowman & Littlefield.

Snyder, S. L. (2006).Disability Studies (entry). In G. Albrecht, J. Bickenbach, D. T. Mitchell, W. O. Schalick, and S. L. Snyder, (Eds.). *Encyclopedia of disability*, 478–490. Thousand Oaks, CA: Sage.

Snyder, S. L. and Mitchell, D. T. (2006). *Cultural locations of disability*. Chicago: University of Chicago Press.

Tennessee v. Lane, 541 U. S. 509. 2004.

Terzi, L. (2008) *Justice and equality in education: A capability perspective on disability and special educational needs*. London and New York: Continuum.

Tremain, S. (Ed.) (2005). *Foucault and the government of disability*. Ann Arbor: University of Michigan Press.

_____. (2004). *Ideology and the Politics of Exclusion*. New York: Peter Lang.

_____. (2009). Disablity studies: No simple splice. To appear in *The handbook of research in the social foundations of education*, edited by Steven Tozer, Bernardo Gallegos and Annette Henry. New York and London: Routledge.

Young, I. M. (1990).*Justice and the politics of difference*. Princeton, NJ: Princeton University Press.

Section Eight

Urban and Rural Diversity

Twenty-Five

No Short Cuts in Urban Education
Metropedagogy and Diversity

Joe L. Kincheloe

I recently had the opportunity to speak to a group of distinguished scientists about several issues concerning educational purpose and the nature of educational success. In the course of the speech, I made several points about the difficulty of being a good teacher in contemporary urban schools. In the public and private discussion that followed my presentation, many of the scientists were quick to take exception to my focus on the difficulty of urban teaching. "The teachers are so bad, so ill-prepared," they told me, "what they need is to understand their subject areas so they will know what to teach." While there is no doubt that there are weak and ill-prepared urban teachers in failing city schools, I told the scientists that I thought the amazing part of the story about contemporary urban education involves how many great teachers continue to teach in such hostile conditions.

They were taken aback by such an argument—I don't think very many of them had ever heard such an assertion. In addition I told them that while knowledge of particular subject matter is always essential to being a good urban teacher, even the most brilliant scientists among us might find themselves failing abjectly in particular urban schools and classrooms. Such knowledge is necessary, but not sufficient—successful urban teaching demands so much more. This "so much more"—the knowledges that the scientists had not considered—are key to what we're attempting to explore in this book. Indeed, the complexity of urban education is a central theme of diversity and multicultural education.

There is difficulty in constructing a rigorous, practical, culturally and socioeconomically sensitive, just, and engaging urban education. Like the scientists in my audience, most people simply don't realize the complexity of this enterprise. As teachers, we must all be students of power, sociocultural context, and justice. My vision of urban education is one that never gives in to the larger forces and processes that operate to undermine the hopes and dreams of urban students from backgrounds marginalized by race, class, and gender. Indeed, hope springs eternal and despite the dark ages for social justice and educational excellence in which we now operate, urban education can be reformed and reformulated to provide marginalized students with a greater chance for profound vocational, personal, and civic achievement.

The Emergence of Urban Education as a Field of Study

Only with the impetus of the Civil Rights Movement of the 1960s did urban education begin to emerge as a distinct field of study. In the urban world that existed around the turn of the twentieth century, urban schools in the United States were touted by many as the best in the world. In merely six decades, such representations of urban schools have become lost memories. By the zenith of the Great Society programs marked by the civil rights legislation of 1964, urban schools were viewed as chaotic, violent, and unjust venues. No place for the timid, urban schools even by the mid-1960s were coming to be viewed as places beyond hope. Such hopelessness would inexorably lead to further neglect and deterioration in the poorest and most non-white urban schools in the following decades. While many wrote of the human damage caused by such neglect, the American public and media would not "discover" urban education until the late 1980s when works such as Jay McLeod's *Ain't No Making It* and the Carnegie Foundation Report would be addressed by a few mainstream journalists.

Since the late 1980s, concerned educators, community groups, and national organizations have worked hard to reform urban education. Metropedagogy emerges from the work of these reformers and from the critical pedagogical tradition in education. In *Metropedagogy: Power, Justice, and the Urban Classroom* (Kincheloe and hayes, 2005), kecia hayes and I refer to a metropedagogy which calls for a rigorous and contextually specific professional education for teachers and administrators who operate in urban settings. Surprisingly, such a proposal has only recently received much support. The dominant position in teacher education has tended to support a one-size-fits-all strategy.[1] Of course, with the advent of standards, standardization, and the test-driven curricula of No Child Left Behind, the one-size agenda again rears its decontextualized head. Such a position assumes that teaching and learning is a culture-free process that has nothing to do with the experiences and identities that teachers and students bring with them to school. A teacher uses the same standardized methods, treats all learners the same, transmits the same knowledges, and seeks the same instructional goals no matter if her students come from the South Bronx or the Upper East Side. Again, urban education or metropedagogy understands that the educational process is much more complex than this.[2] Urban teachers must be practically engaged scholars who possess a wide variety of knowledges and experiences about urban education.

The Critical Foundations of Metropedagogy:
Challenging Deficit Assumptions about Low-Status Urban Students

As kecia and I and many other critical scholars have written elsewhere, a critical pedagogy appreciates that every aspect of schooling and every form of educational practice are politically contested spaces.[3] Shaped by history and challenged by a wide range of interest groups, educational practice is a fuzzy concept as it takes place in numerous settings, is shaped by a plethora of often invisible forces, and can operate even in the name of democracy and justice to be totalitarian and oppressive. Many urban teacher education students often have trouble with this political dimension and the basic notion that schooling can be hurtful to particular students. They often embrace the institution of education as "good" because, in their own experience, it has been good to them. Thus, the recognition of these political complications of schooling is a first step for critical pedagogy-influenced educators and advocates of a metropedagogy in developing an intellectual, social activist teacher persona. As teachers gain these insights, they understand that culture, race, class, and gender forces have shaped all elements of the acts of teaching and learning. They also discover that a central aspect of a just and democratic education involves addressing these dynamics as they systematically manifest themselves.[4]

These critical political concerns play themselves out quite clearly in deficit representations of urban students from economically poor and non-white backgrounds. In work that comes from many corners of educational, social, and psychological research, prospective urban teachers are taught that not all students can learn. This is the deficit model of psychology and pedagogy that undermines so many young lives. The academic and social failure that results from such oppressive assumptions is viewed as a *personal* failing.[5] This regressive pedagogical personalization of failure is viewed outside of any larger social or cultural context and then is used to construct a crisis of youth. In this context, Kathryn Herr describes the growth industry of "kid fixing," with its emphasis on different types of intervention for different categories of young people. For middle-class children/youth with health insurance, therapy is offered; for poor and minority young people, prison is increasingly the solution of choice.

Advocates of metropedagogy insist that politicians and many educational leaders must avoid framing the problems of urban education and its most marginalized students as only psychological (individual) in nature, and not socially constructed. Such a form of psychologization works simply to blame the victims of larger cultural problems for their sticky and disempowering predicaments. Such approaches illustrate yet again the decontextualizing tendencies of particular academic ways of seeing the world, as they substitute individual remedies for larger social problems. Scot Evans and Isaac Prilleltensky[6] maintain that educators and psychologists must learn how social violence is manifested in the lives of individual young people. Such a task is difficult, however, in school systems that are obsessed with testing, labeling, and categorizing children and young people. In such a context, advocates of metropedagogy maintain many "experts" and school leaders simply ignore the way that categories of child and youth pathology and "risk" are socially constructed.

In the pathologizing and victim-blaming deficit model of contemporary urban education, the hurtful practices of such an approach to the discipline can be seen with crystal clarity. Indeed, the reasons many urban students fail, our critical metropedagogy asserts, rest more in the social, philosophical/epistemological, cultural, economic, and political configurations of the society than in these attributions of individual deficiencies. How is failure defined? How is aptitude constructed? What is the process by which success gains its meaning in diverse cultures? As critical urban educators operating as multidisciplinary scholars attempt to answer these questions, we begin to understand the complex ways that such meanings gain widespread acceptance.

In the right-wing political climate of the early twenty-first century, many people believe that the only way to deal with these deficit-inscribed urban students is to "make them shape up" through discipline, regulation, order, and low-level rote memorization of basic academic skills. While not denying that many young people need stability and predictability in their lives, such a call is ultimately an affirmation of "deficitism." This order paradigm gives educators an excuse not to present urban students marginalized by race or class with a challenging curriculum or to expect more from them academically. Teachers implementing a critical metropedagogy avoid such assumptions, as they understand the social and psychological forces that undermine their students' achievement. Such teachers transcend the signifiers of urban as otherness, danger, chaos, and violence—representations that contribute to the marginalization of urban students by way of fear.[7]

Philip Anderson and Judith Summerfield[8] tie deficitism and the fear of urbanness to the macro-context of contemporary American life. Such representations work to counter attempts to understand that contemporary American society is entering a globalized, multicultural, multiracial, multireligious, and multiclassed domain. Urban America stands as the gateway to this multilogical emergent society and, as such, must be resisted. The multiplicity of the urban is inferior to the monologicality of the rural or suburban. Carry me back to Disney's Celebration community in Florida where even the rats are white and all children score above average on standardized tests. In this right-wing monoculturalist representation, the city is not the emergent culture but is one that must be destroyed before it destroys "us."

The Work of Metropedagogy: Getting Beyond Deficitism and Short-Term Crisis Management

The effort to understand the origins of this deficitism and its influence in the twenty-first century is central to any effort to implement a rigorous, just, contextually sensitive, empowering metropedagogy. There are no short cuts, no magic bullets, no one miraculous method that will eliminate the hard work such a process entails. Until such complex understandings are widely cultivated, city students in high-poverty schools will continue to find little opportunity to experience rigorous schoolwork with contextually savvy urban teachers. Without such insights, the term urban itself will continue to be used as a dirty word, deployed to denote dangerous and objectionable conditions characterized by trashy people, drugs, violence, dysfunctional families, and filth.[9] Implicit in the representation is that individuals, through their own human inadequacy, have chosen to live in such conditions. Their dilemma is their own fault—no matter how young they may be—and there is nothing we can do about it.

Because of such "unworthy" clientele and the widespread belief nothing can be done to address urban distress, urban education always finds itself in a crisis. Even, for example, if urban schools were equally funded, such monies would not be sufficient to address basic infrastructural needs—for example, repairs for school buildings or city teacher salaries that approach the pay scale of suburban teachers. The crisis would continue. Thus, the omnipresence of deficitism in urban education is always surrounded by frenetic efforts to solve the next short-term crisis. An observation of frenzied school principals attempting to fill several teacher vacancies on August 24th, two days before the beginning of the new school year, is sobering to the uninitiated onlooker. The idea of a calm group of urban teachers reflecting on their goals for the upcoming school year during the week before school begins is almost humorous to those teachers scrambling to solve today's new emergency.

This perpetual crisis machine of urban education has moved mayors and state legislatures to disband school boards and experiment with new forms of school governance. In some cities, elected school councils now hire and fire principals and other administrative personnel. Much of the time, such councils are responding to short-term demands only and not a long-term vision of what a just, democratic, rigorous, and empowering urban education system might involve. Such emergency responses have sometimes broken the chains of political gridlock that stifled innovation and responsibility—a positive step, no doubt. However, because those charged with implementing changes in the urban systems have had little knowledge of the interaction of social, political, economic, cultural, and other structural forces with urban students and the processes of teaching and learning, the everyday life of schools has too often floundered in such new structures.

Indeed, in their effort to reform failing systems, so many new rules and policies are thrust upon urban schools that individual administrators and teachers are stymied in their efforts to operate as professionals. They and their students are terrorized by bureaucratic micromanagement.[10] Here rests the importance of metropedagogy. This is what a critical pedagogy of urban education brings to the table—insight into how all of these complex components work together to produce particular patterns of failure and institutional pathology. As teachers, we must begin to understand the wide bodies of diverse knowledges that are needed to make a positive difference in these complex educational situations. And, importantly, despite the level of difficulty, we will devote our lives to making these conditions better for the worthy, brilliant, and resilient students who populate these urban schools.

It is difficult to be a great urban educator—whoops, I said it again. No one should go into the field without this understanding deeply embedded into his or her consciousness. The purpose of metropedagogy is to walk a fine line that avoids, on one side, an acknowledgment of difficulty that leads to facile excuses for one's own failure while on the other side, avoids a view that the job can be easily accomplished. All who enter urban teaching will experience moments of failure where what one does rarely seems to work. Concurrently, there are great rewards and contributions to be made by dedicating oneself to this challenging task. One who engages in the metropedagogy promoted here will sometimes be punished for the stands he or she takes in support of students. Such urban educators must be psychologically prepared to understand the reasons for, and to deal with, such punishment as a part of the larger sociopolitical context. Such teachers must also develop the ability to compromise and choose battles wisely—flexibility is a complex, albeit necessary, quality for the successful urban teacher. Making an intractable moral stand that helps no one in particular and undermines one's ability for future intervention, is not usually a judicious path in metropedagogy.

The Fundamental Premises of Metropedagogy

Metropedagogy constructs its philosophical foundation on notions of empowered, professionalized teachers working to cultivate the intellect and enhance the socioeconomic mobility of marginalized urban students. Teachers in a critical metropedagogy conduct research into social and educational problems, design curricula around multiple macro-knowledges of education and the contexts in which it operates and the micro-situations in which their students find themselves in their communities and their schools. Such teachers build coalitions of scholars in urban education and other related areas, teachers, parents, students, community members, professional social service providers, and sociopolitical organizations. In this context, teachers who enact a metropedagogy are serious students of education who apply their insights to promote new educational psychologies/learning theories, new cultural studies of urban communities and the young people who live in them, and subjugated knowledges derived from organic intellectuals who live and operate in urban neighborhoods. Such teachers are motivated by the power of ideas to reshape the world in which we operate, the notion that human beings can become far more than they presently are, and the belief that ultimately the fate of humanity is related to these ideas.

Metropedagogy's Sense of Purpose

The urban education we promote is concurrently a rigorous academic enterprise and a highly pragmatic, hands-on endeavor. Advocates of metropedagogy maintain that they must use these fundamental premises to build a clear, pragmatic, and transformative sense of purpose. What should we be attempting to accomplish in urban education? As cities deteriorated in the middle of the twentieth century, urban schools lost their sense of direction. With few shared values and little discussion of larger goals, urban educators retreated to their private hells. In the midst of such fragmentation, deliberation about the intellectual, social, and political goals of urban education never took place. School reforms came and went without ever answering the questions:

- What are the intellectual goals of urban education—what does it mean to be an educated person?
- What are the social goals of urban education—what social changes in the domain of race, class, language, and power need to take place so that urban education can be improved?
- What are the political goals of urban education—how do urban educators and their allies build coalitions that are strong enough to circumvent the obstacles to systematic reform in city schools?

Advocates of metropedagogy must develop ways of answering these questions that help school leaders, community members, teachers, parents, and students articulate a powerful multilogical (informed by numerous perspectives and concerns) conception of urban school purpose.[11] In the spirit of valuing the power of different perspectives, therefore, advocates of metropedagogy seek not only new knowledges but search for ways of seeing that provide new vantage points on a particular phenomenon. As opposed to many dominant power inscribed mainstream urban educators, metropedagogy values the voices of the subjugated and marginalized that are too often banished from the conversation about the goals of urban education. Thus, the idea of subjugated knowledge is central to the work of metropedagogy. With such an idea in mind, critical urban educators do not assume that experts in the disciplines possess the final word on a domain of study.

Sometimes what such experts report needs to be reanalyzed in light of the insights of those operating outside the frameworks of dominant power. As a scholar of education, I have often observed how some of the most compelling insights I have encountered concerning pedagogy come from those individuals living and operating outside the boundaries of educational scholarship. Sometimes such individuals are not formal scholars at all, but individuals who have suffered at the hands of educational institutions. Such experiences provided them a vantage point and set of experiences profoundly different than more privileged scholars. This phenomenon is not unique to the study of urban education but can be viewed in a variety of domains.[12]

Critical communities of diverse stakeholders understand that there are no shortcuts to the reform of urban education. Permanent but flexible reform strategies must be devised that are supported by a wide range of groups and individuals. Efforts to reform urban education cannot go back to the beginning each time a new regime enters the superintendent's office. Armed with their literacy of power with its understanding of the insidious ways dominant power blocs operate to promote the interests of the privileged, their commitment to democratic and socially just goals, and the worth of investing social resources to cultivate the intellect of urban students, proponents of metropedagogy push ahead. They have good times—they have bad times. They get depressed—they get over it. Such educators know they have to work hard every day with the understanding that all improvements in urban education require long-term efforts. Not only do they require continuing labor, but such reforms also necessitate a form of restructuring that gets beyond merely rearranging the furniture of urban education.

Metropedagogy's Vision:
Connecting Students, Teachers, Families, Communities, and Schools

Unfortunately, the cure for urban education in contemporary reform has often served to make the patient worse—in a sense, it has rewarded the victim of cancer with a case of polio. While urban education waits in the emergency room, metropedagogy assembles a team to save the patient. Critical educators understand that the condition of urban education can improve only when working relationships are established among students, teachers, families, communities, and schools. Because the problems of urban education emanate from diverse social, cultural, political, economic, health, transportation, linguistic, and psychological contexts, solutions must be sought in the complex interaction of all of these domains. Individuals involved in these diverse areas must work together to coordinate their efforts in ways that support the work of urban schools. Thus, advocates of metropedagogy consider health and human services departments, civic organizations, advocacy groups, neighborhood organizations, businesses, labor unions, and religious institutions to be important agencies of urban education.

As the bonds between the work of city teachers and the members of these agencies are established, urban educators are granted a unique opportunity to engage diverse individuals in an analysis of the intellectual, social, and political goals of our metropedagogy. The curse of deficitism can be exposed for what it is, while new visions of human potential and social justice, and their relationship to urban education, can be introduced. These complex coalitions can become learning organizations where everyone learns from everyone else. In such a context, the understanding emerges that schools are intricate social institutions where all problems and solutions are connected to many larger forces. In most contemporary urban educational reform, this interrelated complexity has not been addressed. This is why promising urban educational reforms that work well in a few classrooms notoriously fail when mandated on a grander scale. First, imbedded in such mandates is a one-size-fits-all mind set that fails to account for the infinite diversity of even ostensibly similar settings. Second, such top-down reforms fail to appreciate the multiple agents and agencies needed to nurture reform. In this context, such reforms are shot down by unanticipated forces. Urban educational reform in its post-mortem confusion returns to square one.

Thus, a central concern of metropedagogy arises in this context: how can urban education help construct conditions which enable students to prosper on many levels in the urban communities where they live? If critical urban educators are to become mediators of change who help create such conditions, then they must operate as agents of these larger networks. Especially in the first years of teaching, efforts to operate as rugged individualist crusaders can be counterproductive to the larger effort to survive in an unfriendly system. Thus, the forging of bonds connecting students, teachers, families, communities, and schools is important for many reasons. To help students prosper in their communities and in schools, urban teachers must not only appreciate the complex interactions that shape these communities and the individual lives of students, but they must also understand the roles that coalitions can play in creating the opportunity for social and individual transformation.

Here, advocates of metropedagogy help engage these coalitions in the larger effort to understand the ways urban communities can be mobilized to facilitate learning among their young people. In this context, metropedagogy embraces a curriculum that grounds itself in these communities, and begins the teaching process on the foundation of what students already know. Such a pedagogy uses the coalitions to help students ground the knowledges they confront in the context of their communities. What does it mean, for example, to know geography in East New York? How can such knowledge be applied in this context? How does it help us find our way? Who in the community can illustrate such knowledge to local young people?

As urban students learning in such a context gain knowledge, advocates of metropedagogy induce them to connect it to the continuing effort to appreciate their own heritage, historical context, and language background. Mr. Ortiz, a well-respected labor organizer in Washington Heights, has written a short history of the Dominican community in New York. A critical metropedagogy engages him and many of his colleagues in the Service Employees International Union (SEIU) to be expert teachers who work with students and teachers throughout the community to engage students in researching historical and many other knowledges important to shaping who they are and where they find themselves in the social web of reality. At the same time, they are engaged in these high-level academic activities, such students are studying the myriad ways social and economic power structures operate to shape their relationship with the school and the city. Such studies are designed to get them intellectually, socially, and psychologically ready to confront the forces that work to disempower them, to keep them "in their place."[13]

Metropedagogy's Vision: Self and Social Transformation

To begin with, metropedagogy works to make sure that schools in the poorest and most marginalized urban communities operate simply to *not* retard the intellectual growth of their students. It may seem silly to make such an assertion, but I believe that a detailed, experiential knowledge of many urban schools in poor communities—despite the efforts of brave, talented, and committed educators—often works to impede students' personal and cognitive development. This pedagogy of poverty[14] or insidious deficitism is supported by the structures we have previously analyzed. A poverty-stricken pedagogy has a similar look and smell no matter where we encounter it. As a student who attended poor schools in rural southern

Appalachia, I watched a hillbilly version of it operate throughout my early life. In the poverty curriculum teaching is routinely separated from connection to the lived world.

Ritual acts are established that emphasize form and compliance over substance. Here information is distributed for later recitation, the ability to follow directions (orders) takes precedence over making meaning, and convergent, one-right-answer questions on tests take on an exaggerated importance. Students in such a pedagogy become unbearably bored, as they see little connection between the pedagogy of poverty and their immediate daily concerns—not to mention the improvement of their lives. They want to scream and flail their arms in the air just to break the deadening monotony of it all. Such students are insulted by the "dumbed down" content they are expected to know and spit back on tests. Such procedures position them as dolts who are biologically incapable of engaging with mature information and the cognitive sophistication it demands.[15]

Our understanding of the urban pedagogy of poverty confronts us head on with the larger philosophical question: what are schools in contemporary society attempting to do—train "compliant workers" or educate discerning, empowered citizens? In my observations of far too many high-poverty urban schools, I think the answer to such a question has little to do with graduating smart citizens for a democratic society. In this context, our metropedagogy is very clear about its intentions. A democratic society demands empowered citizens who can work to make sure it does not continue to subvert egalitarian and democratic principles. In an era unfriendly to both political and economic notions of democracy, the future of our political institutions depends on the success of this venture. In addition, it is necessary for individual students to develop through their schooling, the power, confidence, creativity, and deportment to forge their own way in the cosmos. This is why our metropedagogy is based on a commitment to social and personal transformation.

Such a commitment means that a metropedagogy embraces a new vision of what it means to be an educated person. In a context where marginalization by race, class, gender, or religion is the norm, an educated person understands that things must change, that she/he must understand and work to overcome the impediments to personal and social progress. Like their teachers, such marginalized students must join with larger groups that can help make these dreams realities. Social and personal transformations are inseparable.[16] Metropedagogy begins this transformative process by making sure that school is never separate from the lived world, from the personal experience of students. While this is important in the larger quest to make education meaningful and useful and more than an empty ritual of compliance, it is also important for other reasons. When academic activity is connected to the world and the lived experience of students, it is, simply put, more damned interesting.

Indeed, it is very important for students (and teachers) to find pleasure in academic work. No matter how long right-wing commentators proclaim that students must be forced to learn boring lessons, I will argue that all great teachers must find ways to make the process of becoming a scholar interesting. In my own life as a scholar, I had to search for a way to make rigorous scholarship interesting in my life. I had to frame it as a pleasurable activity. I had watched too many would-be scholars fail to become the researchers they wanted to be because they could not make the process interesting for themselves. The same is even more germane for elementary and secondary students from high poverty and racially marginalized backgrounds. We operate in a media-driven, hyper-real world that has successfully represented academic work as intrinsically boring and irrelevant. A critical metropedagogy refuses to accept such constructions and works to make intellectual labor a source of personal satisfaction. Social and personal transformation is not possible without this important step.

In this affective context, I don't believe it is inappropriate for advocates of metropedagogy to devote much time and energy to developing education for enjoyment and personal satisfaction.[17] Neither do I find it out of place to engage urban students in conversations about what it might mean to be a scholar in their own sociohistorical context. The metropedagogy supported here promotes a redefinition of the role of intellectual for marginalized urban students. Indeed, I talk unabashedly with students about a demilitarized, life-affirming, gender-inclusive notion of a warrior-intellectual. Such a concept situates the quest for personal and social transformation in the mean streets of our cities. Warrior-intellectuals are tough young men and women who

- develop the ability to think critically and analytically
- cultivate their intellects
- understand the world as it is, in relation to what it could be
- interpret and make sense of the world around them by understanding the invisible forces at work in shaping particular situations
- employ their creative ability to get beyond ritualized but failed practices in school and society
- use their imagination to transcend the trap of traditional gender, racial, sexual, and class-based stereotypes and the harm they can cause in their individual lives and in the larger society
- reconceptualize the role of "good citizen" in a way that speaks and acts in relation to dominant power and the ways it oppresses those around them
- develop the ability to teach themselves what they need to know to take on a particular task
- cultivate a humility that allows them to be both good leaders and good members of diverse learning communities
- devote themselves to never-ending, life-long growth as citizens, parents, workers, teachers, scholars, researchers, and lovers

This is a pedagogy worth living for, an educational orientation that holds profound consequences for the way we view ourselves and the world. It asks how the world and our lives intersect. Who am I, who are we in relation to the world? Metropedagogy is an approach to urban education that is always close to the world. Knowledge and academic skills are important as they connect us to everyday life—not as they turn us into monks and remove us from reality. Thus, metropedagogy is not an effort to save the "poor children." It is not an attempt to remove them from the mean streets and remake them in the image of their middle class, and often, white saviors. Metropedagogy does not try to emulate Mr. Clean—it is not a whitening agent. In this context, the critical curriculum engages the subjugated knowledges of urban communities, making use of repressed historical memories and alternative frameworks of understanding.[18] Such constructs are not just simply accepted or rejected but are engaged in relation to other knowledges and other ways of making sense of the world. Such explorations set up questions that teachers, students, and, hopefully, community members may carry with them for the rest of their lives.

Metropedagogy's Vision: Why Teach This to Those Students?

Metropedagogy never teaches anything simply because it's in the curriculum. Such a bold proclamation doesn't mean, however, that it ignores knowledges demanded by standardized curricula and mandated tests. When confronted with such requirements, metropedagogy looks behind the epistemological curtain. It asks why these knowledges and not others. It traces the imprint of dominant ideology on such information and explores alternative, repressed perspectives on the topics in question. Dominant ideology refracts meaning so information is more supportive of existing power relations. Thus, a critical metropedagogy develops a deep relationship with curricular knowledge. It is suspicious of all required subject matter and understands that critical knowledge is constructed when particular information intersects the lived worlds of teachers and students. That is, knowledge becomes meaningful when it is viewed in relation to people's lives.

I remember as a young person in the process of getting drafted to serve in the Vietnam War how relevant to my life were the writings of the Frankfurt School of critical theory. As I read Max Horkheimer, Theodore Adorno, and Herbert Marcuse writing about the rational irrationality of modern societies and their ability to construct the consciousness of their citizens so they would serve the needs of dominant power, I understood very clearly the ways schools and other social institutions had attempted to shape my consciousness. The knowledge of critical theory gave me the courage to fight for my convictions and to transcend the angry responses my perspectives elicited in school and other domains of my life. Taking this understanding and applying it to my teaching was a central component of any success I have achieved in that role. Obviously, the life concerns that motivated me could not be transferred to other students in other times and places. The pedagogical key involved understanding that my students had their own life concerns rooted in particular *zeitgeists* and cultural localities. My role as a teacher was to discover and integrate those concerns into my interactions with my students, into the curriculum that they and I would construct.

Obviously, understanding the lifeworlds of students and connecting the curriculum to such insight is a complex, time-consuming task. It is not a job for the uncommitted. Such a pedagogical maneuver takes much practice and cannot be implemented the first week one begins teaching. Making this all-important connection demands that teachers be scholar researchers who possess such a good content background that they have insight into what is significant about curricular knowledge. This question of significance is profoundly complex and important. I ask and answer the question from a critical perspective—what may be significant could involve how misleading and reductionistic a particular dimension of the curriculum might be. Or it might pertain to the relevance of a particular historian's perspectives to a particular student's ethical dilemma. The point is, as John Dewey pointed out decades ago, that advocates of metropedagogy are able to gauge the consequences of particular knowledges and interpretive frameworks. Does this knowledge have use value in this context and if so, for whom and specifically in what way?

As metropedagogy addresses these issues, it escapes from the gravitational pull of traditional pedagogical efforts to improve urban education. Metropedagogy is not a technical adjustment of urban teaching—its focus is not on developing new teaching materials, innovative ways to arrange the classroom, improved standardized tests, or fresh and attractively packaged (and marketable) lessons. While some of these novelties may have facilitated the work of some teachers, they ignored larger questions of power and justice and the relationship between school knowledges and student lives.[19] They were typically uninterested in the intellectual, social, and political goals of schooling. Indeed, they were indifferent to the metropedagogical effort to connect students, teachers, families, communities, and schools in meaningful, transgressive ways. Technical adjustments of urban education assume that if we state clearly and simply what we expect teachers to do and students to learn, urban schools will be improved. While there is no doubt that urban education must be as clear as possible about its goals, this technicist desire for clarity can often be simplistic and reductionistic.

The reason that such reforms are naïve involves the inherent complexity of the pedagogical process. In the language of standardization, students will make great progress in academic achievement because the objectives of the curriculum will be clear to them, and the work of teachers in urban schools will be focused on the attainment of these goals. Such proclamations ignore the complications of connecting the knowledges of schools to the lives of students in meaningful and motivating ways. They snub questions of power and regulation and the ways dominant culture works to reproduce the political relationships of the status quo. They disregard the ideological intent of existing curricula. Do not mistake this plea to understand the complexity of the process as a justification for a failure to convey to students what is expected of them. Clarity in the midst of complexity and consistent but context-specific goals in the belly of chaos represent the metropedagogical position. Here critical teachers work hard to remind students of the larger goals of the metropedagogical curriculum and why such objectives are important in all of our lives.

Metropedagogy's Struggle to Situate Urban Education: Attending to the Social, Cultural, Political, and Economic Setting

One of the biggest problems metropedagogy fights to address is the tendency of urban educational reform to remove teaching and learning from the social conditions that shape them. All educational activity, urban education included, must be examined in its social, cultural, political, and economic settings. Educators, political leaders, and informed citizens cannot grasp either the problems or solutions of urban education without viewing city schooling as ecologically entrenched institutions that mirror the troubles and advantages of their adjacent neighborhoods, not to mention larger contexts both spatial and conceptual. Metropedagogy is focused on understanding and making connections with the diverse structures and forces that help produce urban educational goals, the content of the curriculum, the consciousness of students, and the pedagogical logics of teachers.[20] With these notions in mind, metropedagogy employs the data and insights of many disciplines, many subjugated forms of knowledge, and diverse ways of seeing and understanding these dynamics.

In this interdisciplinary approach, advocates of metropedagogy examine urban schooling from as many angles as possible. How do these structures and social forces shape urban student performance? What shapes the inequities that separate marginalized and privileged urban students? How do these inequities help construct the lives of diverse urban students? How can educators make use of urban resources and urban communities to rethink and reshape urban education?[21] Such interdisciplinary, multilogical ways of viewing urban education avoid one of the most profound mistakes made by leaders of city schooling over the past several decades: the exclusive reliance upon educational psychology in the effort to produce knowledge about, and make sense of, the domain.[22]

Especially when making use of the more mechanistic dimensions of educational psychology, urban educators obtain a very narrow and socially decontextualized view of urban classrooms and students. In such a decontextualized context deficitism abounds, as problems that are socially constructed are too often deemed to be the product of individual deficiency. An urban teacher education grounded on a critical metropedagogy transcends this monolithic view of teaching and learning, immersing professional education students in a rigorous study of urban students and the contexts that shape them. In this process, psychological insights into pedagogy are studied in tandem with the impact of culture, economics, politics, and history.

***

Thus, teacher education students in this framework come to understand the macro-, meso-, and micro-dimensions of urban education, and the multiple ways such dynamics intersect in the teaching and learning process. Learning is not simply an individualistic process. Contemporary sociocognitive theory appreciates the way that learning is always contingent on the relationships connecting the learner to other people and larger contexts. Lev Vygotsky understood this process in the 1930s, as he conceptualized and researched the notion of the zone of proximal development (ZPD)—the context learners make use of to extend their knowledge and insight into particular aspects of the world around them. Students, like all humans, are shaped in relationship to the world—they are not separate, abstracted atoms.[23] Yet, when educators fail to make use of multiple perspectives, multidisciplinary viewpoints on the forces at work in urban settings, students are viewed as atoms operating in isolation from the rest of the world.

The Power of Contextual Understandings in Urban Education

Teaching and learning, as well as the study of teaching and learning, have to do with exploring the context in which they take place. And this context, advocates of metropedagogy maintain, is always complex and multidimensional. Insight into the context allows researchers and educators an insight into the complicated processes that operate to shape urban education. Take, for example, historical processes. In a metropedagogy, it is believed that teachers are ill-equipped to teach in urban schools without a profound understanding of the history of urban education, the history of urbanization and the evolution of urban areas, the history of social policies in relation to urban life, the history of racism and class bias in various societies, the history of urban youth culture, and so on.

These historical dynamics constantly shape what goes on in schools and in the lives of urban students. In the grotesquely unequal socioeconomic conditions that exist in most urban areas, poor students confront realities that undermine their readiness for learning. If urban educators are not aware of how these processes work, they are unprepared to deal with the lived realities they produce. When such educators don't understand these processes, they often resort to easy attributions of individual blame. Juan and Jasmine don't do well in school, such teachers tell their colleagues, because they are so damned lazy. Such an explanation is oblivious to the social forces shaping these students' fatigue in the teacher's class. Juan and Jasmine may be up all night taking care of younger brothers and sisters while their single mother works the graveyard shift at the local factory. I have seen urban students spend their nights in ways that are far more exhausting than babysitting. For many, babysitting all night might look like a good option.

What a difference understanding Juan and Jasmine's nighttime activities might make on the way a particular teacher views them as human beings or interprets their academic performance. Advocates of metropedagogy understand the larger concept at work in such a context: knowledge of anything in the world is contingent on the context in which we view it.[24] Knowing takes place in particular micro-situations, specific cultural contexts, and certain moments in history. Change the situation, context, or moment, and the knowledge produced and the meaning ascribed it will be forever modified. Such an understanding is a key element of higher orders of cognition—and metropedagogy in this context perpetually seeks to move practitioner thinking to more rigorous and complex domains.

Thus, those of us attempting to implement a metropedagogy always work to understand urban classrooms as part of a larger system. We cannot think of our purpose as urban educators outside of this set of connections. Thus, in the most generic pedagogical sense, critical urban educators never teach anything without considering the context in which they and their students are operating. Teaching academic skills in the context of developing higher-order thinking abilities, in relation to problems important to the everyday lives of urban students, is quite different than learning fragments of information by rote.[25] The former reflects the spirit of metropedagogy; the latter replicates the logic of rational irrationality found in educational reforms such as Success for All and No Child Left Behind.

Implementing a metropedagogy is a complex cognitive activity that well-educated, experienced teachers are quite capable of enacting in their professional lives. Armed with historical, social, cultural, economic, political, philosophical, and pedagogical insight, critical urban teachers observe, reflect on their experiences, connect these observations and reflections to their contextual and subject matter knowledges, and act accordingly. These are high expectations for professionals so demeaned by politicians, academicians, and many others—but they are not unrealistic. The public has yet to comprehend the complexity and multidimensionality of urban education reform. Thus, an important dimension of a metropedagogy involves engaging the public in the complexity of the urban educational context, helping lay people understand the great strengths many urban teachers bring to their teaching, and what is needed to improve urban education.

Even within the teaching profession itself, the understanding of the problems unique to the urban educational context is lost on some of those who are teaching in affluent suburban school districts. Indeed, in recent conversations I've had with some school leaders, the assertion was made that if urban and suburban schools simply exchanged faculties, the problems of urban education would be solved. The decontextualized illogic embedded in such a comment is disturbing. The metropedagogical notion of connecting school purpose and the process of teaching and learning to the context of school, family, community, city, and society is absent in such reductionistic assertions. The need for an appreciation of the situated, contextual dimension of all interpretations, all knowledge is apparent.

Bob Dylan, contemplating the situated nature of song writing, expresses this concept from a unique angle: "I would have liked to been able to give him [record producer Daniel Lanois] the kinds of songs that he wanted, like 'Masters of War,' 'Hard Rain,' 'Gates of Eden,' but those kinds of songs were written under different circumstances, and circumstances never repeat themselves (pp. 218–19)."[26]

Viewing the concept of situatedness in relation to artificial intelligence (AI) provides further insight. After decades of frustrating efforts to design a computer that understands human language, AI researchers have come to the realization that computers have great difficulty understanding human language in any significant sense. The reason for such problems is that language is situated in a matrix of tacit ideological, social, and cultural assumptions that always help construct the meanings intended and received. Such situated assumptions cannot be programmed into the computer, thus, undermining the complexity of the linguistic process.[27] All knowledge production, all human transaction takes place in multiple contexts, for example, ideological, epistemological, discursive. Urban education, and the ways we come to understand it and act on those understandings, is always situated in these multiple contexts. Metropedagogy labors to understand these circumstances and apply such understandings to every element of urban pedagogy.[28]

Connecting Urban Education to Urban Communities

In metropedagogy's call for contextualization and situated teaching and learning, a central dimension of our vision of urban education emerges: the connection of all aspects of the pedagogical process to students' lives, their families, their communities, and the larger sociopolitical domain. Making such connections requires that teachers develop a profound understanding of urban communities and the multiple contexts in which schools are located. Here teachers gain a deep phenomenological understanding of what life is like for students and their families living in poor city neighborhoods. Drawing upon these insights, such teachers learn to empathize with such families—an ability that enhances their attempts not only to develop curricula that are useful to students from these families but also prepares them to effectively communicate with such individuals. Such communication helps parents understand the larger purposes of a critical metropedagogy and what they can do to facilitate their children's learning.

Such knowledge also helps urban teachers engage parents, students, and community members in understanding the often invisible forces that shape their social and educational lives. Once such structures and processes have been named and analyzed, cognitive explosions often take place. Teachers working with students, parents, and concerned individuals in the community pool their talents and resources to construct pedagogies that engage and empower everyone associated with them. Research projects, for example, can be devised that engage students and community resource people in the exploration of why certain problems plague the neighborhood and the reasons no one does anything about them. In the process of coming to understand and solve such problems, students learn academic skills that will serve them well in their educational, vocational, and civic futures.

In this context, critical metropedagogues learn to transform diverse forms of knowledge, subjugated insights, and academic subject matter in ways that make them immediately useful to students.[29] Students gain the ability to evaluate the knowledges they encounter in relation to larger ideological concerns, for such information is always inscribed by race, class, and gender relationships. They learn to value the knowledges that brilliant people in the local community surrounding the school have developed and employed for personal and social transformation. Every teacher who understands the principles of metropedagogy searches the local community for such individuals and works to involve them in the school. Urban teachers should always cultivate a stable of local geniuses with the ability to do things that can connect to and extend the academic curriculum. Such connections will enhance the quality of teachers,' students,' and the local geniuses' lives while building strong school–community bonds.

When such school–community relationships are well established, critical urban teachers can draw upon multiple resources to help their students in countless ways. A sixth grade student who is very interested in rap music, for example, is thrilled when a budding rap group comes to school to work with him on his rhymes. It doesn't take a brain surgeon to recognize the ways a savvy sixth grade teacher could use this circumstance to engage the child in reading and writing skill improvement. Such a context could help build a lifelong disposition to value words and spoken and written language. The possibilities embedded in this and literally millions of other examples of school–community connections are very exciting. They remind us of why we wanted to go into teaching in the first place. Great urban teachers can orchestrate diverse relationships connecting their students to inspirational individuals living close to their school. It has been my experience that these community connections often mean more to students in the poorest urban schools than in other educational settings. The same is true with the meaning ascribed to being asked to work in the schools by people in poor urban communities.

In this community-based context, metropedagogy constructs a curriculum of place.[30] A curriculum of place takes our understandings of community and context and uses them to shape and situate the course of study. A curriculum of place is grounded on the history and culture of the urban community in which the school is located but is also a maker of history, a catalyst for historical change. Employing a variety of knowledges including information indigenous to the local urban community, metropedagogy's curriculum of place refracts all data through the lenses of the local. For example, if a class is studying the history of the Depression of the 1930s, the teacher and the students examine its impact in the local community. What was it like to live in Washington Heights in the 1930s? Who lived during those times who can talk to us about it? How do we go about researching the Depression in Washington Heights? In such pedagogical contexts, students come not only to learn more about their community but to get a richer, deeper picture of larger concepts.

In addition, metropedagogy's curriculum of place is always attuned to the connections between the political economy of the city and what goes on in schools. Such political economic concerns revolve around issues of ghettotization of urban neighborhoods, the decline of the manufacturing base in urban areas, the decentralization of cities, the changing structure of urban labor markets, the impact of globalization on urban populations, free market macroeconomic policies, and so on. All of these socioeconomic dynamics have adversely affected family and community resources, have led to increased class and ethnic segregation, and have altered the playing field on which urban schooling takes place. When we view statistics indicating that the United States leads the world in children growing up in poverty, how is it possible to separate these contextual insights from urban student performance?[31] Such changes are central issues in the curriculum of place.

A key dimension of the curriculum of place, vis-à-vis concerns with political economic forces shaping the lives of students and their families, involves the delicate interplay of these structural dynamics with issues of human agency—the ability of humans to shape their own lives. Many scholars who study urban education in relation to political economic structures fall into the trap of determinism.[32] In this deterministic context, they see no hope for educational change and empowering school experience until a more just redistribution of socioeconomic resources is achieved. While I am passionately committed to such economic justice, I assert that great strides toward social and individual transformation can be made in existing urban schools. Indeed, I watch brilliant urban teachers accomplish such goals year after year.[33] Thus, a metropedagogy continues to work for political, social, and economic change, while pursuing everyday victories at the classroom and the individual level. As long as critical urban teachers continue to connect their classrooms to the local community and enact a curriculum of place, these victories can be won.

As critical urban teachers use their diverse social, cultural, political, economic, and contextual knowledges to help connect the school and community in the curriculum of place, they should understand both the power and the limitation of such insights. Contextual insights provide a conceptual backdrop that helps teachers understand what's happening in their classrooms and in their students' lives. Such contextual information does not—much to the consternation of many teachers and teacher education students—provide specific ways of teaching, surefire methods designed to work every time. As I have written elsewhere, professional educational knowledge is simply too complex for such directives.[34] Contextual information should not be used, on one extreme, to blame the victims of social and economic injustice for their academic problems or on the other extreme to absolve them of any personal responsibility for their actions in school.

As always, the hermeneutic circle provides us with important insights into how we use such data. We always view students as individuals in relation to the group(s) and contexts to which they are connected. We always look at group experience in light of the idiosyncratic differences we find among individuals considered part of particular groups. Urban teachers understand, in this context, that seeing, say, an African American student as a member of only one group—African Americans—can be very misleading. An African American student may see him-/herself as a member of multiple groups and as influenced by diverse sociocultural contexts.[35] She may be middle class, a Muslim, an athlete, and the like. This back-and-forth, circular dynamic engaging the macro- and the micro-, and the general and specific that is common to hermeneutic analysis, informs urban teachers in complex, multilogical ways. Such hermeneutic facilities are important teacher skills in a metropedagogy, as teachers attempt to make sense of and connect to the world around them and their students. Here urban teachers are much better equipped to help build the school-neighborhood learning communities that are necessary to developing an urban curriculum of place.

Disempowering Urban Contexts: Overcoming Marginalization, Asserting Agency

The sociopolitical and cultural dynamics that frame urban education, to say the least, are not conducive to personal and social transformation. Indeed, it is not a stretch to maintain that such dynamics operate to undermine the life chances of marginalized students. This is the stark reality that faces all urban educators. As previously maintained, we can, with great commitment and effort, overcome its effects with individual students in specific classrooms, but there is nothing simple and easy about the process. When the success of right-wing political alliances over the last twenty-five years is added to this sobering mix, efforts for just, democratic reform of urban education becomes even more difficult.[36] The goals of the right-wing coalition—maintaining dominant power relations, enhancing international competition, increasing corporate profit margins, and strengthening the social regulation of the "dangerous" poor and non-white—do not provide more hope for poor urban students.

Activists in urban communities can help teachers in city schools connect their curricula to such ideological understandings. For students to grasp these concepts, interpretive frameworks must be constructed in close relationship with their collective lifeworlds and a community-based historical consciousness. Such a relationship creates an ideological zone of proximal development (ZPD) where new meanings emerge in dialogue with stories from the community. These interpretive frameworks and new meanings constitute a much-needed ideological shield against the assault on learning which poverty unleashes on urban students. Boys and girls from poor urban neighborhoods need this ideological shield to fight off the effects of poverty and racism:

- anger that works to subvert efforts to socially survive in school
- low expectations to succeed in school
- hopelessness concerning life expectations
- resentment of the middle class that makes it impossible to cooperate with many teachers
- rejection of the possibility that education may be worth pursuing
- equation of getting an education with "selling out" one's friends and neighbors.[37]

When many sociologists characterize inner-city schools as being populated by those left behind, ensnared in hopelessness by their economic unimportance, then the time has come for a dramatic change. In less than sixty years, these urban schools have moved from white, middle-class bastions with a broad tax base, to low-income, minority systems with an ever-shrinking share of economic resources and political power. In what many call the metropolitan problem, well-to-do urban and suburban districts have not been willing to provide shared resources and financial aid to help those caught in this urban briar patch. In the electronic hyperreality of the last three or so decades, racial inscriptions ideologically frame discussions of urban issues such as these.[38]

Overcoming Marginalization, Asserting Agency in Hyperreality

Hyperreality is a term used to characterize the way the contemporary cultural landscape is saturated by electronic information. On such a terrain, people begin to lose touch with traditional notions of time, community, self, and history. A feeling of alienation and displacement creeps into the collective consciousness. When such hyperreal dislocation is coupled with the disaffection of urban poverty, an explosive cocktail is produced. Those who live and work in the city can feel this estrangement in the anger we sometimes sense on the street. Many times while riding a subway through Brooklyn, I've watched emotions explode and fights break out over what, on the surface, seemed to the naïve observer to be the most trivial of issues. Dig an inch below the epidermis and one begins to discern the sense of humiliation and abandonment so many marginalized urban dwellers feel. Like DeNiro's character, Travis, in *Taxi Driver*, it doesn't take much to provoke an explosive psychotic breakdown. Don't cut that guy off in traffic, he'll shoot you.

The alienation of hyperreality is a topic that must be addressed in the curriculum of metropedagogy. How are we to deal with the bombardment of information from TV, radio, movies, videos, the Internet, IPods, computers, and the like? How are we to make sense of our lives when we have so many information producers telling us how we are supposed to be, and what we are supposed to think and feel? Critical urban teachers want their students to be agents who understand and thus, are able to negotiate their environments—not casualties of evolving social circumstances.[39] As I have maintained elsewhere,[40] many traditional pedagogies and epistemologies are unable to address issues of poverty, alienation, complexity, ideology, changing information environments, and social and cultural displacement. We have to transcend traditional disciplinary arrangements with their tendency for fragmentation and technicism and move to a more interdisciplinary and critical way of seeing. Such a critical interdisciplinarity views problems in multiple contexts and asks *what is* in relation to *what could be*. It produces rigorous and usable knowledges that help us solve the social problems that plague us—in particular, the most marginalized among us.[41]

We must move our ways of thinking about knowledge, modes of interpretation, notions of the social construction of selfhood, and teaching and learning into a hyperreal digital era. It views schooling in context, understanding that education no longer takes place in an oral culture but in a cyber cosmos interfacing with an alienated brick and mortar urban world. The world of hyperreality is a corporatized environment, as information technology has allowed the purveyors of power to gain greater power to promote their best interests. Ideologically charged messages promoting corporations as the providers of the good things of life reach us in public spaces and in our most private domains around the clock. Walk into any urban school and look at the corporate logos embraced by urban students who are wearing them on their tee shirts, hats, and other paraphernalia.

Corporate media representations construct and refract the ways people view public issues and social concerns. In this context, one of the reasons many individuals have written off urban students involves the way the media represent them as incompetent and frightening beings better off incarcerated than educated. As these representations seep into the public consciousness and shape public policies such as funding for urban education, the analytical structures that dominate the schools are unable to even acknowledge that such a process of consciousness construction, of ideological regulation is taking place. Thus, the insidious process goes unchallenged, and teaching and learning go on as if nothing has changed in the world surrounding the school. Urban teachers who understand these covert dynamics and work to address them often find themselves stymied by protectors of the status quo. Such administrators many times use the specter of content standards to justify their censorship of such a critical curriculum. Not only do most schools not address changes in knowledge work and information production in a cyber-era, most educational institutions still haven't understood the need for media literacy.

Such is the case despite our understanding that such sources of knowledge production play a profound role in shaping individual identity and new forms of community. Examine the role of Internet cafes in the everyday world of many urban students and the changes they effect in their social, interpersonal lives. In hyperreality, culture is produced and consumed in ways unfamiliar to many educational experts operating in an older world. These multidimensional changes in the conditions of knowledge production have multiple consequences. Certainly one of the most important involves the ways control of knowledge in hyperreality enhances the influence of dominant power. Given this, an important dimension of the curriculum of metropedagogy involves developing a student's ability to "read" visual images—to understand the conditions of their production and the ways they are used to evoke particular responses.

Concurrently, metropedagogy in hyperreality appreciates the need for urban students to become critical knowledge workers who appreciate the multiple dimensions of visual and cyber imagery. Students in such a curriculum learn to use knowledge tools to accomplish their goals of individual and social transformation, while at the same time understanding the many ways such technologies are used for manipulative and antidemocratic objectives. Urban students live in a different world of knowledge and information technology—a critical urban education must stay ahead of these spiraling changes. New media and information technologies exert a profound social, cultural, political, and economic impact. A metropedagogue knows that such a force must always be a central focus in any critical curriculum. The skills and knowledges learned in this context are tools that will help marginalized urban students escape their oppression and assert agency over their lives.

Metropedagogy and the Knowledge Needed by Urban Teachers: Constructing a Critical Urban Teacher Education

Because there are no short cuts to crafting a high-quality urban education, there are no short cuts to educating high-quality urban teachers. The foundation for educating effective urban teachers involves building a rigorous, multidimensional academic framework that includes the ability to conduct research and engage in complex knowledge work. All teachers must base their pedagogies on a well-developed intellectual power. This alone will not suffice in the complicated daily lives of urban schooling, but without it, teachers are lost. Urban teachers—like all educators—must have the tools to teach themselves, to create learning communities, and to operate as lifelong learners in collaboration with other practitioners. In these contexts, urban teachers can continue their study of the contexts in which urban education takes place and the forces that help shape the failures and triumphs of urban students. Here they can work to reimagine and reconstruct schools as learning organizations where teachers and students are rewarded for participation in the life of the mind.

Schools as learning organizations always work to problematize the act of curriculum development, viewing it as an ongoing, never completed process that changes with our enhanced understanding of the complex interaction of academic knowledges, our understanding of the social and cultural context in which the school operates, student and community knowledges, and the evolution of educational purpose. The same is true of pedagogical method and assessment, as teachers work to know more and more about such complicated processes. In these ways, teacher educators hand schools as learning organizations the torch of continuing practitioner professional education. Schools of education and schools as learning organizations both work to connect scholarship to professional action. When such an academic foundation is neglected, teacher education can sometimes degenerate into a technical focus on the *delivery* of the prescribed curriculum. Questions about the relationships connecting teaching and learning to the larger macro-context and the community around the school are rarely asked in this technicist mode of teacher education.

One caveat that needs to be addressed in relation to technicist tendencies in some schools of education involves the role in teacher education played by arts and sciences colleges/departments in universities. While technicist orientations in professional education must addressed, the ways that arts and sciences programs often dispense knowledge with little emphasis on the process of knowledge production and disciplinary analysis are equally troubling. Such "lecture and recite" types of pedagogies simply do not prepare teachers for the rigorous types of academic work required of educational practitioners. Arts and sciences programs have escaped critique for their role in the miseducation of teachers for much too long. All aspects of university teacher education must be committed to rigorous and challenging academic experiences for educators.[42]

Teacher education is always a contentious topic because there is little agreement—despite claims to the contrary—about the form it should take. A search of the literature focused on urban teacher education will reveal a plethora of positions, ranging from technicist to critical, and from high context to low context. By high context, I am referencing a call to engage urban professional education students in learning about the urban context and its relationship/impact on teaching and learning. By low context, I am referring to the belief among many teacher educators that such contextual understandings of the urban setting are not relevant or helpful to prospective teachers. The multiple dimensions—multiethnic, multiracial, multireligious, multiclass, multigendered, multinational, multidimensional—of urban life delineated by Anderson and Summerfield[43] are not viewed as something worthy of study in the low context articulation of teacher education. Only recently has the notion gained much traction that city teachers need to be specifically educated to teach in the urban context. Those who oppose such a proposition still operate in schools of professional education, higher education in general, and in the political domain.

Metropedagogy, of course, is wedded to the notion that urban educators need to understand teaching and learning in the urban context. There is much to learn about this context and the larger struggle to become a great urban teacher—it is a complex, involved process. Because they teach students with such diverse needs, urban teachers must possess a wide variety of teaching strategies. They need a deep and contextualized understanding of the subject areas they teach so that they can appreciate the central ideas of the diverse domains and connect such ideas to the lives of their students. As previously argued, they need a detailed understanding of the different contexts in which urban education takes place so they can appreciate the forces that shape their students' lives and relationships to school. With these abilities in place, urban teachers then need to be researchers who use such skills for curriculum development, to mentor other teachers, and to study the conditions of their students' lives.

When advocates of metropedagogy argue that teachers should understand their subject areas, they move this capability far beyond traditional assumptions about what that might mean. Not only do teachers need to cultivate a current understanding of scholarship in a discipline, they also need to understand the historical construction of a field, its discursive rules, paradigmatic conflicts within the discipline, and the diverse schools of thought operating within it. The same holds true for developing curricula. Practitioners of a metropedagogy go far beyond the traditional notion of writing a curriculum consisting of key ideas from a particular domain of knowledge. The critical urban educator constructs a curriculum that uses diverse knowledges—subjugated knowledges included—that speaks specifically to the needs, concerns, fears, problems, and successes of their many students. Such a situated curriculum is quite different from what is too often found in urban schools—on one extreme, urban teachers teach a traditional college prep curriculum or, on the other, they teach a course of study that includes nothing but drill on basic skills. Either way, students are turned off and bored. Developing a rigorous, situated curriculum is a demanding task, but the rewards involving student learning and motivation to engage in the life of the mind make it well worth the effort.

Thus, teachers as scholar researchers work constantly to connect their larger sense of purpose to the everyday tasks of teaching. As respected practitioners who work for individual and social transformation, critical urban educators expect forms of professional development that are engaged in critical diversity and social justice. Metropedagogy demands pre-service and in-service modes of teacher education that are appropriate for respected scholars. Too often, urban teacher education reflects the same biases that are found in deficit pedagogies. In this context, issues of social justice vis-à-vis concerns with racism, class bias, and gender bias come directly into focus. Urban teachers realize that such concerns directly affect not only their students, but also urban teachers themselves, as a wide range of deficit assumptions begin to emerge about teachers who would choose urban teaching as their career. Teachers, as scholar researchers, are much better equipped to address such prejudiced assumptions than their less able colleagues.

Urban Teachers as Knowledge Workers

In technicist teacher education programs, teachers are not expected to be scholar researchers. Such approaches to professional education assume that teachers, especially urban teachers, are incapable of high-level conceptual thinking and, as a result, should learn reductionistic predefined curricular knowledge, gimmicks to motivate students, and prespecified classroom discipline techniques. The idea of teachers studying questions of educational purpose, becoming students of context, cultivating critical reflection, examining the ideological dimensions of social and educational institutions, and developing unique ways of accomplishing particular goals is alien in the technicist context. In urban contexts, such skills become extremely important, for urban students don't react very well to canned discipline methods, traditional ways of doing things in the classroom, and rote forms of learning. Simple transmission of knowledge methods fail miserably as such students see through their meaninglessness, their irrelevance to the world outside the school.

Critical urban teachers as knowledge workers respect the need for the curriculum to be useful and resonant with the lived world. They refuse to insult their students by simply providing them with fragments of knowledge that have little meaning except on a test. In this context, such urban teachers work to create classroom learning communities where everyone is a researcher who strives to learn and teach meaningful information and methods of interpreting it. The construction of such learning communities subverts the bureaucratic relationship between truth-providing teachers and empty-vessel students that characterizes many urban schools. When students and teachers are knowledge producers who learn from one another, the power-saturated hierarchy between them begins to melt away into the ether. Such a disappearance opens a new range of possibilities in the negotiation of productive, respectful relationships between urban students and teachers. As scholars who construct knowledge that is useful in the community, teachers, students, and community members learn sophisticated interpretive and analytical skills that can be used for positive effect for the rest of their lives.

In this context, marginalized urban students begin to view schools as less bizarre and uncomfortable places. Producing useful knowledges along with their teachers and peers, they begin to see value in an institution many thought was hopelessly archaic and out of touch with their worlds. Metropedagogy promotes a school culture where teachers, students, and community members are dedicated to the promotion of new knowledge, and all view pedagogy as intimately connected to researching, interpreting, thinking, and creating. In this frame, critical teacher educators in urban contexts work to create situations where such productive processes can flourish.

Though the situation is changing to some extent, there is not enough published by teacher educators and teachers themselves working in an urban context—there are just not enough knowledge workers operating in this field. Those entering urban education need a wide variety of knowledges that help them understand the complexity of teaching and learning in the city. A majority of urban teachers report that when they first enter the classroom, they feel unprepared to accomplish numerous required and complex tasks. When teachers are educated in professional development schools specially designed to educate teachers planning to work in urban schools, nine out of ten teachers report they were adequately prepared to negotiate the complications of urban classrooms. When teachers are respected as knowledge workers and are specially educated to work in urban schools, a new day has dawned for urban education.

In critical diversity, metropedagogy makes it clear that simply because a particular curriculum has worked in one context doesn't mean it will work in all contexts—this is the case no matter how well one controls the so-called variables. How one or more teachers implemented a particular curriculum and how they fared can no doubt inform other teachers. But no study can guarantee the success of a particular approach. Assuring the public that particular approaches are "scientifically valid" is the modus operandi of contemporary right-wing urban educational reformers who claim there is great consensus on how to reform urban education via standardization. The epistemological basis of these guarantees rests on the problematic belief that knowledge is a static and inert entity that can be simply "delivered" intact and complete from the teacher to the student.

In this epistemological and ideological configuration, the static and inert knowledge in question comes from the official Eurocanon that teaches traditional Western values. Excluded here are the "distorted" beliefs of multiculturalists, feminists, and critical pedagogues. Diversity, as represented in this right-wing epistemological and ideological framework, is an effort to "oppress" students by making them listen to alien viewpoints with which they disagree. What an amazing rhetorical reversal: exposing students and potential teachers to a wide range of viewpoints is refracted by the right wing in a manner that represents such actions as a violation of white students' rights. Critical teachers as knowledge workers in their appreciation of the complexity of all educational data understand that research produced on teaching in urban schools does more to raise important questions than it does to provide correct answers.

They understand that any data transferred to them by any teacher or knowledge producer should always be questioned for the belief structures on which it is based, the epistemological and ideological assumptions that support it, the location of the producer in the sociocultural web of reality, the context in which it was produced and so on. Thus, one of the primary responsibilities of teachers and students who operate as knowledge workers in a metropedagogy is to formulate good questions about the knowledge with which they are confronted. Having unanswered questions after reading a text, taking an urban education methods class, or listening to a teacher or professor give a lecture is not the mark of an unsuccessful learner—it is a characteristic of an active mind. Right-wing pedagogies and "evidence-based research" are designed to resolve all questions. In this context, certainty, mastery, and full data banks are the knowledge signifiers for triumphant teaching and learning.[44] We have the answer—hold all further questions. That's why it's called *positivism*.

Urban Teachers and Misleading Pronouncements about Teaching and Learning

In the complex context of urban schools, the socioeconomic, cultural, political, and organizational dynamics that we have previously referenced exacerbate all of these complications of knowledge production about education. "Sure fire methods," guaranteed like carnival snake oil to work miracles, are even less helpful in poverty-stricken urban schools than in more affluent classrooms. Practitioners promoting a metropedagogy in this context attach importance to understanding their own location in the web of reality and how it helps shape the way they see their classrooms, schools, and students. Such critical teachers study the way this sociocultural location, this positionality, affects their research and knowledge work. Urban teachers, especially those from dominant cultural locations, must understand self vis-à-vis others. If they are white, they must understand their whiteness in relation to these issues. When their identities are different from their students, critical teachers work especially hard to understand who they are in relation to their students. This is an increasingly important aspect of our metropedagogy because in the twenty-first century, an overwhelming majority of teacher education students are white, middle-class women from suburban/rural backgrounds, while an ever-growing percentage of urban students are of color.

In the ideological climate of the last half of the first decade of the twenty-first century, middle-/upper-middle-class students are exposed to more and more information that represents poor urban students of color as pathological and undeserving of help and educational attention. There are indications that white middle-/upper-middle-class students have grown angrier, more fearful, and more condemning of poor urban students of color as a result of these omnipresent representations. A metropedagogical teacher education will have to work especially hard to address these dynamics in the coming years. Such teacher educators will have to deal with those students who, on one end of the continuum, view urban students as unworthy and on the other end of the scale, view them as lost souls in need of salvation. Neither perspective is accurate, and critical teacher educators will have to work hard to model alternatives for those who fall into the two constructions.

Teachers operating in the regressive ideological climate of the twenty-first century will have to overcome the right-wing politics of knowledge that has poisoned the well of public information. This reality makes our metropedagogy more important than ever. In such a toxic information environment, it is necessary to prepare urban teachers to be responsible for their own learning, to become rigorous knowledge workers who can cut through the ideological haze of popular information, and to become curriculum developers who can design compelling, connected, and independent courses for their students. In this way, they will not have to rely on the ideologically inscribed, packaged curricula so prevalent in contemporary urban schools. With these abilities, teachers can take responsibility for the conceptualization and execution of their teaching.

Such teachers become self-directed professionals who make their own decisions and refuse to blindly follow the standardized dictates of their superiors. These urban professionals understand the nature of knowledge production and delivery in the contemporary era and how this plays out in education.[45] They understand the hidden forms of indoctrination inscribed in standardized curricula and scripted lessons. Such officially approved lessons are highly politicized with their erasure of power and inequality. Standardization hides its politics while concurrently making it seem that anyone who objects to its indoctrination is the person who is attempting to politicize the curriculum. Advocates of metropedagogy point out these misleading dynamics and work to provide alternatives to the pseudo-objectivity of the dominant curriculum.

In addition to these curricular dynamics, urban teachers as knowledge workers study their students' lives and everyday experiences. Often, middle-/upper-middle-class teachers find it difficult to understand the motivations, feelings, and emotions of the urban students they teach. In such a context, it becomes even more important for teachers to research their students' lives and the relationship between the students and their teachers. Here, metropedagogues begin to tie their contextual understandings and insights into power to their understanding of their students and their relationships with them. As I have pointed out numerous times in this chapter, there is nothing simple about this process—it, like so many other aspects of urban education, is profoundly complex. Urban teachers, as knowledge workers, examine all of this information in an effort to construct positive and production relationships between themselves and their students.

Too often in urban education and professional education in general, scholars will make the claim that becoming a teacher is all about human relations. While there is no doubt that being able to establish positive human relations in a classroom is extremely important, the argument for the importance of the process is often depoliticized and decontextualized. Thus, maintaining good human relations in the urban education classroom becomes merely a technical act removed from the sociopolitical forces marginalized urban students have to confront.[46] Teachers must connect with their students but always within a larger contextual understanding of the problems they face. So, in metropedagogy, we are referring to a contextualized mode of establishing positive connections with urban students. Such productive human interaction always comes with a vision of where we might go pedagogically once such good relationships are established.

Metropedagogy's notion of establishing good human relations between teachers and students involves creating connections to students in their lives both in and out of school. Sometimes one has to understand the student's life outside of school to get a good sense of who he or she is. In my own teaching, I have found that until I understood students in their out-of-school lives, I held a naïve conception of the amazing things they were capable of accomplishing. In this context, teachers as knowledge workers who are researchers of their students, explore the impact of media on their students, especially the ways it constructs their view of self and world. Many times, critical teachers explore with students what they have learned from media and how it has shaped their ideological orientations.[47] Elizabeth Quintero[48] engages urban students in this context to write about their lives. In such lessons, teachers as researchers of their students can find out in very specific ways the impact of electronic media on not only the construction of student consciousness but on how young people learn in hyperreality.

Metropedagogy, Power, and Teacher Professionalization

Metropedagogy's concerns with the power dimensions of criticality and student culture, much to my consternation, often do not play well in some colleges of education. In these organizations, power relations are hidden under vague references to social justice and diversity that do more to muddle teacher education students' understanding of the forces that undermine marginalized students' academic performance than to clarify them. The outcome of such so-called social-justice based teacher education is the promotion of the status quo and the maintenance of existing power relations. Advocates of metropedagogy are saddened by this situation, as such arrangements work to undermine the importance of the critique of how we study urban education and how we prepare teachers for urban settings. Such critique of these teacher education institutions is often positioned as an affront to the consensus claimed about the goals and purposes of urban education.

In this context, those who engage in such critique are often punished and positioned as outsiders to the real work of the college. I have seen this happen too many times over my years in teacher education. Advocates of metropedagogy must keep fighting to make sure that questions of asymmetrical power relations and oppression are viewed as central dimensions of the work of urban teacher educators. When such questions are ignored or repressed, the work of urban teacher education degenerates into one-dimensional technical concerns with methods of information delivery. The decontextualized technicist focus on teacher "competencies" finds fertile soil in schools of education that punish those who raise "impractical" questions of educational purpose and grounded inquiries about justice in relation to race, class, gender, sexuality, and language.[49]

Critical urban teachers always conduct inquiry into whose interests are being promoted, and whose needs are being addressed in schools and whose are not. So often, in the demands of state and other forms of teacher education accreditation, questions such as the preceding are viewed as out-of-bounds and contrary to technical models of what is relevant to good teaching. Questions of ethics and purpose have been replaced by state mandated, fragmented topics that don't merit inclusion in a university curriculum. In lieu of urban teachers studying the connections between the city context and student performance, standards-regulated teacher education has emphasized reductionistic proficiencies taken from the assumed duties of practitioners transmogrified into the language of behavior objectives. "The teacher will post the state objectives on the board in four-inch letters before each lesson." Questions of inequality, of political economics, of ideology, of poor urban communities are viewed here as crass interruptions to the real demands of teaching.[50]

One does not have to look far to find pressure being put on teacher education programs—especially urban ones—to use scripted curriculum packages in the "training" of teachers.[51] Scripted lessons help mitigate the damage of incompetent urban teachers, the conservative reformers assert, and work to bring about the order, discipline, fundamental skills, and traditional values that radical teachers lacking family values have neglected. With such lessons, the conservative reformers proclaim, "we'll make sure that secular educators don't force their multicultural agenda on parents and their children."

With the help of corporate benefactors funding political campaigns and right-wing think tanks, ideas such as these have come to dominate many dimensions of teacher education and urban school reform. With vast financial resources, right-wing groups have more power now to shape urban educational policy and practice than at any other time in history. Despite protestations by corporate and business groups that they want the schools to graduate critical thinking, independent, ethical, and creative workers, they fund groups that promote modes of teaching and evaluation that encourage the production of conformist, power-dependent, and compliant students—and teachers.[52] Metropedagogy understands these problems and knows that the fight for a socially and personally transformative urban education will be contentious and prolonged.

One of the most disturbing dimensions of this struggle involves a fundamental ideological disagreement between progressive forces who advocate a professionalized teaching corps and right-wing groups who don't believe such professionalization is necessary. The right-wing position sees nothing problematic about knowledge and its production. In this regressive context, knowledge is simply a static, fixed body of truths that the teacher transfers directly from the approved textbook to the minds of students. Calls for the teaching of ideas and insights of diverse peoples around the world are positioned in the right-wing universe as anti-Western, anti-American and anti-Christian threats to our "civilization." With rigid content standards, prepared scripts for teachers, and strict monitoring of teacher fidelity to the prepackaged curriculum, advocates of the right-wing position believe they are succeeding in taking back schooling from those multiculturalists who would destroy the nation. One can understand that in such a framework, highly educated, contextually savvy practitioners of metropedagogy capable of sophisticated forms of research are the Right's worst nightmare. Such urban teachers might think for themselves.

Even when the deprofessionalizers don't win a total victory (at least not yet) in destroying the infrastructure of teacher education, they win major battles in the war. With growing influence in state legislatures, they have convinced many states to remove the types of contextual understandings discussed here from teacher education. Included in these contextual understanding are issues of diversity and concerns with racism, class bias, and sexism. Pushed by right-wing forces, more and more states are now promoting alternative routes to teacher education with six-week programs focusing on low-level technical issues. The idea that teaching is an intellectual pursuit is anathema to the deprofessionalizers. Advocates of metropedagogy maintain that the right-wing position reflects a fundamental misconstruction of the work of educators in a democratic society. Education in democratic societies is, first and foremost, a public domain designed to promote the public good through the production of an educated citizenry as well as the creation of pragmatic knowledge. Indeed, metropedagogy is based on a belief in a civically courageous public education for all urban students.

The privatized right-wing vision rejects these public dynamics, focusing on education as an individualized dynamic to aid people in the competition for private commodities. A key strategy of the Right has involved the redefinition of what involves a public concern in a democratic society. The vision of a cooperative, interconnected, and humane society is erased from the right-wing construction of an isolated individuals competing for limited resources. Advocates of metropedagogy don't believe the time has come to return to a social Darwinist universe with its winners and losers. The basis of the pedagogical act involves caring for everyone and an ethic of inclusion and opportunity. The watchword of education in a democratic context is not competition but collaboration. Advocates of metropedagogy understand the way schools operate. The winners in the right-wing model are already determined—and the urban poor are not on the list. Yet, in urban district after urban district, the failure of reform strengthens the position of the privatizers who have persuaded some cities to charter private corporations to administer their schools. The future of public education is undoubtedly in jeopardy.

Conclusion: The Struggle Continues

In this highly political context, we advocate critical diversity—a metropedagogy that understands that we have a fight on our hands. We appreciate the strength of dominant power wielders and their campaign to produce an ethnocentric and monolithic curriculum that relegates marginalized urban students to low-level learning, social regulation, and futures with little hope for social mobility and civic participation. Despite the power of such politicos, advocates of metropedagogy believe that our ideas and values are more powerful. As long as we don't get discouraged and give up, we believe that modes of schooling dedicated to democratic ideals, the capacity of all students to learn, rigorous scholarship that explores multiple viewpoints and knowledges from around the world, the professional sanctity of the career of teaching, the right of urban communities to control their own destinies, and education as the foundation of a humane, egalitarian society will prevail.

Notes

Parts of this chapter were taken from *Metropedagogy: Power, Justice, and the Urban Classroom* (2005). Kincheloe, J. and hayes, k., editors. Rotterdam: Sense Publishers.

1. M. Carvan, A. Nolen, & R. Yinger. Power through Partnership: The Urban Network for the Improvement of Teacher Education, 2002. http://www.urbannetworks.net/documents/tacte%20article,%20final%20revision %201-14-02.pdf.
2. J. Kincheloe, *Critical Constructivism* (New York: Peter Lang, 2005).
3. S. Steinberg, *Multi/intercultural Conversations: A Reader* (New York: Peter Lang, 2001); P. McLaren, *Life in Schools: An Introduction to Critical Pedagogy in the Foundations of Education*. 4th ed. (Boston: Allyn and Bacon, 2002); J. Kincheloe, *Critical Pedagogy* (NY: Peter Lang, 2004).
4. Noone, L. & P. Cartwright, "Doing a Critical Literacy Pedagogy: Trans/forming Teachers in a Teacher Education Course," 2002. http://www.atea.schools.net.au/ATEA/96conf/noone.html; M. Knobel, *Everyday Literacies: Students, Discourse, and Social Practice* (New York: Peter Lang, 1999); M. Gergen & K. Gergen, "Qualitative Inquiry: Tensions and Transformations." In N. Denzin & Y. Lincoln (Eds.) *Handbook of Qualitative Research*. 2nd ed. (Thousand Oaks, CA: Sage, 2000); P. McLaren, *Che Guevara, Paulo Freire, and the Pedagogy of Revolution* (Lanham, MD: Rowman & Littlefield, 2000); J. Kincheloe, *Getting beyond the Facts: Teaching Social Studies/Social*

Sciences in the Twenty-First Century. 2nd ed. (New York: Peter Lang, 2001); W. Crebbin, "The Critically Reflective Practitioner," 2001, http://www.ballarat.edu.au/~wcrebbin/TB780/Critreflect.html; J. Grinberg, "Only the Facts?" In J. Kincheloe & D. Weil (Eds.) *Critical Thinking and Learning: An Encyclopedia for Parents and Teachers* (Westport, CT: Greenwood, 2004).

5. K. Herr, "Problematizing the 'Problem' Teen: Reconceptualizing Adolescent Development." In J. Kincheloe & R. Horn (Eds.) *Educational Psychology: An Encyclopedia* (Westport, CT: Greenwood, 2005).

6. S. Evans & I. Prilleltensky, "Literacy for Wellness, Oppression, and Liberation." In J. Kincheloe & R. Horn (Eds.) *Educational Psychology: An Encyclopedia* (Westport, CT: Greenwood, 2005).

7. S. Henke, "Representations of Secondary Urban Education: Infusing Cultural Studies into Teacher Education," Dissertation, Miami University, 2000; S. Fuhrman, "Urban Education: Is Reform the Answer?" http://www.urbanedjournal.org/archive/issue%201/featurearticles/article0004.html.

8. P. Anderson & J. Summerfield, "Why Is Urban Education Different than Rural and Suburban Education?" In S. Steinberg & J. Kincheloe (Eds.) *19 Urban Questions: Teaching in the City* (New York: Peter Lang, 2004).

9. NWREL (North West Regional Educational Laboratory), "Lessons from the Cities, Part 2: The Strengths of City Kids," 1999, http://www.nwrel.org/nwedu/winter99/lessons2.html; A. Ciani, "Teacher Education Issues for Urban Middle Schools," 2002, http://www.nmsa.org/about/urban.teachered.pdf

10. J. Halford, "Urban Education: Policies of Promise," 1996, http://www.ascd.org/publications/infobrief/issue5.html; K. Louis & B. Smith, "Teacher Engagement and Real Reform in Urban Schools." In B. Williams (Ed.) *Closing the Achievement Gap: A Vision for Changing Beliefs and Practices* (Alexandria, VA: ASCD, 1996); P. Hill & M. Celio, *Fixing Urban Schools* (Washington, D.C.: Brookings Institute Press, 1998); E. Kozleski, "Educating Special Education Teachers for Urban Schools," *Urban Perspectives Newsletter*, 2002, http://www.edc.org/collaborative/summer02.txt; S. Steinberg & J. Kincheloe (Eds.) *19 Urban Questions: Teaching in the City* (New York: Peter Lang, 2004).

11. J. Bamburg, "Raising Expectations to Improve Student Learning," 1994, http://www.ncrel.org/sdrs/areas/issues/educatrs/leadrshp/ie0bam.htm; K. Peterson, "Building Collaborative Cultures: Seeking Ways to Reshape Urban Schools," 1994, http://www.ncrel.org.sdrs/areas/issues/educatrs/leadrship/le0pet.htm; Hill & Celio, *Fixing Urban Schools;* MDRC (Manpower Demonstration Research Corporation) for the Council of the Great City Schools, "Foundations for Success: Case Studies of How Urban School Systems Improve Student Achievement," 2002, http://www.cgcs.rg/reports/foundations.html.

12. J. Pickering, "The Self Is a Semiotic Process," *Journal of Consciousness Studies.* **6** (4), (1999): 31–47; E. O'Sullivan, *Transformative Learning: Educational Vision for the Twenty-first Century* (NY: Zed, 1999); E. Malewski, "Administration—Administrative Leadership and Public Consciousness: Discourse Matters in the Struggle for New Standards." In J. Kincheloe & D. Weil (Eds.), *Standards and Schooling in the United States: An Encyclopedia*, 3 vols. (Santa Barbara, CA: ABC-Clio, 2001); B. Thayer-Bacon, *Transforming Critical Thinking: Thinking Constructively* (New York: Teachers College Press, 2000); B. Thayer-Bacon, *Relational "(E)pistemologies,"* (New York: Peter Lang, 2003).

13. M. Wang & J. Kovach, "Bridging the Achievement Gap in Urban Schools: Reducing Educational Segregation and Advancing Resilience-Promoting Strategies." In B. Williams (Ed.), *Closing the Achievement Gap: A Vision for Changing Beliefs and Practices* (Alexandria, VA: ASCD, 1996); USSR (Urban Schools Symposium Report), "Relationship, Community, and Positive Reframing: Addressing the Needs," 1998, http://www.inclusiveschools.org/procsho.htm; NWREL (North West Regional Educational Laboratory), "Lessons from the Cities, Part 2: The Strengths of City Kids," 1999, http://www.nwrel.org/nwedu/winter99/lessons2.html; Carvan, Nolen, & Yinger, "Power through Partnership."

14. M. Haberman, "Urban Education: The State of Urban Schooling at the Start of the Twenty-First Century," *EducationNews.org*, 2004, http://www.educationnews.org.

15. J. Kincheloe, S. Steinberg, & A. Gresson (Eds.), *Measured Lies: The Bell Curve Examined* (New York: St. Martin's Press, 1996).

16. USSR, "Relationship, Community, and Positive Reframing"; J. Cuello, "Reconstructing the Paradigm for Teaching and Learning at the University: Lessons from the Field of an Urban Campus," 1999, http://www.culma.wayne.edu/obs/reconstructing.htm; D. Hurley, "Developing Students as Change Agents: Urban Education and Reform," 2003, http://www.eastern.edu/publications/emme/2003spring/hurley.html.

17. Cuello, "Reconstructing the Paradigm."

18. Henke, "Representations of Secondary Urban Education."

19. Hill & Celio, *Fixing Urban Schools*; E. Morrell, "Legitimate Peripheral Participation as Professional Development: Lessons from a Summer Research Seminar." *Teacher Education Quarterly*, 2003, http://www.findarticles.com/p/articles/mi_qa3960/is_200304/ai_n9166599.

20. Wang & Kovach, "Bridging the Achievement Gap in Urban Schools."

21. M. Haberman, "Achieving 'High Quality' in the Selection, Preparation and Retention of Teachers," *Education-News.org*, 2002, http://www.educationnews.org.

22. C. Bingham, "Knowledge Acquisition." In J. Kincheloe & D. Weil (Eds.) *Critical Thinking and Learning: An Encyclopedia for Parents and Teachers* (Westport, CT: Greenwood Press, 2004).

23. S. Harding, *Is Science Multicultural? Postcolonialisms, Feminisms, and Epistemologies.* (Bloomington: Indiana University Press, 1998).

24. D. Weil, "World Class Standards? Whose World, Which Economic Classes, and What Standards?" In J. Kincheloe & D. Weil (Eds.) *Standards and Schooling in the United States: An Encyclopedia*, 3 vols. (Santa Barbara, CA: ABC-Clio, 2001).

25. B. Dylan, *Chronicles: Volume One* (New York: Simon & Schuster, 2004).

26. F. Capra, *The Web of Life: A New Scientific Understanding of Living Systems* (New York: Anchor Books, 1996).

27. T. May, *Between Genealogy and Epistemology: Psychology, Politics, and Knowledge in the Thought of Michel Foucault* (University Park, PA: Penn State Press, 1993).

28. J. Kincheloe & W. Pinar (Eds.), *Curriculum as Social Psychoanalysis: Essays on the Significance of Place* (Albany, NY: State University of New York Press, 1991).

29. Wang & Kovach, "Bridging the Achievement Gap in Urban Schools."

30. J. Irvine, "The Education of Children Whose Nightmares Occur Both Night and Day," 1999, http:///www.emory.edu/senate/facultycou/fac_cmtes/dfl_irvine.htm

31. W. Holder, "How Can Urban Students Become Writers?" In S. Steinberg & J. Kincheloe (Eds.), *19 Urban Questions: Teaching in the City* (New York: Peter Lang, 2004).

32. J. Kincheloe, "The Knowledges of Teacher Education: Developing a Critical Complex Epistemology." *Teacher Education Quarterly* 31 (1), (2004): 49–66; J. Kincheloe, A. Bursztyn, & S. Steinberg (Eds.), *Teaching Teachers: Building a Quality School of Urban Education* (New York: Peter Lang, 2004).

33. G. Madison, *The Hermeneutics of Postmodernity: Figures and Themes* (Bloomington: Indiana University Press, 1988); L. Weiner, *Urban Teaching: The Essentials* (NY: Teachers College Press, 1999); Kincheloe, *Getting beyond the Facts*; Carvan, Nolen, & Yinger, "Power through Partnership."

34. J. Kincheloe, *Classroom Teaching: An Introduction* (New York: Peter Lang, 2005).

35. M. Apple, "The Politics of Official Knowledge: Does a National Curriculum Make Sense?" *Teachers College Record* 95 (2), (1993): 222–41; M. Apple, "Dominance and Dependency: Situating *The Bell Curve* within the Conservative Restoration." In J. Kincheloe, S. Steinberg, & A. Gresson (Eds.), *Measured Lies: The Bell Curve Examined* (New York: St. Martin's, 1996); M. Apple, *Power, Meaning, and Identity: Essays in Critical Educational Studies* (New York: Peter Lang, 1999).

36. Z. Leonardo, "Race." In J. Kincheloe & D. Weil (Eds.) *Critical Thinking and Learning: An Encyclopedia for Parents and Teachers* (Westport, CT: Greenwood, 2004).

37. S. Lester, "Learning for the Twenty-First Century." In J. Kincheloe & D. Weil (Eds.) *Standards and Schooling in the U.S.: An Encyclopedia*, 3 vols. (Santa Barbara, CA: ABC-Clio, 2001).

38. Kincheloe, *Critical Constructivism*.

39. Kincheloe, *Critical Pedagogy*.

40. R. Novick, "Actual Schools, Possible Practices: New Directions in Professional Development." *Education Policy Analysis Archives* 4 (14), (1996); USSR, "Relationship, Community, and Positive Reframing"; R. Blunden, "Reflective Teaching and the Beginning Teacher Morality and Methodology." *Research and Reflection: A Journal of Education Praxis* 1 (1), (1998); A. Edwards, "Researching Pedagogy: A Sociocultural Agenda" Inaugural Lecture, University of Birmingham, 2000, http://www.edu.bham.ac.uk/SAT/Edwards1.html.

41. D. Ferguson, On Reconceptualizing Continuing Professional Development: A Framework for Planning, 2000, http://www.edc.org/urban/op_rec.htm.

42. Noone & Cartwright, "Doing a Critical Literacy Pedagogy"; Hill & Celio, *Fixing Urban Schools*; Cochran-Smith, "The Outcomes Question in Teacher Education."

43. Anderson & Summerfield, "Why Is Urban Education Different."

44. Weiner, *Urban Teaching*; Haberman, "Achieving 'High Quality' in the Selection, Preparation and Retention of Teachers."

45. Carvan, Nolen, & Yinger, "Power through Partnership"; V. Domine, "How Important Is Technology in Urban Education?" In S. Steinberg & J. Kincheloe (Eds.) *19 Urban Questions: Teaching in the City* (New York: Peter Lang, 2004).

46. E. Quintero, "Can Literacy Be Taught Successfully in Urban Schools?" In S. Steinberg & J. Kincheloe (Eds.) *19 Urban Questions: Teaching in the City* (New York: Peter Lang, 2004).

47. I. Snook, "Teacher Education: Preparation for a Learned Profession," 1999, http:www.aare.edu.au/99pap/sno99148.htm; Edwards, "Researching Pedagogy."

48. J. Goodlad, *Educational Renewal: Better Teachers, Better Schools* (San Francisco, CA: Jossey-Bass, 1994); L. Cary, "Redemption, Desire, and Discourse: The Unapparent Teacher in Education." Paper Presented to the LSU Internationalizing the Curriculum Conference, 2000, Baton Rouge, Louisiana; Cochran-Smith, "The Outcomes Question in Teacher Education."

49. *California Educator*, "Scripted Learning: A Slap in the Face?" 6, 7 (2002) http://ww.cta.org/californiaeducator/v6:7feature_4.htm.

50. G. Getzel, "Humanizing the University: An Analysis and Recommendations," 1997, http://humanism.org/opinions/articles.html; Snook, "Teacher Education"; Cochran-Smith, "The Outcomes Question in Teacher Education."

51. Kincheloe, Bursztyn, & Steinberg (Eds.), *Teaching Teachers: Building a Quality School of Urban Education.*

52. S. Steinberg, & J. Kincheloe (Eds.) *What You Don't Know about Schools* (New York: Palgrave, 2006).

Twenty-Six

Lost in the Shuffle
Re-calling a Critical Pedagogy for Urban Girls

Venus Evans-Winters and Christie Ivie

In this chapter, we draw from the multicultural, social justice, and feminist literature to explore the possibilities of a critical feminist pedagogy for urban girls. We use the term "urban girls" to refer to young women being educated in central cities or high-poverty communities, who are economically disadvantaged and/or members of racial/ethnic minority groups. These are young women who have been marginalized or excluded from society and from discussions of equal educational opportunity in the United States. In 1992, the American Association of University Women (AAUW) released to the nation a report on the state of education for American girls. The widely received report suggested that schools were shortchanging girls.

In particular, the AAUW (1991) authors cited findings that girls were falling behind their male peers in the areas of math and science, had lower self-esteem and less confidence about themselves and their abilities, and were called on less by teachers in class (Orenstein, 1994; AAUW, 1991). For both the general public and the education community, the report suggested that girls were not allowed the same economic and social opportunities in our society as boys due to being left behind and excluded in the early school years, and more so, in the middle-school grades. Unfortunately, the AAUW report was not as inclusive in detailing the educational experiences of young women of color and girls from economically disadvantaged groups.

Other feminists and female scholars of color have noted the unique educational experiences of young women of color, urban female students, and those students from economically disadvantaged groups (Evans-Winters, 2005; Fine, 1991; Fordham, 1996; O'Conner, 1997; Smith, 1982). Students from racial/ethnic minority groups, economically disadvantaged backgrounds, and minority-language students are more likely to live in central cities. These groups of students are more likely to be from single-parent households; to attend high-poverty or under-funded schools or schools with high dropout rates; to live in hyper-segregated communities; and to encounter teachers who are from racial and social classes different from their own. Unlike their white female and male middle-class counterparts, many girls attending schools in urban communities are more likely to experience racism, sexism, classism, and other forms of discrimination at school. In the 1980s and early 1990s, at the height of multicultural paradigms in education, scholars (Smith, 1982; Ladner, 1987; Leadbeater & Way, 1996) attempted to call attention to the social and educational needs of urban girls.

More recently, however, the educational and pedagogical needs of urban girls have been ignored or overlooked because of the attention from the scholarly community and public being given to the educational experiences of boys in American schools. The new argument in academia and by the masses is that boys are being left behind and shortchanged by our schools. People inside and outside of academia point to the high reading and writing competencies of girls compared to boys; the closing gap between boys and girls in standardized scores in math and science; and the fact that girls are less likely than boys to repeat a grade, be placed in a special education classroom, and be reported for problem behavior in the classroom (see Pollack, 1998; Kunjufu, 2005; Sommers, 2000; Wilgoren, 2001). Scholars and educational advocates of color also point out the disparity between black males and females, with black girls making up the majority of classrooms, graduating from high school, and outnumbering black men in the attainment of higher-education degrees (Wilgoren, 2001). The reports and research findings over the last fifteen years have raised much debate about the schooling of both boys and girls in the United States and inspired much discussion about the best practices for educating boys, girls, and students from marginalized groups.

Unfortunately, in this boys-versus-girls debate, the educational needs of urban girls have been left out of the discussion. By focusing exclusively on gender, researchers, theorists, and practitioners fail to acknowledge the unique needs and potential of urban girls. Much of the debate centered on the educational accomplishments or failures of boys and girls overlooks the role that race and class play in the educational experiences and outcomes of many girls. In the past, feminists have looked to feminist classrooms and pedagogies as a possible solution to close the gap between boys and girls. Other scholars, interested in positive educational development for boys, have called for separate classrooms for males and females, male role models in the classrooms, and mentors outside of the school environment. In this discussion, we look to pedagogies grounded in the multicultural, social justice, and feminist' literature to call for pedagogical practices that work to improve the educational experiences of urban girls and prepare them to be change agents in the social world.

Feminist Pedagogy

The concept of feminist pedagogy has its roots in the second wave of feminism in the United States in the 1960s and 1970s. During this time of extreme social change, leaders of the feminist revolution like Betty Friedan advocated education as the key to women's liberation. The idea of consciousness-raising or talking about women's oppression and liberation, became popular as women across the nation created safe spaces for themselves and one another to discuss sexism and resistance strategies (Fisher, 2001). As women began to gain access to the academy, they began to apply the principle of consciousness-raising in higher education classrooms, especially in women's studies classrooms and programs. By exploring political and social issues through discourse, both teachers and students were able to reach new levels of understanding about the teaching and learning process and society. Thus, the concept of feminist pedagogy began to grow and take shape at institutions of higher education.

The goals of feminist pedagogy in higher education, like the definitions, are fluid and highly context specific. First, the concept of mutual learning is a goal for both students and professors in feminist classrooms. In this paper, we use the term "feminist classroom" as a classroom in which the instructor has a concept of feminist pedagogy which s/he deliberately applies to teaching. While these instructors may lecture or employ other traditional teaching techniques, the students' input is also valued, and learning becomes a dynamic process. Typically this means that the students benefit from the wider knowledge of the professor, and the professor benefits from the fresh perspectives provided from the students. Once a space for mutual learning has been established, the students can explore gender, identity, power structures, and social justice issues in relation to the subject matter. A second objective is to cultivate personal engagement in the material among the students in an attempt to analyze their own positions in society and to achieve a better understanding of one another. A third goal of a feminist classroom in higher education is to teach students how to thrive in the larger society, while simultaneously challenging that social order in which they were taught to succeed (Fisher, 2001, p. 27). This social change includes, but is not limited to, working toward gender equality.

Certainly no universal model of feminist pedagogy exists because the concept has as many diverse meanings and applications as feminism itself. It is highly contingent on a teacher's "political and educational values, the models of teaching and learning she [or he] has encountered and adopted, and the institutional and social conditions under which she [or he] teaches" (Fisher, 2001, p. 25). Despite the many difficulties involved in defining feminist pedagogy, feminist scholars have attempted to understand and share their own meanings. Fisher (2001) describes it as "teaching that engages students in political discussion of gender injustice" (p. 44). A more inclusive conceptualization is articulated by Maher and Tetreault (2001), who seek "an education that is relevant to their [the students'] concerns, to create their own voices in relation to the material" (p. 4). A common theme found throughout the literature on feminist pedagogy is "collective and cooperative learning" (Fisher, 2001, p. 38). Consistent with its foundation in consciousness raising, feminist teaching emphasizes learning through open discussion, self-disclosure, and active listening without judgment. Students and teachers are encouraged to understand and analyze oppression and power imbalances and explore the meanings of social justice. Ideally, this understanding will inspire activism and social change; thus, it can be described as action oriented (Fisher, 2001). Although the meanings given to feminist pedagogy seem to have certain values that serve as guidelines, it is important to remember that actual techniques vary within different contexts.

Also, because many administrators, teachers and parents feel that educators should not impose their values on students, many teachers are hesitant to enact their feminist values in the classroom. Another challenge in reaching a universal concept of feminist pedagogy is the contestable nature of traditional white Western liberal feminism, which is sometimes viewed as a "private white cult" (Maher & Tetreault, 2001, p. 7). A common criticism of traditional mainstream feminism is that it overlooks race, sexuality, age, and class-based inequalities, with the presumed intention of not distracting from the central issue of gender inequality (Davis, 1983; hooks, 1990; Collins, 1990). Unfortunately, the needs of urban girls have been lost in the shuffle, between efforts to save middle-class white girls and boys and latest efforts to save young black boys from dropping out and being pushed out of school.

Multicultural and Social Justice Education

Obviously, as pointed out by Evans-Winters (2005) in her book *Teaching Black Girls: Resiliency in Urban Classrooms*, any feminism or pedagogy that avoids issues of racism, sexism, and classism renders itself inapplicable to urban school communities and classrooms. This outdated notion of gender as being separate and above other forms of oppression and social justice struggles has prevented a unified concept of feminism in today's world, let alone feminism's application to diverse urban educational systems. As pointed out above, research has looked at the contribution of feminist pedagogy and teaching practices in colleges and university settings, and over the last few years, more research has looked at the application of feminist pedagogy in K–12 classrooms.

However, very little research exists about its relevance to urban K–12 classrooms. What are the possibilities/possible benefits of a feminist curriculum in elementary and secondary education? What would it "look like"? What are some practical suggestions for integrating race, class, gender and social justice issues into K–12 education? To begin to answer these questions, we must look to the multicultural and social justice literature. In the *Handbook of Research on Multicultural Education* (Gay, 2004) defines multicultural education "as a set of beliefs and explanations that recognize and value the importance of ethnic and cultural diversity in shaping lifestyles; social experiences; personal identities; and educational opportunities of individuals, groups, and nations" (p. 33). Furthermore, multicultural education furthers principles of social justice because it uses critical pedagogy as its underlying philosophy and focuses on knowledge, reflection, and action (Gay, 2004, p. 34). Traditionally, scholars and advocates of multicultural and social justice education have centered on the needs of students from marginalized groups.

According to Banks (2004), a major goal of multicultural education is to reform educational institutions so students from diverse racial, ethnic, and social class groups will experience quality education and to give male and female students opportunities for academic success. In the following excerpt, Banks (2004) provides an even more comprehensive view of the underpinnings of multicultural education:

> There is a general agreement among most scholars and researchers that, for multicultural education to be implemented successfully, institutional changes must be made in the curriculum; the teaching materials; teaching and learning styles; the attitudes, perceptions, and behaviors of teachers and administrators; and the goals, norms, and culture of the school. (p. 4)

Scholars have pointed out the tensions between multiculturalism and feminism, with claims that multiculturalism ignores struggles for gender equality and women's everyday realities (Ladson-Billings, 2004). We add to this recognized and acknowledged tension that both multiculturalism and feminism, with their commitments to social justice in mind, fail to contribute to discourse and practice on improving the state of education for urban female children and adolescents. However, it is the authors' belief that, together, feminism and multiculturalism have the potential to shape curriculum, practice, and policy that serve to enhance the educational, social, economic, and cultural opportunities for urban girls. From a social justice perspective, we also argue by increasing the educational and social opportunities for urban girls, educational communities are also contributing to the overall empowerment of all those living and being schooled in urban school communities.

Toward a Critical Multicultural Feminism

Fisher (2001, pp. 46–52) identifies six values around which she centers her knowledge of feminist pedagogy: access, caring, community, transmission, performance, and critical thinking.

- Access: including, accommodating, and benefiting all students equally
- Caring: showing genuine interest in a student's emotional, social, and intellectual well-being
- Transmission: passing on knowledge and skills to students
- Performance: awareness of one's own interpretation of education and her/his role of educator
- Critical thinking: reasoning and problem solving

The first value expressed by Fisher (2001) is access, which is ideally achieved by ensuring that the material, method of teaching, environment, educator, classroom, and the overall climate are not causing any students to feel excluded. An example might be teaching abstinence-only education to sexually active teens, thus depriving them of knowledge about their own sexuality and sexual health and denying them chances to make informed, healthy decisions. Another example would be ensuring that all students, regardless of gender, language abilities, mental and physical abilities, etc., are fully included in the social, cultural, educational experiences of the classroom and school environment. Such a focus on full access is especially important at a time when more research is detailing the number of students of color, especially African American males and females, being segregated within schools into special education classrooms or lower ability tracks, being more likely to be suspended and expelled, and less likely to have access to higher quality teaching (Harry & Anderson, 1994; Serwatka, Deering, & Grant, 1995; Cooper, 2002). A critical multicultural classroom and curriculum theorized here will assure that all students will have full access to culturally relevant (Ladson-Billings, 1994) teaching practices and methods, with a central focus on the intersection of race, class, and gender.

Fisher's (2001) second value is caring. Effective teachers embrace a meaningful pedagogy that places caring and the student's well-being at the center of pedagogy. Angela Valenzuela (1999) explores this topic in her research on U.S.-Mexican youth and their experiences with education. She found that many Latino/a students prefer a process of schooling based on respectful and caring relations. Yet, the students in the study felt that the teachers did not care for them, while the teachers felt that the students did not care about school. This cultural incongruence caused many of the Mexican and Mexican American students in her study to resist schooling. Her study suggests that urban high school classrooms would benefit from increased caring based on mutual understanding.

Valenzuela (1999) argues that "the most important step is to introduce a culture of authentic caring that incorporates all members of the school community as valued and respected partners in education" (p. 99). The value of community is defined as creating an environment of mutual responsibility and care, group cohesion (Fisher, 2001, p. 48). This value aims to fulfill the students' need of belonging (p. 49) and combat the anonymity that so many students feel today especially in large culturally and ethnically diverse urban schools.

The third value of feminist pedagogy, according to Fisher (2001), is transmission or "the process of passing knowledge and disciplinary skills that lie at the center of our own academic identities" (p. 49). For many feminist teachers, the preferred method of transmission is mutual or cooperative learning. Nancy Barnes (2000), in her essay "Teaching Locations," explores alternate techniques of transmission as she teaches her college students how to position themselves as teachers in urban schools. In the process, she challenges the students' belief in the importance of personal experience and encourages them instead to investigate the perspectives of the high school students themselves. This type of exercise in pre-service teacher education could prove particularly valuable in multicultural urban classrooms where the teacher's personal experience may differ significantly from that of his/her students.

Performance, the fourth value defined above, can be described as awareness of the "dramaturgical performance" of education. Meaning, by examining the "complex selves" (p. 51) urban teachers bring to the classroom, teachers can better analyze our own biases and how they affect teachers' approaches to teaching and pedagogy (and students' multiple identities). Douglas E. Foley (1990) explored the role of dramaturgical performances in the school setting and how they contribute to cultural reproduction. In his study of a Texas high school, he found that those students who mastered performing their different roles were ultimately the ones who succeeded in sports, academics, and the real world. For educators, analyzing their own performance can help determine which aspects of each of them to bring to the classroom (and, possibly, which to suppress), for the benefit of the development of the student. Even more, a multicultural feminism would assist and encourage students to reflect on, critique, and embrace their own multiple identities. Such self-reflection is critical for urban children and adolescents because too often, others (e.g., researchers, school administrators, policymakers, and the media) are defining, constructing, and exploiting their identities for them.

Critical thinking is the next value that shapes Fisher's (2001) theory and practice of feminist pedagogy. Critical thinking is the mental process of acquiring information, then evaluating it to reach a logical conclusion or answer. The Bush administration enacted No Child Left Behind (NCLB) in 2001, which aims to standardize and narrow the curriculums of elementary and secondary public schools. Schools are pressured to perform well on standardized tests and face budget deductions if they do not. Many scholars have argued that standardized tests and curriculum have only contributed to devaluing critical thinking in classrooms, especially urban classrooms with economically disadvantaged students and students from racial/ethnic minority groups (Apple, 1993; Kozol, 2006; Ladson-Billings, 2004). Unfortunately, this means that children in K–12 classrooms are being deprived of opportunities for creativity and self-expression, especially poor and minority students, who are more likely to be affected by the mandates of NCLB. A multicultural feminist curriculum and pedagogy, although quite possibly incompatible with the principles of NCLB, would encourage young students to use critical thinking and problem-solving techniques.

Implications for Practice

Using these applications of Fisher's (2001) six values of feminist pedagogy to elementary and secondary education, we have hypothesized several possibilities/possible benefits of their integration into K–12 curricula, focusing specifically on urban classroom settings. An important benefit would be the creation of spaces for identity work and self-expression (Fine & Weis, 2000). While college students in many liberal institutions of higher education are asked to analyze the intersection of race, class, and gender, and how these variables shape their experiences, younger students are not given the same opportunity. Thus, they are often robbed of chances to (re)create and explore their own identities. In addition, a curriculum based on social justice underpinnings would better meet the social, emotional, and cultural needs of younger students.

Another possibility of multicultural feminist pedagogy in K–12 classrooms is to increase the level of student engagement, by allowing female and male students to teach *and* be taught. This concept of mutual learning, when applied to children and youth, could empower students by encouraging them to value, question, and expand their own innate knowledge. Furthermore, a multicultural feminist curriculum would work toward the development of a social consciousness and sense of community in all students. The possibility to prepare students to be socially responsible citizens and work together toward gender and racial equality and social justice would prove invaluable in today's society. A significant thematic thread runs throughout all these possible benefits, and that is the idea of reaching students earlier.

Given these possibilities/possible benefits of a critical multicultural feminist curriculum in elementary and secondary education, what might a sample curriculum "look like" in the urban K–12 classroom? First of all, there would be plenty of opportunities for self-expression through media such as art, writing, and discussion. The students would further develop their own voice and social imagination through open, relevant discussions of social roles, stereotypes, and inequalities. These conversations can be used to address racism, classism, sexism, heterosexism, ageism, and help the students make sense of conflicts and power imbalances in their own lives.

With increased opportunities for the students to expound on their own knowledge, there would be less "banking" and more interactive learning. Banking refers to Freire's theory that the teaching and learning process in classrooms becomes an act of depositing, in which the students are the depositories and the teacher is the depositor (Freire, 2007). Ideally, in a feminist classroom, the environment, subject matter, language, and material would be accessible and context specific to meet needs of urban children and adolescents, keeping in mind the realities in which they live, work, and play. In addition, there would be less "busy work," and more critical-thinking exercises. Most importantly, themes of gender equality, social justice, and social activism would be woven throughout any and all materials.

With these possibilities, goals, and expectations in mind, we have merged the tenets of multicultural education and feminist-based discourse to locate and create some practical suggestions for curriculum activities that would integrate the values and goals of multicultural feminist pedagogy into K–12 curricula. For practicality purposes, we have separated secondary and elementary education into three levels: K–5th grade (primary school), 6th–8th grade (secondary/middle school), and finally, 9th–12th grade (high school). Some suggestions for K–5 are:

- Field trips to local arts/cultural events
- Learn about different cultures
- Conflict narratives

- Gender narratives
- Learn about and volunteer time/money as a class/grade/school project to a worthy cause (e.g., Habitat for Humanity, Heifer International)
- Class discussion of gender issues. Sample questions: Why is it important for boys and girls to be friends? Do you ever feel like you are expected to act a certain way (play with certain toys, etc.) because you are a girl/boy? Have you ever been called a hurtful name like faggot or tomboy? How did it make you feel?

Conflict narratives, as defined in the essay "Narrative Sites for Youths' Construction of Social Consciousness" by Colette Daiute (2000), are narratives that serve "to develop social consciousness rather than being a passive reflection of social capacity or risk" (p. 211). In these exercises, students write about a conflict they have faced and how it was solved. After several months, the young students in Daiute's study (2000) began to show more depth and develop a social consciousness or what Freire (2007) calls *conciencizacion*. They begin to analyze their own role as well as other participants' and move past an aggressor/victim model. This creative approach to conflict resolution could be especially useful in schools with high incidences of neighborhood or community conflict. Gender narratives, as suggested by McClure (1999), help children identify and confront gender inequalities. One example she gives for this activity is as follows:

> Recall an event in your childhood, one which is clearly etched in your memory. Write a brief but detailed narrative of the experience. Rewrite the narrative, changing your gender. Review both texts, highlighting or underlining the passages that were altered because of the gender change. (p. 80)

These exercises, like conflict narratives, aim to promote the child's social imagination. As students move on to higher grade levels and stages of development, the activities also can become more complex by building on previous knowledge and activities. Some suggestions for 6th–8th grades are:

- Relevant class discussions of social roles, expectations, stereotypes
- Sexuality education as part of sex education
- Have students choose and research a social justice group
- Writing assignments. Sample topics: What does racism mean to you? Pick a classmate that you admire and write about why. Identify a "clique" that you feel exists at school (Do not use specific names of classmates). How would it feel to be a member of that group for a day?
- Study contributions of both genders in core subjects, like famous women in math, physics, biology, etc.
- Have students conduct research reports on well-known African Americans, Latino/as, Native Americans, etc.
- Have students conduct oral histories with a female relative
- Institute a rites of passage program at your school for young men and women

Sexuality education as part of sex education could be very controversial. However, consistent with the goals of analyzing and discussing oppression through feminist pedagogy, it would be an important step forward in reaching out to gay, lesbian, bisexual and transgendered youth, and combating heterosexism beginning at an earlier age. It should be noted that writing and oral communication are both valuable in the multicultural feminist classroom, and gender is an intricate part of class discourse. Gender-based discussions and observations are not simply add-ons in the curriculum, and neither are topics of race and class. Some suggestions for 9th–12th grade questions and activities are:

- Field trip to local women's shelter, home for battered women, etc.
- Watch a movie as a class and identify race/class/gender stereotypes and inequalities portrayed.
- Work with a partner of the opposite sex and write ten adjectives describing him/her. How many are gender specific? How many are positive?
- Research a social issue (affirmative action, reproductive rights, etc.) and lead a class discussion on your topic.
- Bring in nontraditional guest speakers to talk about their experiences after graduation (teen mother, army veteran, stay-at-home father, female factory worker, policeman/woman, etc.).
- Write a paper examining your childhood and how different events shaped your personality/biases.
- Write about a time you felt like a valued member of a group and a time you felt you were on the "outside."
- Emphasize critical thinking and creative expression in all disciplines.
- Have students organize girls-only groups at their school
- Require students to participate in community service projects.
- Attend a school board meeting and have students analyze issues of power

In order to make educational experiences more relevant to the lives of the students, it would be helpful to bring in classroom visitors whose life chances resembled those of the student participants. For example, in school neighborhoods with high teenage pregnancy rates, it may be beneficial to bring in a single parent to talk about her goals, dreams, and challenges. Similarly, it is important to invite other community members in the classrooms, who have (or are) overcoming societal challenges and barriers. The goal of multicultural classrooms is to place at the center of pedagogy the experiences of those social actors who we want to most benefit from a more just society.

The possibilities/possible benefits for feminist pedagogy for urban multicultural classrooms at the K–12 level are endless; however, they need to be explored. The authors are the first to admit the limitations of the suggested classroom practices and curricula; however, we know what it is like to yearn for a classroom that embraces all of our identities (hooks, 1990). We yearn for a pedagogy that considers place and urbanicity, race and racism, sexuality and sexism, social class and classism, voice and language, history and tradition, family and individualism, age and agency in educational spaces. We argue that although the students would benefit from applying the principles of access, caring, community, transmission, performance, and critical thinking, teachers too would benefit. By creating a caring community within a class, teachers could feel more connected to their students. A multicultural feminist curriculum would also alleviate the pressure currently placed on teachers to "teach to the test" and allow them more flexibility and creativity. By making the material relevant to the experiences of the students, we can assume that the students would become more excited about education; therefore, teaching might become a more rewarding process for all the participants in the teaching and learning process. Multicultural feminist pedagogy at the K–12 level has the possibility of creating a more caring, community-based, engaging, and socially just concept of education, especially for those who otherwise may be lost in the shuffle.

References

American Association of University Women. (1991). *How schools shortchange girls: A study of major findings on girls and education.* Washington, DC: AAUW Educational Foundation, The Wellesley College Center for Research on Women.

Apple, M.W. (1993). *Official knowledge: Democratic education in a conservative age.* New York: Routledge.

Banks, J.A. (2004). Multicultural education: Historical development, dimensions, and practice. In J.A. Banks & C.A. Banks (Eds.), *Handbook of research on multicultural education* (3rd ed., pp. 3–29). New York: Wiley.

Barnes, N. (2000). Teaching locations. In Fine, M. & Weis, L. (Eds.), *Construction sites: Excavating race, class and gender among urban youth* (pp. 196–210). New York: Teachers College Press.

Collins, P.H. (1990). *Black feminist thought: Knowledge, consciousness, and politics of empowerment.* London: Unwin Hyman.

Cooper, P. (2002). Does race matter? A comparison of effective black and white teachers of African American students. In J.J. Irvine (ed.), *In search of wholeness: African American teachers and their culturally specific classroom practices* (pp. 47–63). New York: Palgrave.

Daiute, C. (2000). Narrative sites for youths' construction of social consciousness. In Fine, M. & Weis, L. (Eds.), *Construction sites: Excavating race, class and gender among urban youth* (pp. 211– 234). New York: Teachers College Press.

Davis, A. (1983). *Women, race and class.* New York: Vintage Books.

Evans-Winters, V. (2005). *Teaching black girls: Resiliency in urban classrooms.* New York: Peter Lang.

Fine, M. (1991). *Framing dropouts: Notes on the politics of an urban high school.* New York: SUNY Press.

Fine, M. & Weis, L. (2000). *Construction sites: Excavating race, class and gender among urban youth.* New York: Teachers College Press.

Fisher, B.M. (2001). *No angel in the classroom: teaching through feminist discourse.* New York: Rowman & Littlefield.

Foley, D.E. (1990). *Learning capitalist culture: Deep in the heart of Tejas.* Philadelphia, PA: University of Pennsylvania Press.

Fordham, S. (1996). *Blacked out dilemmas of race, identity, and success at Capital High.* Chicago, University of Chicago Press.

Freire, P. (2007). *Pedagogy of the oppressed.* New York: Continuum.

Gay, G. (2004). Curriculum theory and multicultural education. In J.A. Banks & C.A. Banks (Eds.), *Handbook of research on multicultural education* (3rd ed., 30–49). New York: Wiley.

Harry, B. & Anderson, M.G. (1994). The disproportionate placement of African American males in special education programs: A critique of the process. *Journal of Negro Education, 63*(4), 602–618.

hooks, b. (1990). *Yearning: Race, gender and cultural politics.* Boston: South End Press.

Kozol, J. (2006). *The shame of the nation: The restoration of apartheid schooling in America.* New York: Three Rivers Press.

Kunjufu, J. (2005). *Keeping black boys out of special education.* Sauk Village, Illinois: African American Images.

Ladner, J.A. (1987). Introduction to tomorrow's tomorrow: The Black woman. In S. Harding (Ed.), *Feminism and methodology* (pp. 74–83). Bloomington, Indiana: Indiana University Press.

Ladson-Billings. (1994). *The dreamkeepers: Successful teachers of African American children.* San Francisco, CA: Jossey-Bass.

———. (2004). New directions in multicultural education: Complexities, boundaries, and critical race theory. In J.A. Banks & C.A. Banks (Eds.), *Handbook of research on multicultural education* (3rd ed., pp. 50–65). New York: Wiley.

Leadbeater, B.J.R., & Way, N. (Eds.). (1996). *Urban girls: Resisting stereotyping, creating identities.* New York: New York University Press.

Maher, F., & Tetreault, M. (2001). *The feminist classroom: Dynamics of gender, race, and privilege.* New York: Rowman & Littlefield.

McClure, L.J. (1999). Wimpy boys and macho girls: Gender equity at the crossroads. *English Journal.* V 88(3), pp. 78–82.

O'Connor, C. (1997). Dispositions toward (collective) struggle and educational resilience in the inner city: A case analysis of six African-American high school students. *American Educational Research Journal,* 34(4), pp. 593-692.

Orenstein, P. (1994). *Schoolgirls: Young women, self-esteem and the confidence gap.* New York: Doubleday.

Pollack, W. (1998). *Real boys: Rescuing Our Sons from the Myths of Boyhood.* New York: Henry Holt.

Serwatka, T.S., Deering, S., & Grant, P. (1995). Disproportionate representation of African Americans in emotion-ally handicapped classes. *Journal of Black Studies,* 25 (4), 492.

Smith, E.J. (1982). The Black female adolescent: A reviw of the educational, career, and psychological literature. *Psychology of Women Quarterly,* 6 (3): 261–288.

Sommers, C.H. (2000). *The war against boys: How misguided feminism is harming our young men.* New York: Simon & Schuster.

NCES (2007). *Statistics and trends in the education of racial and ethnic minorities.* Washington, D.C.: U.S. Department of Education Institute of Educational Sciences.

Valenzuela, A. (1999). *Subtractive schooling: U.S. Mexican youth and the politics of caring.* New York: SUNY Press.

Wilgoren, J. (2001). *Girls rule.* New York Times Upfront, 133 (13), pp. 8–13.

Twenty-Seven

Rurality, Locality, and the Diversity Question

Paul Theobald and Wade Herley

Most Americans tend to think of the U.S. countryside, the "Heartland," as an overwhelmingly homogeneous, "white" place. To say that this is an erroneous conception is an understatement, as our analysis in this chapter will demonstrate. America's rural places are significantly diverse along racial, ethnic, religious, and socioeconomic lines. This diversity exists not only within rural places, but between them, as we shall shortly see. As America has grown increasingly urban and suburban, "rurality," or the status of dwelling in a rural locale, has gradually garnered a second-class or second-rate cultural status. To be rural in America is to be a "hick," a derogatory nickname given to the backwoods supporters of U.S. President Andrew Jackson, or "Old Hickory," as he was often called. In today's culture, a hick lacks the wherewithal to make his or her way to urban/suburban America, where success ostensibly resides. It is this last element of rural diversity that we will explore first.

Rurality in an Increasingly Urban Society

In the United States, it is perfectly permissible for anyone to make a joke at the expense of rural dwellers for any reason. A car dealer dresses up like a "hillbilly," another common derogatory term for rural dwellers, to shoot a television commercial designed to convince viewers that he is so dimwitted that he sells his cars for far less than they are worth. A comedian entertains the guests at a comedy club by relaying stories of the ridiculous behaviors he supposedly observed growing up in a rural place. An entire genre of comedy called "redneck humor" has become immensely popular in the United States. But rural dwellers have not always been the butt of jokes; they have not always been labeled backward, uneducated, and unsophisticated. There is a history to this cultural development that is worth exploring.

Today we commonly assume that the locus of power in the United States is its urban centers: Washington, DC, New York City, Chicago, Los Angeles, and so on. This was not always the case. There was a time when the locus of power was the complete inverse of what we know it as today. In the larger scope of history, an urban locus of power is a relatively recent phenomenon. If we look at medieval Europe, we see that power resided in a rural aristocracy for centuries. Changes in the seventeenth and eighteenth centuries, particularly those that advanced industrial pursuits, meant that urban areas would eventually vie for the power previously held near-exclusively by rural interests.

The shift from rural to urban as the locus for authority began in England during the late seventeenth century, and it is worth a short digression in order to fully understand the lingering cultural dynamics related to what it means to be rural. The 1690s saw the development of two unprecedented and far-reaching financial devices that proved to be the death knell of feudalism and changed the nature of economics—and regional power—forever. Years of military struggle with France had left the government of William III near a state of financial disaster. But William was blessed with able finance ministers who conceived of a way out of trouble. Working with a small group of London's wealthiest merchants, they acquired huge loans on the understanding that taxes would be levied to pay back the loans. In return, the merchants were given a charter to create what became the Bank of England in 1694. In this way the concept of a funded public debt was created, along with a large, commercial, centralized bank that played an enormous role in the generation and management of government resources. These unprecedented developments resulted in a huge variety of new investment strategies and an expanded money market, which spurred the growth and development of industrial manufacturers, overseas colonialism, trade, shipping, and banks and insurance houses. The government was transformed as administrative offices multiplied at every level. All of these were urban developments.

Over the course of the seventeenth century, the English monarchy had been significantly humbled. The civil war of the 1640s had removed the monarchy entirely, and while it was to return, Parliament effectively determined the line of succession. While the so-called Glorious Revolution of 1688 saw William III emerge as king, parliament ensured that this new monarchy would not be a return to absolute rule. By the 1720s, however, under the reign of George I, the monarchy gradually re-asserted itself with the compliance of finance-oriented prime ministers like Robert Walpole. Each successive reign of Georges grew in power and authority, but it was aligned not with the rural aristocracy, but with the emerging urban commercial class.

Rural residents were opposed to these new developments. The nobles and gentry believed that the countryside was the wellspring of virtue required to ensure the nation's wellbeing. The land itself, they argued, was the true source of wealth, and there was something too ephemeral about profit that emerges from the mere manipulation of money. They didn't have to search far for evidence to support their case. The filth, poverty, and misery of growing industrial centers like Manchester were prime examples of what was wrong with the new urban England according to the rural aristocracy. The more they used the Houses of Lords and Commons to express their concern through the introduction of rural-oriented policy measures, the more the king, prime minister, and urban politicians rallied to push them back.

Increasingly, rural members of parliament were dubbed backward, or unwilling to change with the times. It was an epithet that would stick.

Gradually, England's "captains of industry," those involved with manufacturing and trade, were elevated to high status while the status of farmers—hillbillies, hicks, bumpkins—dropped precipitously. William Cobbett, England's fiery journalist and advocate of parliamentary reform during the first three decades of the nineteenth century, remarked that he had witnessed the transition in the status of rural dwellers during his own lifetime. Said Cobbett, "by degrees beginning about 50 years ago the industrious part of the community, particularly those who create every useful thing by their labour, have been spoken of by everyone possessing the power to oppress them in any degree in just the same manner in which we speak of the animals which compose the stock upon a farm. This is not the manner in which the forefathers of us, the common people, were treated." Identifying the switch from "the commons of England" to such phrases as "the lower orders," frequently used by David Hume and countless other elites, Cobbett blamed this development on "tax-devourers, bankers, brewers, and monopolists of every sort." He noted further that one could hear these sorts of pejorative designations not only from the wealthy upper class, but also from "their clerks, from shopkeepers and waiters, and from the fribbles stuck up behind the counter" (Hammond & Hammond, 1912, p. 211).

It is significant to note this status reversal was fully accepted by Karl Marx, as well as by mainstream English academics and politicians. Said Marx:

> The bourgeoisie has subjected the country to the rule of the towns. It has created enormous cities, has greatly increased the urban population as compared with the rural, and has thus rescued a considerable part of the population from the idiocy of rural life (Marx, 1848, p. 208).

Over a hundred years later an American scholar borrowed the phrase, "the idiocy of rural life," for the title of an essay in *The New Republic* written to expose the conception of farming as a lifestyle as mere myth (Pasley, 1986). The assignment of a backward status to the rural dwellers of England was well in place by the time the American colonists were making their bid for independence. Once that was achieved, America's leaders had to sort through the pros and cons of urban versus rural power. In reality, though, there wasn't much of a choice. Thomas Jefferson was clearly an advocate of trying to promote a rural republic based on the rights of man, freedom, and equality, but he was opposed by many. In the minds of most of America's leaders, the rejection of feudalism was one and the same as the acceptance of the high finance techniques of Walpole and the industrial, banking, and insurance interests that followed in its wake. Alexander Hamilton lobbied hard for the creation of a bank of the United States modeled after the Bank of England and got his way. From the start, America's cultural development closely mirrored similar developments in England. Rural dwellers in this country garnered the derogatory labels similar to those Cobbett heard in England.

Locality and Multiculturalism

At least one sociologist has argued that circumstances have developed to the point where rural dwellers in the United States now constitute a cultural minority (Atkin, 2003). He argues that rural people value ways of life and living that are out of step with the majority of society, and this puts them into a category of "others" who seek legitimation for their history and for the ways that they are different from the majority of Americans. Given the way mainstream society characterizes rural people and ignores them in policy creation, locality should be added to the list that makes people different, a list that currently includes religion, gender, disability, sexuality, race, and ethnicity. Rural people stand in need of the same kind of respect, recognition, and legitimation as other marginalized groups. They seek the same thing members of these other groups seek: the survival and vitality of their ways of life and living. In the case of rural dwellers, it's the survival and vitality of what we might call "small-town life." The vitality of small-town life in this country has been heavily damaged, and in many instances destroyed, by policies created in the name of state neutrality (related to ways of living) and individual rights (especially regarding making money via a free market).

What rural dwellers need is recognition of their legitimacy and significance to the whole of American society in the same way as African Americans or other racial and ethnic groups. This suggests that the nation ought to embrace multicultural perspectives that include the ramifications of locality in modern society. This has obvious implications for the curriculum of rural schools, but we will say more about this later. Rural dwellers also need to embrace a community-focused politics that raises small-town community survival—a collective pursuit—to the same level of legitimacy and protection as the pursuit of individual aims and desires.

Our current social and political system, on the whole, rejects the pleas of various cultural groups for survival but does promise equal protection of the rights of individuals regardless of race, ethnicity, gender, and religion. We believe that *sometimes* this difference-blind approach to policy should be abandoned so that the state can recognize the particularities of cultural groups and raise their level of protection above that which is in place to defend individual rights. In other words, rural dwellers pursuing what they define as the good life, small-town life, should not be held hostage to the individual's right to profit from its destruction. Note that we emphasize the word *sometimes*. This elevation of collective cultural pursuits cannot be done haphazardly. In our view, it should hinge on two things, one stemming from multicultural theory, the other from communitarian theory.

Elevating the collective pursuit of survival for Native Americans or African Americans would be merited according to a multicultural test advanced by the Canadian philosopher Charles Taylor: "all human cultures that have animated whole societies over some considerable stretch of time have something important to say to all human beings" (Taylor & Gutmann, 1995, p. 66). Has African American or Native American culture animated whole societies? Of course. And they have done so for centuries. Do they have something to contribute to the human conversation related to collaborative, nonhierarchical, democratic decision-making? Few would deny this possibility. To apply this test to rural dwellers we need to ask if rural cultures have animated whole societies over considerable periods. The answer is obviously yes on both counts. This test answers critics of multiculturalism who claim that not all cultures are "equal" in terms of their contribution to humanity and therefore, not all cultures deserve respect. These claims are certainly true, for some cultures go through periods of decadence where they offer little to humanity. German culture has made great contributions, though it also contributed Nazism for a short period. Nazi culture does not meet the test of something that has animated a whole society over a considerable period of time. Nazi subcultures such as skin-heads do not meet the criteria set up by this test.

However, cultures that pass this test are worthy of study and deserve respect in both school curriculum and the public curriculum advanced by corporate media. A second test is derived from communitarian thought: Will the survival of a particular culture, in this case small-town life, contribute positively to the well-being of the larger polity? Should we elevate the collective right of rural people to maintain vital and vibrant communities? Or should we continue to fashion policy based on the individual right to pursue profit (largely at the cost of rural culture)?

It is difficult to judge the societal contribution of our individual rights-oriented, difference-blind policies. To be sure, we have created an affluent society, and we have healed suffering (though we have created it, too). We have eased the burden of work, though it is unclear whether the absence of heavy work has made us or the majority culture healthier. We have created comfort and greatly expanded entertainment options. None of these accomplishments should be taken lightly, nor would any rational person wish them away. It is legitimate, however, to question whether policy choices geared toward the survival and vitality of various cultural groups, rural dwellers included, would diminish these accomplishments. It is doubtful they would.

Resources would be distributed differently, however. School consolidation would cease or become very rare. Busing to achieve racial integration would become rare, too. In place of these policy choices, new resources would need to be infused to make rural and urban schools legitimate counterparts of suburban schools. This couldn't be accomplished via the largely nineteenth-century funding formula in place in most states. It would require tapping other resources. This makes it controversial, but what would American society gain for this new investment?

In the case of rural schools, the investment would contribute directly to the vitality of rural communities. This has merit on many counts, but one in particular rises above all others. History has yet to supply an example of a democratic society that does not depend heavily on a healthy rural culture. As our policy choices continue to erode small-town life in this country, there is every reason to believe that American society will be assuredly less animated by democratic practices and values. This fact has been recognized by many American scholars, but it has yet to result in a new policy trajectory. There were signs earlier in our history that this might happen. Liberty Hyde Bailey, John Dewey, Lewis Mumford and others recognized the practical value of a healthy rural culture and took steps to promote its survival and vitality. However, depression and two world wars seem to have washed over and effectively ended their efforts. But they could be picked up again. We believe they should be.

What is the connection between healthy rural communities and the health of democracy in the larger society? The answer to this is an accumulation of many circumstances. One such circumstance is that rural locales tend to be the site of what are often called "extractive enterprises": farming, mining, logging, ranching, etc. Historically, extractive industries have been the source of the most grievous exploitation, and consequently rural dwellers have a heightened sensitivity to questions of social and economic justice. In other words, the rural voice has historically demanded democratic treatment. Marty Strange has observed that until midway through the twentieth century, farmers were behind every substantive movement for social and economic reform (Strange, 1996).

A second circumstance has to do with the locus of food production. The Russian revolutionary Trotsky argued that any and every society is a mere three days from revolution. Shut down the food supply and there will be blood in the streets. It takes very little to imagine such a possibility. This suggests that any policy that consolidates a nation's food supply into fewer hands is a policy inimical to the practice of democracy. The possibility of people holding and wielding power—which is theirs by virtue of living in a democracy—is trumped by the loss of a stable, dependable food supply. Agriculture is a concern on another level as well. On this question there has been no more a committed and passionate spokesperson than Wendell Berry. History demonstrates that if agriculture is done poorly, deserts are created. When this happens, the ability to generate the food supply can be obliterated through human ignorance. What is our best safeguard against this possibility?

This is an increasingly important question. We now know beyond a shadow of a doubt that the earth is getting warmer. What impact will this have on agriculture throughout the world? Returning to the previous question, what is our best safeguard against human malpractice in the agricultural realm, especially considering the climatic changes already upon us? Should we turn the nation's farms over to multinational corporations motivated by maximizing profit? Or would it make more sense to turn it over to independent owner/operators who can farm on a size and scale that allows them to practice their craft with care and skill? If we are interested in guaranteeing a food supply throughout our increasingly warm world, we would do better to distribute production efforts over as large a population as possible. This would revitalize rural communities and ensure the extension of democracy over time.

Available, affordable energy ranks alongside food supply in terms of influencing the quality of the nation's democratic arrangements. We can no more claim to be defenders of democracy and allow ourselves to become totally dependent on a few multinational corporations than we can on a few foreign powers. Once again, the vitality of the countryside may be crucial in this regard. Deriving energy uses from crops is just one obvious example of the way rural locales contribute to energy independence. Gradually the use of wind power on "wind farms" will make an even greater contribution.

Another circumstance has to do with the many questions surrounding an ever-urbanizing society. Food supplies and energy concerns aside, a centralizing population makes the possibility of undemocratic and unaccountable "control" a much easier proposition. This circumstance seems like one that ought to be avoided if it is reasonably possible. Another concern relates to health and the proliferation of viruses and bacteria emanating from the impoverished conditions of the global urban sprawl.

Many scholars believe we have painted too rosy a picture of our urban future. The societal ideal of a house in the suburbs with a two-car garage is a piece of public curriculum that has proved detrimental to rural places through its legitimation of antirural community policy choices and implanting this image of success in the minds of rural youth. The message is that success exists in the urban or suburban locale, not in my hometown. It is an increasingly dubious, if not sinister, message.

There are pieces of rural culture itself that are worth promoting in the interest of both rural and nonrural society. One piece is the notion of ethical neighborliness. Rural neighbors may not always like one another, but on some fundamental level they have been responsible to and for one another. This is a sharp contrast to other areas, particularly suburban society, where most residents cannot tell you the names of their neighbors. Once again, if our interest is in the promotion of democracy and overall democratic practices in society, elevating the survival of rural culture is an excellent way to help ensure this. To encourage democratic practice everywhere we need to maximize the presence of responsible neighborliness throughout society.

There is much more to consider, but we have made our point. There is a strong connection between healthy rural communities and a healthy democratic society. Said differently, orchestrating the survival of rural small-town life meets the test of contributing to the health of the whole. In creating policy that promotes the survival and vitality of small-town life, our individual rights-oriented, difference-blind polity should make an exception. This should be done for rural people, but done for all.

Currently, the state goes this far with respect to race, ethnicity, religion, gender, and even locality: each individual will be allowed to pursue his or her own unique identity with the full protection of the law related to individual rights. From a legal standpoint, a black man will not be denied admission to law school because he is black, and a Hispanic woman will not be turned down for a job because she is Hispanic. What the state does not do is create policies that respect the ways that various groups define themselves through various activities and practices. There is no protection for the traditions that individuals from different groups use to define themselves.

Multicultural theorists have noted for some time that this is the real problem. By not legitimating a marginalized group's way of life, real harm is done to the development of individual identities within a group. In the absence of policies legitimizing the histories and cultures of different groups, demeaning, oppressive stereotypes can flourish in society. Young men and women grow up internalizing diminished conceptions of their worth based on these widely disseminated stereotypes.

"Black face" minstrel shows depicted blacks as slow and dimwitted. Television Westerns depicted Native Americans as violent and savage. Cartoons depicted Mexican Americans as lazy and lethargic. Dick and Jane readers depicted girls as passive observers of actions undertaken by males. While the advent of multiculturalism has curbed the worst abuses of this sort in public and school curriculum, they have not been eradicated. Few multiculturalists have recognized how rural Americans have been subjected to demeaning—even oppressive—stereotypes, though examples abound. Last fall, an auto body shop in Lincoln, Nebraska, broadcast a radio advertisement for the football games of the University of Nebraska-Lincoln's Cornhuskers. "It's that time of year again, and you never know who's going to be in town," says the narrator, followed by a mock hillbilly voice exclaiming, "Why, lookey there, a stoplight." This is followed by a crash and the narrator explains that the company was prepared to do the necessary collision repairs made by ignorant rural dwellers unfamiliar with the stoplights of the big city. This advertisement is a piece of the public curriculum that teaches Americans about the worth of rural residents.

Television has been a prime vehicle for disseminating negative stereotypes of rural people. *The Bob Newhart Show* is a classic example of this. The stars of the show, Larry, Daryl, and Daryl, were a group of disheveled, barely literate brothers from backwoods Vermont. The *Beverly Hillbillies, Green Acres,* and the *Dukes of Hazzard* were other television programs built upon the idea of rural ignorance. Lest anyone think that these are examples from the past that no longer apply, reruns of all of these programs still air daily in the United States. Two prime time television networks had attempted to produce "reality" remakes of *Green Acres* and the *Beverly Hillbillies*. The premise was to put "real" rural people in urban situations where their ineptitude served as a punch line for viewers. Rural protest stopped the development of these programs, but plenty of more insidious depictions of rural people still exist. The rural dwellers in the 1972 film *Deliverance* were depicted as depraved, illiterate, and prone to violent aggression. But *Deliverance* is just one of many movies set in the rural South where rural dwellers are depicted as evil and ignorant.

The point, of course, is that this negative stereotyping does real damage. These characters are not harmless fictions for the sake of entertainment. They feed into a cultural assumption that suggests that, in all cases, bigger is better than smaller. Big cities are better than small towns. Big farms are better than small farms. Big schools are better than small schools. Students from big schools are better than students from small schools. Freshman survey data reported by the Higher Education Research Institute at UCLA indicate that rural students attending publicly supported comprehensive colleges perceive their academic ability and their self-confidence to be significantly lower than their urban and suburban peers at similar institutions across the country (Higher Education Research Institute, 2002).

Many teachers measure professional success by the size of their school. The tacit assumption is that I am better than those who teach in small schools by the virtue of being hired to teach in a large one. Sometimes students graduating from teacher education programs compete to see who will receive a position in a large urban or suburban district versus those who are only able to find a job in a small rural school.

In textbooks commonly used by teacher preparation programs, the antirural bias frequently comes out. Usually it exists merely as omission; the idea that some schools are small and rural never emerges as a topic for study or discussion. But sometimes it is more obvious and insidious. One text on the social foundations of education, discussing immigration in the United States, claims "The refugees came from all strata of society. Some were wealthy; others were poverty stricken. Some were widely traveled and sophisticated; others were farmers and fishing people who had never before left their small villages" (Sadker & Sadker, 2003, p. 488). The obvious implication is that sophisticated individuals do not farm or fish for a living. We routinely accept this stereotype because it is deeply engrained in our culture. We give no consideration to how this colors the aspirations of rural youth, despite the fact that this generalization does not stand up to even minimal scrutiny.

The *Chronicle of Higher Education* recently touted a feature story about dramatic performances in rural colleges and universities. The front page description of the article read "In rural areas, arts programs at colleges provide a rich diet for culture-starved residents" (Fogg, October 26, 2007, p. B1). "Culture-starved," at least for this author, is synonymous with hick, hillbilly, and any other derogatory epithet for rural people. It never occurred to the author that rural dwellers possess their own culture and don't sit around waiting for someone to bring culture to them. However, another recent *Chronicle* article, allegedly exposing significant contributions by scholars and artists born and raised in Appalachia, noted that "hillbillies may be the last tolerated American stereotype" (Biggers, May 23, 2008, B3).

The lessons multiculturalists have taught us about how school and corporate-produced public curriculum can demean individuals, how they can even constitute a form of oppression, can be readily applied to the case of rural residents in this country. Further, the lessons communitarians have taught us about the absence of community as a value in policy creation directly connects to the question of respect not only for individual rights, but for the traditions, history, and culture of various groups.

Diversity Within

The perception that rural America is largely white is a product of the fact that the rural areas of northern and midwestern states were settled while blacks were held in bondage and Native Americans sequestered on "reservations." Because of these circumstances, northern and midwestern rural communities are quite racially homogeneous, as the following ethnic demographic breakdown demonstrates.

Demographic Table of Rural U.S. Population

Race	Total Pop.	% of Pop.
White	40,711,020	81.5
Black	4,197,536	8.4
Native American	940,981	1.9
Asian	466,102	0.9
Mixed Race	483,893	1
Hispanic	3,129,034	6.3

Source: USDA, using U.S. Census Bureau county population estimates.

In contrast, however, the rural areas of the South and Southwest were and are far more racially diverse. Still, the northward migration of many rural southern blacks during the twentieth century added to the perception that rural areas were predominantly white. But this perception was wrong, and it is becoming increasingly apparent. Rural America has changed greatly in the last hundred years. A drain on the population that started in the 1920s and continues today has strained many communities.

The population drain on rural America has been going on since the mechanization of the farm. Machines increased the productivity per acre so only a few people are now needed to operate massive, highly productive farms that would have been too labor-intensive before mechanization. Mechanization has changed rural communities so much that only 6.5% of the workforce is engaged in farming today (Johnson, 2006).

The east and west coasts of America have been experiencing a population boom while the Midwest and Great Plains continue to lose people. Retirees like to move to warmer climates, and immigrants like faster-growing economies for jobs. According to the Carsey Institute (Johnson, 2006), immigration accounted for 31% of population growth in rural areas. Most of the growth in rural communities, by percentage, comes from Hispanic and mixed races. Blacks have the second highest percentage of the population in rural communities, with the highest concentration in the south. Racial diversity within rural communities will continue to grow. Non-Hispanic white populations have added little to new growth in rural areas. In fact, most new growth will be seen from Hispanic, black, and mixed races (Johnson, 2006).

Diversity within rural communities encompasses many issues including, but not limited to, economy, society, and education. They all weave together to form the socioeconomic structure that allows a community to evolve and grow. The social and economic health of a community must be in good order for the community to survive.

The outflow of the rural population for the last hundred years suggests that opportunity and preferred lifestyle seemingly exists in the urban environment. If that is the case, how can one explain the need for suburban communities to seemingly fill a desire for an urban lifestyle with a country feel? The suburb is a direct descendant of rural communities, fueled by the desire to escape life in the "big city," and the stresses accompanying it have given rise to urban sprawl. The expansion of cities outward to decrease population per square mile and even square foot support the theory of a natural tendency that people increasingly prefer to live the "small-town" life. The desire to be part of a community and make differences in that community is a powerful one. A safe environment for rearing a family that is close to nature also drives the desire to live the "small-town life" as well (Johnson, Nucci, & Long, 2006).

The people who first settled and founded the many rural communities in the United States were the pioneers, adventurers of their time. They were risk takers willing to bet everything they had for the chance to tame the land and forge a self-sufficient existence in rural America. The very essence of what it means to be an American comes from their "can-do spirit" that has been passed down from generation to generation.

Diversity Between

As noted earlier, rural communities were generally built around a few core extractive industries: farming, fishing, ranching, mining, or logging. While agricultural communities dominated the rural landscape in this country, there nevertheless have been significant differences between them. Policy concerns for one rural community were often at odds with the concerns of another community. Even those communities dominated by a single industry like agriculture differed over what might be beneficial to one versus another. Corn-growing regions might successfully lobby for price subsidies that reduce what is available for cotton subsidies. These inherent differences between rural communities have often inhibited the success of efforts to tie together the interests of a rural occupational group. Historically, attempts to organize farmers have proved inordinately difficult. The same has generally been true for miners, loggers, and fishermen in various parts of the country.

It should be noted, though, that larger interests have been opposed to the successful organization of various rural occupational groups. Mining companies fought unionization efforts at every turn throughout the twentieth century. Many farmer organizations, such as the Farm Bureau, have been co-opted by larger agri-business interests. Family fishing operations have been unmercifully crowded out by corporate operations. These circumstances are directly related to the urban-rural contest for power. In each industry that was historically—that is to say, at one time, of necessity—rural, the largest share of profit now accrues to urban-based corporate entities. Every attempt by rural occupational groups to prevent this development has failed. As one might expect in a society marked by pronounced racial and ethnic inequalities, the few localities where ethnic minority groups once maintained a substantial presence in rural occupational groups, such as black-owned farms in the rural south, the disappearance of family-owned operations has accelerated at a rate much faster than that of white-owned family farms. Where industrial techniques cannot be applied to agricultural production, such as in the harvesting of fruits and vegetables, the work has been relegated largely to Hispanic migrant workers since, as George W. Bush claimed, "Americans won't do that kind of work."

Conclusion

Wendell Berry once noted that "the stereotype of the farmer as rustic simpleton or uncouth redneck is, like most stereotypes, easily refuted: All you have to do is compare it with a number of real people." He goes on to say, however, that the stereotype of the small farmer or small-town dweller as "obsolete, clinging to an obsolete kind of life," is not as easy to deal with. It stems, as Berry says, from a more complicated prejudice, one that "begins with the idea that work is bad, and that manual work outdoors is the worst of all" (Berry, 2002, p. 23). He links this sentiment to the American experience with slavery—with the idea some work is "beneath" self-respecting individuals. For Berry, this is a central dynamic to the perpetuation of racism in American society, and it constitutes what he calls the "hidden wound" of racism—a wound that whites inflict upon themselves when they discriminate against racial minorities (Berry, 1970).

The prejudice against small-town life in this country is indeed complicated. Elements of it go back to the urban-rural power struggle that eventually ended feudalism in the modern world. The prejudice is monolithic, as we have seen, and it disregards vast differences that exist within rural communities and between them. Still, rural or small-town culture has made significant contributions to humankind, and the ease with which small towns give citizens a political role to play with their lives makes them a vital democratic agent. For these reasons, if no others, small-town, rural life merits special consideration in the face of policy choices that all too willingly contribute to its destruction.

References

Atkin, C. (2003). Rural communities: Human and symbolic capital development, fields apart. *Compare* 33(4), 507–518.

Berry, W. (1970). *The hidden wound*. Boston: Houghton Mifflin.

Berry, W. (April 2002). The prejudice against country people. *The Progressive*, 21–24.

Biggers, J. (2008). "They came down from these hills and made history." *The Chronicle of Higher Education*, May 23.

Fogg, P. (2007). A special role for rural community colleges. *The Chronicle of Higher Education*, October 27.

Hammond, J. L., & Hammond, B. (1912). *The village labourer 1760–1832*. London: Longmans, Green, and Company.

Higher Education Research Institute. (2002). *First-time, full-time freshmen at Wayne State College, 2001–2002*. Technical Report published by the University of California at Los Angeles.

Johnson, K. M. (2006). *Reports on rural America. Volume 1, Number 1*. Carsey Institute, University of New Hampshire at Durham, New Hampshire.

Johnson, K. M., Nucci, A., & Long, L. (2006). *Population trends in nonmetropolitan America: The rural rebound and beyond*. Population Research and Policy Review.

Marx, K. [1848] (1983). Manifesto of the communist party. In Eugene Kamenka, ed., *The Portable Karl Marx*. New York: Penguin Books.

Pasley, J. L. (December 8, 1986). The idiocy of rural life. *The New Republic*, 24.
Sadker, M. P. & Sadker, D. M. (2003). *Teachers, schools, and society*. Sixth edition. New York: McGraw-Hill.
Strange, M. (1996). *Family farming: A new economic vision*. Lincoln: University of Nebraska Press.
Taylor, C., & Gutmann, A. (1995). *Multiculturalism*. Princeton, NJ: Princeton University Press.

Section Nine

Diversity, Multiculturalism, and Leadership

Twenty Eight

Diversity and Educational Leadership
Democratic Equality and the Goals of Schooling

Larry Daffin and Gary L. Anderson

While diversity training and diversity offices are common today in many organizations, understanding how recent this focus is in education and in American society requires a historical framework. Diversity did not gradually evolve with the evolution of the American educational system and the influx of Jewish, Irish, or Italian immigrants. Nor did it appear as northern philanthropists began to build southern schools for the "rural Negro." By and large, education was assimilationist at best and exclusionary at worse.

The history of education, then, is not one of unconditional inclusion but rather a continual debate about its purpose and the mechanisms by which to obtain its objectives. Reform within this continual struggle can be seen as conceptual victories along the path of improvement for common schools. In their 1995 book, *Tinkering Toward Utopia: A Century of Public School Reform*, Tyack and Cuban highlight the struggle over competing views that have always guided public school policy. From its creation, the aims of education have involved a contentious battle among social mobility, social efficiency, and democratic equality: social mobility being the perception of education as an avenue for individuals to overcome or transcend class barriers, social efficiency being the process of producing citizens who have the skills necessary to contribute to our economy, and democratic equality being the method by which America maintains an educated constituency capable of continuing the virtues deemed essential to the constitution.

In this chapter, we will discuss the ongoing struggle to keep the goal of democratic equality central to education and to educational leadership. First, we will provide some historical background to the current debates about diversity and the ways this debate was belatedly taken up in educational leadership. While diversity is often viewed as cultural, ethnic, or racial diversity, its meaning has expanded to include other types of difference, such as gender, class, sexual orientation, disability, religion, and language. Diversity concerns have also expanded to include not merely an appreciation of difference but also an analysis of how difference is immersed in complex relations of power and domination. Finally, we will provide ways that educational leadership might more effectively link issues of diversity to the goal of democratic equity, particularly in a era that promotes individual mobility and international competition as the primary goals of schooling.

The Long Road to Cultural Diversity

Cultural, ethnic, and racial diversity was not an early objective of education. As Kaestle and Foner (1983) note in *The Pillars of the Republic: Common Schools and American Society, 1780–1860*, assimilation was the guiding principle in the early expansion of common schools. Assimilation was, and to a great extent, still is the core of American ideology. It has always been America's intent to create citizens who are reflective of a community desired by its forefathers. In essence, public policy has consistently been the driving force behind the implementation and reformation of the American educational system.

It is thus understandable that policy (through the arm of the legislative branch) would lead to diversity as an objective for common schools. In the historical decision in *Brown v. Board of Education*, the United States Supreme Court forced America to acknowledge the neglect and shame of a "separate but equal" school system. While *Brown* did not generate a unified commitment to diversity, it did provide the basis from which the conception of diversity grew.

By acknowledging the separate and unequal treatment of blacks, *Brown* not only called on America to correct its unjust actions but also empowered a people by providing them with a voice that had historically been muted. *Brown* is often criticized for its ineffectiveness in bringing about educational equality for the African American community, especially given the rate of implementation in light of the courts mandate to move with "all deliberate speed." However, credit must be given to Thurgood Marshall and the NAACP for producing a body of legislative work that would ultimately lead to the successes of the Civil Rights Movement of the 1960s.

In *Brown v. Board of Education: A Civil Rights Milestone and Its Troubled Legacy*, James T. Patterson chronicles the tumultuous times of America before and after the 1954 decision. Patterson's work is profound in that it positions *Brown* within the crux of its historical perspective. *Brown* was not an isolated case within the history of the Supreme Court, but rather a ruling that forever changed the social construct of America. *Brown* forced America to realize that it could not and should not maintain its segregated school system and led, not only to the end of segregated schools but also to the legalized segregation of America under the laws of Jim Crow. In his conclusion, Patterson quotes Jack Greenberg as assessing the influence of *Brown* better than anyone. In 1994 Greenberg wrote, "Altogether, school desegregation has been a story of conspicuous achievements, flawed by marked failures, the causes of which lie beyond the capacity of lawyers to correct. Lawyers can do right, they can do good, but they have their limits. The rest of the job is up to society" (p. 223).

The troubled patterns of integration not only heightened the sense of difference between whites and blacks but also led to the distinction of Hispanic Americans as a non-white minority. In *Brown, Not White: School Integration and the Chicano Movement in Houston*, Guadalupe San Miguel, Jr. expounds upon the mindset of Hispanics who, spurred by resentment as their schools became integrated under the mandate of desegregation while most non-Hispanic white schools remained segregated, sought to be identified not as white, but as a separate minority group within America. Their campaign for a separate identity within the legal system, as well as the energy generated during the Civil Rights Movement, saw an unparalleled growth of ethnic pride in the marginalized minority communities of that time. No longer was assimilation seen as the only means by which to function in America. The turmoil of the sixties had given birth to a mindset of diversity. Minority groups began to embrace and seek acceptance of their diversity within the majority culture rather than follow the historic path of assimilation.

Thus the implementation of *Brown* in an era of ethnic pride produced the early forms of diversity within education; diversity amongst the student body as well as diversity within the curriculum. Diversity within the curriculum, however, has been a slow, gradual process. Despite such gestures as the 1968 Bilingual Education Act, the decades following *Brown* saw little transformation within curriculum. American schools had become diversified and to some extent bilingual, but their method of educating remained primarily one of assimilation. The expectations of minorities entering into desegregated schools were in many ways similar to those of first-generation Irish, Italian, or Jewish immigrants of the nineteenth century, as they, too, were expected to embrace and embody the dominant culture of America.

In "Approaches to Multicultural Curriculum Reform," James Banks illustrates four approaches that have been used to address the diversity of culture within American schools since the late sixties. His methods are semi-hierarchical in nature, requiring an increased level of commitment and respect to diversity as schools increase the level of input from their minority constituency. The approaches are: the "contributions approach," the "ethnic additive approach," the "transformative approach," and the "decision-making and social action approach."

The contributions approach does not yield change to the traditional curriculum; it simply acknowledges diversity by highlighting the contributions of heroic minorities. The celebration of Cinco de Mayo and Martin Luther King's birthday are examples of the contribution approach. The approach is a primarily trivial appeasement, for it marginalizes the role of minorities within the historical framework of America and the world.

Similar to the contributions approach is the ethnic additive approach. The ethnic additive approach seeks to introduce the concepts, themes, and perspectives of minority cultures into the curriculum. While this approach acknowledges the historical context of minorities, it does little to alter or change the traditional curriculum. Ethnic content is simply added to material that is already being presented, often in support of, or from the perspective of, the dominant culture.

Fundamental change within the curriculum is achieved in the transformative approach. Instead of presenting concepts, issues, and themes solely from the perspective of the dominant culture, students are challenged to comprehend the various perspectives of multicultural groups within America. This shift allows students to gain a better appreciation and understanding of the complex and diverse relationships that have historically shaped their society.

The fourth and most complex approach is the decision making and social action approach. It not only encompasses the elements of the transformative approach, but also seeks to develop critical thinking and decision making skills within students, challenging them to empower themselves and acquire a sense of political efficacy. The decision making and social action approach seeks to create a citizenry that will identify, analyze, and develop a course of action that can mitigate or eliminate social problems that exist in their society.

The contributions approach is by far the most common choice made by schools to combat the issue of diversity. It requires the least amount of effort as it does not affect or challenge the status quo. As schools move closer to the decision making and social action approach, underlying assumptions and basic ideology about the purpose of schooling begin to surface. The changes in curriculum required for implementing a decision making and social action approach challenge the fundamental purpose of school: is it social efficacy, mobility, or democratic equality? The answer to that question will determine the level of support such a change will receive.

Decision making and social action is a direct departure from assimilation. It does not attempt to reinvent or encourage the dominant viewpoints of a monolithic culture but rather invokes students to realize the diverse mixture of cultures and viewpoints within society and seek to obtain a solution that is reflective of all. The difficulty in obtaining such a curriculum is highlighted by the views of Jim Cummins in "Empowering Minority Students: a Framework for Intervention." Initially published in 1986, the *Harvard Educational Review* chose to reprint his article in 2001 as part of their Classic Series. Although the article is over two decades old, its theoretical and practical approaches to addressing diversity, as defined by the minority achievement gap, remain relevant.

Cummins' article provides a critique of the numerous educational reform measures proposed and implemented in response to the 1983 National Commission on Excellence in Education report entitled, *A Nation at Risk*. The report had generated a sense of "crisis" as the nation began to seek reforms that would counteract the perceived failure of public schools.

Cummins (2001) predicted the failure of these reforms and others because of the following inherent flaws: "(a) empirical data relating to patterns of educational underachievement that challenge the current ideological mindset are systematically ignored or dismissed; (b) there is a deep antipathy to acknowledging that schools tend to reflect the power structure of the society and that these power relations are directly relevant to educational outcomes" (p. 650). In his reprint, he echoed sentiments that only grew stronger in the subsequent years, stating his conviction that reformers need to challenge the exclusion of human relationships from the understanding of what constitutes effective education:

> In short, current reform efforts selectively highlight empirical data linking individual student characteristics to underachievement while simultaneously ignoring much stronger empirical relationships between achievement and social educational inequities. The implicit assumption underlying these (and previous) reform efforts is that instructional interventions can remediate student "deficits" while ignoring the associated social and educational inequities. There is little evidence of serious inquiry into why thirty years of reform initiatives, each with its claim to scientific legitimacy, should have yielded such paltry results. (p. 652)

The framework for change offered by Cummins is reflective of Banks' decision making and social action approach. Both advocate the empowerment of minority students and their communities in an effort to address diversity and the gap in achievement. Both also illustrate what Cummins calls an "additive approach," which emphasizes that additive, collaborative, interactive/experiential, and advocacy-oriented curriculum leads to empowered students, whereas subtractive, exclusionary, transmission, and legitimization-oriented curriculum disables them.

We tend to think that diversity issues entered the field of education in the 1970s and 1980s as educators in schools and universities were becoming more diverse by race and gender. However, there were periods in American history in which these issues surfaced briefly. The Reconstruction period after the Civil War saw gains in race relations, and the Harlem Renaissance saw a flowering of the arts in the black community. A first wave of feminism occurred during the early twentieth century, and social class gains were made, primarily through the labor struggles of the 1930s that led to the creation of the welfare state. Advocacy by the LGBT community and people with disabilities did not occur until more recently. Throughout history members of oppressed groups have always struggled to change power relations, but as James C. Scott documents in *Domination and the Arts of Resistance*, these underground struggles are usually relegated to the hidden transcripts of history. At various points, they surface as a collective concern, usually through successful social movements.

Academic researchers for the most part ignored issues of diversity or tended to pathologize those who were different. In education, for instance, throughout the 1960s and 1970s, non-white students and families were openly referred to as "culturally disadvantaged." Much as Native American children were taken from their families and communities and placed in boarding schools, non-white and poor students, their families, and communities were viewed only through a deficit lens. With regard to gender, major researchers in psychology such as Erik Erikson, who studied human development, used male samples and generalized to women. This tendency was most famously challenged by Carol Gilligan in her book *In a Different Voice*.

As issues of race, class, and gender became legitimate subjects of scholarship in the academy, scholars became concerned that researchers studied them in isolation. They felt that in most social settings, race, class, and gender are all relevant analytic categories that intersect in complex ways (Apple & Weiss, 1983; McCarthy, 1993). There is also a growing concern that diversity fails to include issues such as the environmental crisis or growing inequalities related to important shifts in our political economy from a welfare state to a neoliberal or competition state. Environmentalists insist that issues of race, class, and gender become irrelevant if we aren't teaching children to be good stewards of the planet. Many link this problem to unregulated capitalism based on constant consumption and growth. The study of diversity then, has broadened to include more issues and has insisted on an interdisciplinary and interconnected approach.

Nancy Fraser in *Justice Interruptus: Critical Reflections on the "Post-Socialist" Condition*, argues that the political left has split between those concerned primarily with recognition based on race, class, gender, and sexual orientation (identity politics) and those concerned primarily with issues of distribution of social resources (social justice). Often those who study identity politics (which are often associated with diversity) may do so in the absence of a critique of a political economy in which the distribution of resources is becoming generally more unequal. Walter Benn Michaels has popularized this idea in his book, *The Trouble with Diversity: How We Learned to Love Identity and Ignore Inequality*, in which he argues that diversity (defined narrowly as identity politics) has been a distraction from the massive inequalities that pro-corporate social policies of the 1980s and 1990s have created.

On the other hand, much of the new scholarship that critiques this new world of un-regulated capitalism fails to discuss the ways it affects subgroups differently. For instance, working-class males have had a harder time adjusting to the post-industrial economy than females, while elite white males are filling the ranks of the new millionaire and billionaire class. In education, Scott (in press) has studied how neo-classical economics has marketized school-ing in urban settings and set about dismantling the education bureaucracy. The impact of these changes, she argues, has been most detrimental to women and people of color.

Diversity and Educational Leadership

If a concern with diversity came late to the field of education, it came even later to educational leadership. Since diversity was initially seen as a curriculum issue, most issues of diversity, to the extent they were addressed at all, were addressed by curriculum theorists.. As Banks sug-gests above, early attention to diversity consisted of the ethnic additive approach that sought to add concepts, themes and perspectives of minority cultures into the curriculum.

Issues of diversity entered the subfield of educational leadership more through a focus on issues of gender than race or class. As more women entered the field, they brought with them an experiential knowledge that affected their work. Two early female scholars of color, Barbara Jackson and Flora Ida Ortiz, produced some of the earliest work on women and ad-ministration. In 1985 Charol Shakeshaft published her book, *Women and Administration*. It had a profound effect on the field and made gender a legitimate topic for research.

Several years before, Shakeshaft had been warned by her dissertation committee that if she wrote her dissertation on gender, she might be marginalized professionally, since gender was such a marginal topic to do research on. However, Shakeshaft broke important ground in the field, not only by documenting gender disparities in percentages of female and male prin-cipals and superintendents but also by demonstrating how most leadership theory had been developed on males and generalized to females. She also documented the unique skills and commitments women brought to leadership and argued that these relational skills were pre-cisely what organizational literature was demanding of effective leaders. At the organizational level, she documented the forms of workplace discrimination women administrators faced in a largely male field.

In the area of culture, ethnicity, and race, Kofi Lomotey (1989), in *African-American Princi-pals: School Leadership and Success*, began to look at how leadership styles and commitments also varied by culture and race. This work later had its parallel among African American scholars who studied effective teaching practices for low-income students of color. Michelle Foster (1997), Geneva Gay (2000), Gloria Ladson-Billings (1995) and others began to document what became known as "culturally responsive pedagogy." This literature, aimed at the classroom, was later translated to the school level (Burns, Keyes & Kusimo, 2005; Johnson, 2002). John-son and Bush (2004) identify the following characteristics of a culturally responsive school:

Demand high academic achievement

Have high expectations of teachers and students

Provide the space for students to critique the dominant culture and power relations

Recognize and validate color, relationships, ways of being, and culture of bicultural students

Bring students closer to who they are as defined in their community, culture, and history

Draw heavily on and affirm the cultural knowledge, language, prior experience, frame of reference, and performance styles of diverse populations

Ensure that cultural relevance permeates and informs classroom management and discipline procedures, instructional strategies and methods, classroom environment, student teacher and parent-teacher relationships, and curriculum content

Exhibit strong leadership

Monitor student progress continually (p. 275)

While cultural, ethnic, and racial diversity is often viewed as an urban phenomenon, it has become increasingly suburban as well. Areas such as Los Angeles, Chicago, Washington, D.C., Houston, and New York have minority suburban populations of about 43% of the total suburban population (Frey, 2001).

Since the aftermath of the Civil Rights Movement, discussions about education have co-mingled issues of class with those of race and gender, with class receiving little attention of its own. Although educators use such codes as SES (socioeconomic status) to identify economically disadvantaged students, dialogue to address issues of disparity often falls along racial lines. While it is difficult to disentangle class from race and gender, differences do exist. Ostrove and Cole highlight those differences in their 2003 article, "Privileging Class: Toward a Critical Psychology of Social Class in the Context of Education." Most notable is the expectation of change from a social mobility perspective. While "passing as white" or displaying "masculine tendencies" can be problematic from a racial and gender perspective, aspiring to change one's social status is often seen as the American dream (p. 682). The paradox of this is that, while our educational system purports opportunities of social mobility, schools themselves often simultaneously reproduce existing class stratification (Anyon, 1997).

While the growing problem of class inequality must be attacked at the level of social policy, leaders can mitigate its effects in schools by interrupting those practices that implicate schools in the social reproduction of class oppression. Eliminating academic tracking or making movement among tracks more fluid is one way leaders can insist that all students have access to a quality education. Many detracking strategies exist, but they generally require professional development that aids teachers in teaching heterogeneous groupings effectively. Leaders who detrack schools should also anticipate resistance from the parents of high track students who will see it as a threat to their students' privileged position in the school (Mehan, Villanueva, Hubbard, Lintz, & Okamoto, 1996).

While issues of disability receive more attention than issues of class, they too have become entangled with issues of gender and race. Males and students of color are disproportionately referred to special education programs. Proponents of inclusion argue that all students, including those with disabilities, English-language learners, and gifted students should be educated together while providing for their needs in regular classrooms (Frattura & Capper, 2007). In addition, LGBT students must be included as respected members of the school community.

LGBT students have higher than average suicide rates in part because of the harassment they receive in schools where leaders allow a climate of homophobia and bullying to prevail.

Because "diversity" has expanded to include all forms of difference as well as issues of political economy and the environment, the term "social justice" has gained popularity in educational leadership. The discourse of social justice in the realm of educational leadership focuses on developing transformational leaders who can identify institutional and social inequities affecting issues of class, disability, gender, race, and sexual orientation. In their 2005 article, "Educating School Leaders for Social Justice," Nelda Cambron-McCabe and Martha McCarthy emphasize the importance of advocacy from school leaders in four areas of reform: the standards movement, selection of leaders, student achievement, and privatization of education. Critical to their analysis is an assessment of current preparation programs: "school leadership programs must prepare new leaders to critically inquire into the taken-for-granted structures and norms that often pose insurmountable barriers for many students' academic success" (p. 204).

Citing Bogotch's (2002) statement that social justice is inseparable from the practices of educational leadership, George Theoharis presents the successful characteristics of social justice leaders in his 2007 article, "Social Justice Educational Leaders and Resistance: Toward a Theory of Social Justice Leadership." Similar to Ladson-Billings' (1995a) article "But That's Just Good Teaching!", Theoharis disputes the claim that social justice leaders simply exhibit good leadership qualities and emphasizes the difference between 'good leaders' and 'social justice leaders.' He cautions us to consider that "decades of good leadership have created and sanctioned unjust and inequitable schools" (p. 253). In the words of Theoharis, social justice leadership is the new definition of good leadership because it succeeds in creating more equitable schools.

No Child Left Behind (NCLB), Leadership, and Diversity

Cummins' (2001) model for the empowerment of minority students called for professional role definitions in schools that included additive forms of cultural/linguistic incorporation, authentic community participation, wholistic and interactive pedagogies, and authentic forms of assessment. He viewed such role definitions as enabling students and their opposite definitions as disabling.

NCLB has taken Cummins' (2001) recommendations in the exact opposite direction. In every case, current reform has moved in the direction of disabling role definitions rather than in empowering ones. Under NCLB, cultural/linguistic incorporation is subtractive in the wake of a one-size-fits-all curriculum. Community participation occurs more at the rhetorical level than in reality. Pedagogies for minority students are more transmission oriented and assessments more standardized and less authentic. However, Cummins' framework is still valid and should be included in any framework for post-NCLB school reform.

While some view NCLB's strong accountability measures and the disaggregation of test scores by race, SES, disability, and language, as a way to call attention to those groups that have been previously ignored (Skrla and Scheurich, 2004), many see the cure as worse than the disease. The National Council of Churches Committee on Public Education (2003) felt a need to speak out from an ethical perspective and has objected to NCLB on the following grounds:

1. The law will discredit public education. Undermining support for public schooling threatens our democracy.
2. The annual progress component fails to acknowledge significant improvements students have made; too many are labeled failures even when they are making strides. Those children labeled failures are disproportionately poor and of color.
3. Schools are ranked by test scores of children in demographic subgroups. A "failing group of children" will know when they are the ones who made their school a "failing" school.
4. Children in special education are required to pass tests designated for children without disabilities.
5. English-language learners are required to take tests in English before they learn English.
6. Schools and teachers are blamed for many challenges that are neither of their making nor within their capacity to change.
7. An emphasis on testing basic skills obscures the role of the humanities, the arts, and child and adolescent development. Children are treated as products to be tested, measured, and made uniform.
8. The law operates through sanctions, it takes federal Title I funding away from educational programming in already overstressed schools and uses funds to bus students to other schools or to pay for private tutoring firms.
9. The law exacerbates racial and economic segregation in urban areas. Because urban schools have more subgroups and more complex demands, they are more likely to be labeled "in need of improvement" than more affluent districts. This labeling of schools and districts encourages families with means to move to wealthy, homogeneous school districts.
10. Demands are made on states and school districts without fully funding those reforms to build the capacity to close achievement gaps (p. 22)

While one could debate some of these assertions, the fact that a national ecumenical Christian organization would endorse such a strong moral objection to NCLB suggests that NCLB's claim that it is an advocate for low-income students and students of color should be viewed with some skepticism. in the NCC's 1999 policy statement, *Churches and the Public Schools at the Close of the Twentieth Century*, contains the following claim:

> Too often, criticism of the public schools fails to reflect our present societal complexity. At a moment when childhood poverty is shamefully widespread, when many families are under constant stress, when schools are often limited by lack of funds or resources, criticism of the public schools often ignores an essential truth: we cannot believe that we can improve public schools by concentrating on the schools alone. They alone can neither cause nor cure the problems we face. In this context, we must address with prayerful determination the issues of race and class, which threaten both public education and democracy in America (p. 4).

Diversity and Democracy: The Goals of Schooling

While the rhetoric of NCLB touts equity, it is essentially informed by an ideology of social efficiency that views schools as institutions producing human capital for a global economy. The human capital theory links schooling with economic growth, arguing that the "new" economy will produce a demand for more highly-skilled workers. What is becoming increasingly clear is that this promised demand for highly-skilled workers has not materialized, largely because of automation and outsourcing. According to economist James K. Galbraith (1998):

> What the existing economy needs is a fairly small number of first-rate technical talents combined with a small superclass of managers and financiers, on top of a vast substructure of nominally literate and politically apathetic working people (pp. 34–35).

If Galbraith is right, then from a social efficiency perspective, a stratified society of highly skilled and creative students alongside a lower track of students who can pass minimum competency exams through the acquisition of basic skills may be highly functional. But it is not only a social efficiency approach that reproduces social inequalities in schools.

Labaree (1997) argues that as the United States continues to promote marketization and competition, Americans will increasingly view schooling from a perspective of excessive individual self-interest. Both social efficiency and individual self-interest make human-capital theory and the economic payoff of schooling the primary goal. Thus, parents begin preparing their children for a competitive world as early as pre-school. As choosing schools becomes more common, those with the cultural, social, and economic capital to compete for the best schools will be the winners. But individual self-interest cannot serve as a national ideal to inspire young people, and, while always a force in American society, it was previously tempered by larger ideals of democracy and equity. Unless our society can find a way to reflect these ideals in our social policies, school leaders will have a difficult job defending them within their schools.

This brings us back to James Banks' fourth approach to curriculum, which has important implications for leaders who wish to be transformative. Just as a transformative curriculum seeks to develop critical thought and a sense of political efficacy in students, transformative leaders will need to develop the same skills. As an important goal of schooling, they will need to prioritize, creating a citizenry that will identify, analyze, and develop responses that mitigate or eliminate the social problems that exist in their schools and in society. These leaders will also have to be the advocates for disenfranchised students both within their schools and through their advocacy for social policies that empower their students and their families.

References

Anyon, J. (1997). *Ghetto schooling: A political economy of urban educational reform*. New York: Teachers College Press.

Apple, M. & Weis, L. (1983). Ideology and practice in schooling: A political and conceptual introduction. In M. Apple & L. Weis (Eds.) *Ideology and practice in schooling*. (pp. 3–33). Philadelphia: Temple University Press.

Banks, James. (1990). Approaches to Multicultural Curriculum Reform. *The Social Studies Texan, 5*(3), 43.

Bogotch, I. (2002). Educational leadership and social justice: Practice into theory. *Journal of School Leadership, 12*, 138–156.

Burns, R., Keyes, M., & Kusimo, P. (2005). *Closing achievement gaps by creating culturally responsive schools*. Institute of Education Sciences (ED), Washington, DC.

Cambron-McCabe, N., & McCarthy, M. M. (2005). Educating school leaders for social justice. *Educational Policy, 19*(1), 201–222.

Cummins, Jim. (2001). Empowering Minority Students: A Framework for Intervention. *Harvard Educational Review, 71*(4), 649–675.

Foster, M. (1997). *Black teachers on teaching*. New York: New Press.

Fraser, N. (1997). *Justice interruptus: Critical reflections on the "postsocialist" condition*. New York: Routledge.

Frattura, E. & Capper, C.A. (2007). *Leadership for Social Justice in Practice: Integrated Comprehensive Services (ICS) for All Learners.* Thousand Oaks, CA: Corwin Press.

Frey,W. (2001). *Melting pot suburbs: A census 2000 study of suburban diversity.* Washington, DC: Brookings Institution.

Galbraith, J. (1998) *Created unequal: The crisis in American pay.* New York: Simon & Schuster.

Gay, G, (2000). *Culturally responsive teaching: Theory, research, & practice.* New York: Teachers College Press.

Gilligan, C. (1986) *In a different voice.* Chicago, MA: Harvard University Press.

Johnson, R. (2002). *Using data to close the achievement gap. How to measure equity in our schools.* Thousand Oaks, CA: Corwin.

Johnson, R. & Bush, L. (2004). Leading the school through culturally responsive inquiry. In F. English (Ed.) *Handbook of Educational Leadership: New Dimensions and Realities.* Thousand Oaks, CA: Sage.

Kaestle, C. F., & Foner, E. (1983). *The pillars of the republic: Common schools and American society, 1780–1860* (1st ed.). New York: Hill and Wang.

Labaree, D. (1997). *How to succeed in school without really learning: The credentials race in American education.* London & New Haven, CT: Yale University Press.

Ladson-Billings, G. (1995a). But that's just good teaching! The case for culturally relevant pedagogy. *Theory into Practice, 34*(3), 159–165.

Ladson-Billings, G. (1995b). Toward a theory of culturally relevant pedagogy. *American Educational Research Journal, 42,* 465–491.

Lomotey, K. (1989). *African-American principals: School leadership and success.* Westport, CT: Greenwood Press.

McCarthy, C. (1993). Beyond the poverty of theory in race relations: Nonsynchrony and social difference in education. In L. Weiss and M. Fine (Eds.) *Beyond silenced voices: Class, race, and gender in United States schools.* (pp. 325–346) Albany: SUNY.

Mehan, H., Villanueva, I., Hubbard, L., Lintz, A., and Okamoto, D. (1996). *Constructing success: The consequences of untracking low achieving students.* London: Cambridge University Press.

Michaels, W. B. (2006). *The trouble with diversity: How we learned to love identity and ignore inequality.* New York: Metropolitan Books.

National Council of Churches (1999). *Churches and the Public Schools at the Close of the Twentieth Century.* New York: National Council of the Churches of Christ, Nov. 11.

National Council of Churches (2003). Ten Moral Concerns in the Implementation of the No Child Left Behind Act. Retrieved June 20, 2007.

Ostrove, J. and Cole, E. (2003). "Privileging Class: Toward a Critical Psychology of Social Class in the Context of Education." *Journal of Social Issues* 59(4) 677–692.

Patterson, James T. (2001). *Brown v. Board of Education: A Civil Rights Milestone and Its Troubled Legacy.* Oxford; New York: Oxford University Press.

San Miguel, G. (2001). *Brown, not white: School integration and the Chicano movement in Houston.* College Station: Texas A&M University Press.

Scott, J. (In Press). Managers of choice: Race, gender, and the political ideology of the "new" urban school leadership. In W. Feinberg & C. Lubienski (Eds.), *School choice policies and outcomes: Philosophical and empirical perspectives on limits to choice in liberal democracies.* Albany: SUNY Press.

Scott, J.C. (1990). *Domination and the arts of resistance: Hidden transcripts.* New Haven, CT: Yale University Press.

Skrla, L. and Scheurich, J. (2004). *Educational equity and accountability.* New York: Routledge

Theoharis, G. (2007). Social justice educational leaders and resistance: Toward a theory of social justice leadership. *Educational Administration Quarterly, 43*(2), 221–258.

Tyack, D. B., & Cuban, L. (1995). *Tinkering Toward Utopia: A Century of Public School Reform.* Cambridge, MA: Harvard University Press.

Twenty-Nine

African-Centered Schools as Sites of Hope
Community Building Through Culture and School Leadership

Kmt G. Shockley and Rona M. Frederick

The education community remains in a quandary about what action to take regarding the difficulties black children continue to experience in the U.S. public education system. For example, according to the National Center for Education Statistics (NCES, 2004), the population of blacks, first-language-Spanish speakers, and Asians enrolled in American public schools grew from 29.7% to 39.5%. However, the teaching force remains overwhelmingly white and female, and the academic achievement gap persists. Furthermore, while black students represent 17% of the total U.S. school population, they are 36% of the students who are suspended from school and 32% of the students who are expelled from school (Department of Education Office of Civil Rights, 2002). Also, black students have lower math and reading scores than do all other cultural groups (NCES, 2004). As Lomotey (1992) explains, it is still true that "...the academic achievement of a large number of Black children across the country—as measured by standardized achievement tests, suspension rates, special education placement rates, and dropout rates has deteriorated considerably over the last twenty years" (p. 455). Over the past thirty years or so, Africentric theorists have called for the black community to consider becoming more knowledgeable about their African past (Akbar, 1992; Asante, 1988, 1990; ben-Jochannan, 1972; Clarke, 1991; Diop, 1987; Karenga & Carruthers, 1986; Obenga, 1986). A related group of scholars and practitioners who refer to themselves as Africentric (a.k.a. Afrocentric/African centered) educators have advanced proposals calling for the institutionalization of cultural reattachment Africentric education for black children (Afrik, 1981; Akoto, 1992; Akoto & Akoto, 1999, 2007; Brookins, 1984; Doughty, 1973; Hilliard, 1997; Kambon, 1992; Lee, 1992; Lomotey, 1978, 1992; Madhubuti, 1973; Ratteray & Shujaa, 1987; Ridley, 1971; Satterwhite, 1971; Shujaa, 1993). Cultural reattachment is a process whereby blacks become familiar with and also practice aspects of indigenous African culture.

For the purpose of capturing the essence of the work of the school leaders who are part of this study, we make a distinction between Africentric educators, who are calling for a relevant and meaningful education for black children that focuses on the accomplishments of people of African descent, and cultural reattachment Africentric educators, who are interested in exposing blacks to specific African cultural groups (such as Asante). Some of the most well-known cultural reattachment Africentric educationists are the founders and/or principals of Africentric schools who are using their institutions to invoke positive change in the community. This study investigates the theories, beliefs, and practices of those Africentric education leaders.

The ideological battle continues between those oriented toward Afrocentrism and those against it (Appiah, 1993; Asante, 2000; ben Jochannan, 1972; Bernal, 1987; Browder, 1992; Early, 1991; Howe, 1998; Lefkowitz, 1996; Schlesinger, 1992; Williams, 1987). Proponents of cultural reattachment Africentric education (such as Akoto & Akoto, 1999; Asante, 1991; Hilliard, 1997; Lee, 1992; Lomotey, 1978, 1993; Murrell, 2002; Shujaa, 1994) are less visible in the mainstream than they were formerly. Since proponents of Africentric education are less visible, the most ardent supporters of major change for black children are only heard as their ideas are transformed to suit mainstream tastes and preferences. That is, Africentric educationists may receive less mainstream public attention and less acceptance of their work in major outlets such as mainstream journals, but they continue to inconspicuously influence the dialogue related to educating black children through their written works and their constant appearances on the lecture circuit in black communities (e.g., Na'im Akbar, Marimba Ani, Julia Hare, Asa Hilliard, Jawanza Kunjufu, Mwalimu Shujaa, etc.). While Africentric education and ideas are becoming more popular among blacks, it still appears true that these ideas are simply unpalatable throughout the U.S. mainstream, as none of the major education conferences in the United States highlights the work and contributions of Africentric education leaders; also, teacher education programs do not focus on methods for teaching and reaching black children (Delpit, 2001; Hilliard, 1991; Murrell, 2002).

The Conceptual Context: Africentric Ideology and the Questions it Raises

While a chapter of this sort brings the work of African-centered scholars to the forefront, scholars of African descent have discussed the difficulty of making their works available to the public in general. Tillman (2006) points out that the academy is often a challenging place for blacks regardless of their research agenda; this difficulty is doubled for scholars who have made a point to focus on issues related to African agency (Asante, 1991). Furthermore, distinguishing African-centered work from work that focuses on blacks in general requires the employment of Africalogy—the African-centered study of phenomena related to blacks (discussed later in this chapter). This distinction is critical because although too narrow a focus can create a certain parochialism, too wide a focus obliterates the cultural reattachment Afrocentric aspect, which in turn silences those educationists whose lifetime contributions have been about the need to use indigenous African cultures to improve the lives of people of African descent. Their efforts are not contrary to, but are, in fact, different than research on blacks that is not grounded in African cultural reattachment. This work considers that distinction in order to provide a true voice for the often-silenced lines of reason emanating from Africentric educationists.

Africentric ideology raises a great many questions, especially for non-Africentric thinkers. Africentric ideology is seen by authors such as Schlesinger (1992) as an attempt to disunite America. While Schlesinger argues that Africentric education is detrimental to American society, Asante (1998) argues that

> Afrocentricity seeks to understand [phenomena] by beginning all analysis from the African person as human agent. In classes, it means that the African American child must be connected, grounded to information presented in the same way White children are grounded when we discuss literature, history, mathematics, and science. Teachers who do not know this information with respect to Africans must seek it out from those who do know it. Afrocentrists do not take anything away from White history except its aggressive urge to pose as universal (p. 16).

Africentric ideology requires a reorientation of thinking on issues pertaining to education because when traditional lenses are used, oftentimes they are insufficient tools for understanding black phenomena. But some scholars are concerned that Africentric education is an overshoot to address academic achievement challenges for black children. The claim is sensible because if academic achievement was the concern, it appears that Africentric educators would be well served to conduct research on the best practices for improving black academic achievement. However, academic achievement (as it is usually referenced in test scores, I.Q. tests, etc.) is to Africentrics what, for example, school violence is to the mainstream education community. That is, the mainstream community views school violence as a problem that is birthed from mounting societal problems and issues, such as parenting issues and the ineffectiveness of the criminal justice system: in other words it is a symptom. Africentrics view mainstream notions of academic achievement similarly—as a problem that is rooted in issues of cultural mismatch and societal racism. Many in the mainstream believe that school violence is best solved by addressing the home/social problems of young people, not by making them prisoners at school. Africentrics view more holistic approaches to understanding academic achievement as an issue that is best addressed by applying a black (African) culture to black students, not by attempting to find best teaching practices, but by bringing the academic achievement problems into context, which requires addressing issues of cultural mismatch and racism.

Some scholars argue that Africentric education is a very hostile version of educational reform for black children. A few educational reform efforts, such as the charter schools movement, are reported to have some benefits for black children. Other movements such as the community control movement have also gained attention as efforts to reform the educational system. It is important to note that the Africentric education effort is not a movement or a reform project. Africentric education is viewed by leading proponents as an expression of culture within education. To explain, the term *Africentric education* is used because it is fitting: education that is centered on Africa and its people. However, the main goal of the group of African-centered educationists in this study is not to push a set of "anti"-Eurocentric values and propositions; the main goal is to advance a culturally relevant experience for black children, and what is commonly known as Africentric education emerges as the expression of that cultural mandate in education. In the aforementioned sense, Africentric educationists do not call for educational reform, they call for black (African) culture for black children. Cultural adoption requires educational experiences that are relevant. For Africentric educationists, reformed American public education is not relevant, nor is it desirable because reformed education is an incomplete attempt to address a problem that is much larger than education.

Lomotey (1978) expresses the sentiment by explaining the principle held by Africentric educationists, "Africa is the home of all people of African descent and all Black people should work for the total liberation and unification of Africa and Africans around the world. . . and schools for African American children should be based upon this principle" (p. 36).

Africentric educationists stress cultural practice as the most important element for empowering and transforming black communities. African cultural practice is understood as the answer to the plethora of challenges faced by black children in education. The belief is that the current cultural order is debilitating and stifling of the growth, development, and chances of black children. Therefore, Africentric educators call for sankofa, which literally means to return and retrieve that which was lost during the period of African destruction (e.g., a loss of independence and culture). Through the process of sankofa, people of African descent are "re-Africanizing," that is, they are re-becoming who they were culturally before slavery and colonization. Many of the efforts to re-Africanize are being guided by the leaders of African-centered schools.

In light of the fact that the Africentric perspective is becoming more commonplace within certain domains, the purpose of this study is to investigate how some schools that use Africentric ideas as organizing themes are impacting their communities. Also this study explores how Africentric themes are used within certain schools and communities to rebuild African culture.

Literatures and Definitions: Toward Understanding Africentric Ideas in Education

Africentric education scholars advance several concepts that constitute the cultural imperatives of Africentric ideas in education. The cultural imperatives are the "main ingredients" of Africentric ideas in education. In other words, certain concepts provide the ideological basis for creating an Africentric experience. The concepts include identity, Pan-Africanism, African/African American culture, African values adoption and transmission, black nationalism, community control/institution building, and education as opposed to schooling (see Shockley, 2007, for a full description of these concepts). In the process of working with children and communities, Africentric educationists incessantly use these concepts: they are the baseline and ostensible "material" of African centeredness.

Identity and Pan-Africanism

Before the experiences of chattel slavery in the Americas and colonialism in Africa, Africans were clear about who they were. After those experiences, the identity of black children became a matter for debate. Black children in the United States have been called many names from Negro to African American. Africentric education leaders often refer to the fact that children in the Caribbean areas are often referred to by the name of their island (e.g., Jamaican or Antiguan). Children on the African continent are often referred to by their national or clan designations (e.g., Ghanaian or Akan). African-centered leaders stress that teaching black children of their African identity is critical for the survival of the black community because it reconnects them with their natural and original foundation and prepares them to act in accordance with their own global self-interests (Akoto, 1992; Akoto & Akoto, 1999; Anwisye, 2006; Hilliard, 1991; King, 2005; Madhubuti, 1973).

African-centered educationists believe that it is in the best interest of blacks to identify Africa as the source and origin of all black people. They also stress that all black people in the world are Africans (Madhubuti, 1973). This idea is known as Pan-Africanism. Black children in the Americas, and particularly in the United States, are members of communities that are unable to connect themselves to their exact and direct ancestors because their predecessors were forced to disperse and completely disconnect from their relatives. This process ultimately blurred African identity to the point of creating widespread identity confusion. By virtue of history, phenotype, and scientific testing (e.g., C. Diop's Dopa Drop Test), it is obvious to Africentric educators that the natural foundation from which blacks come is the continent of Africa. African-centered educators are concerned that the difficulty and/or inability to identify the exact and direct ancestral lineage of blacks represents a unique circumstance that takes away some of the communal and personal power that other groups who have this knowledge are able to enjoy (Anderson, 2001). The identification of black children (and people) as displaced Africans (not Negroes and not labeled by color and citizenship such as "black Americans") is not only historically correct but provides a much-needed link to their African past as a way to move forward toward understanding and reattaching to specific African cultures (Akoto, 1992; Akoto & Akoto, 1999; Lomotey, 1978).

African Cultural and Values Infusion and Transmission

Africentric educationists purport that the long-standing tradition of blacks using African culture to sustain themselves and bring order to their lives and communities is threatened because blacks are not educated about African cultures (Akoto & Akoto, 1999; Anwisye, 2006). Cultural reattachment is a process that includes blacks becoming (re)familiarized with specific African cultural beliefs and practices for the purpose of readopting those beliefs and practices into one's life. Many education researchers have stressed that this infusion process is critical because considering the conditions in black communities (e.g., black children's disproportionately high special education placement rates) the status quo is not working for blacks (Ani, 1994; Hale-Benson, 1982; Hilliard, 1997; King, 2005; Ladson-Billings, 1994; Lee, 1992; Lomotey, 1978; Nobles, 1986).

Knowledge of one's culture teaches him (or her) the values that are a part of familial tradition. Africentric educationists refer to an African axiology (e.g., Njia—a *kiswahili* word meaning "the way through our values"), which is the fourth imperative of African-centered education. Njia (Karenga, 1980) is one example of an African value system. Njia originates from indigenous African culture and is a system of cultural values practiced mostly by African descendants in the United States. Africentric educationists are concerned that the modern cultural and value system of blacks is frivolous because cultural connections to Africa are lost. A solution to this frivolity is the inclusion of African ethos into the educational process for black children. African cultural groups naturally include value systems that speak to the importance of ancestor veneration, respect for elders, and socialization practices for children that are unique to each cultural group (Hilliard, 1997). Africentric educationists call for re-Africanization (Akoto & Akoto, 1999; Anwisye, 2006), which principally includes reattachment to African cultural ethos for the purpose of the transmission of African values. Indigenously speaking, African cultural groups are largely essentialist (there are certain cultural practices and values that *are* and *are not* Yoruba or Zulu, for example). Historically, African cultural groups have taken great pride in the maintenance of their own beliefs and practices (Akoto, 1992, 1999; Anwisye, 2006; Asante, 1991, 1988; Hilliard, 1997). Africentric educationists wish to reestablish this pride in tradition by encouraging an African nationalistic sentiment that offers cultural substance.

Black/African Nationalism

African (or black) nationalism is the fifth construct and refers to the idea that all blacks, regardless of their specific location on the planet, constitute a "nation." This concept is important in research on black education because minor differences between black groups in various locales have been exploited and blacks have been made the "pawns and playthings of those who are directed and powerful" (Akoto, 1992, p. 4). That is, people of African descent have found themselves unable to use their in-group diversity to their advantage; instead, in-group diversity has been manipulated and blacks have experienced mayhem as "divide and conquer" strategies have been used against them (Akoto, 1992; Akoto & Akoto, 1999) In the past African groups were able to somewhat successfully be nationalistic toward their own cultural beliefs and practices (Clarke, 1991; Williams, 1987), but in more modern times those differences are leading to black destruction because the indigenous African cultural component of black life is being neutered throughout the globe by European hegemony (Akoto & Akoto, 1999, Asante, 2007; Hilliard, 1996, 1997, 2002; James, 1954). The destabilization of individual African nations (e.g., Bakongo, Khoi San, Zulu, etc.), as well as the failure of the Western-derived principles (such as liberty and individualism) (Ani, 1994; Hilliard, 2003) justify the need for Pan-African nationalism. That is, the establishment of Pan-African nationalism reestablishes the African cultural emphasis on togetherness via collectivism and self-determination and teaches black children of their responsibility to the group, not just to themselves individually. By focusing on group needs and "self" (group)-determination, African-centered educators simultaneously call for an education for black children that instills the desire for ownership and control of the institutions needed for survival within the black community—the sixth imperative of African-centered education.

Community Control and Institution Building

Community control involves making important decisions about the institutions that exist in one's community. Institution building involves creating the necessary agencies that are designed to "impart knowledge, skills, values and attitudes that are necessary [for a community] to survive and progress" (Doughty, 1973, p. 3). Independent black institutions (IBIs), mostly private and charter schools, were designed for the purpose of creating the necessary agencies to serve the interests of the black community. The importance of black community control and institution building was highlighted by the decentralization movement, which began in the 1960s. Particularly, the Ocean Hill–Brownsville, New York, incident sparked a national campaign for community control (Podair, 2002). African-centered educationists stress that blacks will be unable to meet their own needs and secure their interests until they own and control the institutions that are needed for their survival (Madhubuti, 1973). While blacks are the top consumers in the United States they own and control less than any other group (Anderson, 2001). African-centered educationists argue that black children are being taught to maintain their status as consumers of virtually everything and owners and controllers of virtually nothing. That is, they argue that black children need an African-centered education that imparts the skills and knowledge needed in order for the children to be productive and to administrate the state.

Education Not Schooling

African-centered educationists claim that black children in America's schools are not educated, instead they are schooled—the final construct of Africentric education. Schooling is a process of creating people who have the necessary skills to maintain the status quo within the society (King, 2005; Shujaa, 1994). To the contrary, education is a process of imparting upon the children all of the things they need to be able to "administrate the state" (Lomotey, 1978), that is, the things they need to provide leadership within their communities and within their nation. Particularly, African-centered educationists desire an education for black children where their African identity is emphasized and clarified, where Pan-Africanism, African nationalism, and African culture and values are emphasized within the curriculum. Finally, they wish for an education that teaches black children to own and control all of the resources within the black community. The inclusion of such imperatives into the curriculum is possible only via true education.

The Ethnographic Africalogical Research Methodology

Investigating African-centered education in practice at both public (via charter) and private institutions requires deep cultural knowledge of people of African descent. The complexities of examining disenfranchised communities by using mainstream research paradigms have objectified and in some cases even overtly disrespected some cultural groups (Asante, 1990; Ani, 1994; Hilliard, 1997). Some black scholars call for appropriate and relevant research methods for examining black phenomena (Asante, 1988, 1990; Doughty, 1973; Hale-Benson, 1982; Hilliard, 1997; Lomotey, 1978, 1992; Richards, 1989; Ridley, 1971). Asante (1990) develops Africalogy as a research genre for analyzing and interpreting black phenomena. *Africalogy* is defined as, "The Africentric study of phenomena, events, ideas, and personalities related to Africa" (p. 14). Asante explains that the "mere study of phenomena of Africa is not Africalogy but some other intellectual enterprise" (p. 14). Therefore, the most important element of Africalogical research is that it be "Africentric." Africentricity literally means "placing African ideals at the center of any analysis that involves African culture and behavior" (Asante, 1998, p. 2). In other words, Africalogical researchers are able to view phenomena with crucial reference to African history, traditions, and culture, which informs analyses and interpretations of events and data. Asante provides insight into the shape of the discipline of Africalogy:

> Centrism, the groundedness of observation and behavior in one's own historical experiences, shapes the concepts, paradigms, theories, and methods of Africalogy. In this way Africalogy secures its place alongside other centric pluralisms without hierarchy and without seeking hegemony. As a discipline, Africalogy is sustained by a commitment to centering the study of African phenomena and events in the particular cultural voice of the composite African people. Furthermore, it opens the door for interpretations of reality based in evidence secured by reference to the African world voice (p. 12).

In this study, the requirement for deep knowledge of the group under study was most beneficial because it helped with the task of interpreting certain cultural rituals and interpersonal behaviors. That is, often there were occurrences that would have been interpreted differently had there only been surface cultural knowledge of the participants' cultural beliefs. Furthermore, the Africalogical requirement for cultural and social immersion over "scientific distance" was proven beneficial as, in this context, deep knowledge is only ascertainable through participation in certain rituals and practices. Asante explains that "[immersion] in itself is extremely difficult because it means that the researcher must have some familiarity with the history, language, philosophy, and myths of the people under study" (1998, p. 27). The Africalogical requirements and suggestions offered tools for analysis that had they not been in place might have caused unintentionally biased and skewed interpretations of events, conversation, and cultural practices that would have come about because of the differing cultural orientations (which will be discussed in detail in the findings section). The participants have a different cultural orientation than do the researchers, in that the researchers consider themselves to be practitioners of western/Americanized culture, whereas the leaders of these schools practice an African culture. Asante's (1990) Africalogical requirements helped the researchers to remain "culturally sensitive" (Tillman, 2006) to the needs and backgrounds of participants. While the tenets of ethnographic work also require certain sensitivities to participants, Asante's Africalogical requirements are pointed at correcting the specific insensitivities that occur when researchers investigate black phenomena.

While the Africalogical requirements helped to frame the research methods of this study by requiring introspection, retrospection, and becoming familiar with the history, myths, and mores of the people under study as prerequisites, at the root of this investigation also lay issues related to social justice. While these leaders are creating institutions that may serve African-American children better, they are also social justice workers who resist the embedded societal structures (Theoharis, 2007). Ethnographic investigations are particularly useful for projects that are aimed to address embedded societal injustices because of the requirement for prolonged field work and "native" understandings of groups' attempts to liberate themselves. That is, Spradley (1980) suggests that ethnography is the work of describing a culture (p. 3).

In many ways the environments that these school communities create is producing a new "culture" that consists of African cultural ethos. Tedlock (2000) clarifies that the goal of ethnography is to grasp the native's point of view in relation to his own life and realize his vision of his own world. Ethnographic data collection is not the act of "studying people," instead, as Spradley (1980) suggests, it is the act of "learning from people" (p. 3). Stake's (2000) position that the "qualitative case study is characterized by researchers spending extended time, on site, personally in contact with activities and operations of the case, reflecting, revising meanings of what is going on" (p. 445) creates a perfect union between the characteristics of ethnographic research and this case. That is, we developed an understanding of our participants' points of view and perspectives by spending extended time with them and actually participating in the cultural activities. We were sensitive to their cultural difference from us and chose to intimately engage with them so that we could understand the world from their perspective.

We were able to glean from school leaders a very holistic understanding of what they believed to be the impact of their schools within the community. Interview questions included the following:

1. In general, what do you notice about the way this school operates within this community?
2. Exactly how do you think Afrocentrism as a concept is used within the school?
3. What is the purpose of hosting so many programs (such as identity awareness conferences, summer cultural experiences, etc.)? Why do you do it?
4. What would you say are the ultimate goals of this school?
5. How do you understand culture?
6. How is culture used and woven into the life of the school?

Interviews and observations of Africentric and "culturally centered" schools were conducted between 2002 and 2007. Schools and school leaders were chosen based on the location of the school, the popularity of the institution and/or its leadership, and the perceived impact of the institution within the community. Not all Africentric education institutions are open to researchers. Our final decision as to which schools to use was based on accessibility, national popularity (we spoke to many people who are part of the Africentric movement), type of school (we wanted to learn from both charter and private institutions), and the school's community outreach reputation.

Approximately seventy formal and informal interviews were conducted with Africentric school leaders at their educational institutions. Formal and informal interview questions were asked intermittently throughout the course of this study. Reported here are the results of formal and informal interviews, observations, researcher participation, and meetings and other forums to which we were given special access. The results of the interview questions above represent the views of some of the most well-established and well-known Africentric education leaders in the United States. They were chosen primarily because of their influence on the Africentric education movement.

Data Collection

The purpose of this study was to investigate how some schools that use Africentric ideas as organizing themes are impacting their communities. In addition, the study explored how Africentric themes are used within certain schools and communities to rebuild culture. Leadership of charter and private schools that use Africentric organizing principles (i.e., African culture, spirituality, and values) were chosen for this study. Three charter schools and one private school were chosen. Two of the charter schools and the private school are in Washington, D.C.; the other charter school is in Boston, Massachusetts. Two of the schools in Washington, D.C. were chosen because they are highly respected within the community for their outreach, which spans some thirty years. In this study one of those schools is called "Africentric Private School" (APS) and the other is called "Africentric Charter Day School" (ACDS). The other D.C. school was chosen because it is a new charter school that has hired and appointed several self-labeled Afrocentrists to key leadership positions. That school is called "New D.C. Charter" (NDC). The school in Boston, hereafter called "Boston Charter" (BC), is important in this study because nowhere in that school's mission or goals do they mention anything Africentric (they use the term "culturally centered"), yet they appointed an extremely well-known self-labeled Africentric educator to a key administrative position in the school, and his African-centered focus has had an immense impact on the institution and its standing and popularity within the community. All four of these schools feature key leaders that deem themselves African centered and use African ethos such as African culture, spirituality, and rituals in their practice. Also, the leadership of all these schools focuses on re-Africanization as the most important idea for educating black children and communities.

This is an ongoing study of Africentric education leadership that began in fall 2002. Data collection began within two of the schools in the fall of 2002. Administrators from all five schools signed informed consents allowing access to relevant components within the schools. In the fall of 2002 classroom observation began. It is difficult to fully understand what takes place in well-established Africentric schools by observing classroom teaching because much of what takes place is culturally coded (it is unable to be fully understood because it comes from a different cultural frame of reference and it takes much time to learn/understand the codes). The cultural differences forced us to conduct many formal and informal interviews of school founders, faculty, and staff to continuously check for meaning. A major difficulty of this study was understanding the complexity of the schools through conversations with people because they often see researchers as "outsiders" and therefore may lack trust. In order to fully understand, we had to participate in the cultural and community activities, and over time we became familiar with the depth of the cultural attempts that are being made within these schools.

We were allowed to join conversations held by the Ndundu (executive body) of the Council of Independent Black Institutions (CIBI) and attended countless board and founders meetings at all of the schools in this study. We also participated in cultural events at all of the schools, and for the past four years we attended the week-long cultural leadership retreat that is organized by private and charter school leaders in D.C. Furthermore, we attended CIBI science fairs, met with charter school boards, and engaged with Africentric education leadership in Boston and D.C. throughout this study by conducting home visits, sitting in on meetings with parents and students, and even studying their ways of settling major disagreements among themselves. The data collection activities have been numerous and time consuming, yet they have been necessary in order to grasp the rather intricate nature of the seemingly humdrum but actually quite extraordinary happenings within these school communities. Data were kept locked and secured in an electronic notebook. The task of coding relationships between and among data was facilitated by the qualitative software program Ethnograph v. 5.0. Coding included sorting data to find the major themes and to understand the relationship between and among data.

Findings

Understanding African-centered schools requires the primary task of understanding culture. That is, although it takes much time to really understand this principle, studying Africentric education requires a deep commitment to studying and understanding the way(s) African cultural groups think, cosmologically speaking. In this instance the commitment requires involvement in and engagement with participants, not scientific distance and objectivity from the participants. One of the reasons that involvement and engagement are so necessary in Africentric contexts is because informants will not offer information until they trust your intentions. Surely this phenomenon is due to the long history of blacks in the United States having many of their efforts to organize themselves thwarted by entities—from the government to private citizens. Our understanding of the importance of these schools to the communities in which they exist only comes through relationship building and direct involvement. Our engagement with Africentric school leaders in this study reveals two important themes. The first theme involves the fact that indigenous African culture, which includes African-derived values, is the substance of Africentric leaders' offerings within the schools and communities in which they work. Attaching to African culture requires a process of re-Africanization. Africentric education leaders work to reestablish African cultural ethos within their schools and communities. The second theme relates to the fact that schools using Africentric organizing principles (i.e., African culture, spirituality and values) stress the importance of family and community building as part of their grassroots efforts to encourage nation building among blacks.

Framing Re-Africanization

The indigenous African cultural knowledge and folkways of people of African descent were virtually erased by two processes: (1) chattel enslavement of blacks in the Americas, and (2) the colonization of blacks throughout Africa. Re-Africanization refers to the systematic process of reorienting Africans with the cosmological, axiological, and ontological knowledge and folkways they lost during enslavement and colonization. Re-Africanization is a multistep and multifaceted process. A first step of the process involves becoming consciously aware of one's African-ness. In most instances, students in Africentric schools (and/or schools with an Africentric focus) are given an African name, which serves to match students' African heritage with their identity. Many children of African descent who attend these schools at first do not have names that match their African-derived identity. Another step of the re-Africanization process within Africentric schools involves creating an environment where respect for elders and tradition is emphasized. Hence, teachers and administrators are usually referred to by African titles such as "Mama" and "Baba," Swahili words that translate to "mother figure" and "father figure." In schools such as BC, the principal is referred to by the title "Queen Mother." But perhaps the most important element to which students are exposed is the African cultural cosmology and values component.

We found that Africentric leaders use African axiological systems such as *Maat* (an ancient African system of cardinal virtues and negative confessions) and *Nguzo Saba* (seven principles of a black value system derived from *Kawaida theory*, a value system based on African ethics) (see Karenga, 1980), which are used as cultural referents within the schools. The principles within those cultural offerings are used to guide student behaviors and staff relations with one another. All of the schools in this study have the Nguzo Saba and Maat posted in hallways and on billboards, and teachers use the substance of the systems to control student behavior and as reminders to students about the achievement expectations when students begin to go astray. As an example, three of the principles of the Nguzo Saba include Kiswahili words such as *ujamaa*, which means "cooperative economics," *nia*, which means "purpose," and *umoja* which means "unity." We found that one must first have an understanding of the overarching concepts such as those discussed above (e.g., Nguzo Saba, etc.) before truly being able to decode the happenings in these schools.

Decoding the Re-Africanization Process

After spending much time at these schools observing how Nguzo Saba, Maat, and other African cultural notions were woven into the educational process, we thought we understood the essence of African-centered education functioning. Early on we had concluded that ACDS, APS, NDC, and BC were essentially just like public schools, with the exception that such schools additionally incorporate certain African cultural rituals and themes.

An example of the difficulty of correctly interpreting data from within these settings follows. The principal of APS stated the following to students during class, "You have to remember to respect those who came before you." This mandate appears as a general request to a student requiring him/her to respect those who are older and/or more experienced. We saw statements such as the one above as general mandates that any teacher or authority figure would expect from students. On another occasion, a teacher at ACDS required that students "behave in unity like the bristles of a broom." He then began humming a song and the children nodded their heads along with him. When we first heard such statements being made we were unable to put them into the cultural contexts in which they belonged. In fact, we did not realize there was a very specific cultural context that needed to be considered. After attending the cultural leadership retreat and a number of other relevant activities such as the Identity Awareness conference, we were able to understand that the statements above are loaded with cultural significance which related to re-Africanization.

The practices at established Africentric schools are only decodable if the observer is clued into the cultural significance of events. On two different occasions and in both Boston and D.C., we watched as the students practiced drumming and dancing. As we watched we initially believed that we were observing a group of people who were simply interested in practicing their culture and having fun. The celebrations featured colorful dresses, African décor, loud pounding drums, and painted faces. We thought about joining in on several occasions. As we watched the celebration at APS, we smiled and turned to Makia, a teacher there, and asked her, "Why aren't you out there dancing?" She did not smile back. She looked at us and said, "You don't just dance because you want to, you dance to send and receive messages." We were curious about Makia's answer, so we questioned other people about it. We found that the dancing is not done for the purpose of having fun. Though it may be fun, each motion has cultural significance. For example, hands are waved in a certain way to ward off certain spirits. Faces are painted to bring certain spirits in or to impersonate an ancestor from the past. Where we thought participants in such rituals were merely having fun, they had actually been possessed by an ancestor, were telling an important story, or were mimicking the behaviors of an ancestor. The Akan people have a saying: "A stranger has eyes but he cannot see." That saying certainly applied to us before engaging deeply in the cultural lives of these leaders.

We found that to understand what was going on, we had to submerse ourselves into the culture. The examples above illustrate the importance of understanding the cultural reasons for behavior. But knowledge of the cultural reasons is not enough, one must submerse oneself to understand from the participants' perspective so that analysis is wholly informed. These understandings came largely via our engagement in the summer cultural experience. What seems like an ordinary interaction between teachers and students is actually a cultural lesson that is intent on helping students to reach a point of re-Africanization. What seems like fun and games is a call to the ancestors and/or a worship session dedicated to the Divine.

Much of what we observed had to be resifted through an African cultural lens so that it could be analyzed from an appropriate cultural perspective. During the summer cultural experience, we were exposed to numerous African philosophies. Among them was one that provided insight into the earlier notion that children should "[behave] in unity like you are the bristles of a broom." During the class, the teacher simply made that statement, but during the summer cultural experience we learned that children are socialized via the use of certain common folk songs:

Praye wo ho ye	The broom as it exists
wo yi baako	When you take one stick
a na ebu	Then it breaks
woka bo mu a	When you put it together
emmbu	It will not break

Had we not attended the summer cultural experience, we would have never known that students were, in fact, being socialized to understand the importance of communal unity through this song about brooms. As the teacher hummed and students nodded, only we (the researchers) were not informed that the lessons of a very ancient and powerful song were being transmitted to students.

While sitting in class one afternoon, Baba Douglas, a teacher at NDC lightheartedly responded to a student who was misbehaving in his class by saying, "If Yaa doesn't stop whining, he will receive the Dagomba treatment!" The students chuckled but we were completely lost. We asked Baba Douglas what it meant, but he only responded by saying it was an "inside joke." During the summer cultural experience, however, we learned the Akan have a proverb, "*Asem a ehia Akanfoo no na Ntafoo de goro brekete*," which translates to "A matter which troubles the Akan people, the people of Gonja take to play the brekete drum." After much decoding this is found to be a proverb that is used to tease the Dagomba people of the northern region to make them feel how important the Akans are. Baba Douglas has re-Africanized and become Akan although he was born an African American from Detroit, Michigan. He taught his students the popular proverb, showed them a video that demonstrated how this "teasing" occurs, and created a culturally relevant "inside joke" that is full of cultural cues and language that is only decodable by investigating the African cultural ethos. Baba Douglas was saying that Yaa was going to be teased by his peers if he did not stop whining.

We saw Mamas (the female teachers) carrying babies on their hips while teaching class. As one infant demands a Mama's attention she also teaches social studies to a group of students. When we first observed the practice of Mamas teaching while holding babies, we were confused about why the infants did not have babysitters. We thought having babies in the classroom was a distraction to everyone. The cultural lens we were using did not allow us to understand that Mamas and Babas are constantly teaching lessons about the importance of family and taking care of the young. Their practice is to demonstrate the notion that the children must be cared for, that they must always be at the center of attention. As we submersed ourselves into the culture through the summer experience and other rituals, we begin to understand Makia's proclamation that, "In Western societies, children are treated as if they are a burden, but in African societies they and the elders are the very focus of our concern."

Seeing these institutions through an African cultural lens is a requisite for understanding practice with the schools. Our initial observations were skewed by our cultural lens. Though we thought we were competent and able, we were in fact, culturally illiterate to understand the context of interactions between students and teachers. We were confused about how these schools were any different from most public schools, and even though we were informed on

Africentric ideology, we were confused about how African cultural philosophy permeated the entire educational experience within the schools.

After participating in the cultural experiences for four years, we found ourselves "culturally literate" enough to understand the essence of Africentric schools. For example, a student named "Kwabena" at BC misbehaved by calling another student a negative name, the teacher stopped and said, "Kwabena, do we want unity in here or disunity?" The student replied, "Unity!" The teacher then said, "Well then, call her a name that shows we want unity and not disunity then." The student then apologized and said that the other student "looked nice" today. The teacher followed up with the whole class saying, "Brothers and sisters look at me, whenever you say something to another brother or sister, make sure you are saying something that promotes umoja, okay?" The students agreed and then the teacher called out "What does umoja mean?" The students said very loudly, in unison, and in cadence, "Umoja means unity!" Our interpretation of events such as this one became more than our initial Western idea of the "importance of unity for unity's sake." Instead, "unity" in the African cultural sense (e.g., Akan vs. Dagomba: the unity of our group as we 'tease' another group because we are larger and have a longer history), as well as *"Praye wo ho ye,"* means that the broom bristles as a metaphor of our need to stick together to get the community's hard work done. African-centered education leaders lead the effort to use these and other African cultural understandings to inform the education of children in Africentric schools.

The use of African value systems such as Nguzo Saba and Maat also guide teachers and administrators in their interactions with one another. Meetings begin with African-derived spiritual sayings that speak to the mindset that is necessary in order for a meeting to be successful. Principal Baba Kojo begins the Ndundu (executive body meeting) meeting at CIBI with the Swahili reminder that, "I am because we are, and we are therefore I am. . . ." This ancient Swahili saying reminds participants to focus on the communal goals and purposes of the gathering, not individual political goals and/or purposes. Disagreements are handled by first reminding participants of the cardinal virtues of Maat. Participants share that they often think of Maat and/or Nguzo Saba while in relations with others.

Participants personally operationalize Maat, Nguzo Saba and a host of other axiological systems. The principal of ACDS, Mama Binta, encouraged two who were in disagreement at the Ndundu that "Maat reminds us that we must have order here. . . ." The axiological systems help to maintain togetherness and unity by encouraging people to "police themselves." Deep knowledge of the value systems, the cultural ethos from which they are derived, and an ability to practically use such cultural knowledge is a necessity for adult members in the community.

Culture is the central ingredient used by Africentric educators in their attempts to work with black children. In the past, school leaders adopted certain general aspects of African culture. That is, they borrowed from the best of what African cultural groups, such as Swahili or Xhosa have to offer. An example of this borrowing is the use of the Nguzo Saba—the language of the Nguzo Saba derives from the East African Kiswahili people. While African-centered leaders are becoming more entrenched in specific African cultural practices, these specificities are not "used" in the schools; instead, they use these cultural forms to inform the direction of the school. Baba Kojo explained how this effort to re-Africanize was operationalized in the development of his school:

Makia (Baba Kojo's wife) studied with a guy named Zulu in New York. He had been organizing since the 50's to establish traditional culture, he had the oldest traditional dance group in the country—using Yoruba in Nigeria. He had a branch in New York. She (Makia) had gone to some of his programs in the city and was impressed with his work here and abroad. This is how Yoruba became the cultural theme of the school. We don't advertise that Yoruba is the cultural theme of the school; Yoruba informs the cultural direction of the school—we don't try to sell that to parents, etc. Our principal motivating factor was the establishment of families. Because, you know, we actually thought about opening things like restaurants, clothing stores. We had organic gardening. We purchased the land in North Carolina, originally to grow crops and farm, etc. Through Makia, Zulu helped us with, you know, some of the cultural issues.

We found that when Africentric educationists speak of using African culture to inform the direction of their institutions, they mean that African epistemology and axiology contain the guiding principles for family, community, and school functioning, and they use the culture as a guide to restore their communities. For example, some school leaders within APS and ACDS draw from Akan tradition, namely the Onyame paradigm or "God's order," and represented within that tradition are practices that we saw within the schools that actually had come from the Akan people of Africa.

Within schools, we noticed some students briefly bowing and/or saluting to certain school leaders. For example, the student might begin to pass Baba Kojo in the hallways and then shake Baba Kojo's hand while doing a quick knee bow. Our first inclination was that the students were too enamored of the community popularity of Baba Kojo and other leaders. Later, we found that both brief bowing and saluting are part of certain African groups' cultural norms. For example with the Akan, when a younger female greets an older person, she places her hands middrift with palms up, slightly bows and offers the greeting "Mi Pawochaw Ete Sen?" which translates to "Person of respect, how are you?" Males who are younger "salute" the older person and offer the same greeting.

African-centered teachers demand that students respect elders. An older adult male visitor walked into the multipurpose room at ACDS and the children continued to chat with one another. Mama Binta looked at the children in dismay and said loudly, "Children! Did you not see Baba Oba walk into this room?" They all stopped and said in unison, "Habari Gani Baba Oba?" (Greetings, what's the news Baba Oba)?

African-centered leaders view academic achievement through a cultural lens. Whereas conventional ideas of academic achievement relate to performance on tests or other measures, Africentric leaders believe that when black children are re-Africanized, they have achieved. Furthermore, they believe that the children can achieve anything they wish to (including meeting conventional and mainstream standards) once they are culturally grounded. While visiting schools with Africentric leadership, one is constantly reminded of the different cultural frame of reference used by these leaders. From the meaning of the phrase "academic achievement" to determining what is seen as "bad behavior," once one decodes, the differences in cultural frames of reference between mainstream public institutions and culturally centered/Africentric institutions are striking. As we witnessed the young children sing "happy birthday" in Swahili to their classmate, the assumption was that they were simply recognizing yet another year of life of that member. But later we learned that birthday recognitions allowed a time to speak to the birthday child about ways that they have and have not been a good citizen within the community throughout the year. At ACDS we saw the students sing happy birthday to Aja, who turned six years old. After the song, students such as Kwame spoke to her about herself saying, "I remember when Aja wouldn't let me play with the ball outside because she was playing with her brother." The teacher said, "Okay Aja, and sometimes you really don't like to let people play when you're playing with your brother. What can you do differently?" Aja said, "I can let them play too." For the purpose of balance, the teacher turned back to Kwame and said, "What else can you say about Aja?" Kwame said, "Aja let me use her coloring book." After the birthday session ended, the teacher summarized things that Aja needs to work on and also reiterated the praise that students offered. The teacher explained to us that this is an African cultural practice that encourages meaningful dialogue and critical feedback among community members. She said, "Doing this *is* achievement for a group of students who don't know who they are [emphasis hers]. They are learning to think and be critical at age four instead of age twenty-four. If they can do this, they can definitely analyze the story problems they get on the [standardized] test." School leaders work tirelessly with parents and other caretakers and community members trying to help them understand the importance of studying and understanding how African cultural ethos is a first step for creating a better and more African-centered community.

Nation Building: The Family and Community Connection

Mama Binta explained to us that Africentric leaders believe educating black children is less about "the three R's" and more about building community. She clarified that

> Organizing life for our families consists of a person deciding to organize his or her own family first. Once the families are organized, you have a clan. The coming together of organized clans makes a nation. A group of functioning families within a unified nation solves the problem of African dependency, dysfunction and cultural disorientation. We believe the problems being faced by Black children in most public schools can be resolved primarily by building families, clans and eventually nations. This is not easy stuff, but there's no short cut for doing the work that's necessary.

Africentric education leaders lead the community toward re-Africanization and nation building by hosting many programs that invite members of the surrounding communities into the schools for functions including conferences on identity awareness, movie nights, and talent shows. During the past several years, attendance at the Identity Awareness Conference, which is held at APS, has grown from fifteen attendees in its early years (1998 through 2000) to 100 attendees in 2006 and 132 attendees in 2007. In 2004 the conference drew participants from other countries for the first time. When the school hosts its monthly movie night members from the surrounding community (including parents) attend. When the movie ends, the principal, Baba Kojo, leads discussions on how subjects related to the movie impact the local community.

After watching *The Joe Clark Story*, parents and other community members asked questions and made comments to school leaders. During the discussions, Duane (an APS parent) asked, "Baba Kojo, you know my other son attends [a public school in Maryland]. Why do you think the public schools can't teach our children anything?" Baba Kojo replied, "The answer to that question is in the question itself. If the school was *yours*, your son would be getting educated, right?" Duane continued, "I see. But what are we supposed to do? [My ex-wife] can't afford to put him in a private school, and there aren't any charter schools in Maryland." Baba Kojo replied, "You'll have to educate him yourself." Many of the parents and community members passionately and desperately asked questions about what to do regarding what they believe are failed public schools. The response from Africentric education leaders is to own and control the schools if you intend to see your children get educated.

The leaders of these schools meet periodically to discuss important issues that are relevant to educating their communities. In response to the overwhelming community concerns, leaders from the schools host an annual week-long leadership academy during the summer for young adults in the community. As researcher/participants in the week-long academy in 2002, 2003, 2004, and 2005, we learned much from these leaders about the relationship between nation building and African-centered education. During the academy these principals and other school leaders become "elders." It is striking how they transition from "principals/bureaucrats" (Lomotey, 1993) to "community elders" who hold immense cultural knowledge and have many practical solutions to community disenfranchisement.

The academy features cultural information including the latest findings on learning styles of the children in their schools and other cultural information that is helpful to their constituency. One aspect of the academy that participants find especially helpful is the relationship forums. Baba San explained that "Education begins in the home, and if the home is dysfunctional your children will be also. Education is not separate and apart from family life." Married couples (many of whom send their children to the schools) attend sessions with the school leaders who have been married for at least twenty years. Singles attend gender-specific sessions and discuss the challenges of their dating lives. School leaders offer their years of experience and counsel to the young adults. The leaders believe that the communities from whence participants come are challenged by what Baba Kojo believes is an "unnecessary dependency upon outsiders and a lack of the basic skills needed to operate a community." Baba Kojo says it is a "lack of sovereignty and learned co-dependency." Mama Binta agrees with Baba Kojo, saying that the community "can be dysfunctional in that people spend so much money on things they want and then are disappointed when they don't have the resources to get what they need." Since they believe that the community is, in many ways, dysfunctional, the school leaders have developed a portion of the academy called *life skills*. Life skills features hands-on opportunities for participants to learn skills such as fixing home appliances, understanding electrical wiring, water supplying, tree trimming, understanding herbs, developing herbal medicines, and understanding the ways animals work in the ecological environment. The academy brochure states that such skills are "essential for nation building, and our children's future depends on it."

Many of the participants take the life skills learned in the academy and develop small businesses that are focused on those skills. The administrator of the life skills department, Mama Yaa (who is also the business manager at APS), explains that, "[participants] are required to develop a small business of any sort [because] the community needs to become interdependent and not so dependent on outsiders." One of the participants developed a tree trimming and pruning business. He and his wife travel to area homes to prune and trim trees and cut grass. Other participants have initiated technology-related businesses, home repair, African dance lessons, professional massage services, and one participant is even attempting to initiate a charter airline that would transport people to different Africentric conferences and other events around the United States. When participants return to the academy each year they are required to report the progress of their small businesses to the leaders. A requirement of all small businesses is that they be culturally relevant to the community.

Africentric education leaders believe that schools should operate as community centers that focus on the totality of the needs that are present within the community. Furthermore, they believe that educating our children in isolation from the needs and interests of the community is backward. Instead, education is a whole-community effort that requires returning to being who we were before being interrupted by outsiders and turning our back on our own culture. Community members attempt to use what they learn about nation building and re-Africanization in their own lives. Networks of African cultural practitioners have been created that seem to cross all of the boundaries within the community. The Africentric leader at BC brought in experts who focused on re-Africanization into the school. He also organized a group of teachers and community members from Boston who traveled to Washington, D.C., for the Identity Awareness Conference. He reported that "the community really supports what we are doing at the school. We need more support from within the school, but we now have an organization that people can join and we're trying to help each other implement what we have learned at the conferences. Most of them didn't know anything about re-Africanization but now they feel like they have something to strive for." Our interactions and involvement with community members in Boston and D.C. indicate that when the people understand the purposes and importance of re-Africanization, they support it and wish to use the inherent principles for their own families.

At the summer leadership academy and during the Identity Awareness Conference Baba Kojo explained that, "the first institution is the family and each of us has the ability and responsibility to develop the first institution before establishing other [institutions]." This statement is constantly reiterated by all of the Africentric education leaders within these academies and conferences. Conference attendees (most of whom have no children within Africentric schools), struggle to understand why there is so much emphasis on family development. One attendee stated, "Why is there so much talk about me having a family? What if I don't want a family but I want to start a school that can help our children?" A principal from an African-centered school in D.C., Mama Kenya, answered saying, "Use your own children as the starting grounds for any school you may choose to start." By the end of the conference, participants begin to understand what Baba San, leader of an African-centered school in St. Louis, Missouri, said in summary: "Family building and righteous living go together. There is no revolution for us to engage in that doesn't start in the home. The ruin of a nation begins in the homes of its people and our homes are in bad shape. When we act righteously we build family and when we build conscious and focused families, we are, in fact nation building." These leaders clarify that for black children, true education is only possible when there is an appropriate focus on the black community's need for nation building and re-Africanization.

Implications

While mainstream efforts appear focused on improving black students' academic prowess, leaders of Africentric schools seek to promote academic success within an African cultural context. The main goal of Africentric education is to reconnect, confirm, and reaffirm students' cultural and communal identities and empower them to transform society by offering them a meaningful and relevant education that prepares them to act as change agents who are concerned about the uplift of their own community. Africentric leaders believe that focusing on the academic problems of black students gets at the symptoms of larger problems (lack of nation building and cultural disorientation) instead of focusing on the problems themselves.

Africentric education leaders are clarifying that if somehow black children begin to perform better in school and on standardized tests, they will still face the larger and more devastating problems of the disillusionment of their families and communities. The question they raise is: What good does it do to improve the academic standing of black students if their families and communities are unable to be sustained? Their work focuses on finding effective ways to ensure that students are taught to build families and communities. Once families and communities are rebuilt, symptoms such as academic failure will be easily resolved because those families and communities will be able to create a relevant education for the youth therein. A critical part of the nation building effort includes helping people of African descent to realize that they have the ability and entitlement to create an education that is relevant for their children. The nation building effort that is led by Africentric school leaders provides an opportunity for people of African descent to take control over their own lives and institutions and to meet their own goal of bringing a stop to rampant dependency on outside forces for their most basic necessities.

Perhaps the most important aspect of what Africentric leaders are attempting to do is to re-Africanize children of African descent. Re-Africanization includes becoming familiar with and even practicing some of the customs, beliefs, and practices of African cultural groups. By re-Africanizing, blacks' ideological confusion via what Du Bois (1903) calls "double consciousness" is addressed, even resolved. When ideological confusion is resolved via African cultural adoption, blacks' children are educated, as opposed to being miseducated away from their own community's needs and interests.

One of the challenges of re-Africanization is the fact that educing culture and values from African societies is more a political than a cultural necessity. Although the practice of searching traditional African culture for answers to modern challenges faced by people in the African diaspora is both political and cultural, the essence of doing so is more a political answer to European hegemony and miseducation. The practice is more political than cultural because African culture has not been "intentionally" developed, in the sense that Africans did not purposely develop, for example, Bantu culture. Bantu culture came about as a result of the daily needs and interactions among (Bantu) people. These Africentric leaders are challenged by their own desire to be traditional African in a modern context, yet responsive to European hegemony, and at the same time naturally emergent and action-oriented as opposed to reactionary.

The response to European hegemony has mandated the necessity of a political stance, using aspects of African culture as a guide but also as a weapon against European imperialism. The political element, which is reactionary, raises the question of whether or not cultural adoption is as authentic as it needs to be to ensure usability and survivability. The lingering question remains: Can a politically charged cultural adoption process, and all of the issues within such a process, wield the changes necessary to advance toward nation building? Africentric education leaders believe that successful re-Africanization is the only answer to the troubles within black communities.

Conclusions

African and culturally centered schools are pioneering new and different possibilities for children who struggle greatly in the U.S. educational system. While they continue struggling to create a comprehensive curriculum that can address the myriad problems created by miseducation, teachers and administrators dedicate many hours to supplementing the traditional curriculum with culturally enriching information and practices. Also, these institutions serve the sociocultural needs of the community and are creating programs and initiating projects designed to increase communal responsibility and reestablish a sense of high morality and values within the community. No other efforts exist that are specifically designed to educate, inspire, and re-Africanize children of African descent. While some would argue against such efforts, it is unarguable that black communities are in a state of emergency. For example, Ladson-Billings (1994) reports that

> Nearly one out of two African American children is poor. The rate of infant mortality among African Americans is twice that of Whites. African American children are five times as likely as White children to be dependent on welfare and to become pregnant as teens; they are four times as likely to live with neither parent, three times as likely to live in a female-headed household, and twice as likely to live in substandard housing. More young African American men are under the control of the criminal justice system than in college (p. 2).

Those startling statistics and information indicate that black children and communities need immediate intervention. Black educators and researchers have been incessantly calling for relevant education for black children (Akoto, 1992; Akoto & Akoto, 1999; Anwisye, 2006; Lee, 1992; Hale-Benson, 1982; Ladson-Billings, 1995, 2002; Lomotey, 1978, 1993; Madhubuti, 1973; Murrell, 2002; Murtadha & Watts, 2005; Shujaa, 1994; Tillman, 2006; Woodson, 1933). While they have made these calls, they have been largely ignored as less confrontational approaches have been applied (such as multiculturalism), but for centuries the more socially acceptable approaches have proven to have little benefit for black children. The findings of this study suggest that because of the comprehensive and community-based approach, more efforts to support African-centered education could lead to improved educational experiences for black children and subsequently improved conditions within black communities. It is crucial that education researchers begin to support the work of African-centered educationists as the problems being faced by black children are beginning to have a devastating effect on the American ecology.

References

Afrik, H. T. (1981). *Institutional development: The need for Black educational models, and is community control of schools still alive?* Chicago, IL: Black Spear Press.

Akbar, N. (1992). *Chains and images of psychological slavery.* Jersey City, NJ: New Mind Productions.

Akoto, K. A. (1992). *Nationbuilding: Theory and practice in Afrikan centered education.* Washington, DC: Pan Afrikan World Institute.

Akoto, K. A. & A. N. (1999). *The Sankofa movement.* Washington, DC: Okoyo Infocom.

Akoto, K. A. & A. N. (2007). Marroonage: Issues in building and sustaining independent community, *Sankofa Pan African Journal of Nationbuilding & ReAfricanization (1)* 07, 5–17.

Anderson, C. (2001). *Powernomics.* Bethesda, MD: Powernomics Corp.

Ani, M. (1994). *Yurugu.* Trenton, NJ: Africa World Press.

Anwisye (2006). "Comfort now or freedom later." Sankofa Pan African Journal of Nationbuilding and ReAfricanization., 22.

Appiah, K. A. (1993). Europe upside down: The fallacies of Afrocentricity. *Sapina Journal*, 5(3).

Asante, M. K. (2000). *The Egyptian philosophers: Ancient African voices from Imhotep to Akhenaten* Philadelphia, PA: Molefi Asante.

Asante, M. K. (1998). *The Afrocentric idea*. Philadelphia, PA: Temple University Press.

Asante, M. K. (1991). Afrocentrism: A valid frame of reference. *Journal of Black Studies (25)* 2, 170–190.

Asante, M. K. (1990). *Kemet, Afrocentricity and knowledge*. Trenton, NJ: African World Press.

Asante, M. K. (1988). *The Afrocentric idea*. Philadelphia, PA: Temple University Press.

Asante, M. K. (2007). *The history of Africa*. London: Routledge.

ben Jochannan (1972). *The black man of the Nile and his family*. Oakland, CA: Alkebulan Books.

Bernal, M. (1987). *Black Athena: Afroasiatic roots of classical civilization: The fabrication of ancient Greece, 1785–1985, Volume 1*. Rutgers, NJ: Rutgers University Press.

Brookins, C. C. (1984). *A descriptive analysis of ten independent Black educational models*. Unpublished master's thesis, Michigan State University, Ann Arbor, MI.

Browder, A. (1992). *Nile Valley contributions to civilization*. Washington, DC: IKG.

Clarke, J. H. (1991) *Africans at the crossroads: Notes for an African world revolution*. Trenton, NJ: Africa World Press.

Delpit, L. (2001). *Other people's children*. New York: The New Press.

Department of Education Office of Civil Rights (2002). Retrieved From http://nces.ed.gov/pubsearch/index.asp Retrieved 3/3/07.

Diop, C. A. (1987). *Black Africa: The economic and cultural basis for a federated state*. Trenton, NJ: Africa World Press.

Doughty, J. J. (1973). *A historical analysis of Black education-focusing on the contemporary independent Black school movement*. Unpublished doctoral dissertation, Ohio State University, Columbus.

DuBois, W.E.B. (1999 reprint). *The souls of Black folk*. New York: Norton.

Early, G. (1991). Understanding Afrocentrism. *Civilization* (magazine of the Library of Congress), pp. 31–39.

Hale-Benson, J. (1982). *Black Children: Their roots, culture, and learning styles*. Baltimore, MD and London: Johns Hopkins University Press.

Hilliard, A. (1992). Behavioral style, culture, and teaching and learning. *Journal of Negro Education, 61*(3), 370–377.

Hilliard, A. (1996). *The Maroon within us: Selected essays on African American community socialization*. Black Classic Press.

Hilliard, A. (1997). *SBA: Reawakening of the African mind*. Gainesville, FL: Makare.

Hilliard, A. (1991). Do we have the will to educate all children? *Educational Leadership (49)*, 31–36.

Hilliard, A. (2002). *African power: Affirming African indigenous socialization in the face of culture wars*. Gainesville, FL: Makare.

Hilliard, A. (2003). No mystery: Closing the achievement gap. In T. Perry, C. Steele & A. Hilliard (Eds.) *Young, gifted and Black: Promoting high achievement among African American students* (pp. 131–165). Boston: Beacon.

Howe, S. (1998). *Afrocentrism*. Oxford: Oxford University Press.

James, G. G. M. (1954). *Stolen legacy*. Chicago: African American Images.

Kambon, K. (1992). *The African personality in America: An African-centered framework*. Tallahassee, FL: Nubian Nation Publications.

Karenga, M. (1980). *Kwanzaa: Origin, concepts, practice*. Los Angeles: Kawaida Groundwork Committee.

Karenga, M. and Carruthers, J. H. (Eds.). (1986). *Kemet and the African worldview: Research, rescue and restoration*. Los Angeles, CA: University of Sankore Press.

King, J. (2005). (Ed.). *Black education: A transformative research and action agenda for the new century*. Washington, DC: American Educational Research Association.

Ladson-Billings (1994). *Dreamkeepers: Successful teachers of African American children*. San Francisco: Jossey-Bass.

Ladson-Billings (1995). Toward a theory of culturally relevant pedagogy. *American Educational Research Journal (32)* 3, 465–491.

Ladson-Billings, G. (2002). Fighting for our lives: Preparing teachers to teach African American students. *Journal of Teacher Education (51)* 3, 206–214.

Lee, C. D. (1992). Profile of an independent Black institution: African-centered education at work. *Journal of Negro Education, 61* (2), 160–177.

Lefkowitz, M. (1996). *Not out of Africa*. New York: Basic Books.

Lomotey, K. (1993). African-American principals: Bureaucrat/administrators and ethno-humanists. *Journal of Urban Education (27)* 395–412.

Lomotey, K. (1992). Independent Black institutions: African-centered education models. *Journal of Negro Education, 61*, 455–462.

Lomotey, K. (1978). Alternative educational institutions: Concentration on independent Black educational institutions. Unpublished master's thesis, Cleveland State University, Cleveland, OH.

Madhubuti, H. (1973). From plan to planet: The need for Afrikan minds and institutions. Chicago, IL: Third World Press.

Murrell, P. C. (2002). *African-centered pedagogy: Developing schools of achievement for African American children.* New York: State University of New York Press.

Murtadha, K. and Watts, D. (2005). Linking the struggle for education and social justice: Historical perspectives of African American leadership in schools. *Educational Administration Quarterly* (41)4.

National Center for Education Statistics (2004). *The digest of education statistics.* Retrieved [2/15/06] from www.nces.ed.gov/programs/digest.

Nobles, W. (1986). *African psychology: Toward its reclamation, re-ascension and revitalization.* Oakland, CA: Institute for the Advanced Study of Black Family Life & Culture.

Obenga, T. (1986). *African philosophy during the period of the pharaohs, 2780-330 bce.* Per Ankh.

Podair, J. (2002). *The Strike That Changed New York: Blacks, Whites, and the Ocean Hill-Brownsville Crisis.* New Haven: Yale University Press.

Ratteray, J. D. and Shujaa, M. J. (1987). *Dare to choose: Parental choice at independent neighborhood schools.* Washington, DC: U.S. Department of Education.

Richards, D. (1989). *Let the circle be unbroken.* New York: DA Publishers.

Ridley, J. A. (1971). *The independent Black (educational) institution: An exploratory study with implications for the institutionalization of American schools.* Unpublished doctoral dissertation, University of Michigan, Flint.

Satterwhite, F. J. (Ed.) (1971). *Planning an independent Black educational institution.* New York: Afram Associates.

Schlesinger, A. (1992). *The disuniting of America.* New York: Norton.

Shockley. K. (2007). Literatures and definitions: Toward understanding African centered education. *Journal of Negro Education.*

Shujaa, M. J. (Ed.) (1994). *Too much schooling too little education: A paradox of Black life in White societies.* Trenton, NJ: Africa World Press.

Shujaa, M. J. (1993). Education and Schooling: You can have one without the other. *Urban Education, 27* (4), 328–351.

Spradley, J. P. (1980). *Participant observation.* New York: Holt, Rinehart and Winston.

Stake, R. E. (2000). Case studies. In N. K. Denzin and Y. S. Lincoln (Eds.) *Handbook of qualitative research* (2nd ed.). Thousand Oaks: Sage.

Tedlock, B. (2000). Ethnography and ethnographic representation. *The handbook of qualitative research.* (2nd ed.). Thousand Oaks, CA: Sage Publications, Inc.

Theoharis, G. (2007). Social justice educational leaders and resistance: Toward a theory of social justice leadership. *Educational Administration Quarterly,* 43(2), 221–258.

Tillman, L. (2006). Researching and writing from an African American perspective: Reflective notes on three research studies, *International Journal of Qualitative Studies in Education, 19*(3), 265–287.

Williams, C. (1987). *The destruction of Black civilization.* Chicago, IL: Third World Press).

Woodson, C. G. (1933). *Mis-education of the Negro.* Washington, DC: Associated Publishers.

Thirty

Administration, Leadership, and Diversity
Reproduction or Transformation?

Carolyn M. Shields

> I hate indifference. Living means taking sides. Indifference means weakness, cowardice, a parasitical attitude. It doesn't belong to life. . . . Indifference is the dead weight of history. . . . It is a lead weight for those with new ideas, a ballast within which the most beautiful enthusiasms can drown, a swamp that defends the old order far better than any warriors or strong defences. . . (Gramsci, in Gonzales, 2003, p. 493)

As one thinks about educational leadership in diverse settings, it is likely that what comes to mind are images of people from different ethnic, cultural, and social backgrounds coming together in one school community. They speak different languages at home, worship differently, have different kinds of abilities and disabilities; they come in different shapes, sizes, and sexual orientations—and have multiple attitudes, practices, preferences, and ideological orientations. Much has been written in recent years about how many of these differences are associated with what has become known as a persistent "achievement gap"—inequities and differences in academic outcomes related to differences in high school completion or drop-outs, to differential school achievement and college attendance, and to life's disparate opportunities and social inequities beyond school.

Here, it is not my purpose to replicate what others have written about the need for educators to attend to issues of race, class, ethnicity, sexual orientation, home language, religious differences, and so forth, because these topics have been extensively addressed. Instead my purpose is to explore ways in which educational leaders may work to transform rather than simply perpetuate and reproduce the current inequities. In the next few paragraphs, however, by way of background, I provide a cursory overview of some of the statistics that argue the need both for transformative leadership and dramatic change.

Recent data indicate, for example, that in the United States, Asian and white students outperform their African American, Native American, and Latino counterparts on almost every academic measure (see for example, Education Trust, 2008; and Figure 30.1). These achievement data correspond in large measure to the poverty statistics gathered through the U.S. Census Bureau. In 2006, for example, 17.4% of the population was found to live in poverty (U.S. Census, 2007) including 10% of the white population, 33% of blacks, and 27% of Hispanics under the age of 18. In 1995, ethnic differences, not surprisingly, were reflected in differences in the graduation rates of 25- to 29-year-olds with a bachelor degree or higher: whites 31%, blacks 18%, and Hispanics 16% (NCES, 1996). Other data tell us that gay and lesbian youth are at greater risk for school failure than heterosexual children: "Academic failure, lack of student involvement and low commitment to school are profound for gay and lesbian youth because schools are neither safe, healthy nor productive places for them to learn" (USDH, 1989). Some estimate the drop-out rate for these students to be as high as 28% (Remafedi, 1987).

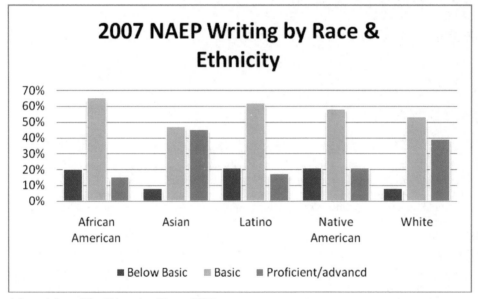

Adapted from The Education Trust, 2008.

To address these differences, educational leaders have been bombarded by the myriad of packaged programs, professional development workshops, and legislative mandates, many of which, in the United States, are associated with the legislation commonly known as No Child Left Behind (NCLB, 2002). The Title I provisions of NCLB offer such programs as Reading First, Early Reading First, and Even Start to address literacy gaps. The phenomenon is not new, however. In 1995, Woods listed twelve different programs including: ways to address school drop-outs including cross-age tutoring through the Coca-Cola Valued Youth Program; targeting neighborhood drop-outs through the Alternative Schools Network in Chicago; or Project Coffee in Oxford, Massachusetts, which offers "comprehensive vocational instruction, integration of academics and occupational training, counseling, job training and work experience, and a school-business and industry partnership."

In this chapter I argue that none of these interventions, no matter how well intentioned, has the potential to do more than perpetuate and reproduce inequities in the status quo. Moreover, I argue that if education is to be more than a mechanism for sorting and selecting students, educators will have to understand their roles as transformative and not as reproductive leaders. They will have to "take sides"—as Gramsci—states in order to lead with courage to overcome the indifference that weighs us down. My starting assumption is that diversity is the norm in educational organizations throughout the world and perhaps particularly so in developed countries such as the United States, Canada, or Britain. A concomitant assumption is that diversity per se is not a problem but, in fact, contributes to the rich fabric of daily life. Nevertheless, disparity and inequity that are often associated with diversity are not only problematic, they must be addressed by school administrators and leaders who want to lead with integrity and justice for the benefit of all students and of society as a whole.

To develop this argument, I advance a theoretical position, because I believe that educational administration and leadership as a field has been remiss in its use of theory and because I am convinced that theory has both explanatory and promissory potential. Throughout, I illustrate the theoretical concepts by using excerpts from a study in which I interviewed educators from minoritized and disadvantaged backgrounds.[1]

In large part, the field of educational administration and leadership has taken up concepts such as culturally relevant pedagogy, or professional learning communities, used them almost as mantras for effective change, without really exploring or understanding their theoretical precepts and grounding. Here, I use Bourdieu's sociological explanations of fields, habitus, cultural capital, and symbolic violence as lenses through which to examine how leadership can serve a reproductive function. Then, drawing on literature related to transformative leadership (Foster, 1986; Quantz, Rogers, & Dantley, 1991; Shields, 2009; Weiner, 2003), I offer an alternative model for leading in diversity—one that will help us to "take sides" and assist in the advancement of "beautiful new ideas." I argue that transformative leadership permits us to challenge and overcome reproduction of inequities in the status quo in that it begins with questions of justice and democracy; it critiques inequitable practices and offers the promise not only of greater individual achievement but of a better life lived in common with others.

Understanding Reproduction

There is little doubt that our education system is not only diverse, it is also both stratified and fragmented in that children and youth do not have equal opportunities for positive educational outcomes. Their experiences, access to programs, and subsequent outcomes and life chances depend largely on their family backgrounds—their economic, ethnic, linguistic, religious, and geographical locations as well as a myriad of other markers including sex and sexual orientation, ability, and disability. Arguably, a major problem with the current situation is that children are treated as widgets or fungible items, each experiencing education in the same way, studying from a common curriculum, and demonstrating learning on the same standardized test. Despite the remarkable differences in backgrounds, beliefs, and practices that students bring to school, in the political contexts of today's North American schools, students are too often expected to conform to the implicit rules and values of schooling in order to pass the required tests that legitimate the actions of teachers and their own school achievements. The problem, however, is that although some students succeed very well, others do not. There is a need for educational leaders to think about how to lead educational organizations in ways that do not attempt to homogenize students but that permit all to achieve to high standards in both academic and intellectual development and in their understandings of their collective responsibilities as democratic citizens.

Power Relations

In this section, I focus on Bourdieu's theoretical constructs that help us to understand—perhaps in new ways—how, instead of being agents of transformation, change, and social mobility, schools are too often instruments of reproduction. This approach permits us to overcome the negativity of so many of our current explanations that either locate the blame and responsibility for school failure in children and families themselves, in teachers and the quality of their preparation, or in a lack of alignment of the curriculum and assessment strategies. Bourdieu's analysis takes us away from a posture of blame and helps to understand a system that persistently but unconsciously legitimizes the privileging of certain groups of children and the marginalizing of others. It helps us to perceive the interconnections between reproduction of the status quo and the inability of current education systems to be an agent of change and social mobility in our society. Here, the intent is to move beyond blame to understanding that has the potential to lead to collective action and transformative leadership.

Bourdieu would have us accept that "power is not a separate domain of study but stands at the heart of all social life" (Swartz, 1997, p. 6). From this belief, it becomes important to analyze how power relations infuse all of Bourdieu's sociological analyses and how various constructs such as fields, habitus, and culture are, in reality, expressions of political content. Bourdieu argues that each field (education, politics, the arts, the church, etc.) has developed its own forms of legitimacy that are related, in complex ways, to other intersecting and overlapping fields that comprise the nation itself. For Bourdieu, fields are "sites of struggle," "sites of resistance as well as of domination," but rarely, according to Swartz (1997), "sites of social transformation" (p. 121). Within each field, Bourdieu and Passeron explain,

> Because they correspond to the material and symbolic interests of groups or classes differentially situated within the power relations, these pedagogic actions always tend to reproduce the structure of the distribution of cultural capital among these groups or classes, thereby contributing to the reproduction of social structure. (1990, p. 11)

Within each field, the struggle is enjoined in large part because of the habitus that has developed over long periods of time. Habitus, Bourdieu explains, develops as a result of the beliefs and attitudes of those who hold power and serves to structure all of the actions that are perceived as acceptable and "normal" within a given field. In somewhat convoluted language, he defines habitus as

> a system of durable, transposable dispositions, structured structures predisposed to function as structuring structures, that is, as principles which generate and organize practices and representations that can be objectively adapted to their outcomes without presupposing a conscious aiming at ends of an express mastery of the operations necessary in order to attain them. (Swartz, 1997, p. 101)

In education, as in the arts, the church, or even family life, there are enduring tendencies or dispositions that shape what are perceived to be acceptable actions—and even those dispositions are basically unconscious and unrecognized. Thus, the dominant dispositions and the consequent organizing principles have, over time, become recognized as legitimate authority. They have also gained authority to impose rules and procedures that are perceived as legitimate because of the implicit but arbitrary and hidden power that underlies the principles themselves. The implication is that educators are not often aware of how power operates to structure the field of education in ways that privilege some students and tend to marginalize others, thereby reproducing social inequity. Thus, if a student seems to break the implicit rules—by wearing a hijab, speaking a language other than English, having multiple body piercings—it is too easy for educators to assume that their unconventionality will also be associated with learning deficits.

Reproducing Failure

For Bourdieu, habitus explains how "schooling seems to assure the privileged of success and the less fortunate of failure" (Swartz, 1997, p. 207). This occurs, in large part, he explains, because different amounts of economic, social, and cultural capital constitute power resources that explain unequal academic achievement. Economic capital, Bourdieu says, "is immediately convertible into money"; social capital "made up of social obligations" is convertible, in certain conditions, into "economic capital" (2004, p. 16). It is, however, to differences in cultural capital that Bourdieu attributes "unequal scholastic achievement of children originating from the different social classes by relating academic success. . . to the distribution of cultural capital between classes and class fractions" (p. 17).

Cultural capital exists in three forms:

> An *embodied* state, i.e., in the form of long-lasting dispositions of the mind and body; in the *objectified* state, in the form of cultural goods (pictures, books, dictionaries, instruments, machines, etc.). . . and in the *institutionalized* state, a form of objectification which must be set apart because, as will be seen in the case of educational qualifications, it confers entirely original properties on the cultural capital which it is presumed to guarantee. (p. 17)

Capital develops first in the home, in its embodied form, as parents and caregivers engage in what Bourdieu calls "pedagogical work." It comprises schemes of appreciation and understanding that an individual develops through early socialization. Thus, simplistically, we can understand that because some children learn to speak in certain ways, to appreciate books and pictures, and to play musical instruments while others learn to cook or build shelves, to listen to different types of music, and to use language in different ways, these cultural differences will be manifested in their attitudes and behaviors when they go to school. Some come to school having already had opportunities to experiment with paints and crayons, for example, while others have not. Although this prior experience does not predispose a child to be a great artist, the cultural benefits they have received from their home experiences may lead teachers to believe they have more aptitude or even are "smarter" than their less advantaged classmates.

Thus, within each field, it is the capital of those in power that tends to be recognized and valued. This is the capital that sets the rules and creates the parameters for attitude and action. When children from other than dominant groups arrive in school, they tend to find themselves in situations in which their home cultures are misrecognized, not valued, and rarely respected or legitimized. This is the dissonance that leads Delpit (1990) to urge that educators must teach all students how to navigate the implicit norms of schooling. Especially important, she says, is making the implicit "rules explicit" for those who do not come from the "culture of power." Indeed, if we fail to do so, the resulting dissonance creates what Bourdieu calls "symbolic violence." He explains that

> A power to exert symbolic violence which manifests itself in the form of a right to impose legitimately, reinforces the arbitrary power which establishes it and which it conceals. (Bourdieu & Passeron, 1990, p. 13)

Doing Violence

In large part, the ways in which schooling is organized to legitimize some practices and marginalize others may be unconscious. Nevertheless, failure is still construed, not as a result of individual deficits or lack of motivation or effort but rather as a result of disparity in the kinds and amounts of capital that children from different social situations bring to school and in the ways in which different forms of capital are recognized and valued. As Bourdieu understands it, this disparity is not simply a gap between home and school—one that can be remediated by intensive tutoring or remediation but is to be perceived as symbolic violence done by the school on children from dominated subgroups. It is important to be explicit here that although symbolic violence may be invisible, it is no less real than physical violence.

Sometimes, however, the violence is not simply symbolic but material. Phoenix (n.d.) reports, for example, that "27% of gay and lesbian youth have been physically hurt by another student" and that "in Seattle, 34% of students who described themselves as gay, lesbian or bisexual reported being the target of anti-gay harassment or violence at school or on the way to or from school, compared to 6% of heterosexual students." The achievement gaps based on ethnicity result in some students and groups of students being considered less capable and often forced to engage in some form of remedial instruction and tutoring. They also create a situation in which large numbers of students from these groups are pushed out of school and in which, disproportionate numbers from these same groups end up in the criminal justice system. Herr and Anderson (2003) argue that violence occurs "when children are labeled in schools, when women are marginalized through various forms of sexism, or when unequal power relations are hidden through attempts to characterize them as natural" (p. 416).

In general, we do violence when we force students to negate their home cultures and to "act white" in order to succeed (Ogbu, 1992). We do violence when we condescendingly provide after-hours tutoring, giving children the message that they cannot learn enough during the regular school day but instead must put in extra hours to succeed. We do violence when we ask students to renounce (or at least repress) their home language, religious beliefs, and cultural practices and to adopt those of the dominant group—never asking, as Bourdieu indicates, how these dominant practices came to be legitimated in the first place.

In 1997, Wallerstein described this legitimation process as a "game of never-ending mirrors." He explained that we need to seek to discover the reality on the basis of which we have constructed reality and argued that when we find this reality, we must then seek to understand how this underlying reality has in turn been socially constructed (in Torres, 1998). Failure to engage in this kind of analysis permits schools to continue their reproduction function without ever considering the harm that is done to individuals, social groups, and society as a whole.[2] Torres (1998) therefore argues that

The challenge for educators, parents, students, and policymakers is to think critically about the failures of the past and about the myriad exclusionary practices that still pervade schooling—hence bringing to the forefront issues of power and domination, class, race, and gender. The validity of the notion of instrumental rationality guiding school reform should also be examined because it gives attention to administration, procedures, and efficiency as the prime criteria for change and progress and because it assumes that there is a common framework structuring the experience of all people. (p. 57)

Torres argues the need to question the rationality of school reform that takes as an unquestioned starting point available data about who is failing and who is succeeding—without ever asking why. These data, he argues, focus on individuals within a specific group or school without ever attending to the broader social inequities and material differences reflected in their lived experience. Rational forms of school reform focus on efficiency and effectiveness—finding ways to ensure that the school ranks well in published lists and league tables, and, certainly in the U.S. context, that it makes adequate yearly progress (AYP).[3]

Outcomes of Reproductive Leadership

This reproductive approach to leadership emphasizes meeting the requirements of NCLB, or its national equivalent elsewhere, and promotes an exclusionary culture of blame and fear. If it weren't for *that* group of students, newly arrived in the school's catchment area, the school would have continued to meet expectations. The attendant implication is that students from *that* group—either lower income, a specific ethnic group, or perhaps refugee and immigrant children—are not as capable as those from the dominant group. They are perceived to have learning deficits, and their culture is seen as deficient in that it impedes their school success; thus, they are treated as second class citizens.

The Failure of Multiculturalism

If the situation of these "failing students" is considered, it is generally in terms of how to address their deficiencies. What kinds of pedagogies, supports, after-school activities, or parental involvement programs could help them to overcome their disadvantages and promote school success? Even the well-intentioned adoption of multicultural programs and culturally relevant pedagogies may simply reproduce the status quo. Often this leads to sanitized multi-cultural fairs that provide superficial and temporary recognition of the food, fun, and fashion of some groups (always to the exclusion of others). Consider the shame of a student who brings samosas, lovingly prepared by his mother, only to hear students making rude comments and to find, at the end of the evening, that the dish has not been touched (see Sayani, 2002). Failure to consider how multiethnic students locate themselves in activities asking them to bring food from "their culture" or to step inside a circle if they are nonwhite (see Mohan, 2008) excludes as many students as it includes. And consider the impact of such activities on the white students, who, once again, may leave believing that they have no culture and no ethnicity (see Kincheloe & Steinberg, 1998; Roman, 1993) and thus that they do not contribute to any of the problems or challenges facing the school. Moreover, the promotion of what I have called elsewhere "a pathology of color-blindness" (Shields, 2003) permits all students to believe that because they all share characteristics as human beings, the differences in their material lived experiences make no difference to the ways in which they understand the world or to the ways in which the world of schooling constructs them. Yet, when Ruth Simmons, African American president of Brown University, tells us she is followed on a regular basis in department stores, or that taxi drivers refuse to serve her, instead locking their doors, it should be a wake-up call. When my own African American doctoral students state that they are still afraid to drive through certain communities within a seventy-mile radius of the university and that if they do, they ensure they have enough gas so they will not have to stop and endure the embarrassment of being refused service, we must begin to acknowledge that our own privileged location may have shielded us from experiences others encounter on a daily basis.

Pretending that equal access provides equity of opportunity and the possibility of equitable outcomes is simply another way of perpetuating social inequality. Pauline, a mixed-race black woman, talks about how her mother always told her to "focus on education, and it would get you where you wanted to go." Yet, she explained that her own experience as well as her parents' belied that statement. She explained that her father grew up in a community where education was "no ladder. You couldn't climb." The reproductive nature of her school system gave her the clear message: "You are at the bottom." Despite being told she only had the ability to be a "hair dresser or clean other people's houses or work in a restaurant," Pauline graduated from a university with a degree in political science and applied to teach in Africa. She explained that although the North American agency had accepted her, she was rejected during the subsequent interviews because "being black, it was not good to go to these countries and, with a background in politics, it was an absolute 'No, no,' because of the influence I would have on the women in the African countries." Her story reminds us of two separate truths. First, even though students from minoritized backgrounds sit in school classrooms, teachers often communicate their belief that the students are less capable than their white peers and should not strive for higher education. Then even if students overcome the barriers of deficit thinking and inappropriate streaming, they are still confronted by assumptions that restrict their career opportunities. These are some of the implicit but very real outcomes of a system that focuses on reproduction.

Leadership Is Political

Educational leaders of diverse institutions (and that means all of us) are faced with some difficult dilemmas. We are often appointed because we have been team players, because of our prior achievements and support for the system within which we work. At the same time, however, we are required to exercise leadership that not only promotes the school or organization but that facilitates the deep learning of all children. For that reason, it is incumbent on all educational leaders to understand how the invisible decisions about what is important and what counts as valid knowledge have come to be accepted as the only legitimate forms of knowledge to be transmitted and assessed in public schools. We must understand, as Herr and Anderson (2003) assert, that

> Just as Bourdieu's theory of symbolic violence involves many forms of capital and many sites of oppression that occur on multiple levels, altering relations of domination will require struggle on many fronts, including, both the critical pedagogical action of committed teachers who understand how symbolic violence operates, and large-scale political struggles. (p. 431)

One way of thinking about altering these relations of domination and violence in order to provide viable learning opportunities for all students is to understand leadership in terms of transformation and not reproduction.

Understanding Transformative Leadership

Leading for transformation takes seriously Freire's (1998) contention "that education is not the ultimate lever for social transformation, but without it transformation cannot occur" (p. 37). Transformative leadership begins with questions of justice and democracy; it critiques inequitable practices and offers the promise not only of greater individual achievement but of a better life lived in common with others. As Foster (1986) posits, leadership "must be critically educative; it can not only look at the conditions in which we live, but it must also decide how to change them" (p. 185). Transformative leadership, therefore, inextricably links education and educational leadership with the wider social context within which it is embedded.

In this section, I draw on a number of theorists who work in the area of transformative leadership, distinguishing it from both transactional and transformational leadership. They clarify that *transformative* leadership is not synonymous with *transformational* leadership—a theoretical construct that addresses specified dimensions of organizational life and work (setting directions, developing people, redesigning the organization and managing the instructional program) (see, e.g., Leithwood, in press). The starting point for transformative leadership is different and the emphasis on social justice and equity goes well beyond attending to improving the school as a whole. It acknowledges, with Bourdieu and many others, that education is a field of struggle and therefore recognizes the need to address issues of power, dominance, and legitimation. Freire (1998) acknowledges these fundamental conflicts, stating:

> I cannot consider myself progressive if I understand school space to be something neutral, with limited or no relation to class struggle, in which students are seen only as learners of limited domains of knowledge which I will imbue with magic power. I cannot recognize the limits of the political-educative practice in which I am involved if I don't know, if I am not clear about in whose favor I work. (p. 46)

The point is, once again, that educators must "take sides" as we make decisions about how to organize the school—sides, however, that promote the welfare of all children as we recognize that continuing disparity is both undemocratic and unacceptable. Green (2001) identifies the need for taking sides and to be motivated by "moral outrage" (p. 176), saying that the outrage must always be directed

> at the disparity between the lives of those who possess an immense superfluity and those of many millions more who lack even a bare sufficiency. . . the disparity can be justified neither by any apparent social necessity nor by any apparent difference in deservingness among the groups who benefit and suffer from it. (p. 176)

Transformative Decisions

If, as still happens often in public schools, classes are organized such that the preponderance of advantaged students are in certain academic or advanced classes, while children from poverty or ethnic minority families are overrepresented in special education and remedial classes, educators must speak out. If, as often happens in elementary schools at least, more parents volunteer in the middle class programs to provide extra support for parties and fieldtrips, it is incumbent on the educational leader to create policies that, for example, reassign parent volunteers to places where they are most needed, or discontinue classroom celebrations in favor of whole school parties and activities. Whether one is taking a relatively small decision such as these or a larger one related to assignment of children and material resources to classes and programs, in every decision, one must ask questions about who is being advantaged or disadvantaged, who is being privileged or marginalized, included or excluded, and whose voices have been heard and whose silenced. This is what it means to lead for diversity; it is to take sides—to ensure that educational decisions no longer perpetuate social inequality.

Other scholars frame in slightly different ways the need to take sides. Capper (1989), recognizing the school as a site of struggle, cites Giroux's and McLaren's definition of a transformative intellectual as one who attempts

> to insert teaching and learning directly into the political sphere by arguing that schooling represents both a struggle for meaning and a struggle over power relations. . . one whose intellectual practices are necessarily grounded in forms of moral and ethical discourse exhibiting a *preferential concern for the suffering and struggles of the disadvantaged and oppressed.* (p. 9, italics added)

Once again, this does not imply a lack of concern for all students, simply a recognition that if schools are to move beyond a sorting, selecting, or reproductive function, we must attend carefully to overcoming the violence perpetuated by the mismatch in valued cultural capital between those from the dominated and the dominating groups.

Using Power Ethically

Just as the distribution of power and power relations is central to reproductive leadership, so too, the moral and ethical use of power is central to transformative leadership. In a relatively early discussion of transformative leadership in education, Quantz, Rogers, and Dantley (1991) outline many of its tenets. They argue that traditional theories of leadership are inadequate for democratic empowerment and that "only the concept of transformative leadership appears to provide an appropriate direction" (p. 96). In words somewhat reminiscent of Bourdieu, they posit that schools are sites of cultural politics that serve both to reproduce and perpetuate the inequities inherent in gender, race, and class constructs and which "confirm and legitimate some cultures while disconfirming and delegitimating others" (p. 98). They go on to argue that because organizations must be based on democratic authority, transformative educational leaders must learn to diminish *"undemocratic power relationships"* (p. 102, italics in original) and use their "power to transform present social relations" (p. 103). Transformative leadership, they assert, "requires a language of critique and possibility" (p. 105); a "transformative leader must introduce the mechanisms necessary for various groups to begin conversations around issues of emancipation and domination" (p. 112).

Weiner (2003) also emphasizes the centrality of power to transformative leadership: "Transformative leadership is an exercise of power and authority that begins with questions of justice, democracy, and the dialectic between individual accountability and social responsibility" (p. 89). He delineates the responsibilities of the transformative leader to instigate structural transformations, to reorganize the political space, to understand the relationship between leaders and the led dialectically (and not hierarchically). He also calls for leaders to confront more than just what is, and work toward creating an alternative political and social imagination that does not rest solely on the rule of capital or the hollow moralism of neoconservatives, but is rooted in radical democratic struggle. (p. 97)

Leading with Moral Imagination

The notion of leading with moral imagination (see also Johnson, 2001) is one way of thinking about seeing "more than what is." In Gramsci's words, cited at the beginning of this chapter, educational leaders need to promote, with "beautiful enthusiasms," some new ideas about how to lead diverse schools. Times have changed; demographics have changed and education too must adapt to the new realities of a global and globalizing world. To do this, I advocate elsewhere that leaders need to break their silence about issues like race and class—silence that tends to pathologize differences; I argued then, and still believe that

> transformative educators and educational leaders must address issues of power, control, and inequity; they must adopt a set of guiding criteria [. . .] to act as benchmarks for the development of socially just education; and they must engage in dialogue, examine current practice, and create pedagogical conversations and communities that critically build on, and do not devalue, students' lived experiences. (Shields, 2003, p. 128)

Breaking the silence and enjoining "courageous conversations" (Singleton & Linton, 2005) about topics that are both difficult and dangerous is a necessary leadership act. It recognizes that if we simply celebrate diversity or promote choice among "individuals with unequal access to cultural as well as material resources" we are "likely to inhibit rather than enhance their chances of emancipation" (Whitty, in Torres, 1998, p. 109).

Fraser (1997) argues that there are two different kinds of impediments that restrict the opportunities of students to participate fully in democratic society:

> I assume that to be a radical democrat today is to appreciate—and seek to eliminate—two different kinds of impediments to democratic participation. One such impediment is social inequality; the other is the misrecognition of difference. Radical democracy, on this interpretation, is the view that democracy today requires both economic redistribution and multicultural recognitions. (pp. 173–174)

Although economic distribution in the wider society may be beyond the reach of leaders in diverse schools, there is little question that we can and must address "multicultural recognition."

Further, if a student is doing well academically, then assuming that there are no problems related to multicultural recognition is false. Annie, a Chinese American school principal who talked about her early years of schooling in America, explains very clearly how being Chinese led to lots and lots of prejudice and definitely lots of insults and definitely lots of bullying and harassing going on in the schools. "Name calling, pushing and shoving, students trying to trip you on stairs as you walked down the stairs, and all of those things. . . ." She continued, "Then there was also the stereotype about us being perfect students, and so that really had an impact. So I set out to prove that I was a perfect student." In her subsequent comments, she explained how, later, that led to a kind of rebellion that also created problems, for as she "started interpreting questions, assignments differently," she "always got smacked for it" although she still did it. As she reflected on her schooling, and on the ways in which schools and educators still think about multiculturalism, Annie stated, "The trouble with multiculturalism is that everything is so nice and sweet, and you never deal with all the racist stuff. . . what we do is we do the nice, fluffy, happy, smiley things. . .. I think what usually happens when there's name calling or pushing and shoving, and you attribute it to a race thing, we immediately put on folk dancing."

The caution is that even well-intentioned programs like multiculturalism, when not examined for implicit power imbalances, can serve to reproduce the unequal status quo, without ever addressing its underlying issues. Her comments remind us that the kind of multicultural recognition advocated by Fraser is not the "smiley, fluffy activities" that lead to avoidance of deeper issues but rather the difficult task of attending to the impediments to social equality—impediments usually ignored by educators who find it much easier to put on folk dancing than to address the deeper issues, such as racism.

Outcomes of Transformative Leadership

There are times—wonderful moments for individual students—when education is transformative, when it opens opportunity to be something one has not dreamed possible and to realize one's potential. I conclude this discussion of transformation with the story of Michael—a successful school principal, whose father is Métis[4] and whose mother was a war bride from Belgium. He described his early home life in these terms:

> A few months after I was born the family bought their first house, and it was very interesting because our back lane was kind of like the city division, so our house was on the other side of the street, literally. So we had a brand new development of professionals behind us, and on my side of the street, we had an outhouse, and we walked to the corner and hauled our water in the winter, and we cut wood, and then we had a slop pile, and we had a real almost rural lifestyle right there, so that's my social construct that I grew up with. Dressed in clothes from the Sally Ann [Salvation Army]. You know, that's the way we grew up.

Despite his home situation, at one point, following some testing, Michael was invited to attend a district program for gifted students. He explains,

> For me, I had to take three buses to get to school. School started at 9 o'clock. So I'd be on the bus at 7:30 in the morning and have lunch at school and take the bus back. We went to school in this basement classroom, and we had a very nice education. I really think that. I mean I really enjoyed it. . .. Our friendships consisted of the hour we spent together on the bus; we were ostracized within the school that we were part of. This wasn't our home community.

As we concluded our interview, Michael reflected that it was a later school experience, a time spent in a theater school where he found out who he was, that had most shaped him. He asserted,

> Education gave me an opportunity to go beyond where I was. It has lifted me socially in terms of classes more than any single thing that I could ever hoped for. Sophistication, I learned from the people I went to the theatre school with because they were all upper crust people because they were the ones who could afford the money to send their kids to the theatre school in the evening. It provided me with an opportunity to be and do things that I could never have hoped to be before. I could not even have realized that they were there.

Here, without being conscious of it, Michael sums up Bourdieu's concept of the pedagogical work of the home in creating a certain kind of cultural capital.

We also find here the surprising outcome that Michael, as a result of his belief in education and the attention of several teachers, mentioned during the course of the interview, was able to experience school as transformative. It not only offered Michael the possibility of things beyond belief, it has shaped his conviction of the importance of his role as an educational leader. He states it simply but eloquently:

> And so, my purpose in staying in education is to demystify it, to make it less an institution, and more an opportunity. It's for everybody. . ...You go to school, and it's oppressing. In order for you to truly become involved, you've got to be heard, know that you're being heard, and that you have to have some impact to let you know where you fit in.

Michael's experience, is unfortunately, too rare. The lessons to be learned are not that if you work hard, you can pull yourself up with your bootstraps, overcome adversity, and be successful. It is his conclusion that it is the role of an educational leader to demystify education that is important here. To become a transformative educator requires demystifying the ways in which the dominant power groups in society have arbitrarily legitimized certain kinds of cultural capital at the expense of others. It necessitates admitting that we arbitrarily value the experiences of the child whose parents have taken her to the theater over those of the child who has learned to haul water and chop wood and take three buses to get to school. It requires understanding the violence done to children through this misrecognition of their intrinsic worth and inherent ability. To reject reproduction and inequity requires transformative leaders to overturn the message that school success is not for the likes of Michael.

Critique and Possibility: Educational Leaders as Agents of Transformation

To lead equitably and effectively in diverse contexts requires educators to be transformative—offering both a critique of the current reproductive emphasis in education and the promise of something better for all students. It requires, as Annie suggested, that educators make consistent and concerted attempts to effect both deep and equitable changes. It requires, as Pauline's experiences demonstrated, both deconstruction and reconstruction of the knowledge frameworks that generate inequity. It requires an acknowledgment of power and privilege, an emphasis on both individual achievement and the public good; a focus on liberation, democracy, equity, and justice, and finally, evidence of moral courage and activism. Although these are not necessarily the only aspects of transformative leadership that might be included in a leader's repertoire, they provide important starting points. Taken together, their presence offers the potential to overcome the reproductive functions illuminated by Bourdieu and to actualize the promise of transformation.

To both administer and lead in contexts of diversity requires educators to acknowledge, with Gramsci, that indifference is "a swamp that defends the old order far better than any warriors or strong defenses" (in Gonzales, 2003, p. 493). To overcome the indifference that reproduces inequities and disparities in the wider society requires us to recognize that schools are truly sites of struggle. If we do not join the struggle, create opportunities for both critique and promise, and stand up for those who are the least advantaged, the struggle will be lost. If, on the other hand, we recognize that the fabric of our school community comprises diversity of race, ethnicity, language, sexual orientation, religious perspective, and differences in ability and disability, we will take a courageous stand. Gonzales (2003, p. 503) cites these lines from Pelagius that sum up this message:

> *In a time of confusion*
> *You must make a stand. There is a chrysalis*
> *Throbbing to disgorge oppression and pessimism,*
> *Proscription, prescription, conscription,*
> *Praying mantises. Cut them down.*

Transformative educational leaders must take a stand, cutting down the oppression and pessimism, and replacing them with liberation and optimism. Only then will education fulfill its promise as an agent of equity and change for our democratic society.

Notes

1. I use the term *minoritized*, rather than the more common word *minority* to indicate the process by which those who are not members of the dominant middle class power group are ascribed characteristics of subordinate groups, whether or not they are in the actual numerical minority in a given school or community. In 1998, in an attempt to understand both the schooling experiences of minoritized individuals who had eventually chosen careers in education, I conducted a study in which I interviewed twelve teachers and school administrators. The comments are taken from their interviews.
2. Here I make the assumption that the reader is well informed about the social and economic costs of school drop-outs, the criminal justice system, the costs of health care for those who are not covered on society as a whole, the lack of political participation by those with less formal education, and so forth. For further reading in this area, see Shields, 2009, chapter 3.
3. AYP requires that all students from all subgroups within the school meet expectations on the specified statewide test—regardless of other indicators of student learning or of whether the test process itself discriminates against them, perhaps because they are still English language learners, or because of identified intellectual conditions requiring accommodation.
4. Métis is the term used in Canada to indicate that someone is of both First Nations and French background.

References

Bourdieu, P. (2004). The forms of capital. In S. J. Ball (Ed.), *The RoutledgeFalmer reader in sociology of education*. New York: RoutledgeFalmer, pp. 13–29.

Bourdieu, P., & Passeron, J-C. (1990).*Reproduction in education, society, and culture*. Thousand Oaks, CA: Sage.

Capper, C. A. (1989). *Transformative leadership: Embracing student diversity in democratic schooling*. ED 305 714.

Delpit, L. D. (1990). The silenced dialogue: Power and pedagogy in educating other people's children. In N. M. Hidalgo, C. L. McDowell, & E. V. Siddle (Eds.), *Facing racism in education*. Reprint Series No. 21 ed. Cambridge, MA: Harvard Educational Review.

Education Trust (2008), *National Center for Education Statistics, NAEP Data Explorer*, http://nces.ed.gov/nationsreportcard/nde/

Foster, W. (1986). *Paradigms and promises*. Buffalo, NY: Prometheus.

Fraser, N. (1997). *Justice interruptus: Critical reflections on the postsocialist condition*. New York: Routledge.

Freire, P. (1998). *Pedagogy of freedom: Ethics, democracy, and civic courage*. Lanham, MD: Rowman and Littlefield.

Gonzalez, M. (2003). Against indifference. *Teaching in Higher Education*, 8(4), 493–503.

Green, P. (2001). Egalitarian solidarity. In S. J. Goodlad (Ed.), *The last best hope: A democracy reader*. San Francisco, CA: Jossey-Bass. pp. 176–193.

Herr, K., & Anderson, G. L. (2003). Violent youth or violent schools? A critical incident analysis of symbolic violence. *International Journal of Leadership in Education*, 6(4): 415–433.

Johnson, M. (2001). Moral imagination. In S. J. Goodlad (Ed.), *The last best hope: A democracy reader*. San Francisco, CA: Jossey-Bass. pps. 194–203.

Kincheloe, J. L., & Steinberg, S. R. (1998). Addressing the crisis of whiteness: Reconfiguring white identity in a pedagogy of whiteness. In J. L. Kincheloe, S. R. Steinberg, N. M. Rodriguez, & R. E. Chennault (Eds.), *White reign: Deploying whiteness in America,* New York: St. Martin's Press.

Leithwood, K., (in press), Transformational school leadership, In E. Baker, B. McGaw, & P. Peterson (eds.), *International Encyclopedia of Education* (3rd Edition). Oxford: Elsevier.

Mohan, E. J. (2008). *Policy implications of a critical analysis of the role of schools in the identity construction of multi-ethnic youth,* Paper presented at the Youth Forum of the Canadian Society for Studies in Education, Vancouver, June.

NCES (1996). *College attendance and attainment.* U.S. Department of Education. National Center for Education Statistics. The Condition of Education 1996, NCES 96–304. Washington, DC: U.S. Government Printing Office, 1996 (based on March Current Population Surveys). http://aspe.hhs.gov/hsp/97trends/ea1-6.htm

Ogbu, J. (1992). Understanding cultural diversity and learning. *Educational Researcher. 21*(8), 5–14.

Phoenix, P. (n.d.) Today's gay youth: The ugly, frightening statistics. Retrieved May 2008 from http://www.pflagphoenix.org/education/youth_stats.html.

Quantz, R. A., Rogers, J., & Dantley, M. (1991). Rethinking transformative leadership: Toward democratic reform of schools, *Journal of Education, 173*(3), pp. 96–118

Remafedi, G. (1987). Male homosexuality: The adolescent's perspective. *Pediatrics, 79.* pp. 326–337.

Roman, L. G. (1993). White is a color! White defensiveness, postmodernism, and anti-racist pedagogy. In C. McCarthy & W. Crichlow (Eds.), *Race, identity, and representation in education.* New York: Routledge.

Sayani, A. (2002). *Narratives of identity: Implications for school leaders.* Unpublished master's project, University of British Columbia, Vancouver, Canada.

Shields, C.M. (2003), Dialogic leadership for social justice: Overcoming pathologies of silence. *Educational Administrative Quarterly,* XI(1), pp. 111–134.

Shields, C. M. (2009), *Courageous leadership for transforming schools: Democratizing practice.* Norwood, MA: Christopher-Gordon.

Shields, C. M. (in press). Leadership: Transformative, In E. Baker, B. McGaw, & P. Peterson (eds.), *International Encyclopedia of Education* (3rd Edition). Oxford: Elsevier.

Singleton, G. E., & Linton, C. (2005). *Courageous conversations about race: A field guide for achieving equity in schools.* Thousand Oaks, CA: Corwin.

Swartz, D. (1997). *Culture and power: The sociology of Pierre Bourdieu.* Chicago: Chicago University Press.

Torres, C. A. (1998). *Democracy, education, multiculturalism.* Lanham, MD: Rowman & Littlefield, Chapter 4, "Citizenship."

U.S. Census, 2007, *Historical poverty tables,* http://www.census.gov/hhes/www/poverty/histpov/hstpov3.html

USDH (1989). *Report of the secretary's task force on youth suicide: Gay male and lesbian youth suicide.* U.S. Department of Health and Human Services, http://www.pflagphoenix.org/education/youth_stats.html

Weiner, E. J. (2003). Secretary Paulo Freire and the democratization of power: Toward a theory of transformative leadership, *Educational Philosophy and theory, 35*(1), 89–106.

Woods, E. L. (1995). *Reducing the dropout rate,* Portland, OR: Northwest Regional Educational Laboratory, School Improvement Research Series.